LIST OF THE OFFICERS OF THE BENGAL ARMY

Printed and bound in Great Britain by Antony Rowe Ltd, Eastbourne

LIST OF THE OFFICERS OF THE BENGAL ARMY

1758—1834

*Alphabetically Arranged and Annotated
with Biographical and Genealogical
Notices by*

MAJOR V. C. P. HODSON
INDIAN ARMY (RETIRED LIST)
AUTHOR OF 'HISTORICAL RECORDS OF THE VICEROY'S BODY-GUARD'

W - Z

W

WADDINGTON, John (1744-1770). Captain, Infantry. *b.* 1744. Cadet 1764. Ensign 7 June 1764. Lieut. 22 Aug. 1765. Capt. 1 Dec. 1767. *d.* Calcutta 29 Dec. 1770.

2nd son of Rev. Joshua Waddington, vicar of Harworth and Walkeringham, Notts., and Anne his wife, youngest dau. of Rev. Thomas Ferrand, vicar of Bingley. Grand-uncle of William Henry Waddington, French Ambassador in London 1883-93.

Services: Posted to 1st Bengal Eur. Regt. 13 Aug. 1765. Resigned during the " Batta mutiny " 1766 ; restored later.

Refs.: Burke's *Landed Gentry*, *s.n.* Ferrand, of St. Ives. *A Hist. of Monmouthshire*, by Joseph A. Bradney, Vol. ii, Pt. ii, p. 388. Will dated 27 Dec. 1770 ; proved 15 Jan. 1771.

WADE, Sir Claude Martine (1794-1861). Colonel, Kt., C.B. 45th N.I. *b.* Bengal 3 Apr. 1794. Cadet 1809. Admitted 15 Dec. 1810. Ensign 20 July 1812. Lieut. 21 Oct. 1815. Capt. 13 May 1825. Major 10 Nov. 1840. Bt. Lt. Col. 23 July 1839. Retired 1 May 1844. Hon. Col. 28 Nov. 1854. *d.* 16 Queen Sq., Bath, 21 Oct. 1861.

bapt. Berhampore 6 July 1795. Son of Joseph Wade, *q.v.*, and Maria Anne his wife. Cousin-german of John Peter Wade, *q.v. m.* Bath 7 Aug. 1845, Jane Selina, eldest dau. of Thomas Nicholl, *q.v.*

Services: See *D.N.B.* Barasat C.C. 6 mos. Cadet d.d. 15th N.I. ; posted to 1/23rd N.I. 1812 ; Adjt. do. 1 Feb. 1816 till 18 Mar. 1823. Third Mahratta War 1817-19 ; Chanda ; Lieut. 1/23rd N.I., with 5th Div. Army of Deccan. Offg. Bde. Major to troops in Oudh 1820-1 ; extra Asst. in office of Surveyor Gen. 1822 ; P.A. at Ludhiana 15 Mar. 1823 till 1839. Had charge of Shah Shuja, and sole charge of negotiations with Ranjit Singh 1827-39. Transfd. to 45th N.I. (late 1/23rd) May 1824. First Afghan War 1838-40 ; sent on a special mission to Peshawar ; forced Khyber Pass and captured Ali Masjid July 1839 ; entered Kabul (Medal). Local Lt. Col. while employed beyond Indus (29 Sept. 1838) 3 Jan. 1839. Resdt. at Indore and P.A. Malwa 31 Mar. 1840 till 1 May 1844. Kt. 11 Dec. 1839. C.B. 20 Dec. 1839. Sikh Order of Bright Star of Punjab. Durani 1 cl. 29 June 1841.

Refs.: Burke's *Landed Gentry of Ireland*, p. 730, *s.n.* Wade, of Clonebraney, co. Meath. *Walford. D.N.B. D.I.B. Boase. G.M.* 1861, ii. 692-3. *The Times*, 23 Oct. 1861.

LIST OF OFFICERS OF THE BENGAL ARMY 363

WADE, Edward Saunders Armigel-Waad Wada (1802-1836).
Lieutenant, Pension Est. Artillery. (503) *b.* Standon, Herts.,
11 Nov. 1802. Cadet 1818. 2nd Lieut. 20 Apr. 1819. Lieut.
7 Mar. 1824. Pensioned 18 Apr. 1829. *d.* Chinsura, Bengal,
16 Oct. 1836.

bapt. Standon 24 Dec. 1802. Son of John Wade, of the I. of Man,
and Helen his wife, dau. of Edward Saunders, M.C.S., sometime
Member of Council at Madras. *m.* Barrackpore 5 May 1831,
Harrietta, dau. of Robert Francis, *q.v.* (She died of cholera 19 Oct.
1844, aged 31.) Addiscombe Cadet 1817-19.

Services : Siege and capture of Bhurtpore ; Lieut. comdg. 4th
Coy. 3rd Bn. Foot Art.

Refs. : *A.J.* N.S. xxii. 292.

WADE, John Peter (1802-1873). Major. 13th N.I. *b.* Calcutta 20 Aug. 1802. Cadet 1819. Admitted 14 June 1820.
Ensign 9 Jan. 1820. Lieut. 11 July 1823. Capt. 8 Oct. 1839.
Retired 15 July 1845. Hon. Major 28 Nov. 1854. *d.* 1 June
1873.

bapt. Calcutta 19 Oct. 1802. Son of John Peter Wade, M.D.,
Surg. Bengal, and Rachel his wife, 2nd sister of Robert Carruthers,
q.v. Ed. Edin. Coll.

Services : Posted Ensign to 2/9th N.I. (? Operations in Oudh
1822 ; capture of Bardgaon ; Ensign 2/9th N.I.) Transfd. to
7th N.I. 1823 ; to 13th N.I. (late 1/7th) May 1824 ; actg. Intr.
& Qmr. do. 14 Mar. 1828 ; do. 30th N.I. 6 Oct. 1828 ; do. 13th N.I.
31 Mar. 1830 ; permanent do. 19 Oct. 1830 till 6 Apr. 1836. Fur.
p.a. 16 Jan. 1837 till 10 Jan. 1840. Attached to 1st L.I. Bn. 1841-2.
Fort Adjt. at Allahabad 6 May till 30 Oct. 1843. Fur. s.c. 16 Feb.
1844 till retirement.

Refs. : Burke's *Landed Gentry of Ireland*, p. 730, *s.n.* Wade, of
Clonebraney, co. Meath.

WADE, Joseph (*d.* 1807). Lieut. Colonel, Bengal Eur. Regt.
Country Cadet 1778. Admitted 9 Mar. 1778. Ensign 1778.
Lieut. 26 Oct. 1780. Capt. 3 Oct. 1796. Major 13 July 1803.
Lt. Col. 17 Oct. 1805. *d.* Ghazipur, U.P., 12 Sept. 1807.

2nd son of Walter Wade, of Dublin, M.D., and Mary Kennedy
his wife. *m.* 9 May 1793, Maria Anne, eldest dau. of Robert Ross,
Lt. Col. R.M. (She died 2 Oct. 1863, aged 88.) Father of Sir
Claude Martine Wade, *q.v.*

Services : Campaign against the Rajah of Benares 1781 ; Benares
21 Aug. ; Lieut. comdg. a Coy. of French Rangers. Lieut. in the

Corps of Foreign Rangers in June 1784. Fur. 2 Oct. 1786 till 3 Feb. 1794. Posted to 4th Eur. Bn. 10 Feb. 1794; as Capt. Lt. to 2nd Eur. Regt. June 1796. Major Bengal Eur. Regt.; transfd. to newly-raised 21st N.I. 1804. Posted Lt. Col. to 13th N.I. 1805; to Bengal Eur. Regt. 1806.

Refs.: Burke's *Landed Gentry of Ireland*, p. 730, *s.n.* Wade, of Clonebraney, co. Meath. *Scottish Antiquary,* iv. 61.

WADE, William Henry (1774-1808). Ensign. Infantry. Afterwards Lieut. 25th Light Dgns. *b.* Brightlingsea, Essex, 3 Mar. 1774. Cadet 1795. Arrived in India 27 Feb. 1797. Ensign 30 Nov. 1796. Resigned 20 Oct. 1797. *d.* Madras 30 Sept. 1808.

Son of William Wade, of Brightlingsea, and Anne his wife. *m.* (?) (She died 8 Oct. 1811.)

Services: Ensign H.M. 76th Ft. 26 Oct. 1797; Lieut. 25th Light Dgns. 22 Nov. 1803.

Refs.: M.I. St. Mary's cemetery, Madras. Intest.; admon. (Madras) 4 May 1809.

WAGSTAFF,[1] **Thomas** (*d.* 1798). Bt. Captain, Engineers. Country Cadet 1781. Ensign Oct. 1781. Lieut. 2 Nov. 1782. Bt. Capt. 7 Jan. 1796. *d.s.p.* Calcutta (? Barrackpore) 14 Dec. 1798.

Elder son of William Wagstaff, of Manchester, apothecary, and Mary his wife, dau. of —— Taylor, of Salford. His sisters *m.* Alexander Kyd and Charles Morgan, *qq.v.*

Services: Apptd. a Cadet for the Engrs. through the influence of his brother-in-law, Edward Hay, B.C.S. Leave s.c. to sea 7 Sept. 1782; fur. 10 Oct. 1785 till 9 Oct. 1789. Clerk of the Works in Ft. Wm. in 1790. Apptd. Sec. and Persian Intr. to Col. Charles Morgan, *q.v.,* 4 Jan. 1792. Fur. 12 Oct. 1794 till 12 Nov. 1798.

Refs.: Manchester School Register, i. 116. *G.M.* 1799, ii. 716. Will dated Cape Town, 7 Dec. 1794; admon. 20 Feb. 1799.

[1] *Note:* The name usually appears in official documents with a final ' e '.

*WAHAB, Henry (1789-1830). Lieutenant. 10th N.I. Afterwards Captain, 37th M.N.I. *b.* Masulipatam, Madras, 11 Jan. 1789.[1] Cadet 1804. Never arrived in Bengal. Ensign 3 Oct. 1805. Lieut. 2 Nov. 1805. Resigned 16 July 1807. *d.s.p.* Kamptee, C.P., 16 June 1830, of inflammation in the bowels.

3rd son of Maj.-Gen. George Wahab, Madras Est., and Catherine his wife, dau. of Henry Brooke, M.C.S., sometime Member of Council

at Madras. *m.* Masulipatam 2 Mar. 1829, Beata (or Beatta), youngest sister of James Towell, Garr. Surg.
Services: Lieut. (Madras) 12 June 1806; Capt. 23 May 1819.
Refs.: The Ulster Branch of the Family of Wauchope, by Dr. Gladys M. Wauchope (1929), pp. 118, 123, Ped. II (where dates of birth and death are given as 11 July 1788 and 5 June 1830). *A.J.* xxviii. 348.
¹ *Note:* This is the date of his birth according to an affidavit sworn by him on 29 Mar. 1805.

WAITE, George (1778-1815). Captain, Invalid Est. 22nd N.I. *bapt.* Lincoln 15 June 1778. Cadet 1798. Arrived in India 6 Sept. 1799. Ensign 17 Dec. 1799. Lieut. 29 May 1800. Capt. 29 July 1813. Invalided 1 Sept. 1814. *d.* 8 Dec. 1815: drowned in the Ganges nr. Patna, *en route* from Calcutta to Chunar: *bur.* Dinapore.¹
Son of Charles Waite and Jane his wife. *m.* Calcutta 22 Dec. 1810, Jane, sister of Charles Kiernander, *q.v.* (She was drowned with him.)
Services: Fur. 29 Oct. 1800 till 23 June 1803. Posted to 2/17th N.I. 15 Apr. 1801; transfd. to newly-raised 22nd N.I. 1804. Fur. 22 Jan. 1806 till 22 Aug. 1808. Capt. Lt. 22nd N.I. 3 Jan. 1812.
Refs.: G.M. 1816, ii. 185.
¹ *Note:* According to the account in *G.M.*, he and his wife were suddenly taken ill, stopped for medical aid at Bankipore, and died within 6 hours of each other.

WAITE, Thomas (*d.* 1771). Cadet, Infantry. Cadet 1770. *d.* Dinapore 1 Sept. 1771.
Services: N.F.P.

WAKE, Charles Hamilton (1808-1872). Major. 34th N.I. *b.* York 4 Sept. 1808. Cadet 1827. Arrived in India 23 Sept. 1828. Ensign 23 May 1828. Lieut. 14 Aug. 1839. Capt. 24 June 1847. Retired 21 Feb. 1852. Hon. Major 28 Nov. 1854. *d. unm.* Ormathwaite House, Keswick, 14 Feb. 1872.
bapt. St. Michael-le-Belfrey, York, 8 Sept. 1808. 2nd son of Baldwin Wake, M.D., of Whitehaven, and Sarah his wife, dau. of James Spedding.
Services: Ensign d.d. 51st N.I. 5 Nov. 1828; posted to 34th N.I. 4 Mar. 1829. Operations against Kols and Chuars 1832-3; Ensign 34th N.I. Leave s.c. to Hills 1 Dec. 1834 till 1 Dec. 1836. Actg. Adjt. 34th N.I. 7 May 1837; actg. Intr. & Qmr. do. 11 Mar. 1839; do. 23rd N.I. 4 Sept. 1839. Fur. p.a. 22 Feb. 1840 till

15 Dec. 1842. Intr. & Qmr. 34th N.I. 16 Feb. 1843 till disbanded for mutiny 20 Mar. 1844. Actg. Intr. & Qmr. 54th N.I. 30 Apr. 1844. Posted to new 34th N.I. (late Inf. of Bundelkhand Legion) July 1846. Second Sikh War; no actions; Capt. 34th N.I. Offg. D.J.A.G. Meerut Div. 5 June 1850.

Refs.: Burke's *Peerage*, 1923, p. 2243, *s.n.* Wake, Bart., of Courteenhall, Northants. *The Times*, 19 Feb. 1872.

WAKE, William Henry (1788-1854). Bt. Colonel, 44th N.I. *bapt.* St. Paul's, Covent Gdn., Middlesex, 1 Sept. 1788. Cadet 1809. Arrived in India 26 Apr. 1811. Ensign 3 Jan. 1812. Lieut. 2 Jan. 1815. Capt. 4 Mar. 1828. Major 8 Oct. 1839. Lt. Col. 10 Jan. 1846. Bt. Col. 20 June 1854. *d.* Dinapore 14 Nov. 1854.

Son of John Wake and Mary Owen his 1st wife. *m.* St. John's, Calcutta, 27 Dec. 1823, Catherine, only dau. of John Bagshaw, of Bourton, co. Warwick, and sister of John Bagshaw, M.P., of Dovercourt. (She died 11 Nov. 1856, aged 55.)

Services: Captured by the French in *Ceylon* Indiaman 3 July 1810 (w.); prisoner at Mauritius till 20 Sept. 1810, when sent to Cape and exchanged; accompanied H.M. 87th as a Vol. against Mauritius and landed Port Louis 3 Dec. 1810. Posted to 1/22nd N.I. 1812. Served in Java with Vol. L.I. Bn. July 1812 till Nov. 1816, sometime as Adjt. Third Mahratta War 1817-18; Lieut. 2/22nd N.I., with Pioneers. Adjt. Gorakhpur L.I. 1818-20; do. Cuttack Legion 24 Jan. 1821; do. Ramgarh L.I. 1824. Transfd. to 44th N.I. (late 2/22nd) May 1824. Leave s.c. to Cape 20 Dec. 1824 till 18 Feb. 1827; fur. p.a. 15 Mar. 1834 till 9 Oct. 1836. In charge of Kumaon Local Bn. 10 Nov. 1842; comdg. in Kumaon 16 Nov. 1843. First Sikh War; Ferozshahr; Major 44th N.I. (Medal). Capture of Kot Kangra Apr. 1846; Lt. Col. 44th N.I. Posted Lt. Col. to 44th N.I.; transfd. to 70th N.I. 26 Dec. 1846; to 33rd N.I. 5 Feb. 1848; to 14th N.I. 12 Apr. 1848; to 44th N.I. Aug. 1851. Posted to 47th N.I. Oct. 1854, but never joined.

Refs.: Boase. *G.M.* 1855, i. 544. Will dated Dinapore 29 Apr. 1852; proved 19 Dec. 1854.

WAKEFIELD, Edward (1799-1861). Lieutenant. 19th N.I. Afterwards Capt. 15th Hrs. *bapt.* Gt. Baddow, Essex, 15 Dec. 1799. Cadet 1818. Ensign 24 July 1819. Lieut. 11 July 1822. Struck off in England 1 Nov. 1825. *d.* Eastbourne Terr., London, 1 May 1861.

Of Gilford, co. Down. Son of Edward Wakefield, of co. Down, and Marian Charlotte his wife, dau. of Commodore John Watson,

THE BENGAL ARMY, 1758-1834

of Bombay. Brother of James Watson Wakefield, *q.v.*, and 2nd cousin of Edward Anthony Hull, *q.v.* (? *m.* Paris Apr. 1826, Frances, only dau. of Rev. D. Davies, D.D.) *m.* 3 Oct. 1843, Mary Jane, eldest dau. of Henry Unett, of Freen's Court, co. Hereford. (*See also* Charles Pratt Kennedy.) Woolwich Cadet.

Services: Ensign d.d. 10th N.I. 1819; posted to 2/1st N.I. 1820; transfd. to 3rd N.I. 1823; to 19th N.I. (late 2/3rd) May 1824. Fur. 1824 till struck off. Lieut. H.M.S. 29 June 1826; Lieut. 15th Light Dgns. (Hrs.) 12 Mar. 1829; Capt. do. 27 June 1834; retired 2 Sept. 1836.

Refs.: Burke's *Landed Gentry*, 5th edn., p. 1429, *s.n.* Unett, of Freen's Court, co. Hereford. *G.M.* 1861, i. 700. *The Times*, 7 May 1861.

WAKEFIELD, James Watson (1802-1826). Lieutenant, Artillery. (497) *bapt.* nr. Lisburn, co. Antrim, 23 June 1802. Cadet 1818. 2nd Lieut. 24 Apr. 1819. Lieut. 18 Oct. 1822. *d.* Ellichpur, Berar, 20 Sept. 1826, aged 23.

Son of Edward Wakefield and Marian Charlotte his wife. Brother of Edward Wakefield, *q.v.* Addiscombe Cadet 1817-19.

Services: 2nd Lieut. 2nd Coy. 1st Bn. Foot Art.; transfd. to 2nd Troop H.A. 1823; to 2nd Troop 3rd Bde. 1824; to 1st Troop 3rd Bde. 1825. Asst. Sec. to Mily. Board 1824. d.d. Nizam's Art. 10 June 1825 till death. Siege and capture of Bhurtpore; Lieut. 1st Troop 3rd Bde.

Refs.: *A.J.* xxiii. 537. Will dated 24 Dec. 1825; admon. 19 July 1827. M.I. Ellichpur.

WAKEFIELD, John Howard (1803-1862). Lieut. Colonel. 3rd Bengal Eur. Regt. *b.* London 2 June 1803. Cadet 1822. Arrived in India 22 Aug. 1823. Ensign 11 July 1823. Lieut. 13 May 1825. Capt. 9 July 1840. Major 1 Sept. 1855. Retired 1 Jan. 1857. Hon. Lt. Col. 1 Jan. 1857. *d.* suddenly at Barnsbury Pk., Islington, 25 June 1862.

bapt. St. Pancras, Middlesex, 19 Jan. 1818. 5th son of Edward Wakefield, of 34 Pall Mall, land surveyor (*D.N.B.*) (who was cousin-german of the wife of William Curphey, *q.v.*), and Susannah his 1st wife, dau. of —— Crash, of Felstead, Essex. Brother of Edward Gibbon Wakefield (*D.N.B.*). *m.* Bareilly 9 Jan. 1832, Miss Maria Suffolk, "a converted Hindu, dau. of the late Vizier of Bussahor, ward of the Rana of Kumasin (India)." (*Foster*) (She died Lahore 8 Aug. 1852.) Ed. Westminster; admitted 29 Apr. 1816; K.S. 1818; elected to Trin. Coll., Camb., 1822; Pensioner 18 May 1822. (Did not reside.)

Services: Posted Ensign to 17th N.I. 1824. Employed on survey work 1838-9. Attached to 2nd Vol. Regt. 29 Apr. 1842 till 1 Mar. 1843, when broken up. First China War 1842; capture of Chinkiang Foo; Capt. 2nd Bengal Vols. (Medal). Cantt. Joint Mgte. at Lahore 26 Mar. 1850 till 1855. Transfd. to newly-raised 3rd Bengal Eur. Regt. Nov. 1853.

Refs.: Foster's *Families of Royal Descent*, ii. 844. *Alumni Westmon. The Times*, 28 June 1862.

WALCOTT, John. Lieutenant. Infantry. Cadet 1781. Ensign 27 July 1781. Lieut. 26 Oct. 1782. Struck off 1788.

Services: Never arrived in India.

WALCOTT, William George (1789-1824). Captain, Artillery. (381) *b.* Christchurch, Hants, 21 Sept. 1789. Cadet 1805. Arrived in India 20 July 1807. Fireworker 7 May 1807. Lieut. 2 Feb. 1808. Capt. 2 Aug. 1819. *d. unm.* Mauritius 7 Mar. 1824.

bapt. Christchurch 16 Nov. 1789. 2nd son of Edmund Walcott, of Winkton House, Hants, Lieut. 2nd D.G., Col. of the Christchurch Vols. (who assumed the name of Sympson, in accordance with the Will of John Sympson, of Cork), and Catherine Anne his wife, dau. of John Lyons, of Thundersley House, Hunts. Cousin-german of Theodore Lyons, *q.v.*

Services: Nepal War 1814-15; Lieut. 2nd Coy. 3rd Bn. Foot Art., with 4th Div. Nepal War 1816 (s.w. at Chiriaghati Pass 16 Feb. when reconnoitring); Adjt. Art. Comy. of Stores Nagpur Subsdy. Force 20 Nov. 1816 (reapptd. 17 Oct. 1818) till death. Third Mahratta War 1818; Seoni 16 Apr.; Chanda; Lieut. 2nd Coy. 3rd Bn., Comy. of Stores.

Refs.: Burke's *Landed Gentry*, 6th edn., p. 1669, *s.n.* Walcott, of Lisfunshion and Coolclough, co. Cork.

WALDRON, John Hamersley (1786-1826). Captain, 46th N.I. *b.* 2 Oct. 1786. Cadet 1806. Arrived in India 25 Nov. 1807. Ensign 7 Oct. 1807. Lieut. 27 Feb. 1812. Capt. 30 May 1824. *d. unm.* Assam 17 Jan. 1826.

bapt. Sedgley, Staffs., 24 Mar. 1791. Son of John Waldron and Sarah his wife.

Services: Barasat C.C. Posted Ensign to 23rd N.I. 1808. With 3rd Gren. Bn. 1815-16. Third Mahratta War 1817-19; Lieut. 1/23rd N.I. Transfd. to 2/23rd N.I.; to 46th N.I. (late 2/23rd) May 1824. First Burma War; Assam 1824; Rangpur; Capt.

THE BENGAL ARMY, 1758-1834

comdg. detachment 46th N.I. Intr. & Qmr. 46th N.I. 21 Jan. till 12 July 1825.
Refs.: Will dated Dinapore 15 Apr. 1822; proved 8 Jan.1827.

WALKER, Charles (1783-1805). Lieutenant, 24th N.I. *bapt.* Chipping Barnet Oct. 1783. Cadet 1800. Arrived in India 21 Aug. 1801. Ensign 23 Oct. 1801. Lieut. 30 Sept. 1803. *d.* Cawnpore 18 June 1805.
Son of Charles Walker and Ann his wife.
Services: Ensign d.d. 16th N.I. in 1802; posted Ensign to 3rd N.I.; transfd. to newly-raised 24th N.I. 1804.

WALKER, Charles Leslie (1792-1816). Lieutenant, 20th N.I. *b.* Barbados 21 Oct. 1792. Cadet 1807. Arrived in India 19 Aug. 1808. Ensign 22 Sept. 1808. Lieut. 12 Apr. 1814. *d.* at sea 29 July 1816: drowned on his passage to Fort Marlbro' in the *Malabar* cruiser.
bapt. St. Michael's, Barbados, 11 Apr. 1793. Son of David Walker, Lieut. 4th Bn. 60th Regt., and Charlotte his wife. Cousin of William Tankerville Monypenny.
Services: Barasat C.C. Posted Ensign to 20th N.I. 1809. Capture of Java 1811; Ensign 1/20th N.I. Transfd. to 2/20th N.I. Served at Bencoolen 1813-16.
Refs.: A.J. iv. 208.

WALKER, Edward Thomas (1787-1820). Lieutenant, 22nd N.I. *b.* Redbourn, Herts., 24 Dec. 1787. Cadet 1805. Arrived in India 11 July 1806. Ensign 16 July 1806. Lieut. 20 Sept. 1808. *d.* C.G.H. 11 Feb. 1820.
bapt. Redbourn 27 Jan. 1788. 4th son of William Walker, of Haileybury, Herts., late Surg. Bengal Est., and Elizabeth his wife, dau. of Capt. William Pye, Madras Est. Brother of William Bensley Walker, *q.v.* Ed. Winchester Coll.; Scholar 1801 till 22 Aug. 1805.
Services: Barasat C.C. Posted Ensign to 22nd N.I. 1807. Nepal War 1816; Lieut. 2/22nd N.I., in 3rd Bde. Centre Column. Leave to Cape 1819.
Refs.: Burke's *Royal Families*, Ped. xcv. *Kirby.*

WALKER, Forster (1781-1843). Major General. Colonel 3rd N.I. *b.* Northallerton, Yorks., 12 Feb. 1781. Cadet 1800. Arrived in India 6 Feb. 1802. Ensign 18 Oct. 1801. Lieut. 13 July 1803. Capt. 13 Aug. 1815. Major 13 May 1825. Lt. Col. 26 Feb. 1829. Col. (22 Jan. 1834) 5 Nov. 1841. Maj. Gen. 23 Nov. 1841. *d.* Calcutta 19 Jan. 1843, of cholera.

Of Stanhope Terr., Hyde Pk. Gdns., London. Son of Rev. Benjamin Walker, vicar of Northallerton, and Isabella Warren his wife, a near relation of John Forster, Govr. of Ft. Wm., Bengal, 1746-8. Uncle of James Lumsdaine Walker, *q.v.*, and cousin-german of the wife of Dalhousie Watherston, *q.v. m.* St. John's, Calcutta, 29 Mar. 1821, Miss Lydia Sarah Pattle. (She died Versailles, France, 7 Dec. 1864.)

Services: Posted Ensign to Bengal Eur. Regt. 13 Nov. 1802. Second Mahratta War; operations in Bundelkhand 1803-4 under Lt.-Cols. G. Martindell and W. D. Fawcett, *qq.v.*; under Lake 1804-5; battle and capture of Deig; Bhurtpore [1]; Lieut. Eur. Regt. Expedn. to Macao 1808-9; Lieut. Vol. Bn. under Capt. T. M. Weguelin, *q.v.* Adjt. Bengal Eur. Regt. 26 Feb. 1809 till 1815. Served in Java and Amboyna with his Regt. 1813-17. Third Mahratta War; Capt. Eur. Regt. Served in Ceylon July 1818 till 1819 as Paymr. to Bengal troops. d.d. Ramgarh Bn. 21 Sept. 1822. Transfd. to newly-raised 33rd N.I. July 1823; to 65th N.I. (late 1/33rd) May 1824. Comdd. 12th Rampura Local Bn. 9 July 1825 till 22 Dec. 1826. Posted Lt. Col. to 65th N.I. 1829. Fur. s.c. 24 Jan. 1831 till 15 Dec. 1833. Transfd. to 33rd N.I. 3 Jan. 1834 and comdd. for 3 yrs. 10 mos. Fur. p.a. 8 Mar. 1838 till 29 Dec. 1840. Transfd. to 28th N.I. 30 Dec. 1840; to 8th N.I. 28 May 1841; as Col. to 3rd N.I. 5 Nov. 1841. Bdr. 2 cl. comdg. Oudh 17 Sept. 1841; do. Barrackpore 19 Dec. 1842.

Refs.: Family information. Will dated North Allerton 3 July 1840; admon. 13 Feb. 1844. M.I. Circular Rd. cemetery, Calcutta.

[1] *Note:* He and an ofr. of H.M. 76th were the only two in the whole force who were engaged in all four storms, in the last of which Walker was blown up and severely injured.

WALKER, Henry Brooks (1811-1838). Lieutenant, Bengal Eur. Regt. *b.* Hampstead 18 Mar. 1811. Cadet 1829. Arrived in India 30 May 1830. Ensign (4 Feb. 1830) 30 May 1830. Lieut. 11 Nov. (? 27 Sept.) 1837. *d.* suddenly Agra 10 Aug. 1838, of apoplexy.

bapt. St. John's, Hampstead, 23 May 1811. Son of Henry Walker and Olivia his wife. *m.* Agra 19 Mar. 1838, Helen Cunningham, 2nd dau. of W. B. Crichton, of Dalkeith. (She died 1851.)

Services: Ensign d.d. 43rd N.I. 7 June 1830; Cadet d.d. 54th N.I. 8 Jan. 1831; Actg. Ensign (having been 2 yrs. in India) 16 July 1832; d.d. 74th N.I. 15 Oct. 1832; posted to Left Wing, Bengal Eur. Regt., 20 Aug. 1833. No record of active service.

Refs.: *A.J.* N.S. xxvii. 232. *G.M.* 1839, i. 223, 333.

THE BENGAL ARMY, 1758-1834 371

WALKER, James (d. 1820). Capt. Lieutenant. Artillery. (140) Cadet 1772. Fireworker 10 Aug. 1776. Lieut. 22 Sept. 1778. Capt. Lieut. 1 Feb. 1784. Resigned on pension 2 Feb. 1784. d. 29 Nov. 1820.

m. July 1785, Wilhelmina, 2nd dau. of Andrew Wight, of Ormiston.

Services: Posted to Art. with New Bde. in dominions of the Nawab-Wazir of Oudh 7 Aug. 1777. Second Mysore War; Lieut. 5th Coy. 2nd Bn. Art. Pensd. on Lord Clive's fund 10 Sept. 1784.

Refs.: Burke's *Landed Gentry*, 11th edn., p. 180, *s.n.* Wight-Boycott, of Rudge Hall, Salop.

WALKER, James Lumsdaine (1817-1865). Lieut. Colonel. 71st N.I. b. Meerut 22 May 1817. Cadet 1833. Arrived in India 1 Dec. 1834. Ensign (13 June 1834) 25 Sept. 1834. Lieut. 22 Mar. 1839. Capt. 1 May 1847. Major 31 May 1857. Lt. Col. 16 Feb. 1861. d. Calcutta 11 Mar. 1865, of sporadic cholera.

Son of Col. George Warren Walker, H.M. 59th Regt., D.A.G. in Ceylon, and Anna Maria his wife, dau. of Robert Patton (1742-1812), *q.v.* Nephew of James Lumsdaine and Forster Walker, *qq.v.*, and cousin-german of Frederick Torrens, *q.v.* m. Calcutta 1 Oct. 1844, Charlotte Fullarton, dau. of James Dunbar and widow of William Little, *q.v.* Addiscombe Cadet 3 Aug. 1832 till 13 June 1834.

Services: Permitted to proceed as a passenger in the *St. George* on certain conditions to see his friends. Ensign d.d. 33rd N.I. 4 Dec. 1834; posted to 71st N.I. 2 Mar. 1835; actg. Adjt. do. 20 Nov. 1839. A.D.C. to Presdt. of Council (Hon. W. W. Bird) 19 Jan. 1844; do. Dy. Govr. of Bengal 28 Feb. 1844; do. Govr. of Bengal 15 June 1844. Adjt. Ramgarh L.I. Bn. 20 Sept. 1844 till Aug. 1847. Fur. s.c. 27 Aug. 1847 till 26 Oct. 1850. Operations on N.W.F. against Mohmands 1851; Capt. comdg. Wing of 71st N.I. under Sir Colin Campbell. Fur. 1858-60. Actg. Bdr. at Barrackpore at death.

Refs.: Family information.

WALKER, John (1796-1820). Lieutenant, 11th N.I. b. 16 Oct. 1796. Cadet 1813. Ensign (25 Nov. 1814) 25 Apr. 1815. Lieut. 5 Aug. 1816. d. Barrackpore 7 June 1820.

bapt. St. James's, Westminster, 21 Nov. 1796. Son of William Walker, of Northaw, Herts., and of Lisson Grove, Paddington, and Mary his wife. m. Calcutta 21 Oct. 1817, Elizabeth, dau. of Roderick Fraser (1763-1818), *q.v.* (See also Harrie Nichelson.) (She re-m. 1 Oct. 1827.)

Services: Posted Ensign to 1/11th N.I. Apr. 1815, and served throughout with that Bn. No record of active service.

Refs.: Will dated Calcutta Aug. 1819; proved 8 July 1820. M.I. S. Park St. cemetery, Calcutta.

WALKER, John Pascal (1808-?). Lieutenant. 47th N.I. *b.* Blackheath 31 May 1808. Cadet 1825. Arrived in India 16 May 1826. Ensign 5 Nov. 1825. Lieut. 21 Mar. 1828. Dismissed by G.C.M. 16 Feb. 1835. *d.* in Australia.

bapt. Lewisham, Kent, 25 June 1808. Eldest son of Adam Walker, M.D., Surg. E.I.C.N.S., formerly R.N., and Eliza his wife, 5th dau. of Capt. Thomas Larkins, Comdr. of the *Warren Hastings* East Indiaman. Cousin-german of Henry Goodwyn, *q.v.* His sister *m.* Richard Tickell, *q.v.*

Services: Posted Ensign to 69th N.I. 1826. Operations against the Bhils 1827; Ensign 69th N.I. Transfd. as Lieut. to 47th N.I. 1828; actg. Adjt. do. 27 Dec. 1830; actg. Intr. & Qmr. do. 1 Jan. 1831. Settled at Lucknow after dismissal, and later in Australia.

Refs.: Family information. *A.J.* N.S. xvii. 240.

WALKER, Richard (*d.* 1801). Lieut. Colonel, Infantry. Cadet 1772. Admitted 3 Oct. 1772. Ensign 8 July 1776. Lieut. 29 June 1778. Capt. 26 Oct. 1792. Major 31 Aug. 1798. Lt. Col. 8 Dec. 1800. *d.* at sea 4 July 1801, on board the *Cornwallis* off C.G.H.

Brother of Thomas and William Walker, of Haileybury House, Herts.

Services: Ensign 30th Bn. Sepoys in 1777 on its transfer to the Coy. from service of Nawab-Wazir of Oudh. Campaign against the Rajah of Benares 1781; Lieut. 23rd N.I. (late 30th Bn.). Lieut. 29th Bn. (late 23rd N.I.) in July 1787 and Dec. 1788. Posted Capt. to 6th Eur. Bn. 22 Nov. 1792; transfd. to 1st Eur. Regt. 1796; to 6th N.I. 1798. Fur. 21 Mar. 1801 till death.

Refs.: *G.M.* 1801, ii. 1053. *M.M.* 1801, p. 473. Will dated Barrackpore 1 Jan. 1801; proved 28 Aug. 1802.

WALKER, Richard Clements (1790-1822). Bt. Captain, 29th N.I. *b.* Manchester 18 Apr. 1790. Cadet 1804. Arrived in India 10 Apr. 1805. Ensign Nov. 1805. Lieut. 17 Sept. 1806. Bt. Capt. 1 Jan. 1819. *d.* Kalpi 23 Aug. 1822.

bapt. St. Mary's, Manchester, 21 May 1790. Son of Richard Walker and Ann his wife. Brother of Sidney Walker, *q.v.*, and nephew of John Pau, of Kirkby Lonsdale. *m.* Cawnpore 19 Jan. 1811, Miss Eliza Howard Morris. (She died Oct. 1849.) His dau.

m. John William Hicks, *q.v.* Ed. Manchester Grammar School; admitted 17 Jan. 1803.

Services : Allowed to proceed to India as a passenger and to be apptd. a Cadet on attaining age of 15 yrs. Posted Lieut. to 4th N.I. 24 Apr. 1807 ; with Mirzapur Bn. in 1814 ; transfd. to newly-raised 29th N.I. 1815 ; Intr. & Qmr. 1/29th N.I. 4 May 1815 till death. Siege and capture of Hathras 1817. Employed on public bldgs. at Bithur 1818 ; do. Cawnpore 1820 ; do. Etawah and Kalpi 1821 till death.

Refs. : Manchester Grammar School Register. Will dated 26 Sept. 1817 ; codicil 29 Oct. 1821 ; proved 21 Mar. 1823.

*WALKER, Robert (1812-1846). Bt. Captain, Invalid Est. Artillery. (615) *b.* 17 Apr. 1812. Cadet 1828. Arrived in India 24 Mar. 1829. 2nd Lieut. 12 June 1828. Lieut. 7 Oct. 1836. Bt. Capt. 12 June 1843. Invalided 2 Feb. 1844. *d.* Agra 17 Nov. 1846.

bapt. St. Pancras, Middlesex, 19 July 1813. Youngest son of William Walker, of Brunswick Sq., London, and of the Inner Temple, barr.-at-law, and Sarah his wife, dau. of William Sleigh, of Whitehall. Brother of Thomas Walker (1809-1841), *q.v. m.* Dum-Dum 18 June 1838, Mary, dau. of William Curling, of Ham, Kent. (She died 22 Oct. 1865.) Ed. Westminster ; admitted 16 Apr. 1821. Addiscombe Cadet 1826-8.

Services : A.D.C. to Maj.-Gen. J. W. Sleigh, H.M.S., comdg. Cawnpore Div., 29 Jan. 1831 ; Adjt. & Qmr. Cawnpore Div. Art. 1832 till 1 Dec. 1834 ; A.D.C. to Maj.-Gen. Sleigh, in Bo. Presdy., 5 Feb. 1835. Posted to 1st Troop 2nd Bde. H. A. 26 Jan. 1837 ; to 4th Coy. 2nd Bn. Foot Art. 25 Apr. 1838. First Afghan War 1838-42 ; Ghazni 1839 (Medal) ; defence of Kalat-i-Ghilzai Nov. 1841 till June 1842 ; Lieut. 4th Coy. 2nd Bn., comdg. Art. (Medal). Adjt. & Qmr. 4th Bn. 5 Jan. 1842 till 3 Dec. 1843.

Refs. : Westminster School List. G.M. 1847, i. 334. Will dated Kalat-i-Ghilzai, 18 Feb. 1842 ; admon. 19 Apr. 1847.

WALKER, Sidney (1794-1826). Captain, 7th N.I. *b.* Manchester 25 Feb. 1794. Cadet 1808. Arrived in India 27 Oct. 1809. Ensign 17 Oct. 1810. Lieut. 16 Dec. 1814. Capt. 3 Mar. 1826. *d.* at sea 16 Mar. 1826, on board the *Princess Charlotte of Wales,* on his passage to England.

bapt. St. Mary's, Manchester. Son of Richard Walker and Ann his wife. Brother of William Walmesley Walker, *q.v.* Marlow Cadet.

Services : Posted to 14th N.I. 1810 ; transfd. to 4th N.I. 1811.

Nepal War 1816; Lieut. 2/4th N.I., in 4th Bde. Centre Column. Fur. 13 Aug. 1817 till 1822. Transfd. to 7th N.I. (late 1/4th) May 1824. Fur. s.c. 1826 till death.

WALKER, Thomas (1786-1808). Lieutenant, 26th N.I. *bapt.* Lower Sapey, Worcs., 4 Oct. 1786. Cadet 1803. Arrived in India 2 Dec. 1804. Ensign 20 Oct. 1804. Lieut. 20 Oct. 1804. *d.* Benares 19 Dec. 1808.

Son of William Walker and Sarah his wife.

Services : Posted Lieut. to newly-raised 26th N.I. 1805. Operations in Bundelkhand 1807; Sehlehuganj; Lieut. 26th N.I. Operations against Gopal Singh 1808; Lieut. 2/26th N.I., with detachment under Lieut. Augustus Thomas Watson, *q.v.*

Refs. : Will dated camp, 9 Oct. 1808; proved 19 June 1809.

WALKER, Thomas (1809-1841). Bt. Captain, 1st N.I. *b.* London 27 Feb. 1809. Cadet 1824. Arrived in India 13 Sept. 1825. Ensign 11 Apr. 1825. Lieut. 24 Nov. 1827. Bt. Capt. 11 Apr. 1840. *d.* Kabul 25 Nov. 1841, of wounds received in action at Bemaru on 23 Nov.

bapt. St. Pancras, Middlesex, 9 Aug. 1810. Son of William Walker and Sarah his wife. Brother of Robert Walker, *q.v.* Ed. Westminster; admitted 19 Feb. 1818.

Services : Posted Ensign to 1st N.I. Adjt. 4th Local Horse 28 Oct. 1829; 2nd in comd. do. 8 Dec. 1829 till death. Leave s.c. 8 mos. to China 13 Mar. 1834. First Afghan War 1839-41; Ghazni 1839; reoccupation of Kalat 3 Nov. 1840, comdg. the Cav. (*Lond. Gaz.* 12 Feb. 1841); operations against Ghilzais Aug. 1841; action at Karatu, nr. Saighan Pass, 5 Aug. (horse kld.), comdg. detachment of 4th Irreg. Cav. with force under Lt.-Col. R. E. Chambers, *q.v.*; outbreak at Kabul; comdg. 1 Sqdn. 4th Irreg. Cav. in 2nd expedn. to village of Bemaru, and received a mortal wound when charging across the plain.

Refs. : Westminster School List. The Times, 14 Mar. 1842. M.I. Afghan Memorial Church, Bombay.

WALKER, Thomas Caldecott (1808-1840). Lieutenant, 26th N.I. *b.* Newbold Grange, nr. Rugby, 23 Dec. 1808. Cadet 1826. Arrived in India 2 June 1827. Ensign 3 Feb. 1827. Lieut. 25 Dec. 1828. *d.* Karnal 25 Nov. 1840.

bapt. Newbold-on-Avon, co. Warwick, 10 Mar. 1809. Son of Thomas Walker, of Newbold Grange, and Letitia Mary his wife. Ed. Rugby; admitted 1819.

Services : Posted Ensign to 26th N.I. 19 June 1827. Fur. p.a.

THE BENGAL ARMY, 1758-1834

6 Feb. 1838 till 29 Oct. 1839 ; leave s.c. 1 yr. to Simla 10 Nov. 1840, and *d.* on his way there. No record of active service.

Refs.: Rugby School Register.

WALKER, William (1791-1824). Bt. Captain, Invalid Est. 26th N.I. *b.* Ecclesgreig, co. Kincardine, 31 Jan. 1791. Cadet 1805. Arrived in India 18 Mar. 1807. Ensign 5 Dec. 1806. Lieut. 20 Dec. 1808. Bt. Capt. 24 May 1821. Invalided 16 Apr. 1822. *d.* Raingarh, nr. Sabathu, Punjab, 17 May 1824.

bapt. 12 Feb. 1791. Eldest son of Rev. William Walker, minister of Ecclesgreig, or St. Cyrus, 1781-97, and Margaret Scott his wife.

Services: Barasat C.C. Posted Ensign to 26th N.I. 1807. (? Operations in Bundelkhand 1809 ; Lieut. 2/26th N.I.) Mily. student at Coll. of Ft. Wm. 1814. d.d. 1st Nassiri Bn. 1816-18. Comdg. Resdt.'s escort at Delhi in 1819. Transfd. to 1/26th N.I.

Refs.: Scott's *Fasti*, v. 482. *S.M.* 1825, i. 255.

WALKER, William Bensley (1780-1839). Lieut. Colonel, Invalid Est. 43rd N.I. *b.* Patna 5 Apr. 1780. Cadet 1797. Arrived in India 30 Oct. 1798. Ensign 21 Sept. 1798. Lieut. 1 Nov. 1798. Capt. 15 May 1810. Major 1 Aug. 1818. Lt. Col. 20 July 1823. Invalided 25 Nov. 1825. *d.* Chunar 19 Sept. 1839.

Eldest son of William Walker, of Haileybury, late Surg. Bengal Est., and Elizabeth his wife, dau. of Capt. William Pye, Madras Est. Brother of Edward Thomas Walker, *q.v. m.* Calcutta 27 June 1801, Miss Charlotte Dickson. His dau. *m.* Christian Hohney, *q.v.*

Services: Lieut. 3rd N.I. ; Adjt. 1/3rd N.I. 1807 till 6 Mar. 1809. (? Operations against Lachman Dawa 1809 ; Rajaoli ; Ajaigarh ; Lieut. 1/3rd N.I.) Capt. 2/3rd N.I. With 5th Vol. Bn. 1815-16. Major 2/3rd N.I. Lt. Col. 43rd N.I. May 1824. Comdg. Patna Provl. Bn. 1825-31 ; do. Eur. Invalids at Chunar 18 Mar. 1834 till death.

Refs.: Burke's *Royal Families*, Ped. xcv. Will dated 24 Jan. 1834 ; codicil 28 July 1835 ; proved 4 Oct. 1839. M.I. at Chunar.

WALKER, William Walmesley (1785-1804). Lieutenant, 2nd N.I. *b.* Manchester 13 July 1785. Cadet 1800. Arrived in India 21 Aug. 1801. Ensign 1 Dec. 1801. Lieut. 30 Sept. 1803. *d.* Sikandra 24 Aug. 1804 : kld. in action.

bapt. St. Mary's, Manchester, 19 Aug. 1785. Son of Richard Walker, of Manchester, merchant, and Ann his wife. Brother of Richard Clements Walker, *q.v.*

Services: Ensign d.d. 16th N.I. in 1802. Operations in Jumna Doab 1803; Sasni; Bijaigarh; Kachaura; Ensign 2/2nd N.I. Second Mahratta War 1803-4; battle of Delhi; Hinglaisgarh; Monson's retreat (kld.); Lieut. 2/2nd N.I.

Refs.: E.I.M.C. ii. 559. Intestate; admon. 30 Apr. 1805.

WALKINSHAW, William (1786-1825). Captain, 34th N.I.
b. Paisley 5 Dec. 1786. Cadet 1804. Arrived in India 10 July 1805. Ensign (?) Lieut. 24 Aug. 1805. Capt. 6 Jan. 1823. *d.* Ghazipur 19 May 1825.

bapt. 10 Dec. 1786. Son of Robert Walkinshaw, of Parkhouse, sheriff clerk of co. Renfrew, and Jean Monro his wife, dau. of Daniel Monro, of Summerfield. Brother of Robert Walkinshaw, of Rancho-del-Oro, Mexico.

Services: Lieut. Edin. Art. Mil. Posted Lieut. to 17th N.I. 1806. Nepal War 1814-15; Lieut. 2/17th N.I., in 3rd Div. Adjt. 2/17th N.I. 25 May 1820 till Jan. 1823. Transfd. to 34th N.I. (late 1/17th) May 1824.

WALL, Frederick (1810-1835). 2nd Lieutenant, Artillery. (614) *b.* Stockton, Salop, 19 Sept. 1810. Cadet 1828. Arrived in India 19 Feb. 1829. 2nd Lieut. 12 June 1828. *d. unm.* Quatt Malvern, Salop, 17 Sept. 1835.

bapt. Stockton 23 Sept. 1810. 5th son of Rev. John Wall, rector of Stockton with Bonninghall, and Elizabeth his wife, 7th dau. of William Whitmore, of Dudmaston, Salop. Addiscombe Cadet 1826-28.

Services: Leave s.c. 2 yrs. to Tasmania 30 Oct. 1833; commuted to fur. s.c.; arrived in England 1 Apr. 1835. No record of active service.

Refs.: Family information. *A.J.* N.S. xviii. 143. M.I. Quatt church.

*WALL, Joseph. Lieutenant. Infantry. Cadet (?) Ensign (?) Lieut. (?)

m. Madras 30 July 1785, Regina (or Reginah) Alexander.

Services: Writes from Benares on 22 Mar. 1782, to say that he is unable to refund his prize money for the capture of Bijaigarh, 10 Nov. 1781, as he has spent it. N.F.P.

WALLACE, Francis (1805-1853). Lieutenant, Invalid Est. 18th N.I. *b.* Negapatam, Madras, 22 Dec. 1805. Cadet 1826. Ensign 7 Jan. 1827. Lieut. 15 Nov. 1828. Invalided 16 Jan. 1834. *d.* Benares 13 July 1853, of cholera.

4th son of John Wallace, M.C.S., Commercial Resdt. at Ingeram

THE BENGAL ARMY, 1758-1834   377

(who was cousin-german of Thomas Wallace, 1st and last Baron Wallace of Knaresdale). *m.* Dinapore 12 Feb. 1844, Mrs. Catherine Cupola, dau. of William Graham.

Services : Posted Ensign to 18th N.I. 19 June 1827. No record of active service.

Refs. : Burke's *Landed Gentry*, 5th edn., p. 1454, *s.n.* Wallace, of Asholme, Northumberland. *I.M.* 20 Sept. 1853, p. 546. *G.M.* 1853, ii. 537.

WALLACE, George Thomas (1784/85-?). Lieutenant. 3rd N.I. *b.* Picardy, France, 1784/85. Cadet 1800. Arrived in India 22 Aug. 1801. Ensign 4 Oct. 1801. Lieut. 14 July 1803. Struck off 30 Mar. 1810.

Son of Thomas Wallace.

Services : Ensign d.d. 17th N.I. in 1802 ; posted Ensign to 3rd N.I. ; served in Ceylon with 2nd Vol. Bn. 1803-4. Fur. s.c. 30 Mar. 1805 till struck off.

WALLACE, John (*d.* 1805). Captain, 15th N.I. Cadet 1783. Arrived in India Aug. 1784. Ensign 4 Apr. 1785. Lieut. 4 May 1793. Capt. 28 June 1804. *d. unm.* Bhurtpore 9 Jan. 1805 [1] : kld. in action.

4th and youngest son of William Wallace, of Cairnhill, co. Ayr, and Jean his wife and cousin, dau. of Archibald Campbell, of Succoth.

Services : Apptd. Cadet 6 Mar. 1783 ; reapptd. 7 Jan. 1784 ; sailed for India in the *Earl of Mansfield* 10 Feb. 1784. Posted to 28th Bn. Sepoys 8 Feb. 1790. Third Mysore War 1790-2 ; Arikera ; operations before Savandrug ; Ramgiri ; Shivanagiri ; Seringapatam ; Ensign 28th Bn. Posted to 5th Bengal Eur. Bn. 26 Jan. 1792 ; to 3rd do. 26 Mar. 1793. Second Rohilla War 1794 ; actg. Qmr. 2nd Bde. Adjt. & Qmr. 15th N.I. 1803-4. Operations in Jumna Doab 1803 ; Sasni ; Bijaigarh ; Kachaura ; Lieut. 15th N.I. Second Mahratta War 1803-5 ; battle of Delhi ; Agra ; Laswari ; battle of Deig ; Bhurtpore (kld. in 1st assault) ; Capt. 15th N.I. Was Bde. Major to Col. Maitland, H.M. 75th Ft., at siege of Bhurtpore.

Refs. : Burke's *Landed Gentry*, 13th edn., p. 1821, *s.n.* Wallace, of Busbie, co. Ayr. Burke's *Colonial Gentry*, p. 250, *s.n.* Wallace, of Cairnhill. *Pester*, p. 170. *The Book of Wallace*, by Rev. Chas. Rogers (1889), p. 103. *G.M.* 1805, ii. 970. *S.M.* 1805, p. 805. Will dated Cawnpore 6 Aug. 1803 ; proved 8 Feb. 1805. M.I. Craigie church.

[1] *Note :* (? *d.* 11 Jan. of wounds received on 9th.)

WALLACE, Newton (1790-1845). Lieut. Colonel, 73rd N.I.
b. Dagenham, Essex, 24 June 1790. Cadet 1805. Arrived in India 13 Nov. 1806. Ensign 12 Oct. 1806. Lieut. 2 Apr. 1811. Capt. 1 Mar. 1824. Major 10 Apr. 1831. Lt. Col. 8 Oct. 1836. *d.* Ferozshahr 22 Dec. 1845 : kld. in action.

bapt. Dagenham 18 July 1790. Son of William Augustus Wallace and Mary his wife. (? Brother of the wife of William Benson, *q.v.*) *m.* 1st, Sourabaya, Java, 17 Oct. 1814, Catherina Maria, eldest dau. of H. C. Van der Hoff. *m.* 2nd, Calcutta 15 July 1831, Constantia Harvey, widow of Francis Dwyer. His daus. *m.* William Wynne Apperley, *q.v.*, and Sir Matthew Richard Onslow, Bart., *q.v.*

Services: Barasat C.C. Dec. 1806 till Jan. 1808. Posted Ensign to 27th N.I. 1 Feb. 1807. Operations in Oudh 1810; Ensign 2/27th N.I. With 4th Bengal Vols. 28 Feb. 1811 till Feb. 1817. Capture of Java 1811; Cornelis; Lieut. 4th Vol. Bn. Capture of Jokyakarta 1812; Lieut. 4th Vol. Bn. Attached to Javanese Corps as Adjt. July 1812. Served in Java, Sumatra and E. Archipelago till Nov. 1816. Adjt. Cuttack Legion May 1817 till Oct. 1820. Leave s.c. to sea 16 Sept. 1819; fur. s.c. from Java 16 Oct. 1820 till 15 July 1822. d.d. Cuttack Legion 14 Sept. 1822; Adjt. Rangpur L.I. (late Cuttack Legion, now 1st Bn. 6th Gurkha Rifles) 18 Sept. 1823 till 18 May 1824. First Burma War; operations on Sylhet and Cachar frontiers and in Assam 1823-4; Lieut. Rangpur L.I. (from May till July, Capt. d.d. 46th N.I,). Transfd. as Capt. to 53rd N.I. (late 1/27th) May 1824. Fur. p.a. 1 Jan. 1828 till 13 Sept. 1830. Posted Lt. Col. to 53rd N.I. 19 June 1837; transfd. to 2nd N.I. 10 Oct. 1838. First Afghan War 1840; conducted (as Bdr. 2 cl. without the rank) with 2nd N.I. a large convoy from Ferozepore Feb. 1840, arrived Jalalabad 10 Apr. 1840; operations against Ghilzais May-July 1840; Lt. Col. 2nd N.I. Fur. s.c. from Bombay 1 Mar. 1841 till 9 Apr. 1842. Transfd. to 19th N.I. 24 May 1842; to 26th N.I. 14 Feb. 1843; to 73rd N.I. 28 Nov. 1844. First Sikh War; Mudki; tempy. Bdr. comdg. 5th Bde. 3rd Div.; Ferozshahr (kld.); tempy. comdg. 3rd Div.

Refs.: *De Rhé-Philipe.* M.I. St. Andrew's, Ferozepore.

WALLACE, Samuel Robertson (1804-1875). Major. 39th N.I. *b.* Bombay 3 Mar. 1804. Cadet 1824. Arrived in India 31 May 1825. Ensign 7 Dec. 1824. Lieut. 16 Sept. 1825. Capt. 17 Oct. 1838. Invalided 30 Jan. 1846. Retired 30 Jan. 1858. Hon. Major 30 Jan. 1858. *d.* Gravesend 12 July 1875.

bapt. Bombay 8 Mar. 1807. Son of Samuel Wallace, Major Bo,

THE BENGAL ARMY, 1758-1834

Eur. Regt., and Elizabeth his wife (who re-m. Martin Hillhouse, of Bristol). Nephew of Margaret Wallace, of Limerick.
Services: Ensign d.d. 28th N.I. 11 June 1825; posted Lieut. to 39th N.I. 1825. Fur. s.c. 17 Mar. 1839 till 4 Feb. 1844. No record of active service.
Refs.: The Times, 17 July 1875.

WALLACE, Thomas (1753/54-1788). Lieutenant, Infantry. *b.* in Scotland 1753/54. Cadet 1781. Ensign 1781. Lieut. 5 Aug. 1782. *d.* Berhampore 23 Apr. 1788.
Services: Apptd. Cadet 15 May 1781, aged 27; sailed for India in the *Blandford* 26 June 1781. Lieut. 16th Bn. Sepoys in 1783; 32nd Bn. in July 1787.
Refs.: S.M. 1789, p. 205.

WALLACE, Thomas (1806-1890). Major. 3rd N.I. *bapt.* Chatham 23 Mar. 1806. Cadet 1825. Arrived in India 24 Sept. 1826. Ensign 15 May 1826. Lieut. 11 Oct. 1827. Capt. 15 Sept. 1839. Retired 1 Jan. 1850. Hon. Major 28 Nov. 1854. *d.* 25 Cambray, Cheltenham, 5 Aug. 1890.
Son of Peter Margetson Wallace, Lt. Col. R.A., and Louisa his wife. Grandson of Sarah Mulcaster. *m.* Trinity Church, Sloane St., London, 26 Nov. 1842, Fanny Teresa, dau. of J. W. Long. (She died 8 July 1890.)
Services: Posted Ensign to 3rd N.I. 9 Nov. 1826; actg. Intr. & Qmr. do. 4 Jan. and 13 Dec. 1832. Shekhawat expedn. 1834; Lieut. 3rd N.I. Adjt. 3rd N.I. 6 July till 1 Nov. 1839. Fur. s.c. 23 Jan. 1840 till 15 Jan. 1843. Second Sikh War; Jullundur Doab 1848-9; Rangar Nagal; Dalla; Capt. 3rd N.I. (Medal).
Refs.: A.J. N.S. xxxix. 451. The Times, 7 Aug. 1890.

WALLACE, formerly JAMES, William James (1803-?). Lieutenant. 68th N.I. *b.* Dublin 24 Feb. 1803. Cadet 1824. Admitted 8 Aug. 1825. Ensign 11 Dec. 1824. Lieut. 7 Apr. 1826. Retired 27 Aug. 1832. (Living in Apr. 1851.)
bapt. St. Bridget's, Dublin, 26 Feb. 1803. Son of Thomas James, of Stephen St., Dublin, and Marianne his wife. Brother of Thomas James (1807-1871), *q.v.*
Services: Acted as Lieut. and Adjt. of the Bencoolen Corps before he was apptd. a Cadet. (Letter from C.D. of 24 Nov. 1824, and G.O. of 9 May 1825.) First Burma War; Arakan 1825; Ensign 68th N.I. (India medal). Actg. Adjt. Sylhet Local Bn. 18 May 1826. Actg. Intr. & Qmr. 68th N.I. 11 June 1828. Fur.

s.c. via Penang and China 30 June 1829 till Aug. 1833, when, in consideration of his having served 9 yrs. in the unhealthy climate of Sumatra and Arakan, he was retired on a special pension of £40 p.a. with effect from 27 Aug. 1832.

WALLER, George (*d.* 1768). Ensign, Infantry. Cadet 1767. Ensign 15 Sept. 1767. *d.* 19 Oct. 1768.

Services : N.F.P.

Refs. : Long's *Selections from Records of the Govt. of India* (1869), i. 460.

WALLER, Matthew (*d.* 1780). Lieutenant, Infantry. Cadet 1769. Ensign 12 Sept. 1769. Lieut. 3 Feb. 1773. *d.* 1780, with the Bombay Detachment.

Services : First Mahratta War 1778-80.

WALLER, Robert (1808-1877). Colonel. Artillery. (587) *b.* psh. of St. Thomas, Dublin, 26 Dec. 1808. Cadet 1826. Arrived in India 13 Aug. 1827. 2nd Lieut. 23 June 1827. Lieut. 29 July 1833. Capt. 3 July 1845. Major 8 June 1856. Bt. Lt. Col. 20 June 1854. Bt. Col. 12 Oct. 1857. Retired 9 Feb. 1858. *d.* The Elms, Shirley, Southampton, 17 Oct. 1877.

3rd son of George Waller, of Prior Park, co. Tipperary, and Elizabeth his 2nd wife, dau. of George Studdert, of Kilkishen, co. Clare. Nephew of Sir Robert Waller, 1st Bart., of Newport. *m.* Karnal 19 Nov. 1839, Anne Caroline, eldest dau. of Charles Griffiths, *q.v.* (She died 24 Mar. 1905, aged 83.) [1] Addiscombe Cadet 1824-6.

Services : Posted to 1st Troop 1st Bde. H.A. 26 Sept. 1832; to 1st Troop 3rd Bde. 28 Feb. 1834. Actg. Adjt. Sirhind Div. Art. 15 Apr. 1839. First Afghan War 1840-2; forcing of Khurd Kabul Pass Oct. 1841; outbreak at Kabul (w. 4 Nov. 1841); retreat from Kabul; hostage with Mohd. Akbar 9 Jan. till 21 Sept. 1842 (*Lond. Gaz.* 6 Dec. 1842); Bt. Capt. 1st Troop 1st Bde. (Medal). Granted gratuity of 12 mos. pay for wound. Adjt. & Qmr. 1st Bde. H.A. 25 Dec. 1843. First Sikh War; Sobraon; Capt. 2nd Troop 1st Bde. (Medal). Served with 2nd Troop 1st Bde. 1846-55. Second Sikh War; Jullundur Doab; Dinanagar; Capt. comdg. 2nd Troop 1st Bde. (Medal). Operations on N.W.F. 1851-2; comdg. 2nd Troop 1st Bde., with force under Sir Colin Campbell (Medal). Fur. s.c. 28 Dec. 1855 till retirement. Posted to 1st Bde. H.A. 9 Oct. 1856.

Refs. : Burke's *Peerage*, 1923, p. 2254, *s.n.* Waller, Bart., of Newport, co. Tipperary. Burke's *Landed Gentry of Ireland*, p. 736,

THE BENGAL ARMY, 1758-1834

s.n. Waller, of Prior Park, co. Tipperary. *De La Ferté,* p. 60. *The Times,* 22 Oct. 1877.

[1] *Note:* She was the last survivor of the Kabul prisoners of 1842. (*The Times,* 28 Mar. 1905, p. 10e.)

WALLINGTON, Charles Arthur Granado (1785-1867). General. Colonel 18th N.I. *b.* Ealing 30 Jan. 1785. Cadet 1802. Arrived in India 13 Feb. 1804. Ensign 13 Feb. 1804. Lieut. 3 June 1804. Capt. 1 Oct. 1815. Major 14 Dec. 1826. Lt. Col. 4 Apr. 1832. Col. 20 Dec. 1843. Maj. Gen. 20 June 1854. Lt. Gen. 4 Mar. 1858. Gen. 12 June 1866. *d. unm.* 18 Feb. 1867.

J.P. and D.L. co. Warwick. Elder son of Rev. Charles Wallington, rector of Hawkwell, Essex, and Frances Russell his wife, dau. of Hamlyn Harris, of Daventry.

Services: Ensign N. Bn. Glos. Mil. Posted Lieut. to 18th N.I. 1804; Adjt. & Qmr. 18th N.I. 21 Apr. 1805 till 1814. Second Mahratta War; operations in Bundelkhand 1805-6. Adjt. & Qmr. to detachment for service in Bundelkhand 12 Jan. 1809. Operations in Bundelkhand 1809; Rajaoli; Ajaigarh; Lieut. 1/18th N.I. Adjt. 1/18th N.I. 1814 till 1 June 1815. Nepal War 1816; Capt. 1/18th N.I., in 1st Bde. Rt. Column (India medal). Cuttack insurrection 1816; operations in Khurda against the Chuars Apr. 1817; Capt. 1/18th N.I. Fur. p.a. 28 Mar. 1818 till 10 June 1822. Operations in Jodhpur 1823; Lamba; Capt. 1/18th N.I. Transfd. to 37th N.I. (late 2/18th) May 1824. Siege and capture of Bhurtpore; Capt. 37th N.I. (clasp to India medal). Major 37th N.I., to take charge of 45th N.I. 7 Sept. 1829. Posted Lt. Col. to 66th N.I. 1 Dec. 1832; to 1st N.I. 19 Feb. 1839; to 61st N.I. 9 Dec. 1840. Fur. s.c. 1 Apr. 1841 till death. Col. 32nd N.I. 6 Mar. 1844; 18th N.I. 30 Mar. 1844 till death.

Refs.: Burke's *Landed Gentry,* 13th edn., p. 1822, *s.n.* Wallington, of Dursley. *Boase.*

WALLIS, Henry (*d.* 1793). Captain, 4th Bengal Eur. Bn. Cadet 1771. Ensign 3 Mar. 1773. Lieut. 23 Mar. 1778. Capt. 16 Oct. 1781. *d.* Chinsura 5 Aug. 1793.

Services: Qmr. of Sepoy Corps in 2nd Bde. 22 Mar. 1780 till 24 Oct. 1781. Capt. 2nd Bengal Eur. Regt. in 1782; Supy. Capt., unposted, in July 1787. Transfd. from 1st to 5th Eur. Bn. 26 Jan. 1792; to 6th do. 22 Nov. 1792.

WALLIS, John Eglonton (1789-1825). Captain, 30th N.I. *b.* Colchester 26 Aug. 1789. Cadet 1804. Arrived in India

10 Sept. 1805. Ensign 24 Oct. 1805. Lieut. 17 Apr. 1806. Capt. 1 Jan. 1819. d. Chittagong 25 Jan. 1825.

bapt. Colchester 23 Sept. 1789. Son of John Eglonton Wallis, of the psh. of St. Martin, Colchester, and Sarah his wife. Ed. Felsted.

Services : Posted Lieut. to 15th N.I. 1806. Nepal War 1814-15; Lieut. 2/15th N.I., in 4th Div. Nepal War 1816; Lieut. 2/15th N.I., in 4th Bde. Centre Column. Siege and capture of Hathras 1817; Lieut. 2/15th N.I. With 1st Ceylon Vol. Bn. 1818-19. Transfd. to 30th N.I. (late 1/15th) May 1824.

WALPOLE, George (1784-1807). Lieutenant, Bengal Eur. Regt. *b.* London 27 Mar. 1784. Cadet 1804. Arrived in India 6 Apr. 1806. Ensign 28 Mar. 1806. Lieut. 1807. *d.s.p.* nr. Patna 10 Apr. 1807.

bapt. St. George's, Hanover Sq., 29 June 1784. 2nd son of Hon. Robert Walpole, a clerk of the privy council, afterwards envoy extraordinary and minister plenipotentiary to Portugal, and Diana his 1st wife, dau. of Walter Grosset.

Services : No record of active service.

Refs. : Burke's *Peerage,* 1923, p. 1716, *s.n.* Orford, E. Will dated 7 Dec. 1805; proved 14 Oct. 1807.

WALSH, Charles Gustavus (1810-1866). Colonel. 14th N.I. Comdt. Ludhiana Regt. *bapt.* Dublin 6 Apr. 1810. Cadet 1827. Arrived in India 28 May 1828. Ensign 25 Dec. 1827. Lieut. 8 Oct. 1839. Capt. 10 Sept. 1848. Major 13 Apr. 1859. Bt. Lt. Col. 20 July 1858. Retired 31 Dec. 1861. Hon. Col. 31 Dec. 1861. *d.* Manor House, Dundrum, co. Dublin, 2 Nov. 1866.

2nd son of John Walsh, of Dublin, and Sarah Hayes his wife. *m.* 1st, Booterstown 10 Sept. 1850, Anna Maria Sarah, youngest dau. of Samuel Pratt Winter and cousin-german of Francis Winter, *q.v.* (She died Jan. 1857.) *m.* 2nd, ——. T.C.D. ; Pensioner 18 Oct. 1824, aged 14.

Services : Posted Ensign to 14th N.I. 4 Nov. 1828. Offg. Intr. & Qmr. 32nd N.I. 7 Nov. 1831. Fur. p.a. 6 July 1838 till 17 Nov. 1839. d.d. Sylhet L.I. 19 Nov. 1841 till Dec. 1843; comdg. at Silchar 13 July 1842. Intr. & Qmr. 14th N.I. 24 Nov. 1843 till 1 Sept. 1846. First Sikh War; Ferozshahr (w. & horse kld.— *Lond. Gaz.* 23 Feb. 1846); Bt. Capt. 14th N.I. (Medal). 2nd in comd. Regt. of Ludhiana (now 2nd Bn. 11th Sikh Regt.) 1 Aug. 1846 till 22 Dec. 1847. Fur. s.c. 16 Jan. 1848 till 4 Jan. 1851. Offg. in P.W.D. 1852-3. Leave s.c. 25 Mar. 1854; fur. s.c. 17 Jan.

THE BENGAL ARMY, 1758-1834

1855 till 21 Aug. 1857. Comdt. Regt. of Ludhiana 18 Feb. 1858 till retirement. Served with Gurkha force under Jang Bahadur 27 Feb. till 9 Apr. 1858. Mutiny campaign 1858; siege and capture of Lucknow; Major comdg. Gurkhas (Medal with clasp). Second China War 1860; Bt. Lt. Col. comdg. Ludhiana Regt., with force for protection of Shanghai against Taiping rebels (Medal).

Refs.: Family information. Burke's *Landed Gentry of Ireland*, p. 774, *s.n.* Winter, of Agher. *Alumni Dub.* *G.M.* 1867, i. 266.

Note : According to *Service A.L., Bengal,* Vol. viii, he was granted a gratuity of 6 mos. pay for wound received in action nr. Kabul on 14 Nov. 1841. As neither he nor his Regt. served in Afghanistan, this would appear to be a mistake.

*WALSH, John Elisha (1750/51-1789). Bt. Ensign, Invalid Est. Infantry. *b.* 1750/51. Bt. Ensign 22 Nov. 1781. Invalided (?) *d.* Chunar 25 July 1789, aged 38.

Services : Apptd. a Bt. Ensign of Mil. from Sergt. of Art.

Refs. : M.I. old cemetery, Chunar.

WALSH, William (*d.* 1785). Lieutenant, 2nd Bengal Eur. Regt. Country Cadet 1781. Ensign 22 May 1781. Lieut. 5 Sept. 1782. *d.* Calcutta 22 Sept. 1785.

Services : Sailed for India as a recruit in the *Fortitude* 13 Mar. 1781, and served as a private in the Carnatic. Apptd. Cadet in Bengal 29 Apr. 1782, " being a young man of respectable connexions "; but was not actually commissioned till 27 Feb. 1785, when he was a Corporal of Art.

Refs. : Will dated —— Sept. 1785; proved 1 Oct. 1785.

WALSHAM, Thomas (1751/52-1786). Lieutenant, Infantry. *b.* London 1751/52. Cadet 1781. Ensign 10 Apr. 1781. Lieut. 1 Aug. 1782. *d.* Cawnpore 1 Feb. 1786.

Services : Apptd. Cadet 26 Jan. 1781; sailed for India in the *Osterley* 13 Mar. 1781, aged 29. First Mahratta War; Lieut. with Goddard's detachment in W. India.

WALTER, Augustus (1792-1820). Lieutenant, 30th N.I. *b.* London 16 Feb. 1792. Cadet 1807. Arrived in India 21 Mar. 1809. Ensign 19 Aug. 1807. Lieut. 29 Nov. 1809. *d.* Tanghi, B. & O., 9 Jan. 1820.

Son of Edward Walter, coroner, and Charlotte his wife. Marlow Cadet.

Services : Posted Ensign to 26th N.I. 1809; transfd. to newly-raised 1/30th N.I. 1815.

Refs.: Will dated Barrackpore 16 July 1818; proved 2 Feb. 1820. M.I. Cuttack cemetery.

WALTER, Francis (1777-1808). Captain, 19th N.I. *b.* 13 Jan. 1777. Cadet 1795. Admitted 10 Nov. 1797. Ensign 19 Nov. 1796. Lieut. 30 Oct. 1797. Capt. 28 Oct. 1806. *d.* Balasore 12 June 1808.

bapt. Lakhipur 12 Feb. 1777. Son of Henry Walter, Senior Merchant, B.C.S., and Ann (or Frances) his 3rd wife, dau. of Francis Peacock. Brother of Charlotte Draper Walter. (*Probably* nephew of Francis William Peacock, *q.v.*) Ed. Charterhouse; admitted Apr. 1790.

Services : Lieut. 12th N.I. in 1798; transfd. to 19th N.I.; Capt. Lt. do. 8 May 1806; Capt. 2/19th N.I. No record of active service.

Refs.: Hickey, iv. 406. Will dated Balasore 11 June 1808; proved 22 June 1808. M.I. Balasore.

WALTER, George (1798-1823). Lieutenant, Engineers. *bapt.* St. Ann's, Blackfriars, London, 8 Dec. 1798. Cadet 1815. Ensign 1 Sept. 1818. Lieut. 10 Oct. 1821. *d.* Calcutta 5 Sept. 1823, of fever.

Son of William Walter, of 34 Devonshire Pl., and Anne his wife. Addiscombe Cadet 1814-16.

Services : Detained in England 1817-18 on a trig. survey, and to learn art of sapping and mining. Posted to S. & M. With Malwa F.F. 1820-23.

Refs.: M.I. in S. Park St. cemetery, Calcutta.

WALTER, James Saddel (or Siddal) (*d.* 1783). Lieutenant, Infantry. Country Cadet 1778. Ensign 27 Apr. 1779. Lieut. 7 Jan. 1781. *d.* 7 Mar. 1783, with the Bombay detachment.

Services : Lieut. Bombay Marine 4 Aug. 1778; apptd. Cadet 10 Sept. 1778. Ensign 2/1st Bengal Eur. Regt. in Oct. 1779. First Mahratta War.

WANE, Wilfred (*d.* 1770). Cadet, Infantry. Cadet 1769. *d.* Apr. 1770.

Services : N.F.P.

WARBURTON, Robert (1812-1863). Lieut. Colonel, Artillery. (651) *bapt.* Coolbanagher, Queen's Co., 8 Mar. 1812. Cadet 1830. Arrived in India 29 Dec. 1831. 2nd Lieut. 9 June 1831. Lieut. 18 Mar. 1840. Capt. 21 Feb. 1849. Bt. Major 13 Mar. 1859. Lt. Col. 5 Jan. 1860. *d.* Peshawar 10 Nov. 1863.

8th son of Richard Warburton, of Garryhinch, King's Co., J.P.

THE BENGAL ARMY, 1758-1834

and D.L., high sheriff Queen's Co. 1801, and Anne his wife, dau. of Thomas Kemmis, of Dublin. *m.* an Afghan lady, formerly wife of a Kabul Sirdar, and said to have been a niece of the Amir Dost Muhammad Khan. Father of Col. Sir Robert Warburton, K.C.I.E. (*D.N.B.*). Addiscombe Cadet 1829-31.

Services : First Afghan War 1839-42 ; Ghazni 1839 (Medal) ; occupation of Kabul ; 2nd Lieut. 2nd Coy. 6th Bn. Art. ; took comd. of Shah Shuja's Own Art. 23 Aug. 1839 ; operations in Kohistan Sept.-Nov. 1840 ; Tutam-dara (*Lond. Gaz.* 9 Jan. 1841) ; Julgah ; Parwandara ; Kabul insurrection. Delivered over 29 Dec. 1841 as a hostage to Nawab Mohd. Zaman Khan ; made over to Mohd. Akbar Khan July 1842 ; released and joined Gen. Pollock at Kabul 21 Sept. 1842. Intr. & Qmr. 6th Bn. 20 Jan. 1843. Gwalior campaign ; Maharajpur ; Bde. Qmr. of Foot Art. (Bronze star). Capt. comdt. 3rd Coy. Art., Gwalior Contingent, 13 Jan. 1844 till Jan. 1852. Fur. Apr. 1857 till 7 Mar. 1860. Posted to 3rd Bn. and to comd. Art. Div. at Amritsar 28 Mar. 1860 till 1863 ; transfd. to R.A. Oct. 1861 ; to comd. R.A. of Peshawar Div. 1863 ; tempy. comdg. Peshawar Bde. June 1863 till death.

Refs. : Burke's *Landed Gentry of Ireland*, p. 746, *s.n.* Warburton, of Garryhinch. Burke's *Colonial Gentry*, ii. 804, *s.n.* Warburton, of Vancouver. *De Rhé-Philipe.* *G.M.* 1864, i. 262. M.I. at Peshawar.

WARD, Andrew George (1798-1846). Captain, 68th N.I. *b.* London 19 May 1798. Cadet 1818. Admitted 5 Sept. 1818. Ensign 21 Apr. 1818. Lieut. 16 Nov. 1818. Capt. 1 Nov. 1830. *d.* Lahore 20 May 1846.

Grandson of John Ward, of Derby, carpenter and builder. (*Probably* son of Thomas Ward.) Nephew of Andrew Mathias, of 11 New Burlington St., London. *m.* St. John's, Calcutta, 5 Apr. 1825, his cousin Hannah, eldest dau. of Rev. William Ward, of Serampore, Bengal, Baptist missionary (*D.N.B.*).

Services : Ensign d.d. 1/9th N.I. Sept. 1818 ; posted to 1/1st N.I. Mar. 1819 ; transfd. to newly-raised 1/34th N.I. 25 Sept. 1823 ; to 68th N.I. (late 2/34th) May 1824. First Burma War ; Arakan 1825 ; Lieut. 68th N.I. d.d. 20th N.I. 26 Mar. till 25 Oct. 1827. Actg. Intr. & Qmr. 68th N.I. 7 Mar. 1828 ; permanent do. 28 Sept. 1829 till 31 Aug. 1831. Jodhpur demonstration 1834 ; Capt. 68th N.I. First Sikh War ; Sobraon ; Capt. 68th N.I., Bde. Major (Medal).

Refs. : *De Rhé-Philipe.* Will dated 8 Aug. 1839 ; proved 6 June 1846. M.I. at Lahore.

WARD, John (1778-1842). Lieut. Colonel. 58th N.I. *bapt.* St. Clement Danes, London, 7 June 1778. Cadet 1799. Arrived in India 1 Dec. 1800. Ensign 1 Oct. 1800. Lieut. 7 Mar. 1802. Capt. 21 Sept. 1814. Major 1 May 1824. Lt. Col. 7 Mar. 1826. Retired 9 Jan. 1833. *d.* Vassal Rd., N. Brixton, 22 May 1842, aged 65.

Son of James Ward and Joanna his wife. *m.* (?)

Services: Posted Ensign to 2/9th N.I. 17 Apr. 1801. Second Mahratta War 1803-5; Agra; Laswari; Gwalior; Monson's retreat (w. at Banas R. 24 Aug. 1804); Bhurtpore; Lieut. 2/9th N.I. Adjt. 2/9th N.I. 1805; do. Chittagong Provl. Bn. 19 June 1806 till 1815. Capt. Lt. 5 Dec. 1812. Capt. 1/9th N.I. Fur. p.a. 29 Jan. 1823 till 8 Oct. 1824. Transfd. as Major to 21st N.I. (late 2/9th) May 1824. Siege and capture of Bhurtpore; Major 21st N.I. Posted Lt. Col. to 21st N.I. 7 Dec. 1826; to 1st Bengal Eur. Regt. 29 Nov. 1828; to 58th N.I. 1829. Tempy. Bdr. 2 cl. in Rohilkhand 15 Nov. till 30 Dec. 1829. Fur. p.a. 21 Jan. 1832 till retirement.

Refs.: *G.M.* 1842, ii. 106. *The Times,* 24 May 1842.

WARD, Thomas (1787-1824). Lieutenant, 45th N.I. *b.* 22 Jan. 1787. Cadet 1808. Arrived in India 27 Oct. 1809. Ensign (20 Mar. 1810) 28 Sept. 1810. Lieut. 16 Dec. 1814. *d.* Gauhati, Assam, 21 Oct. 1824.

bapt. Tong, Salop, 28 Jan. 1787. Eldest son of John Ward and Mary Andrews his wife. *m.* 16 Jan. 1815, Miss Matilda Elizabeth Rouband. (She died 14 Dec. 1876, aged 80.) His dau. *m.* Charles Lloyd Edwards, *q.v.*

Services: Barasat C.C. Posted to 23rd N.I. 1810; Lieut. 1/23rd N.I. Served with 5th Vol. Bn. in Java 1814-16, sometime d.d. Colonial Eur. Hrs. Third Mahratta War 1817-19; Lieut. 2/23rd N.I. Intr. & Qmr. 2/23rd N.I. 20 Nov. 1819 till May 1824. Transfd. to 45th N.I. (late 1/23rd) May 1824; Intr. & Qmr. do. 17 June 1824 till death. First Burma War; Chittagong and Assam 1824; Lieut. 45th N.I.

WARDE, Arthur (1787-1838). Lieut. Colonel, 3rd L.C. *b.* 25 Nov. 1787. Cadet 1803. Arrived in India 4 Sept. 1804. Cornet 11 Mar. 1805. Lieut. 5 Dec. 1807. Capt. 1 Jan. 1819. Major 24 July 1828. Lt. Col. 30 Dec. 1833. *d.* Landour 12 Nov. 1838.

bapt. New Woodstock, Oxon., 18 Dec. 1787. 2nd son of Charles Warde, of Westerham, Kent, and Anne his wife, eldest dau. of Arthur Annesley, of Bletchington, Oxon. Brother of Henry

THE BENGAL ARMY, 1758-1834

William Warde, *q.v.*, and cousin-german of William Warde, *q.v.*
m. Allahabad 15 Sept. 1816, Anne, dau. of Thomas Denson, of
Ellesmere, Salop. (She died London 20 June 1853, aged 53.)

Services: Posted Cornet to 3rd N.C. 1806. (? Operations in
Bundelkhand 1809; Rajaoli; Ajaigarh; Lieut. 3rd N.C.) Adjt.
3rd N.C. 29 May 1810 till 20 Nov. 1818. Siege and capture of
Hathras 1817; Lieut. 3rd N.C. Third Mahratta War 1817-18;
Jawad; Bt. Capt. 3rd N.C. Leave s.c. to sea 9 Oct. 1819 till
27 Jan. 1822. Operations in Jodhpur 1823; Lamba; Capt. 3rd
L.C. Comdt. 5th Local Horse 15 Dec. 1825 till 1 Nov. 1832. Fur.
p.a. 10 Feb. 1833 till 11 Dec. 1835. Posted Lt. Col. to 1st L.C.
10 Sept. 1834; to 10th L.C. 25 Nov. 1834; to 6th L.C. 31 Oct.
1835; to 3rd L.C. 26 Dec. 1835. Leave s.c. to Mussoorie 15 May
1838.

Refs.: Burke's *Landed Gentry*, 13th edn., p. 1831, *s.n.* Warde,
of Squerryes Court, Kent. *Howard & Crisp*, iv. 55, *s.n.* Warde.
A.J. N.S. xxvii. 142. M.I. Westerham, Kent, and Landour
cemetery.

WARDE, Henry William (1788-1819). Captain, 6th L.C. *b.*
Bucknell, Oxon., 22 Oct. 1788. Cadet 1804. Arrived in India
16 July 1806. Cornet 4 Apr. 1806. Lieut. 18 Dec. 1813. Capt.
13 Dec. 1818. *d.* at sea 30 Aug. 1819, on board the *David Scott*.

bapt. ptely. 27 Oct. 1788; publicly at Bucknell 16 Nov. 1788.
3rd son of Charles Warde and Anne his wife. Brother of Arthur
Warde, *q.v.* Ed. Rugby; admitted Jan. 1800.

Services: Barasat C.C. Posted Cornet to 6th N.C. 1807 and
served throughout with that Regt. Settlement of Hariana 1809;
Bhawani. Qmr. 6th N.C. 19 Oct. 1813 till Dec. 1818. Third
Mahratta War 1817-18; Sitabaldi; Nagpur; Chanda.

Refs.: Burke's *Landed Gentry*, 13th edn., p. 1831, *s.n.* Warde,
of Squerryes Court, Kent. *Howard & Crisp*, iv. 55, *s.n.* Warde.
Rugby School Register.

WARDE, William (1788-1858). Lieut. Colonel. 5th L.C. *b.*
Bradfield House, Berks., 9 Feb. 1788. Cadet 1805. Arrived in
India 13 Nov. 1806. Cornet 2 Jan. 1807. Lieut. 27 Feb. 1812.
Capt. 13 May 1825. Major 14 Dec. 1835. Retired 1 Mar. 1836.
Hon. Lt. Col. 28 Nov. 1854. *d.* 19 Grosvenor Pl., Bath, 23 Jan.
1858.

bapt. Bradfield 3 Mar. 1788. 3rd son of Gen. George Warde, of
Woodland Castle, co. Glam., and Charlotte his wife, dau. of Rt.
Rev. Spencer Madan, Bishop of Peterborough. Cousin-german of
Arthur Warde, *q.v. m.* 1st, Dinapore 18 June 1815, Isabella, eldest

dau. of Innis Delamain, *q.v.* (*See also* John William Gibbs.) (She died Nagpur 29 Nov. 1835.) *m.* 2nd, Manchester 25 July 1838, Catherine, dau. of Edward Hawkins, of Court Herbert, co. Glam. (She died Bath 4 Apr. 1866, aged 77.) Ed. Westminster; left Dec. 1805.

Services : Posted Cornet to 5th N.C. 1807 ; comdd. a troop of 5th N.C. as escort to G.G. (the Earl of Moira) on tour, Oct. 1814 ; Intr. & Qmr. 5th N.C. 2 Dec. 1814 till 27 Feb. 1821. Third Mahratta War 1817-19 ; Lieut. 5th N.C. Leave s.c. 12 mos. to Presdy. 19 Apr. 1820. Dy. Paymr. Hoshangabad 26 Feb. 1821 ; do. Benares 21 Jan. 1825 till 6 Feb. 1828. Mily. Asst. to Resdt. at Nagpur Apr. 1829 ; offg. Head Asst. do. 9 Apr. 1832 ; permanent do. 15 Jan. 1835 till 24 Feb. 1836.

Refs.: Burke's *Landed Gentry*, 13th edn., p. 1831, *s.n.* Warde, of Squerryes Court, Kent. *Howard & Crisp*, iv. 58, *s.n.* Warde. *Westminster School Register. Pte. Journal of the Marquess of Hastings*, p. 101. *G.M.* 1858, i. 337. Will dated 11 Dec. 1856 ; codicil 10 Aug. 1857 ; admon. 14 Jan. 1859.

WARDEN, George (1783-1831). Lieut. Colonel, 71st N.I. *b.* British Factory, Lisbon, 12 Dec. 1783. Cadet 1798. Arrived in India 8 June 1800. Ensign 16 Dec. 1799. Lieut. 29 May 1800. Capt. 16 Dec. 1814. Major 18 Oct. 1822. Lt. Col. 1 May 1824. *d.* Saugor 23 Aug. 1831.

3rd son of George Warden and Elizabeth Barclay his 1st wife. Nephew of Francis Warden, Dir. E.I. Co. 1838-51. *m.* Benares 29 Nov. 1801, Matilda, dau. of Francis Wilford, *q.v.* (*See also* William Baker (1775-1825).) (She died 29 May 1868, aged 83.) Father of William Ellison Warden, *q.v.*

Services : Posted to 2/16th N.I. 15 Apr. 1801. Transfd. to newly-raised 27th N.I. 1805. Adjt. Benares Provl. Bn. 1807-8. Operations in Oudh 1810 ; Lieut. 2/27th N.I. Adjt. 2/27th N.I. 31 Jan. 1811 till 4 May 1815. Fur. p.a. 16 Nov. 1817 till 1 July 1820. Posted Lt. Col. to 54th N.I. (late 2/27th) May 1824 ; to 46th N.I. 1826 ; to 27th N.I. 3 Apr. 1828 ; to 71st N.I. 28 Aug. 1829.

Refs.: *A.J.* N.S. vii. 159. Will dated 17 Aug. 1831 ; proved 24 Oct. 1834. M.I. old cemetery, Saugor.

WARDEN, William Ellison (1810-1857). Bt. Major, 23rd N.I. *b.* Cawnpore 28 Feb. 1810. Cadet 1826. Arrived in India 5 Oct. 1827. Ensign 20 May 1827. Lieut. 23 Feb. 1836. Capt. 8 Aug. 1847. Bt. Major 20 June 1854. *d.* Mhow 12 June 1857.

bapt. Cawnpore 3 Apr. 1811. Eldest son of George Warden, *q.v.*

m. Lucknow 28 Sept. 1847, Priscilla Amelia, eldest dau. of John Lloyd, Comdr. R.N., and niece of George William Aylmer Lloyd, *q.v.*
Services : Posted Ensign to 23rd N.I. 3 Jan. 1828. Operations against Afridis in Kohat Pass Feb. 1850 ; Capt. 23rd N.I.
Refs. : Burke's *Landed Gentry of Ireland*, p. 411, *s.n.* Lloyd, of Lloydsboro'. *I.M.* 17 Sept. 1857, p. 593. *G.M.* 1857, ii. 347. M.I. Mhow old cemetery.

WARDLAW, Thomas (1787-1863). Colonel. 69th N.I. *b.* Dunfermline 12 Oct. 1787. Cadet 1805. Arrived in India 13 Dec. 1806. Ensign 6 Dec. 1806. Lieut. 7 Feb. 1809. Capt. 1 May 1824. Major 8 June 1832. Lt. Col. 27 Jan. 1839. Retired 2 Feb. 1842. Hon. Col. 28 Nov. 1854. *d.* 22 May 1863. *bapt.* Dunfermline 21 Oct. 1787. Eldest son of Henry Wardlaw, brewer in Dunfermline, and Euphan Chalmers his wife. *m.* Aberdeen 23 Sept. 1835, Margaret, 3rd dau. of James Davidson, M.D., of Marischal Coll., Aberdeen. (She died 23 Nov. 1869.)
Services : Barasat C.C. 8 mos. Posted Ensign to 23rd N.I. 1807. (? Settlement of Hariana 1809 ; Bhawani ; Lieut. 2/23rd N.I.) Third Mahratta War 1817-19 ; Lieut. 2/23rd N.I. ; actg. S.A.C.G. with force under Lt.-Col. J. W. Adams, *q.v.*, in Betul valley Feb. 1819. Junior Asst. to A.G.G. Saugor 19 Feb. 1821 ; Principal do. 12 Sept. 1823 till 24 Sept. 1824. Transfd. to 45th N.I. (late 1/23rd) May 1824. Fur. p.a. 20 Feb. 1834 till 11 Nov. 1836. Posted Lt. Col. to 45th N.I. 19 Mar. 1839 ; to 69th N.I. 30 Oct. 1841.
Refs. : The Wardlaws in Scotland, by J. C. Gibson (Edin. 1912), p. 111, *s.n.* Wardlaw, of Wester Luscar.

WARDLAW, William (1772-1812). Capt. Lieutenant. Artillery. (294) *b.* Burntisland 3 Dec. 1772. Cadet 1791. Admitted 2 Dec. 1791. Fireworker 8 Feb. 1792. Lieut. 6 Nov. 1800. Capt. Lt. 25 Aug. 1804. Resigned 26 Mar. 1807. *d.s.p.* 27 Aug. 1812.
Eldest son of William Wardlaw, Capt. R.N., and Elizabeth Balfour his wife, dau. of Robert Balfour Ramsay, of Balbirnie.
Services : Apptd. Cadet 13 Apr. 1791 ; sailed for India in the *Airly Castle* 10 May 1791. Posted to 2nd Bn. Art. 23 Mar. 1792. To Madras Aug.-Oct. 1793 for siege of Pondicherry ; Lieut. F. d.d. 5th Coy. 3rd Bn. Fur. 8 Dec. 1801 till resignation.
Refs. : Burke's *Landed Gentry*, 12th edn., p. 1577, *s.n.* Wardlaw-Ramsay, of Whitehill, Midlothian. *The Wardlaws in Scotland*, by J. C. Gibson, p. 179, *s.n.* Wardlaw, of Abden.

WARDROPER, Frederick Bayley (1809-1883). Major. 3rd Bengal Eur. Regt. *b.* Midhurst, Sussex, 7 July 1809. Cadet 1828. Arrived in India 2 Oct. 1829. Ensign (17 Feb. 1829) 14 Sept. 1829. Lieut. 24 Nov. 1839. Capt. 15 Nov. 1853. Retired 15 Oct. 1854. Hon. Major 28 Nov. 1854. *d.* 27 May 1883.

bapt. Midhurst 4 Aug. 1809. Son of Richard Wardroper, of Midhurst, solicitor, and Frances his wife. *m.* Calcutta 17 Dec. 1833, Frances Mary, sister of Charles Herbert White, *q.v.* (She died Calcutta 19 Dec. 1841.)

Services: Posted Supy. Ensign to 6th N.I. 1829. Leave s.c. to Mauritius 14 June 1832 till 20 Nov. 1833. Transfd. to 69th N.I. 24 Sept. 1835; to 6th N.I. 10 Aug. 1836; to 25th N.I. 21 Nov. 1837. Disturbances in Bundelkhand 1840-2; Jigni Mar. 1840; Chirgaon Apr. 1841; Intr. & Qmr. and Legion Staff, Bundelkhand Legion. Fur. p.a. 11 Feb. 1843 till 1846. Second Sikh War; passage of Chenab; Sadulapur; Chilianwala; Gujerat; Bt. Capt. 25th N.I. (Medal with 2 clasps). S.S.O. at Darjeeling 8 Nov. 1850. Posted to newly-raised 3rd Bengal Eur. Regt. 15 Nov. 1853.

Refs.: *I.N.* Vol. i, p. 12.

WARE, Charles (1740-1803). Major General. Colonel 6th N.I. *b.* 1740. Cadet 1765. Ensign 11 Aug. 1765. Lieut. 28 Dec. 1766. Capt. 17 May 1770. Major 12 Jan. 1781. Lt. Col. 17 July 1787. Col. 1 Mar. 1794. Maj. Gen. 3 May 1796. *d.* Laswari 1 Nov. 1803: kld. in action.

2nd son of Richard Ware, of Harefield, and Catherine his wife (? *née* Gam). Brother of Richard and Thomas Ware. *m.* (?) (She died Calcutta 11 Mar. 1780.)

Services: 2nd Lieut. newly-raised 85th, Crawford's Vols., 6 Aug. 1759; 1st Lieut. do. (?), till its disbandment in May 1763; h.p. do. till death. Served at capture of Belleisle in 1761, and in Portugal. Apptd. Lieut. on the Bombay Est. 1764; sailed for India in the *Asia* 16 May 1764; resigned and went to Bengal 1765; permitted to remain in India as a free merchant 23 Oct. 1765. Ensign 3rd Bengal Eur. Regt. in 1766. Apptd. to comd. 24th Bn. Sepoys (late 8th Bn. of Nawab-Wazir's troops) in New Bde. 7 Aug. 1777; to comd. 17th N.I. 1 Jan. 1781; comdd. 7th Bn. Sepoys till 31 May 1786; Major in 4th Bde. on 1 July 1787; comdg. 2nd Eur. Bn. in Dec. 1788; comdg. 3rd Bde. Sepoys at Dinapore in July 1789. Apptd. to comd. 6th Eur. Bn. 1 Feb. 1790; to comd. 2nd (later altered to 1st) Bde. of Army for service in Rohilkhand 17 Oct. 1794. Second Rohilla War 1794; battle of Bitaurah;

THE BENGAL ARMY, 1758-1834 391

Col. comdg. Rt. Bde. Second Mahratta War; battle of Delhi (w.); Agra; Laswari (kld.—head shot off by a cannon-ball).
Refs.: Family information. *E.I.M.C.* ii. 442 *n.* Will dated Agra fort 17 Oct. 1803; proved 10 Feb. 1804.

SCOTT-WARING, Charles Edward Hastings (1786-1813). Lieutenant, 7th N.C. *b.* Oct. 1786. Cadet 1803. Arrived in India 14 Aug. 1804. Cornet 11 Mar. 1805. Lieut. 4 Nov. 1810. *d.* Calcutta 2 Feb. 1813.

bapt. Bromley, Kent, 2 Nov. 1786. 2nd son of John Scott-Waring, *q.v.*, and Elizabeth his 1st wife. Nephew of Henry Scott, *q.v.*, cousin-german of Jonathan Scott (1788-1838), *q.v.*, and uncle of Edward Stokes Scott-Waring and Henry Jonathan Reade, *qq.v.* Ed. Shrewsbury; admitted 1799.

Services: Posted Cornet to 7th N.C. 1805. Fur. 2 Aug. 1807 till 3 Oct. 1810. Apptd. to G.G.B.G. 1811. Capture of Java 1811; Lieut. G.G.B.G. Adjt. G.G.B.G. 15 Feb. 1812 till death.

Refs.: Burke's *Landed Gentry*, 13th edn., p. 1569, *s.n.* Scott, of Betton, Salop. *Shrewsbury School Register. V.B.G.* Will dated 1 Apr. 1811; proved 27 Apr. 1813. M.I. in S. Park St. cemetery, Calcutta.

SCOTT-WARING, Edward Stokes (1809-1851). Captain. 6th L.C. *b.* Stockton-on-Tees 4 Oct. 1809. Cadet 1825. Arrived in India 16 May 1826. Cornet 5 Nov. 1825. Lieut. 10 Apr. 1831. Capt. 1 Mar. 1844. Cashiered 3 Apr. 1848. *d.* Meerut 16 Feb. 1851.

bapt. Redmarshall, co. Durham, 28 Oct. 1809. Younger son of Edward Warren Hastings Scott-Waring, B.C.S., and Mary his wife, *née* Maclean, widow of Capt. Smith. Grandson of John Scott-Waring, *q.v.* Ed. Charterhouse; admitted 1820, left Mar. 1823.

Services: Posted Cornet to 6th L.C. 1826. d.d. 4th L.C. 6 Jan. 1832 till 15 Jan. 1833. Fur. s.c. 9 May 1842 till June 1845. No record of active service.

Refs.: Burke's *Landed Gentry*, 2nd edn., p. 1198, *s.n.* Scott, of Betton, Salop. *Misc. Gen. et Her.*, 3S. iv. 58. *A Record of the Redes*, pp. 72-3. *Charterhouse School List. I.M.* 2 June 1848, pp. 325-6; 17 Apr. 1851, p. 222. Portrait by Masquerier.

SCOTT-WARING, John (1747-1819). Major. Infantry. *b.* Charlton Hall, Salop, 24 Oct. 1747. Cadet 1767. Ensign 14 Aug. 1767. Lieut. 4 Oct. 1769. Capt. 3 Jan. 1778. Major 21 Feb. 1781. Resigned 1781. *d.* Half Moon St., Piccadilly, 5 May 1819. Assumed the additional surname of Waring 17 Nov. 1798. Eldest son of Jonathan Scott, of Shrewsbury, and Mary his wife. Brother of Henry Scott, *q.v.* *m.* 1st, Calcutta 22 June 1772, Elizabeth, dau. of Alexander Blackrie, of Bromley, Kent. (She died 26 Oct. 1796, aged 50.) Father of Charles Edward Hastings Scott-Waring, *q.v.*, and grandfather of Edward Stokes Scott-Waring, *q.v.* *m.* 2nd, 1796, Mary, dau. of Samuel Hughes, of Seskin, co. Tipperary. (She was found dead at the bottom of the staircase at his house in Fulham 6 Feb. 1812.) *m.* 3rd, 15 Oct. 1812, Harriet Pye, dau. of —— Bennet, a tanner of Tooting, formerly wife of Lieut. James Esten, R.N., and sometime an actress at Covent Gdn. Theatre. (She died 29 Apr. 1865, a reputed centenarian.)

Services : See *D.N.B.* Sailed for India as a Cadet for Bombay in Mar. 1766; transfd. to Bengal Est. 1767. Adjt. 1st Bengal Eur. Regt. First Rohilla War 1774 ; battle of St. George. Apptd. A.D.C. to Warren Hastings 19 Sept. 1778 ; to comd. 12th Bn. Sepoys at Chunar May 1780. Sent by Hastings to England as his agent, and arrived London 17 Dec. 1781. M.P. for West Looe 1784-90 ; M.P. Stockbridge, Hants, 1790. Pub. 1782, " Short Review of Transactions in Bengal during the last ten Years," etc.

Refs. : Burke's *Landed Gentry*, 13th edn., p. 1569, *s.n.* Scott, of Betton, Salop. *Misc. Gen. et Her.* 3S. iv. 58-9 ; 4S. v. 246-7. *D.N.B. D.I.B. E.I.M.C.* ii. 242-7. Holzman. *S.M.* 1819, i. 586. Portrait by J. J. Masquerier—engraved J. Turner—pub. 27 Feb. 1802.

WARLOW, Thomas (1797-1839). Captain, Engineers. *b.* Haverfordwest 1 Sept. 1797. Cadet 1815. Admitted 27 Sept. 1816. Ensign 15 Dec. 1817 (? 4 July 1818). Lieut. 1 Oct. 1819. Capt. 28 Sept. 1827. *d.* Meerut 2 Feb. 1839.

bapt. St. Martin's, Haverfordwest, 27 Dec. 1797. Eldest son of John Warlow, of Castle Hall, co. Pembroke, wine and brandy merchant, and Catherine his wife, 4th dau. of Thomas Picton, of Poyston, co. Pembroke. Nephew of Lt.-Gen. Sir Thomas Picton, G.C.B. (*D.N.B.*). *m.* Nagpur 27 Apr. 1824, Mary Prudence Ord. (She *re-m.* Laurence Fyffe, M.D., and died his widow 20 Oct. 1877, aged 77.) Addiscombe Cadet 26 Feb. 1812 till 10 Nov. 1814.

Services : Siege and capture of Hathras 1817 ; Asst. Field Engr. Third Mahratta War ; Mandala (*Lond. Gaz.* 7 Dec. 1818) ; Asirgarh (ib. 30 Aug. 1820) ; Asst. Field Engr. 3rd Div. Field Engr. with Nagpur Subsdy. Force 21 July 1820 till 19 Jan. 1824. District Bk. Mr. Cawnpore Div. 24 Dec. 1823. Fur. s.c. 4 Jan. 1830 till 28 Dec. 1833. Comdt. Corps of S. & M. 4 Jan. 1834. Shekhawat

THE BENGAL ARMY, 1758-1834

expedn. 1834; offg. Field Engr., Capt. comdg. S. & M. Field Engr. Upper Provinces 24 Feb. 1835; Garr. and Executive Engr. at Delhi 28 Apr. 1835 till 10 Sept. 1836; do. N.W.P. 6 Dec. 1837.
Refs.: Burke's *Landed Gentry*, 13th edn., p. 1782, *s.n.* Turbervill, of Ewenny Priory, co. Glam. *Hist. of the Warlow Family*, by G. H. Warlow, London, 1926. *A.J.* xxvii. 216; xxviii. 78; N.S. xxix. 63. M.I. at Meerut.

WARNER, Goodwin (1779-1812). Captain, 22nd N.I. *b.* 1779. Cadet 1794. Arrived in India 26 Sept. 1795. Ensign 14 Oct. 1795. Lieut. 15 Feb. 1797. Capt. 6 June 1805. *d.* Fatehgarh 2 Jan. 1812, aged 32.

Of Carlow. (*Probably* of the same family as the next.) *m.* Calcutta 3 Jan. 1801, Marian Grace, dau. of Sir Henry White, K.C.B., *q.v.* (*See also* James Scott (1778-1820).)

Services: Apptd. Cadet 22 Apr. 1795; sailed for India in the *Lord Thurlow* 24 May 1795. Ensign 6th Bengal Eur. Bn. in Feb. 1796; Lieut. 5th N.I.; transfd. to newly-raised 22nd N.I. 1804; Capt. 2/22nd N.I.

Refs.: M.I. Fatehgarh fort cemetery.

WARNER, John Henry (1783-1861). Captain, Pension Est. 6th N.I. *b.* Dublin Sept. or Oct. 1783. Cadet 1799. Arrived in India 23 Oct. 1800. Ensign 24 Aug. 1800. Lieut. 8 Jan. 1801. Capt. 31 May 1813. Pensioned in India 1 Sept. 1815. *d.* Rajshahi, Bengal, 27 July 1861, aged 77.

Only son of Charles Warner, of Carlow, and Florinda his 1st wife, dau. of John Higginbotham, of the Manor of Grangeford, co. Kildare. *m.* 1st, Calcutta 7 Dec. 1813, Miss Charlotte Blechynden. (She died Bauleah 2 Oct. 1833.) *m.* 2nd, Calcutta 3 Mar. 1835, Sarah Caroline, eldest dau. of B. Orde, of Long Ridge House, Northumberland.

Services: Sailed for India in the *Kent* 3 May 1800, and was wounded in action when she was captured by *La Confiance* off the Sand Heads, 7 Oct. 1800. Posted to 1/6th N.I. 17 Apr. 1801. Disturbances in Ganjam, Madras, 1801; Lieut. 6th N.I. Capt. Lt. 6th N.I. 12 May 1811. Nepal War 1814-15; Kalanga; Capt. 1/6th N.I., in 2nd Div. After transfer to Pension Est. was for some time employed as Executive Ofr., 4th Div., P.W.D.

Refs.: Family information. *A.A.R.*, ii. 142-4.

*WARNER, Paul. Lieut. Fireworker. Artillery. Fireworker 1766.

Services : *Probably* commissioned from the ranks in May 1766 in order to fill a vacancy caused by the " Batta mutiny." N.F.P.
Refs. : B.M. Add. MS. 6050, p. 90.

WARNER, Thomas. Ensign. Infantry. Cadet 1783. Ensign 17 May 1785. Struck off 1788.

Services : Apptd. Cadet 19 Mar. 1783 ; should have sailed for India in the *Middlesex* 27 Dec. 1783. Shown as on fur. in July 1787, but probably never arrived in India.

WARNER, William Kerby (1811-1856). Bt. Lieut. Colonel, Artillery. (628) *b.* Kensington 15 Oct. 1811. Cadet 1829. Arrived in India 17 Feb. 1830. 2nd Lieut. 12 June 1829. Lieut. 17 Nov. 1837. Capt. 31 Mar. 1847. Bt. Major 7 June 1849. Bt. Lt. Col. 1 May 1855. *d.* at sea 21 Jan. 1856, on board the *Malta*, between Bombay and Aden.

bapt. 21 Nov. 1811. 4th and youngest son of Joseph Warner and Laura Elizabeth his 2nd wife, dau. of Robert Hoadley Ashe, D.D. *m.* St. Mary Abbots, Kensington, 3 Aug. 1841, Frederica Elizabeth, 7th dau. of George Battye, of Campden Hill. (She died 13 Feb. 1886, aged 64.) Addiscombe Cadet 2 May 1827 till 12 June 1829.

Services : Cadet d.d. Foot Art. at Cawnpore 7 Jan. 1832 ; Actg. 2nd Lieut. (having been 2 yrs. in India) 12 Mar. 1832. Posted to 1st Coy. 6th Bn. 12 Jan. 1838 ; to 4th Troop 1st Bde. H.A. 7 Sept. 1838 ; to 2nd Troop 1st Bde. 5 Feb. 1840. Fur. s.c. 26 Mar. 1839 till 29 July 1842. Adjt. & Qmr. 4th Bn. 3 Dec. 1843 till 17 June 1846. Gwalior campaign ; Maharajpur ; Lieut. & Adjt. 4th Bn. (Bronze star). First Sikh War ; Ferozshahr (w.), Sobraon ; Bt. Capt. & Adjt. 4th Bn., Comy. Ord. (Medal with clasp). Comdd. 1st Troop 3rd Bde. H.A. 1848-55. Second Sikh War ; Ramnagar ; Sadulapur ; Chilianwala ; Gujerat ; Capt. 1st Troop 3rd Bde. (Medal with 2 clasps). Fur. p.a. 30 Mar. till 22 Dec. 1855 ; s.c. 6 mos. Jan. 1856.

Refs. : Burke's *Landed Gentry*, 4th edn., p. 1614, *s.n.* Warner, of Antigua. Oliver's *Hist. of Antigua*, iii. 186. *I.N.* No. 17, p. 398. *I.M.* 4 Mar. 1856, p. 131. Intestate ; admon. 17 Apr. 1857.

WARRE, William. Lieutenant, Infantry. Cadet 1775. Ensign 4 Mar. 1777. Lieut. 2 Aug. 1778.

Services : Apptd. Cadet 22 Nov. 1775 ; sailed for India in the *Nassau* 9 Jan. 1776. Second Mysore War.

Refs. : Will dated Nellore, 9 July 1781 ; proved (Madras) 8 Apr. 1783.

WARREN, Benjamin William (1759/60-1787). Lieutenant, Infantry. *b.* Surrey 1759/60. Cadet 1779. Ensign 12 Feb.

THE BENGAL ARMY, 1758-1834 395

1780. Lieut. 22 Feb. 1781. *d.* at sea 22 May 1787 : drowned on board the *Ganges* in Balasore roads.

Son of Ann Warren. Brother of Augustus and Peter Francis Warren.

Services: Apptd. Cadet 28 Jan. 1779; sailed for India in the *True Briton* 16 June 1779, aged 19. Was Adjt. 10th N.I. in Mar. 1786. Was on sick leave, together with Adam Nuttall, *q.v.*, when he met his death.

Refs.: Will dated 30 Mar. 1787; proved 28 May 1787.

WARREN, Frederick (1799-1818). 2nd Lieutenant, Artillery. (471) *b.* 21 Dec. 1799. Cadet 1816. 2nd Lieut. 25 Sept. 1817. *d.* Calcutta 10 May 1818.

bapt. Bangor 25 Feb. 1800. 4th son of Very Rev. John Warren, dean of Bangor 1793-1838, and Elizabeth his wife, *née* Crooke, of Preston, Lancs. Brother of Maj.-Gen. Sir Charles Warren, K.C.B. (*D.N.B.*), and cousin-german of Pelham Donnithorne Warren, *q.v.* Addiscombe Cadet 1814-16.

Services: No record of active service.

Refs.: Peds. of Anglesey and Carnarvon Families, by J. E. Griffiths, 1914, p. 388. M.I. at Dum-Dum.

WARREN, George (1802-1884). General. Colonel 1st Eur. Bengal Fus. *b.* Madras 15 Aug. 1802. Cadet 1818. Admitted 19 June 1819. Ensign 6 Oct. 1818. Lieut. 30 Apr. 1820. Capt. 13 Apr. 1830. Major 25 Feb. 1837. Lt. Col. 6 Aug. 1843. Col. 5 Dec. 1853. Maj. Gen. 28 Nov. 1854. Lt. Gen. 6 Apr. 1863. Gen. 23 Aug. 1869. *d.* 1 Brandon Terr., Southsea, 22 June 1884.

bapt. Vepery, Madras, 25 July 1803. Son of George Warren and Elizabeth Eleanora his wife. Brother of William and Frederick Warren. *m.* 1st, Madras Presdy. 1 May 1824, Miss Clara Jessy Connell. (She died Agra 25 Oct. 1838.) *m.* 2nd, Calcutta 15 Aug. 1840, Isabella Barry, dau. of William Barry Fitzgerald, of Dublin. (She died Southsea 15 Jan. 1900, aged 80.)

Services: Ensign d.d. Bengal Eur. Regt.; posted to do. 7 July 1820; d.d. Gorakhpur L.I. 19 Aug. 1822 till 14 Jan. 1823. Fur. 27 Jan. 1823 till 19 May 1824. Siege and capture of Bhurtpore (s.w. 3 times—lost 3 fingers of left hand—*Lond. Gaz.* 4 July 1826); Lieut. Bengal Eur. Regt. (India medal). Adjt. Mhairwara Local Bn. 8 May 1826. Leave s.c. to Singapore 14 Aug. 1837 till 1 June 1838. First Afghan War 1839; Ghazni (s.w. 3 times—ib. 30 Oct. 1839); Major 1st Eur. Regt. (Medal). Offg. Town Major Ft. Wm. 17 Feb. 1840. Leave s.c. 6 mos. to sea 14 Apr. 1841. Town and

LIST OF THE OFFICERS OF

Fort Major Ft. Wm. 5 Mar. 1842 till 1851. Posted Lt. Col. to 1st Eur. L.I. 11 Sept. 1843; to 17th N.I. 1849; to 1st Eur. Fus. Nov. 1849. Bdr. 2 cl. comdg. Barrackpore 4 Nov. 1851 till May 1854. Second Burma War 1852; Rangoon; Bdr. comdg. Bengal Bde. under Gen. Godwin (Medal). Transfd. to Benares Bde. May 1854. Fur. s.c. 4 Aug. 1854 till 1859; fur. 2 yrs. 9 Nov. 1859. Col. 1st Eur. Bengal Fus. 1854-69. Durani 3 cl. 15 Feb. 1842. Hon. A.D.C. to G.G. 12 Jan. 1848 till 1855.

Refs.: Boase. *The Times*, 25 June 1884, p. 7.

WARREN, Isaac Eyles (1736/37-1809). Captain. Artillery. (39) *b.* 1736/37. Cadet 1762. 2nd Lieut. 3 Dec. 1763. Lieut. 25 Jan. 1765. Capt. Lt. Feb. 1767. Capt. 4 Mar. 1770. Resigned 18 Jan. 1772. Pensd. on Lord Clive's fund 15 July 1772. *d.* Warham, Norfolk, 16 Oct. 1809, aged 72.

(*Perhaps* son of Isaac Warren, Acct. Gen. to the Coy. in England, and Anne his wife.) *m.* (?)

Services: Was a Volunteer at the siege of Quebec, "and it was his solemn task to support on the rock (12 Sept. 1759) and witness the last moments of the Immortal Wolfe." (M.I.) "He was presented with one of the rifle balls which gave that great soldier his death wound." (*M.M.*)

Refs.: *M.M.* 1809, p. 642. M.I. in churchyard of Warham All Saints', Wells, Norfolk.

WARREN, Pelham Donnithorne (1812-1837). Lieutenant, 19th N.I. *b.* 25 Sept. 1812. Cadet 1831. Arrived in India 27 Oct. 1832. Ensign 19 May 1832. Lieut. 21 Sept. 1835. *d.* Cuttack 18 June 1837.

bapt. Nottingham 20 Nov. 1812. Only son of Robert Warren, Bk. Mr. of Warley, Essex, sometime Capt. 4th D.G., and Mary his wife, eldest dau. of Rev. Thomas Donnithorne, of Holme-Pierrepont. Cousin-german of Frederick Warren, *q.v.* Ed. Repton; admitted Feb. 1822. Winchester Scholar 1825-30. Addiscombe Cadet 12 Feb. 1830 till 8 Dec. 1831.

Services: Cadet d.d. 13th N.I. 22 Nov. 1832; posted Ensign to 19th N.I. 19 Dec. 1833. Actg. Intr. & Qmr. 43rd N.I. 11 Apr. 1835; Intr. & Qmr. 19th N.I. 29 July 1835 till death. Rising in Cuttack July 1836; Lieut. 19th N.I.

Refs.: *Peds. of Anglesey and Carnarvon Families*, p. 388. *Repton School Register. Kirby. A.J.* N.S. xxv. 37. M.I. at Cuttack.

WARTON, John (1779-?). Captain. 16th N.I. *bapt.* Milton Abbas 8 Oct. 1779. Cadet 1793. Arrived in India 24 Feb. 1796.

THE BENGAL ARMY, 1758-1834

Ensign 16 Oct. 1794. Lieut. 13 Sept. 1796. Capt. 21 Sept. 1804. Resigned in India 16 Oct. 1810.
Son of Rev. John Warton and Elizabeth his wife.
Services: Lieut. 10th N.I. in 1798.

WARWICK, Francis (1802-1857). Lieutenant, Pension Est. 5th N.I. *bapt.* Warwick, Cumberland, 18 May 1802. Cadet 1819. Ensign 7 Apr. 1820. Lieut. 11 July 1823. Pensioned in India 2 Feb. 1827. *d.* Moradabad 4 June 1857: kld. by mutineers.
Son of Robert Warwick, of Warwick Hall, Cumberland,[1] and Mary Anderson his wife.
Services: Posted to 2/30th N.I. 1820; transfd. to 2nd N.I. July 1823; to 5th N.I. (late 1/2nd) May 1824. No record of active service. Was Postmr. at Moradabad when kld.
Refs.: A.J. xxiv. 79. *Naval & Mily. Mag.*, ii. 677-8.
[1] *Note:* A descendant of Edward, Lord of Arley, whose family had held Warwick Hall since the Conquest.

WATERFIELD, John[1] (1812-1858). Major, 38th N.I. *b.* London 9 Aug. 1812. Cadet 1828. Arrived in India 29 May 1829. Ensign 20 Jan. 1829. Lieut. 30 Mar. 1837. Capt. 24 Jan. 1845. Major 25 May 1857. *d.* Firozabad, nr. Agra, 14 May 1858: kld. by mutineers.
bapt. ptely. 1812; publicly at St. John Evang., Westminster, 14 Oct. 1818. 5th and youngest son of William Waterfield, of Barton St., Westminster, accomptant, Exchequer Bill Office, and Elizabeth Weekes Patey his wife. *m.* Benares 11 July 1837, Helen Ellenor, dau. of Sir Robert Blair, *q.v.* (*See also* Henry Clayton.) Ed. Westminster; admitted 24 Sept. 1819.
Services: Ensign d.d. 33rd N.I. 13 July 1829; posted to 9th N.I. 13 Mar. 1830; transfd. to 38th N.I. 2 July 1832; actg. Adjt. do. 12 Oct. 1838. Adjt. 3rd Recruit Depot Bn. 7 Sept. 1839 till 19 Oct. 1840. Actg. Adjt. 38th N.I. 24 Apr. 1841. First Afghan War 1840-2; operations against Ghilzais; action at Ilmi 29 May 1841 (w.—*Cal. Gaz.* 7 July 1841); operations of Kandahar force; Baba-Wali 25 Mar. 1842 (*Lond. Gaz.* 4 Sept. and 24 Nov. 1842); actg. A.D.C. to Maj.-Gen. Nott 15 May 1842; Ghazni; Kabul; Lieut. 38th N.I., with Nott's force (Medal). Adjt. 38th N.I. 21 June 1843 till 30 May 1844. Comdt. 2nd Bn. Bundelkhand Legion 9 Apr. 1844. Fur. s.c. 21 Feb. 1847 till Nov. 1849. Offg. Bde. Major at Ludhiana 18 May 1850; permanent do. 1 Aug. 1850; do. Meerut Nov. 1850 till Sept. 1855; D.A.A.G. Meerut Div.

28 Sept. 1855 till May 1857. Mutiny campaign 1857-8. Apptd. to comd. at Aligarh 1858, and was travelling thither by *dak* at night when he was surrounded by mounted mutineers and murdered.

Refs.: Family information. *Westminster School List.* I.M. 5 July 1858, p. 551. Name on Westminster School Memorial Column.

¹ *Note:* Name given in family Bible as John Bothamley Waterfield.

WATERHOUSE, Robert Jephson (1788-1805). Ensign, 12th N.I. *bapt.* Brinny, co. Cork, 12 Jan. 1788. Cadet 1802. Arrived in India 6 Sept. 1803. Ensign 10 Sept. 1803. *d.* Bhurtpore 9 Jan. 1805 : kld. in action.

Son of Robert Waterhouse and Philippa Jephson his wife.

Services: Second Mahratta War 1804-5; Bhurtpore (kld. in 1st assault); Ensign 2/12th N.I.

WATERS, Edmund Frederick (1783-1866). General, C.B. Colonel 68th N.I. *b.* London 16 Dec. 1783. Cadet 1799. Arrived in India 10 Dec. 1800. Ensign 1 Nov. 1800. Lieut. 1 July 1803. Capt. 1 Sept. 1815. Major 11 July 1823. Lt. Col. 13 May 1825. Col. 16 Nov. 1835. Maj. Gen. 23 Nov. 1841. Lt. Gen. 11 Nov. 1851. Gen. 17 Sept. 1861. *d.* Wyvenhoe rectory, Essex, 2 May 1866.

bapt. St. James's, Westminster, 13 Apr. 1790. Eldest son of Edmund Waters, of Kingsbury, Middlesex, and Ann his wife. *m.* 26 Oct. 1819, Eliza Stephens, dau. of T. S. Aldersey, of Lisson Grove. (She died 30 Dec. 1857, aged 65.)

Services: Posted Ensign to 2/17th N.I. 17 Apr. 1801. Operations in Jumna Doab 1803. Second Mahratta War 1803-6; Aligarh; battle and defence of Delhi; pursuit of Holkar; Lieut. 2/17th N.I. (India medal). Adjt. 1/17th N.I. 18 Jan. 1805; do. 2/17th 1 Aug. 1813 till 4 May 1815. Leave s.c. 6 mos. to sea Feb. 1806. Nepal War 1814-15; Jitpur; Lieut. 2/17th N.I., in 3rd Div. (clasp to India medal). Capt. 2/17th N.I. Fur. u.p.a. 4 Dec. 1815 till May 1820. Comdd. Rangpur Local Bn. 28 Sept. 1822; do. Dinajpur Local Bn. 1824 till 12 July 1825. First Burma War; Assam 1824-5; action at Hautgong 28 Oct. 1824; Rajachokey 2 and 5 Nov. 1824 (*Lond. Gaz.* 19 Apr. 1825); occupation of Rangpur Jan. 1825, succeeding Lt.-Col. Alfred Richards, *q.v.*, on the latter being wounded (ib. 19 July 1825); Major comdg. Dinajpur Bn. (clasp to India medal). Transfd. to 34th N.I. (late 1/17th) May 1824. To comd. newly-raised 4th Extra N.I. 21 May 1825; transfd. to 59th N.I. 28 Dec. 1826; to 66th N.I. 24 Sept. 1828;

to 47th N.I. 16 Dec. 1830. Operations in Cuttack 1833 ; Lt. Col.
comdg. 47th N.I. Fur. p.a. 5 Feb. 1834 till 11 Nov. 1839. Transfd.
to 63rd N.I. 7 Dec. 1833 ; to 29th N.I. 26 Aug. 1834. Posted Col.
to 27th N.I. 31 May 1836 ; to 46th N.I. 29 Nov. 1839 ; to 68th N.I.
1840. Bdr. 2 cl. comdg. troops in Rohilkhand and Kumaon Aug.
1840 till Feb. 1845. Fur. p.a. 21 Feb. 1845 till death. C.B.
20 July 1838.
Refs.: *E.I.M.C.* iii. 393-8. *Boase. G.M.* 1866, i. 928. *The
Times,* 4 May 1866.

WATHERSTON(E), Dalhousie. Captain. Infantry. Cadet
1770. Ensign 19 Nov. 1771. Lieut. 1 Aug. 1776. Capt.
24 Feb. 1781. Resigned Nov. 1782. (*d.* before 1803.)
Of Manderston, Berwick ; M.P. Boston, Lincs., 1784. Brother
of Lt.-Col. Robert Watherstone (Robert Witherston(e), *q.v.*), Mrs.
Christiana Landels, and Elizabeth, wife of William Tait, of Pirn,
and grand-uncle of the fourth wife of William Henry Penrose, *q.v.*
m. Jane, dau. of Rev. Thomas Walker and cousin-german of Forster
Walker, *q.v.* (She *re-m.* 5 June 1810, Gen. Hon. William Mordaunt
Maitland, 4th son of James, 7th Earl of Lauderdale, and died 5 Sept.
1854.)
Services : Adjt. of Sepoys in 3rd Bde. in 1777 ; posted to Nawab-
Wazir of Oudh's troops 30 Apr. 1777. First Mahratta War 1778-82 ;
Paymr. to Bombay detachment under Col. Goddard.
Refs.: Burke's *Peerage,* 1923, p. 1346, *s.n.* Lauderdale, E.
Holzman. *Misc. Gen. et Her.* N.S. i. 413.

WATKINS, Alexander (*d.* 1831). Major. Artillery. (227)
Country Cadet 1781. Admitted 5 Nov. 1781. Fireworker
28 July 1782. Lieut. 10 July 1788. Capt. Lt. 8 Jan. 1796.
Capt. 19 Feb. 1802. Major 7 May 1806. Retired 29 Sept. 1808.
d. Upper Baker St., London, 7 Jan. 1831.
m. Anne. (She died 18 Apr. 1841, aged 54.)
Services : Lieut. 3rd Bn. Art. in July 1787. Fur. 5 Mar. 1804
till 17 Mar. 1808. No record of active service.
Refs.: *G.M.* 1831, i. 281.

WATKINS, Hutton (1789-1818). Lieutenant, 1st N.I. *b.*
Linlithgow 21 Dec. 1789. Cadet 1804. Arrived in India 10 Sept.
1805. Ensign 13 Nov. 1805. Lieut. 17 Sept. 1806. *d.* Kalpi,
U.P., 18 Nov. 1818.
bapt. 10 Jan. 1790. Son of Thomas Watkins, merchant, and
Christian his wife, dau. of John Hutton, J.P. for co. Lanark.
Brother of James Watkins, *q.v. m.* 21 Oct. 1814, Maria, dau. of

William Henry Cooper, *q.v.*, and sole legatee of Acheson Maxwell, *q.v.* (*See also* Gordon Caulfeild and J. B. Robinson.)

Services : Posted Lieut. to 1st N.I. 1806, and served throughout with that Regt. (? Operations in Bundelkhand 1807 ; Chamir ; Sehlehuganj. Operations against Lachman Dawa 1809 ; Rajaoli ; Ajaigarh ; Lieut. 2/1st N.I.) Nepal War 1814-15 ; Lieut. 2/1st N.I., in 1st Div. Siege and capture of Hathras 1817 ; Lieut. 2/1st N.I. Third Mahratta War 1817-18 ; Dhamoni ; Lieut. 2/1st N.I.

Refs.: Burke's *Landed Gentry*, 13th edn., p. 1843, *s.n.* Strang-Watkins, of Shotton, Salop. *S.M.* 1819, i. 584.

WATKINS, James (1787-1871). Colonel. 67th N.I. *b.* Linlithgow 12 Apr. 1787. Cadet 1804. Arrived in India 10 Sept. 1805. Ensign 25 Oct. 1805. Lieut. 17 Apr. 1806. Capt. 11 July 1823. Major 4 May 1831. Lt. Col. 9 Mar. 1837. Retired 21 Jan. 1838. Hon. Col. 28 Nov. 1854. *d.* 6 Buckingham Terr., Edinburgh, 7 Jan. 1871.

Of Calderbank, co. Lanark ; *s.* to Shotton Hall, Salop, Dec. 1849. *bapt.* 22 Apr. 1787. Son of Thomas Watkins and Christian his wife. Brother of Hutton Watkins, *q.v. m.* 1st, Middle 18 Jan. 1825, his cousin Mary Ann, dau. of Watkin Watkins, of Shotton. (She died Almora, U.P., 13 Aug. 1828.) *m.* 2nd, 1843, Helen, dau. of John Buchanan, of Catter. (She died 11 Sept. 1882.)

Services : Posted Lieut. to 14th N.I. 1806. Intr. & Qmr. 1/14th N.I. 1 July 1814 till 28 Jan. 1822. Leave s.c. to Mauritius 31 Jan. till 30 Oct. 1817. Third Mahratta War 1818 ; Dhamoni ; Mandala ; Garhakota ; Lieut. 1/14th N.I. Fur. s.c. 24 Jan. 1822 till 17 Sept. 1825. Transfd. as Capt. to newly-formed 31st N.I. July 1823 ; to 62nd N.I. (late 2/31st) May 1824. d.d. 23rd N.I. 30 July till 1 Dec. 1828. Fur. p.a. 7 Feb. 1832 till 19 Sept. 1835. Comdd. 3 Coys. 62nd N.I. in Apr. 1836 in a punitive expedn. against the Jat insurgent Golab Singh at the village of Baloowalee in Ludhiana district. Posted Lt. Col. to 67th N.I. 21 Aug. 1837.

Refs. : Burke's *Landed Gentry*, 13th edn., p. 1843, *s.n.* Strang-Watkins, of Shotton, Salop. *A.J.* N.S. xxi. 100. *The Times*, 10 Jan. 1871.

WATKINS, Joseph (*d.* 1762). Lieutenant, Infantry. Cadet 1760. Ensign 1 Mar. 1760. Lieut. 8 July 1762. *d.* Calcutta 15 Oct. 1762.

Services : N.F.P.

Refs. : Will dated 12 Oct. 1762 ; proved 26 Oct. 1762.

THE BENGAL ARMY, 1758-1834

WATKINS, Rice (1745/46-1784). Bt. Ensign, Infantry. b. 1745/46. Bt. Ensign 15 Aug. 1783. d. Chunar 5 (or 15) Nov. 1784, aged 38.

m. Hannah.

Services: "Agreed that Rice Watkins, Serjt.-Major in the G.G.B.G., who has served the Coy. above 16 years and is much disabled by Wounds which he has received in the Service, be apptd. a Brevet Ensign of Militia." (M.C. 15 Aug. 1783.)

Refs.: V.B.G. Will dated Chunar 3 Nov. 1784; proved 22 Mar. 1785. M.I. Lower Lines, Old Cemetery, Chunar.

*WATKINS, William. Cadet. Deserted at Madras 1769.

Services: Tried by G.C.M. at Fort St. George, 23 Aug. 1769, for desertion. Sentenced to be "drummed through the Ranks with a halter about his neck, and to be confined till an opportunity offers of sending him hence to England." (Cons., Fort St. Geo., 25 Aug. 1769.)

WATSON, Alexander (1786-1806). Lieutenant, 5th N.I. b. St. Ninian's, co. Forfar, 28 Aug. 1786. Cadet 1803. Arrived in India 14 Aug. 1804. Ensign 31 Aug. 1804. Lieut. 21 Sept. 1804. d. St. Helena 8 Mar. 1806, on board the *Carmarthen*.

Son of James Watson and Agnes Scott his wife. m. Calcutta 20 Jan. 1806, Miss Mary Mattocks.

Services: Posted Lieut. to 5th N.I. Fur. 31 Nov. 1805 till death.

Refs.: S.M. 1807.

WATSON, Archibald (1779-1855). Lieut. General. Colonel 1st L.C. b. Rhynd, co. Perth, Jan. 1779. Cadet 1794. Arrived in India 4 Mar. 1797. Cornet 8 Nov. 1795. Lieut. 28 Apr. 1797. Capt. 11 Mar. 1805. Major 18 Aug. 1814. Lt. Col. 4 May 1823. Col. 5 June 1829. Maj. Gen. 28 June 1838. Lt. Gen. 11 Nov. 1851. d. Abbethune 22 Aug. 1855.

Eldest son of James Watson, younger, of E. Rhynd, afterwards of Tipperty, and Anne his wife, 6th dau. of Robert Scott, of Dunninald and Usan, M.P. co. Forfar. Cousin-german of the wife of J. H. Salmond, q.v., and of the mother of W. S. Dodgson, q.v. m. 1st (?) m. 2nd, Inchbrayock Cottage, Montrose, 30 July 1821, his cousin Anne, dau. of Archibald Scott, of Usan, and aunt of Charles Scott (1814-1847), q.v. His daus. m. R. G. Macgregor, q.v., Murray Mackenzie, q.v., and James Remington, q.v.

Services: Apptd. Cadet 6 Apr. 1796. Posted to 1st N.C. 1797. Served in Rohilkhand 1798; in Oudh and Rohilkhand 1802. Capt. Lt. 1st N.C. 22 Jan. 1802. Qmr. 1st N.C. 29 May 1800 till 1803.

Operations in Jumna Doab 1803; Kachaura; comdg. Sqdn. 1st N.C. Second Mahratta War 1803-5; Aligarh; Agra; Laswari; Shamli; capture of Deig; Bhurtpore; Capt. Lt. 1st N.C. (India medal). Operations in Bundelkhand 1810-11; Bichaund; in comd. of a detached force against Lachman Singh and Omrao Singh; successful action on 19 Nov. 1810 at Bhamori, and other minor actions; Capt. 1st N.C. Reduction of Kalinjar 1812; Capt. 1st N.C. Third Mahratta War 1817-18; against the Bhattis of Hariana 1818; Major 1st N.C. Fur. Dec. 1819 till 29 Oct. 1823. Posted Lt. Col. to 7th L.C. 1823; Lt. Col. Comdt. do. 13 May 1825. Comdd. garr. of Monghyr 31 Oct. 1827 till 11 Apr. 1828. Posted Col. to 7th L.C. 1829; to 10th L.C. 6 June 1833; to 1st L.C. 22 Apr. 1835; to 11th L.C. 2 Apr. 1844; 1st L.C. 6 Dec. 1847 till death. Comdt. Allahabad fort 22 July 1840 till 6 Dec. 1847. Fur. 13 Jan. 1850 till death.

Refs.: *Memorials of Four Old Families*, by Capt. D. Wimberley (Inverness, 1893), p. 125. Burke's *Heraldic Illustrations* (1853), iii. plate cx. *E.I.M.C.* i. 387-94. *Boase*. *I.M.* 31 Aug. 1855, p. 498. *G.M.* 1855, ii. 443.

WATSON, Augustus Thomas (1778-1832). Lieut. Colonel, 40th N.I. *bapt.* Carlton Parva (St. Cross), Lincs., 6 Mar. 1778. Cadet 1796. Arrived in India 7 Nov. 1798. Ensign 15 Oct. 1797. Lieut. 10 Sept. 1798. Capt. 27 Apr. 1809. Major 13 Jan. 1822. Lt. Col. 1 May 1824. *d.* Aligarh 29 Oct. 1832.

Son of Thomas Watson and Elizabeth his wife. *m.* Dinapore 5 Mar. 1806, Elizabeth Hepzebah, reputed dau. of Richard Henry, *q.v.* (*See also* Henry Philipps.) (She died 5 Oct. 1855, aged 69.)

Services: Lieut. 11th N.I. Leave s.c. 6 mos. to sea 3 Mar. 1803. Transfd. to newly-raised 23rd N.I. 9 Nov. 1803; to 26th N.I. 1805; Capt. Lt. do. 30 Dec. 1807. Operations against Gopal Singh; successful surprise of enemy at Santi, nr. Mohar, 4 Oct. 1808; comdg. detachment 26th N.I. Capt. 2/26th N.I. Third Mahratta War 1818; Dhamoni; Satanwara (s.w. cheek and shoulder, horse shot—*Lond. Gaz.* 20 Jan. 1821); Capt. 1/26th N.I.[1] Successful attack on a party of *Grassias* (professional robbers) at Bhopal Mar. 1820; Capt. comdg. party of 2/26th N.I. Transfd. as Lt. Col. to 52nd N.I. (late 2/26th) May 1824. (? First Burma War; Cachar 1825; Lt. Col. 52nd N.I.) Transfd. to 42nd N.I. 1826; to 36th N.I. 2 May 1828; to 40th N.I. 3 Oct. 1831.

Refs.: M.I. Aligarh.

[1] *Note:* His widow unsuccessfully claimed the reward of £2,000 offered by Govt. for the discovery of the Pindari chief Chitu.

WATSON, Brook (1787-1817). Lieutenant, 24th N.I. *bapt.*
Brixton, Devon, 13 Mar. 1787. Cadet 1804. Arrived in India
25 Mar. 1806. Ensign 17 Mar. 1806. Lieut. 1 Feb. 1807. *d.
unm.* Calcutta (? Barrackpore) 11 Oct. 1817, aged 30.
Son of John Watson and Rebecca his wife.
Services: Barasat C.C. Posted Lieut. to 24th N.I. 1807.
Capture of Java 1811 ; Lieut. 6th Vol. Bn. Served with 6th Vols.
in Java till 1816. In charge of Pay and Comst. Depts. at Weltervreden 1815-16.
Refs.: Will dated Calcutta 20 Mar. 1817 ; proved 6 Dec. 1817.
M.I. S. Park St. cemetery, Calcutta.

WATSON, Edward John (1800-1859). Lieut. Colonel. 59th
N.I. *b.* co. Bedford 27 May 1800. Cadet 1820. Admitted
20 Aug. 1821. Ensign 4 Apr. 1821. Lieut. 11 Sept. 1823.
Capt. 4 Feb. 1833. Major 29 Aug. 1851. Retired 8 May 1853.
Hon. Lt. Col. 28 Nov. 1854. *d.* Bucksbridge, Wendover, 2 Mar.
1859.
Eldest son of Maj.-Gen. Sir James Watson, K.C.B., sometime
comdg. Presdy. Div., and Sarah his wife. Nephew of John Watson,
Capt. R.N. His sister *m.* Joseph Graham, *q.v. m.* 1st, Allahabad,
31 Jan. 1834, Jane Campbell, 3rd dau. of Robert Moseley Thomas,
of Calcutta, atty. (*See also* Sir Henry Byng Harington.) (She
died Ludhiana 14 Dec. 1840, aged 25.) *m.* 2nd, Egham, Surrey,
24 June 1855, Louisa Elizabeth, dau. of George Frederick Furnivall,
of Egham.
Services: Posted Ensign to 2/3rd N.I. 1821 ; transfd. to 2/7th
N.I. 23 May 1822 ; to 30th N.I. July 1823 ; to 59th N.I. (late
1/30th) May 1824. d.d. Hill Rangers 27 Mar. 1826. A.D.C. to
his father, Provl. C.-in-C. Bengal, 8 Apr. till 5 Sept. 1835. Comdt.
Arakan Local Bn. 6 May 1836 till 13 Mar. 1837. Comdt. 3rd
Depot Bn. at Aligarh 4 Mar. 1842 till 1 Mar. 1843, when broken
up. With Army of Reserve (for Afghanistan) Oct. 1842 till Jan.
1843 ; Capt. 59th N.I., Bde. Major 3rd Inf. Bde. Fur. p.a. 17 Mar.
1843 till 1846. No record of active service.
Refs.: Howard & Crisp, vi. 47, *s.n.* Thomas. *I.M.* 3 July 1855,
p. 370. *G.M.* 1859, i. 440. *The Times,* 8 Mar. 1859.

WATSON, Gilbert [1] (1790-1859). Major. 41st N.I. *b.* 10 May
1790. Cadet 1805. Arrived in India 11 July 1806. Ensign
28 July 1806. Lieut. 23 Nov. 1807. Capt. 1 Nov. 1823. Retired
18 Nov. 1834. Hon. Major 28 Nov. 1854. *d.* 16 July 1859.
bapt. Southwell, Notts., 14 May 1790. Son of William Watson,

q.v., and Catherine his wife. Brother of Richard Augustus Clay Watson, *q.v.*

Services: Barasat C.C. 1806-7. Posted Ensign to 21st N.I. 1807. Lieut. 2/21st N.I. "Conduct most conspicuous in transactions before Fort Beety in the Vizier's territory." (*Cons.* 19 Dec. 1817.) Transfd. to 41st N.I. (late 1/21st) May 1824. To take charge of 3rd Extra Regt. 24 May 1825. (? Siege and capture of Bhurtpore; Capt. 41st N.I.[2]) Sub-Asst. in Stud Dept. 17 Dec. 1828 till 22 Dec. 1829. Fur. p.a. 13 Apr. 1830 till 7 Jan. 1832.

[1] *Note:* His Commission as Bt. Capt., dated 27 Mar. 1821, gives his christian names as Gilbert William.

[2] *Note:* His name figures in Bhurtpore P.R. but not in M.R. for India medal. It is possible that he was with Left Wing of 41st N.I., which remained behind at Muttra.

WATSON, Henry (1737-1786). Lieut. Colonel. Engineers. Chief Engr., Bengal. *b.* Holbeach, Lincs., 1737. Capt. 1 May 1764. Major Sept. 1769. Lt. Col. 19 Jan. 1775. Resigned 16 Jan. 1786. *d.* Dover 17 Sept. 1786.

Son of a grazier at Holbeach. *m.* Calcutta 28 June 1780, Maria Theresa, sister of Thomas Kearnan, *q.v.* (*See also* Richard Humfrays or Humphreys.) (She *re-m.* Alexander Nowell, *q.v.*) His only dau. and heiress (with a fortune of £6,000 *p.a.*) *m.* George Evans, 4th Baron Carbery.

Services: See *D.N.B.* Ensign H.M. 52nd Ft. 27 Dec. 1755; Lieut. 50th Ft. 25 Sept. 1757. R.M.A. Woolwich. Sub-Engr. and Lieut. R.E. 17 Mar. 1759; H.M. 97th Ft. 23 Feb. 1762; promoted to a Coy. in H.M. 104th Ft. 4 Feb. 1763. Served at siege and capture of Belleisle June 1761; Sub-Engr. with expedn. to Havana 1762. Sailed for India in the *Prince of Wales* 17 May 1764. Went to Calcutta 1764 and was apptd. Field Engr. from 1 May; engaged on defences of Ft. Wm.; built vessels and commenced docks at Kidderpore, nr. Calcutta. Resigned May 1772; readmitted Aug. 1774. Apptd. by C.D. in England, 15 Mar. 1776, Chief Engr. for Bengal with rank of Lt. Col. Returned from fur. Nov. 1777. Chief Engr. Bengal 1778 till 16 Jan. 1786, when he returned to England. Pub. 1776, a translation of Euler's "Compleat Theory of the Construction and Properties of Vessels . . ."

Refs.: D.N.B. D.I.B. Hickey, ii, iii. *G.M.* 1786, ii. 996. *Eur. Mag.* Dec. 1786, p. 497 (portrait, engraved T. Prattent, pub. J. Sewell, 1787). (? Portrait by John Smart.)

WATSON, Holland (1809-1838). Lieutenant, Bengal Eur. Regt. *b.* Astbury, co. Chester, 12 Apr. 1809. Cadet 1827.

THE BENGAL ARMY, 1758-1834

Arrived in India 15 Oct. 1828. Ensign 16 Apr. 1828. Lieut. 5 Dec. 1833. *d.* Agra 20 July 1838.

bapt. Astbury 23 Aug. 1809. Son of Holland Watson, of Stockport (of Congleton), and Harriott his 2nd wife, only dau. of Richard Powell, of Stanedge.

Services: Ensign d.d. 13th N.I. 20 Nov. 1828; posted to 1st Bengal Eur. Regt. 4 Mar. 1829; to Rt. Wing Eur. Regt. Jan. 1830. No record of active service.

Refs.: Burke's *Landed Gentry*, 6th edn., p. 1299, *s.n.* Powell, of Brandlesome Hall, Lancs. A.J. N.S. xxvii. 232.

WATSON, James (*d.* 1773). Ensign, Infantry. Cadet 1772. Ensign 1 Mar. 1773. *d.* 1773: drowned.
Services: N.F.P.

WATSON, James (*d.* 1786). Captain, 1st Bengal Eur. Regt. Cadet 1771. Ensign 10 Jan. 1773. Lieut. 4 Apr. 1777. Capt. 29 Mar. 1781. *d.* 1786.

Son of Isobel Watson, of Duns. Brother of Jean Stewart, of Duns.

Services: Leave s.c. to sea Nov. 1784. N.F.P.

Refs.: Will dated 4 Aug. 1784; proved 27 June 1786.[1]

[1] *Note:* His exors. were Robert and Dalhousie Watherstone, of Manderston, *q.v.*

WATSON, John Edward (1796-1868). Major. 59th N.I. *b.* 25 Apr. 1796. Cadet 1811. Admitted 20 Mar. 1813. Ensign 11 Oct. 1814. Lieut. 3 Jan. 1818. Capt. 3 Apr. 1826. Invalided 14 May 1832. Retired 19 Sept. 1837. Hon. Major 28 Nov. 1854. *d.* 22 May 1868.

bapt. Wellingborough, Northants, 14 July 1796. Son of Rev. Joseph Watson and Sarah his wife. *m.* Dinapore 26 Feb. 1820, Caroline Trueman, widow of Anthony Daffy Swinton, *q.v.* (She died Herne Bay 18 Mar. 1869.)

Services: Posted Ensign to newly-raised 2/30th N.I. 1815; d.d. Mirzapur Bn. 1815. Offg. Intr. & Qmr. 2/30th N.I. 19 Oct. 1820; d.d. Champaran L.I. 25 Jan. 1822 till 17 Aug. 1826. First Burma War; Assam 1824; capture of stockade at Baragaon 19 Mar.; surprised party of enemy at (?) Dickaree Oct. 1824 (*Lond. Gaz.* 19 Apr. 1825); Lieut. Champaran L.I. Transfd. to 59th N.I. (late 1/30th) May 1824. Fur. s.c. 13 Feb. 1827 till 14 May 1831.

WATSON, Joseph Yelloly (1793-1817). Ensign, 26th N.I. *b.* Warren House, Bamburgh, Northumberland, 30 Sept. 1793. Cadet 1811. Ensign 21 Apr. 1814. *d.* Banda 18 Oct. 1817.

Son of William Watson, of Warren House and Adderstone, Belford, Northumberland. Heir to Adam Yelloly (who *d. unm.* Chesterhill, nr. Belford, 24 Feb. 1810). Brother of William Watson, of Adderstone House.

Services: Posted to 1/26th N.I. 1814; attached to Champaran L.I. 1814 till death. Nepal War 1814-15, and 1816; Ensign Champaran L.I., with 1st Bde. Rt. Column.

Refs.: Burke's *Landed Gentry*, 13th edn., p. 1844, *s.n.* Watson, of Adderstone Hall, Belford, Northumberland. Will dated 21 Feb. 1817; proved 2 May 1818.

WATSON, Richard Augustus Clay (1783-1824). Lieut. Colonel, 44th N.I. *bapt.* Southwell, Notts., 9 June 1783. Cadet 1798. Arrived in India 6 Nov. 1799. Ensign 6 Nov. 1799. Lieut. 29 May 1800. Capt. 3 Jan. 1812. Major 28 July 1820. Lt. Col. 1 May 1824. *d.* Dacca 2 Oct. 1824.

2nd son of William Watson, *q.v.*, and Catherine his wife. Brother of William Mitchell Watson, *q.v. m.* 1st, (?) (She died 15 Mar. 1821.) *m.* 2nd, Bankipore, B. & O., 19 June 1824, Miss Anne Weston, 3rd dau. of Charles Weston. (She died London 28 Aug. 1826.)

Services: Minor Cadet 28 June 1784; struck off 3 May 1786. Posted Ensign to 17th N.I.; transfd. to 18th N.I.; to 2/11th N.I. 15 Apr. 1801; to newly raised 2/22nd N.I. in 1804, and spent the remainder of his life with that Bn. Adjt. 1804 till 30 July 1810. Second Mahratta War; battle and capture of Deig; Bhurtpore (w. in 2nd assault 21 Jan. 1805). Fur. 10 Nov. 1810 till 1814. Capt. Lt. 11 Mar. 1811. Nepal War 1816; Makwanpur; in 3rd Bde. Centre Column. Posted Lt. Col. to 44th N.I. (late 2/22nd) May 1824.

Refs.: *E.I.M.C.* ii. 365. *A.J.* xix. 721. Will dated Dacca, 17 Sept. 1824; proved 21 Oct. 1824. M.I. Dacca.

WATSON, Samuel (1748/49-1814). Lieut. General. Colonel 3rd N.I. *b.* 1748/49. Cadet 1769. Admitted 27 July 1769. Ensign 26 July 1769. Lieut. 10 Nov. 1772. Capt. 19 Nov. 1780. Major 1 Mar. 1794. Lt. Col. 27 July 1796. Col. 29 May 1800. Maj. Gen. 25 Apr. 1808. Lt. Gen. 4 June 1813. *d.* Dinapore 11 July 1814, aged 65.

Son of Lovegood Watson, 6th Ft., afterwards 65th Ft., and Anne Pipe his wife. Uncle of Thomas Colclough Watson, *q.v.*

THE BENGAL ARMY, 1758-1834

m. 1st, Calcutta 7 Oct. 1773, Eleanor Fielding. (She died Calcutta 19 Oct. 1776, aged 25.) *m.* 2nd (in England before Feb. 1778) Mary. (She died Calcutta 22 May 1813, aged 55.) Father of William Larkins Watson, of the wife of Thomas Morgan, and of the mother of Sulivan Harington Steer, *qq.v.*

Services: Returned from fur. s.c. Aug. 1778. Lieut. 2/3rd Bengal Eur. Regt. in Oct. 1779. First Mahratta War. Capt. 2nd Bengal Eur. Bn. in July 1787; apptd. to comd. 4th Bn. Sepoys 31 Oct. 1787. Lt. Col. 2/12th N.I. Posted Col. to 18th N.I. 29 May 1800; to 11th N.I. Jan. 1801; 3rd N.I. 1804 till death. Comdg. Dinapore Div. June 1810 till 1813.

Refs.: Will dated Diggah, 27 Jan. 1814; proved 16 Aug. 1814. *S.M.* 1815, p. 237.

WATSON, Samuel (1789-1838). Lieut. Colonel, 65th N.I. *bapt.* Watford, Herts., 23 Feb. 1789. Cadet 1803. Arrived in India 11 Dec. 1804. Ensign 24 Oct. 1804. Lieut. 24 Oct. 1804. Capt. 8 Jan. 1820. Major 13 Dec. 1830. Lt. Col. 11 July 1836. *d.* at sea 18 Feb. 1838, on board the *Adelaide*, the day before she arrived in the Downs.

Son of Thomas Watson and Mary his wife. Nephew of James Smith. *m.* Wilton Mar. 1823, Miss Hannah Nickleson, dau. of E. B. Metford, of Flook House, Taunton. (She died Chittagong 9 July 1837.)

Services: Posted Lieut. to Bengal Eur. Regt. 1805. Served in Java with his Regt. 1812 till Feb. 1817, part of the time as actg. Adjt. Operations against the Rajah of Boni, in Celebes, 1816; assault of Baliangan Pass 8 June (w.); actg. Adjt. Eur. Regt. Posted to newly-raised 1/28th N.I. 1815, but did not join till end of 1817. Third Mahratta War 1818; Madhurajpura; Lieut, 1/28th N.I. Leave s.c. 10 mos. to sea 24 Dec. 1819; fur. p.a. 2 Nov. 1820 till 8 Oct. 1823. d.d. 1/34th N.I. 25 Nov. 1823 till 4 Nov. 1824. Transfd. to 55th N.I. (late 1/28th) May 1824. Tempy. charge of Delhi Provl. Bn. 1 Oct. 1827. Posted Lt. Col. to 55th N.I. 21 Oct. 1836; to 65th N.I. 9 Oct. 1837. Fur. s.c. 1 Sept. 1837 till death.

Refs.: *A.J.* N.S. xxv. 199.

*WATSON, Thomas (or John). Lieutenant. Infantry. Cadet 1777. Never arrived in India. Ensign 1778. Lieut. 19 Oct. 1778. Struck off ——.

Services: Apptd. Cadet 28 Jan. 1777; was to have sailed in the *Union*, Danish East Indiaman.

LIST OF THE OFFICERS OF

WATSON, Thomas Colclough (1787-1834). Lieut. Colonel, 53rd N.I. b. (*probably* in Canada) 20 June 1787. Cadet 1801. Arrived in India 17 July 1802. Ensign 10 Aug. 1802. Lieut. 30 June 1804. Capt. 1 June 1818. Major 21 June 1826. Lt. Col. 3 Nov. 1831. d. Dacca 30 Apr. 1834, of cholera.

Of Mount Anna, nr. Wexford. Eldest son of Col. Jonas Watson, H.M. 13th, formerly 65th Regt., A.D.C. to H.R.H. Duke of Kent (who was kld. by rebels May 1798), and Harriett his wife, 2nd dau. of Rev. Thomas Colclough, of Kilmagee, co. Kildare, rector of Cleenish. Brother of Henry Watson (Appendix A) and cousin-german of William Larkins Watson, *q.v.* m. (? 7 Oct.) 1817, Sarah James, of Ballycrystal, co. Wexford, sister of Thomas James (1807-1871), *q.v.* (She died 18 June 1874, aged 76.)

Services: Posted Lieut. to Bengal Eur. Regt. May 1804. Second Mahratta War; battle and capture of Deig; Bhurtpore (w. in 2nd assault 21 Jan. 1805); Lieut. Eur. Regt. Expedn. to Macao 1808-9. A.D.C. to his uncle, Maj.-Gen. Samuel Watson, *q.v.*, comdg. Dinapore Div., 1810; d.d. 2/15th N.I. at Dinapore 1811; extra A.D.C. to Hon. Thomas Stamford Raffles (*D.N.B.*), Lt. Govr. of Java, 31 Mar. 1813 till 1815. Capt. Lt. 28 July 1816. Fur. from Anger, Java, 15 Jan. 1817. d.d. troops in Bencoolen 3 May 1819; comdd. Bencoolen Local Corps 1 Jan. 1820 till 1822 [1]; do. Cawnpore Inf. Levy 4 Oct. 1822; Bde. Major Presdy. 12 Nov. 1823 till 4 June 1824. Transfd. to newly-raised 2nd Bengal Eur. Regt. May 1824; apptd. in Mar. 1825 Comr. for handing Bencoolen over to the Dutch, but the proceedings had terminated before his arrival. Fur. s.c. 21 Nov. 1827 till 11 Oct. 1830. Posted Lt. Col. to 53rd N.I. 11 June 1832.

Refs.: Foster's *Families of Royal Descent*, ii. 812. *Hist. of the Hawtrey Family*, i. 214-15. Burke's *Landed Gentry of Ireland*, p. 120, *s.n.* Colclough, of Tintern Abbey. *G.M.* 1834, ii. 558. Will dated on board *Roxburgh*, 27 Aug. 1830; proved 30 May 1834. M.I. in Templeshando church, co. Wexford, and in Dacca cemetery.

[1] *Note*: In July 1821 he left Bencoolen in the *Hastings* for Bengal, via Madras, having been sent back under arrest by the Lt. Govr. of Bencoolen for disrespect. No proceedings were taken against him; he was released from arrest Sept. 1822, and resigned comd. of Bencoolen Local Corps on 23 Dec. 1822.

WATSON, William (*d.* 1815). Major. 3rd Bengal Eur. Regt. Lieut. 3 Sept. 1768. Capt. 7 July 1776. Major 1 Feb. 1781. Struck off 1793. d. Southwell, Notts., 1815.

J.P. and D.L. Notts. for 28 yrs. "Descendant of a very respectable family long residing at Farnsfield, Notts., and grandson of Sir Beaumont Dixie, Bart." *m.* Catherine. Father of Gilbert Watson, Richard Augustus Clay Watson, William Mitchell Watson, *qq.v.*, and of the wife of Hugh Ross, *q.v.*

Services: Ensign H.M. 54th Ft. 10 May 1760; Lieut. 49th Ft. 13 Sept. 1760; Lieut. 34th Ft. 7 Nov. 1762; h.p. 1763 till death. " Served in almost every island in West Indies with H.M. 34th Ft." (*E.I.M.C.*) Entered H.E.I.C.S. as Lieut. Sept. 1768. Apptd. Adjt. and actg. Chaplain 3rd Bengal Eur. Regt. shortly after arrival in India. First Rohilla War 1774; battle of St. George; Lieut. Bengal Eur. Regt. Fur. Jan. 1777 till Sept. 1783. Comdd. 3rd Eur. Regt. 1783-4. Major comdg. 4th Bn. Sepoys in Apr. 1786; transfd. to 2nd Eur. Bn. 1787. Fur. 1787 till struck off.

Refs.: *E.I.M.C.* ii. 365. *G.M.* 1816, i. 378.

WATSON, William Larkins (1784-1852). Lieut. Colonel, C.B. 53rd N.I. *b.* in India 1784. Cadet 1799. Arrived in India 9 Dec. 1800. Ensign 9 Nov. 1800. Lieut. 30 Sept. 1803. Capt. 2 Jan. 1815. Major 1 May 1824. Lt. Col. 23 Feb. 1827. Retired 9 May 1830. *d.* Harwood House, Cheltenham, 6 Apr. 1852, aged 67.

bapt. Calcutta 26 Mar. 1785. Son of Samuel Watson, *q.v.*, and Mary his 2nd wife. *m.* Meerut 12 Mar. 1808, Sarah, dau. of Sir Dyson Marshall, *q.v.* (*See also* Christopher D'Oyly Aplin.) (She died Harwood House 4 Dec. 1852, aged 65.)

Services: Minor Cadet Nov. 1784; struck off 2 May 1786. Posted to 2/8th N.I. 17 Apr. 1801; transfd. to 11th N.I.; to newly-raised 22nd N.I. 1804. Second Mahratta War 1804-5; Bhurtpore (w. in 2nd assault 21 Jan. 1805); Lieut. 2/22nd N.I. Bde. Major at Karnal 1809-13; do. Delhi and Rewari 1813-14. Capt. Lt. 22nd N.I. 1 Sept. 1814. Nepal War 1814-15; Capt. 2/22nd N.I., A.A.G. 4th (Dinapore) Div. Nepal War 1816; A.A.G. (India medal). 1st A.A.G. of the Army 1 Feb. 1816. Transfd. to 1/22nd N.I. 1st D.A.G. of the Army (with official rank of Major) 1818; A.G. (with official rank of Lt. Col.) 29 Apr. 1825 till 1828. Transfd. to 43rd N.I. (late 1/22nd) May 1824. Siege and capture of Bhurtpore; A.G. (clasp to India medal). Posted Lt. Col. to 27th N.I. 1827; to 2nd Eur. Regt. 3 Apr. 1828; to 43rd N.I. 10 Sept. 1828; to 53rd N.I. 1829. Fur. 1828 till retirement. C.B. 2 Jan. 1827.

Refs.: *I.M.* 4 May 1852, p. 276.

WATSON, William Mitchell (1778/79-1811). Captain, 18th N.I. *b.* 1778/79. Cadet 1793. Arrived in India 30 Oct. 1795.

Ensign 2 Oct. 1794. Lieut. 8 Jan. 1796. Capt. 22 Mar. 1804. d. Moradabad 12 July 1811.

Eldest son of William Watson, q.v. Brother of Gilbert Watson, q.v. m. Harriet.

Services : Apptd. Minor Cadet Oct. 1783, aged 4 yrs.; struck off 2 May 1786. Apptd. Cadet 20 Mar. 1795; sailed for India in the *Woodcot* 18 June 1795. Posted to 1st Bengal Eur. Regt. June 1796; transfd. to 1/18th N.I. 29 May 1800. Second Mahratta War 1803-4; Bundelkhand 1803; Kapsa; Narnaul; Kanun; defeat of Rajah Ram Singh; capture of Jaitpur; Capt. 18th N.I. Fur. 12 Mar. 1806 till 19 Aug. 1808. (? Operations in Bundelkhand 1809; Rajaoli; Ajaigarh; Capt. 1/18th N.I.)

WATT, Alexander (1804-1851). Major, 27th N.I. *b.* Liff and Benvie, co. Forfar, 17 Apr. 1804. Cadet 1820. Admitted 31 May 1821. Ensign 13 Jan. 1821. Lieut. 11 July 1823. Capt. 7 Feb. 1833. Major 31 Dec. 1845. *d.* Edinburgh 18 Apr. 1851.

Son of Isaac Watt, of Dundee, merchant. *m.* (before 1831) Susanna. (She died Landour 22 Aug. 1842, aged 35.) Ed. Dundee Acad.

Services : Posted Ensign to 2/28th N.I. 1821; transfd. to 13th N.I. July 1823; to 26th N.I. (late 1/13th) May 1824. First Burma War; Arakan 1825; Lieut. 26th N.I.[1] Transfd. to 27th N.I. 3 June 1825. Fur. s.c. 8 Dec. 1825 till 14 Jan. 1829. S.A.C.G. 12 Dec. 1829; D.A.C.G. 2 cl. 3 Dec. 1834; 1 cl. 12 Apr. 1837. Comst. Ofr. 1st Div., Army of Indus, 13 Sept. 1838 till 6 Jan. 1839. First Afghan War 1839-40; Ghazni; Capt. 27th N.I., Comst. Ofr. (Medal). A.C.G. 2 cl. 9 Mar. 1840; 1 cl. 24 Jan. 1845 till Feb. 1846. First Sikh War; no actions; Major 27th N.I. Deputed in 1849 to inspect Comst. offices in Lower Provinces. Fur. s.c. Jan. 1850 till death. Durani 3 cl. 7 Sept. 1841.

Refs. : I.M. 30 July 1851, p. 447.

[1] *Note :* Died just before issue of India medal.

WATT, Edward (1803-1864). Lieut. Colonel. 6th L.C. Bdr. Gen. in Turkey. *b.* Derryloran, co. Tyrone, 19 May 1803. Cadet 1819. Admitted 29 July 1820. Ensign 4 Mar. 1820. Cornet 3 Jan. 1823. Lieut. 13 May 1825. Capt. 28 Dec. 1838. Bt. Major 11 Nov. 1851. Retired 31 Dec. 1851. Hon. Lt. Col. 28 Nov. 1854. *d.* Dublin 3 Apr. 1864.

bapt. Derryloran 24 May 1803. Son of John Watt, of Belfast, excise ofr. *m.* Sultanpur, Benares, 26 Aug. 1841, Elizabeth, dau. of Sir Henry Worsley, G.C.B., q.v.

Services: Posted Ensign to 16th N.I. ; transfd. to Cav. 8 Sept. 1823 ; posted Cornet to 6th L.C. Siege and capture of Bhurtpore ; Lieut. 6th L.C. (India medal). Adjt. 6th L.C. 14 July 1825 till 5 Jan. 1833. Leave s.c. to N.S.W. 20 Dec. 1830 till 13 Aug. 1832 ; fur. s.c. 9 Sept. 1832 till 22 Oct. 1836. 2nd in comd. 1st Cav., Oudh Auxy. Force, 29 Jan. 1837 till 25 Oct. 1839. Reduction of Jhansi 1838-39 ; Capt. 6th L.C. Fur. s.c. 3 Feb. 1847 till 25 Nov. 1849. Was a Dir. of N.W. Bank in 1850. Crimean War ; Bdr. Gen. in Turkey.

Refs.: G.M. 1864, ii. 812. *The Times*, 5 May 1864.

WATTELL, Christopher (1750-1789). Lieutenant. Infantry. *b.* Hants 1750. Cadet 1780. Arrived in India Mar. 1781. Ensign 1780. Lieut. 12 Aug. 1781. Resigned on h.p. 10 Feb. 1785. *d.* Pall Mall, London, 16 Sept. 1789, aged 38.

m. (?)

Services: Sailed for India in the *Bellmont* 3 Apr. 1780, aged 30. Dy. Paymr. to 2nd Bde. 1782-4. Granted fur. for 3 yrs. on h.p. 10 Feb. 1785.

Refs.: Eur. Mag. 1789, ii. 251. G.M. 1789, ii. 956.

WATTS, Edward Raphael (1798-1881). Major. Artillery. (463) *bapt.* Malmesbury, Wilts., 6 June 1798. Cadet 1815. Admitted 17 Aug. 1816. Fireworker 14 Aug. 1817. Lieut. 1 Sept. 1818. Capt. 19 May 1832. Retired 24 Aug. 1842. Hon. Major 28 Nov. 1854. *d.* 12 Jan. 1881.

Son of Edward Watts and Simha his wife. Related to Solomon Franco, of Old Burlington St., London, merchant. *m.* Leckhampton 6 Sept. 1848, Maria, 2nd dau. of George Swiney, *q.v.* Ed. Christ's Hospital. Addiscombe Cadet 1813-16.

Services: Adjt. & Qmr. Saugor Div. Art. 26 Jan. 1825. Leave s.c. 11 Oct. 1828 till Oct. 1829 ; fur. s.c. 9 Sept. 1832 till 5 Sept. 1835. Transfd. from 4th Coy. 4th Bn. Foot Art. to 4th Troop 1st Bde. H.A. 1 Nov. 1836. Fur. s.c. 1 Apr. 1840 till retirement. No record of active service.

WATTS, Elias (*d.* 1770). Ensign, Infantry. Cadet 1770. Ensign 19 Sept. 1770. *d.* Dinapore 1770.

Services: N.F.P.

WATTS, James (1741-1770). Captain, Infantry. *b.* London 16 Apr. 1741. Cadet 1763. Ensign 1 Feb. 1763. Lieut. 7 Oct. 1763. Capt. 1768. *d.* " Byampore " (? Berhampore) 12 Mar. 1770 : drowned.

bapt. St. Stephen's, Coleman St., 18 Apr. 1741. Son of John

Watts and Hannah his wife. Ed. Merchant Taylors' Oct. 1750-Mar. 1755. Eton; K.S. 20 July 1755. Peterhouse, Camb.; admitted sizar 8 Feb. 1759. Exeter Coll., Oxon.; matric. 10 Nov. 1760; exhibitioner 1760-2.
Services : Sailed for India in the *Walpole* 5 Mar. 1762. Lieut. 1st Bengal Eur. Regt. in 1765-6. Resigned his Commission during the "Batta mutiny" in May 1766 and went home; restored to the Service by C.D. in England 22 Feb. 1769.
Refs. : Robinson. Eton Coll. Register. Alumni Oxon. Broome, pp. lix, lxxi.

WATTS, Joseph (1778-1806). Lieutenant, 13th N.I. *b.* London 6 June 1778. Cadet 1799. Arrived in India 7 Dec. 1800. Ensign 24 Oct. 1800. Lieut. 28 Oct. 1801. *d.* at sea 10 Mar. 1806, on board the *Sir William Bensley*, on his passage to India.
bapt. St. John Evang., Westminster, 30 June 1778. Son of Thomas Watts and Susan his wife. (? *m.* Juliet Rosetta.)
Services : Posted to 1/13th N.I. 17 Apr. 1801. Fur. 2 Nov. 1803 till death.
Refs. : G.M. 1806, i. 478.

WATTS, Robert (1756/57-?). Lieutenant. Infantry. *b.* Warwick 1756/57. Cadet 1780. Ensign 1780. Lieut. 10 July 1781. Struck off 1788.
Services : Should have sailed for India in the *Hillsborough* 27 July 1780, aged 23. Shown as on fur. in Mar. 1786, but probably never arrived in India.

WATTS, Thomas (1765-?). Lieutenant. 9th Bn. Sepoys. *bapt.* Calcutta 6 May 1765. Cadet 1782. Ensign 21 Jan. 1783. Lieut. 15 Mar. 1789. Resigned 7 Dec. 1790.
Son of Hugh Watts, of Lovell's Hill, Berks., high sheriff 1776, sometime Member of the Bengal Council, and Elizabeth Fenwick his wife. Grandson of "Begum" Frances Johnson.
Services : Sailed for India in the *Worcester* 6 Feb. 1782, aged 16. Posted to 3rd Bengal Eur. Regt. 28 Feb. 1783; Ensign do. in July 1787; transfd. from 1st do. to 9th Bn. Sepoys 5 Feb. 1790.

WAUGH, Sir Andrew Scott (1810-1878). Major General, Kt. Engineers. Surveyor Gen. of India. *b.* Cannanore, Madras, 3 Feb. 1810. Cadet 1828. Arrived in India 25 May 1829. 2nd Lieut. 13 Dec. 1827. Lieut. 13 Dec. 1827. Capt. 19 Feb. 1844. Local Lt. Col. 3 Dec. 1847. Major 3 Aug. 1855. Lt. Col.

20 Sept. 1857. Col. 18 Feb. 1861. Retired 12 Mar. 1861. Hon. Maj. Gen. 6 Aug. 1861. *d.* 7 Petersham Terr., Queen's Gate, London, 21 Feb. 1878.

Eldest son of Maj.-Gen. Gilbert Waugh, Mily. Auditor Gen. Madras, and Charlotte his wife, 2nd sister of Henry Wahab, *q.v.* Nephew of Capt. Sir Murray Maxwell, Kt., R.N. (*D.N.B.*). *m.* 1st, Calcutta 8 June 1844, Josephine Morison, dau. of Dr. William Graham, of Edinburgh. (She died 1866.) *m.* 2nd, 1870, Cecilia Eliza Adelaide, dau. of Sir Thomas Whitehead, *q.v.* (*See also* Sir George Hall Macgregor.) (She died London 9 Feb. 1884.) Ed. Edin. High School. Addiscombe Cadet 1827-8 ; Chatham 1828.

Services : See *D.N.B.* d.d. S. & M. at Aligarh 13 July 1829 ; offg. Executive Engr. 6th (Allahabad) Div. 11 June 1830. Leave p.a. 6 mos. to Penang 13 Oct. 1830. Adjt. Engrs. 13 Apr. 1831 till 21 Sept. 1833. Sub.-Asst. in Gt. Trig. Survey 2 July 1832 ; Supt. do., and Surveyor Gen. of India, 16 Dec. 1843 till retirement. No record of active service. Author of " Memorandum on the Mutiny of the Bengal Native Army," London, 1857 ; " Instructions for topographical surveying," 1861. Kt. 10 Dec. 1860. F.R.S. 3 June 1858.

Refs. : *D.N.B. Boase. D.I.B. Thackeray,* p. 158. *The Times,* 22 Feb. 1878. *I.L.N.,* xli. 567-8 (portrait).

WAUGH, George (1749/50-1812). Captain. Infantry. *b.* 1749/50. Cadet 1769. Ensign 4 Sept. 1769. Lieut. 1 Feb. 1773. Capt. 16 Nov. 1780. Struck off 1793. *d.* Outwood, Yorks., Feb. 1812, aged 62.

m. Thalia. (She died 1 Sept. 1877, aged 96.)

Services : First Mahratta War 1778-84 ; Capt. comdg. 6th N.I., with Bombay detachment under Col. Goddard. Fur. 21 Oct. 1785 till struck off.

Refs. : *Williams,* p. 99. *M.M.* 1808, i. 144 ; 1812, i. 188.

WAUGH, Nicholas Dobree (*d.* 1794). Lieutenant, 4th Bengal Eur. Bn. Cadet 1783. Ensign 30 Mar. 1785. Lieut. 8 Aug. 1793. *d. unm.* at sea 13 Aug. 1794, with the Bengal Squadron.

Son of Capt. John Waugh, of Guernsey, and Elizabeth his wife. Brother of Lieut. Daniel Waugh and of Mrs. Elizabeth Le Marchant.

Services : Apptd. Cadet 31 Dec. 1782 ; sailed for India in the *Duke of Kingston* 11 Mar. 1783. Examiner in Mily. Dept. of Inspection in Dec. 1788. Brought on full pay from Supy. Ensign and posted to 35th Bn. Sepoys 15 Feb. 1790. Served from Nov. 1793 till death with a detachment sent with Commodore Mitchell's fleet for service against French cruisers in the Bay of Bengal and E. Archipelago ; Lieut. 4th Eur. Bn.

Refs.: Will dated Ft. Wm. 18 Nov. 1793 ; admon. 25 Nov. 1794.

WAUGH, Patrick Young [1] (1788-1829). Captain, 10th L.C. *b.* Dublin 11 Aug. 1788. Cadet 1804. Arrived in India 12 Sept. 1805. Cornet 1 Feb. 1804. Lieut. 12 Oct. 1806. Capt. 4 May 1823. *d.* camp Shahpura 28 Feb. 1829, as the result of an accident a few days earlier.

Son of Robert Waugh and Jesse his wife. Brother of John Middleton Waugh, Lieut. R.N., Mrs. Jesse Delamain, and Mrs. Elizabeth Hollings Ferrier, and cousin of James Tod, *q.v.* Marlow Cadet.

Services : Posted Lieut. to 1st N.C. 1806. Operations in Bundelkhand 1810-11 ; Bichaund ; Lieut. 1st N.C. Adjt. 1st N.C. 28 Feb. 1817 till 3 Apr. 1821. Third Mahratta War 1817-18 ; Lieut. 1st N.C., in Rt. Div. Operations against the Bhattis of Hariana 1818. Comdg. Resdt.'s escort at Udaipur 1819 ; Asst. to P.A. Mewar and Haraoti 1820 ; comdg. Udaipur escort 1821 ; Asst. to P.A. Mewar 1821 ; P.A. Mewar 1822-3. Fur. 1823-6. Transfd. to newly-raised 2nd Extra Cav. (became 10th L.C.) 17 June 1825.

Refs.: *A.J.* xxviii. 495. Will dated camp Shahpura, 26 Feb. 1829 ; proved 11 Apr. 1829. M.I. Mowa, Bhilwara district.

[1] *Note :* He signs both his Cadet Papers and his Will without the ' Young.'

WAVELL, Arthur Goodall (1785-1860). Lieutenant. 8th N.I. Subsequently Maj. Gen. in the Venezuelan service. *b.* Edinburgh 20 Mar. 1785. Cadet 1804. Arrived in India 10 Dec. 1805. Ensign 30 Sept. 1805. Lieut. 20 Oct. 1805. Struck off in England 28 Oct. 1811. *d.* Ladbroke Grove, London, 10 July 1860.

bapt. St. Benet's, Gracechurch St., London, 7 Dec. 1785. Younger son of Dr. William Wavell, M.B., of Barnstaple,[1] and Mary Garratt his wife, dau. of William Smith, of Guildford. *m.* 1825, Anne, 5th and youngest dau. of Sir William Paxton, of Middleton Hall, co. Carmarthen, and sister of George Augustus Paxton, *q.v.* (She died Almorah Lodge, Surbiton, 7 Feb. 1882, aged 79.) Grandfather of F.M. Lord Wavell, Viceroy of India. Ed. Winchester ; Scholar 1798 ; superannuated 1804.

Services : Posted Lieut. to 8th N.I. 1806. Fur. 28 Apr. 1809 till struck off in 1816 with effect from $2\frac{1}{2}$ yrs. after quitting India. Volunteered his services in Spain ; battle of Barrosa 5 Mar. 1811 ; assault on the French lines before Tarragona 16 June 1811, A.D.C. to the Spanish General Sarsfield. Col. in the Spanish service. Kt.

of San Fernando and of Carlos III (R.L. 16 Feb. 1818). Gen. in the Venezuelan service. Author of " Tactica de la Infantirea de Linea, etc.," 1819. F.R.S. 24 May 1827. K.F., K.C.S. Maj. Gen.

Refs.: Family information. *Kirby.* Burke's *Landed Gentry,* 5th edn., p. 1062, *s.n.* Paxton, of Cholderton, Wilts. *The Times,* 11 July 1860.

[1] *Note:* After whom the mineral Wavellite, first discovered nr. S. Molton in 1805, was named.

WEALE, William Wheler. Lieutenant. Infantry. Cadet 1776. Ensign 14 Mar. 1777. Lieut. 11 Aug. 1778. Resigned 1 Apr. 1782.

m. (before July 1781) A—— E——.

Services: Apptd. Cadet 17 Nov. 1775; sailed for India in the *Nassau* 9 Jan. 1776. (? Second Mysore War 1781-2.)

WEAR,[1] **Daniel** (*d.* 1776). Major, Infantry. Capt. 17 June 1765. Major 2 Oct. 1769. *d.* Bombay 15 May 1776.

Services: Ensign (Madras) 26 Jan. 1759; Lieut. do. 1 June 1761; Capt. do. 18 June 1765; transfd. to Bengal Est. 1766. Assault of Madura 26 June 1764 (w.); Lieut. Madras Est. Leave s.c. to Bombay Oct. 1775.

Refs.: Admon. (Bombay) 17 June 1776.

[1] *Note:* Weare in bur. register; sometimes Ware or Weir.

WEAVER, Henry (1818-1842). Lieutenant, 54th N.I. *b.* Gloucester 27 Mar. 1818. Cadet 1834. Arrived in India 4 Feb. 1835. Ensign 15 Sept. 1834. Lieut. 23 July 1838. *d.* Gandamak 13 Jan. 1842: kld. in action during the retreat from Kabul.

bapt. Gloucester 13 Apr. 1818. Son of Charles Weaver, of Gloucester, pinmaker, and Maria his wife, eldest dau. of Thomas Palin, of Wotton Villa, Gloucs. Cousin-german of Robert William Palin, *q.v. m.* Blagdon, Somerset, 21 May 1839, Marianne, eldest dau. of John Baker, of Woodlands, Somerset. Addiscombe Cadet 10 Aug. 1832 till 13 June 1834.

Services: Posted to 54th N.I. 2 Mar. 1835. Fur. s.c. 7 Feb. 1837 till 11 Nov. 1839. First Afghan War 1840-2; outbreak at Kabul; retreat from Kabul (kld.); Lieut. 54th N.I.

Refs.: M.I. Afghan Memorial Church, Bombay.

WEBB, Charles (*d.* 1783). Captain, Invalid Est. Infantry. Cadet 1770. Ensign 3 Dec. 1771. Lieut. 12 Aug. 1776. Capt. 3 Mar. 1781. Invalided Mar. 1781. *d.* Chunar 2 Jan. 1783.

Services: First Mahratta War 1778-9; returned sick to Bengal from Bombay Apr. 1779.

WEBB, Henry (1784-?). Lieutenant. 3rd N.I. *b.* London 15 Oct. 1784. Cadet 1799. Arrived in India 9 Dec. 1800. Ensign 25 Sept. 1800. Lieut. 8 Sept. 1802. Resigned in India 30 Apr. 1814.

bapt. St. James's, Westminster, 24 Nov. 1784. Son of William Webb and Ann his wife.

Services: Posted Lieut. to 2/3rd N.I. 17 Apr. 1801. Fur. 25 Mar. 1805 till 15 Dec. 1809. With Mirzapur Bn. 1813-14. No record of active service.

WEBB, Henry (1792-1818). Lieutenant, Artillery. (419) *b.* Hillingdon, Middlesex, 17 May 1792. Cadet 1809. Arrived in India 2 Aug. 1810. Fireworker 2 Aug. 1810. Lieut. 25 Sept. 1817. *d.* nr. Cawnpore 21 Apr. 1818 : drowned.

bapt. Hillingdon 22 July 1792. Son of John Webb, proctor, and Dorothy his wife. Woolwich Cadet; nominated 20 Jan. 1808.

Services: Reduction of Kalinjar 1812. Third Mahratta War; (*probably* Taragarh); Lieut. 4th Coy. 1st Bn. Foot Art.

WEBB, Nathaniel Spencer (1787-1833). Major, Artillery. (345) *bapt.* Wexford 31 Mar. 1787. Cadet 1804. Admitted 7 Nov. 1805. Lieut. 5 May 1805. Capt. Lt. 11 Dec. 1810. Capt. 25 Sept. 1817. Major 24 Oct. 1824. *d.* Nasirabad 21 Oct. 1833.

Son of John Spencer Webb, Lieut. H.M. 15th Ft., and Elizabeth his wife, dau. of William Robinson, of Wexford. *m.* St. Pancras, Middlesex, 31 July 1829, Harriet, dau. of Rev. Henry Fry, D.D., vicar of Willesden, and afterwards sub-dean of St. Paul's. (She died 17 Mar. 1884, aged 91.) Woolwich Cadet 8 July 1802 till 22 Dec. 1804.

Services: Reduction of Kalinjar 1812. Nepal War 1814-15; operations against Amar Singh; Malaun; Jaithak (*Lond. Gaz.* 16 Nov. 1815); Capt. Lt. 4th Coy. 2nd Bn., in 1st Div. Fur. s.c. 23 Jan. 1818 till 19 Feb. 1821. To comd. Art. proceeding to S. frontier of Chittagong against Burmese Oct. 1823 till July 1824. To comd. Art. at Karnal 23 Sept. 1825. Fur. s.c. 24 Jan. 1827 till 20 Feb. 1830. Transfd. to 3rd Bn. 10 Oct. 1833.

Refs.: A.J. N.S. xiii. 223. M.I. at Nasirabad.

WEBB, William Spencer (1784-1865). Captain. 56th N.I. *b.* Lamb's Conduit St., London, 2 Dec. 1784. Cadet 1800. Arrived in India 26 Aug. 1801. Ensign 20 Nov. 1801. Lieut. 30 Sept. 1803. Capt. 9 Dec. 1818. Retired 29 June 1824. *d.* Clarendon Gdns., Maida Hill, London, 4 Feb. 1865.

THE BENGAL ARMY, 1758-1834

bapt. St. George the Martyr, Queen's Sq., 30 Dec. 1784. Son of William Webb and Mary his wife. Ed. R. Maths. School, Christ's Hospital.

Services: Passed exam. at Trinity House and joined H.M.S. *Amazon* at sea for 2 yrs. Ensign d.d. 3rd N.I. in 1802; posted Ensign to 10th N.I. Second Mahratta War 1805-6; Lieut. 10th N.I. Employed surveying in Upper Provinces 1808-11. Fur. 1811-14. Transfd. to newly-raised 28th N.I. 1815. Nepal War 1814-15; Lieut. 2/28th N.I., Bde. Major (India medal). In charge of survey in Kumaon 1815 till July 1821. Capt. 2/28th N.I. Fur. 1822 till retirement. Transfd. to 56th N.I. (late 2/28th) May 1824. Author of " Altitudes of Places and Stations in Kumaon, from Barometrical Observations."

Refs.: *G.M.* 1865, i. 396. *The Times,* 7 Feb. 1865.

WEBBER, Charles (1766-1822). Lieut. Colonel. 5th N.C. b. 10 Apr. 1766. Cadet 1782. Admitted 15 Aug. 1783. Cornet 1 Mar. 1783. Lieut. 16 Feb. 1790. Capt. 17 July 1801. Major 11 Mar. 1805. Lt. Col. 27 Feb. 1812. Invalided 18 Aug. 1814. Retired 7 May 1817. d. *unm.* Braunton, Devon, 22 Feb. 1822.

bapt. 13 Apr. 1766. 3rd son of Philip Rogers Webber, of Buckland, J.P. and D.L. Devon, and Mary his wife, eldest dau. and co-heir of John Incledon, of Buckland, nr. Braunton. His niece *m.* Henry Colvin Jackson, *q.v.*

Services: Apptd. Cadet 6 June 1782; sailed for India in the *Montagu* 11 Sept. 1782. Ensign 1st Eur. Bn. in Dec. 1788; transfd. to 21st Bn. Sepoys 5 Feb. 1790; from 2nd Eur. Bn. to 6th Bn. Sepoys 26 Mar. 1793. Lieut. and Bt. Capt. 3rd N.C.; transfd. as Capt. Lt. to 5th N.C. 29 May 1800. Second Mahratta War 1803-4; defeat of Rajah Ram Singh 2 July 1804; Capt. 5th N.C. Operations in Bundelkhand 1805-6; Major 5th N.C. Posted Lt. Col. to 5th N.C. Fur. 1815 till retirement.

Refs.: Burke's *Landed Gentry,* 12th edn., p. 1986, *s.n.* Incledon-Webber, of St. Brannock's, Devon. Vivian's *Visitations of Devon,* p. 812. Portrait in oils in possession of Mrs. W. B. Incledon-Webber, Buckland House, Braunton. M.I. at Braunton.

WEBBER, James (*d.* 1808 ?). Bt. Major. Bengal Eur. Regt. Major General H.M.S. Bt. Capt. 3 Jan. 1776. Bt. Major 1 July 1777. Resigned 19 Jan. 1780. (? *d.* 1808.[1])

Services: Ensign 58th Ft. 15 Mar. 1759; Lieut. do. 27 June 1762; h.p. of reduced Coy. do. 1763; Lieut. 58th Ft. 25 Dec. 1765; Capt. do. 23 July 1773; h.p. of Capt. late 95th Ft. (reduced 1763) 3 Apr. 1777 till 1794. A.D.C. to Gen. Clavering, C.-in-C.

in India, 1775. Raised and comdd. a Regt. of Cav. for the service of the Nawab-Wazir of Oudh 1776-7 ; comdd. 2nd Regt. Cav. 7 Aug. 1777 till 6 Apr. 1778. Granted on 3 Jan. 1776 a Bt. Commission of Capt. in Coy.'s service, from 7 June 1773, " being the date of his commission in the King's service, and this commission is to endure only so long as he shall continue in the Nabob's employ." Promoted Major by brevet in England. Adjt. Gen. in Bengal 1778. Bt. Lt. Col. 1 Mar. 1794 ; Bt. Col. 1 Jan. 1798 ; Maj. Gen. 1 Jan. 1805. Capt. of a new Independent Coy. and Unattached Ofrs. in 1795 ; h.p. of same till death.

Refs.: Forrest, ii. 475. *V.B.G.*, p. 12.

[1] *Note:* His name appears in the British *A.L.* for 1808 for the last time.

WEBBER, Mark Carter (1785-1853). Colonel, 55th N.I. *b.* Deptford 10 Sept. 1785. Cadet 1803. Arrived in India 31 Aug. 1804. Ensign 15 Aug. 1804. Lieut. 21 Sept. 1804. Capt. 1 Aug. 1818. Major 13 May 1825. Lt. Col. 8 Mar. 1830. Col. 26 Dec. 1841. *d.* Serampore, Bengal, 11 July 1853.

bapt. St. Paul's, Deptford, 10 Jan. 1786. Son of Arthur Webber, of Butt Lane, Lieut. R.N., and Margaret his wife. *m.* 1st, Calcutta 1 May 1811, Miss Julia Heale. (She died at sea 16 June 1813.) *m.* 2nd, Burdwan 27 Mar. 1816, Miss Amelia Blenkinsop. (*See also* Edward FitzGerald.) (She died Stockwell 28 Jan. 1873.)

Services: Posted Lieut. to 17th N.I. 1804. A.D.C. to Lord Minto, the G.G., 13 Jan. 1809 till 1813, and accompanied him to Madras Aug. 1809 till May 1810. Capture of Mauritius 1810-11 ; Lieut. 1st Vol. Bn. Actg. Asst. Accounts Soo., Mily. Board, 1 Mar. 1812 ; actg. S.A.C.G. 24 July 1813. Comdd. Burdwan Provl. Bn. 18 Sept. 1813 till 1819 ; do. Patna Provl. Bn. 13 Feb. 1819 till Apr. 1825. Capt. 1/17th N.I. ; transfd. to 34th N.I. (late 1/17th) May 1824. Leave s.c. 12 mos. to Mauritius 7 Apr. 1825. Posted Lt. Col. to 34th N.I. 9 July 1830 ; to 28th N.I. 1 Dec. 1832 ; to 53rd N.I. 9 July 1834 ; to 65th N.I. 15 Jan. 1835 ; to 55th N.I. 9 Oct. 1837. Leave s.c. to Simla 15 Feb. till 15 Dec. 1834. Transfd. to 74th N.I. 25 Feb. 1840 ; to 68th, 17th, 19th, 34th N.I. Posted Col. to 19th N.I. 19 Jan. 1842 ; 55th N.I. 11 Mar. 1842 till death. Bdr. 2 cl. comdg. Agra 30 Sept. 1842 ; do. Lucknow 10 Dec. 1842 till 5 May 1847. Fur. 13 Apr. 1847 till 1848.

Refs.: Boase. I.M. 30 Aug. 1853, p. 506. Will dated Serampore 18 Aug. 1852 ; proved 15 July 1853.

WEBSTER, Alexander (1803-1842). Captain, 43rd N.I. *b.* Nassau, W.I., 14 Nov. 1803. Cadet 1820. Arrived in India

THE BENGAL ARMY, 1758-1834 419

16 Jan. 1822. Ensign 21 June 1821. Lieut. 9 Oct. 1823. Capt. 10 Dec. 1834. *d.* in camp nr. Nowshera 17 Nov. 1842, whilst returning from Kabul.

Eldest son of James Webster, of Cheltenham, formerly a merchant in Liverpool and sometime Speaker of the House of Assembly at the Bahamas, and Honora Tucker his wife. Ed. Edin. Coll.

Services: Ensign d.d. Bengal Eur. Regt. 31 Jan. 1822; posted to 22nd N.I. 1822; transfd. to 43rd N.I. (late 1/22nd) May 1824. First Burma War; Arakan 1825; Lieut. 1st Gren. Bn. Actg. Intr. & Qmr. 43rd N.I. 19 Nov. 1828. Fur. p.a. 23 May 1834 till 28 Dec. 1836. First Afghan War 1838-42; Ghazni 1839; Capt. 43rd N.I. (Medal).

Refs.: *G.M.* 1843, i. 555. *The Times,* 11 Feb. 1843. M.I. Afghan Memorial Church, Bombay.

WEBSTER, Charles (1787-1816). Lieutenant, 5th N.I. *b.* Forfar 17 Dec. 1787. Cadet 1803. Arrived in India 2 Dec. 1804. Ensign 12 Oct. 1804. Lieut. 12 Oct. 1804. *d.* Saharanpur, U.P., 4 Nov. 1816, of a bilious fever.

bapt. Forfar 22 Dec. 1787. 2nd son of Charles Webster, merchant, provost of Forfar, and Clementina Binny his wife. Brother of Thomas Webster, *q.v.*

Services: Posted Lieut. to 5th N.I. 1805. Reduction of Kalinjar 1812; Lieut. 2/5th N.I. Nepal War 1815; operations in Kumaon Feb.-Apr.; Sitauli; capture of Almora; Lieut. 2/5th N.I.

Refs.: *S.M.* 1817, i. 584. Will dated 18 Apr. 1815; proved 3 Jan. 1817.

WEBSTER, Henry (*d.* 1784). Ensign, 3rd Bengal Eur. Regt. Cadet 1782. Arrived in India 22 Jan. 1783. Ensign 3 Apr. 1783. *d.* Cawnpore 15 Apr. 1784.

Services: Apptd. Cadet 23 Jan. 1782; sailed for India in H.M.S. *Inflexible.* Posted to 3rd Eur. Regt. 28 Feb. 1783.

WEBSTER, John Ernestus (1785-1822). Captain, 22nd N.I. *b.* psh. of St. Thomas the Apostle, London, 18 Dec. 1785. Cadet 1804. Arrived in India 10 Sept. 1805. Ensign 6 Sept. 1805. Lieut. 7 Sept. 1805. Capt. 9 Oct. 1818. *d.* Calcutta 20 Jan. 1822. Son of John Webster.

Services: Posted Lieut. to 22nd N.I. 1806; Adjt. 2/22nd N.I. 4 May 1815 till 6 Nov. 1818. Nepal War 1816; Lieut. 2/22nd N.I., in 3rd Bde. Centre Column.

Refs.: Will dated 12 Jan. 1822; proved 18 Feb. 1822. M.I. S. Park St. cemetery, Calcutta.

WEBSTER, Robert (1778-1800). Lieutenant, 12th N.I. *bapt.*
Fowlis 17 Sept. 1778. Cadet 1795. Arrived in India 15 Feb.
1797. Ensign 3 Oct. 1796. Lieut. 30 Oct. 1797. *d.* Chunar
22 Nov. 1800.

2nd son of Robert Webster, in Mains of Fowlis (of Cransley),
and Margaret his wife, dau. of James Hunter, of Inchture.

Services : Served throughout with 12th N.I.

Refs. : Burke's *Landed Gentry*, 2nd edn., iii. 309, *s.n.* Webster,
of Balruddery, co. Forfar.

WEBSTER, Thomas (1793-1865). Major. 59th N.I. *b.* Forfar 25 May 1793. Cadet 1808. Arrived in India 20 July 1809.
Ensign 17 Jan. 1810. Lieut. 16 Dec. 1814. Capt. 2 Sept. 1825.
Retired 1 Dec. 1837. Hon. Major 28 Nov. 1854. *d.* Charlecombe
Villa, Bath, 11 May 1865.

bapt. Forfar 2 June 1793. Son of Charles Webster and Clementina
Binny his wife. Brother of Charles Webster, *q.v.* *m.* 1st, St.
John's, Calcutta, 29 June 1822, Miss Ann Davidson Rice. *m.* 2nd,
Selina, dau. of Dr. French, of Walmer, Kent. (She died 9 May 1878,
aged 78.)

Services : Barasat C.C. Posted Ensign to 11th N.I. 1810.
Reduction of Kalinjar 1812; Ensign 11th N.I. Transfd. to
newly-raised 1/30th N.I. 1815. Leave s.c. to Cape and N.S.W.
29 Feb. 1820 till 1822. d.d. Gorakhpur L.I. 26 Sept. 1822; Adjt.
do. 22 June 1824 till 28 Sept. 1825. Transfd. to 59th N.I. (late
1/30th) May 1824. Fur. u.p.a. 3 Jan. 1826 till 8 May 1829.

Refs. : *G.M.* 1865, i. 805. *Bath Chron.* 18 May 1865.

WEDDERBURN, Charles (*d.* 1778). Captain, Infantry. Ensign 13 Oct. 1766. Lieut. 9 Dec. 1767. Capt. 4 Apr. 1773.
d. Boggah (? Bogra, Bengal) 1 Jan. 1778.

Son of Charles Wedderburn.

Services : Permitted to proceed to India as a free mariner 6 Apr.
1763. *Probably* commissioned owing to the "Batta mutiny."

Refs. : *The Wedderburn Book*, by Alexander Wedderburn (2 vols.,
privately printed 1898), i. 383. Admon. 6 Apr. 1778.

WEDDERBURN, Charles (1748-1829). Captain. Infantry.
b. Pearsie, co. Forfar, 1 Aug. 1748. Cadet 1770. Ensign 29 Nov.
1771. Lieut. 9 Aug. 1776. Capt. 1 Mar. 1781. Resigned 8 Jan.
1785. *d.s.p.* Pearsie 15 Feb. 1829.

Of Pearsie. 2nd son of Robert Wedderburn, of Pearsie, and
Isobel his wife, dau. and heiress of David Edward, of Pearsie.
Brother of John Wedderburn, *q.v.* *m.* 1st, Dundee 11 Sept. 1787,

Anne, dau. of Capt. John Read, of Cairney, co. Angus. (She died 20 Nov. 1789.) *m.* 2nd, Fintry, co. Forfar, 5 Dec. 1797, Eliza, dau. of David Rattray, M.D., of Coventry, co. Warwick, niece of William Rattray (1759-1819), *q.v.*, and aunt of Charles Rattray, *q.v.* (She died Daventry 25 Feb. 1833.) Ed. St. Andrews Univ.; matric. 1762.

Services: Asst. Surg. Bengal 1772; removed to Inf. 24 Dec. 1772. Sometime A.D.C. to his kinsman, Bdr.-Gen. David Wedderburn, Comdr. of the Forces, Bombay. Was serving at Chakai, Monghyr district, on 30 Sept. 1777, and signed a medical cert. there, so he was still doing some medical work. Was probably at home in 1779. Capt. comdg. 31st Bn. Sepoys in Sept. 1783.

Refs.: *The Wedderburn Book*, i. 325-6 (portrait). Burke's *Peerage*, 1923, p. 2281, *s.n.* Wedderburn, Bart., of Ballindean, co. Perth. *Roll of the I.M.S.*, No. B. 191. Will dated 8 Feb. 1821; proved in London May 1829.

*WEDDERBURN, Henry (1722-1777). Captain comdg. a Coy. of Vols. Afterwards Master Attendant at Calcutta. *bapt.* Dunfermline 19 July 1722. Lieut. (Militia) 1756. Capt. 1756 or 1757. *d.* Calcutta 17 Nov. 1777, aged 46.

Of Gosford. 2nd son of Charles Wedderburn, of Gosford, and Mary his wife and cousin-german, dau. of Sir Henry Wardlaw, of Pitreavie, co. Fife, Bart. Brother of Sir John Wedderburn-Halkett, of Pitfirrane, 4th Bart. of Gosford. Cousin-german of Peter Carstairs, *q.v. m.* 1st (*probably c.* 1747), Alice. (She died 1766/7.) His dau. *m.* Sir John Cumming, *q.v. m.* 2nd, Edinburgh 31 Jan. 1768, Mary, dau. of John Belsches, of Innermay, co. Perth. (She died Calcutta 28 July 1771.) *m.* 3rd, Calcutta 4 Mar. 1773, Alice, sister of James Tetley, *q.v.* (She died before 1806.) His dau. *m.* James Murray (1779-1847), *q.v.*

Services: Bred to the sea and settled at Bengal as a free mariner soon after 1740. Apptd. Lieut., and later Capt., of the Gren. Coy. of the Mil. during the siege of Calcutta. Fled to Fulta, thus escaping the Black Hole. Apptd. Master Attendant of Marine at Calcutta in 1758, but held this post a short time only. Served against the Dutch under Col. Forde 1759, after which he returned to the sea as Capt. of a trading vessel. On outbreak of war with Mir Muhammad Kasim in 1763, he raised a Coy. of Vols. from amongst the Calcutta Mil. This Coy., which he comdd. as Capt., left Calcutta in charge of a fleet of store boats and continued to perform that duty to the close of operations in 1765. At home 1766-8. Restored in 1769 to post of Master Attendant, which he held till his death.

Refs.: The *Wedderburn Book*, i. 383-4. *Hill's Calcutta. Hill. Broome*, p. 369. *S.M.* 1778, p. 221. Will dated 13 May 1777; proved in London 3 May 1780. M.I. S. Park St. cemetery, Calcutta.

WEDDERBURN, John (1744-1787). Lieut. Colonel, 2nd Bengal Eur. Bn. Comdt. at Chunar. *b.* 28 July 1744. Cadet 1764. Ensign 7 Mar. 1765. Lieut. 14 Dec. 1766. Capt. 15 Oct. 1769. Major 10 Jan. 1781. Lt. Col. 14 Feb. 1787. *d. unm.* Calcutta 15 July 1787.

Eldest son of Robert Wedderburn, of Pearsie, and Isobel his wife. Brother of Charles Wedderburn (1748-1829), *q.v.*, and grandson of Sir Alexander Wedderburn, 4th Bart.

Services : " It is possible that before going out he was apprenticed to the mercantile house of Websters in London, as a John Wedderburn was so occupied in 1757." (*Wedderburn*) Sailed for India in the *Success* 17 May 1764. Posted to 1st Bengal Eur. Regt. 13 Aug. 1765; 2nd Eur. Regt. in 1766. Resigned during the " Batta mutiny " ; readmitted later. Was Capt. in 2nd Eur. Regt. in Mar. 1775, when he applied for fur. s.c. Pensd. as Capt. on Lord Clive's fund in England 16 Apr. 1776 ; surrendered his pension and returned to India. Capt. comdg. 1/1st Eur. Regt. on 26 Aug. 1780 ; apptd. to comd. 32nd Bn. Sepoys 2 Nov. 1780 ; to comd. 25th N.I. 1 Jan 1781. Second Mysore War 1781-5 ; Major comdg. 25th N.I., with Col. Pearse's detachment. Comdg. 2nd Eur. Bn. and Comdt. at Chunar on 1 July 1787.

Refs.: The *Wedderburn Book*, i. 325. Burke's *Peerage*, 1923, p. 2281, *s.n.* Wedderburn, Bart., of Ballindean, co. Perth. *S.M.* 1788, p. 206. *G.M.* 1788, i. 366.

WEDGWOOD, Charles (1800-1820). Ensign, Infantry. *b.* 25 Nov. 1800. Cadet 1819. Ensign (?) *d.* Berhampore 16 Sept. 1820.

bapt. Westbury-on-Trym, Gloucs., 24 Dec. 1800. 3rd son of John Wedgwood, banker and master potter (who was eldest son of Josiah Wedgwood, F.R.S., master potter of Etruria—*D.N.B.*), and Louisa Jane his wife, dau. of John Bartlett Allen. Woolwich Cadet.

Services : An unposted Ensign. No record of active service.

Refs. : Burke's *Landed Gentry*, 15th edn., p. 2393, *s.n.* Wedgwood, of Etruria. *A Hist. of the Wedgwood Family*, by Josiah C. Wedgwood, M.P., London, 1908.

WEGUELIN, Thomas Matthias (1763/64-1828). Lieut. Colonel Comdt., 41st N.I. *b.* Moorfields, London, 1763/64.

THE BENGAL ARMY, 1758-1834

Cadet 1781. Arrived in India 12 Apr. 1782. Ensign 16 June 1781. Lieut. 22 Sept. 1782. Capt. 10 Aug. 1801. Major 3 Mar. 1808. Lt. Col. 6 Mar. 1814. Lt. Col. Comdt. 20 July 1823. *d.* 25 Montagu Sq., London, 23 May 1828, aged 64.

Eldest son of John Christopher Weguelin and Elizabeth his 2nd wife. Brother of George Weguelin. *m.* 1st, Calcutta 26 Jan. 1814, Miss Mary Cooper. *m.* 2nd, Mary. (She *re-m.* Thomas Willis, M.D., of Leamington, and died 15 Sept. 1856.) His natural dau., by Elizabeth Shaw, *m.* Francis Rowcroft, *q.v.*

Services: See *D.N.B.* Apptd. Cadet 20 Mar. 1781, aged 17. Posted Ensign to 3rd Bengal Eur. Regt. 1782; transfd. as Lieut. to 1/22nd N.I. (became 28th Bn. Sepoys) Nov. 1782. Third Mysore War 1790-2; Arikera; Seringapatam; Lieut. 28th Bn., with Col. Cockerell's detachment. Transfd. as Bt. Capt. to 1/13th N.I. Dec. 1797; to 1st Bengal Eur. Regt. 1799; Capt. Lt. do. 29 May 1800. Second Mahratta War; Gwalior; Bhurtpore; Capt. Eur. Regt. J.A.G. in the field Sept. 1804 till Mar. 1808. Comdd., with local rank of Col., the expedn. against Macao June 1808 till Feb. 1809. Apptd. Dy. Comy. Gen. 1 Feb. 1810, on the establishment of the Comst. Dept. Expedn. to Mauritius 1810; as head of the Comst., and afterwards Comy. Gen. Mauritius and Bourbon; returned to Bengal Mar. 1812. Comy. Gen., with rank of Lt. Col., 26 June 1812 till 31 Dec. 1820. Nepal War 1814-15, and 1816. Third Mahratta War 1817-18. Posted Lt. Col. to 2/30th N.I.; transfd. to 2/17th N.I.; to 2/1st N.I. Fur. Jan. 1822 till death. Lt. Col. Comdt. 56th N.I. May 1824; 41st N.I. 28 Dec. 1826.

Refs.: *D.N.B. E.I.M.C.* i. 180-92. *D.I.B. G.M.* 1828, ii. 180. Will dated 27 Apr. 1828; proved 23 Oct. 1828. M.I. Marylebone church.

WELCHMAN, Frederick (1793-1838). Captain. 58th N.I. *b.* 2 May 1793. Cadet 1808. Arrived in India 6 Dec. 1809. Ensign 30 June 1811. Lieut. 1 Sept. 1814. Capt. 21 Jan. 1826. Retired 1 Jan. 1837. *d. unm.* Ampthill, Beds., 15 Jan. 1838: accidentally shot.[1]

bapt. Kineton, co. Warwick, 12 May 1793. Son of Edward Welchman, of Kineton, surgeon, and Mary his wife. Brother of John Welchman, *q.v.* Ed. Rugby; admitted 1806.

Services: Barasat C.C. Posted Ensign to 3rd N.I. 1811; transfd. to newly-raised 2/29th N.I. 1815; to 58th N.I. (late 2/29th) May 1824. Served with Pioneers 1815-35; actg. Adjt. do. 28 Apr. 1829; Comdt. do. 23 Oct. 1831.

Refs.: Rugby School Register. A.J. N.S. xxv. 127. *G.M.* 1838, i. 218.

¹ *Note :* A young nephew handed him a cocked gun, muzzle first, through a hedge when out shooting. He died in about 2 hours.

WELCHMAN, John (1803-1870). Major General, C.B. 1st Eur. Bengal Fus. *bapt.* Kineton, co. Warwick, 15 Sept. 1803. Cadet 1820. Arrived in India May 1821. Ensign 1 June 1821. Lieut. 11 July 1823. Capt. 5 Mar. 1835. Major 28 Mar. 1848. Lt. Col. 14 July 1853. Col. (28 Nov. 1854) 21 Apr. 1863. Maj. Gen. 25 June 1864. *d.* Leamington 8 Aug. 1870.

Son of Edward Welchman, surgeon, and Mary his wife. Brother of Frederick Welchman, *q.v. m.* Calcutta 25 July 1838, Harriet Alzelia, youngest dau. of John Woodhouse Martin, Asst. Surg. H.M.S. (*See also* Edward Lacon Ommanney.) (She died 18 Mar. 1885, aged 65.)

Services : Posted Ensign to 1/30th N.I. 1821 ; transfd. to 7th N.I. July 1823 ; to 10th N.I. (late 2/7th) May 1824. d.d. 2/29th N.I. 1822 ; tempy. charge of 6th Coy. Pioneers 22 Nov. 1822 ; do. 5th Coy. 2 Aug. 1823. Adjt. 10th N.I. 17 Nov. 1828 till 14 Mar. 1835. 2nd A.A.G. of the Army 16 Mar. 1835 ; 1st do. 22 Feb. 1838 till 1 Nov. 1842. Leave to Cape 28 Feb. till 20 Dec. 1840. Comdt. Kumaon Local Bn. 1 Nov. 1842 till 5 Nov. 1847. Rejoined and comdd. 10th N.I. tempy. in Sind 1843. Fur. 20 Feb. 1848 till 16 Dec. 1850. Second Burma War 1852-3 ; relief of Pegu 1852 ; operations of Martaban Column Jan. 1853 ; Gongoh ; Tonghoo ; Lt. Col. 1st Eur. Bengal Fus., with 10th N.I. (Medal). Posted Lt. Col. to 10th N.I. Sept. 1853 ; to 1st Eur. Bengal Fus. Feb. 1854 till 1864. Mutiny campaign 1857 ; Badli-ki-Serai ; Sabzi Mandi 23 June 1857 (s.w.) ; Bt. Col. 1st Eur. Bengal Fus. (Medal). Fur. 1858 till 30 Jan. 1860. Bdr. 2 cl. comdg. Gwalior district 17 July 1860 ; Maj. Gen. comdg. Presdy. Div. 11 Oct. 1865 till Jan. 1868. Fur. s.c. 10 July 1867 till death. C.B. 21 Jan. 1858.

Refs.: Boase. *The Times,* 15 Aug. 1870. M.I. in Winchester cathedral.

WELDON, Dennis (*d.* 1790). Lieutenant, 4th Bengal Eur. Bn. Cadet 1782. Ensign 29 Jan. 1783. Lieut. 10 Dec. 1789. *d.* Benares 16 Sept. 1790.

Services : Sailed for India in the *Duke of Athol* 11 Sept. 1782. Posted Ensign to 1st Bengal Eur. Regt. ; transfd. to 3rd Eur. Bn. 1785 ; to 6th do. ; to 4th do. 5 Feb. 1790.

Refs.: M.I. Benares.

WELFORD, Henry Pyke (1808-?). Ensign. 30th N.I. *b.* Marlborough, Wilts., 24 Mar. 1808. Cadet 1826. Ensign 10 Mar. 1827. Resigned in India 18 Apr. 1828.

bapt. St. Mary the Virgin, Marlborough, 2 May 1808. Son of Richard Welford, of Marlborough, solicitor, and Sarah his wife.
Services : Posted to 30th N.I. 1827. No record of active service.

WELLAND, Charles (1796-1821). Lieutenant, 12th N.I. *b.* Lympstone, Devon, 24 Dec. 1796. Cadet 1813. Ensign 16 Dec. 1814. Lieut. 29 Sept. 1816. *d.* Jubbulpore 1 Dec. 1821.

bapt. Lympstone 5 Mar. 1799. Son of Richard Welland, of Gittisham House, Devon, formerly R.N., and Emily his wife, cousin of George Higgins Raban, *q.v.* Brother of Walter Palk Welland and kinsman of Walter Palk, *qq.v.*
Services : Posted Ensign to 21st N.I. ; transfd. to 1/12th N.I. 1815 ; Lieut. 1/12th N.I. No record of active service.
Refs. : Devonshire Parishes, by Charles Worthy, ii. 328.

WELLAND, Walter Palk (1793-1847). Captain. 55th N.I. *b.* Tooting Graveney, Surrey, 25 Feb. 1793. Cadet 1808. Arrived in India 27 Oct. 1809. Ensign 22 Mar. 1810. Lieut. 16 Dec. 1814. Capt. 14 Jan. 1826. Retired 1 Dec. 1836. *d.* Devonport 18 May 1847.

bapt. Tooting Graveney 26 Mar. 1793. Eldest son of Richard Welland, of Gittisham House, Devon, Lieut. R.N., and Emily his wife, *née* Evans. Brother of Charles Welland, *q.v.*, and gt.-nephew of Sir Robert Palk, 1st Bart., Govr. of Madras 1763-7. Ed. Blundell's 15 Aug. 1803 till 29 June 1807.
Services : Barasat C.C. Posted Ensign to 22nd N.I. 1810; transfd. to newly-raised 2/28th N.I. 1815. Third Mahratta War 1818 ; Dhamoni ; Lieut. 2/28th N.I. Transfd. to 1/28th N.I. Adjt. Cawnpore Provl. Bn. 1819 ; tempy. comd. do. 25 Apr. 1823 ; Adjt. Murshidabad Provl. Bn. 25 Jan. 1825 till Feb. 1826. Transfd. to 55th N.I. (late 1/28th) May 1824. Fur. s.c. 11 Feb. 1826 till 18 Feb. 1831.[1] Leave s.c. 18 mos. to Singapore and Tasmania 14 Aug. 1833.
Refs.: Blundell's School Register. Will dated 31 Jan. 1826 ; admon. 22 Aug. 1848.

[1] *Note :* Having exceeded 5 yrs. absence from India, was reinstated by C.D. from 18 Feb. 1831. (G.O. 1 May 1832.)

WELLER, Joseph Alexander (1812-1881). Colonel. Engineers. *b.* London 13 Sept. 1812. Cadet 1829. Arrived in India 1 July 1830. 2nd Lieut. 12 Dec. 1828. Lieut. 20 May 1839.

Capt. 12 Dec. 1843. Major 11 Aug. 1857. Lt. Col. 27 Aug. 1858. Retired 31 Dec. 1858. Hon. Col. 31 Dec. 1858. *d.* Bedford 17 June 1881.

bapt. Marylebone 27 Sept. 1812. Only son of Joseph Hume Weller and Maria his wife. *m.* Landour 22 Aug. 1849, Alice, 4th sister of Thomas Wilson Oldfield, *q.v.* (*See also* Richard Cautley.) (She died Bedford 5 Dec. 1878, aged 59.) Addiscombe Cadet 1827 till 12 Dec. 1828.

Services: d.d. S. & M. 10 July 1830; Asst. to Supt. Delhi-Allahabad road 28 June 1833 till 1840. Executive Engr. Kumaon Div. 20 Jan. 1841; Asst. Comr. in Kumaon 9 Feb. 1842 till 1 June 1843. Apptd. to Army of Exercise 24 Nov. 1843. Gwalior campaign; Maharajpur; Capt. Engrs. (Bronze star). Executive Engr. in Sind 25 July 1845; in charge of Bombay road from Agra 28 Nov. 1845; Comdt. Sappers & Pioneers 28 Sept. 1849 till Oct. 1856. Suptg. Engr. 2nd circle (N.W.P.) 24 Oct. 1846 till retirement. Mutiny campaign; defence of Agra 1858.

Refs.: The Times, 20 June 1881.

WELLS, Edmund (1755/56-1794). Lieutenant, 13th Bn. Sepoys. *b.* 1755/56. Cadet 1780. Ensign 6 Oct. 1780. Lieut. 6 July 1781. *d.* Rampur, U.P., 12 Nov. 1794, of wounds received in action on 26 Oct.

Son of —— Wells, of Stratford-on-Avon.

Services: Sailed for India in the *Contractor* 3 Apr. 1780, aged 24. Was Adjt. 14th Bn. Sepoys in Mar. 1786 and in July 1787 A.D.C. to Col. John Fullarton, *q.v.*, till 5 Feb. 1790. Third Mysore War 1790-2; Bde. Major to Lt.-Col. Cockerell's detachment. Comdg. troops in Andaman Is. 1793 till Mar. 1794, and sometime offg. Supt. of the Andamans. To d.d. 14th Bn. 9 Oct. 1794. Actg. Bde. Major of 1st Bde. for service in Rohilkhand 17 Oct. 1794. Second Rohilla War; battle of Bitaurah (s.w.); Bde. Major 1st Bde. Apptd. Bde. Major on the Est. 31 Oct. 1794. Transfd. from 6th to 13th Bn. Sepoys 11 Nov. 1794.

Refs.: G.M. 1795, ii. 792. M.I. in St. John's churchyard, Calcutta. Will dated 1 Jan. 1792; codicil 5 Mar. 1793; proved 9 Jan. 1795.

WELLS, Luke (1749/50-1786). Bt. Ensign, Invalid Est. Infantry. *b.* 1749/50. Bt. Ensign 9 Aug. 1782. *d.* Calcutta 12 Sept. 1786, aged 36.

Services: Apptd. a Bt. Ensign from Sergt.
Refs.: M.I. S. Park St. cemetery, Calcutta.

THE BENGAL ARMY, 1758-1834

WELSH, George (*d.* 1806). Major, 1st N.C. Cadet 1782. Admitted 4 Feb. 1783. Cornet 4 Feb. 1783. Lieut. 1 Jan. 1790. Capt. 16 June 1800. Major 11 Mar. 1805. *d. unm.* Calcutta 31 Jan. 1806.

Younger son of Thomas Welsh, of Edinburgh, carver and gilder. Brother of Thomas Welsh and of the mother of David Allan, *qq.v.*

Services: Apptd. Cadet 20 Dec. 1781; sailed for India in the *Alfred* 6 Feb. 1782. First Mahratta War; Cadet with Bengal detachment under Col. Charles Morgan, *q.v.* Ensign 2nd Bengal Eur. Bn. in July 1787. Posted to 6th Eur. Bn. 16 Jan. 1790; transfd. to 13th Bn. Sepoys 5 Feb. 1790. Third Mysore War 1790-2; Arikera; operations before Savandrug; Seringapatam; Lieut. 13th Bn. Fur. 6 May 1798 till 15 Mar. 1804. Lieut. and Bt. Capt. 1st N.C.; Capt. Lt. do. 29 May 1800. Second Mahratta War 1804-5; Major 1st N.C. "Distinguished himself greatly in Lord Lake's campaign." (*S.M.*) Was on the eve of embarking on fur. when his death occurred.

Refs.: Stubbs, i. 277. *S.M.* 1806, p. 565. Will dated London, 12 Feb. 1803; proved 6 Feb. 1806.

WELSH, John (1789-1815). Lieutenant, 27th N.I. *b.* Drumelzier, co. Peebles, 26 Feb. 1789. Cadet 1805. Arrived in India 10 July 1807. Ensign 8 July 1807. Lieut. 4 Mar. 1812. *d.* Saharanpur, U.P., 29 Apr. 1815.

bapt. Drumelzier 13 Mar. 1789. 2nd son of Rev. William Welsh, minister of Drumelzier, and Sarah Ballantyne his 2nd wife.

Services: Barasat C.C. Posted Ensign to 27th N.I. 1808. (? Operations in Oudh 1810; Ensign 2/27th N.I.)

Refs.: Scott's *Fasti,* i. 269.

WELSH, Thomas (*d.* 1822). Colonel. 2nd N.C. Cadet 1769. Admitted 12 Sept. 1769. Ensign 12 Sept. 1769. Lieut. 2 Feb. 1773. Capt. 18 Jan. 1781. Major 1 Mar. 1794. Lt. Col. 6 Aug. 1797. Col. 29 May 1800. Retired 13 Aug. 1800. *d.* 11 Apr. 1822.

Elder son of Thomas Welsh, of Edinburgh. Brother of George Welsh, *q.v. m.* Brit. Embassy, Paris, 14 Dec. 1788, Ann Martha, sister of Irwin Maling, *q.v.* (She died London 25 Jan. 1850.)

Services: With Nawab-Wazir of Oudh's troops at Lucknow in Nov. 1777; posted to Cav. 6 Apr. 1778. First Mahratta War 1778-84; Capt. 1st Regt. Cav., with Bengal detachment under Goddard. Presented with a sword by Warren Hastings in June 1784 in recognition of his services in the late campaign. Fur.

5 Jan. 1787 till 6 Aug. 1790. Transfd. from 1st to 5th Bengal Eur. Bn. 30 Jan. 1791. Third Mysore War 1791-2; Bangalore; Arikera; operations before Savandrug; Ramgiri; Shivanagiri; Seringapatam; Capt. comdg. 1st Bn. Bengal Vols.; succeeded John Scrymgeour, *q.v.*, in comd. of 28th Bn. Sepoys 5 Oct. 1791. Expedn. to Assam 1793; recapture of Gauhati; Capt. comdg. the force consisting of 15 Coys. Inf. Posted Lt. Col. to 2nd N.C. 2 June 1797, when the Cav. was separated from the Inf. and declared a distinct Corps. Formed the Calcutta Mil. Cav. in 1798. Fur. 11 Jan. 1799 till retirement.

Refs.: Gen. *Memoirs of John Knox*, by Rev. Charles Rogers, p. 156. *E.I.M.C.* i. 71-5. *Cardew*, pp. 57, 60, 63. *Williams*, p. 89.

WELSH, Thomas Henry (1774-1799). Lieutenant, 7th N.I. *b.* Plymstock, Devon, 13 June 1774. Cadet 1794. Arrived in India 18 Feb. 1795. Ensign 13 Sept. 1794. Lieut. 10 June 1796. *d.* Gaya, B. & O., 11 Jan. 1799.

bapt. Plymstock 29 Oct. 1775. Son of John Welsh and Anna Maria his wife.

Services: Apptd. Cadet 17 June 1794; sailed for India in the *Lascelles* 14 Aug. 1794. Ensign 6th Bengal Eur. Bn. in Feb. 1796; posted Lieut. to 1st Bengal Eur. Regt. June 1796; transfd. to 7th N.I.

WEMYSS, James (1807-1865). Major. 44th N.I. *b.* Calcutta 11 Jan. 1807. Cadet 1824. Arrived in India 27 May 1825. Ensign 19 Jan. 1825. Lieut. 3 May 1826. Capt. 8 Oct. 1839. Retired 27 May 1845. Hon. Major 28 Nov. 1854. *d.* 27 June 1865.

bapt. Calcutta 15 Dec. 1807. Eldest son of James Wemyss, B.C.S., Collector of Cawnpore, and Caroline Charlotte his wife, 5th dau. of Rev. Henry Binfield, vicar of Albrighton. Brother of William Binfield Wemyss, *q.v. m.* 1st, Sulkea, Pabna, 27 July 1836, Miss Bella Driver. (She died Gauhati, Assam, 31 Aug. 1840, aged 30.) *m.* 2nd, Gauhati 11 Sept. 1841, Helen Maria, dau. of James Reilly. (She died Port Said 30 Mar. 1898, aged 75.)

Services: Ensign d.d. 66th N.I. 10 June 1825; posted to 2nd Extra Regt. 1825; transfd. to 44th N.I. 1826; actg. Intr. & Qmr. do. 5 June 1827. d.d. Talain Corps 16 June 1825; d.d. Assam L.I. 27 Jan. 1826; actg. Adjt. do. 1 Aug. 1837 till 2 Feb. 1839. Junior Asst. to A.G.G., N.E. frontier, 4 Feb. 1839; Principal Asst. to Comr. of Assam 1 Apr. 1839 till 26 Jan. 1842. No record of active service.

Refs.: Burke's *Peerage*, 1923, p. 2293, *s.n.* Wemyss, E.

WEMYSS, John (1742/43-?). Captain. Artillery. (114) *b.* 1742/43.¹ Cadet (Inf.) 1770. Fireworker 14 Mar. 1771. Lieut. 27 Oct. 1773. Capt. Lt. 16 Sept. 1779. Capt. 15 Apr. 1781. Resigned on pension 1 Sept. 1783.

Services: Fur. 13 Jan. 1780 till 12 Nov. 1782. Left India in the *Resolution* 20 Sept. 1783, arrived in England 12 Nov. 1784, and pensd. on Lord Clive's fund from that date.

¹ *Note:* Aged 41 in 1784.

WEMYSS, William Binfield (1810-1890). General. 1st Bengal Eur. L.C. *b.* in India 15 Feb. 1810. Cadet 1825. Arrived in India 27 Oct. 1826. Cornet 22 May 1826. Lieut. 3 Dec. 1828. Capt. 10 Oct. 1836. Major 2 Oct. 1851. Lt. Col. 28 Nov. 1854. Bt. Col. 20 July 1859. Maj. Gen. 3 July 1867. Lt. Gen. 6 Feb. 1875. Gen. 1 Oct. 1877. Retired List 15 Feb. 1880. *d.* Highfield House, Guildford, 24 May 1890.

bapt. Calcutta 22 Nov. 1811. 2nd son of James Wemyss, B.C.S., and Caroline Charlotte his wife. Brother of James Wemyss and cousin-german of A. R. J. Swinton, *qq.v.* *m.* Nimach 24 Mar. 1832, Martha Rose Diana, eldest dau. of Samuel Smith (1783-1852), *q.v.* (*See also* Charles Garrett.) (She died 23 Oct. 1876, aged 63.)

Services: Posted Cornet to 9th L.C. 9 Nov. 1826; actg. Adjt. do. 5 Dec. 1829; permanent do. 11 Dec. 1830 till 10 June 1833. Leave s.c. to Simla 1 Nov. 1838 till 1 Nov. 1839. Campaign in Sind 1843; Miani; Hyderabad; Capt. 9th L.C. (Medal). Bde. Major Meerut 16 May 1845 till Oct. 1850; Supt. Remount Depot at Karnal 31 Oct. 1850 till 1851. Posted Lt. Col. to 9th L.C. Apr. 1855; to 10th L.C. 2 Jan. 1857. Fur. s.c. 30 Dec. 1856 till 12 Dec. 1859. Transfd. to newly-raised 4th Bengal Eur. L.C. May 1858; to 1st do. 28 Dec. 1859 till 1864. Fur. 10 Dec. 1867 till retirement.

Refs.: Burke's *Peerage*, 1923, p. 2293, *s.n.* Wemyss, E. *Boase.* I.L.N. 7 June 1890, p. 708 (portrait). *The Times*, 27 May 1890.

WEST, formerly LUCADOU,¹ James Louis (1761-1819). Lieutenant. Infantry. *b.* London 2 Nov. 1761. Cadet 1780. Ensign 4 Dec. 1780. Lieut. 18 Aug. 1781. Struck off 1791. *d.* Aug. 1819.

Of Countisbury, Devon. Eldest son of John Daniel Lucadou,² of Grove Pl., Hackney, and of Lombard St., banker, and Mary Anne his wife, dau. of Rev. David Duval. Changed his name to West 13 May 1816.

Services: Sailed for India in the *Bridgwater* 12 Feb. 1780, aged 19. Fur. 3 yrs. on full pay 20 Feb. 1786 till struck off. Became a banker in Lombard St.; elected a Dir. of the French Hospital in London 9 July 1788.

Refs.: Genealogist, N.S. xxvii. 230. Agnew's *French Protestant Exiles*. Will dated 14 Oct. 1818; proved 20 Oct. 1819.

¹ *Note*: His name is given as James Lewis Lucadon (Luccadon in *D. & M.*) in all official records, and his brother in B.C.S. as George Lucadon.

² *Note*: Naturalized by Act of Parliament 33 Geo. II (1759).

WEST, Martin Thomas (1803-1849). Ensign. 21st N.I. Subsequently Lieut. Govr. of Natal. *b*. London 9 July 1803. Cadet 1821. Ensign 9 Dec. 1821. Resigned in India 31 Oct. 1823. *d*. Natal, S.A., 1 Aug. 1849.

Eldest son of Gilbert Harvey West, of Marylebone, senior clerk in H.M. Treasury Office, and Fanny Mary his wife, eldest dau. of Sir Martin Browne ffolkes, 1st Bart. Nephew of Sir Edward West, C.J. Bombay. *m.* Bombay, Albinia, dau. of —— Sullivan. Univ. Coll., Oxon.; matric. 22 Mar. 1820.

Services: Posted to 4th N.I. 1822; transfd. to 21st N.I. 1823. No record of active service. Sometime Civil Comr. of Albany, S.A.; Lieut. Govr. of Natal 30 Dec. 1845 till death.

Refs.: Family information. Burke's *Landed Gentry*, 5th edn., p. 1491, *s.n.* West, of Braywick Lodge, Berks. *Alumni Oxon*.

*WEST, William (*d.* 1763). Cornet. Cavalry. Cornet (?) *bur*. Calcutta 1 Dec. 1763.

m. Dorothy.

Services: "Late Cornet of Horse at Bengal." (M.C. 18 Mar. 1768.)

Refs.: Will dated 24 Sept. 1763; proved 13 Dec. 1763.

Note: Qy. whether strictly eligible for inclusion.

WESTERN, James Roger (1812-1871). Colonel. Engineers. *b.* London 28 Feb. 1812. Cadet 1829. Arrived in India 6 Oct. 1830. 2nd Lieut. 12 Dec. 1828. Lieut. 20 May 1839. Capt. 24 Aug. 1847. Bt. Major 7 June 1849. Retired 23 Jan. 1855. Lt. Col. 11 May 1855. Hon. Col. 1856. *d.* 12 Park St., Regent's Pk., London, 13 Jan. 1871.

4th son of James Western, of Bath, and of London, solicitor, and Charlotte his wife, eldest dau. of Rev. Robert Hallifax, vicar of Standish, Gloucs. Nephew of William Brydges Western, *q.v. m.* Calcutta 25 Nov. 1847, Catherine Laura, 3rd dau. of Charles Samuel Goodwyn, of Blackheath. (She died Jullundur 27 Feb.

1850, aged 27.) Ed. Uppingham Feb.-June 1827. Addiscombe Cadet 1827-8.

Services: Attached to office of Surveyor Gen. 5 Jan. 1831; employed with Gt. Trig. Survey 15 July 1831 till 6 Sept. 1834; posted to S. & M. at Delhi 22 Sept. 1834. (? Shekhawat expedn. 1834.) Executive Engr. 2nd (Berhampore) Div., P.W.D., 28 Oct. 1840. Fur. p.a. 13 Feb. 1841 till 8 Oct. 1842. Executive Engr. Arakan Div. 24 Oct. 1842; do. Rajputana Div. 22 May 1843; do. Dacca 18 Aug. 1843. Second Sikh War; Multan, conducting Engr. (*Lond. Gaz.* 7 Mar. 1849); Gujerat (ib. 19 Apr. 1849); Capt. Engrs. (Medal with 2 clasps). Executive Engr. Jullundur Doab Div. 30 May 1849; offg. Comdt. S. & M. 2 Nov. 1852; Executive Engr. 11th (Meerut) Div. 18 Nov. 1853 till retirement.

Refs.: Burke's *Peerage*, 1905, p. 1655, *s.n.* Western, Bart., of Rivenhall, Essex. Ruvigny's *Plantagenet Roll of the Blood Royal*, Essex Vol., p. 312. *Uppingham School Register. The Times*, 14 Jan. 1871.

WESTERN, William Brydges (1779-1818). Captain, 6th L.C. *b.* 12 Nov. 1779. Cadet 1798. Arrived in India 1 Sept. 1799. Cornet 2 June 1800. Lieut. 17 July 1801. Capt. 15 Apr. 1816. *d. unm.* Lohargaon, C.I., 26 Oct. 1818, on his way to the sea coast for the benefit of his health.

bapt. Walcot, Somerset, 15 Dec. 1779. 7th and youngest son of Thomas Western, of Gt. Abington, Cambs., and Jane his wife, dau. of Felix Calvert, of Albury Hall, Herts., M.P. for Wendover. Uncle of James Roger Western, *q.v.*, and of Sir Thomas Burch Western, 1st Bart.

Services: Operations in Jumna Doab 1803; Sasni; Bijaigarh; Kachaura; Lieut. 6th N.C. Second Mahratta War 1803-6; Laswari; relief of Delhi; Shamli; pursuit of Holkar; Lieut. 6th N.C. Qmr. 6th N.C. 26 Jan. 1804 till 1812. Operations against Dhundia Khan 1807; Lieut. 6th N.C. Settlement of Hariana 1809; Bhawani; Lieut. 6th N.C. Capt. Lt. 6th N.C. 1 Nov. 1809. Fur. 1812 till 20 Aug. 1815. Third Mahratta War; Sitabaldi; Nagpur; Chanda; Capt. 6th N.C.

Refs.: Burke's *Peerage*, 1923, p. 2298, *s.n.* Western, Bart., of Rivenhall, Essex (extinct 1 Feb. 1917). *G.M.* 1819, ii. 88. Will dated 17 Dec. 1814; proved 13 Nov. 1818.

WESTMACOTT, George Edward (1807-1841). Captain, 37th N.I. *b.* London 23 Feb. 1807. Cadet 1822. Arrived in India 24 Aug. 1823. Ensign 11 July 1823. Lieut. 13 May 1825. Capt.

18 Sept. 1833. *d.* nr. Kabul 10 Nov. 1841 : kld. in action at the retaking of Rikabashi fort.

bapt. Paddington 22 Mar. 1807. Eldest son of George Westmacott, clerk in H.M. Stamp office at Somerset House, and Ann Knightery his wife. (*Probably* nephew of Sir Richard Westmacott, the sculptor (*D.N.B.*), who was one of a family of 24 children.)

Services: Posted Ensign to 36th N.I.; transfd. as Lieut. to 37th N.I. May 1824. Siege and capture of Bhurtpore; Lieut. 37th N.I. Intr. & Qmr. 37th N.I. 21 Dec. 1827 till 3 Dec. 1833. Junior Asst. to A.G.G., N.E. frontier, 19 Oct. 1833. Fur. s.c. 30 Mar. 1835 till 20 Mar. 1839. Rejoined 37th N.I. in Sind Apr. 1839. First Afghan War 1839-41; D.J.A.G. to troops in Afghanistan 14 Dec. 1840; do. to Shah Shuja's troops 17 Mar. 1841; outbreak at Kabul; recapture of Rikabashi fort (kld.); Capt. 37th N.I. Author of "The Present and Future Prospects of our Indian Empire," 8vo, London, 1838.

Refs.: *G.M.* 1842, i. 677. M.I. Afghan Memorial Church, Bombay.

WESTON, Charles (1735/36-1769). Ensign. Infantry. *b.* London 1735/36. Cadet 1765. Ensign 10 Aug. 1765. Resigned May 1766. *d.* Calcutta 27 Sept. 1769.

Services: Should have sailed for India in the *True Briton* 26 May 1761, aged 25, but was "not on board when the ship sailed." Was already in Calcutta when apptd. Cadet (G.O. 17 Apr. 1765). *Probably* resigned his Commission during the "Batta mutiny."

WESTON, Charles Thomas Gustavus (1786-1828). Captain, 66th N.I. *b.* London 13 Nov. 1786. Cadet 1806. Arrived in India 14 Oct. 1807. Ensign 25 Oct. 1807. Lieut. 7 Apr. 1813. Capt. 1 May 1824. *d.* Calcutta 27 May 1828, of cholera.

bapt. St. Anne's, Westminster, 13 Sept. 1787. Son of Charles Gustavus Weston, of Brompton and New Clement's Inn. His sister *m.* John Lewis Stuart, *q.v.* *m.* Chunar 23 Dec. 1823, Miss Charlotte Jane Arnold.

Services: Barasat C.C. Posted Ensign to 14th N.I. 1808. Capture of Mauritius 1810-11; Ensign 2nd Vol. Bn. Adjt. Rangpur Bn. 18 Sept. 1813; do. 2/14th N.I. 13 Dec. 1816 till 1819. Adjt. & Qmr. Eur. Invalids at Chunar, and sometime, in addition, Sub-Dir. telegraphic communication, 1819-24. Transfd. to 29th N.I. (late 2/14th) May 1824; to 66th N.I. 1824. Supt. & Dir. telegraphic communication 1824 till death.

Refs.: *A.J.* xxvi. 740. Will dated 14 Oct. 1824; proved 25 July 1828.

THE BENGAL ARMY, 1758-1834

WESTON, Frederick Alexander (1782-1836). Lieut. Colonel, Invalid Est. 11th N.I. *b.* Lausanne, Switzerland, 14 Feb. 1782. Cadet 1799. Admitted 23 Oct. 1800. Ensign 21 Dec. 1799. Lieut. 29 May 1800. Capt. 18 Nov. 1808. Major 11 July 1823. Lt. Col. 7 Nov. 1824. Invalided 11 Apr. 1828. *d.* Almora, U.P., 11 July 1836.

bapt. Lausanne 21 Mar. 1782. 3rd son of Henry Perkins Weston, of W. Horsley, Surrey, and Marianne his 1st wife, dau. of Sebastian Bergier de Rovereaz, of Lausanne. Half-brother of John Samuel Henry Weston, *q.v.* Ed. Eton; in 3rd Form, Lower School, in 1793.

Services: Posted Lieut. to 1/2nd N.I. 15 Apr. 1801. Operations in Jumna Doab 1803; Sasni; Lieut. 1/2nd N.I. Second Mahratta War 1803-5; battle of Delhi; battle and capture of Deig; Bhurtpore; Lieut. 1/2nd N.I. Adjt. & Qmr. 2nd N.I. 1805 till 8 July 1809. Capt. 1/2nd N.I. Fur. 17 Nov. 1812 till 1818. Actg. Bde. Major Presdy. Div. 1820; permanent do. 1821-4. Transfd. to 5th N.I. (late 1/2nd) May 1824. Comdg. Burdwan Provl. Bn. 1824. Posted Lt. Col. to 8th N.I. 18 Feb. 1825; to 5th N.I. 1825; to 35th N.I. 30 Oct. 1826; to 11th N.I. 29 Feb. 1828. To comd. 2nd Bn. Native Invalids at Chunar 1 May 1828; do. Delhi Provl. Bn. 5 Feb. 1829; do. Eur. Invalids at Chunar 14 Dec. 1833.

Refs.: Burke's *Landed Gentry*, 13th edn., p. 1863, *s.n.* Weston, of West Horsley, Surrey. *Eton School Lists. Pester, passim. A.J.* N.S. xxii. 118. Will dated 28 Feb. 1831; codicil Delhi 13 Aug. 1834; proved 1 Feb. 1837.

WESTON, Henry (1786-1828). Lieut. Colonel, 3rd N.I. *bapt.* Witney, Oxon., 6 Mar. 1786. Cadet 1800. Arrived in India 16 Oct. 1801. Ensign 15 Nov. 1801. Lieut. 30 Sept. 1803. Capt. 16 Dec. 1814. Major 1 May 1824. Lt. Col. 30 Sept. 1827. *d.* Lohoo Ghat, Kumaon, 21 Sept. 1828.

Son of Rev. Phipps Weston, rector of Witney, afterwards preby. of Durham, and Mary his wife. Brother of John Weston, *q.v.*, and nephew of John Wilton, of 11 Devonshire Pl., London, formerly B.C.S., sometime sheriff of Calcutta.

Services: Ensign d.d. 2nd Eur. Regt. in 1802; posted Ensign to 19th N.I. 1803. Adjt. & Qmr. 19th N.I. 2 Apr. 1807 till 1814. Nepal War 1814-15; Capt. 1/19th N.I., in 1st Div. Intr. & Qmr. 1/19th N.I. 1815. Fur. 1816-20. Transfd. to 2/19th N.I. Comdg. 2nd Nassiri Bn. 1822-8. Transfd. to 39th N.I. (late 2/19th) May 1824. Posted Lt. Col. to 3rd N.I. 3 Apr. 1828.

Refs.: A.J. xxvii. 482. Will dated Lohoo Ghat 21 Apr. 1825; proved 11 Dec. 1828.

LIST OF THE OFFICERS OF

WESTON, John (1780-1819). Lieut. Colonel, 20th N.I. *b.* Witney 23 Sept. 1780. Cadet 1794. Arrived in India 6 Feb. 1797. Ensign 29 Oct. 1795. Lieut. 25 Apr. 1797. Capt. 10 May 1804. Major 12 Apr. 1814. Lt. Col. 30 June 1818. *d.* at sea 31 July 1819, on board the *Eliza.*

bapt. 18 Oct. 1780. Son of Rev. Phipps Weston and Mary his wife. Brother of Henry Weston, *q.v.*, and cousin of Rev. Charles Gerard. Magdalen Coll., Oxon.; matric. 25 July 1794, aged 13; demy 1794-96.

Services: Apptd. Cadet 20 Jan. 1796; sailed for India in the *Manship* 12 Apr. 1796. Lieut. 2nd Bengal Eur. Regt., comdg. Resdt.'s escort with Sindhia 1798-1802; transfd. to newly-formed Marine Regt. (became 20th N.I.) 1802. At P.W.I. in 1803; A.D.C. to Govr. of P.W.I.; do. to G.G. 1 Mar. 1806. Fur. 6 Sept. 1806 till 7 Dec. 1809. Capture of Java 1811; Capt. 20th N.I. Asst. Professor of Arabic and Persian at Coll. of Ft. Wm. 18 Dec. 1813 till 1818. Leave s.c. to Cape Apr. 1816 till 18 Mar. 1818. Serving in Ceylon in 1818.

Refs.: Alumni Oxon. Will dated 10 Aug. 1818; proved 28 Aug. 1819. M.I. in St. John's church, Calcutta.

WESTON, John Samuel Henry (1791-1850). Bt. Colonel, C.B., 73rd N.I. *b.* Lausanne 9 Jan. 1791. Cadet 1809. Arrived in India 3 Oct. 1810. Ensign 25 Apr. 1812. Lieut. 13 June 1817. Capt. 18 Jan. 1826. Major 20 Dec. 1838. Lt. Col. 2 Feb. 1845. Bt. Col. 28 Mar. 1850. *d.* Paris 8 Oct. 1850.

Of West Horsley, Surrey. *bapt.* St. Francis, Lausanne, 15 Feb. 1791. 4th son of Henry Perkins Weston, of West Horsley, and Jeanne Marie his 2nd wife, dau. of Joseph Samuel Bergier du Mont, of Lausanne. Half-brother of Frederick Alexander Weston, *q.v. m.* 1st, Sarah, natural dau. of James Murray MacGregor, *q.v.* (*See also* Hon. Patrick Campbell Sinclair.) (She died 16 Oct. 1825.) *m.* 2nd, Saugor 22 Nov. 1826, Margaret, sister of Malcolm Nicolson, *q.v.* (*See also* James Nesbitt Jackson.) (She died 1838.) *m.* 3rd, Meerut, 29 Apr. 1840, Jessie Macdonald, 2nd dau. of George Playfair, M.D., Bengal Medical Est., and niece of Sir Hugh Lyon Playfair, *q.v.* Ed. Eton 1805-8.

Services: Barasat C.C. Cadet d.d. 2nd N.I. 1811; posted Ensign to 2/2nd N.I. 1812. (? Operations in Baghelkhand 1813; Entauri; Ensign 2/2nd N.I.) With 2nd Gren. Bn. 1815-16. Transfd. Lieut. to 1/15th N.I. 1817. Third Mahratta War; siege and capture of Asirgarh 1819; Lieut. 1/15th N.I. Actg. Bk. Mr. Sikraul Div. 31 July 1819; offg. Sec. and Persian Intr. to

THE BENGAL ARMY, 1758-1834   435

O.C. Narbada F.F. 20 Dec. 1820; D.J.A.G. Nagpur Subsdy. Force 23 Oct. 1821 till Jan. 1825. Transfd. to 31st N.I. (late 1/15th) May 1824. D.J.A.G. Saugor Div. 12 Jan. 1825; do. Meerut Div. 4 May 1832; do. Saugor Div. 6 Oct. 1838 till 5 Aug. 1839. Rejoined 31st N.I. for service Sept. 1838. First Afghan War 1838-40; Ghazni (Medal); capture of Kalat (*Lond. Gaz.* 13 Feb. 1840); Major comdg. 31st N.I. Gwalior campaign; Maharajpur (ib. 8 Mar. 1844); Bt. Lt. Col. comdg. 31st N.I. (Bronze star). Bdr. 2 cl. for service in Army of Gwalior 22 Jan. 1844. Posted Lt. Col. to 31st N.I. 17 Apr. 1845; transfd. to 12th N.I. 1846; to 44th N.I. 1849; to 73rd N.I. 1850. Fur. s.c. Jan. 1850 till death. C.B. 3 Apr. 1846. Durani 3 cl. 15 Aug. 1840.

Refs.: Burke's *Landed Gentry*, 13th edn., p. 1863, *s.n.* Weston, of West Horsley, Surrey. *Eton School Lists*. *G.M.* 1850, ii. 679.

WESTON, Richard. Lieutenant, Infantry. Cadet 1780. Ensign 29 Jan. 1781. Lieut. 5 Oct. 1781. *d.* Madras Presdy. 1783: kld.

Services: Second Mysore War.

WHALLEY, Frederick Elidor (1810-1830). Cornet, 6th L.C. *b.* Calcutta 29 Aug. 1810. Cadet 1826. Cornet 2 Oct. 1828. *d.* Sultanpur, Benares, 22 Oct. 1830, of apoplexy.

bapt. Calcutta 3 Feb. 1811. Son of Charles Whalley, of Calcutta, atty.-at-law, and Sarah his wife, 2nd dau. of John Lewis, of Harpton Court, co. Radnor.

Services: Cadet d.d. 6th L.C. 22 Jan. 1828; posted Cornet to 6th L.C. 26 Jan. 1829. No record of active service.

Refs.: Burke's *Landed Gentry*, 2nd edn., p. 727, *s.n.* Lewis, of Harpton Court, co. Radnor. *A.J.* N.S. iv. 215. M.I. Chunar (Sultanpur).

WHARTON, Robert (1788-1819). Lieutenant, 7th N.C. *b.* London 24 Dec. 1788. Cadet 1810. Cornet (30 Sept.) 23 Nov. 1815. Lieut. 1 Sept. 1818. *d.* Muttra 25 July 1819.

bapt. St. George's, Hanover Sq., 30 Jan. 1789. Son of Samuel Wharton, of H.M. Household, of Chelsea, and Mary Killick his wife.

Services: Barasat C.C. Cadet d.d. 8th N.C. 1811-13. Posted Cornet to 7th N.C. Nov. 1815. Siege and capture of Hathras 1817; Cornet 7th N.C. Third Mahratta War 1817-19; Dhamoni; Mandala; Lieut. 7th N.C.

WHARTON, Thomas (1758-1802). Lieut. Colonel, 5th N.C. *b.* 13 Mar. 1758. Cadet 1777. Admitted 26 Feb. 1778. Cornet

16 Feb. 1778. Lieut. 25 Sept. 1778. Capt. 14 Feb. 1796. Major
1 Nov. 1798. Lt. Col. 29 May 1800. d. 21 Jan. 1802 : drowned
when crossing the Kali Nadi in flood.[1]
Eldest son of Thomas Wharton (of the family of Barons Wharton),
of Lauriston, Edin., Comr. of Excise in Scotland, and Judith his
1st wife, dau. of Capt. Charles Massey. Step-nephew of Sir
Alexander Mackenzie, 6th Bart. of Coul, *q.v.* m. Cawnpore 12 Aug.
1789, Sarah Paulina, dau. of Samuel Skardon, *q.v.* (*See also*
Richard Ramsay.) (She died Ghazipur 22 Jan. 1838, aged 63.)
Father of Thomas Ramsay Wharton, *q.v.*, and grandfather of the
wife of William Payne, *q.v.*
Services : Sailed for India in the *Europa* 9 Feb. 1777. Lieut.
35th Bn. Sepoys in July 1787 and in Dec. 1788. Transfd. to 1st
Cav. Regt. Adjt. 36th Bn. Sepoys 31 Oct. 1791 till 1794. Second
Rohilla War ; battle of Bitaurah ; Lieut. Cav., 2nd in comd. to
his brother-in-law. Major 3rd N.C. Apptd. 29 May 1800 to comd.
5th N.C. which he had just raised at Ghazipur.
Refs. : Temple's *Thanage of Fermartyn*, p. 122. *Fatehgarh
Camp 1777-1857*, by C. L. Wallace, M.C., I.C.S. (1934), p. 120.
S.M. 1802, p. 708. *G.M.* 1803, i. 86.

[1] *Note :* A tall pyramid and two tombs, believed to be those of
himself, his horse and dog, drowned with him, still stand on a hill
overlooking the spot where the Kali Nadi used to flow into the
Ganges, and 2 miles east of Serai Miran, U.P.

WHARTON, Thomas Ramsay (1791-1849). Ensign. 20th
N.I. Afterwards Lieut. 8th (K.R.I.) Light Dgns *b.* Dinapore
31 July 1791. Cadet 1808. Arrived in India 19 July 1809.
Ensign 21 Nov. 1809. Resigned 25 Feb. 1812. *d.* Patna 19 Aug.
1849.

bapt. Dinapore 7 Feb. 1792. Son of Thomas Wharton, *q.v.*, and
Sarah Paulina his wife. Nephew of Charles Ramsay Skardon and
cousin-german of Samuel Lowis Thornton, *qq.v.* m. 1st, Madelina
Elizabeth Maria Frances, eldest dau. of Joseph Jeremiah Le
Marchand, of Muddiford House, Christchurch, Hants. (She died
Ghazipur 2 Dec. 1827, aged 36.) m. 2nd, Chapra 18 July 1832,
Miss Anne Smith.
Services : Posted Ensign to 20th N.I. 1809. Capture of Java
1811 ; Ensign 1/20th N.I. Cornet 24th Light Dgns. 5 Dec. 1811 ;
Lieut. 17th Light Dgns. 1 Sept. 1813 ; h.p. of Lieut. 21st Ft. 25 Feb.
1816 ; Lieut. 8th Light Dgns. 28 May 1818 ; retired 1823. At date
of death was 1st Surveyor in Opium Dept.
Refs. : Will dated 14 Feb. 1834 ; proved 4 Dec. 1849.

THE BENGAL ARMY, 1758-1834

WHEATLEY, Arthur (1807-1881). Major General. 4th Bengal Eur. L.C. *b.* Much Hadham, Herts., 2 Feb. 1807. Cadet 1823. Arrived in India 3 May 1824. Cornet 9 Jan. 1824. Lieut. 13 May 1825. Capt. 3 Dec. 1838. Major 16 Apr. 1850. Lt. Col. 14 Nov. 1853. Bt. Col. 28 Nov. 1854. Retired 31 Dec. 1861. Hon. Maj. Gen. 31 Dec. 1861. *d.* 13 Sept. 1881.
bapt. Much Hadham 19 Oct. 1807. 3rd son of John Wheatley, barr.-at-law, formerly of Calais, France, later of Calcutta, and Georgiana his wife, dau. of William Lushington, of Cobham Place, Kent. Brother of George Hampden Wheatley, *q.v. m.* Mainpuri 8 Nov. 1827, Charlotte, 6th dau. of Goddard Richards, *q.v.* (*See also* George Burges.) (She died Wimbledon 12 Apr. 1881, aged 70.) His dau. *m.* Charles Grant (1808-1887), *q.v.*
Services : Posted Cornet to 5th L.C. ; Adjt. do. 14 June 1827 till 9 Apr. 1836. Leave s.c. to Hills 1 Feb. till 1 Dec. 1834. Offg. A.D.C. to Govr. of Agra 20 Mar. 1835 ; Town and Fort Major at Allahabad Mar. 1835 till 13 Apr. 1836, when the appt. was abolished. Asst. to A.G.G., Saugor & Narbada territories, 16 Mar. 1836 ; 1st Junr. Asst. to Comr. of Saugor Div. 27 Mar. 1840 till 1843. Gwalior campaign ; Paniar ; Capt. 5th L.C. (Bronze star). Leave s.c. 2 yrs. to Cape 13 Nov. 1844. Second Sikh War ; Ramnagar (w.) ; Sadulapur ; Chilianwala ; Gujerat ; Capt. 5th L.C. (Medal with 2 clasps). Posted Lt. Col. to 5th L.C. May 1854 ; to 3rd L.C. Oct. 1855 ; to 6th L.C. May 1856. Fur. s.c. 9 May 1856 till 1859. Transfd. to newly-raised 4th Bengal Eur. L.C. May 1858.
Refs. : Burke's *Landed Gentry*, 13th edn., p. 1870, *s.n.* Wheatley, of Gwersyllt Park, co. Denbigh. *A.J.* xxv. 683.

WHEATLEY, George Hampden (1804-1822). Actg. Ensign, Engineers. *bapt.* Sunninghill, Berks., 29 July 1804. Cadet 1821. Actg. Ensign (?) *d.* Calcutta 15 Oct. 1822, aged 18.
2nd son of John Wheatley and Georgiana his wife. Brother of Arthur Wheatley, *q.v.* Addiscombe Cadet 1818-20.
Services : Detained in England till 1822 to learn the art of sapping and mining.
Refs. : Burke's *Landed Gentry*, 13th edn., p. 1870, *s.n.* Wheatley, of Gwersyllt Park, co. Denbigh. M.I. in N. Park St. cemetery, Calcutta.

WHEELER, Sir Hugh Massy (1789-1857). Major General, K.C.B. Colonel 48th N.I. Comdg. Cawnpore Div. *b.* Clonbeg, co. Tipperary, 30 June 1789. Cadet 1803. Arrived in India 17 Mar. 1805. Ensign 17 Mar. 1805. Lieut. 5 Apr. 1805. Capt. 1 Jan. 1819. Major 18 July 1829. Lt. Col. 27 June 1835. Col.

1 Apr. 1846. Maj. Gen. 20 June 1854. *d.* Cawnpore 27 June 1857 : massacred at the Ghat.

Son of Capt. Hugh Wheeler, H.E.I.C.S., and Margaret his wife, 2nd dau. of Hugh, 1st Lord Massy, of the Irish peerage, and widow of Godfrey Evan Baker, *q.v. m.* Agra 6 Mar. 1842, Frances Matilda, widow of Thomas Samuel Oliver, *q.v.* (She was massacred with him.) Ed. Bath Grammar School.

Services : See *D.N.B.* Posted Lieut. to 2/24th N.I. 1805. With 2nd Ceylon Vol. Bn. 1818-19. On service with 2 Coys. 2/24th N.I. against the freebooter Diraj Singh Dec. 1824. Transfd. to 48th N.I. (late 2/24th) May 1824. Posted Lt. Col. to 48th N.I. 11 Dec. 1835. First Afghan War 1839-40 ; Ghazni (*Lond. Gaz.* 20 Dec. 1839) ; Kabul ; against the Waziris Aug. 1840 ; capture of Kajja fort (ib. 19 Jan. 1841) ; Lt. Col. 48th N.I. (Medal). To comd. 2nd Inf. Bde., Army of the Sutlej, 13 Dec. 1845. First Sikh War ; Mudki (s.w.) (ib. 23 Feb. 1846) ; Aliwal ; Bdr. comdg. 2nd Bde. (Medal with clasp). Capture of Kot Kangra Apr. 1846 ; comdg. the force. Bdr. Gen. 1 cl. comdg. Jullundur Doab F.F. 29 Apr. 1846 till 1852. Posted Col. to 48th N.I. 1846. Second Sikh War 1848-9 ; operations in Jullundur Doab ; comdg. the force (Medal). Fur. p.a. 8 Apr. 1853 till Nov. 1855. Maj. Gen. comdg. Presdy. Div. 25 Apr. 1856 ; do. Cawnpore Div. 30 June 1856 till death. Mutiny campaign ; defence of the " Wheeler entrenchments " at Cawnpore 6-26 June 1857, when he surrendered to the Nana Sahib on terms. C.B. 20 Dec. 1839. K.C.B. 17 Aug. 1850. Durani 2 cl. 26 Feb. 1842. A.D.C. to the Queen 3 Apr. 1846.

Refs. : Burke's *Peerage*, 1923, p. 1525, *s.n.* Massy, B. *D.N.B.* Boase. *D.I.B. G.M.* 1857, ii. 460.

WHEELHOUSE, Henry (*d.* 1775). Cadet, Artillery. (143) Cadet 1775. *bur.* Calcutta 9 Feb. 1775.

Services : N.F.P.

WHELER, Sir Francis, tenth baronet (1801-1878). Lieut. General, C.B. 1st Bengal Eur. L.C. *b.* Crakemarsh Hall, Staffs., 9 Nov. 1801. Cadet 1818. Admitted 22 Jan. 1819. Cornet 18 Aug. 1819. Lieut. 30 June 1821. Capt. 7 July 1833. Major 15 Dec. 1851. Lt. Col. 28 Nov. 1854. Bt. Col. 28 Nov. 1854. Maj. Gen. 21 July 1861. Lt. Gen. 25 June 1870. *d.* The Roccles, Sydenham, 4 Apr. 1878.

10th Bart., of Leamington Hastings, co. Warwick. *s.* his brother, Sir Trevor Wheler, 9th Bart., 6 Sept. 1869. *bapt.* Uttoxeter 9 Dec. 1801. 2nd son of Sir Trevor Wheler, 8th Bart., and Harriet his wife, dau. of Richard Beresford, of Ashbourne, co. Derby. Nephew of William Beresford, *q.v.*, and cousin-german of Henry Trevor Wheler, *q.v. m.* 1st, Nasirabad 3 Feb. 1827, Caroline, dau. of Rev. William Palmer, chaplain at Nasirabad, and sister of Henry Palmer, *q.v.* (*See also* J. W. J. Ouseley.) (She died Leamington Priors, co. Warwick, 13 Jan. 1833, aged 28.) *m.* 2nd, Lucknow 16 Nov. 1841, Elizabeth, dau. of William Bishop, of Grayswood, Surrey. (*See also* Thomas Bradridge Studdy.) (She died Southport, Lancs., 16 Mar. 1900, aged 80.) Ed. Rugby; admitted 1810. Haileybury 1818.

Services: Transfd. from Inf. to Cav. 15 May 1820; posted to 2nd L.C. Post Adjt. at Lohargaon 4 June 1821. Adjt. 2nd L.C. 3 May 1822; Intr. & Qmr. do. 28 Aug. 1823 till Jan. 1831. Fur. p.a. 3 Jan. 1831 till 21 Jan. 1834. Jodhpur demonstration 1834; Capt. 2nd L.C. Bde. Major Meerut 24 Feb. 1836 till 11 Nov. 1838; do. Cav. Bde., Army of Indus, 30 Sept. 1839. First Afghan War 1839-40; Ghazni; pursuit of Dost Mohd. Khan 1839; Capt. 2nd L.C. (Medal). D.J.A.G. to troops remaining in Afghanistan 2 Oct. 1839; returned to India 16 Dec. 1840. Comdt. 7th Irreg. Cav. 6 May 1841 till 1 Jan. 1852.[1] Second Sikh War; Multan; Surajkhund; Bt. Major comdg. 7th Irreg. Cav. (Medal). Posted Lt. Col. to 1st L.C. 1854. Bdr. 2 cl. comdg. Oudh Irreg. Force 12 Feb. 1856; Bdr. 1 cl. comdg. Saugor district 28 Oct. 1857 till 11 Oct. 1861. Mutiny campaign 1857-9; action at Zalimpur 28 Feb. 1858; Bdr. comdg. Saugor (Medal). Transfd. to newly-raised 1st Eur. Bengal L.C. May 1858. Maj. Gen. comdg. Meerut Div. 11 Oct. 1861 till 5 Aug. 1865. C.B. 27 Jan. 1862. Durani 3 cl. 24 Sept. 1841.

Refs.: Burke's *Peerage,* 1923, p. 2311, *s.n.* Wheler, Bart. *Howard & Crisp,* viii. 84, *s.n.* Wheler. Glover's *Derbyshire,* ii. 46. *Rugby School Register. D.I.B. Boase. The Times,* 10 Apr. 1878.

[1] *Note:* This Regt., which he raised at Bareilly in 1841, later became 5th Bengal Cav. and is now 3rd Cavalry.

WHELER, Henry Trevor (1804-1860). Lieutenant. 45th N.I. Subsequently rector of Berkley, Somerset. *b.* Leamington Hastings, co. Warwick, 9 Aug. 1804. Cadet 1823. Ensign 16 Jan. 1824. Lieut. 13 May 1825. Resigned 29 Jan. 1829. *d.* Berkley 28 Apr. 1860.

bapt. Leamington Hastings 8 Sept. 1804. 4th son of Charles John Wheler, of The Spring, Kenilworth, and Isabella his wife, dau. of John Close, of Easby, Yorks. Brother of Stephen Glynne Wheler, *q.v.*, and cousin-german of Sir Francis Wheler, Bart., *q.v.*

m. Polebrook, Northants, 11 Dec. 1834, Charlotte, 4th dau. of Rev. Charles Euseby Isham, rector of Polebrook. (She died Windsor 30 Aug. 1885, aged 77.) Ed. Rugby; admitted 1814 and 1818. Jesus Coll., Oxon.; matric. 25 Apr. 1828. Postmaster Merton Coll. 1828-31; B.A. 1832; M.A. 1833.

Services: Posted Ensign to 45th N.I. Fur. s.c. 13 July 1826 till resignation. No record of active service. Took holy orders. Deacon and Priest 1831. Vicar of Pillerton-Hersey, co. Warwick; Rector of Berkley, Somerset, 1834 till death.

Refs.: Burke's *Peerage*, 1923, p. 2311, *s.n.* Wheler, Bart. Howard & Crisp, ix. 14. *Rugby School Register. Alumni Oxon. The Times,* 1 May 1860. Will dated 4 July 1847; proved at Wells 26 May 1860.

WHELER, Stephen Glynne (1802-1865). Major General. 19th N.I. *b.* Charlotte St., Bloomsbury, 28 Mar. 1802. Cadet 1817. Admitted 19 Sept. 1818. Ensign 15 Sept. 1818. Lieut. 20 Aug. 1819. Capt. 7 Apr. 1828. Major 23 June 1842. Lt. Col. 21 Nov. 1848. Col. 27 Aug. 1858. Retired 8 Oct. 1858. Hon. Maj. Gen. 8 Oct. 1858. *d.* Chitaura, nr. Agra, 8 May 1865.

bapt. St. Swithin and St. Mary Bothaw, London, 28 May 1802. 3rd son of Charles John Wheler and Isabella his wife. Brother of Thomas Trevor Wheler, *q.v.* Ed. Rugby; admitted 1810.

Services: Posted to 1/17th N.I.; transfd. to 34th N.I. (late 1/17th) May 1824. Operations against the Kols 1832; Capt. 34th N.I. Transfd. to new 34th N.I. (late Inf. of Bundelkhand Legion) Mar. 1844 on disbandment of 34th N.I. for mutiny. Leave s.c. to Cape 25 Feb. 1849. Posted Lt. Col. to 1st Eur. Bengal Fus. 1849; transfd. to 18th N.I. May 1850; to 71st N.I. 3 Feb. 1851; to 37th N.I. 1853; to 31st N.I. Feb. 1856; to 34th N.I. 1856 [1]; to 19th N.I. 24 June 1857.

Refs.: Burke's *Peerage*, 1923, p. 2311, *s.n.* Wheler, Bart. Howard & Crisp, ix. 13, *s.n.* Wheler. *Rugby School Register.* Boase. M.I. Agra Cantt. cemetery.

[1] *Note:* Three Coys. of this Regt. mutinied at Chittagong; H.Q. and 7 Coys. were at Barrackpore, comdd. by Wheler, when, on 29 Mar. 1857, Sepoy Mangal Pandy shot the Adjt. and Sergt. Major of the Regt. Lord Canning was of opinion (see his Minute of 9 Apr. 1857) that the outbreak was due in great measure to Wheler's attempts to convert his sepoys to Christianity.

WHELER, Thomas Trevor (1809-1847). Captain, 56th N.I. *b.* Leamington Hastings 1 Dec. 1809. Cadet 1825. Arrived in India 22 Oct. 1826. Ensign 21 May 1826. Lieut. 19 Feb.

THE BENGAL ARMY, 1758-1834   441

1833. Capt. 4 Mar. 1845. *d. unm.* Kenilworth, co. Warwick, 28 Dec. 1847.

bapt. Leamington Hastings 22 Dec. 1809. 5th son of Charles John Wheler and Isabella his wife. Brother of Henry Trevor Wheler, *q.v.* Ed. Rugby; admitted 1822.

Services: Posted Ensign to 56th N.I. 9 Nov. 1826. d.d. Ramgarh L.I. 30 June 1838 till Mar. 1840; Adjt. 5th Local Horse 25 Mar. 1840 till 16 Feb. 1842; Comdt. Cav. of Malwa Contingent 15 Dec. 1841 (acted as Adjt. till the comd. was vacant 1 May 1842) till 12 Sept. 1846. Fur. s.c. 1846 till death. No record of active service.

Refs.: Burke's *Peerage*, 1923, p. 2311, *s.n.* Wheler, Bart. Howard & Crisp, ix. 15, *s.n.* Wheler. *Rugby School Register.*

WHICHCOT(E), George or Thomas. (*See* **WITCHCOT, George.**)

WHINFIELD, Charles Rabett (1796-?). Lieutenant. Artillery. (451) *b.* Harwich 25 Feb. 1796. Cadet 1813. Admitted 5 Aug. 1814. Fireworker 17 Feb. 1815. Lieut. 1 Sept. 1818. Resigned 13 Sept. 1829. (Living in 1851.)

bapt. St. Nicholas, Harwich, 31 Mar. 1796. Son of Rev. William Whinfield, vicar of Dovercourt cum Harwich, and of Ramsey, Essex, chaplain to Duke of Manchester, afterwards chaplain at Bencoolen, and Susan his wife, *née* Baggott. Brother of William Henry Whinfield, *q.v.* Addiscombe Cadet 1811-14.

Services: Siege and capture of Hathras 1817; Lt. F. 4th Coy. 3rd Bn., d.d. from 7th Coy. 1st Bn. Third Mahratta War (*probably* Taragarh and Madhurajpura); Lieut. 5th Coy. 1st Bn. Served with Rocket Troop 1820-6; Bde. Major to Div. of Horse and Light Field Batteries, Bhurtpore Force, 6 Dec. 1825. Siege and capture of Bhurtpore; Bde. Major (India medal). Fur. p.a. 10 Jan. 1827 till resignation. Employed at Addiscombe 2 July 1828 till 25 June 1831. Bt. Capt. 8 June 1831; subsequently cancelled on his resignation being accepted (M.C. 2 Nov. 1831) with effect from 13 Sept. 1829.

WHINFIELD, William Henry (1794-1825). Captain, 30th N.I. *b.* Ramsey, Essex, 22 Jan. 1794. Cadet 1808. Arrived in India 19 July 1809. Ensign 23 Dec. 1809. Lieut. 15 Sept. 1814. Capt. 13 May 1825. *d.* Midnapore 28 Sept. 1825.

bapt. Ramsey 23 July 1794. 2nd son of Rev. William Whinfield, vicar of Ramsey, and Susan his wife. Brother of Charles Rabett Whinfield, *q.v.*

Services: Barasat C.C. Posted to 15th N.I. 1810; with 6th Gren. Bn. 1815-16. Nepal War 1815; operations in Kumaon; capture of Almora; Lieut. 6th Gren. Bn. d.d. 1/24th N.I. 11 Oct. 1817; Adjt. 1/15th N.I. 13 Jan. 1818 till 1822. Third Mahratta War; Asirgarh; Lieut. 1/15th N.I. Adjt. 2/15th N.I. 1822 till May 1824; transfd. to 30th N.I. (late 1/15th) May 1824.

Refs.: Will dated Midnapore 16 Sept. 1825; proved 11 Nov. 1825. M.I. at Midnapore.

WHINYATES, Thomas (1755-1806). Major, 24th N.I. *b.* 18 Sept. 1755. Cadet 1780. Arrived in India Sept. 1781. Ensign 1780. Lieut. 1 June 1781. Capt. 1 Nov. 1798. Major 15 Aug. 1803. *d.* Allahabad 24 Mar. 1806.

Of Abbotsleigh and Pasture, Devon. Eldest son of Rev. Thomas Whinyates, of Abbotsleigh and Pasture, rector of Charleton, Devon, and Margaret his wife, eldest dau. of Rev. John Salter, rector of Stoke Fleming, Devon. *m.* Walcot, Bath, 1 July 1777, Catherine, 4th dau. of Adm. Sir Thomas Frankland, 5th Bart., of Thirkleby Park, Yorks. (She died Allahabad 30 Mar. 1806, aged 47.) His dau. *m.* James Robertson (*c.* 1775-1810), *q.v.* Wadham Coll., Oxon.; matric. 17 May 1774; left midsummer 1777.

Services: Cornet 2nd D.G. (Queen's Bays) 9 Feb. 1778; sold out Mar. 1780. Sailed for India in the *Hillsborough* 28 July 1780; captured by combined French and Spanish fleets 9 Aug., taken to Cadiz and eventually exchanged. Arrived in Bombay Sept. 1781; in Calcutta 27 Feb. 1782. Apptd. 1 Apr. 1784 to comd. a newly-raised Sebundy corps at Kishenagar, established for the service of the Salt Dept.; corps disbanded 1 Mar. 1785. Qmr. 4th Bde. Sepoys June 1786 till 1793; offg. Fort Adjt. at Chunar 16 Nov. 1792; permanent 15 Aug. 1793. Lieut. 1st Bengal Eur. Regt. in 1796; Capt. 6th N.I. in Nov. 1798. Comdd. 1st Bn. Invalids at Allahabad; Dy. Postmaster at Allahabad; Fort Major Allahabad. Major 6th N.I.; transfd. to newly-raised 25th N.I. 1804; to 24th N.I. 1805.

Refs.: Whinyates Family Records, by Maj.-Gen. F. T. Whinyates, late R.H.A., 3 vols., 25 copies privately printed, 1894-6. Burke's *Peerage*, 1923, p. 939, *s.n.* Frankland, Bart. *Genealogist*, N.S. viii. 54. *Alumni Oxon.*

WHISH, George Palmer (1813-1902). General, *u.s.l.* 60th N.I. *b.* Fatehgarh 30 June 1813. Cadet 1829. Arrived in India 15 May 1830. Ensign 19 Nov. 1829. Lieut. 1 Dec. 1836. Capt. 15 Nov. 1849. Major 18 Feb. 1861. Lt. Col. 18 Feb. 1863. Bt. Col. 4 June 1860. Maj. Gen. 9 Dec. 1867. Lt. Gen. 29 May

THE BENGAL ARMY, 1758-1834 443

1875. Gen. 1 Oct. 1877. *d.* 54 Nevern Sq., London, 31 Jan. 1902.

Eldest son of Sir William Sampson Whish, *q.v.*, and Mary his wife. *m.* 1st, Mhow 15 Mar. 1836, Maria, only dau. of John Tulloch, *q.v.* (She died Calcutta 4 Jan. 1855.) *m.* 2nd, Benares 16 Mar. 1869, Anne Wemyss, dau. of James Black, of Edinburgh, and widow of W. Wright.

Services : Cadet d.d. 29th N.I. 27 May 1830; d.d. 60th N.I. 18 Oct. 1831; Actg. Ensign (having been 2 yrs. in India) 2 July 1832; posted to 60th N.I. 20 Aug. 1833; Adjt. do. 25 Apr. 1837 till 18 Jan. 1848. First Afghan War 1842; Lieut. 60th N.I., with Pollock's force (Medal). A.D.C. to his father 18 Jan. 1848. Second Sikh War; Multan; Gujerat; Bt. Capt. 60th N.I., A.A.G. to Multan F.F. and to 1st Inf. Div., Army of Punjab (Medal with 2 clasps). Fur. 25 Dec. 1851 till Dec. 1854. Bde. Major at Meerut 28 Sept. 1855 till Mar. 1863. Transfd. to Staff Corps 18 Feb. 1861. Mily. Sec. to Presdt. of Council 19 Mar. 1863 till 1864. Bdr. Gen. comdg. Dinapore 26 Oct. 1866 till Feb. 1868. Fur. 15 Feb. 1871 till death.

Refs. : The Times, 3 Feb. 1902.

WHISH, Sir William Sampson (1787-1853). Lieut. General, K.C.B., Artillery. (332) *b.* Northwold, Norfolk, 27 Feb. 1787. Cadet 1803. Arrived in India 2 Sept. 1804. Lieut. 21 Aug. 1804. Capt. Lt. 13 May 1807. Capt. 29 Dec. 1815. Major 1 May 1824. Lt. Col. 28 Sept. 1827. Col. 25 Apr. 1838. Maj. Gen. 23 Nov. 1841. Lt. Gen. 11 Nov. 1851. *d.* Claridge's Hotel, Brook St., London, 25 Feb. 1853.

bapt. Northwold 4 Apr. 1787. Son of Rev. Richard Whish, rector of W. Walton, vicar of Wickford, Essex, preby. of Salisbury, and Philippa his wife, dau. of William Sandys, of Helston, and sister of William Sandys (1759-1829), *q.v. m.* Calcutta 9 Jan. 1809, Mary, sister of Charles George Dixon, *q.v.* (She died 9 Aug. 1861, aged 71.) Father of George Palmer Whish, *q.v.*, and of the wife of E. W. S. Scott, *q.v.*

Services : See *D.N.B.* Woolwich Cadet; nominated 23 Apr. 1802; obtained his certificate 14 Mar. 1804. Siege and capture of Hathras 1817; Capt. comdg. Rocket Troop H.A. Third Mahratta War 1817-18; Capt. comdg. Rocket Troop. Bde. Major at Meerut 26 July 1820. Fur. 26 Feb. 1823 till 5 Apr. 1825. Siege and capture of Bhurtpore; Major comdg. 1st Bde. H.A. (India medal). Transfd. to 2nd Bde. H.A. 1826. To comd. Karnal and Sirhind Div. Art. 23 Dec. 1826; comd. Art. at Saugor 9 July 1827;

do. Sirhind 24 Dec. 1827. Transfd. from 3rd to 1st Bde. H.A. 22 Oct. 1830; posted Col. to 2nd Bde. 25 July 1838. Comdt. Art., with rank of Bdr., and M.M.B. 21 Dec. 1838. To comd. Presdy. Div. Art. Feb. 1839. Fur. s.c. 9 Jan. 1842 till 7 Dec. 1847. Transfd. to 6th Bn. Foot Art. 24 July 1845. To comd. Punjab Div. at Lahore 23 Jan. 1848; do. Multan F.F. Aug. 1848. Second Sikh War; siege and capture of Multan; comdg. the force (*Lond. Gaz.* 23 Mar. 1849); capture of fort Chiniot 9 Feb. 1849; Gujerat; comdg. 1st Div. (ib. 19 Apr. 1849) (Medal with 2 clasps). Transfd. to Presdy. Div. Mar. 1849; to Cis-Jhelum Div. Oct. 1851. Fur. s.c. 11 Dec. 1851 till death. C.B. 20 July 1838; K.C.B. 9 June 1849.

Refs.: D.N.B. Boase. D.I.B. *The Times*, 28 Feb. 1853. *G.M.* 1853, i. 436. *I.M.* 3 Mar. 1853, p. 112. Will dated 16 Nov. 1851; codicil 22 Nov. 1852; admon. 6 Sept. 1853.

WHISTLER, Gabriel Henry (1811-1848). Captain, Invalid Est. 72nd N.I. *b.* Newtimber, Sussex, 8 Nov. 1811. Cadet 1827. Arrived in India 10 June 1828. Ensign 20 Feb. 1828. Lieut. 19 Nov. 1837. Capt. 20 Feb. 1843. Invalided 6 June 1845. *d.* nr. Rajmahal, B. & O., 20 Mar. 1848 : drowned in the Ganges, occasioned by the taking fire of the Benares steamer.

bapt. Hastings 11 Nov. 1811. Youngest son of Rev. Webster Whistler, rector of Hastings and Newtimber (who was cousin of Sir Godfrey Webster, Bart., of Battle Abbey), and Mary his 2nd wife, dau. of George Lashmer, of Shipley, Sussex. *m.* Calcutta 15 Dec. 1842, Charlotte Anna Maria, dau. of W. J. Duncan, partner in the firm of Mackenzie, Lyall & Co., Calcutta. (She died Hammersmith 17 Nov. 1877.)

Services: Ensign d.d. 13th N.I. 25 July 1828; posted to 8th N.I. 4 Nov. 1828. Jodhpur demonstration 1834; Ensign 8th N.I. Transfd. to 72nd N.I. 28 June 1836. Fur. p.a. 15 Jan. 1840 till 28 Oct. 1842. Comdd. a detachment consisting of 2 Coys. 72nd N.I. and 150 men of 3rd Irreg. Cav. employed against town of Kaithal, Karnal district, Apr. 1843 (w.—reported kld.); Capt. 72nd N.I. Fur. s.c. 26 June 1845 till 22 Dec. 1847. Posted to Eur. Invalid and Veteran Coy. at Chunar 11 Feb. 1848, and was on his way to join when he met his death.

Refs.: Burke's *Landed Gentry*, 8th edn., p. 2188, *s.n.* Whistler, of Elton. Burke's *Colonial Gentry*, i. 8, *s.n.* Smith, of Gordon Brook, N.S.W. *Cardew*, pp. 197-8. *I.M.* 2 June 1848, p. 345. *Patrician*, v. 102.

WHITAKER, Thomas (1776-1803). Lieutenant, 9th N.I. *bapt.* St. Mary's, Manchester, 12 Jan. 1776. Cadet 1794. Arrived

THE BENGAL ARMY, 1758-1834

in India 17 Feb. 1795. Ensign 15 Oct. 1794. Lieut. 13 Sept. 1796. *d.* in camp before Agra 10 Oct. 1803, of wounds received in action the same day.[1]

Son of Daniel Whitaker[2] and Esther his wife. Brother of George Whitaker and brother-in-law of Benjamin Satterthwaite, of Church St., Lancaster.

Services: Apptd. Cadet 30 Apr. 1794; sailed for India in the *Lascelles* 14 Aug. 1794. Posted to 1st Bengal Eur. Regt. June 1796; Lieut. 9th N.I. in 1798. Second Mahratta War; Agra (s.w.); Lieut. 2/9th N.I. "The death of this officer was particularly lamented, as it was occasioned by his gallant and humane exertions to carry off another wounded officer (Lieut. Robert Grant, *q.v.*) of the same Corps." (*Pester*)

Refs.: Pester, p. 200. Will dated camp before Agra 6 Oct. 1803; proved 5 Apr. 1804.

[1] *Note:* Pester (op. cit.) states that his death took place on 12th Oct. His name sometimes appears as Whittaker.

[2] *Note:* One of this name was borough-reeve of Manchester in 1778.

WHITAKER, William (1798-1835). Lieutenant. 60th N.I. *b.* 28 May 1798. Cadet 1818. Ensign (?) Lieut. 1 Jan. 1821. Cashiered by G.C.M. 30 Jan. 1830. *d.* Whalley Abbey, Lancs., Nov. 1835.

bapt. Holme, Lancs., 25 June 1798. 2nd son of Rev. Thomas Dunham Whitaker (*D.N.B.*), vicar of Whalley and Blackburn, J.P., and Lucy his wife, dau. of Thomas Thoresby, of Leeds.

Services: Ensign d.d. Bengal Eur. Regt. 1819-20; posted Lieut. to 1/25th N.I. 1821; transfd. to 30th N.I. July 1823; to 60th N.I. (late 2/30th) May 1824. Siege and capture of Bhurtpore; Lieut. 60th N.I. d.d. Pioneers 1826 till 29 Aug. 1829.

Refs.: Burke's *Landed Gentry*, 12th edn., p. 2007, *s.n.* Master-Whitaker, of The Holme, Lancs. *A.J.* N.S. ii. 156. *G.M.* 1835, ii. 665.

WHITE, Adam (1791-1839). Lieut. Colonel, 61st N.I. Comdt. Assam L.I. P.A. Upper Assam. *b.* 18 Aug. 1791. Cadet 1807. Arrived in India 14 Sept. 1808. Ensign 7 Oct. 1808. Lieut. 16 Dec. 1814. Capt. 15 Dec. 1824. Major 3 Mar. 1832. Lt. Col. 3 Oct. 1838. *d.* Sadiya, Upper Assam, 29 Jan. 1839: kld. in action against the Kamptis.

bapt. S. Leith 2 Sept. 1791. Son of Adam White, of Fens, cooper in Leith and sometime provost of that port, and Catherine his wife, sister of William Ogilvy, merchant in Leith.

Services: Barasat C.C. 6½ mos. Posted Ensign to 26th N.I. 1809; transfd. as Lieut. to newly-raised 1/30th N.I. 1815. Fur. p.a. 20 Feb. 1821 till 12 Nov. 1823. Transfd. to 59th N.I. (late 1/30th) May 1824; Intr. & Qmr. do. 17 June 1824 till 7 June 1825. Asst. to A.G.G., N.E. frontier, 24 Jan. 1826; Comdt. Assam L.I. Bn. (now 1st Bn. 6th Gurkha Rifles) and P.A. Upper Assam 1831 till death. Major 59th N.I. Operations against Duffa Gaum and the Singphos Oct.-Nov. 1835. Posted Lt. Col. to 61st N.I. 3 Dec. 1838. Kld. (9 spear and 4 *dah* wounds) in repelling a night attack on the cantt. of Sadiya by a party of Kamptis, Singphos and other tribes. Author of "Considerations on the State of British India," 1822.

Refs.: D.I.B. A.J. N.S. xxix. 13, 63, 91. *Atlas*, 4 May 1839. Will dated Sadiya, 6 Feb. 1837; codicil 6 Apr. 1837; proved 1 July 1839. M.I. St. Paul's, Dibrugarh, Assam.[1]

[1] *Note:* His remains were interred beneath St. Paul's church, Dibrugarh, when the first stone was laid 23 Mar. 1846.

WHITE, Andrew (*d.* 1790). Lieutenant, Artillery. (206) Country Cadet 1779. Fireworker 2 Oct. 1780. Lieut. 29 May 1786. *d.* Calcutta 25 Mar. 1790.

Services: Apptd. Cadet 20 Mar. 1779. Lieut. 3rd Bn. Art. in July 1787 and Dec. 1788.

WHITE, Charles (1762/63-1806). Major, 17th N.I. *b.* London 1762/63. Cadet 1781. Admitted 4 June 1782. Ensign 1781. Lieut. 18 Sept. 1782. Capt. 29 May 1800. Major 23 Sept. 1804. *d.* Dec. 1806, on his passage to India, in the wreck of the *Skelton Castle*. Struck off with effect from 5 Nov. 1806. (See note to David Allan.)

Son of Henry White and Mary Ann his wife. Brother of Evan Marsh White, M.C.S.[1]

Services: Apptd. Cadet 29 Mar. 1781; sailed for India in the *Deptford* 26 June 1781, aged 18. Lieut. 36th Bn. Sepoys in July 1787 and Dec. 1792; Bt. Capt. 2/6th N.I. in July 1798. Transfd. to newly-raised 17th N.I. 1798; Capt. 2/17th N.I. Fur. 4 Apr. 1801 till death.

[1] *Note:* "He fell a sacrifice to the incautious use of castor oil nuts." (M.I. in Guntoor cemetery, erected by his brother Charles.)

WHITE, Charles Edward (1806-1850). Captain. 4th L.C. *b.* London 30 Sept. 1806. Cadet 1825. Arrived in India 28 June 1826. Cornet 13 Feb. 1826. Lieut. 18 June 1835. Capt. 28 Oct. 1848. Retired 30 July 1849. *d.* Brighton 16 Aug. 1850.

THE BENGAL ARMY, 1758-1834 447

bapt. St. Pancras, Middlesex, 14 Jan. 1807. Son of Matthew White, of Bedford Sq., and Sarah his wife.
Services : Posted Cornet to 4th L.C. 1826, and served throughout with that Regt. Shekhawat expedn. 1834; Cornet 4th L.C. Gwalior campaign; Maharajpur; Bt. Capt. 4th L.C. (Bronze star). First Sikh War; Mudki; Ferozshahr; Sobraon; Bt. Capt. 4th L.C. (Medal with 2 clasps). Fur. s.c. 30 Jan. 1847 till retirement.
Refs. : *The Times,* 19 Aug. 1850.

WHITE, Charles Herbert (*d.* 1798). Lieut. Colonel, Infantry. Cadet 1768. Admitted 28 Aug. 1768. Ensign 24 Jan. 1769. Lieut. 23 May 1770. Capt. 18 Sept. 1778. Major 6 Feb. 1784. Lt. Col. 1 Mar. 1794. *d.* Barrackpore 30 June 1798.
Related to William Chauncey Lawrence, *q.v.*
Services : Capt. 1/1st Bengal Eur. Regt. in Oct. 1779. Second Mysore War 1781; Chilambram 18 June (w.); Capt. 2/1st Eur. Regt. Apptd. to comd. 16th Bn. Sepoys 31 May 1786, and was still in comd. in 1792.

WHITE, Charles Herbert (1801-1850). Captain. 8th L.C. *b.* Totnes, Devon, 2 July 1801. Cadet 1819. Admitted 14 June 1820. Cornet 14 Nov. 1819. Lieut. 1 May 1824. Capt. 31 May 1835. Invalided 20 Feb. 1838. Retired 6 May 1844. *d.* Ambleside, Westmorland, 25 Mar. 1850.
bapt. Epsom 5 Mar. 1802. Son of Charles White, of Ambleside, Post Capt. R.N., and Sophia James his wife. His sister *m.* Frederick Bayley Wardroper, *q.v. m.* St. Giles-in-the-Fields, London, 9 May 1831, Georgiana Jubilee, 4th sister of Samuel Robinson Bagshawe, *q.v.* (She died 20 Apr. 1873, aged 63.) Ed. Shrewsbury 1816-18.
Services : Posted Cornet to 8th L.C. and served throughout with that Regt. Siege and capture of Bhurtpore (s.w.—*Lond. Gaz.* 4 July 1826); Lieut. 8th L.C. Intr. & Qmr. 14 Feb. 1826 till 25 July 1827. Fur. p.a. 31 July 1830 till 20 Nov. 1833; leave s.c. 20 Feb. 1836 till 20 Feb. 1838; fur. s.c. 9 Apr. 1841 till retirement.
Refs. : Burke's *Landed Gentry,* 13th edn., p. 60, *s.n.* Bagshawe, of Oakes and Wormhill. *Shrewsbury School Register. Bath Chron.* 26 May 1831. *I.M.* 2 Apr. 1850, p. 211.

WHITE, Francis Sellon (1780-1850). Captain. 4th N.I. *b.* 22 Aug. 1780. Cadet 1800. Arrived in India 22 Aug. 1801. Ensign 28 Nov. 1801. Lieut. 30 Sept. 1803. Capt. 22 June 1816. Retired 6 Feb. 1819. *d.* 4 Leonard Pl., Kensington, 19 July 1850.
bapt. Worksop, Notts., 4 Sept. 1780. 2nd son of Rev. Stephen

White, of Castor, Northants, rector of Conington, Hunts., and Elizabeth Anna his wife, dau. of Rev. William Sellon, of Hurley, Berks. Cousin-german of Sir Thomas Woollaston White, 1st Bart. *m.* 18 Nov. 1818, Joanna, dau. of Charles Goldney Rees, of Cross Hall, Lancs. (She died 1870.) Ed. Westminster; in school list 1795.

Services: Ensign d.d. 2nd Eur. Regt. in 1802; posted Ensign to 4th N.I. Second Mahratta War 1803-4; Aligarh; (? defence of Delhi); Lieut. 4th N.I. Surveying in the Doab 1811-13; do. Delhi 1814-15. Capt. Lt. 2/4th N.I. 19 Jan. 1816; Capt. 2/4th N.I. Fur. 13 Jan. 1816 till retirement.

Refs.: Burke's *Landed Gentry*, 13th edn., p. 1875, *s.n.* White, of Castor, Northants. Foster's *Baronetage*, p. 653, *s.n.* White, Bart., of Wallingwells, Notts. *Westminster School Register. G.M.* 1850, ii. 336. *I.M.* 1 Aug. 1850, p. 467.

WHITE, George Henry (1802-1825). Lieutenant, 68th N.I. *bapt.* Walcot, Somerset, 29 May 1802. Cadet 1818. Ensign (?) Lieut. 1 Jan. 1821. *d.* Calcutta 16 Apr. 1825.

Son of Henry White, of Bath, J.P. Somerset, and Barbara his wife, *née* Dicken. Ed. Eton 1811-17; K.S. 1814.

Services: Ensign d.d. Bengal Eur. Regt. 1819-20. Posted Lieut. to 2/4th N.I. 1821. Operations in Oudh 1822; Bardgaon; Lieut. 2/4th N.I. Transfd. to newly-raised 34th N.I. 11 July 1823; to 68th N.I. (late 2/34th) May 1824.

Refs.: Eton School Lists.

WHITE, Sir Henry (1741/42-1822). Major General, K.C.B. Colonel 11th N.I. *b.* 1741/42. Cadet 1772. Admitted 1 Aug. 1772. Ensign 25 July 1776. Lieut. 12 July 1778. Capt. 21 Mar. 1793. Major 31 July 1798. Lt. Col. 21 Feb. 1801. Col. 25 July 1810. Maj. Gen. 4 June 1813. *d.* Bath 7 Nov. 1822, aged 80; *bur.* Bath Abbey 15 Nov.

An Irishman. Brother of Mark White, *q.v. m.* (?) His daus. *m.* James Scott (1778-1820), *q.v.*, and Goodwin Warner, *q.v.*

Services: Apptd. Cadet 1 Aug. 1772, "at a more advanced age than usual." (*A.J.*) Operations against the Mahrattas 1773. First Rohilla War 1774; battle of St. George; Cadet in the Select Picket. Apptd. Ensign 14th Bn. Sepoys July 1776; transfd. to 2nd Bengal Eur. Regt. 1776; Adjt. do. 1776-7; transfd. to 26th Bn. 1777. First Mahratta War 1780-1; Lieut. 18th Bn. Second Mysore War 1782-4; Cuddalore; Lieut. comdg. 1/12th N.I. Lieut. 12th Bn. Sepoys in July 1787; 7th Bn. in Dec. 1788. Third Mysore War 1790-2; Bangalore; Arikera; Savandrug; Nandidrug; Utradrug; Seringapatam; Lieut. 14th Bn., with Col.

Cockerell's detachment. Comdd. 14th Bn. on death of John Archdeacon, *q.v.*, until its return to Bengal 1793. Posted Capt. to 2nd Eur. Regt. Fur. 10 Jan. 1798 till 22 Aug. 1801. Major 10th N.I. Posted Lt. Col. to 2nd Eur. Regt. Suggested, *c.* 1801, the formation of the Marine Regt. and was apptd. to comd. one of its two Bns. Second Mahratta War 1803-4; Agra; Laswari (w.); Lt. Col. 2/16th N.I.; capture of Gwalior; comdg. the force. Apptd. Bdr. Gen. Nov. 1803. Comdt. Gwalior fort 1804-6. Transfd. to 2/14th N.I. 1807. Leave s.c. to Cape 1807; fur. from Cape 25 Feb. 1809 till death. Col. 11th N.I. 1811 till death. K.C.B. 7 Apr. 1815.

Refs.: *E.I.M.C.* i. 24-37. *D.I.B. Williams*, p. 148. *A.J.* xv. 1-6. *S.M.* 1822, ii. 752. M.I. in Bath Abbey.

WHITE, Henry Lewis (1788-1850). Colonel, 42nd N.I. *bapt.* St. Andrew's, Holborn, 23 Apr. 1790, "said to be 18 mos. old." Cadet 1803. Arrived in India 17 Mar. 1805. Ensign 7 Apr. 1805. Lieut. 8 Apr. 1805. Capt. 11 July 1823. Major 25 Mar. 1828. Lt. Col. 14 June 1833. Col. 26 Dec. 1844. *d.* Glos. Gdns., Hyde Pk., London, 28 Mar. 1850.

Son of Samuel White, of Shoe Lane, and Mary his wife. *m.* Calcutta 25 Jan. 1815, Catherine, dau. of William Browne, of Howrah, Calcutta. (She died London 18 Jan. 1850.)

Services: Posted Lieut. to 18th N.I. Operations in Bundelkhand 1805-6; Lieut. 18th N.I. (? Settlement of Hariana 1809; Bhawani; Lieut. 2/18th N.I.) Nepal War 1816; Lieut. 2/18th N.I., 8th Gren. Bn., in 2nd Bde. Left Column. Actg. Adjt. 2/18th N.I. 1817. Cuttack insurrection 1817 (s.w. in head). Offg. Bde. Major Cuttack 31 Aug. 1817; do. Dinapore Sept. 1821 till Feb. 1824; do. troops on Chittagong frontier 6 Mar. 1824. First Burma War; Chittagong 1824; d.d. 2/20th N.I., offg. Bde. Major. Transfd. to 36th N.I. (late 1/18th) May 1824. Bde. Major 1st Bde. Chittagong 25 Oct. 1824 till 4 Jan. 1825; tempy. charge of Jaghirdar Est. 6 Apr. 1825; actg. Bde. Major Chittagong 4 July 1826; Bde. Major on the Est. at Barrackpore 22 Dec. 1826 till 6 Aug. 1828. Fur. s.c. 12 Dec. 1828 till 10 Nov. 1831. Posted Lt. Col. to 36th N.I. 7 Dec. 1833. Fur. p.a. 11 Apr. 1835 till 3 Dec. 1838. Transfd. to 67th N.I. 30 May 1838; to 56th N.I. 1840. Fur. s.c. 17 Aug. 1840 till death. Posted Col. to 42nd N.I. 13 Mar. 1845.

Refs.: *I.M.* 2 Apr. 1850, p. 211. *G.M.* 1850, i. 551.

WHITE, Henry Sainthill (1790-1816). Cornet, 2nd N.C. *b.* London 7 Jan. 1790. Cadet 1807. Arrived in India 21 Mar.

1809. Cornet 26 Mar. 1809. Resigned 31 Dec. 1809. Re-admitted as Cadet and former rank cancelled 20 Aug. 1811. Cornet 23 Apr. 1815. d. Karnal 25 Dec. 1816.

bapt. St. Botolph, Bishopsgate, 11 Feb. 1790. Son of Edward White and Esther his wife.

Services: Barasat C.C. 1809. Cadet d.d. 2nd N.C. 1811-13. Posted Cornet to 2nd N.C. 1815.

Refs.: G.M. 1817, ii. 183. M.I. Karnal.

WHITE, Henry Vansittart (1763/64-1835). Lieut. Colonel. 15th N.I. *b.* co. Ayr 1763/64. Cadet 1780. Admitted 8 Mar. 1781. Ensign 1780. Lieut. 31 Aug. 1781. Capt. 6 Feb. 1799. Major 28 Sept. 1804. Retired 27 July 1808. Lt. Col. (?) *d.* Leamington Spa 8 Oct. 1835; *bur.* St. Cuthbert's, Edinburgh.

Of Milton. Eldest son of Martin White (*d.* 1776), *q.v.* Brother of Martin White, *q.v.*, and uncle of William Paterson (1791-1819), *q.v.* Glasgow Univ.; matric. 1777.

Services: Sailed for India in the *Rochford* 3 June 1780, aged 16. Lieut. 1st Bn. Sepoys in July 1787. Capt. 15th N.I. Fort Adjt. at Ft. Wm. 1 Oct. 1799 till 1803. Apptd. A.D.C. to G.G. 11 Feb. 1800; actg. Mily. Sec. to G.G. Aug.-Dec. 1802. Agent for mily. stores 1804-5. Supy. A.D.C. to G.G. 28 Mar. 1804. Fur. 18 Feb. 1806 till retirement. Retired as Major; promoted Lt. Col. after retirement on some date before 1812.

Refs.: A.J. N.S. xviii. 195. M.I. in St. Cuthbert's psh. churchyard, Edinburgh.

WHITE, James (1800-1825). Lieutenant, 6th Extra Regt. N.I. (49th N.I.) *b.* Glasgow 5 Aug. 1800. Cadet 1818. Ensign 20 May 1819. Lieut. 8 Aug. 1821. *d.* Arakan 24 Aug. 1825. 2nd son of James White, of Glasgow, merchant, and Janet Muir his wife. Ed. Glasgow Univ.[1]

Services: Ensign d.d. Bengal Eur. Regt. 1819-20; posted to 2/25th N.I. 1820; transfd. to 49th N.I. (late 1/25th) May 1824. First Burma War; Arakan 1825; Lieut. 49th N.I. Transfd. to newly-raised 6th Extra Regt. May 1825, but never joined.

Refs.: Will dated 20 Jan. 1825; proved 3 Oct. 1825. M.I. in S. Park St. cemetery, Calcutta, on his brother William's tomb.

[1] *Note:* Not in the matriculation roll, though two of his brothers are recorded therein.

WHITE, John (1729/30-1794). Colonel, Infantry. *b.* 1729/30. Cadet 1758. Ensign 1758. Lieut. 20 Sept. 1759. Capt. 15 Oct.

1763. Major 27 Oct. 1773. Lt. Col. 2 Dec. 1781. Col. 31 May 1786. *d.* Chunar 6 Oct. 1794, aged 64.

m. Sarah —— (? Lee), a cousin of Warren Hastings, through her mother, a Mosley. (? She died in England 19 Feb. 1815.) His dau. *m.* Richard Boswell Armstrong, *q.v.*

Services: Raised 15th Bn. Sepoys at Monghyr Oct. 1763. This Bn., which became 12th N.I. in May 1824 and mutinied in June 1857, was called after him "*Hote-ki-Paltan.*" Fur. s.c. Jan. 1766 till 1773. "Capt. John White, formerly Bengal, be permitted to return and take rank as the youngest Major." (M.C. 3 Feb. 1773.) Comdg. 1/1st Bengal Eur. Regt. at Berhampore in Sept. 1777; apptd. to comd. 6th N.I. 1 Jan. 1781. Campaign against the Rajah of Benares 1781; was present on a visit at Benares on the outbreak on 21 Aug.; comdg. 6th N.I. at Chunar. Comdd. Invalid Corps 17 Dec. 1781 till Nov. 1783; comdg. 2nd Bengal Eur. Regt. in May 1784. Apptd. to comd. 6th Bn. Eur. Inf. 31 May 1786; Col. comdg. troops at Dinapore in July 1787 and in Dec. 1788; comdg. at Fatehgarh 1790-2; at Berhampore in 1793.

Refs.: Patrician, vi. 405. *Grier,* p. 141. *Cardew,* pp. 22, 23. *Williams,* p. 163. Will dated 24 Aug. 1794; proved 12 Feb. 1795. M.I. old cemetery below Chunar fort.

WHITE, John (1757/58-1778). Lieutenant, Infantry. *b.* Durham 1757/58. Cadet 1778. Ensign Oct. 1778. Lieut. 30 Nov. 1778. *d.* Cawnpore Dec. 1778: shot dead in a duel by Lieut. George Wilson (*d.* 1790), *q.v.*

Services: Sailed for India in the *Gatton* 27 Apr. 1778, aged 20.

WHITE, John B——[1] (*d.* 1784). Lieutenant, Bengal Eur. Regt. Cadet 1777. Ensign 23 Feb. 1778. Lieut. 29 Sept. 1778. *d.* Calcutta 24 July 1784: kld. in a duel.

Services: Apptd. Cadet 19 Dec. 1777. 1/1st Bengal Eur. Regt. in Oct. 1779.

Refs.: Cal. Gaz. 29 July 1784. Will dated, "Thursday, 12 o'clock"—; proved 5 Aug. 1784.

Note: He signs his Will "I. B. White." The second name is omitted from all official records.

WHITE, John Holt (1789-1854). Captain. 10th L.C. *bapt.* Newington, Oxon., 30 Jan. 1789. Cadet 1806. Arrived in India 3 Oct. 1807. Cornet 1 Aug. 1807. Lieut. 1 Sept. 1818. Capt. 13 May 1825. Invalided 25 Dec. 1831. Retired 25 Jan. 1833. *d.* Sandwich St., Burton Cresc., London, 27 Jan. 1854.

2nd son of George White, of Newington House, Oxon., and Elizabeth Mary his wife. *m.* 1st, Benares 31 May 1821, Miss Mary Satterthwaite. (*See also* George Thornton.) His dau. m. Charles Fleeming Bruere, *q.v.* *m.* 2nd, Madras 9 Mar. 1832, Eliza, widow of Dr. Thomas Luxmoore, Bengal Medical Est., and formerly widow of —— Perrot, of Lucknow. (She died 10 Feb. 1856.) Ed. Westminster; at the school *c.* 1801-4.

Services: Barasat C.C. Applied to resign the Service in 1808; permitted to withdraw his resignation 10 Oct. 1808; posted Cornet to 1st N.C. 24 Oct. 1808. Operations in Bundelkhand 1810-11; Bichaund; Cornet 1st N.C. Leave s.c. to N.S.W. 15 Mar. 1813 till 23 Sept. 1815. Third Mahratta War 1817-18; Lieut. 1st N.C., in Rt. Div. Actg. Adjt. 1st N.C. 1818. Operations against the Bhattis of Hariana 1818. Transfd. to newly-raised 2nd Extra Cav. (became 10th L.C.) 17 June 1825. Fur. s.c. 19 Feb. 1832 till retirement. Retired on a pension of 10/6 *p.d.*

Refs.: Westminster School Register. G.M. 1854, i. 334.

WHITE, Kenneth John (1810-1858). Lieutenant. Artillery. (592) *b.* Dacca 24 July 1810. Cadet 1826. Arrived in India 24 Sept. 1827. 2nd Lieut. 28 Sept. 1827. Lieut. 10 Feb. 1834. Retired 29 July 1840. *d.* Paris 2 Mar. 1858.

bapt. Calcutta 21 Dec. 1810. Son of Martin White, *q.v.*, and Frances Mellish his wife. Brother of Martin Thomas White, *q.v.* Addiscombe Cadet 1825-6.

Services: Apptd. A.D.C. to his father, comdg. Benares Div., 24 Nov. 1831. Posted to 1st Coy. 4th Bn. Foot Art. 8 Nov. 1834. Fur. p.a. 29 Jan. 1838 till retirement. No record of active service.

Refs.: Bath Chron. 18 Mar. 1858. *The Times,* 6 Mar. 1858. Will dated 15 Nov. 1856; admon. 26 Apr. 1860.

WHITE, Mark (*d.* 1798). Captain, 8th N.I. Country Cadet 1777. Admitted 19 May 1777. Ensign 24 Sept. 1777. Lieut. 7 Oct. 1778. Capt. 19 Mar. 1796. *d.* Chunar 8 Aug. 1798.

Brother of Sir Henry White, *q.v.*

Services: Apptd. Adjt. 33rd Bn. Sepoys 22 Mar. 1780; Adjt. 26th Sepoys till 21 Dec. 1782. Lieut. 26th Bn. Sepoys in July 1787. Third Mysore War 1790-2; Bangalore; Arikera; operations before Savandrug; Utradrug; Seringapatam; Lieut. 26th Bn. Capt. 1/8th N.I.

Refs.: M.I. at Chunar.

WHITE, Martin (*d.* 1776). Captain. Bengal Eur. Regt. Lieut. 30 Dec. 1757. Capt. 27 July 1759. Resigned 11 Sept.

1761. *d*. 5 June 1776: drowned when bathing in R. Clyde nr. his house, about 3 miles above Hamilton.

Of Milton. Father of Henry Vansittart White and Martin White, *qq.v*.

Services: Sent with a detachment of Bengal Eur. Bn., some Sepoys and Art., to subdue the province of Midnapore in Nov. 1760, and in Birbhum the following month; action against the Rajah of Burdwan 29 Dec.

Refs.: *Broome*, pp. 319-20. *Innes*, p. 129. *S.M.* 1776, p. 340.

WHITE, Martin (1766/67-1856). General. Colonel 22nd N.I. *b*. 1766/67. Cadet 1782. Arrived in India 28 Dec. 1782. Ensign 2 Mar. 1783. Lieut. 17 Feb. 1790. Capt. 30 Sept. 1803. Major 28 Apr. 1812. Lt. Col. 10 Aug. 1816. Lt. Col. Comdt. 1 May 1824. Col. 5 June 1829. Maj. Gen. 10 Jan. 1837. Lt. Gen. 9 Nov. 1846. Gen. 20 June 1854. *d*. Sydney Pl., Bath, 18 July 1856, aged 89.

Son of Martin White, *q.v.* Brother of Henry Vansittart White, *q.v. m.* Chittagong 30 May 1807, Frances Mellish, sister of Kenneth Archibald John Murchison, *q.v.* (She died Tunbridge Wells 18 Sept. 1851.) Father of Kenneth John White and Martin Thomas White, *qq.v.*, and of the wife of Col. Sir Henry Yule, K.C.S.I. (*D.N.B.*)

Services: Apptd. Cadet 7 Nov. 1781; sailed for India in the *Calcutta* 6 Feb. 1782. Posted to 1st Bengal Eur. Regt. 28 Feb. 1783. Ensign 3rd Eur. Bn. in Dec. 1788 and in 1790; transfd. to 1st Bn. Sepoys in Feb. 1790. Capt. Lt. 2nd N.I. 15 Aug. 1802. Operations in Jumna Doab 1803; Sasni; Bijaigarh; Kachaura; Capt. Lt. 2nd N.I. Transfd. to newly-raised 24th N.I. 1804. Comdd. Provl. Corps at Etawah 1804-6; do. Chittagong 1807-9; do. Dacca 4 Aug. 1809 till 31 Oct. 1812. Major 1/24th N.I. Posted Lt. Col. to 1/2nd N.I. 1816. Hon. A.D.C. to G.G. 2 Nov. 1816 till 1819. Supt. of Mysore Princes 1817-18. Transfd. to 17th N.I. 1819; to 1/3rd N.I. 1820. Leave p.a. to Cape 13 Nov. 1819 till 11 Jan. 1821; fur. p.a. 20 Feb. 1821 till 11 Oct. 1824. Posted Lt. Col. Comdt. to 61st N.I. May 1824; to newly-raised 2nd Extra Regt. (became 70th N.I.) May 1825. Fur. 1826-9. Posted Col. to 70th N.I. 1829; to 22nd N.I. 30 Nov. 1830 till death. Bdr. on Est. comdg. troops in Bundelkhand 19 Jan. 1831; Bdr. Gen. comdg. Benares Div. 24 Nov. 1831 till 24 Nov. 1836. Leave s.c. to Simla 1 Feb. till 20 Dec. 1834; fur. p.a. 29 Jan. 1838 till death.

Refs.: *Boase*. *G.M.* 1856, ii. 391.

WHITE, Martin Thomas (1809-1841). Lieutenant, Invalid Est. 37th N.I. *b*. Calcutta 18 July 1809. Cadet 1826. Arrived in India 24 Sept. 1827. Ensign 30 Jan. 1828. Lieut. 4 Apr. 1832. Invalided 22 Aug. 1833. *d.* Moulmein, Burma, 21 Jan. 1841.

bapt. Calcutta 21 Dec. 1810. Son of Martin White, *q.v.*, and Frances Mellish his wife. Brother of Kenneth John White, *q.v.*

Services : Posted Ensign to 63rd N.I. 1827 ; transfd. to 37th N.I. 30 Jan. 1828. Fur. s.c. 13 Apr. 1830 till 26 Oct. 1832. d.d. 66th N.I. at Benares (where his father was comdg.) 16 Apr. 1833. No record of active service. Permitted to reside at Benares 19 Oct. 1833 ; do. at Amherst Town, Burma, 23 Mar. 1840.

WHITE, Matthew George (1801-1866). Lieut. Colonel. 66th N.I. *b.* Arcot, Madras, 16 May 1801. Cadet 1817. Arrived in India 31 July 1818. Ensign 23 Feb. 1818. Lieut. 1 Aug. 1818. Capt. 26 June 1830. Major 7 Nov. 1840. Retired 16 May 1844. Hon. Lt. Col. 28 Nov. 1854. *d.* Boulogne-sur-Mer, France, 3 Sept. 1866, of cholera.

Son of John Douglas White, Surg. Madras Est., later Member of the Madras Medical Board. Brother of Robert Dennis White, *q.v.*

Services : Arrived at Madras 31 July 1818 and was permitted to serve as Ensign of Madras Inf. till Court's pleasure be known ; arrived Bengal 23 June 1821. Posted Lieut. to 1/23rd N.I. 1819 ; transfd. to newly-raised 33rd N.I. July 1823, but remained with 1/23rd till 15 Feb. 1824. d.d. 2/10th Madras N.I. embarking for Rangoon Mar. 1824 ; returned from Rangoon 4 Dec. 1824 (India medal). Transfd. to 66th N.I. (late 2/33rd) May 1824 ; Adjt. do. 23 Aug. 1825 till 26 May 1829. Asst. to Local Supt. of Arakan 15 May 1829 till 1838. Fur. p.a. 5 Jan. 1838 till 11 Oct. 1841. Offg. Principal Asst. to Comr. of Arakan 17 June 1842 ; Principal Asst. to A.G.G. and Comr., N.E. frontier, 1 Nov. 1842 till retirement.

Refs. : The Times, 11 Sept. 1866.

WHITE, Richard (1762/63-?). Lieutenant. Infantry. *b.* 1762/63. Cadet 1780. Ensign 27 Sept. 1780. Lieut. 20 Aug. 1781. Struck off 1788.

Services : Should have sailed for India in the *Lascelles* 12 Feb. 1780, aged 17. Shown as on fur. in Mar. 1786, but probably never arrived in India.

WHITE, Robert Dennis (1802-1867). Lieut. Colonel. 69th N.I. *b.* Seringapatam, Mysore, 18 June 1802. Cadet 1817. Admitted 11 Jan. 1819. Ensign 18 July 1818. Lieut. 19 Jan. 1820. Capt. 29 June 1835. Bt. Major 9 Nov. 1846. Retired

THE BENGAL ARMY, 1758-1834

29 May 1848. Hon. Lt. Col. 28 Nov. 1854. *d.* 1 Clarendon Villas, Penge, Kent, 21 Aug. 1867.

Son of John Douglas White, Surg. Madras Est. Brother of Matthew George White, *q.v.* *m.* (?)

Services: Ensign d.d. 14th N.I. 1819; posted to 2/12th N.I. 1820; transfd. to newly-raised 2/33rd N.I. July 1823; to 66th N.I. (late 2/33rd) May 1824. Adjt. of Major P.C. Gilman's Levy (64th N.I.) 14 Sept. 1824. Transfd. to 1st Extra Regt. (became 69th N.I.) May 1825. Adjt. newly-raised 8th Extra Regt. 21 May 1825 till reduced 1826. Apptd. to 8th Coy. Pioneers 22 Sept. 1826; actg. Adjt. do. 10 June 1832. Offg. Bde. Major Meerut 29 Oct. 1835; A.D.C. to Sir. T. Anbury, *q.v.*, 24 Nov. 1836 and joined 19 Jan. 1837. Offg. D.J.A.G. Saugor 17 Apr. 1838; Postmr. at Saugor 15 Oct. 1838. Demonstration against Jhansi 1838-39; A.D.C. Offg. D.J.A.G. Sukkur 25 July 1844; A.D.C. to Maj.-Gen. E. H. Simpson, *q.v.*, 18 Jan. 1845. Fur. 1847 till retirement. Started after retirement the firm of White, Ludlow & Co., E.I.U.S. Agency, 53 Charing Cross, London.

Refs.: The Times, 24 Aug. 1867.

WHITE, Samuel (*d.* 1806). Captain, 22nd N.I. Cadet 1781. Admitted 1781. Ensign 3 Sept. 1781. Lieut. 16 June 1783. Capt. 6 May 1803. *d.* Calcutta 8 Sept. 1806.

Services: Apptd. a Vol. by Sir Eyre Coote 13 Mar. 1781, and served as such with the Bengal detachment during Second Mysore War. Lieut. 15th Bn. Sepoys in July 1787 and in Dec. 1792; Bt. Capt. 7th N.I. in June 1798; transfd. to 6th N.I. 1798. Disturbances in Ganjam, Madras, 1801; Bt. Capt. 6th N.I. Capt. Lt. 6th N.I. 8 Dec. 1800. Transfd. to newly-raised 22nd N.I. 1804.

WHITE, Thomas Russell (*d.* 1803). Lieutenant, 6th N.C. Cadet 1796. Arrived in India 15 Mar. 1798. Cornet 1 Nov. 1798. Lieut. 29 May 1800. *d.* Chandausi, U.P., 25 July 1803.

Services: Posted Cornet to 4th N.C.; transfd. as Lieut. to newly-raised 6th N.C. May 1800. Operations in Jumna Doab 1803; Sasni; Bijaigarh; Kachaura; Lieut. 6th N.C.

WHITE, William (1789-?). Bt. Captain. 15th N.I. *bapt.* St. Clement Danes, Middlesex, 12 Sept. 1789. Cadet 1806. Arrived in India 1 Aug. 1807. Ensign 19 Aug. 1807. Lieut. 25 Apr. 1810. Bt. Capt. 28 Feb. 1822. Struck off in England 26 Aug. 1822. (Living in 1845.)

Son of William White and Ann his wife. *m.* Berhampore 19 Nov.

1813, Caroline, dau. of Charles Brietzcke, *q.v.* (*See also* John Frederick Sanford.) (She died Berhampore 21 June 1816, aged 18.)
Services : Barasat C.C. Posted Ensign to 15th N.I. 1808. Adjt. Murshidabad Provl. Bn. 13 Sept. 1813 till 1818. Third Mahratta War 1819 ; Asirgarh ; Lieut. 2/15th N.I. Fur. 25 Feb. 1820 till struck off. Author of " A Political history of the . . . events which led to the Burmese war," map, London, 1827 ; " *Mirza Kaiwan Jah* ; or the Deposed King of Oude in Chains," 1838 ; " Indian Cookery ; or Fish Curries [1] ; . . ." London, 1845.

[1] *Note :* " Capt. White's curry paste " may have been named after him.

JERVIS-WHITE, Humphrey (1797-1849). Lieut. Colonel, 50th N.I. *b.* 25 Dec. 1797. Cadet 1817. Admitted 19 Sept. 1818. Ensign 25 May 1818. Lieut. 24 Aug. 1819. Capt. 21 June 1830. Major 7 July 1842. Lt. Col. (30 Apr. 1844) 4 Jan. 1849. *d.* Delhi 15 Dec. 1849.

bapt. St. Thomas, Dublin, 30 Jan. 1798. 2nd son of Thomas Jervis Jervis-White, of Ferns, co. Wexford, and Frances his wife, dau. of Sir John Meredyth, 1st Bart., of Garlandstown. Nephew of Sir John Jervis-White-Jervis, 1st Bart., of Ballyellis, of John Canning, *q.v.*, and of Arthur Tisdal Meredyth, *q.v.*, and cousin-german of Joseph Liddell Farrer, *q.v. m.* Calcutta 28 Mar. 1835, Elizabeth, only dau. of Capt. William Bury, H.M. 35th Regt. (She died 15 Jan. 1879.) Sandhurst Cadet.

Services : Posted to 2/25th N.I. ; Adjt. do. 1 Oct. 1823. Apptd. Asst. and Pte. Sec. to his uncle, Major John Canning, P.A., 24 Mar. 1824, and joined him in Rangoon 15 July 1824. Rejoined 50th N.I. (late 2/25th) Feb. 1825. Fur. s.c. 28 Jan. 1832 till 30 Jan. 1835. Comdd. 50th N.I. June till 20 Oct. 1836, and 8 Nov. 1841 till 30 Aug. 1842. Gwalior campaign ; Paniar (*Lond. Gaz.* 8 Mar. 1844) ; Major comdg. 50th N.I., and took 2nd Bde. into action on Bdr. Joseph Anderson, H.M. 50th, being wounded (Bronze star). Posted Lt. Col. to 50th N.I. 1849. Second Sikh War ; Lt. Col. comdg. 50th N.I. in garr. at Lahore (Medal).

Refs.: Burke's *Landed Gentry of Ireland*, p. 766, *s.n.* Jervis-White, of Ferns. Burke's *Peerage*, 1923, p. 1254, *s.n.* Jervis-White-Jervis, Bart., of Bally Ellis. *I.M.* 9 Mar. 1850, p. 145.

WHITEFOORD, James (1807-1876). Major. Artillery. (585) *b.* London 14 Jan. 1807. Cadet 1825. Arrived in India 2 Jan. 1827. 2nd Lieut. 16 June 1826. Lieut. 25 July 1833. Capt. 3 July 1845. Retired 31 July 1854. Hon. Major 28 Nov. 1854. *d.* Gloucester 7 Oct. 1876.

bapt. Marylebone 10 Feb. 1807. Son of Sir John Rousselet Whitefoord, Kt., of Ghent, and Deborah his wife. *m.* Carphin House, Fife, 25 Aug. 1835, Louisa Jane, youngest dau. of Capt. Impett, of Ashford, Kent. Addiscombe Cadet 1824-6.

Services : Fur. s.c. 8 Jan. 1834 till 28 May 1836 ; leave s.c. 15 mos. to Singapore 7 Aug. 1837. Adjt. 6th Bn. Foot Art. 13 Apr. 1840 till 1845. Gwalior campaign ; Maharajpur ; Bt. Capt., Adjt. 6th Bn. (Bronze star). Fur. 1853 till 6 Mar. 1854.

Refs. : G.E.C. *Barts.* iv. 401, note (c). *A.J.* N.S. xviii. 143. *The Times,* 10 Oct. 1876.

WHITEFORD, Joseph (1799-1840). Captain, 65th N.I. *b.* Plymouth 24 Dec. 1799. Cadet 1820. Arrived in India Sept. 1821. Ensign 5 May 1821. Lieut. 11 Sept. 1823. Capt. 14 Apr. 1839. *d.* at sea 17 Mar. 1840, on board the *Lord Hungerford.*

Elder son of Joseph Whiteford, of Plymouth, solicitor, and Martha Pitman his wife, 4th dau. of Abraham Lovell. *m.* St. John's, Calcutta, 25 Oct. 1824, Jane, sister of John Howard Rice, *q.v.*[1] (She *re-m.* Edward Thomas Tierney, *q.v.*)

Services : Posted Ensign to 1/22nd N.I. ; transfd. to 33rd N.I. July 1823 ; to 65th N.I. (late 1/33rd) May 1824. Fur. u.p.a. 6 Aug. 1825 till 13 Aug. 1827. Intr. & Qmr. 65th N.I. 21 Aug. 1829 till 29 May 1839. Offg. Asst. in *Thagi* Dept. at Murshidabad 19 Mar. 1838 ; permanent do. 26 Nov. 1839. Leave s.c. 2 yrs. to Cape 25 Jan. 1840. No record of active service.

Refs. : Burke's *Landed Gentry,* 6th edn., p. 1731, *s.n.* Whiteford, of Thornhill, Devon. *Misc. Gen. et Her.* 2S. ii. 264.

[1] *Note :* His name is given in the marriage register as Joseph Charles Whiteford.

WHITEHEAD, John (1773-1797). Lieutenant, Infantry. *bapt.* Ulverston, Lancs., 6 July 1773. Cadet 1794. Arrived in India 22 Feb. 1796. Ensign 19 Nov. 1795. Lieut. 30 Oct. 1797. *d.* Kumurmela, C.P., 29 Dec. 1797.

Son of Joseph Whitehead, of Ulverston.

Services : Apptd. Cadet 22 Apr. 1795 ; sailed for India in the *Triton* 9 July 1795. N.F.P.

WHITEHEAD, Sir Thomas (1777-1851). Lieut. General, K.C.B. Colonel 2nd Bengal Eur. Fus. *bapt.* Eccleston, Lancs., 25 May 1777. Cadet 1794. Arrived in India 16 Feb. 1795. Ensign 19 Sept. 1794. Lieut. 8 Jan. 1796. Capt. 21 Sept. 1804. Major 21 Sept. 1814. Lt. Col. 21 Oct. 1818. Lt. Col. Comdt.

1 May 1824. Col. 5 June 1829. Maj. Gen. 10 Jan. 1837. Lt. Gen. 9 Nov. 1846. *d.* Uplands Hall, Lancs., 7 Apr. 1851, aged 73; *bur.* Eccleston.

Of Uplands Hall. Eldest son of Rev. Thomas Whitehead, rector of Eccleston, and Margaret Hannah Shaw his wife, of Preston. *m.* 4 Nov. 1816, Charlotte, dau. of James Burdett Ness, of Osterley Hall, Yorks. His daus. *m.* Sir George Hall Macgregor, *q.v.*, and Sir Andrew Scott Waugh, *q.v.*

Services : Apptd. Cadet for Madras 21 May 1794; exchanged to Bengal; sailed for India in the *Lascelles* 14 Aug. 1794. Lieut. 9th N.I. in 1798. Second Mahratta War; Lieut. 9th N.I. (? Operations against Dhundia Khan 1807; Komona; Ganauri; Capt. 1/9th N.I.) Settlement of Hariana 1809; Bhawani (w.); Capt. 1/9th N.I. Operations in Oudh 1809-10; Pragpur; Capt. 1/9th N.I. Fur. p.a. 12 Dec. 1813 till 11 Oct. 1816. Major 1/9th N.I. Posted Lt. Col. to 9th N.I. 1818; to 1/21st N.I. 1821; Lt. Col. Comdt. to 41st N.I. (late 1/21st) May 1824. To comd. 4th Inf. Bde. for Bhurtpore 3 Dec. 1825. Siege and capture of Bhurtporē (*Lond. Gaz.* 12 June & 7 Oct. 1826); Lt. Col. Comdt. 41st N.I., Bdr. comdg. 4th Bde. To comd. 4th Bde. 1st Inf. Div. 4 Feb. 1826. Transfd. to 68th N.I. 12 Oct. 1826. Fur. p.a. 18 Jan. 1827 till death. Col. 68th N.I. 1829; 2nd Bengal Eur. Regt. Oct. 1839 till death. C.B. 18 June 1827. K.C.B. 20 July 1838.

Refs.: *Manchester School Register*, i. 80. *Howard & Crisp's Ireland*, i. 92, *s.n.* Massy-Westropp. Foster's *Lancs. Peds. Boase. G.M.* 1851, i. 683. *A.R.* (1851), 278.

WHITELOCKE, George Frederick (1804-1879). Lieut. Colonel. 13th N.I. *bupt.* St. Thomas, Winchester, 28 Dec. 1804. Cadet 1825. Arrived in India 24 Sept. 1826. Ensign 15 May 1826. Lieut. 13 Aug. 1835. Capt. 24 Jan. 1845. Major 28 Nov. 1854. Retired 28 Feb. 1855. Hon. Lt. Col. 11 May 1855. *d.* 5 Prince's Bldgs., Clifton, 19 Jan. 1879, aged 74.

Son of Dr. James Whitelocke, Bt. Inspector Gen., Insp. of Hospitals at Boulogne, and Elizabeth his wife. Brother of John Gilbert Whitelocke, *q.v.*

Services : Ensign d.d. 57th N.I. 7 Oct. 1826; posted to 13th N.I. 9 Nov. 1826. Actg. Intr. & Qmr. 72nd N.I. 12 Aug. 1832; do. 44th N.I. 5 July 1834. Intr. & Qmr. 13th N.I. 27 Apr. 1836 till 14 May 1839. Fur. s.c. 23 Dec. 1839 till 8 July 1842. Intr. & Qmr. 8th L.C. 16 Oct. 1843. Offg. Bde. Qmr. Left Column, 1st Div., Army of Exercise 26 Dec. 1843. Gwalior campaign; Paniar; Bt. Capt. 13th N.I., Bde. Qmr. (Bronze star). Second Sikh

THE BENGAL ARMY, 1758-1834

War; passage of Chenab; Gujerat; Capt. 13th N.I. (Medal with clasp).
Refs.: *The Times*, 22 Jan. 1879.

WHITELOCKE, John Gilbert (1803-?). Ensign. 22nd N.I.
b. Stoke, Devon, 5 May 1803. Cadet 1824. Arrived in India 29 June 1825. Ensign 8 Jan. 1825. Resigned in India 19 May 1826.

Son of Dr. James Whitelocke. Brother of George Frederick Whitelocke, *q.v.*
Services: Posted Ensign to 44th N.I. 1825; transfd. to 22nd N.I. 1826. No record of active service.

WHITESMITH, Leonard (1784-1811). Lieutenant, 7th N.I.
b. Bawtry, Yorks., 14 Oct. 1784. Cadet 1800. Arrived in India 14 Oct. 1801. Ensign 16 Nov. 1801. Lieut. 30 Sept. 1803. *d.* on the expedn. to Java 26 Aug. 1811.

bapt. 17 Oct. 1784. Son of Thomas Whitesmith and Mary his wife. *m.* (?)
Services: Ensign d.d. 4th N.I. in 1802; posted Ensign to 7th N.I. Second Mahratta War; operations in Cuttack 1803-4; capture of Balasore; Lieut. 2/7th N.I., with 1st Vol. Bn. At P.W.I. 1805; Adjt. P.W.I. Mil. 1806-8. Capture of Java 1811; Lieut. 4th Vol. Bn.

WHITFIELD, Charles (1780-1808). Lieutenant, 26th N.I.
bapt. Astbury, co. Chester, 11 Jan. 1780. Cadet 1798. Arrived in India 24 Feb. 1800. Ensign 11 Dec. 1799. Lieut. 29 May 1800. *d.* Berhampore 13 Mar. 1808.

Son of John Whitfield and Ellen his wife. *m.* Fatehgarh 6 Feb. 1803, Ann, dau. of Simpson Dubois, *q.v.* (*See also* Thomas Hall (1770/71-1856).) (iii. 791.)
Services: Posted to 2/13th N.I. 15 Apr. 1801; transfd. to newly-raised 26th N.I. 1805. Operations in Bundelkhand 1807; Sehlehuganj; Lieut. 26th N.I.

WHITFIELD, Charles Howard (1807-1849). Captain. 46th N.I. *b.* London 28 Nov. 1807. Cadet 1823. Arrived in India 19 May 1824. Ensign 17 Jan. 1824. Lieut. 13 May 1825. Capt. 26 May 1835. Retired 1 Aug. 1838. *d.* 18 May 1849.

bapt. Dulwich 3 Aug. 1808. Son of George Whitfield, of 85 Gt. Surrey St., Blackfriars, and Elizabeth Holston his wife. *m.* Calcutta 2 Sept. 1828, Anne Olivia, dau. of Archibald Duff, of Calcutta, atty.
Services: Posted Ensign to 46th N.I. and served throughout

with that Regt. Actg. Intr. & Qmr. 29 July 1829. Fur. s.c. 3 Apr. 1837 till retirement. No record of active service.

Refs.: A.J. xxvii. 358.

WHITFORD, George (1764/65-1791). Lieutenant, 33rd Bn. Sepoys. *b.* 1764/65. Cadet 1782. Arrived in India Jan. 1783. Ensign 23 Feb. 1783. Lieut. 12 Feb. 1790. *d.* at sea in Madras roads; *bur.* Madras 11 Oct. 1791, aged 26.

Services: Apptd. Cadet 16 Nov. 1781; sailed for India in the *Royal Henry* 6 Feb. 1782. Posted to 1st Bengal Eur. Regt. 28 Feb. 1783. Was Adjt. 33rd Bn. Sepoys in Mar. 1787 and in Jan. 1791. Third Mysore War 1790-1.

Refs.: M.I. (" Whiteford ") St. Mary's cemetery, Madras.

WHITTAL, Joshua (*d.* 1777). Lieutenant, Infantry. Country Cadet 1769. Ensign 31 Mar. 1769. Lieut. 19 Sept. 1770. *d.* Berhampore Aug. 1777.

Services: Apptd. Cadet 28 Feb. 1769. N.F.P.

***WHYTE, Andrew Mark** (1762/63-1783). Lieutenant, Infantry. *b.* in Ireland 1762/63. Cadet 1781. Arrived in India 15 May 1782. Ensign 17 Apr. 1781. Lieut. 8 Aug. 1782. *d.* Madras 22 Nov. 1783.[1]

(*Perhaps* son of Mark Whyte, by Elizabeth his wife, dau. of John Edwards, of Old Court, co. Wicklow.)

Services: Apptd. Cadet 7 Feb. 1781; sailed for India in the *Hinchinbrooke* 13 Mar. 1781, aged 18. Granted leave s.c. to sea Aug. 1783.

Refs.: (? Burke's *Landed Gentry of Ireland*, p. 771, *s.n.* Whyte, of Newton Manor, co. Leitrim.)

[1] *Note:* Buried as " Lieut. Mark White."

***WICK(S),** ——. Lieutenant. Bengal Eur. Regt. Ensign (Madras) (?) Lieut. (Bengal) 7 Feb. 1757.

Services: Served in Bengal under Clive 1757; battle of Plassey; Ensign in Capt. G. F. Gaupp's Coy. of Madras Inf. Transfd. to Bengal Est. as Lieut. in 1757. Expedn. to N. Circars 1758; battle of Condore (w.); Lieut. Bengal Eur. Regt. Not in List of 1760.

Refs.: Orme *MSS.*—India, xiii. 3639. *Forde*, pp. 64, 66.

WICKENS, John (1747/48-1790). Lieutenant, 20th Bn. Sepoys. *b.* 1747/48. Country Cadet 1779. Ensign 30 Sept. 1779. Lieut. 12 May 1781. *d.* Hazaribagh, B. & O., 30 Sept. 1790, aged 42.

Services: Apptd. Cadet 19 Aug. 1779. Lieut. 20th Bn. Sepoys in July 1787.

Refs.: M.I. in Hazaribagh old cemetery.

THE BENGAL ARMY, 1758-1834

WIDENHAM, John (1737-1767). Captain, Infantry. *b.* Limerick 1737. Cadet 1763. Ensign 22 June 1763. Lieut. 8 Feb. 1764. Capt. 8 July 1766. *d.* 6 Oct. 1767.

Services : Sailed for India in the *Plassey* 2 Jan. 1763, aged 25. Battle of Buxar Oct. 1764. Apptd. to act as Adjt. of Sepoys 13 Feb. 1765. Was Dy. Judge Advocate at Ramgarh camp on 18 May 1767.

WIGGENS, John (*d.* 1773). Lieutenant, Artillery. (111) Cadet 1769. Fireworker 1770. Lieut. 19 May 1772. *d.* Kalpi 6 Oct. 1773.

Services : Sailed for India in the *Pigot* 2 Jan. 1769.

WIGGINS or WIGGENS,[1] **Charles Henry** (1804-1828). Lieutenant, Artillery. (513) *b.* Calcutta 27 June 1804.[2] Cadet 1820. Arrived in India June 1821. 2nd Lieut. 19 Dec. 1820. Lieut. 1 May 1824. *d.* Calcutta 1 Jan. 1828.

bapt. Calcutta 24 Feb. 1806. Son of Lewis Wiggins, *q.v.* Brother of Douglas Kinnaird Wiggins, *q.v.* Addiscombe Cadet 1819-20.

Services : 2nd Lieut. 5th Coy. 3rd Bn. Foot Art. Posted to 3rd Troop 2nd Bde. H.A. 1825. Siege and capture of Bhurtpore ; Lieut. 3rd Troop 2nd Bde. Leave s.c. 5 mos. to Singapore 28 Aug. 1826. Transfd. to 4th Troop 1st Bde. 1826 ; to 1st Troop 2nd Bde. 1827.

Refs. : A.J. xxv. 825.

[1] *Note :* The grandfather, Thomas, M.P., appears to have spelt his name Wiggins, but the sons and grandsons seem to have used either spelling indifferently.

[2] *Note :* This is the date as given in his Cadet Papers. In the baptismal register (where the name is spelt Wiggens) he is stated to have been *b.* 27 Jan. 1805.

WIGGINS or WIGGENS, Douglas Kinnaird (1807-1847). Lieutenant. 7th L.C. *b.* Calcutta 7 May 1807. Cadet 1823. Arrived in India 19 May 1824. Cornet (?) Lieut. 4 Feb. 1825. Retired 3 Sept. 1838. *d.* 12 Dec. 1847.

Son of Lewis Wiggins, *q.v.* Brother of Charles Henry Wiggins, *q.v. m.* 1st, Grace Edgecumbe. (She died off Kasipur 7 Aug. 1834, aged 22.) *m.* 2nd, Augusta Matilda. (She died Clapham 4 June 1838, aged 23.) Ed. Charterhouse July 1818-Aug. 1821.[1]

Services : Posted to 3rd L.C. ; transfd. to 7th L.C. 24 Dec. 1825. Siege and capture of Bhurtpore ; Lieut. 7th L.C., d.d. 6th L.C. Leave s.c. to N.S.W. 3 Mar. 1829 till 12 Apr. 1831 ; fur. s.c. 31 Mar.

1831 till 25 Dec. 1833 ; s.c. 26 Jan. 1837 till retirement. Retired on h.p., viz., 4/- *p.d.*
Refs.: Charterhouse School List. A.J. N.S. xxii. 127.
[1] *Note:* He appears as Douglas Robert Kinnaird Wiggins in School List.

WIGGINS, Francis Smith (1788-1832). Captain, 31st N.I. *bapt.* Danbury, Essex, 10 Mar. 1788. Cadet 1808. Arrived in India 4 Nov. 1809. Ensign 8 Dec. 1810. Lieut. 15 Sept. 1814. Capt. 25 Jan. 1825. *d.* Queen's Row, Pentonville, London, 30 July 1832, aged 44 : cut his throat in a fit of temporary insanity. Son of John Wiggins and Elizabeth his wife.
Services: Barasat C.C. Posted to 10th N.I. 1810 ; transfd. to 1/15th N.I. 1811. Fur. 5 Sept. 1811 till 30 Sept. 1815. Pindari War 1817-18 (w.) ; Lieut. 1/15th N.I. Attacked and severely wounded by Mahrattas (? Pindaris) nr. Lucknow in Nov. 1817. With 1st Ceylon Vol. Bn. Oct. 1818 till Mar. 1820. Intr. & Qmr. 1/15th N.I. 3 Feb. 1821 till 17 June 1824 ; transfd. to 31st N.I. (late 2/15th) May 1824, but remained with 30th N.I. on Chittagong frontier till the following Nov. Adjt. & Qmr. Eur. Invalids at Chunar 31 May 1824 (joined 25 Nov.) till 14 July 1825. Siege and capture of Bhurtpore ; Capt. 31st N.I. Suspended by G.C.M. from rank and pay for 4 mos. 18 June 1827. Fur. s.c. 21 Oct. 1830 till death.
Refs.: A.J. N.S. ix. 51. *The Times,* 2 Aug. 1832, p. 3*d.*

WIGGINS or WIGGENS, George William (1781-1808). Captain, 17th N.I. *b.* Taplow 5 Oct. 1781. Cadet 1796. Arrived in India 17 July 1797. Ensign 9 Oct. 1797. Lieut. 10 Sept. 1798. Capt. 1807. *d.* Cuttack 7 Jan. 1808.
bapt. St. George's, Hanover Sq., London, 13 Nov. 1781. Son of Thomas Wiggins, M.P. for Okehampton, and Hon. Margaret his wife, 3rd and youngest dau. of Charles, 6th Baron Kinnaird. Brother of Lewis Wiggins, *q.v. m.* Calcutta 20 Oct. 1800, Miss Caroline Collins. (She *re-m.* Henry Edward Gilbert Cooper, *q.v.*) Ed. Winchester ; K.S. 1793-6.
Services: Ensign 7th N.I. ; transfd. as Lieut. to newly-raised 17th N.I. ; Capt. Lt. do. 20 Oct. 1805.
Refs.: Burke's *Peerage,* 1923, p. 1302, *s.n.* Kinnaird, B. *Kirby.* Will dated 1 June 1807 ; proved 15 Mar. 1808. M.I. at Cuttack.

WIGGINS or WIGGENS, Lewis (1784-1826). Lieut. Colonel, 62nd N.I. *b.* London 12 Apr. 1784. Cadet 1798. Arrived in India 27 Mar. 1800. Ensign 24 Sept. 1799. Lieut. 28 Oct. 1799.

THE BENGAL ARMY, 1758-1834

Capt. 19 May 1808. Major 6 July 1818. Lt. Col. 11 July 1823. d. Arakan 14 Jan. 1826.

bapt. St. George's, Hanover Sq., 30 May 1784. Son of Thomas Wiggins and Hon. Margaret his wife. Brother of George William Wiggins, cousin-german of Charles Patrick Dana, and uncle of the wife of Charles Short, *qq.v.* m. Calcutta 21 Feb. 1805, Miss Maria McArthur. (She died London 11 Dec. 1847.) Father of Charles Henry Wiggins and Douglas Kinnaird Wiggins, *qq.v.*, and of the wives of Anthony Highmore Jellicoe, Francis Edward Manning, and Andrew Gildart Reid, *qq.v.*

Services: Posted Ensign to 2nd Bengal Eur. Regt. 15 Apr. 1801; transfd. to Marine Regt. (became 20th N.I.) 1803. Operations in Ceylon 1803-4; Lieut. 20th N.I., with 2nd Vol. Bn. Capt. Lt. 20th N.I. 14 Nov. 1805. At P.W.I. in 1806. Capt. 1/20th N.I.; Supy. A.D.C. to G.G. Apr. 1808. Dy. Paymr. at Chunar 9 Jan. 1809 till 1812; do. at Benares 1812; Asst. Mily. Auditor Gen. 1 Jan. 1813 till 1823. Transfd. to newly-raised 1/30th N.I. 1815; Lt. Col. 62nd N.I. May 1824. First Burma War; Arakan 1825; Lt. Col. 62nd N.I.

Refs.: Burke's *Peerage*, 1923, p. 1302, *s.n.* Kinnaird, B.

*WIGHT, Alexander (1787-1805). Cadet, Infantry. *b.* St. Andrew's psh., Edinburgh, 8 June 1787. Cadet 1804. Never arrived in India. *d.* 5 Feb. 1805: lost at sea in the wreck of the *Earl of Abergavenny* off Portland. (See note to Charles Davis or Davies.)

Son of Alexander Wight, of Edinburgh, W.S. (who was cousin-german of Hercules Skinner, *q.v.*), and Jane (Jean) his 1st wife, dau. of William Macconochie or McOnochie, wright in Edinburgh.

WIGHT, Arthur (1788-1847). Major. 23rd N.I. *b.* 4 Jan. 1788. Cadet 1805. Arrived in India 13 Dec. 1806. Ensign 16 Dec. 1806. Lieut. 22 Dec. 1811. Capt. 1 May 1824. Major 19 June 1831. Retired 28 July 1833. *d.* Braboeuf Manor, nr. Guildford, 9 May 1847.

Of Braboeuf. *bapt.* St. Nicholas, Guildford, 17 June 1788. 2nd son of John Wight, of Braboeuf Manor, and Sarah Spencer his wife. m. Jane More, (? half-) sister of Thomas More Molyneux, *q.v.* (She *re-m.* Rev. Henry Shrubb and died 26 Feb. 1868.)

Services: Barasat C.C. 8 mos. Posted Ensign to 4th N.I. 1807. Nepal War 1815; operations in Kumaon; capture of Almora (s.w. 24 Apr.—*Lond. Gaz.* 16 Nov. 1815); Lieut. 1/4th N.I. Adjt. Kumaon Local Bn. 21 July 1815 till Jan. 1818. Intr. & Qmr.

2/4th N.I. 30 Jan. 1818 till 17 June 1824. Transfd. to 23rd N.I. (late 2/4th) May 1824. D.A.Q.M.G. 1st Div. Bhurtpore force 1 Dec. 1825. Siege and capture of Bhurtpore; Capt. 23rd N.I., D.A.Q.M.G.[1] Fur. p.a. 28 Jan. 1832 till retirement. Retired on pension of 16/– *p.d.*

Refs.: Burke's *Landed Gentry*, 7th edn., p. 1986, *s.n.* Wight, of Braboeuf Manor, Surrey. *G.M.* 1847, ii. 108.

[1] *Note:* Bt. Major for distinguished service at Bhurtpore (*Lond. Gaz.* 1 Aug. 1834).

WIGNEY, Frederick (1793-?). Lieutenant. 15th N.I. *b.* Newington, Surrey, 4 Sept. 1793. Cadet 1808. Arrived in India 24 July 1809. Ensign 22 Oct. 1809. Lieut. 15 May 1814. Invalided 16 June 1819. Struck off in England 9 July 1825.

bapt. St. Mary's, Newington, 27 Nov. 1793. Son of Joseph Wigney and Elizabeth his wife.

Services: Barasat C.C. 1809-10. Posted Ensign to 2/15th N.I. 1810. Nepal War 1814-15; Barharwa Nov. 1814; (? Parsa Jan. 1815); Lieut. 2/15th N.I., in 4th Div. Nepal War 1816; Makwanpur; Lieut. 2/15th N.I., in 4th Bde. Centre Column. Siege and capture of Hathras 1817; Lieut. 2/15th N.I. (? Third Mahratta War; Lieut. 2/15th N.I.) Fur. 1823 till struck off.

WILCOX, George (1809-1827). Lieutenant, 64th N.I. *b.* West Ham, Essex, 17 May 1809. Cadet 1824. Ensign 13 May 1825. Lieut. 21 May 1827. *d.* Benares 8 Oct. 1827.

bapt. West Ham 24 June 1812. Son of Richard William Wilcox, linendraper, and Jane his wife. Brother of Joshua Wilcox, *q.v.*, and nephew of John Shore.

Services: Posted Ensign to 64th N.I. No record of active service.

WILCOX, Henry (*d.* 1774). Ensign, Infantry. Cadet 1771. Ensign 29 Dec. 1772. *bur.* Madras 10 Nov. 1774.[1]

Services: N.F.P.

[1] *Note:* Dodwell & Miles say "*d.* Dec. 9, 1774, on the coast of Tanjore." The date given here is taken from the burial register of St. Mary's, Madras.

WILCOX, John Theodore (1808-1841). Lieutenant. 49th N.I. *b.* London 19 May 1808. Cadet 1826. Arrived in India 11 June 1827. Ensign 13 Feb. 1827. Lieut. 7 Jan. 1836. Dismissed by G.C.M. 11 Jan. 1837. *d.* in India Jan. 1841.

bapt. St. Clement Danes 13 Mar. 1809. Eldest son of Rev. John Wilcox, rector of Stonham Parva, Suffolk, sometime minister of the Episcopal chapel, Broad Court, Drury Lane, London, and Charlotte his wife. *m.* Lucknow 23 Sept 1829, Miss Maggy Ellen Rainey. (? She died Serampore 10 Aug. 1853.)

Services: Posted Ensign to 49th N.I. 1827. Attached to Sylhet L.I. 5 Sept. 1832 till 7 Dec. 1833. (? Demonstration against Jodhpur 1834; Ensign 49th N.I.)

Refs.: *A.J.* N.S. xxiii. 133-4. *G.M.* 1841, ii. 110.

WILCOX, Joshua (1807-1859). Lieut. Colonel. 4th N.I. *b.* London 15 July 1807. Cadet 1823. Arrived in India 9 June 1824. Ensign 21 Feb. 1824. Lieut. 2 June 1826. Capt. 24 Jan. 1845. Bt. Major 11 Nov. 1851. Retired 14 Feb. 1852. Hon. Lt. Col. 28 Nov. 1854. *d.* 20 Jan. 1859.

bapt. St. Mary's, Whitechapel, 3 Sept. 1807. Son of Richard Wilcox, of Lemon St., Whitechapel, linendraper, and Jane his wife. Brother of Richard Wilcox, *q.v. m.* Ludhiana 20 Sept. 1828, Clarissa Mary Grace, sister of Peter Arnold Torckler, *q.v.*

Services: Posted Ensign to 4th N.I. and served throughout with that Regt. Fur. s.c. 25 Dec. 1836 till 14 Nov. 1839. Second Sikh War; Jullundur and Bari Doabs 1848-9; Capt. 4th N.I. (Medal).

Refs.: *A.J.* xxvii. 481.

WILCOX, Richard (1802-1848). Lieut. Colonel, 68th N.I. Astronomer to King of Oudh. *b.* London 31 May 1802. Cadet 1817. Admitted 14 Nov. 1818. Ensign 28 June 1818. Lieut. 7 Dec. 1819. Capt. 18 June 1831. Major 3 Oct. 1838. Lt. Col. 23 Dec. 1844. *d.* Cawnpore 26 Oct. 1848.

bapt. St. Mary's, Whitechapel, 14 Oct. 1802. Son of Richard Wilcox, woollendraper in the Strand, and Jane his wife. Brother of George Wilcox, *q.v. m.* Ghazipur 29 July 1833, Susan Jane, eldest dau. of George Wilson, of Ghazipur.

Services: Ensign d.d. 18th N.I. 1819; posted to 2/30th N.I. 1820. Mily. student at Coll. of Ft. Wm. Sept. 1820 till Feb. 1822. d.d. 1/19th N.I. 21 Apr. 1822. Transfd. to 59th N.I. (late 1/30th) May 1824. Asst. Revenue Surveyor 12 Feb. 1824 till July 1832. First Burma War 1824; Surveyor attached to F.F. in Assam and Chittagong. Leave s.c. 5 mos. to Java 10 Apr. 1829. Surveyed Brahmaputra R. 1831. Transfd. to Gt. Trig. Astronomical Survey 23 July 1832. Permitted to enter service of King of Oudh for purpose of suptg. an observatory in city of Lucknow 5 Feb. 1835. Astronomer to King of Oudh Sept. 1835 till death. Posted Lt. Col. to 72nd N.I. 13 Mar. 1845; transfd. to 68th N.I. 1846.

Refs.: *Delhi Gaz.*, 1 Nov. 1848. Will dated 25 Oct. 1848; proved 15 Jan. 1849.

WILCOXON, Charles (1789-1806).   Cadet (? Ensign), Infantry.
b. London 2 Mar. 1789.   Cadet 1805.   Arrived in India 19 Sept. 1806.   (? Ensign 10 Oct. 1806.)   *d.* Barasat C.C. 17 Dec. 1806.
bapt. St. Edmund King & Martyr, London, 5 Apr. 1789.   Eldest son of Arthur Wilcoxon, of Lombard St., London, and Mary his wife.
Services :   Barasat C.C.   Not yet posted to any Regt.
Refs. :   *G.M.* 1807, i. 586.

WILD, Charles Frederick (1786-1846).   Colonel, C.B., 56th N.I.   *b.* Bex, Switzerland, 15 May 1786.   Cadet 1805.   Arrived in India 7 Apr. 1807.   Ensign 9 Apr. 1807.   Lieut. 25 Jan. 1809.   Capt. 17 Jan. 1821.   Major 10 May 1828.   Lt. Col. 19 Sept. 1833.   Col. 28 Mar. 1845.   *d.* Bern, Switzerland, 1 Apr. 1846.
bapt. Bex 27 May 1786.   Son of Francis Samuel (von) Wild, of Bern, Capitaine des Mines d'Etat, and Dame Catherine Marguerite Mary de Trachswald his wife.   Naturalized 1822.[1]   Cousin-german and brother-in-law of Frederick Rodolphus Muller, *q.v.*   *m.* Bern 1823, Julia Catharina von Graffenreid.   (She died Gerzensee 11 June 1873, aged 76.)
Services :   Barasat C.C. 6 mos.   Posted Ensign to 8th N.I. 1807.   Intr. & Qmr. 2/8th N.I. 1 July 1814 till 3 Feb. 1821.   Nepal War 1816 ;   Lieut. 2/8th N.I., in 4th Bde. Centre Column.   Third Mahratta War 1817-18 ;   Nagpur ;   Lieut. 2/8th N.I.   Fur. p.a. 23 Jan. 1821 till 2 June 1824.   Transfd. to 24th N.I. (late 2/8th) May 1824.   Took charge of 26th N.I. 24 Sept. 1828 ;   do. 8th N.I. 7 Sept. 1829 ;   do. 42nd N.I. 17 Oct. 1829 till Feb. 1834.   Posted Lt. Col. to 62nd N.I. 22 Feb. 1834 ;   to 30th N.I. Jan. 1837.   Bdr. 2 cl. to comd. 1st Bde. Inf. for Jodhpur demonstration 5 Aug. till 14 Oct. 1839.   Rejoined 30th N.I. 20 Mar. 1840.   First Afghan War 1842 ;   Bdr. 2 cl. comdg. reinforcements proceeding to Peshawar 5 Jan. 1842 ;   repulse in Khyber Pass 19 Jan. (w. cheek and neck) ;   to comd. 3rd Bde. Inf. under Pollock 23 Feb. 1842 ;   forcing of Khyber 5 Apr. (s.w.—*Lond. Gaz.* 7 June 1842) ;   disaster to rear guard of his Bde. nr. Garhi Lala Beg 3 Nov. ;   Bdr. comdg. 3rd Bde. (Medal).   Transfd. to 12th N.I. 1843 ;   to 22nd N.I. 16 Aug. 1843.   Fur. s.c. 18 Apr. 1843 till death.   Posted Col. to 56th N.I. 6 Aug. 1845.   Granted 12 mos. pay for each wound.   C.B. 27 Dec. 1842.
Refs. :   *Almanach Généalogique Suisse*, ii. 542, *s.n.* Wild and von Wild, of Berne.   *Dict. Biog. Genevois & Vaudois*, ii. 641.   *Fortescue*, xii.   *A.J.* N.S. xxi. 100.   *G.M.* 1846, ii. 222.   Will dated Ferozepore 18 Oct. 1841 ;   admon. 19 Dec. 1846.

[1] *Note :* Name appears as De Wild in *E.I.R.* down to 1820, but as Wild only in *A.L.* pub. in India.

WILDING, Benjamin (1733-1780). Lieut. Colonel, Infantry. Comdg. Sepoy Corps of 2nd Bde. *b.* London 22 Aug. 1733. Cadet 1759. Ensign 10 Dec. 1759. Lieut. 10 Dec. 1761. Capt. 21 Oct. 1763. Lt. Col. 4 Sept. 1768. *d.* Calcutta 30 Aug. 1780. *bapt.* St. Mary Woolnoth, Lombard St., 16 Sept. 1733. Eldest son of Benjamin Wilding, of Tokenhouse Yard, wine merchant, and Hannah his wife. Brother of Warner Wilding, *q.v.*, and of Rebecca, 2nd wife of Philip Milner Dacres, B.C.S., presdt. of the Board of Trade in 1777. (He left a sum of £5,000 upon trust for Millicent Jane, wife of Horton Briscoe, *q.v.*) Ed. Rugby; admitted 23 Jan. 1743/4; Merchant Taylors' Feb. 1745/6–Mar. 1747.

Services: Storm of Masulipatam 8 Apr. 1759 (? as Cadet or Vol. with Bengal Eur. Bn.); apptd. one of the four prize agents, and tried by C.M. for accepting bribes. Battle of Buxar 1764; Capt. comdg. 13th Bn. Sepoys. Resigned his Commission during the "Batta mutiny" in May 1766 and went home; readmitted and returned to India. Writes on 8 Feb. 1769 requesting leave to resign and sail for England in the *Salisbury*; returned to India in the *Lord Holland*, sailing 14 May 1771. Apptd. to comd. at Chunar 28 May 1772; comdg. at Monghyr in Dec. 1775; comdg. 2/1st Bengal Eur. Regt. at Dinapore in Sept. 1777; comdg. at Fatehgarh in 1778; comdg. Sepoy Corps of 2nd Bde. at death.

Refs.: Rugby School Register. Robinson. Broome, p. 490. *Macpherson*, p. 94. Will dated 3 Mar. 1780; proved 19 Dec. 1780. M.I. in S. Park St. cemetery, Calcutta.

WILDING, Warner (1746-1764). Ensign, 13th Bn. Sepoys. *b.* in Ireland 1746. Cadet 1764. Ensign 9 Dec. 1764. *d.* in camp 15 Dec. 1764, of wounds received in action 4 Dec.

4th son of Benjamin Wilding and Hannah his wife. Brother of Benjamin Wilding, *q.v.*

Services: Sailed for India in the *Fort William* 17 May 1764, aged 18. Assault of Chunar fort (s.w.); Cadet in the Cadet Coy. Posted to his brother's Bn. 5 Dec. 1764, and promoted Ensign by Major Hector Munro 9 Dec., for his gallant conduct at Chunar.

Refs.: Broome, p. 490.

WILFORD, Francis (1760/61-1822). Bt. Lieut. Colonel, Invalid Est. Engineers. *b.* 1760/61. Country Cadet 1781. Admitted 12 Dec. 1781. Ensign 21 Dec. 1781. Lieut. 4 Nov. 1782. Capt. Lt. 15 Dec. 1798. Capt. 1 Jan. 1806. Bt. Major 25 Apr. 1808. Invalided 1 July 1812. Bt. Lt. Col. 4 June 1814. *d.* Benares 3 Sept. 1822, aged 61.[1]

Said to have been of either Swiss or Hanoverian extraction. His daus. by Khanum Sahib *m.* William Baker (1775-1825), Henry Pelham Davies, William Pickersgill, and George Warden, *qq.v.*

Services : Apptd. Cadet 1781 on the recommendation of Henry Watson, *q.v.*, by whom he had perhaps been employed at the Kidderpore docks. On survey work from 1782 ; was Asst. to Surveyor Gen. in Feb. 1786 and in 1790. Was at Benares in 1788, where he resided for the rest of his life. Permitted in June 1794 to remain at Benares and prosecute his researches into Hindu literature and geography. In 1800, became Sec. to the Committee which took over the management of Jonathan Duncan's (*D.N.B.*) new Sanskrit Coll. at Benares. "Scholar, and learned and indefatigable cultivator of the Asiatic History and Literature of the Hindus." (*G.M.*)

Refs. : *G.M.* 1823, i. 568. Will dated 5 Apr. 1815 ; codicils dated 1 Aug. 1821, 27 June 1822 ; proved 12 Sept. 1822. M.I. in old civil cemetery, Benares.

[1] *Note :* His age at death is variously given as 61 and 71.

WILKIE, David (1809-1894). Colonel. 4th N.I. *b.* Dacca 10 Apr. 1809. Cadet 1825. Arrived in India 18 Mar. 1826. Ensign 28 Sept. 1825. Lieut. 22 Aug. 1827. Capt. 31 Mar. 1845. Major 15 Nov. 1853. Lt. Col. 26 Apr. 1858. Retired 31 Dec. 1861. Hon. Col. 31 Dec. 1861. *d.* Ashbourne, co. Derby, 18 Dec. 1894.

Of Ashbourne. *bapt.* Dacca 24 June 1809. Son of John Wilkie, *q.v.*, and Margaret his wife. *m.* 1st, Cawnpore 25 Sept. 1841, Emily, youngest dau. of William Bishop, of Grayswood, Haslemere. (*See also* Thomas Bradridge Studdy.) (She died Indore 5 May 1843.) *m.* 2nd, Indore 2 Sept. 1847, Fanny Ann, dau. of Frederick Walpole Anson, *q.v.* (She died Nasik 3 Feb. 1851, aged 20.) *m.* 3rd, Chelsea 28 Oct. 1854, Amelia Wilde, dau. of Capt. Ford, 79th Highlrs., of the Royal Hospital, Chelsea. Addiscombe Cadet 17 Mar. 1824 till June 1825.

Services : Posted Ensign to 4th N.I. 1826 ; actg. Intr. & Qmr. do. 4 Aug. 1835 ; do. 58th N.I. 2 Jan. 1837. Actg. Asst. to Resdt. at Lucknow 13 Dec. 1838 ; offg. 2nd Asst. to Resdt. at Indore 15 Apr. 1842 ; offg. Asst. in Nimar 9 Dec. 1842. Apptd. to Pol. Dept. 25 Apr. 1843 ; 2nd in comd. Malwa Bhil Corps 2 June 1843 till 1846 ; Bhil Agent at Indore 18 July 1845 till 1851. Fur. 3 Apr. 1851 till 13 May 1855. Was comdg. Rt. Wing of 4th N.I. at Nurpur on outbreak of Mutiny. This Wing remained loyal. Posted Lt. Col. to 4th N.I. 24 July 1858. No record of active service.

Refs.: Some old Families, by H. B. McCall. *The Times*, 21 Dec. 1894.

WILKIE, James (1786-1845). Major. 8th N.I. *b.* Montrose 20 June 1786. Cadet 1804. Arrived in India 10 July 1805. Ensign 22 Aug. 1805. Lieut. 23 Aug. 1805. Capt. 1 July 1821. Major 1 Nov. 1830. Retired 20 July 1832. *d.* 13 May 1845. Of Easter Bush. Son of Robert Wilkie and Jean Johnston his wife. *m.* Kilpunt, co. Linlithgow, 12 Mar. 1839, Catherine, youngest dau. of William Keir, of Milnholme, co. Dumfries.

Services: Posted Lieut. to 9th N.I. 1806. Operations against Dhundia Khan 1807; Komona (s.w. 18 Nov.); Lieut. 1/9th N.I., d.d. Pioneers. Adjt. Ramgarh Bn. 1810-12. Served with Pioneers 1812-25. Nepal War 1814-15; Lieut. 1/9th N.I., 7th Coy. Pioneers, in 4th Div. Capt. 2/9th N.I. Transfd. to 8th N.I. (late 1/9th) May 1824. First Burma War; Arakan 1825 (*Lond. Gaz.* 1 Oct. 1825); Capt. Pioneers. Comdd. Pioneers 28 June till 26 Sept. 1825. Offg. Army Clothing Agent, 1st Div., Fatehgarh, 3 Sept. 1825; permanent do. 30 Dec. 1825 till Jan. 1832. Fur. s.c. 28 Jan. 1832 till retirement. Retired on pension of 16/- *p.d.*

Refs.: A.A.R. x. 21. *A.J.* N.S. xxix. 79.

WILKIE, John (1782-1824). Captain, 49th N.I. *b.* Cults, co. Fife, 13 Aug. 1782. Cadet 1800. Arrived in India 22 Aug. 1801. Ensign 21 Oct. 1801. Lieut. 13 July 1803. Capt. 21 May 1816. *d.* Dinapore 10 Aug. 1824.

Eldest son of Rev. David Wilkie, minister of Cults 1774-1812, and Isabella his 3rd wife, dau. of James Lister, farmer, Pitlessie Mill. Brother of Sir David Wilkie, R.A. (*D.N.B.*), the painter. *m.* Calcutta 6 Aug. 1806, Margaret, eldest dau. of Rev. Andrew Walker, minister of Collessie 1772-1820. (She died Oct. 1828, aged 46.) Father of David Wilkie, *q.v.*, and of the wives of Cosby Burrowes, *q.v.*, and William Riddell, *q.v.*

Services: Ensign d.d. 7th N.I. in 1802. Posted Ensign to 3rd N.I.; transfd. to newly-raised 1/25th N.I. 1804; Adjt. do. 18 Jan. 1805 till 4 May 1815. Second Mahratta War 1805; Adalatnagar. Operations against the Rana of Gohad 1806; capture of Gohad. Capt. Lt. 1/25th N.I. 16 Dec. 1814. Siege and capture of Hathras 1817; Capt. 1/25th N.I. Third Mahratta War 1817-18; Capt. 1/25th N.I. Transfd. to 49th N.I. (late 1/25th) May 1824. His death occurred " in the course of a severe and fatiguing march with his Regt." from Agra to take part in the First Burma War in Arakan.

Refs.: Some old Families, by H. B. McCall, p. 249. Scott's *Fasti*, v. 135, 139. Will dated 12 May 1812; proved 23 Oct. 1824.

WILKINS, Robert Bateman (1788-1862). Major. 42nd N.I. *b*. Marston Bigott, Somerset, 25 Feb. 1788. Cadet 1804. Arrived in India 16 May 1806. Ensign 27 Apr. 1806. Lieut. 19 Nov. 1807. Capt. 1 Jan. 1819. Invalided 17 Oct. 1824. Retired 3 Nov. 1831. Hon. Major 28 Nov. 1854. *d*. Thames Ditton, Surrey, 18 Mar. 1862.

Son of Robert Wilkins and Frances his wife. Nephew of Sir Charles Wilkins, the orientalist (*D.N.B.*).

Services: Barasat C.C. Posted Lieut. to 1/21st N.I. 1807. Capt. 1/21st N.I. Fur. 10 Feb. 1820 till 1822. Transfd. to 41st N.I. (late 1/21st) May 1824. Comdd. Eur. Invalids at Chunar 1826-30. Fur. p.a. 24 Dec. 1830 till retirement. No record of active service.

Refs.: The Times, 22 Mar. 1862.

WILKINSON, Benjamin (1740/41-1784). Lieutenant, 16th N.I. *b*. in Ireland 1740/41. Cadet 1776. Ensign 4 Apr. 1777. Lieut. 11 Aug. 1778. *d*. Cawnpore 2 Sept. 1784.

m. Elizabeth ——, of Tremiton (?), Cornwall. (She died 1820.)
Services: Sailed for India in the *Duke of Cumberland* 29 Mar. 1776, aged 35. With Ramgarh L.I. Bn. 1781-2.

Refs.: Will dated Kaisabad 2 Jan. 1784; proved 7 Dec. 1786.

WILKINSON, Christopher Dixon (1794-1879). General, C.B. 6th Bengal Eur. Inf. *b*. 24 Apr. 1794. Cadet 1810. Admitted 27 Aug. 1811. Ensign (16 Aug. 1811) 8 June 1813. Lieut. 1 Mar. 1816. Capt. 14 June 1825. Major 26 June 1833. Lt. Col. 26 Mar. 1840. Col. 28 Sept. 1850. Maj. Gen. 28 Nov. 1854. Lt. Gen. 12 Mar. 1865. Gen. 25 June 1870. *d*. 112 Belgrave Rd., London, 4 Apr. 1879.

bapt. Campton-cum-Shefford, Beds., 27 June 1794. Son of Rev. Thomas Wilkinson, rector of Armthorpe, nr. Doncaster, and Jane his wife. *m.* Berhampore 19 Dec. 1825, Miss Catharine Beaty, dau. of Henry Beaty. (She died 30 July 1865, aged 56.) His dau. *m.* Peregrine Powell Turner, *q.v.*

Services: Cadet d.d. 23rd N.I. 1811; posted to 2/14th N.I. 1813. Intr. & Qmr. 1/14th N.I. 17 Dec. 1823 till 29 July 1825. Transfd. to 28th N.I. (late 1/14th) May 1824. Posted Lt. Col. to 28th N.I. 24 Aug. 1840. Leave s.c. 2 yrs. to Cape 8 Feb. 1841. Transfd. to 54th N.I. 30 Dec. 1840; to 73rd N.I. 16 May 1843; to 4th N.I. 28 Nov. 1844; to 69th N.I. May 1845; to 63rd N.I. 16 Oct. 1845.

THE BENGAL ARMY, 1758-1834 471

First Sikh War; Ferozshahr; Lt. Col. 63rd N.I.; Sobraon; Bdr. comdg. 6th Inf. Bde. (Medal with clasp). Transfd. to 28th N.I., 38th, 23rd, 7th N.I. 13 Aug. 1850; Col. 7th N.I. Dec. 1850 till 1858. Bdr. 2 cl. comdg. Delhi 4 Nov. 1851; do. Cawnpore Jan. 1854; do. Sind Sagar Feb.-Sept. 1854. Fur. s.c. Jan.-Nov. 1856. Transfd. to newly-raised 6th Eur. Inf. 1858. Fur. 3 yrs. 8 Mar. 1860. C.B. 27 June 1846.

Refs.: Boase. *The Times*, 8 Apr. 1879; 9 Apr., p. 11.

WILKINSON, George (1788-1811). Lieutenant, 1st N.I. *b.* Halesworth, Suffolk, 19 Aug. 1788. Cadet 1804. Arrived in India 4 Aug. 1806. Ensign 29 Apr. 1806. Lieut. 1 May 1808. *d.* Calcutta 20 Aug. 1811.

bapt. 4 Sept. 1788. Son of John Wilkinson, gent., and Jane his wife, née Brettingham.

Services: Barasat C.C. Posted Lieut. to 1st N.I. 1807 and served throughout with that Regt.

WILKINSON, Henry (1809-?). Lieutenant. 30th N.I. *bapt.* Wrexham 26 Feb. 1809. Cadet 1824. Arrived in India 5 Sept. 1825. Ensign 9 Apr. 1825. Lieut. 1 Nov. 1827. Struck off in India 21 June 1833.

Son of Joseph Wilkinson, surgeon, and Hannah his wife.

Services: Posted Ensign to 30th N.I. Suspended 12 Mar. 1832 pending decision of C.D. No record of active service. He was granted a pension of £30 *p.a.* by the Indian Govt. 10 Sept. 1834, but C.D. refused to sanction this.

Refs.: *A.J.* N.S. ii. 158; N.S. v. 34, 216.

WILKINSON, Henry William (1779-1829). Lieut. Colonel, 22nd N.I. *b.* London 9 Aug. 1779. Cadet 1799. Arrived in India 1 Dec. 1800. Ensign 12 Sept. 1800. Lieut. 22 Sept. 1801. Capt. 5 Dec. 1812. Major 15 Feb. 1824. Lt. Col. 2 Nov. 1825. *d.* Kaitha, U.P., 26 Aug. 1829.

bapt. Trinity Minories, Tower of London, 3 Sept. 1779. Son of William Wilkinson and Sarah his wife. *m.* 1st, Burdwan district 1 Aug. 1805, Charlotte Elizabeth, eldest dau. of James Gray, Capt. R.N. and sometime Muster Master to King's Troops in Bengal, sister of James Clarke Charnock Gray, *q.v.*, and widow of Sir Arthur Hesilrige, 9th Bart., B.C.S. ("Her mother was sister to Sir Home Popham's lady.") (She died at sea 8 Jan. 1817, aged 34.) Father of Henry William James Wilkinson, *q.v. m.* 2nd, St. John's, Calcutta, 17 Jan. 1822, Susan Eliza, natural dau. of Charles Holloway, Ft. Marlbro' C.S., and half-sister of Charles Holloway

(Appendix A). (*See also* William Henry Hewitt.) (? Ed. Charterhouse.[1])

Services: Posted Ensign to 1/9th N.I. 17 Apr. 1801. Adjt. Moradabad Provl. Bn. 1804-6. Second Mahratta War 1805; operations against Amir Khan; Lieut. Moradabad Provl. Bn. Adjt. Chittagong Provl. Bn. 1807; do. Dacca 1808-13; comdg. Murshidabad Provl. Bn. 1815. Capt. 2/9th N.I. Leave s.c. to sea 1815-16. Fort Adjt. at Ft. Wm. (and sometime, in addition, Adjt. Town Gds.) 1818-24. Leave to China in 1822. Transfd. to 8th N.I. (late 1/9th) May 1824; posted Lt. Col. to 44th N.I. 1825; to 22nd N.I. 5 Mar. 1828.

Refs.: Hickey, iii. 188. *G.M.* 1830, i. 478.

[1] *Note:* One of this name admitted June 1792.

WILKINSON, Henry William James (1806-1847). Captain, Invalid Est. 6th N.I. *b.* Cawnpore 29 May 1806. Cadet 1821. Arrived in India 14 Jan. 1823. Ensign 11 Feb. 1823. Lieut. 1 May 1824. Capt. 20 Dec. 1843. Invalided 6 Mar. 1846. *d.* Bareilly 11 Dec. 1847.

Son of Henry William Wilkinson, *q.v.*, and Charlotte Elizabeth his 1st wife. *m.* Cuttack 4 Apr. 1838, Jane Wetherell. (She died Dehra Dun 19 June 1847, aged 36.)

Services: Posted Lieut. to 3rd N.I. 1823; transfd. to 19th N.I. (late 2/3rd) May 1824; to 6th N.I. (late 1/3rd) 13 May 1825. Siege and capture of Bhurtpore; Lieut. 6th N.I. Actg. Intr. & Qmr. 53rd N.I. 17 May 1831 till 18 Feb. 1832; Intr. & Qmr. 6th N.I. 9 Feb. 1833 till Dec. 1843. First Afghan War 1842; Bt. Capt. 6th N.I., on L. of C. (Medal).

WILKINSON, James (1758/59-1792). Captain, Artillery. (145) *b.* 1758/59. Cadet 1776. Fireworker 14 May 1777. Lieut. 25 Sept. 1778. Capt. Lt. 3 July 1784. Capt. 28 May 1786. *d.* Calcutta 16 June 1792, aged 33.

m. Fatehgarh 3 June 1786, Mary Tomkyns (*probably* sister of John Tomkyns, *q.v.*). (She died 22 July 1850.)

Services: Apptd. Cadet 25 Oct. 1775; sailed for India in the *Greenwich* 7 Jan. 1776. Second Mysore War 1781-5; Lieut. 4th Coy. 2nd Bn. Capt. 1st Bn. in July 1787.

Refs.: Will dated 2 July 1790; proved 20 June 1792. M.I. in S. Park St. cemetery, Calcutta.

WILKINSON, Sir Thomas (1795-1867). Lieut. Colonel, K.C.S.I. 6th L.C. *bapt.* Crosby-Ravensworth, Westmorland, 15 Mar. 1795. Cadet 1810. Admitted 15 Dec. 1810. Cornet

THE BENGAL ARMY, 1758-1834

18 Apr. 1816. Lieut. 1 Sept. 1818. Capt. 13 May 1825. Bt. Major 28 June 1838. Retired 1 Mar. 1844. Hon. Lt. Col. 28 Nov. 1854. *d*. 23 Hanover Sq., London, 7 Apr. 1867, aged 72.

Eldest son of James Wilkinson, of Flass, and Nanny his wife, late Eggleston.

Services: Cadet d.d. 9th N.I. 1811-13; posted to 6th N.C. 1816. Third Mahratta War 1817-18; Nagpur; Chanda; comdd. column of Auxy. Horse in action 18 Sept. 1818 (*Lond. Gaz.* 1 Mar. 1819); Lieut. 6th N.C. (India medal). Served with Nagpur Auxy. Horse 1819 till June 1830, when it was broken up and he received a donation of 6 mos. pay. Leave s.c. to Cape 4 Feb. 1824 till 10 Jan. 1826. Offg. P.A., S.W. frontier, and tempy. comdg. Ramgarh Local Bn. 3 Apr. 1830; 2nd in comd. do. 8 Feb. 1832; P.A., S.W. frontier, and comd. do. 17 Sept. 1832 till Mar. 1836. Comr. of Chota Nagpur; A.G.G., S.W. frontier, Mar. 1836; Resdt. at Nagpur 15 May 1839 till 30 Sept. 1843. K.C.S.I. 24 May 1866.

Refs.: Boase. *The Hearseys*, p. 327. *N. & Q.* 10S. iv. 46. *G.M.* 1867, i. 690. *The Times*, 9 Apr. 1867.

WILLETT, Thomas (1759/60-1807). Lieut. Colonel, 24th N.I. *b*. London 1759/60. Cadet 1777. Admitted 18 Dec. 1777. Ensign 24 Feb. 1778. Lieut. 30 Sept. 1778. Capt. 15 Feb. 1796. Major 21 Apr. 1800. Lt. Col. 13 July 1803. *d*. Cawnpore 10 July 1807.

Of Brookend, Gloucs. Brother of Mary Osborn. *m*. (?)

Services: Sailed for India in the *Duke of Kingston* 24 Mar. 1777, aged 17. Leave s.c. to sea 13 Nov. 1784. Adjt. 11th Bn. Sepoys 1786-94; Capt. 15th N.I. in 1798. Was comdg. the Bengal detachment in Hyderabad in Feb. 1800. Major 1/15th N.I. Fur. 8 Mar. 1803 till 22 July 1806. Posted Lt. Col. to 8th N.I. 1803; to 26th N.I. 1805; to 2/24th N.I. 1807.

Refs.: Will dated 17 Apr. 1805; proved 27 Jan. 1808.

WILLIAMS, Ballantyne (1803-1823). 2nd Lieutenant, Artillery. (501) *b*. Walthamstow, Essex, 7 Apr. 1803. Cadet 1818. 2nd Lieut. 28 Apr. 1819. *d*. Kamptee, C.P., 3 Jan. 1823.

bapt. St. Mary's, Walthamstow, 23 Apr. 1811. Son of James Williams, of Walthamstow, merchant, and Harriet his wife. Addiscombe Cadet 1817-19.

Services: 2nd Lieut. 6th Coy. 1st Bn. Foot Art. No record of active service.

WILLIAMS, David. Captain. Infantry. Cadet 1769. Ensign 28 June 1770. Lieut. 22 Mar. 1773. Capt. 21 Jan. 1781. Resigned 5 Feb. 1785.

Services : Posted to New Bde. stationed in dominions of Nawab-Wazir of Oudh 7 Aug. 1777. (? First Mahratta War.) Capt. 1st Bengal Eur. Regt. in 1782. Leave s.c. to sea Aug. 1783.

WILLIAMS, David (1800-1852). Lieut. Colonel, 5th N.I. *b.* 23 Nov. 1800. Cadet 1819. Arrived in India 22 Aug. 1820. Ensign 3 Apr. 1820. Lieut. 11 July 1823. Capt. 29 Oct. 1830. Major 1 May 1844. Lt. Col. 28 July 1850. *d.* Mian Mir, Punjab, 10 July 1852.

bapt. Pen-Bre, otherwise Pembrey, co. Carmarthen, 22 June 1801. Son of R. Williams, of Moreb, and Elizabeth his wife. Brother of R. B. Williams, of Llandilo.

Services : d.d. Bengal Eur. Regt. 25 Aug. 1820. Posted Ensign to 2/2nd N.I. Jan. 1821; transfd. to 2/23rd N.I. 25 Sept. 1823; Adjt. do. 21 Oct. 1823 till May 1824. First Burma War; Assam 1824; Lieut. 2/23rd N.I. (India medal). Transfd. to 45th N.I. (late 1/23rd) May 1824, but remained with 46th N.I. (late 2/23rd) in Assam till Oct. 1824. Adjt. 45th N.I. 17 June 1824 till Mar. 1826. Siege and capture of Bhurtpore; actg. D.A.C.G. (clasp to India medal). Supy. S.A.C.G. Mar. 1826; permanent do. May 1826. Leave s.c. to Cape Jan. 1829 till May 1830. Senior Asst. to Supt. of Arakan 4 Sept. 1834 till Mar. 1849. To rejoin 45th N.I. for service 4 Oct. 1848. Second Sikh War; passage of Chenab; Chilianwala; Gujerat; Major comdg. 45th N.I. (Medal with 2 clasps). Posted Lt. Col. to 65th N.I. Aug. 1850; to 5th N.I. 19 July 1851.

Refs. : De Rhé-Philipe. Boase. *I.M.* 1 Sept. 1852, p. 478. M.I. in R.A. cemetery, Lahore.

WILLIAMS, George Thomas (1793-1814). Lieutenant, 3rd N.I. *b.* Wells, Somerset, 17 July 1793. Cadet 1808. Arrived in India 27 Oct. 1809. Ensign 15 May 1810. Lieut. Apr. 1814. *d.* nr. Ramgarh 27 Nov. 1814 : kld. in action.

bapt. St. Andrew's cathedral, Wells, 13 Aug. 1793. Son of John Williams,* *q.v.*, and Mary his wife. Brother of John Samuel Williams, *q.v.*

Services : Barasat C.C. Posted to 3rd N.I. 1810. Nepal War 1814; operations against Amar Singh (kld.); Lieut. 2/3rd N.I.; in 1st Div.

WILLIAMS, George Walter (1810-1890). Colonel, C.B. 29th N.I. Comdt. Mily. Police, N.W.P. *b.* Kumarkhali, Bengal, 3 May 1810. Cadet 1825. Arrived in India 25 Sept. 1826. Ensign 15 May 1826. Lieut. 21 Aug. 1832. Capt. 24 Jan.

1845. Major 15 June 1857. Lt. Col. (official rank) 29 Jan. 1859. Retired 31 Dec. 1861. Hon. Col. 31 Dec. 1861. *d.* at his residence, Wye Vale, Monmouth, 16 Apr. 1890.

Son of Henry Williams, B.C.S., Commercial Resdt. at Kumarkhali, and Nancy his wife, dau. of George Burrington, *q.v.* Brother of Henry Cinamon Williams, *q.v.*, and of the wives of Frederick Knyvett and Henry John McGeorge, *qq.v.* *m.* Chinsura, Bengal, 23 July 1846, Elizabeth Ann, dau. of Miarah Hill.

Services: Ensign d.d. 40th N.I. 7 Oct. 1826; posted to do. 9 Nov. 1826; actg. Intr. & Qmr. do. 17 Mar. 1827; do. 67th N.I. 29 July 1831. Exchanged to 29th N.I. 21 Aug. 1832. Leave s.c. 2 yrs. to Tasmania 3 Sept. 1834; fur. s.c. 15 July 1836 till 29 Jan. 1840. Asst. to Resdt. in Nepal and comd. escort 27 Jan. 1841 till 21 Feb. 1842. Offg. Comdt. Calcutta Native Mil. 15 Apr. 1842; Adjt. 29th N.I. 21 Nov. 1843 till Jan. 1845. Actg. Asst. in *Thagi* Dept. 22 Mar. 1847. Fur. s.c. 2 Feb. 1851 till Nov. 1853. Joint Cantt. Mgte. at Agra 31 Jan. 1854 till June 1857. Extra Asst. in *Thagi* Dept. 19 Dec. 1855 till 1857. Comdt. Agra Police Corps 11 June 1857; Supt. Police Bn., N.W.P., 29 Oct. 1857; Comdr. of Mily. Police, and Mily. Sec. to Lt. Govr., N.W.P., 8 Feb. 1859. C.B. (Civil) 18 May 1860.

WILLIAMS, Henry (*d.* 1767). Captain, Infantry. Lieut. 19 Nov. 1764. Capt. 28 May 1767. *d.* 9 Sept. 1767.

Services: Probably transfd. from H.M.S.; *possibly* the following: (? Commissioned as 1st Lieut. in (new) 85th Ft. (raised in Wales) 23 Aug. 1759; renewed by George III in 1760; left the Regt. 8 Sept. 1761.)

WILLIAMS, Henry Cinamon (1802-?). Lieutenant. 47th N.I. *b.* Dedham, Essex, 2 Dec. 1802. Cadet 1818. Ensign (?) Lieut. 22 Oct. 1820. Removed from the effective list in England 6 July 1828.

bapt. Dedham 16 June 1807. Son of Henry Williams, B.C.S. Brother of Stephen Williams, *q.v.*, and nephew of Rev. Gervas Holmes, rector of Copford, Essex.

Services: Ensign d.d. 18th N.I. 1819; posted to 2/24th N.I. 1820; transfd. to 47th N.I. (late 1/24th) May 1824; to newly-raised 69th N.I. (became 47th N.I.) Nov. 1824. Fur. 1825 till struck off. No record of active service.

WILLIAMS, John (1741/42-1809). Captain. 2nd Bn. Sepoys. *b.* 1741/42. Cadet 1771. Admitted Apr. 1772. Ensign 14 Apr. 1772. Lieut. 16 Aug. 1776. Capt. 6 Mar. 1781. Invalided

15 Feb. 1792. Retired 26 Jan. 1809. *d.* at sea nr. Westward Is. 20 June 1809, on board the *Northumberland*, aged 67.

Brother of George Williams, of 64 Grafton St., Dublin. (*Probably* brother of Trevor Williams, of Drogheda, and of Rose Anne, wife of William Beere, of Dublin.) *m.* 1st, Mary, widow of —— D'Auvergne and mother of Robert D'Auvergne, *q.v.* (She died Calcutta 23 July 1788, aged 43.) His dau. *m.* Thomas Jaffray, *q.v. m.* 2nd, 17 Nov. 1789, Miss Jane Dale. (She died Monghyr 29 July 1798, aged 33.) Father of the wife of George Nugent, *q.v.*, and of Edward Ellerker Williams (*D.N.B.*), friend of the poet Shelley. *m.* 3rd, Calcutta 5 Jan. 1801, Mary, widow of William Sibbald, *q.v.* (She died Monghyr 17 Feb. 1803.) *m.* 4th, Mary Anne ——. (She survived him.)

Services : Served (? as a private) in the detachment of Marines comdd. by Capt. Maurice Wemyss at the battle of Buxar, 1764.[1] Adjt. 3rd Bengal Eur. Regt. ; apptd. Adjt. of Eur. Mil. at Calcutta 21 Nov. 1778 ; to comd. Mil. sepoys at Purnea 28 Nov. 1780, and was still comdg. in Aug. 1781 ; Capt. 1st Bengal Eur. Bn. in July 1787. Apptd. to comd. 2nd Bn. Sepoys 15 Feb. 1792, and was transfd. to the Invalid Est. the same day. Comdg. Invalid Bn. at Monghyr. Fur. 21 Dec. 1803 till 23 Sept. 1806. Author of " An Historical Account of the Rise and Progress of the Bengal Native Infantry, from its first formation in 1757, to 1796, . . .," London, John Murray, 1817.

Refs. : Will dated Monghyr 11 Sept. 1808 ; proved 9 Apr. 1810. M.I. at Monghyr.

[1] *Note :* See footnote on p. 33 of his *History.*

WILLIAMS, John (1756/57-1816). Major General, Invalid Est. 5th N.I. *b.* London 1756/57. Cadet 1778. Admitted 2 Oct. 1778. Ensign 2 Oct. 1778. Lieut. 26 Oct. 1778. Capt. 7 Jan. 1796. Major 12 Nov. 1799. Lt. Col. 1 Jan. 1803. Bt. Col. 1 Jan. 1812. Invalided 1 June 1813. Maj. Gen. 4 June 1814. *d. unm.* Chunar 31 July 1816.

Services : Apptd. Cadet 17 Dec. 1777 ; sailed for India in the *Nassau* 1 Mar. 1778, aged 21. Lieut. 16th Bn. Sepoys in July 1787 ; Capt. 7th N.I. in 1798. Posted Lt. Col. to 5th N.I. Comdd. 2nd Bn. Native Invalids at Chunar 1813 till death.

Refs. : Will dated 31 July 1816 ; admon. 16 Oct. 1816. M.I. new cemetery, Chunar (where age at death is given as 62).

*WILLIAMS, John (1759/60-?). Lieutenant. Infantry. *b.* Somerset 1759/60. Cadet 1780. Ensign 1780. Lieut. 14 Aug. 1781. Struck off after 1795.

THE BENGAL ARMY, 1758-1834

m. Mary. Father of George Thomas Williams, *q.v.*, and John Samuel Williams, *q.v.*

Services: Apptd. Cadet 26 Apr. 1780; sailed for India in the *Lord Holland* 3 June 1780, aged 20. Fur. on h.p. 2 Oct. 1786 till struck off. (? Bt. Capt. 7 Jan. 1796.)

WILLIAMS, John. Fireworker. Artillery. (242) Cadet 1783. Fireworker 10 Mar. 1785. Struck off 1788.

Services: Apptd. Cadet for the Art. (Order of the Court dated 14 Apr. 1784). Never arrived in India.

WILLIAMS, John Samuel (1792-1861). Lieutenant, Pensioner on Lord Clive's fund. 3rd L.C. *b.* Clifton 6 Feb. 1792. Cadet 1807. Arrived in India 16 Nov. 1808. Ensign (Inf.) 7 Nov. 1808. Struck off 21 Mar. 1810. Cadet 1810. Cornet 10 June 1816. Lieut. 1 Sept. 1818. Pensioned 3 Oct. 1821. *d.* Bath 27 Jan. 1861.

Sometime of Herringstone House, Tunbridge Wells. *bapt.* St. Andrew's cathedral, Wells, 13 Aug. 1793. Son of John Williams,* *q.v.*, and Mary his wife. Brother of George Thomas Williams, *q.v. m.* Walcot, Bath, 18 Jan. 1823, Harriet, 2nd dau. of Sir Thomas Swinnerton Dyer, 8th Bart., of Tottenham, Middlesex, Capt. R.N. (She died 11 Aug. 1889, aged 85.)

Services: Barasat C.C. Dismissed by C.D. 21 Mar. 1810, for having obtained his appt. by improper means; reapptd. 23 May 1810, but had sailed for England before his new nomination to Cav. had arrived. Posted Cornet to 3rd N.C. 1816. Fur. 7 July 1816 till 1819; fur. from Madras 3 Feb. 1821 till pensioned. No record of active service.

Refs.: G.M. 1823, i. 272; 1861, i. 351. M.I. Clifton churchyard.

WILLIAMS, Richard (1802-1824). Lieutenant, Artillery. (494) *b.* 2 July 1802. Cadet 1818. Arrived in India Sept. 1819. 2nd Lieut. 21 Apr. 1819. Lieut. 12 Dec. 1821. *d.* Ludhiana 29 Oct. 1824.

bapt. St. Sepulchre, Northampton, 5 Aug. 1802. Son of Rev. Richard Williams, of Haughton, nr. Northampton, and Charlotte his wife. Addiscombe Cadet 1818-19.

Services: Served throughout with Foot Art. Leave s.c. Feb. 1824 till death. No record of active service.

Refs.: De Rhé-Philipe. M.I. at Ludhiana.

WILLIAMS, Robert (*d.* 1768). Cadet, Infantry. Cadet 1768. *d.* Berhampore 1768.

Services : Qmr. H.M. 17th Ft. 25 Feb. 1757; Ensign 20 Mar. 1758; resigned as Qmr. 2 Apr. 1759; Lieut. 15 May 1760. Served at Louisburg 1758. Left the Regt. 29 Aug. 1767. Apptd. Cadet in England 19 Feb. 1768; sailed for India in the *Salisbury* 21 Mar. 1768.

WILLIAMS, Samuel (1778-1804). Lieutenant, 2nd N.I. *b.* Bow, Middlesex, 19 Feb. 1778. Cadet 1798. Admitted 26 Nov. 1799. Ensign 30 Nov. 1799. Lieut. 29 May 1800. *d.* Calcutta 27 Aug. 1804, in the insane hospital.

Son of John Williams, of Bow, tin-plate worker.

Services : Posted Lieut. to 2/2nd N.I. 15 Apr. 1801. (? Operations in Jumna Doab 1803; Sasni; Bijaigarh; Kachaura; Lieut. 2/2nd N.I.)

WILLIAMS, Stephen (1805-1857). Bt. Colonel, 56th N.I. *b.* Copford, Essex, 4 Mar. 1805. Cadet 1820. Arrived in India 17 Sept. 1821. Ensign 5 May 1821. Lieut. 15 Feb. 1824. Capt. 18 Feb. 1841. Major 21 June 1850. Lt. Col. 20 Feb. 1856. Bt. Col. 28 Nov. 1854. *d.* Cawnpore 27 June 1857, of apoplexy.[1]

bapt. Copford 14 Sept. 1812. Son of Henry Williams, B.C.S. Brother of George Walter Williams, *q.v. m.* Cawnpore 4 July 1829, Mary Amanda, 2nd dau. of William Blanchard, indigo planter in the Dacca district. (*See also* Joseph Ferris.) (She was massacred by mutineers at Cawnpore 15 July 1857.) Ed. Bury St. Edmunds Grammar School.

Services : Posted Ensign to 7th N.I.; transfd. to 1/21st N.I. 1821; d.d. 2/13th N.I.; transfd. to do. 1 Apr. 1822; to 9th N.I. 1823; to 8th N.I. (late 1/9th) May 1824. First Burma War; Chittagong 1824; Ensign 2/13th N.I. (India medal). Actg. Intr. & Qmr. 8th N.I. 16 July 1829. d.d. 20th N.I. Oct. 1832 till Oct. 1833. Second Sikh War; siege of Multan and operations in the vicinity; Major 8th N.I.; Gujerat; comdg. 8th N.I. (Medal with 2 clasps). Posted Lt. Col. to 56th N.I. 1856, and was comdg. this Regt. at Cawnpore when it mutinied 6 June 1857.

Refs. : Boase. *A.J.* N.S. vii. 155-6. *I.M.* 16 Oct. 1857, p. 677. M.I. All Sts. Memorial Church, Cawnpore.

[1] *Note :* *d.* 8 June, according to some accounts.

WILLIAMS, Thomas (1787-1852). Bt. Major. 70th N.I. *b.* Yspytty Ystradmeurig, co. Cardigan, 15 June 1787. Cadet 1807. Arrived in India 20 Nov. 1807. Ensign 22 Nov. 1808. Lieut. 23 Oct. 1812. Capt. 8 Sept. 1825. Bt. Major 28 June 1838. Retired 30 Apr. 1839. *d.* Aberystwith 9 Jan. 1852.

bapt. 16 June 1787. Son of Rev. John Williams, for 40 yrs. Master of Ystrad Meurig school (*D.N.B.*), and Jane his wife, dau. of Lewis Rogers, of Gelli, high sheriff co. Cardigan 1753. Brother of Ven. John Williams, archdeacon of Cardigan (*D.N.B.*).
Services : Barasat C.C. 8½ mos. Posted Ensign to 23rd N.I. 1809. Served with Pioneers 1811-12 ; with 5th Bengal Vol. Bn. in Java 1813-16 ; sometime Asst. Conservator of Forests in Java. Transfd. to newly-raised 2/29th N.I. 1815. Operations against the Bhattis of Hariana 1818. Offg. Bk. Mr. Karnal district 1 Nov. 1821. Intr. & Qmr. 2/29th N.I. 16 Dec. 1823. Transfd. to 58th N.I. (late 2/29th) May 1824 ; offg. Adjt. do. 13 Dec. 1824. Transfd. to newly-raised 2nd Extra Regt. (became 70th N.I.) May 1825 ; Intr. & Qmr. do. 12 July 1825 till 6 Jan. 1826. Leave s.c. to Cape 1 Feb. 1826 till 16 Aug. 1827 ; fur. s.c. 31 Dec. 1829 till 7 Feb. 1833, and 1 Jan. 1836 till 13 Dec. 1837.
Refs. : *G.M.* 1837, i. 209-12 ; 1852, i. 313. *N. & Q.* 10S. ii. 175.

WILLIAMS, Walter (1759/60-?). Lieutenant. 6th Bengal Eur. Bn. Afterwards Lieut. H.M. 76th Ft. *b.* in Wales 1759/60. Cadet 1781. Ensign 23 June 1781. Lieut. 27 Sept. 1782. Resigned 3 Nov. 1788.
Of Penycoed, St. Clears, co. Carmarthen. *m.* (before 1806) Anne. *Services :* Apptd. Cadet 16 Jan. 1781 ; sailed for India in the *Locko* 13 Mar. 1781, aged 21. First Mahratta War ; Lieut. with Goddard's detachment in W. India. Lieut. 22nd Bn. Sepoys in July 1787 ; transfd. to 6th Bengal Eur. Bn. 15 Dec. 1787. Lieut. H.M. 76th Ft. (9 July 1783) 3 Nov. 1788 till Jan. 1805.

WILLIAMS, William. Ensign. Engineers. Country Cadet 1782. Ensign 21 July 1782. Resigned 22 Jan. 1784.
Services : Apptd. Cadet 15 Mar. 1782. N.F.P. (? Became partner with William Tulloh, auctioneer at Calcutta, and *d.* there Apr. 1789. Will dated 7 Apr. 1789 ; proved 21 Apr. 1789.)

WILLIAMS, William (1785-1804). Lieutenant, 8th N.I. *bapt.* Montgomery 17 Feb. 1785. Cadet 1799. Arrived in India 8 Dec. 1800. Ensign 17 Aug. 1800. Lieut. 16 Nov. 1800. *d.* Sikandra 24 Aug. 1804 : kld. in action.
Natural son of Robert Williams, of the firm of Williams & Hohler, Calcutta, by Elizabeth Astley.
Services : Posted Lieut. to 2/8th N.I. 17 Apr. 1801. Operations in Jumna Doab 1803 ; Sasni ; Bijaigarh ; Kachaura ; Lieut. 2/8th N.I. Second Mahratta War 1803-4 ; Laswari ; Tonk

Rampura; Monson's retreat (kld.); Lieut. 2/8th N.I., actg. A.D.C. and Persian Intr. to Monson.

Refs.: E.I.M.C. ii. 559. Intest.; admon. 13 Dec. 1805.

LLOYD-WILLIAMS, Henry (1789-1825). Lieutenant. 3rd N.I. Subsequently Senior Chaplain, Bengal Ecclesiastical Est. *b.* Benares 2 Oct. 1789. Cadet 1804. Arrived in India 13 May 1806. Ensign 1 Apr. 1806. Lieut. 23 July 1807. Resigned 31 Aug. 1814. *d.* Cawnpore 30 Jan. 1825.

3rd son of John Lloyd Williams, of Gwernant Park, co. Cardigan, formerly Surg. Bengal Est., and Martha Louisa his wife, 2nd dau. of Morley Pendred Saunders, of Saunders Grove, co. Wicklow. *m.* 1815, Louisa, 3rd dau. of Rev. Gilbert Parke, of Highnam Court, Gloucs. (She died 1873.) Wadham Coll., Oxon.; matric. 1 Apr. 1811; B.A. 1814.

Services: Barasat C.C. Posted Lieut. to 3rd N.I. 1807. Fur. 22 Jan. 1810 till resignation. Took holy orders. Apptd. chaplain Bengal 12 June 1815; at Patna 1817-18; at Cawnpore 1819 till death.

Refs.: Burke's *Landed Gentry*, 13th edn., p. 1901, *s.n.* Lloyd-Williams, of Gwernant, co. Cardigan. *Alumni Oxon. G.M.* 1825, ii. 475. Will dated 9 July 1824; proved 17 Mar. 1825.

WILLIAMSON, Alfred Arkell (1801-1831). Captain, 25th N.I. *b.* London 6 Nov. 1801. Cadet 1819. Admitted 27 Mar. 1820. Ensign 20 Sept. 1819. Lieut. 26 Aug. 1822. Capt. 30 May 1828. *d.* Gauhati, Assam, 3 July 1831, of jungle fever.

bapt. St. Giles-in-the-Fields, Middlesex, 13 June 1808. Son of Cornelius Williamson, of Woburn, and Anne his wife (who *re-m.* —— Reddall). *m.* 27 Feb. 1826, Janet Elizabeth Rosalie, only dau. of Archibald Mearns, Surg. A.M.D., formerly 3rd Gds. (She died 12 Sept. 1861.)

Services: Posted Ensign to 1/20th N.I.; transfd. to 25th N.I. (late 1/20th) May 1824. Served at P.W.I. Dec. 1821 till 1823. Fur. s.c. 22 Apr. 1823 till 21 Oct. 1826. No record of active service.

Refs.: A.J. xxi. 557; N.S. vii. 42.

WILLIAMSON, David (1785-1855). Major General. Colonel 39th N.I. *b.* Pencaitland, co. Haddington, 4 Mar. 1785. Cadet 1804. Arrived in India 13 May 1806. Ensign 24 Mar. 1806. Lieut. 27 Sept. 1807. Capt. 11 July 1823. Major 18 June 1833. Lt. Col. 28 Feb. 1840. Col. 2 Aug. 1850. Maj. Gen. 28 Nov. 1854. *d.* Maismore Sq., Peckham, Surrey, 7 May 1855.

bapt. Pencaitland 17 Mar. 1785. Son of James Williamson and Helen Douglas his wife. *m.* Chandernagore 31 Mar. 1814, Eleanor Mary, dau. of Jacques Grand-Jean de Fouchy, of Chandernagore. (*See also* Henry Hodgson.) (She died 30 Nov. 1854.) His daus. *m.* Christopher George Fagan, *q.v.*, Henry Edward Pearson, *q.v.*, and George Ramsay, *q.v.*

Services : Present as Cadet at capture of Cape Jan. 1806. Barasat C.C. Posted Ensign to 21st N.I. Comdd. a detachment of 1/21st N.I. Dec. 1811 and Apr. 1812 for protection of some villages on N. frontier of Gorakhpur against incursions of Nepalese. Actg. Adjt. 8th Gren. Bn. 1815; permanent do. 1816. Nepal War 1816; Lieut. 8th Gren. Bn., in 2nd Bde. Left Column (India medal). Intr. & Qmr. 2/21st N.I. 12 Dec. 1817 till 1823; actg. Adjt. do. 4 Oct. 1821 till 1 Oct. 1823; transfd. to 41st N.I. (late 1/21st) May 1824. Leave s.c. to N.S.W. 5 Mar. 1825. Siege and capture of Bhurtpore; Capt. Rt. Wing 41st N.I. (clasp to India medal). Fur. s.c. 1 Feb. 1831 till 10 Dec. 1833. Posted Lt. Col. to 41st N.I. 9 Aug. 1840; to 45th N.I. 8 Mar. 1845; to 14th N.I. 12 Sept. 1846; to 22nd N.I. 11 Oct. 1847. Leave s.c. 2 yrs. to Cape 28 Jan. 1848. Transfd. to 52nd N.I. May 1850; as Col. to 39th N.I. 21 Oct. 1850 till death. Fur. Apr. 1854 till death.

Refs. : Burke's *Royal Families*, ped. lxii. *Boase. I.M.* 19 May 1855, p. 275. *G.M.* 1855, ii. 662. Will dated 2 Jan. 1846; admon. 26 Mar. 1856.

WILLIAMSON, Edward (*d.* 1771). Ensign, Infantry. Cadet 1769. Ensign 12 Apr. 1770. *d.* Monghyr 26 Jan. 1771.
Services : N.F.P.

WILLIAMSON, Francis Alexander (1806-1855). Bt. Major, 63rd N.I. *b.* Edinburgh 19 July 1806. Cadet 1824. Arrived in India 19 Jan. 1826. Ensign 13 May 1825. Lieut. 21 Jan. 1829. Capt. 10 Dec. 1847. Bt. Major 11 Nov. 1851. *d. unm.* Mussoorie, U.P., 17 Apr. 1855.

Elder son of Joseph Williamson, principal clerk, Court of Teinds, and Sarah his 2nd wife, dau. of Henry Francis Dove, Capt. R.N., and widow of —— Lyme. Half-brother of Joseph Williamson, *q.v.*

Services : Posted Ensign to 63rd N.I. 1826; offg. Intr. & Qmr. do. 21 July 1829 and 14 Jan. 1830; permanent do. 9 Aug. 1831 till Dec. 1847. Reduction of Jhansi 1838-9; Lieut. 63rd N.I. With Army of Reserve (for Afghanistan) Oct. 1842 till Jan. 1843; Bt. Capt. 63rd N.I. First Sikh War; Badhowal; Ferozshahr;

Aliwal; Sobraon; Bt. Capt. 63rd N.I. (Medal with 2 clasps). Offg. in Comst. Dept. in 1852.

Refs.: I.M. 1 June 1855, p. 282. *Her. and Gen.* vii. 229. M.I. Mussoorie.

WILLIAMSON, George (1786-1841). Lieut. Colonel, 58th N.I. Comdg. at Barrackpore. *b.* Perth 8 June 1786. Cadet 1802. Arrived in India 17 Feb. 1803. Ensign 17 May 1803. Lieut. 30 Sept. 1803. Capt. 15 Apr. 1816. Major 13 May 1825. Lt. Col. 26 Aug. 1829. *d.s.p.* Barrackpore 17 Sept. 1841.

Only child of Col. William Williamson, of Dundee, and Jane his wife, sister of Sir Mark Wood, Bart., *q.v. m.* (?) (She died 17 Oct. 1831.)

Services: Barasat C.C. Posted Lieut. to 3rd N.I. 1803. Capture of Java 1811; Cornelis; Lieut. 3rd Vol. Bn., Bde. Major to his uncle, Sir George Wood, *q.v.* Returned from Java 27 Nov. 1811. Capt. Lt. 1/3rd N.I. 12 Apr. 1815. A.D.C. to Maj.-Gen. Sir G. Wood 1 Jan. 1817. Leave s.c. to N.S.W. 11 May 1822 till 11 Apr. 1825. Transfd. to 19th N.I. (late 2/3rd) May 1824; as Major to newly-raised 1st Extra Regt. (became 69th N.I.) May 1825. Fur. s.c. 4 Dec. 1825 till 14 Jan. 1829. To take charge of 46th N.I. 5 Feb. 1829; posted Lt. Col. to do. 20 Apr. 1830; to 45th N.I. 15 Sept. 1832; to 57th N.I. 17 Jan. 1833. Fur. p.a. 20 Feb. 1834 till 29 Nov. 1837. Comdd. 19th N.I. Mar. 1838 till Apr. 1840. Leave p.a. to Mussoorie 25 Apr. 1840 till Nov. 1841. Bdr. 2 cl. comdg. Barrackpore 27 Nov. 1840 till death. Transfd. to 58th N.I. 31 Mar. 1841.

Refs.: Memorials of the Woods of Largo, p. 78. M.I. at Barrackpore.

WILLIAMSON, James (1752-1792). Captain, 1st Bengal Vols. Comdt. Bangalore Fort. *b.* 1752. Cadet 1771. Ensign 4 Feb. 1773. Lieut. 23 Feb. 1778. Capt. 10 June 1781. *d.s.p.* Bangalore 20 Feb. 1792.

3rd son of James Williamson, of Cardrona, and Isabella his wife, dau. of Charles Balfour, of Broadmeadows, co. Selkirk. *m.* Elizabeth Lidderdale, niece of Lt.-Gen. Robert Fullerton, of Dudwick. (*See also* James Brown (*d.* 1788).)

Services: Second Mysore War 1781-5; siege of Cuddalore (w. 24 June 1783); Capt. comdg. 24th N.I. Employed at Madras in May 1784 in recruiting troops for Coy.'s Service from H.M. Regts. ordered home. Capt. 7th Bn. Sepoys in July 1787; 5th Eur. Bn. in Dec. 1788. Transfd. from 3rd to 4th Bengal Eur. Bn. 30 Jan. 1791; apptd. to comd. 1st Bn. Bengal Vols. 9 Oct. 1791. Third

THE BENGAL ARMY, 1758-1834

Mysore War 1791-2 ; Bangalore ; Capt. 1st Bengal Vol. Bn. Apptd. Comdt. of Bangalore fort.

Refs. : Burke's *Landed Gentry*, 11th edn., p. 1820, *s.n.* Williamson, of Cardrona, co. Peebles. *Williams*, p. 116. *Cardew*, p. 47. *G.M.* 1792, ii. 761. *S.M.* 1792, p. 413. Will dated 25 May 1791 ; proved 28 Apr. 1792. M.I. in Bangalore fort.

WILLIAMSON, James (1791-1820). Lieutenant, 4th N.I. *b.* Lethendy, co. Perth, 17 Jan. 1791. Cadet 1808. Arrived in India 12 Dec. 1809. Ensign 13 Aug. 1811. Lieut. 14 July 1815. *d.* Muttra 8 Oct. 1820.

Only child of Rev. Robert Williamson, minister of Lethendy 1756-91, and Helen his wife, eldest dau. of John Freer, of Easter Essendy. Nephew of Dr. Robert Freer, Professor of Medicine, Glasgow Univ.

Services : Barasat C.C. Posted to 4th N.I. 1811. Nepal War 1815 ; operations in Kumaon ; Sitauli ; capture of Almora ; Lieut. 1/4th N.I., under Col. Jasper Nicolls.

Refs. : Scott's *Fasti*, iv. 166. Will dated Bareilly, 18 Feb. 1818 ; proved 17 May 1822.

WILLIAMSON, Joseph (1783-1828 ?). Lieutenant. 25th N.I. *b.* Edinburgh 7 Feb. 1783. Cadet 1799. Admitted 11 Dec. 1800. Ensign 22 Aug. 1800. Lieut. 4 Jan. 1801. Retired 4 Nov. 1807. (? *d.* 1828.) [1] *unm.*

2nd son of Joseph Williamson, one of the principal clerks of Court of Teinds, and Joanna (Jacky) his 1st wife, dau. of John Neilson, of St. Cuthbert's, Edinburgh. Half-brother of Francis Alexander Williamson, *q.v.*

Services : Posted Lieut. to 2/13th N.I. 17 Apr. 1801 ; transfd. to newly-raised 23rd N.I. 1804 ; to 25th N.I. 1805. Fur. 5 Mar. 1804 till retirement. No record of active service. (? Subsequently one of the principal clerks of Teinds.)

Refs. : *Her. and Gen.* vii. 229.

[1] *Note :* Half pay drawn up to 1827, when he was transfd. to pension warrant ; name removed from *E.I.R.* after Jan. 1829.

WILLIAMSON, Thomas (*d.* 1770). Lieutenant, Infantry. Cadet 1768. Ensign 11 Jan. 1769. Lieut. 19 Dec. 1769. *d.* 1770.
Services : N.F.P.

WILLIAMSON, Thomas [1] (1758/59-1817). Captain. 17th N.I. *b.* London 1758/59. Cadet 1778. Ensign 1778. Lieut. 29 Oct. 1778. Capt. 1 June 1796. Retired 18 Mar. 1801. *d.* Paris Oct. 1817.

m. (before 1803) Sarah. (She died London 23 June 1854.)

Services : Sailed for India in the *Stafford* 27 May 1778, aged 19. Lieut. 2/3rd Bengal Eur. Regt. in Oct. 1779 ; apptd. Adjt. 3rd Eur. Regt. 28 Apr. 1781 ; 30th Bn. Sepoys in July 1787. Expedn. to Kedah, Penang, 1791 ; action against pirates at Point Pria fort 12 Apr. (w.) ; Lieut. comdg. the force of 2 Coys. 30th Bn. Posted Capt. to 3rd Eur. Regt. June 1796 ; Capt. 2/13th N.I. in Mar. 1798 ; transfd. to 17th N.I. 1798. Suspended (Cons. 4 May 1798) for writing a letter criticizing the Govt.'s mily. policy, signed ' Mentor,' which appeared in the Calcutta *Telegraph* of 17 Mar. 1798, the Board considering " his conduct highly criminal and of a dangerous tendency." He was ordered home, and three years later the C.D., though refusing to reinstate him, decided to let him retire on the h.p. of his rank. Author of various works, including, " Oriental Field Sports," 1807 ; " The East India Vade-mecum," London, 1810, etc., etc.

Refs.: Cardew, p. 56.   *A.J.* iv.   *G.M.* 1817, ii. 637.

[1] *Note :* Or Thomas George Williamson.

WILLIAMSON, Thomas (1764-1799). Captain, Infantry. *b.* Bengal 1764. Cadet 1778. Admitted 10 Dec. 1778. Ensign 1778. Lieut. 17 Nov. 1778. Capt. 1 June 1796. *d.* Allahabad 2 Jan. 1799.

bapt. Calcutta 3 Feb. 1765. Son of George Williamson, the Coy.'s " Vendu Master " (auctioneer) in Calcutta, and Eleanor his wife, *née* Howett.

Services : Sailed for India in the *Shrewsbury* 7 Mar. 1778, aged 14. Lieut. 1/2nd Bengal Eur. Regt. in Oct. 1779 ; 12th Bn. Sepoys in July 1787 and in 1792 ; comdg. at Jaleswar, B. & O., in Apr. 1789.

WILLIM, John (G——) [1] (1777/78-1864). Captain. 18th N.I. *b.* 1777/78. Cadet 1796. Arrived in India 14 Mar. 1798. Ensign 10 Oct. 1797. Lieut. 10 Sept. 1798. Capt. 4 Nov. 1804. Retired 22 May 1811. *d.* St. John's Wood, London, 9 Feb. 1864, aged 86.

Services : Lieut. 1st Bengal Eur. Regt. in 1798 ; transfd. to 9th N.I. ; to 2/18th N.I. 29 May 1800. Second Mahratta War ; operations in Bundelkhand 1803 ; capture of Gwalior 1804 ; defeat of Rajah Ram Singh ; capture of Jaitpur ; Lieut. 2/18th N.I. Fur. 21 Sept. 1806 till retirement.

Refs.: E.I.M.C. iii. 307-8.   *G.M.* 1864, i. 405.   *The Times,* 11 Feb. 1864.

[1] *Note :* His name is given as John G. Willim in *D. & M.,*

THE BENGAL ARMY, 1758-1834

E.I.M.C., and *E.I.R.*, but as John only in obit. notices. As his Cadet Papers are missing from the I.O. this point cannot be determined.

WILLIS, Alfred Leonard (1806-1832). Lieutenant, 32nd N.I. *b.* London 9 Aug. 1806. Cadet 1824. Admitted 9 May 1825. Ensign 11 Dec. 1824. Lieut. 4 July 1826. *d.* Calcutta 30 Apr. 1832, of fever.[1]

bapt. St. Magnus, London Bridge, 4 Sept. 1806. Son of Richard Willis and Ann his wife. *m.* Calcutta cathedral 22 Aug. 1826, Miss Maria Cuppage, reputed dau. of William Cuppage, *q.v.*, by Elizabeth Ramsay.

Services: Enlisted in H.C. Art. 17 June 1824, and embarked for Calcutta in June with a detachment. Apptd. Cadet (Gen. letter from C.D. of 24 Nov. 1824). Ensign d.d. 28th N.I. 23 May 1825; posted to 23rd N.I. 1825. Siege and capture of Bhurtpore; Ensign 23rd N.I. Transfd. to 32nd N.I. 1826; actg. Intr. & Qmr. do. 16 Dec. 1829. Leave u.p.a. 6 mos. to Calcutta 26 Dec. 1831.

Refs.: *A.J.* N.S. ix. 142. M.I. in S. Park St. cemetery, Calcutta.

[1] *Note:* He *d.* in Calcutta gaol, where he had been confined for debt for the past ten days.

WILLIS, Henry (1767-1790). Lieutenant, Artillery. (209) *b.* London 1767. Cadet (Inf.) 1781. Arrived in India Aug. 1783. Ensign 6 June 1781. Lieut. 17 Sept. 1782. Fireworker (Art.) 17 Oct. 1785. Lieut. 6 Sept. 1786. *d.* Fort Marlbro' 15 July 1790, " of Schirrhus of ye Liver and Putrid Fever," aged 22.

Services: Apptd. Cadet 4 Apr. 1781, aged 14; to remain in England till next year (Minute dated 5 Apr. 1781); sailed for India in the *Winterton* 11 Sept. 1782. Lieut. 1st Bn. Art. in July 1787; at Bencoolen in Dec. 1788.

WILLIS, John (*d.* 1770). Captain, Infantry. Capt. 1766. *d.* Bankipore, B. & O., 30 July 1770.

Services: Transfd. from H.M.S. 2nd Lieut. 108th Coy. Marines 11 Apr. 1758 till 27 June 1760. (? Ensign 11th Ft. (in Germany) 4 Feb. 1760; h.p. 1761.)

WILLIS, John (1786-1806). Cadet, Infantry. *b.* Kingston, Jamaica, 22 Nov. 1786. Cadet 1805. Never arrived in India. *d.* Dec. 1806, on his passage to India, in the wreck of the *Skelton Castle*. Struck off with effect from 5 Nov. 1806. (See note to David Allan.)

Son of John Willis.

WILLIS, Paul Wynch (1807-1866). Colonel. Engineers. *b.* 26 May 1807. Cadet 1824. Arrived in India 20 Mar. 1826. 2nd Lieut. 16 Oct. 1824. Lieut. 31 Aug. 1827. Capt. 20 May 1839. Major 1 Dec. 1847. Lt. Col. 1 Aug. 1854. Retired 21 Aug. 1854. Hon. Col. 16 Mar. 1855. *d.* Gt. Malvern 2 Mar. 1866, of apoplexy.

bapt. Freshwater, Hants, 14 Aug. 1810. Youngest son of James Willis, of Hampton Court Palace, and Flora his wife. (*Probably* related to Alexander Wynch, Govr. of Madras 1773-6, and to Joseph McVeagh, *q.v.*) *m.* Kings Nympton, Devon, 17 July 1832, Anne, youngest sister of Charles Patch, *q.v.* (She died Weston-super-Mare 4 Sept. 1885.) Addiscombe Cadet 1822-4.

Services: Posted to S. & M. 25 Apr. 1826. Executive Engr. at Mhow 25 Apr. 1829. Fur. s.c. 28 Feb. 1830 till 29 July 1833. Executive Engr. 13th (Rajputana) Div., P.W.D., 10 Jan. 1834; do. 3rd (Dinapore) Div. 13 Oct. 1835; do. 5th (Benares) Div. 29 Aug. 1836. Fur. s.c. 8 Nov. 1838 till 9 Oct. 1841. Offg. Executive Engr. Delhi Div. 12 Jan. 1842; Supt. of Benares road 14 Jan. 1843; do. Grand Trunk road 1847-52. Fur. s.c. 21 Feb. 1852 till retirement. No record of active service.

Refs.: A.J. N.S. viii. 227. G.M. 1866, ii. 607. *The Times*, 7 Mar. 1866.

WILLMOTT,[1] **John.** Fireworker. Artillery. (155) Cadet 1778. Fireworker 1778. Resigned 5 Oct. 1778.

Services: Apptd. Cadet in India 27 Feb. 1778.

[1] *Note:* Or Wilmot.

WILLOUGHBY, James (1750-1792). Lieutenant, 16th Bn. Sepoys. *b.* 10 July 1750. Cadet 1781. Ensign 30 Apr. 1781. Lieut. 17 Aug. 1782. *d. unm.* Barrackpore 9 Apr. 1792.

7th son of Edward Willoughby, of Cossall and Aspley, Notts. (of a junior branch of the family of Barons Middleton), and Margaret his wife, dau. of Francis Bird, of London. Brother of Richard Willoughby, *q.v.*

Services: Apptd. Cadet 19 Dec. 1780, aged 30; sailed for India in the *Latham* 16 Mar. 1781. First Mahratta War, from Mar. 1782; Ensign in Goddard's detachment. Lieut. 2nd Bengal Eur. Bn. in July 1787; 16th Bn. Sepoys in Dec. 1788.

Refs.: Family information. M.I. at Barrackpore.

WILLOUGHBY, Richard (1748-1825). Lieut. Colonel, Invalid Est. 5th N.I. *b.* 4 Jan. 1748. Cadet 1781. Admitted 4 June 1782. Ensign 1 May 1781. Lieut. 18 Aug. 1782. Capt. 12 Nov.

1799. Major 31 Mar. 1807. Invalided 25 Jan. 1808. Lt. Col. 4 June 1813. *d. unm.* Patna Aug. 1825.

6th son of Edward Willoughby and Margaret his wife. Brother of James Willoughby, *q.v.* Reputed father of Francis Willoughby (see Appendix A).

Services : Apptd. Cadet 18 Apr. 1781; sailed for India in the *Blandford* 26 June 1781. Lieut. 10th Bn. Sepoys in July 1787; 16th Bn. in Dec. 1788; 10th Bn. in 1790. Fur. 27 Mar. 1797 till 27 Mar. 1800. Capt. 5th N.I. Regulating Ofr. of Invalid Tannah Ests. at Chittagong in 1805. Comdd. Native Invalids at Patna 1808 till death.

Refs. : Family information. Will dated 3 Aug. 1805; proved 15 Dec. 1825.

WILLSON, Hill (1774-1846). Lieutenant. Engineers. *b.* Rasharkin, co. Antrim, 22 Mar. 1774. Cadet 1793. Arrived in India 25 Oct. 1794. Ensign 18 Oct. 1794. Lieut. 21 Feb. 1801. Retired 5 Oct. 1803. *d.* 29 Oct. 1846.

Son of James Willson, M.P. for co. Antrim 1776-83, and Sophia his wife, dau. of Rev. Skeffington Bristow, preby. of Rasharkin. *Re-m.* (they having been already *m.* to each other) St. George's, Hanover Sq., 18 Apr. 1807, Isabella Kinnaird.

Services : Apptd. Cadet 5 Mar. 1794; sailed for India in the *Lord Camden* 2 May 1794. Fur. 9 Oct. 1800 till retirement.

*****WILMERS, Diedrich Adolph** (1725/26-?). Capt. Lieutenant. Artillery. *b.* Lon (or Son), Germany, 1725/26. Cadet 1758. Fireworker 6 Jan. 1759. 2nd Lieut. 14 Sept. 1761. Lieut. 17 Sept. 1763. Capt. Lt. 2 Dec. 1763. Resigned 21 Jan. 1765. (Living at Hamburg in 1772.)

Services : Corporal in Capt. J. Pattison's Coy. of 1st Bn., R.A. Apptd. Lieut. F. in letter from C.D., dated London, 12 May 1758; sailed for India in the *Bombay Castle* in 1758, aged 32. Granted a Commission by the Presdt. of Council, Ft. Wm., 18 Jan. 1759. Writes from Calcutta, 21 Jan. 1765, asking leave to resign on account of injustice done to him through his supersession by Fleming Martin, *q.v.*

EARDLEY-WILMOT, Edward Revell (1814-1899). 2nd Lieutenant. Artillery. (642) Subsequently Canon of Worcester. *b.* 11 Feb. 1814. Cadet 1829. Arrived in India 14 Jan. 1831. 2nd Lieut. 11 June 1830. Resigned 5 Feb. 1838. *d.* Clarina, Kenilworth Rd., Leamington, 30 May 1899.

bapt. Leek Wootton, co. Warwick, 22 July 1814. 3rd son of

Sir John Eardley-Wilmot, 1st Bart., Govr. of Van Dieman's Land, M.P. for N. Warwickshire 1832-43, and Elizabeth Emma his 1st wife, dau. of Caleb Hillier Parry, M.D., of Bath. *m.* 1st, Little Risington, Gloucs., 4 Aug. 1840, Frances Anne, youngest sister of Charles Ekins, *q.v.* (She died 11 Apr. 1846.) *m.* 2nd, Ham, Surrey, 8 Feb. 1848, Emma Hutchinson, dau. of William Lambert, B.C.S. (She died Leamington 14 Feb. 1907.) Addiscombe Cadet 1828-30. Trinity Hall, Cambs.; B.A. 1840; M.A. 1847.

Services: Apptd. Actg. 2nd Lieut. 9 Feb. 1833. Posted to 2nd Coy. 3rd Bn. Foot Art. 3 June 1835. Fur. s.c. 5 Aug. 1835 till resignation. Granted h.p. of Ensign (viz. 3/- *p.d.*) 20 Apr. 1838. No record of active service. Took holy orders. Deacon 1840; Priest 1841. Vicar of Kenilworth 1846-55; Rector of All Souls', Langham Pl., 1855-72; Rector of Waddingham, Lincs., till 1881. Hon. Canon of Worcester cathedral 1850.

Refs.: Burke's *Peerage*, 1923, p. 2334, *s.n.* Eardley-Wilmot, Bart., of Berkswell Hall, co. Warwick. *Howard & Crisp*, xviii. 126, *s.n.* Ekins. *Boase. Crockford. Graduati Cantab. The Times,* 31 May 1899, p. 9.

WILSON, Alexander (1789-1813). Lieutenant, 8th N.I. *bapt.* St. Mary's, Carlisle, 7 June 1789. Cadet 1805. Arrived in India 19 Sept. 1806. Ensign 14 Oct. 1806. Lieut. 24 May 1808. *d.* Serampore 2 Aug. 1813.

Son of Alexander Wilson, of Castle St., Carlisle, mercer, and Catharine his wife, *née* Beck.

Services: Sailed for India in the *Lady Burges* 30 Mar. 1806; she was lost at sea 20 Apr. 1806. Barasat C.C. Posted Ensign to 8th N.I. 1807. Capture of Mauritius 1810-11; Lieut. 2nd Vol. Bn. Lieut. 1/8th N.I.

WILSON, Alexander (1800-1842). Captain, 64th N.I. *b.* Beith, co. Ayr, 14 May 1800. Cadet 1818. Admitted 27 Mar. 1820. Ensign 20 Sept. 1819. Lieut. 11 July 1823. Capt. 3 Mar. 1831. *d.* Khyber Pass 24 Jan. 1842: kld. in action.

bapt. Beith 18 May 1800. Son of John Wilson, of the Saracen's Head Inn, Beith, vintner, and Jean his wife, dau. of James Wark, of Hazelhead. Nephew of Mrs. Aitkin and uncle of Martha Muir Houston. *m.* Catherine Robertson. (She *re-m.* 7 July 1853, and died Dec. 1854.)

Services: Posted Ensign to 2/10th N.I.; transfd. to newly-formed 1/32nd N.I. July 1823; to 64th N.I. (late 2/32nd) May 1824; Adjt. do. 10 Aug. 1825 till 12 Mar. 1829. Fur. s.c. 26 Feb. 1829 till 23 June 1832. Offg. A.D.C. to Bdr.-Gen. W. Richards, *q.v.*, comdg. Dinapore Div., 12 Aug. till 7 Nov. 1834. Fur. p.a. 13 Dec. 1837 till 21 Jan. 1841. First Afghan War 1842; retreat from Ali Masjid through Khyber (Kafir Jangi) Pass (kld.); Capt. 64th N.I.

Refs.: *The Wilsons of Beith, Ayrshire*, by W. A. Cadbury, LL.D., privately printed, 1933. *A.J.* N.S. xxxvii. 317. Will dated Ferozepore 1 Sept. 1841; proved 6 Apr. 1842. M.I. Afghan Memorial Church, Bombay, and in Beith Church.

WILSON, Andrew Thomas Alexander (1803-1844). Captain, 2nd Bengal Eur. Regt. *b.* 49 Gower St., London, 23 Aug. 1803. Cadet 1818. Admitted 27 Mar. 1820. Ensign 20 Sept. 1819. Lieut. 5 Mar. 1823. Capt. 12 May 1830. *d.* Simla 10 July 1844.

bapt. St. Giles-in-the-Fields, Middlesex, 22 Sept. 1803. Son of Thomas Wilson, of St. Thomas's, Exeter, and Betsey Isabel his wife. Brother of James Dickson Wilson, *q.v.* *m.* Hazaribagh, B. & O., 14 Sept. 1840, Margaret, youngest sister of Ralph Smith, *q.v.* (She *re-m.* 16 Dec. 1845, Lieut. Thomas Fourness Wilson, 13th B.N.I.)

Services: Ensign d.d. Bengal Eur. Regt. Mar. 1820; d.d. 1/16th N.I. Aug. 1820; posted to 1/8th N.I. Jan. 1821; transfd. to 24th N.I. (late 2/8th) May 1824. Apptd. to 1st Gren. Bn. 5 Sept. 1825. First Burma War; Arakan 1825; Lieut. 1st Gren. Bn. Operations against the Chuars 1832-3; Capt. 24th N.I., with Jungle Mehals F.F. Fur. p.a. 18 Dec. 1833 till 4 Dec. 1836. Transfd. to newly-raised 2nd Bengal Eur. Regt. 8 Oct. 1839. With Army of Reserve (for Afghanistan) Oct. 1842 till Jan. 1843. Leave s.c. to Simla Apr. 1844 till death.

Refs.: De Rhé-Philipe. *I.M.* 4 Oct. 1844, p. 564. Will dated Simla 6 July 1844; proved 3 Sept. 1844. M.I. at Simla.

WILSON, Sir Archdale, first baronet (1803-1874). Lieut. General, G.C.B., Artillery. (483) *b.* and *bapt.* Kirby Cane, Norfolk, 3 Aug. 1803. Cadet 1818. Arrived in India Sept. 1819. 2nd Lieut. 10 Apr. 1819. Lieut. 7 July 1820. Capt. 15 Oct. 1834. Major 3 July 1845. Lt. Col. 1 Jan. 1848. Col. 14 Oct. 1858. Maj. Gen. 14 Sept. 1857. Lt. Gen. 6 Mar. 1868. *d.s.p.* 22 Park Cresc., London, 9 May 1874.

1st Bart., of Delhi. *cr.* 8 Jan. and 8 July 1858. 5th son of Rev. George Wilson, of Kirby Cane, rector of Diddington (who was youngest brother of 9th Lord Berners), and Anna Maria his wife, dau. of Rev. Charles Millard, chancellor of Norwich. Brother of Charles Wilson, *q.v.* *m.* Dum-Dum 4 July 1842, Ellen, 2nd dau.

of W. H. L. Frith, *q.v.* (*See also* George Henry Swinley.) Ed. Norwich Grammar School. Addiscombe Cadet 1818-19.

Services: See *D.N.B.* Siege and capture of Bhurtpore; Lieut. comdg. 2nd Coy. 4th Bn. Foot Art. (India medal). Adjt. Nimach Div. Art. 6 May 1828. Offg. A.A.G. of Art. 2 Oct. 1837. Comdd. Art. at Lucknow 1839. Actg. Supt. of Kasipur gun foundry 12 Aug. 1840; permanent do. 11 Nov. 1841 till 10 Aug. 1845. Fur. 1845 till 7 Dec. 1847. Second Sikh War; Jullundur Doab 1848-9; Kalalwala; Dalla (*Lond. Gaz.* 7 and 20 Mar. 1849); Lt. Col. 1st Bn. (Medal). Comdt. Art. at Dum-Dum Jan. 1854. Fur. p.a. 21 Apr. 1855 till Mar. 1856. Tempy. comdg. Meerut Div. on outbreak of Mutiny 9 May 1857. Mutiny campaign 1857-8; Badli-ki-Serai; assault and capture of Delhi; capture of Lucknow (Medal with 2 clasps). Selected to comd. at siege of Delhi 17 July 1857, and promoted Maj. Gen. for special service 29 July (ib. 13 Oct. 1857). Comdd. Art. at siege and capture of Lucknow Mar. 1858. Fur. 1858 till death. Col. Comdt. F. Bde. R.H.A. 1866. C.B. 11 Nov. 1857; K.C.B. 14 Nov. 1857; G.C.B. 13 Mar. 1867. Granted a special pension of £1,000 *p.a.* D.C.L., Oxon., 6 July 1859.

Refs.: Burke's *Peerage*, 1905, p. 1879, *s.n.* Wilson, Bart., of Delhi. *D.N.B. D.I.B. Boase. Walford. Alumni Oxon. The Times*, 12 May 1874. *I.L.N.* xxxi. 333, 334 (portrait). Portrait, from a photo., pub. J. S. Virtue.

WILSON, Charles (1802-1842). Captain, Invalid Est. Bengal Eur. Regt. *b.* Kirby Cane, Norfolk, 2 May 1802. Cadet 1818. Admitted 10 Feb. 1820. Ensign 16 Aug. 1819. Lieut. 18 Jan. 1822. Capt. 13 June 1828. Invalided 5 Mar. 1838. *d. unm.* in England 9 Oct. 1842.

4th son of Rev. George Wilson and Anna Maria his wife. Brother of Sir Archdale Wilson, Bart., *q.v.* Sandhurst Cadet.

Services: Posted Ensign to Bengal Eur. Regt.; exchanged to 2nd Bengal Eur. Regt. 18 June 1824. First Burma War; Arakan 1825; Lieut. 2nd Bengal Eur. Regt., with Left Wing at Cheduba. Fur. s.c. 30 Sept. 1826 till 25 Sept. 1829; p.a. 12 Feb. 1842 till death.

Refs.: Burke's *Peerage*, 1905, p. 1679, *s.n.* Wilson, Bart., of Delhi.

WILSON, Charles Child (*d.* 1810). Major, 23rd N.I. Cadet 1783. Admitted 16 Oct. 1783. Ensign 4 Feb. 1785. Lieut. 19 Oct. 1791. Capt. 1 Oct. 1803. Major 7 Feb. 1809. *d.* Mainpuri, U.P., 27 Sept. 1810.

(Said, according to family tradition, to have been related to

Robert Child, the banker, of Temple Bar.) *m.* Calcutta 23 June 1792, Ann,[1] dau. of Christopher Green, *q.v.* (*See also* Charles Brietzcke.) His dau. *m.* William Clark, *q.v.*

Services: Apptd. Cadet 19 Feb. 1783; sailed for India in the *Pigot* 11 Mar. 1783. Posted to 1st Bengal Eur. Bn. 5 Feb. 1790; Lieut. to 4th do. 26 Jan. 1792; to 6th do. July 1793; 2nd N.I. in 1798. Operations in Jumna Doab 1803; Sasni; Lieut. 1/2nd N.I. Second Mahratta War 1803; battle of Delhi; Agra; Lieut. 1/2nd N.I. Transfd. as Capt. to newly-raised 23rd N.I. 9 Nov. 1803. (? Operations against Dhundia Khan 1807; Komona; Ganauri; Capt. 1/23rd N.I.) Major 1/23rd N.I.

Refs.: Family information.

[1] *Note:* She, having been left behind at Shikohabad when her husband was on service, was taken prisoner by M. Fleury when he attacked the cantt. in Sept. 1803, and carried off to Agra fort. (*Pester*, p. 159.)

WILSON, Edward Pitches (1773-1833). Colonel, 14th N.I. Bdr. comdg. Rajputana F.F. *b.* London 28 Mar. 1773. Cadet 1794. Arrived in India 26 Feb. 1796. Ensign 26 Sept. 1795. Lieut. 25 Apr. 1797. Capt. 19 Nov. 1804. Major 3 Mar. 1814. Lt. Col. 1 June 1818. Lt. Col. Comdt. 1 May 1824. Col. 5 June 1829. *d.* Nasirabad 14 June 1833.

bapt. St. Dunstan-in-the-East 25 Apr. 1773. Son of Edward Wilson, of Thames St., London, brandy merchant, and Jane his wife. Brother of Maria Charlotte, of Millgate, Richmond, Yorks. *m.* Juanpur May 1801, Miss Jane Dubois. (She died Nasirabad 18 Dec. 1858.) His dau. *m.* John Peter Ripley, *q.v.* Ed. Merchant Taylors' Mar. 1786 till Mar. 1790. Queen's Coll., Oxon.; matric. 25 Mar. 1790; B.A. from St. John's Coll. 1793.

Services: Apptd. Cadet 13 Mar. 1794; sailed for India in the *Berrington* 9 July 1795. Posted to 1st Bengal Eur. Regt. June 1796; Lieut. 16th N.I. in 1798; Adjt. & Qmr. do. 1801-5. Operations in Bundelkhand against Gopal Singh 1810; action at Parari 18 Feb.; Jhargarh Mar. 1810; Capt. 1/16th N.I., comdg. the detachment. Nepal War 1814-15; Kalanga (s.w. 31 Oct. 1814— *Lond. Gaz.* 17 May 1815); Major 2/16th N.I., comdg. L.I. Bn. in 2nd Div. Posted Lt. Col. to 2/16th N.I. 1818; transfd. to Bengal Eur. Regt. 1819; Lt. Col. Comdt. do. May 1824. To comd. 3rd Bde. on E. frontier 27 Nov. 1824. Transfd. to 15th N.I. 1825; to 17th N.I. 28 Dec. 1826; to 33rd N.I. 22 Dec. 1827; to 42nd N.I. 13 Apr. 1829. Bdr. comdg. Rajputana F.F. 28 Nov. 1827 till death. Posted Col. to 42nd N.I. 1829; to 14th N.I. 1 Mar. 1831.

Refs.: *Robinson. Alumni Oxon. A.J.* N.S. xii. 238. Will dated Nasirabad 25 Feb. 1830; proved 30 May 1834. M.I. at Nasirabad.

WILSON, Ezekiel Davys (*d.* 1778). Lieutenant, Infantry. Country Cadet 1777. Ensign 31 Dec. 1777. Lieut. 9 Sept. 1778. *d.* Cawnpore 9 Dec. 1778.

Son of Ezekiel Davys Wilson, M.P. for Carrickfergus, and Elizabeth his wife, sister of Joseph McVeagh, *q.v.* Cousin-german of Thomas Shaw (1761-1841), *q.v.*

Services: Arrived in India in a private capacity in Sept. 1775; apptd. Cadet 19 Dec. 1776.

WILSON, Frederick. Lieutenant. Infantry. Country Cadet 1779. Ensign 28 Aug. 1779. Lieut. 15 Apr. 1781. Struck off in England 1793.

Services: Apptd. Cadet 19 Aug. 1779. Posted Ensign to 2/2nd Bengal Eur. Regt. 1779; Dy. Paymr. 2nd Bde. in 1780; to comd. native Mil. at Bhagulpur 4 May 1781. Leave s.c. to sea 15 Dec. 1781; fur. s.c. 16 Oct. 1785 till struck off.

WILSON, George (*d.* 1763). Captain, 5th Bn. Sepoys. Cadet 1757. Ensign 5 June 1757. Lieut. 1 July 1758. Capt. 16 Sept. 1761. *d.* 5th, 6th or 11th Oct. 1763: massacred at or near Patna by order of Nawab Mir Muhammad Kasim. (See note to Henry Somers.)

Son of Elspeth Grant. Brother-in-law of James Ferguson.

Services: Raised in Dec. 1758, 5th Bn. Sepoys and comdd. till death. This Bn., called after him "*Wilson-ki-Paltan*," was destroyed at Patna in 1763. Wounded at assault of Patna 25 June 1763.

Refs.: *Broome,* p. 365. *Firminger,* p. 71. Will dated Patna, 30 May 1763; proved 13 Dec. 1763.

WILSON, George (*d.* 1790). Captain, 6th Bengal Eur. Bn. Cadet 1771. Ensign 20 Dec. 1772. Lieut. 19 Mar. 1777. Capt. 18 Mar. 1781. *d.* Chandernagore 24 Oct. 1790.

Brother of Lieut. James Wilson.

Services: Transfd. from Inf. to Cav. 5 Aug. 1778. Acquitted by a G.C.M. at Cawnpore on a charge of murder after shooting John White (*d.* 1778), *q.v.* First Mahratta War 1780; storm and capture of Gwalior; Lieut. in Cav. with detachment under Major William Popham, *q.v.*; Lieut. comdg. Cav. during Camac's operations against Sindhia Feb.-Mar. 1781. Capt. 6th Eur. Bn. in July 1787.

Refs.: *Stubbs,* i. 61. *India Gazette,* 31 Mar. 1781.

WILSON, George (1802-?). Lieutenant. 24th N.I. *bapt.*
Allendale, Northumberland, 14 Feb. 1802. Cadet 1820. Ensign
16 Jan. 1821. Lieut. 11 July 1823. Retired 28 Nov. 1824.
" His name has been removed from the list as he has not been heard
of for several years and is presumed to be dead." (*India List*,
Jan. 1894.)

Son (twin with Henry) of John Wilson, of Nenthall, Alston Moor,
Cumberland, proprietor and manager of lead mines, and Malley
his wife.

Services: Posted to 2/16th N.I. 1821; transfd. to 8th N.I.
July 1823; to 24th N.I. (late 2/8th) May 1824. Fur. 1824 till
retirement. No record of active service.

WILSON, Henry (1807-1877). Major. 4th N.I. *b.* I. of St.
Kitts 10 Oct. 1807. Cadet 1823. Arrived in India 25 June
1824. Ensign 14 Jan. 1824. Lieut. 13 May 1825. Capt. 16 Apr.
1844. Retired 1 July 1848. Hon. Major 28 Nov. 1854. *d.*
23 Paragon, Ramsgate, 9 Aug. 1877.

Of Sion Hill, Bath. Son of John William Delap Wilson, planter,
Presdt. of Council at St. Kitts, and Selina his wife, eldest dau. of
James Irwin, B.C.S., Dir. E. I. Co., and grand-dau. of Robert
Brooke, *q.v.* Nephew of Louisa Davis and ward of John Ford
Davis. *m.* Beechingstoke 10 Oct. 1848, Mary, widow of Charles
Ralfe, *q.v.* (She died 15 Oct. 1882.)

Services: Posted Ensign to 4th N.I. and served throughout with
that Regt. Actg. Bde. Major in Rohilkhand and Kumaon 10 Nov.
1841. Adjt. 4th N.I. 17 Feb. 1842 till 11 July 1844. No record of
active service.

Refs.: *The Times*, 11 Aug. 1877.

WILSON, Henry Thomas John Richard (1780-1815). Lieutenant. 23rd N.I. *b.* London 1 May 1780. Cadet 1798.
Arrived in India 23 Nov. 1799. Ensign 20 Jan. 1800. Lieut.
29 May 1800. Retired 31 Jan. 1806. *d.* 2 Apr. 1815.

bapt. St. George's, Hanover Sq., 4 June 1780. Son of Richard
Wilson, of Tyrone, and Hon. Anne his wife, only dau. of Rt. Hon.
Charles Townshend (who was younger brother of George, 1st
Marquess Townshend).

Services: Posted Lieut. to 1/11th N.I. 15 Apr. 1801. Fur.
1803 till retirement. No record of active service.

Refs.: Burke's *Peerage*, 1923, p. 2189, *s.n.* Townshend, M.

WILSON, Hugh (1789-1826). Captain, 68th N.I. *b.* Gamrie,
co. Banff, 16 June 1789. Cadet 1805. Arrived in India 19 Sept.

1806. Ensign 29 Sept. 1806. Lieut. 11 Aug. 1808. Capt. 1 May 1824. d. N.S.W. 7 Apr. 1826.

2nd son of Rev. Thomas Wilson, minister of Gamrie 1771-1830, and Elizabeth his wife, dau. of Rev. Theodore Gordon, minister of Kennethmont.

Services: Barasat C.C. Posted Lieut. to 20th N.I. 1807; at Fort Marlbro' 1810-11. Capture of Java 1811; Lieut. 20th N.I. Transfd. to newly-raised 1/30th N.I. 1815. Fur. 1818-20. Transfd. to newly-raised 34th N.I. July 1823; to 68th N.I. (late 2/34th) May 1824.

Refs.: Scott's *Fasti*, vi. 260.

WILSON, Hugh Campbell (1804-1855). Captain. 25th N.I. b. Sornbeg, co. Ayr, 29 Oct. 1804. Cadet 1823. Arrived in India 3 Sept. 1824. Ensign 13 Apr. 1824. Lieut. 13 May 1825. Capt. 7 Aug. 1834. Invalided 5 July 1837. Retired 23 Dec. 1839. d. 12 Merton Rd., Kensington, 27 Feb. 1855.

bapt. Galston, co. Ayr, 21 Nov. 1804. Son of Hugh Wilson, of Kilmarnock, and Euphemia his wife and cousin, elder dau. of Hugh Campbell, of Barquharrie, co. Ayr. m. St. Andrew's, Calcutta, 23 June 1831, Miss Eliza Falconer. (*See also* Alexander Davidson.) (She died Cheltenham 17 June 1883.)

Services: Posted Ensign to 40th N.I. 1824. First Burma War; Lieut. 40th N.I. (India medal). Transfd. to 25th N.I. 2 Mar. 1827; actg. Intr. & Qmr. do. 27 July 1828; actg. Adjt. do. 25 Nov. 1828; permanent do. 25 Apr. 1831 till 4 Jan. 1834. District Staff Ofr. in Arakan Oct. 1833. Fur. s.c. 11 Feb. 1834 till 16 Nov. 1836, and 16 July 1837 till retirement.

Refs.: Burke's *Landed Gentry*, 4th edn., p. 203, *s.n.* Campbell, of Barquharrie, co. Ayr. *I.M.* 21 Mar. 1855, p. 147. *G.M.* 1855, i. 446.

WILSON, James Dickson (1806-1880). Lieut. Colonel. 10th N.I. b. Hackney, Middlesex, 7 Oct. 1806. Cadet 1824. Arrived in India 16 Sept. 1825. Ensign 18 Apr. 1825. Lieut. 18 Jan. 1828. Capt. 21 May 1841. Bt. Major 11 Nov. 1851. Retired 25 June 1852. Hon. Lt. Col. 28 Nov. 1854. d. Rotunda Terr., Cheltenham, 30 Aug. 1880.

bapt. Hackney 25 Dec. 1806. Son of Thomas Wilson and Betsey Isabel his wife. Brother of Andrew Thomas Alexander Wilson, *q.v.*

Services: Posted Ensign to 10th N.I. Rising in Cuttack July 1836; Lieut. 10th N.I. Fur. s.c. 29 Mar. 1839 till 31 Dec. 1841. With Army of Reserve (for Afghanistan) Oct. 1842 till Jan. 1843.

Leave s.c. to Cape 6 Apr. 1845 till 1846. Comdd. Left Wing 10th N.I. and one Wing of 2nd Oudh Local Inf. in expedn. against fort Bihta, 20 m. E. of Lucknow, 29 Mar. 1850 : the casualties in this affair amounted to 17 (including one Ofr.) kld. and 47 wounded.

Refs.: I.M. 4 June 1850, p. 314. *The Times,* 2 Sept. 1880.

WILSON, John (*d.* 1767). Cadet, Infantry. Cadet 1767. *d.* 22 Oct. 1767.

Services: N.F.P.

WILSON, John (1788-1844). Bt. Major, 2nd Bengal Eur. Regt. *b.* 17 Oct. 1788. Cadet 1807. Arrived in India 14 Aug. 1808. Ensign 15 Sept. 1808. Lieut. 20 Aug. 1813. Capt. 1 May 1824. Bt. Major 28 June 1838. *d.* Ludhiana 25 Sept. 1844.

bapt. Kelso, co. Roxburgh, 28 Oct. 1788. Son of Dr. Andrew Wilson, M.D., physician in Kelso, and Jean Hood his wife.

Services: Barasat C.C. 7½ mos.; wounded in a duel at Barasat (*Cons.* 27 Feb. 1809). Posted Ensign to 11th N.I. 1809. (? Reduction of Kalinjar 1812; Lieut. 2/11th N.I.) Siege and capture of Hathras 1817; Lieut. 2/11th N.I. Third Mahratta War 1817-19; Lieut. 2/11th N.I. Leave s.c. 6 mos. to sea 13 Apr. 1819. Served with Hill Bildars 8 Apr. 1823 till his Coy. was disbanded 22 Nov. 1825; transfd. to 17th N.I. (late 2/11th) May 1824; served with Pioneers 24 Dec. 1825 till 1827. Actg. Bde. Major Rajputana F.F. 28 Mar. till 4 Dec. 1835. Bde. Major to troops forming escort to G.G. 3 Nov. 1838. Transfd. to newly-raised 2nd Bengal Eur. Regt. Oct. 1839. Fur. s.c. 23 Feb. 1841 till 24 Dec. 1842.

WILSON, John Neale (1789-1819). Lieutenant, 25th N.I. *b.* Alnwick, Northumberland, 7 May 1789. Cadet 1806. Arrived in India 25 Nov. 1807. Ensign 6 Nov. 1807. Lieut. 26 Oct. 1813. *d.* Lucknow 12 Sept. 1819.

Son of William Wilson, clothier, and Ann his wife.

Services: Barasat C.C. Posted Ensign to 25th N.I. 1808. Capture of Mauritius 1810-11; Ensign 1st Vol. Bn. Nepal War 1814-15; Lieut. 2/25th N.I., with 4th Div. Nepal War 1816; Chirriaghati; Makwanpur; Lieut. 2/25th N.I., with 3rd Bde. Centre Column. Intr. & Qmr. 2/25th N.I. 28 Nov. 1816 till death. Third Mahratta War 1817-18; Lieut. 2/25th N.I., with Centre Div. Grand Army.

WILSON, Malcolmson (1806-1860). Lieutenant. 27th N.I. *bapt.* Shankill, co. Armagh, 21 Dec. 1806. Cadet 1825. Arrived in India 18 Mar. 1826. Ensign 28 Sept. 1825. Lieut. 30 Dec. 1826. Retired 23 July 1837. *d.* close of 1860.

Son of Joseph Wilson and Mary his wife, sister of John Cuppage Douglas, M.D.,

Services : Posted Ensign to 27th N.I. 1826. Fur. s.c. 21 Jan. 1831 till 10 Feb. 1834, and 23 Jan. 1835 till retirement. No record of active service.

WILSON, Patrick (*d.* 1770). Cadet, Infantry. Cadet 1770. *d.* Berhampore June 1770.

Services : N.F.P.

WILSON, Robert Boyd (1793-1832). Captain, Artillery. (432) *b.* Lochlitter, Urquhart, Inverness, 16 May 1793. Cadet 1810. Admitted 27 Aug. 1811. Fireworker 18 Aug. 1811. Lieut. 25 Sept. 1817. Capt. 28 Sept. 1827. *d.* Inverness 30 Mar. 1832.

Son of Major Wilson, of Polmaily. Nephew of John Wilson. Woolwich Cadet. Addiscombe Cadet 1809-10.

Services : Nepal War 1815 ; conquest of Kumaon ; capture of Almora (*Lond. Gaz.* 16 Nov. 1815) ; Lt. F. 2nd Coy. 2nd Bn., in charge of mortars under Col. Jasper Nicolls. Siege and capture of Hathras 1817 ; Lt. F. 2nd Coy. 2nd Bn. Third Mahratta War ; Lieut. 2nd Coy. 2nd Bn. Served at P.W.I. June 1819 till Jan. 1822 ; offg. Engr. and Civil Architect P.W.I. 7 July 1821. Leave s.c. to Cape 23 Aug. 1825 till 26 Sept. 1827 ; fur. p.a. 21 Jan. 1829 till death.

Refs. : *A.J.* N.S. viii. 58.

WILSON, Roger Williamson (1790-1857). Major General, C.B. Colonel 65th N.I. *b.* London 26 Jan. 1790. Cadet 1808. Admitted 6 Nov. 1809. Ensign 16 June 1811. Lieut. 16 Dec. 1814. Capt. 2 Nov. 1827. Major 1 Aug. 1839. Lt. Col. 10 June 1845. Col. (17 Mar. 1851) 8 Mar. 1855. Maj. Gen. 28 Nov. 1854. *d.* Brighton 15 Sept. 1857.

bapt. St. Benet, Gracechurch St., 3 Feb. 1790. Son of Joseph Wilson and Sarah his wife. *m.* Muttra 28 Jan. 1817, Miss Eliza Gibson. (She died 10 Jan. 1874, aged 85.)

Services : Captured by French in Bay of Bengal on passage out, 19 Nov. 1809. Barasat C.C. Posted to 5th N.I. 1811. Nepal War 1814-15 ; Kalanga (w.—*Lond. Gaz.* 19 Aug. 1815) ; reduction of Kumaon 1815 ; Sitauli ; Almora (ib. 16 Nov. 1815) ; Lieut. 2/5th N.I. Transfd. to newly-raised 1/29th N.I. 1815. Siege and capture of Hathras 1817 ; Lieut. 1/29th N.I. Third Mahratta War 1817-18 ; Lieut. 1/29th N.I. Adjt. Mainpuri Inf. Levy

1819-23. Transfd. to newly-raised 1/33rd N.I. (became 65th) 1823; Adjt. do. 1 Oct. 1823 till 22 Feb. 1826. Comdd. Agra Provl. Bn. 22 Aug. 1829 till 1 July 1831, when disbanded. Offg. Dy. Paymr. at Agra 29 Oct. 1832 till 24 Feb. 1835. Comdt. Delhi Palace Gds. 28 Mar. 1836 till Aug. 1839. Apptd. Paymr. to force for China 11 Mar. 1840. First China War 1840-2; Canton (*Lond. Gaz.* 8 Oct. 1841), on staff of Sir H. Gough; capture of Amoy; Chinhae; Ningpo; Chin-kiang Foo; investment of Nankin (Medal). Directed to remain in China as Paymr. 1 Apr. 1843. Posted Lt. Col. to 30th N.I. Sept. 1845. First Sikh War; Aliwal; Lt. Col. 30th N.I., comdg. 10th Inf. Bde. (Medal). Transfd. to 48th N.I.; to 65th N.I. Aug. 1847; to 41st N.I. Jan. 1850; to 14th N.I. Feb. 1854. Fur. p.a. 24 Feb. 1850 till 29 Oct. 1852. Bdr. 2 cl. comdg. Multan 4 May 1853 till 27 Feb. 1856. Fur. s.c. 30 Nov. 1855 till death. Col. 65th N.I. May 1855 till death. C.B. 24 Dec. 1842. Edited the *Delhi Gazette*, c. 1837-9.

Refs.: Boase. *G.M.* 1857, ii. 570.

WILSON, Thomas (1779-1856). Lieut. General, C.B. Colonel 2nd N.I. *b.* 13 Mar. 1779. Cadet 1795. Arrived in India 26 Sept. 1796. Ensign 9 Dec. 1796. Lieut. 17 Dec. 1797. Capt. 30 Dec. 1807. Major 1 July 1819. Lt. Col. 1 May 1824. Col. 13 Dec. 1830. Maj. Gen. 28 June 1838. Lt. Gen. 11 Nov. 1851. *d.* Fronderw, Llanrwst, co. Denbigh, 2 Apr. 1856.

Of Beaurepaire. *bapt.* Scone, Perth, 14 Mar. 1779. 2nd son of Rev. Charles Wilson, D.D., minister of Scone 1777-81, afterwards professor of church history at St. Andrews, and Elizabeth his wife, dau. of Rev. Thomas Stark, of Ballindean, minister of Balmerino. Cousin-german of Thomas Barron, *q.v.*, and of Harry Stark, *q.v.* St. Andrews Univ.; matric. 21 Feb. 1793.

Services: Posted Ensign to 2nd Bengal Eur. Regt. 1796. d.d. 5th N.I. 1800; Lieut. 1/10th N.I. in 1801. Adjt. 1/10th N.I. and A.D.C. to Maj.-Gen. Hon. F. St. John, H.M.S., 1804. Second Mahratta War; Aligarh; Delhi; Laswari (India medal). Transfd. to newly-raised 2/26th N.I. as Adjt. 1805. Capt. Lt. 2/26th N.I. 2 May 1805. Operations in Bundelkhand 1807; Sehlehuganj (w.)[1]; Capt. Lt. 2/26th N.I. Operations in Bundelkhand against Lachman Dawa 1809; Rajaoli; Capt. 2/26th N.I., actg. Staff Ofr. to Lt.-Col. James Lawtie, *q.v.* Civil architect in Rohilkhand in 1813; do. Bengal and B. & O. 6 Nov. 1813 till 4 Dec. 1814, when he rejoined 2/26th N.I. for service. Nepal War 1814-15; Capt. 2/26th N.I., with L.I. Bn. (clasp to India medal). Operations against Bhattis of Hariana 1818; Capt. 2/26th N.I. Fur. s.c.

2 Dec. 1821 till 9 Dec. 1825. Posted Lt. Col. to 31st N.I. May 1824.
Siege and capture of Bhurtpore (*Lond. Gaz.* 12 June, 7 Oct. 1826);
Lt. Col. 31st N.I., comdg. a detachment (clasp to India medal).
Transfd. to 28th N.I. 1826; to 59th N.I. 12 Jan. 1829. Col. 2nd
N.I. 7 Jan. 1831 till death. Fur. s.c. 8 Aug. 1826 till 31 Aug. 1831,
and 4 Oct. 1831 till death. C.B. 2 Jan. 1827.
Refs.: Scott's *Fasti*, vii. 432. Boase. *G.M.* 1856, i. 550.
[1] *Note*: Granted a wound pension on 4 May 1826, retrospective from 25 Dec. 1811.

WILSON, Thomas (1776/77-1824). Lieutenant. Engineers.
b. 1776/77.[1] Cadet 1797. Arrived in India 7 Sept. 1798. Ensign 13 Jan. 1801. Lieut. 10 May 1807. Retired 4 Mar. 1808.
d. Petrograd 15 Oct. 1824.
Of Haydon Sq., Trinity Minories, London.
Services: Fur. 2 Apr. 1805 till retirement. N.F.P.
[1] *Note*: Swears on 19 Jan. 1798, that he was above 21 and under 22 yrs. of age.

*WILSON, William (*d.* 1785). Cadet. Infantry. Subsequently Sergt. Major. Cadet 1778. *bur.* Calcutta 13 Nov. 1785.
Services: Was Sergt. Maj. 2/30th N.I. at Chunar in Nov. 1783, when he wrote to the Board at Calcutta:—" In 1778 I had the honour of being nominated a Cadet for this Est., but from a dispute with my friends I very imprudently resigned the appt. in Apr. 1779, much against the advice of Sir Jacob Wilkinson, of Abchurch Lane, London, who took particular pains to prevent my doing it—I enlisted as a Private; arrived Apr. 1780." Was Sergt. Maj. of Supernumeraries at death.

WILSON, William (1784-1831). Lieut. Colonel, 31st N.I. *b.* Wapping 30 June 1784. Cadet 1799. Arrived in India 11 Dec. 1800. Ensign 27 Jan. 1800. Lieut. 22 Aug. 1800. Capt. 16 Dec. 1814. Major 1 May 1824. Lt. Col. 21 Jan. 1826. *d.* at sea 23 May 1831, on board the *Catherine*, on his passage to England.
bapt. St. Paul's Shadwell, 31 Aug. 1784. Son of William Wilson, of Wapping Walls, coal factor, and Ann his wife. Nephew of George Wilson, of Walthamstow. *m.* (?) His dau. *m.* Alban Thomas Davies, *q.v.*
Services: Posted to 2/16th N.I. 15 Apr. 1801. (? Second Mahratta War 1803; Agra; Laswari; Lieut. 2/16th N.I.) Capture of Gohad 1806; Lieut. 2/16th N.I. Operations in Bundelkhand 1809-10; Lieut. 2/16th N.I. Capt. Lt. 4 Aug. 1811. (? Capture

of Java 1811; Capt. Lt. 2/16th N.I.) Qmr. Javanese Corps 13 Feb. 1812. Transfd. to newly-raised 2/29th N.I. 1815. Fur. s.c. 21 Nov. 1818 till 12 Nov. 1821. Tempy. comd. Benares Provl. Bn. 8 Sept. 1823; transfd. to 58th N.I. (late 2/29th) May 1824; in charge of Native Invalid Bn. at Chunar 10 Nov. 1824 till 11 June 1825; comdd. newly-raised 11th Extra Regt. 21 May 1825 till reduced 1826. Posted Lt. Col. to 57th N.I. 1826; to 31st N.I. 1828. Fur. s.c. 9 May 1831.

Refs.: *G.M.* 1831, i. 477. Will dated 1 Jan. 1831; proved 8 May 1832.

WILSON, William Feuilleteau (1785-1821). Captain, Invalid Est. 5th N.I. *b.* London 21 June 1785. Cadet 1803. Arrived in India 27 Sept. 1804. Ensign 20 Sept. 1804. Lieut. 21 Sept. 1804. Capt. 1 Jan. 1819. Invalided 30 Dec. 1820. *d.* Chunar 2 July 1821.

bapt. Marylebone 20 July 1785. Son of Richard Wilson and Margaret his wife. Ward of William Feuilleteau. *m.* Sourabaya, Java, 5 Jan. 1815, Olymphia Maria, dau. of S. J. Bouberg.

Services: Posted Lieut. to 5th N.I. 1805. Capture of Java 1811; Lieut. 7th (L.I.) Vol. Bn. With L.I. Vol. Bn. 1812-16. Capture of Jokyakarta 1812; Lieut. L.I. Vol. Bn. Qmr. of Javanese Corps and S.A.C.G. at Jokyakarta in 1815. Lieut. 1/5th N.I.; transfd. to 2/5th N.I. 1817.

Refs.: A.J. xiii. 96. Will dated 29 Mar. 1811; proved 12 July 1821. M.I. old cemetery below Chunar fort.

WILSON, William McMurdo (1792-1814). Lieutenant, 26th N.I. *bapt.* Dumfries 17 June 1792. Cadet 1808. Admitted 26 Oct. 1809. Ensign 8 July 1810. Lieut. 16 Dec. 1814. *d.* Jampta, nr. Nahan, 27 Dec. 1814: kld. in action.

Son of William Wilson, grocer, and Isabella his wife.

Services: Barasat C.C. till Jan. 1811. Posted to 2/26th N.I. 4 Sept. 1810; attached to L.I. Bn. Oct. 1814. Nepal War 1814; Kalanga; Jaithak (kld.) [1]; Lieut. 2/26th N.I., with L.I. Bn. in 2nd Div.

Refs.: *De Rhé-Philipe.* M.I. at Nahan.

[1] *Note:* See note to Thomas Thackeray.

WILTON, George (1763-1833). Lieut. Colonel. 18th N.I. *b.* 1763. Country Cadet 1778. Admitted 29 Sept. 1778. Ensign 27 Mar. 1779. Lieut. 30 Jan. 1781. Capt. 30 Oct. 1797. Major 30 Sept. 1803. Lt. Col. 14 Nov. 1805. Retired 13 Sept. 1809. *d.* London 27 Apr. 1833, aged 70.

Younger son of Joseph Wilton, of Snaresbrook, Essex, and of Hammersmith, Middlesex, the sculptor (*D.N.B.*), and Frances his wife, reputed dau. of Lord Orford (Sir Robert Walpole). His sister *m.* Sir Robert Chambers, Kt., C.J. Bengal (*D.N.B.*). *m.* Calcutta 28 Sept. 1793, Miss Margaret Simpson. (She died 26 July 1859, aged 84.) Father of George Robert Wilton and Thomas Collins Wilton, and uncle of George Wilton, *qq.v.*

Services: Apptd. Cadet 29 Sept. 1778; posted Ensign to 17th Bn. Sepoys 14 July 1779. Served in Khairabad district, U.P., 1779; afterwards in the Mahratta country against Sindhia. Adjt. 23rd N.I. A.D.C. to Warren Hastings 1782-5; afterwards to Sir John Macpherson and Lord Cornwallis. Adjt. 10th Bn. Sepoys in July 1787; Adjt. & Qmr. 2nd Bde. Sepoys 31 Oct. 1787 till 1795; Adjt. 20th Bn. 1795. Asst. to John Hutchinson, *q.v.*, Regulating Ofr. of the Jaghirdar institution at Patna, 1795 till 18 May 1801, when he succeeded him till Feb. 1807. Capt. and Major Bengal Eur. Regt. Posted Lt. Col. to 2/18th N.I. in 1805. Fur. 23 Feb. 1807 till retirement.

Refs.: Family information. *E.I.M.C.* i. 238-9. *A.J.* N.S. xi. 96. *G.M.* 1833, i. 563. M.I. Holy Trinity, Marylebone.

WILTON, George (1794-1817). Ensign, Engineers. *b.* Wooler, Northumberland, 4 May 1794. Cadet 1810. Ensign 7 Dec. 1812. *d.* Rangpur, Bengal, 24 Apr. 1817.

bapt. Wooler 11 Oct. 1794. Son of Rev. William Joseph Wilton, of Newcastle-on-Tyne (who was elder brother of George Wilton, *q.v.*), and Mary his wife. Addiscombe Cadet 1810.

Services: Suptg. works at Ichapur, and actg. Adjt. Corps of Engrs. in 1816. No record of active service.

Refs.: Family information.

WILTON, George Robert (1796-1845). Major, Invalid Est. 4th N.I. *b.* Bankipore, B. & O., 6 Nov. 1796. Cadet 1811. Admitted 20 Mar. 1813. Ensign (?) Lieut. 16 Dec. 1814. Capt. 25 June 1826. Major 16 Apr. 1844. Invalided 31 Mar. 1845. *d.* at sea 19 Aug. 1845, on board the *Madagascar.*

bapt. Bankipore 16 Feb. 1797. Son of George Wilton, *q.v.*, and Margaret his wife. Brother of Thomas Collins Wilton, *q.v.*

Services: Nepal War 1814-15; Lieut. 2/1st N.I., in 1st Div. Siege and capture of Hathras 1817; Lieut. 2/1st N.I. Third Mahratta War 1817-19; Dhamoni; Asirgarh; Lieut. 2/1st N.I. Transfd. to 4th N.I. (late 2/1st) May 1824; actg. Adjt. do. 23 June 1824; actg. Intr. & Qmr. do. 2 Aug. 1826 and 10 Feb. 1827. Operations against the Bhils 1824. Fur. s.c. 17 Aug. 1845.

WILTON, Thomas Collins (1803-1841). Captain, Invalid Est. 38th N.I. *b.* Bhagulpur, B. & O., 7 Oct. 1803. Cadet 1819. Admitted 14 June 1820. Ensign 10 Jan. 1820. Lieut. 11 July 1823. Capt. 22 Sept. 1836. Invalided 25 Sept. 1837. *d.* Delhi 21 May 1841.
Son of George Wilton, *q.v.*, and Margaret his wife. Brother of George Robert Wilton, *q.v.*
Services: Posted Ensign to 2/15th N.I.; transfd. to 19th N.I. July 1823; to 38th N.I. (late 1/19th) May 1824. (? Operations against the Kols 1832; Lieut. 38th N.I.)

WINBOLT, William (*d.* 1804). Bt. Captain, Artillery. (279) Cadet (Inf.) 1783. Admitted 16 Oct. 1783. Ensign (Inf.) 6 Feb. 1785. Fireworker (Art.) 6 Feb. 1789. Lieut. 5 Dec. 1794. Capt. Lt. 1 Mar. 1803. Bt. Capt. 8 Jan. 1798. *d.* 24 Aug. 1804: drowned in Banas R. during Monson's retreat.
(*Perhaps* son of Gale Winbolt, Accountant and Sec. at East India House, and Sarah his wife.)
Services: Apptd. Cadet 20 Nov. 1782; sailed for India in the *Atlas* 11 Mar. 1783. Third Mysore War 1790-2; Satiyamangalam (w.); Seringapatam; Lieut. F. 3rd Coy. 2nd Bn. Served in Ceylon 1795-?; Lieut. 5th Coy. 1st Bn. Second Mahratta War 1803-4; Shikohabad Sept. 1803 (w.); taken prisoner on capitulation of the garr.; sent to Cawnpore; Monson's retreat (kld.); Capt. Lt. 2nd Coy. 1st Bn.
Refs.: Pester, pp. 157, 159, 161. Intestate; admon. 26 Jan. 1805.

WINCH, William (1780-1806). Captain, 1st N.I. *b.* London 22 Feb. 1780. Cadet 1795. Arrived in India 15 Feb. 1797. Ensign 13 Oct. 1796. Lieut. 30 Oct. 1797. Capt. 15 Dec. 1804. *d. unm.* Supa, Bundelkhand, 3 Aug. 1806.
bapt. St. Andrew Undershaft, London, 19 Mar. 1780. Son of William Winch, of 38 St. Mary Axe, London, and Elizabeth his wife.
Services: Lieut. 1st N.I. in 1798. Second Mahratta War; operations in Bundelkhand 1804-6; Capt. 1/1st N.I.
Refs.: Will dated Jhansi 3 Oct. 1805; proved 23 Sept. 1806.

***WINCLEBECK, Theodore** (1729/30-1760). Ensign, Bengal Eur. Regt. *b.* Basle, Switzerland, 1729/30. Cadet 1758. Ensign (?) *d.* Masimpur, nr. Patna, 9 Feb. 1760: kld. in action.
Services: Sailed for India in the *Prince George* May 1758, aged

28. War with Shah Alam 1760; battle of Masimpur (kld.); Ensign Bengal Eur. Regt.

Refs.: Innes, p. 112.

WINDSOR, Charles (1808/09-1842). Bt. Captain, 53rd N.I. *b*. 1808/09.[1] Cadet 1826. Arrived in India 15 Aug. 1827. Ensign 7 Jan. 1827. Lieut. 13 Sept. 1834. Bt. Capt. 7 Jan. 1842. *d.* Jalalabad, Afghanistan, 17 June 1842.

Services: Posted Ensign to 30th N.I. 19 June 1827; transfd. to 53rd N.I. 1827; actg. Adjt. do. 4 Oct. 1834. Fur. p.a. 1 Sept. 1837 till 10 Aug. 1840. First Afghan War 1842; Bt. Capt. 53rd N.I., with Pollock's force.

Refs.: *G.M.* 1843, i. 554. M.I. Afghan Memorial Church, Bombay.

[1] *Note:* Aged 17 when passed for Cadet on 19 Dec. 1826.

WINFIELD, James Stainbank (1797-1842). Captain. 47th N.I. *b.* Chester 8 Jan. 1797. Cadet 1813. Admitted 21 Oct. 1814. Ensign (16 Dec. 1814) 15 July 1815. Lieut. 12 Oct. 1817. Capt. 20 Apr. 1833. Retired 15 Dec. 1838. *d.* Lancaster 19 Feb. 1842.

bapt. St. Oswald's, Chester, 20 June 1797. Son of Rev. James Winfield, of Chester, and Martha his wife. *m.* 1st, Residency House, Kumarkhali, 12 Jan. 1825, Eliza Maria, eldest sister of Sir John Larkins Cheese Richardson, *q.v.* (She died 22 June 1828.) *m.* 2nd, Saugor 12 Nov. 1830, Sophia Mary, widow of Cosby Burrowes, *q.v.* (She died 10 June 1899, aged 91.)

Services: Posted to 19th N.I. 1814. Nepal War 1814-15; capture of Almora (*Lond. Gaz.* 16 Nov. 1815); Ensign 19th N.I. Transfd. to 1/24th N.I. 1815. Third Mahratta War 1817-18; Ensign 1/24th N.I. Intr. & Qmr. 2nd Ceylon Vol. Bn. 13 Oct. 1818 till 18 May 1819. Transfd. to 47th N.I. (late 1/24th) May 1824; Adjt. do. 17 June till Nov. 1824, when it mutinied at Barrackpore. Transfd. to newly-raised 69th N.I. (became 47th in 1828) Nov. 1824; Adjt. do. Nov. 1824 till 18 Sept. 1826. Comdt. Reformed Bhopal Contingent of Horse and Foot 21 July 1826 till retirement.

Refs.: *A.J.* N.S. xxxvii. 263. *G.M.* 1842, i. 451. Will dated 10 Sept. 1841 (P.C.C. 5 Apr. 1842); proved in Calcutta 26 May 1843.

WINGFIELD, Watkin (1803-1886). Lieutenant. 10th L.C. *b.* 7 June 1803. Cadet 1822. Arrived in India 13 Jan. 1824. Cornet 21 May 1823. Lieut. 13 May 1825. Retired 6 June 1835. *d.* 65 Chester Sq., London, 23 Sept. 1886.

bapt. Ruabon 16 Aug. 1803. 2nd son of Rev. Rowland Wingfield, of Rhysnant, co. Montgomery, vicar of Ruabon, co. Denbigh, and Margaret his wife, only dau. and heir of Clopton Prhys, of Llandrinio Hall, co. Montgomery. *m.* Anna Hester, 2nd dau. of Felix Vaughan Smith. (She died London 3 Feb. 1902.) Ed. Rugby; admitted 1814.

Services: Ensign 23rd Madras N.I. 27 Apr. 1822; transfd. to Bengal Cav. 21 May 1823; d.d. 2nd L.C. 30 Jan. 1824; Intr. & Qmr. do. 1 July 1824. Transfd. to newly-raised 2nd Extra Cav. (became 10th L.C.) 17 June 1825. Siege and capture of Bhurtpore; Lieut. 10th L.C. (India medal). Adjt. 10th L.C. 25 Nov. 1826; do. G.G.B.G. 23 Mar. 1827 till 15 Nov. 1831. Leave s.c. to China and St. Helena 4 Sept. 1828 till 30 May 1830; fur. p.a. 13 Jan. 1833 till retirement.

Refs.: Burke's *Landed Gentry*, 13th edn., p. 1914, *s.n.* Wingfield, of Onslow, Salop. *V.B.G. Rugby School Register. The Times*, 24 Sept. 1886.

WINGRAVE, John Hanmer (*d.* 1799). Bt. Captain, 15th N.I. Country Cadet 1781. Admitted 24 May 1781. Ensign 26 Sept. 1781. Lieut. 30 June 1783. Bt. Capt. 7 Jan. 1796. *d. unm.* 13 Dec. 1799, on board the *Guide* pilot schooner at Diamond Harbour.

Services: Lieut. 23rd Bn. Sepoys in July 1787; transfd. to 6th Bengal Eur. Bn. 24 Oct. 1792; to 6th Bn. Sepoys 21 Sept. 1793. Fur. s.c. Dec. 1799.

Refs.: Will dated Chunar 9 Oct. 1799; proved 16 Jan. 1800.

*WINKLE, William (*d.* 1763). Cornet, 1st Troop of Horse. Cadet (?) Cornet (?) *d. unm.* Calcutta Aug. 1763.

Services: N.F.P.

Refs.: Will dated Calcutta 20 Aug. 1763; proved 26 Aug. 1763.

WINSTON, John (1785-1808). Lieutenant, 10th N.I. *bapt.* All Saints, Hereford, 7 Sept. 1785. Cadet 1800. Arrived in India 19 Aug. 1801. Ensign 12 Oct. 1801. Lieut. 30 Sept. 1803. *d.* Calcutta 30 June 1808.

Son of John Winston and Mary his wife. *m.* Meerut 27 Dec. 1806, Mary, 2nd dau. of Sir Dyson Marshall, *q.v.* (*See also* Christopher D'Oyley Aplin.) (She *re-m.* William James (1785-1855), *q.v.*)

Services: Ensign d.d. 13th N.I. in 1802. Posted Ensign to 10th N.I. Second Mahratta War 1805-6; Lieut. 10th N.I. Adjt. 2/10th N.I. 1807 till death.

WINTER, Francis (1805-1893). Major. 59th N.I. *b.* Agher Pallas (Agherpallis), co. Meath, 24 Nov. 1805. Cadet 1821. Arrived in India 25 June 1822. Ensign 19 Jan. 1822. Lieut. 25 Nov. 1824. Capt. 1 Dec. 1837. Retired 31 Mar. 1848. Hon. Major 28 Nov. 1854. *d.* 17 May 1893.

4th son of John Pratt Winter, of Agher, of the Irish Bar, and Anne his wife, youngest dau. of Capt. Arthur Gore, E.I.C.S. His cousin-german *m.* Charles Gustavus Walsh, *q.v. m.* 18 Apr. 1850, Anna Julia, eldest dau. of Col. John Caulfeild, of Bloomfield, co. Westmeath, and niece of James Caulfeild, *q.v.* (She died 29 Jan. 1909.)

Services : Posted Ensign to 30th N.I. 1822; transfd. to 59th N.I. (late 1/30th) May 1824. First Burma War; Arakan 1825; Lieut. 2nd L.I. Bn. (India medal). Actg. Intr. & Qmr. 2nd L.I. Bn. 30 Sept. 1825; do. 11th N.I. 27 July 1829; do. 54th N.I. 14 Aug. 1830. Offg. Fort Adjt. Allahabad 29 Oct. 1831. Intr. & Qmr. 59th N.I. 3 Apr. 1832 till 25 Jan. 1834. Fur. p.a. 13 Jan. 1834 till 13 June 1837. Bde. Major 3rd Inf. Bde., Army of Reserve (for Afghanistan) 14 Oct. 1842; D.A.Q.M.G. 2nd Div. do. 9 Nov. 1842 till Jan. 1843. Actg. 2nd in comd. Jodhpur Legion 8 Apr. 1843; Legion Staff Capt., Bundelkhand Legion, 13 June 1844; Comdt. 3rd Inf. Regt., N.W.F. Bde., 14 Dec. 1846 till 1848.

Refs.: Burke's *Landed Gentry of Ireland*, p. 774, *s.n.* Winter, of Agher, co. Meath. Burke's *Colonial Gentry*, ii. 793. Burke's *Peerage*, 1923, p. 486, *s.n.* Charlemont, V.

WINTLE, Edmund (1800-1881). Major General. 24th N.I. *b.* Jessore, Bengal, Nov. 1800. Cadet 1818. Admitted 27 Mar. 1820. Ensign 20 Sept. 1819. Lieut. 25 Apr. 1822. Capt. 5 Feb. 1835. Major 9 July 1846. Lt. Col. 10 July 1852. Bt. Col. 28 Nov. 1854. Retired 31 Dec. 1861. Hon. Maj. Gen. 31 Dec. 1861. *d.* 29 Royal Cresc., Bath, 8 Apr. 1881.

bapt. Bhagulpur Sept. 1802. Son of James Wintle, B.C.S., senior judge of the court of appeal and circuit, Calcutta, afterwards of Cheltenham, later of Lansdown Cresc., Bath, and Sarah Jennings his 2nd wife. Brother of Henry Wintle, *q.v. m.* Chunar 20 Oct. 1824, Miss Frances Wilkinson, 2nd dau. of Capt. J. B. Wilkinson, H.M.S. (She died 24 Sept. 1889, aged 82.) St. John's Coll., Camb. Lincoln's Inn; admitted 12 Mar. 1819.

Services : Posted to 2/21st N.I.; transfd. to 41st N.I. (late 1/21st) May 1824. Actg. Fort Adjt. Monghyr 4 Sept. 1824. Transfd. to newly-raised 3rd Extra Regt. (became 71st N.I.) May 1825; Adjt. do. 20 Aug. 1828 till 18 July 1832. Offg. Bde. Major Mhow 7 Dec.

1838; do. Meywar F.F. 29 Mar. 1839; attached to 1st Bde. Inf. for field service in Marwar 5 Aug. till Oct. 1839. Comdt. 4th Depot Bn. at Bareilly 4 Mar. 1842 till broken up 1 Mar. 1843. Offg. Bde. Major Barrackpore 25 Nov. 1843; actg. 2nd Asst. Sec., Mily. Board, 1845; Bde. Major in Rohilkhand 4 Mar. till 24 July 1846. Second Sikh War; Jullundur Doab 1848-9; Major 71st N.I., with force under Bdr. Wheeler (Medal). Fur. s.c. 10 Feb. 1850 till Feb. 1853. Posted Lt. Col. to 8th N.I. Sept. 1852; to 65th N.I. Mar. 1853; to 39th N.I. Nov. 1853; to 29th N.I. Aug. 1854; to 24th N.I. 18 May 1856 till retirement. Fur. s.c. 10 Jan. 1856 till 10 Jan. 1859, and 1860 till retirement.

Refs.: Boase. *The Times*, 14 Apr. 1881.

WINTLE, Henry (1807-1826). 2nd Lieutenant, Artillery. (570) *b.* Calcutta 29 Aug. 1807. Cadet 1824. 2nd Lieut. 16 Dec. 1824. *d.* Dum-Dum 5 May 1826.

bapt. Calcutta 12 Jan. 1809. 4th son of James Wintle, of Lansdown Cresc., Bath, B.C.S., and Sarah Jennings his 2nd wife. Brother of Edmund Wintle, *q.v.* Addiscombe Cadet 1823-5.

Services: No record of active service.

Refs.: G.M. 1826, ii. 647. M.I. at Dum-Dum.

WINTOUR, Charles Henry (1802-1834). Captain, 53rd N.I. *b.* Clewer, Berks., 8 Apr. 1802. Cadet 1817. Admitted 5 Sept. 1818. Ensign 21 Apr. 1818. Lieut. 16 Dec. 1818. Capt. 10 Apr. 1831. *d.* Dacca 13 Sept. 1834.

bapt. Clewer 14 May 1802. Son of Henry Wintour and Mildred his wife. *m.* Calcutta 25 Apr. 1832, Miss Caroline Nisbet Verner, sister of Charles Farquhar Trower, *q.v.* (She died 5 Jan. 1885, aged 70.) Addiscombe Cadet 1816-17.

Services: Posted Lieut. to 15th N.I.; transfd. to 2/27th N.I. 24 Mar. 1820; Intr. & Qmr. do. 1 Nov. 1822. Offg. Fort Adjt. at Allahabad 17 Apr. 1823. Transfd. to 53rd N.I. (late 1/27th) May 1824; actg. Intr. & Qmr. do. 4 Nov. 1824; Adjt. do. 2 Nov. 1825; Intr. & Qmr. do. 25 July 1827 till 1831. d.d. 31st N.I. 4 May till 1 Oct. 1832. No record of active service.

Refs.: A.J. N.S. xvi. 196. M.I. Dacca cemetery.

WINWOOD, John Jones [1] (*d.* 1791). Lieutenant, 14th Bn. Sepoys. Cadet 1776. Ensign 4 Mar. 1777. Lieut. 2 Aug. 1778. *bur.* Madras 18 Oct. 1791.

Related to Richard Kinchant. (*Probably* son of Ralph Winwood, *q.v.*)

Services: "Eldest Cadet," apptd. 25 Oct. 1775; sailed for

India in the *Nassau* 9 Jan. 1776. Lieut. 1/2nd Bengal Eur. Regt. in Oct. 1779. Campaign against the Rajah of Benares 1781. Lieut. 14th Bn. Sepoys in July 1787. Third Mysore War 1790-1; Arikera; Lieut. 14th Bn.

Refs.: Intestate; admon. 15 Dec. 1791.

¹ *Note*: His second name appears as ' Jones ' in Cadet appts. and in admon. of his estate, as ' James ' in *D. & M.* and in MS. *A.L.* of 1 July 1787. In the burial register of St. Mary's, Madras, his initials (J. J.) merely are given.

WINWOOD, Ralph (*d. c.* 1800). Lieut. Colonel. Artillery. (8) Cadet (?) Fireworker 10 Nov. 1757. 2nd Lieut. 19 Sept. 1758. Lieut. 11 Dec. 1758. Capt. Lt. 26 May 1760. Capt. 2 Nov. 1761. Major 23 Dec. 1765. Lt. Col. (4 Sept. 1768) 6 Nov. 1769. Resigned 21 Sept. 1770. *d.* in England *c.* 1800.

m. 1st, Madras 15 Aug. 1756, Eleanor Wood. (She died Calcutta 22 Sept. 1766, aged 22 [*sic*].) *m.* 2nd, Calcutta 2 July 1770, Elizabeth Quinchant, only dau. of Capt. Jean Jenvre Quienchant, and widow of Rev. William Parry, chaplain Bengal. (She died *c.* 1800.)

Services: Assault on Chunar fort Dec. 1764; Capt. 2nd Coy. Art. Apptd to comd. 2nd Coy. Art., attached to 2nd Eur. Regt., 5 Aug. 1765. Comdt. Bengal Art. Mar. 1766 till Mar. 1768, when he returned to England. Apptd. by C.D. in England, 8 Feb. 1769, Bt. Lt. Col., next below Matthew Leslie, *q.v.*, and to succeed to comd. of the Art. when it becomes vacant; sailed for India in the *Anson* 22 Mar. 1769.

Note: Both *D. & M.* and *Stubbs* give him the rank of Major (19 Oct. 1765) and Lt. Col. (4 Sept. 1768) in the Inf. in addition to his rank in the Art. At date of resignation he appears to have been Lt. Col. in 1/1st Bengal Eur. Regt.

Refs.: *Quienchant vel Quinchant vel Kinchant*, by Maj.-Gen. J. C. Kinchant, privately printed, London, 1917.

WISE, William (1800-1845). Captain, 29th N.I. *b.* 6 Jan. 1800. Cadet 1820. Admitted 10 Sept. 1821. Ensign 14 Feb. 1821. Lieut. 11 July 1823. Capt. 4 July 1836. *d.* Dinajpur, Bengal, 6 Dec. 1845.

bapt. Dundee 10 Feb. 1800. Son of Thomas Wise, of Hillbank, and of Clearmount, Jamaica, and Ann Chalmers his wife.

Services: Was already in India when apptd. Cadet. Posted Ensign to 1/18th N.I. (? Operations in Jodhpur 1823; Lamba; Ensign 1/18th N.I.) Transfd. as Lieut. to 14th N.I. July 1823; to 29th N.I. (late 2/14th) May 1824; actg. Adjt. do. 16 Aug. 1825 and 22 June 1830. Fur. p.a. 16 Dec. 1831 till 29 Feb. 1836. Tempy.

THE BENGAL ARMY, 1758-1834

comdg. 2nd Regt. Oudh Local Inf. 19 May 1841; offg. Fort Adjt. Ft. Wm., and Supt. Gent. Cadets, 10 Sept. 1842. Fur. u.p.a. without pay 12 Aug. 1843 till 27 Sept. 1844.

WISHART, Thomas (1784-1817). Lieutenant, 5th N.I. *b.* St. Andrews, Fife, 31 Jan. 1784. Cadet 1804. Arrived in India 13 May 1806. Ensign 3 Feb. 1806. Lieut. 2 Feb. 1807. *d.* Delhi 28 May 1817.

bapt. St. Andrews 8 Feb. 1784. Son of John Wishart, of St. Andrews, merchant, and Anne Armit his wife. Brother of Anne, wife of Mr. Arnott, farmer, of Elphinstone Pl.

Services : Served for some time with a corps in H.M.S.; probably an Ofr. of Mil. or Fenc. Barasat C.C. till 1 Feb. 1807. Posted Lieut. to 1/5th N.I. Feb. 1807. Operations against Gopal Singh 1810; Tirowa. Operations in Baghelkhand 1813-14; Entauri; Lieut. 1/5th N.I., with Rewah F.F.

Refs. : De Rhé-Philipe. Will dated 28 May 1817; proved 20 June 1817. M.I. in old cemetery nr. P.O., Delhi.

WITCHCOT, George. Captain. Comdt. 5th Bn. Sepoys. Capt. 25 June 1763. Resigned 17 Feb. 1765.

m. (in England before 1761) Mary.

Services : Ensign H.M. 31st Ft. 14 Apr. 1756; Lieut. 2nd Bn. 31st Ft. 30 Sept. 1757; Capt. 84th Ft. 30 June 1760. Sailed for Calcutta in 1761. Exchanged with John Freake, *q.v.*, into Bengal Army in June 1763; comdd. Troop of Eur. Hrs. 1763; raised 17th Bn. Sepoys at Burdwan Oct. 1763. This Bn., which became 5th in 1764, 7th N.I. May 1824, mutinied at Dinapore 25 July 1857. For the sum of Rs. 10,000 he resigned the Service in Feb. 1765 in favour of Capt. William Macpherson, Bo. Est., *q.v.* This roused a protest on the part of the Bengal Ofrs., several of whom were tried by C.M. in May 1765.

Refs. : Williams, p. 93. *Cardew*, pp. 22, 23.

Note : His christian name is given as George in Court Minutes of 29 Apr. 1761, Brit. *A.L.* 1763, and in Orders of 17 Feb. 1765; as Thomas in *D. & M.*

WITHERSTON(E), John (1752/53-1830). Lieut. Colonel. Infantry. *b.* 1752/53. Cadet 1768. Arrived in India 12 Apr. 1770. Ensign 19 Sept. 1769. Lieut. 13 Mar. 1773. Capt. 10 Jan. 1781. Major 1 Mar. 1794. Lt. Col. 25 Apr. 1797. Retired 25 Oct. 1797. *d.* Bexhill, Sussex, 27 Apr. 1830, aged 77.

m. (before 1790) ?

Services : Apptd. Cadet Oct. 1768; sailed for India in the *Prince of*

Wales 24 Mar. 1769. Ordered to Allahabad with one of the Nawab-Wazir of Oudh's Bns. 4 Feb. 1773; apptd. to Nawab's Inf. 9 Apr. 1777. Resigned to go home on fur. 19 Nov. 1782; readmitted ——. Capt. 4th Bengal Eur. Bn. in July 1787; comdg. 32nd Bn. Sepoys in Dec. 1788; 33rd Bn. in 1792.

Refs.: A.J. N.S. ii. 119. *G.M.* 1830, i. 477.

Note: This name and the following also appear as Wetherston(e) and Weatherston(e): it is possibly merely a local variant of Watherston(e).

WITHERSTON(E), Robert (*d.* 1806). Lieut. Colonel, 16th N.I. Asst. Surg. 1 July 1774. Country Cadet 1778. Admitted 9 Mar. 1778. Ensign 1778. Struck off list of Asst. Surgeons 3 Nov. 1780. Lieut. 14 Feb. 1779. Capt. 1 June 1796. Major 8 Jan. 1801. Lt. Col. 30 Sept. 1803. *d.* Cawnpore 7 May 1806. Brother of Dalhousie Watherston(e), *q.v.*

Services: Apptd. A.D.C. to Lt.-Col. Thomas Goddard, *q.v.*, 28 June 1778. First Mahratta War 1778-84; Lieut. Inf., with detachment under Col. Goddard. 1/1st Bengal Eur. Regt. in Oct. 1779; apptd. Adjt. of Sepoy Corps in 1st Bde. 28 Apr. 1781. Apptd. A.D.C. to Col. Christian Knudson, *q.v.*, comdg. 4th Bde., 5 July 1786; posted to 34th Bn. Sepoys 15 Dec. 1787. Capt. 8th N.I. Operations in Jumna Doab 1803; Sasni; Bijaigarh; Kachaura; Major 2/8th N.I. Posted Lt. Col. to 1/16th N.I.

Refs.: Crawford, i. 243. *Roll of I.M.S.*, No. B. 202. *Pester*, p. 225. Will dated Barrackpore 22 Sept. 1804 ("I positively direct that my body shall be burned to Ashes."); proved 5 June 1806.

WITTIT, Charles (*d.* 1804). Bt. Lieut. Colonel, Artillery. (166) Country Cadet 1778. Admitted 11 Aug. 1778. Fireworker 22 Sept. 1778. Lieut. 29 Jan. 1781. Capt. 12 Nov. 1791. Major 1 Mar. 1803. Bt. Lt. Col. 25 Sept. 1803. *d.* in camp in Bundelkhand 27 May 1804.

Elder son of James Wittit, of Bartlett's Bldgs., psh. of St. Andrew, Holborn, formerly of Calcutta, merchant. Brother of John Wittit, *q.v.*, and of Rebekah, wife of Dr. Benjamin Lyon, of Holborn. Nephew of Mrs. Mary Wittit, of Stirling.

Services: Fur. 27 Oct. 1785 till 16 Dec. 1789. Third Mysore War; Bangalore; Lieut. 4th Coy., afterwards 5th Coy. 2nd Bn. Art. To Madras Aug.-Oct. 1793 for siege of Pondicherry; Capt. 5th Coy. 3rd Bn. Comdd. 5th Coy. 3rd Bn. sent to Bombay in 1802.

Refs.: G.M. 1804, ii. 1168. Will dated camp in Bundelkhand 7 Nov. 1803; proved 27 June 1804.

THE BENGAL ARMY, 1758-1834

WITTIT, John (*d.* 1795). Lieutenant, Artillery. (226) Country Cadet 1781. Fireworker 27 July 1782. Lieut. 9 July 1788. *d. unm.* Cawnpore 9 Sept. 1795.

Younger son of James Wittit. Brother of Charles Wittit, *q.v.*

Services: Apptd. Cadet 5 Nov. 1781. Lieut. F. 1st Bn. Art. in July 1787. To Madras Aug.-Oct. 1793 for siege of Pondicherry; Lieut. 5th Coy. 3rd Bn., transfd. tempy. from 3rd Coy. 1st Bn.

Refs.: G.M. 1796, i. 442. Will dated 9 Aug. 1793; proved 9 Jan. 1796.

WITTIT, William (*d.* 1779). Fireworker, Artillery. (181) Country Cadet 1778. Fireworker 7 Oct. 1778. *bur.* Calcutta 14 June 1779.

Services: Apptd. Cadet 11 Aug. 1778. N.F.P.

WOLLASTON, Charles (1806-1882). Lieut. Colonel. 8th L.C. *b.* Lincoln 18 Oct. 1806. Cadet 1825. Arrived in India 7 July 1826. Cornet 15 Mar. 1826. Lieut. 1 Feb. 1836. Capt. 21 Nov. 1848. Bt. Major 20 June 1854. Retired 31 Dec. 1854. Hon. Lt. Col. 16 Mar. 1855. *d.* 112 Northgate St., Bury St. Edmunds, 13 Jan. 1882.

bapt. Lincoln 21 Oct. 1806. 3rd son of Rev. Henry John Wollaston, rector of Scotter, Lincs., and Louisa his wife, 2nd dau. of William Symons, of Bury St. Edmunds. Brother of William Wollaston, *q.v. m.* London 11 July 1878, Katharine Maria, eldest dau. of Sir Robert Affleck, of Daleham Hall, Suffolk, 6th Bart. (She died Territet, Switzerland, 26 Jan. 1895.) Exeter Coll., Oxon.; matric. 23 Oct. 1823; Scholar 1823-6.

Services: Cornet d.d. 8th L.C. 26 Sept. 1826; posted to 8th L.C. 1826. Asst. Central Stud 12 Feb. 1835; 2nd Asst. do. 4 Aug. 1841; 1st do. 7 July 1843; Supt. C.P. 16 Aug. 1853; Dy. Supt. N.W.P. May 1854. (? Insurrection in Bundelkhand 1842-3; Bt. Capt. 8th L.C.)

Refs.: Burke's *Landed Gentry*, 13th edn., p. 1922, *s.n.* Wollaston, of Shenton, Leics. *Howard & Crisp*, xviii. 122, *s.n.* Wollaston. Burke's *Peerage*, 1923, p. 76, *s.n.* Affleck, Bart. *Alumni Oxon. The Times*, 18 Jan. 1882. Will dated 26 Oct. 1881; proved (Prin. Reg. 158, 82) 8 Feb. 1882.

WOLLASTON, William (1810-1831). Lieutenant, 57th N.I. *b.* Scotter Parsonage 2 Mar. 1810. Cadet 1825. Arrived in India 4 Sept. 1826. Ensign 15 Apr. 1826. Lieut. 27 Feb. 1829. *d.* Mhow 3 July 1831, of spasmodic cholera.

bapt. Scotter 3 Mar. 1810. 5th son of Rev. Henry John Wollaston and Louisa his wife. Brother of Charles Wollaston, *q.v.*
Services : Posted Ensign to 57th N.I. 5 Oct. 1826. No record of active service. Promoted Lieut. posthumously (G.O. 2 Sept. 1831).
Refs. : Burke's *Landed Gentry*, 13th edn., p. 1922, *s.n.* Wollaston, of Shenton, Leics. *Howard & Crisp,* xviii. 122, *s.n.* Wollaston. *G.M.* 1831, ii. 574. M.I. at Mhow.

***WOLLEN, William Kelly** (1815-1869). Colonel. 19th N.I.
b. Burdwan, Bengal, 26 June (? 17 July) 1815. Cadet 1833. Arrived in India 24 June 1834. Ensign (4 Jan. 1834) 24 June 1834. Lieut. 22 Sept. 1836. Capt. 24 Jan. 1845. Major 26 Aug. 1856. Lt. Col. 12 Dec. 1859. Retired 31 Dec. 1861. Hon. Col. 31 Dec. 1861. *d.* Eleanor Villas, Tollington Pk., Islington, 19 Jan. 1869.
bapt. Calcutta Dec. 1815. Son of William Wollen, B.C.S., judge of the *Diwani Adalat* at Purnea, and Mary his 1st wife, dau. of John Kelly, of Calcutta. *m.* Jullundur 7 June 1852, Maria, dau. of George Cole. Ed. Sherborne; left 1830.
Services : d.d. 33rd N.I. 7 July 1834 ; posted to 19th N.I. 5 Nov. 1834, and served throughout with that Regt. Rising in Cuttack July 1836 ; Ensign 19th N.I. Fur. 21 Feb. 1848 till 1850.
Refs. : *Sherborne School Register.* *The Times,* 22 Jan. 1869.

WOLLOCOMBE, Thomas (1782-1829). Captain, Invalid Est. 65th N.I. *b.* Devon 14 Sept. 1782. Cadet 1801. Arrived in India 22 July 1802. Ensign 7 July 1802. Lieut. 1 Apr. 1804. Capt. 4 Nov. 1817. Invalided 2 Nov. 1827. *d. unm.* Chandernagore, Bengal, 7 Aug. 1829.
bapt. Gt. Torrington, Devon, 1 Sept. 1784. Eldest son of Thomas Stafford Wollocombe, Lt. Col. Unattached, formerly 2nd Ft., Col. Devon Mil., and Mary his wife, dau. of John Hiern, of Torrington.
Services : Posted Lieut. to 14th N.I. 1804. Nepal War 1816 ; Lieut. 5th Gren. Bn., in 2nd Bde. Left Column. Capt. Lt. 1/14th N.I. 1 Mar. 1816. Third Mahratta War 1818 ; Dhamoni ; Mandala ; Garhakota ; Capt. 1/14th N.I., with Left Div. Transfd. to newly-raised 33rd N.I. July 1823 ; to 65th N.I. (late 1/33rd) May 1824.
Refs. : Vivian's *Visitations of Devon*, p. 797, *s.n.* Wollocombe, of Combe. *A.J.* N.S. i. 96. Will dated P.W.I. 30 Sept. 1826 ; proved 18 May 1830.

WOOD, Andrew Hunter (1790-1834). Captain, 15th N.I.
bapt. Maybole, co. Ayr, 5 Aug. 1790. Cadet 1805. Arrived in India 20 July 1807. Ensign 11 July 1807. Lieut. 22 May 1810. Capt. 1 May 1824. *d.* Cawnpore 31 May 1834, of apoplexy.

THE BENGAL ARMY, 1758-1834

Son of William Wood and Anne Hunter his wife. Brother of David Peebles Wood, *q.v.* *m.* Isabella. (She died 23 Dec. 1860, aged 70.)

Services: Barasat C.C. 12 mos. Posted Ensign to 11th N.I. 1808. Reduction of Kalinjar 1812; Lieut. 1/11th N.I. Fur. s.c. 16 June 1814 till 1818. Intr. & Qmr. 2/11th N.I. 1 Mar. 1821 till 17 June 1824. Transfd. to 15th N.I. (late 1/11th) May 1824. Siege and capture of Bhurtpore; Capt. 15th N.I.

Refs.: *A.J.* N.S. xv. 227. *G.M.* 1835, i. 221.

WOOD, Browne (1798-1835). Captain, 10th N.I. *b.* Lewisham, Kent, 7 Mar. 1798. Cadet 1819. Admitted 27 Mar. 1820. Ensign 26 Oct. 1819. Lieut. 11 Jan. 1822. Capt. 2 Oct. 1828. *d.* Barrackpore 29 Aug. 1835.

bapt. Lewisham 15 Apr. 1798. Son of Capt. John William Wood, Comdr. of the *Wycombe* East Indiaman, and Arabella his wife. Brother of Henry John Wood, *q.v.*

Services: Posted Ensign to 1/7th N.I. 1820. With Benares Levy 1820-1; Adjt. do. 6 Jan. 1823. Transfd. to 10th N.I. (late 2/7th) May 1824; Adjt. do. 22 June 1824 till 17 Nov. 1828. Fur. p.a. 1 Apr. 1830 till 18 Nov. 1833. Actg. Agent for family money, and Paymr. of Native pensioners at Barrackpore, 25 June 1835 till death.

Refs.: *A.J.* N.S. xix. 149. M.I. at Barrackpore.

WOOD, David Peebles (1795-1836). Captain, 17th N.I. *b.* 11 May 1795. Cadet 1811. Arrived in India 3 Oct. 1810. Ensign 7 Sept. 1813. Lieut. 28 July 1816. Capt. 15 Oct. 1832. *d.* Edinburgh 29 Mar. 1836.

bapt. Maybole 11 May 1798. Son of William Wood, in Ballony, and Anne Hunter his wife. Brother of Andrew Hunter Wood, *q.v.* Ed. Edinburgh.

Services: Permitted to proceed to Bengal as a passenger, to be apptd. Cadet on attaining age of 16 yrs. (Order of Court 16 Jan. 1810). (? Barasat C.C.) Cadet d.d. 11th N.I. 1811-12; posted Ensign to 1/11th N.I. 1813. Actg. Adjt. Eur. Invalids at Chunar 6 Feb. 1821; offg. Bde. Major Malwa F.F. 19 Nov. 1823, and 8 Sept. 1824. Intr. & Qmr. 1/11th N.I. 27 Jan. 1824; transfd. to 17th N.I. (late 2/11th) May 1824; Intr. & Qmr. do. 17 June 1824 till 2 Aug. 1833. Fur. s.c. 8 Jan. 1835 till death. No record of active service.

Refs.: *A.J.* N.S. xx. 59.

WOOD, Sir George (*d.* 1824). Lieut. General, K.C.B. Colonel 27th N.I. Country Cadet 1771. Admitted 8 Oct. 1771. Ensign 22 May 1773. Lieut. 19 May 1778. Capt. 14 Jan. 1784. Major 30 Oct. 1797. Lt. Col. 29 May 1800. Lt. Col. Comdt. 27 Sept. 1807. Col. 25 Apr. 1808. Maj. Gen. 4 June 1811. Lt. Gen. 19 July 1821. *d.* at his house, Clifford St., London, 1 Mar. 1824.

Of Ottershaw Park, Surrey. 3rd son of Alexander Wood, of Burncroft, co. Perth, J.P. and Procurator Fiscal of Perthshire, and Jean his wife, dau. of Robert Ramsay, of the Ramsays of Banff. Brother of Sir Mark Wood, Bart., *q.v.*, and of Adm. Sir James Atholl Wood, K.C.B. (*D.N.B.*). Cousin-german of Thomas Wood, *q.v.*, and uncle of George Williamson, *q.v.* *m.* Madras 19 Oct. 1810, Frances Vic, dau. of John Remington, of Barton End, Gloucs., D.L. of that co. (She died 7 Mar. 1860, aged 71.)

Services : On service in Rohilkhand 1772-6. First Rohilla War 1774 ; battle of St. George ; Ensign 2nd Bengal Eur. Regt. Employed on survey work in 1777. " Personally employed 1778-9 in comd. on the river below Calcutta on various duties, for which I received some commendation from Govt. ; continued with 3rd Eur. Regt., to which I had been removed in Ft. Wm. till Aug. 1778." (*Autobiog.*) First Mahratta War 1780 ; capture of Lahar, Staff Adjt. ; Gwalior, A.D.C. to Major William Popham, *q.v.* ; capture of Sipri 1781 by Lt.-Col. Camac's force. Apptd. A.Q.M.G. to Camac's detachment 15 Feb. 1781 ; employed in Malwa 1781-2. Capt. 2nd Bn. Sepoys in July 1787 ; Major 2/6th N.I. in July 1798. " Employed 1804-7 with my Bn. (2/19th) for cover of Mirzapur during latter part of Mahratta War." (ib.) Col. 27th N.I. 1808 till death. Fur. 17 Feb. 1808 till 29 Nov. 1810. Capture of Java 1811 ; Cornelis ; Col. comdg. Bengal Div. (Gold medal). Nepal War 1815 ; sent up from Calcutta to take comd. of 4th (Dinapore) Div. abandoned by Bennet Marley, *q.v.* ; took over comd. 19 Feb. Maj. Gen. comdg. Dinapore Div. 1815-16 ; comdg. at Benares 1816-18. Leave to Cape 1816-18 ; fur. 1819 till death. K.C.B. 7 Apr. 1815. Known in the Army as 'the Royal Bengal Tiger.'

Refs. : Memorials of the Woods of Largo, by Mrs. F. M. Montague, privately printed 1863. Burke's *Landed Gentry*, 13th edn., p. 1928, *s.n.* Brodie-Wood, of Keithick, Cupar Angus. *G.M.* 1824, i. 460. Will dated Calcutta 26 Dec. 1818 ; proved 20 Mar. 1827.[1]

[1] *Note :* He left nearly 20 lacs.

WOOD, George (1789-1808). Lieutenant, 13th N.I. *bapt.* St. Columb's, Londonderry, 21 Mar. 1789. Cadet 1804. Arrived in India 6 Apr. 1806. Ensign 6 Apr. 1806. Lieut. 13 June 1807. *d.* Muttra 8 Sept. 1808 : drowned crossing the Jumna R.

THE BENGAL ARMY, 1758-1834

Son of George Wood and Jane his wife.
Services: (? Barasat C.C.) Posted Lieut. to 13th N.I. 1807. No record of active service.

WOOD, George (1799-?). Ensign. 24th N.I. *b.* Manchester 16 Mar. 1799. Cadet 1820. Arrived in India Oct. 1821. Ensign 21 Mar. 1821. Resigned in India 28 Feb. 1823.

bapt. Unitarian chapel, Moseley St., Manchester, 8 May 1799. 3rd son of Ottiwell Wood, of Edge Hill, nr. Liverpool, and Grace his wife, 3rd dau. of Samuel Grundy, of Balderstone, Lancs.
Services: Posted Ensign to 1/24th N.I. 1821. No record of active service.
Refs.: Hunter's *Familiæ Minorum Gentium*, iv. 1225.

WOOD, Henry (1782-1871). Ensign. Engineers. Subsequently B.C.S., Accountant Gen. Calcutta. *b.* 11 Aug. 1782. Cadet 1797. Arrived in India 7 Sept. 1798. Ensign 31 July 1800. Transfd. to B.C.S. 27 Sept. 1804. *d.* Torquay 13 Jan. 1871.

Of Woodhill, in Send, Surrey. *bapt.* Missenden Abbey, Bucks., 14 Sept. 1782. 4th son of Thomas Wood, of Littleton, Middlesex, and Mary his wife, dau. and heir of Sir Edward Williams, of Gwernyfed, co. Brecon, Bart. *m.* Calcutta 7 Oct. 1809, Margaret Elizabeth, dau. of Thomas Templeton, atty. of the supreme court, Calcutta, and niece of Hercules Skinner, *q.v.* (She died Woodhill 18 Sept. 1879, aged 89.)
Services: Apptd. Asst. in Accountant Gen.'s office 20 Nov. 1804. Accountant Gen., a Dir. of the Bank of Bengal, and Member of the Mint and Sinking Fund Committees, 4 Dec. 1822. Retired 1 May 1832.
Refs.: *Howard & Crisp*, xi. 110, *s.n.* Wood. *The Times*, 17 Jan. 1871. Will dated 5 Oct. 1865; proved 25 Feb. 1871.

WOOD, Henry John (1791-1858). Major General, C.B., Artillery. (421) Comdg. Allahabad Bde. *bapt.* Lewisham, Kent, 7 July 1791. Cadet 1809. Fireworker 13 Sept. 1810. Lieut. 25 Sept. 1817. Capt. 30 May 1824. Major 1 Mar. 1841. Lt. Col. 3 July 1845. Col. 25 Feb. 1853. Maj. Gen. 6 Dec. 1856. *d.* suddenly in a rly. stn., Edinburgh, 12 Nov. 1858, aged 68.

Of Croom's Hill, Greenwich. Son of Capt. John William Wood, of Sydenham, Comdr. H.C.S. *Earl of Wycombe* 1792-7, and Arabella his wife. Brother of William Henville Wood, *q.v. m.* Cawnpore 27 July 1818, Margaret, 2nd sister of William Bell, *q.v.* (She died

Rampur Boalia 4 Dec. 1845, aged 51.) Woolwich Cadet ; nominated to R.M.A. 20 May 1807.

Services : Served in Alwar 1813 ; in Java 1814-15 ; Lieut. F. 1st Coy. 2nd Bn. Foot Art. Siege and capture of Hathras 1817 ; Lieut. F. 7th Coy. 3rd Bn., Adjt. & Qmr. Foot Art. Apptd. Bde. Qmr. Foot Art. with Centre Div. 18 Nov. 1817. Third Mahratta War ; Lieut. 7th Coy. 3rd Bn., Bde. Qmr. Adjt. & Qmr. 1st Bn. Art. 18 Apr. 1818 till 23 Nov. 1824. Siege and capture of Bhurtpore ; Capt. comdg. 1st Troop 3rd Bde. H.A. (India medal). To comd. Art., Saugor Div., 30 Dec. 1842. First Sikh War ; Sobraon (Medal) ; Kangra 1846 ; Lt. Col. 6th Bn., comdg. Art. under Bdr. H. M. Wheeler, *q.v.* Fur. 18 Mar. 1848 till 8 Jan. 1850 ; s.c. 5 Feb. 1852 till death. Col. 6th Bn. 1853 till death. C.B. 27 June 1846.

Refs. : Boase. *G.M.* 1858, ii. 652. *The Times*, 17 Nov. 1858.

WOOD, John (1743/44-1766). Ensign, Infantry. *b.* in Ireland 1743/44. Cadet 1764. Ensign 18 Oct. 1765. *d.* Calcutta 22 Aug. 1766.

Services : Sailed for India in the *Fort William* 17 May 1764, aged 20. Posted to 1st Bde. 1766 ; resigned during the " Batta mutiny " ; reinstated 1766.

WOOD, John Asprey (1806-1833). Lieutenant, 25th N.I. *b.* Shifnal, Salop, 18 Feb. 1806. Cadet 1822. Arrived in India 16 Jan. 1824. Ensign 18 Aug. 1823. Lieut. 13 May 1825. *d.* Cherrapunji, Assam, 22 June 1833.

bapt. Shifnal 22 Feb. 1806. Son of John Wood, of Seale, Surrey, farmer, and Mary his wife. *m.* Calcutta 23 July 1827, Frances Harriet, elder dau. of Charles Patrick Dana, *q.v.* (She died 27 Apr. 1861.) Addiscombe Cadet 1821-3.

Services : Posted Ensign to 25th N.I. ; offg. Adjt. do. 27 Nov. 1829. Offg. 2nd in comd. Assam L.I. 12 Dec. 1831. No record of active service.

Refs. : *A.J.* xxv. 266. M.I. at Cherrapunji.

WOOD, Jonathan (*d.* 1803). Lieut. Colonel, 2nd N.I. Cadet 1772. Admitted 31 Dec. 1772. Ensign 30 Mar. 1773. Lieut. 29 May 1778. Capt. 23 Feb. 1784. Major 1 July 1798. Lt. Col. 29 May 1800. *d.* Calcutta 23 Jan. 1803.

Son of Mrs. Wood, of Kennington Lane, Surrey. Uncle of William Henville Wood, *q.v.* Father of Elizabeth, wife of James Bruce, of Patna, merchant. Ed. Merchant Taylors' Oct. 1760 till Mar. 1761.

Services : Capt. 35th Bn. Sepoys in July 1787. Resigned (for fur.) 22 Feb. 1792; readmitted ——. Major 2nd N.I. in 1798; posted Lt. Col. to 2/2nd N.I. 29 May 1800. Granted fur. s.c. Jan. 1803, but did not live to embark.

Refs.: Robinson. G.M. 1803, ii. 788. Will dated Fatehgarh 17 Nov. 1802; proved 5 May 1803.

Note: One of this name was commissioned as Ensign on the Bombay Est. 1 Oct. 1769, aged 21. His name is absent from the Bombay MS. A.L. dated 20 Nov. 1770.

WOOD, Sir Mark, first baronet (1750-1829). Colonel. Engineers. b. 16 Mar. 1750. Cadet 1770. Ensign 7 July 1772. Lieut. 20 Dec. 1774. Capt. 24 Jan. 1779. Major 13 Feb. 1786. Lt. Col. 15 Nov. 1788. Resigned 14 Feb. 1793. Col. 26 Feb. 1795. d. Pall Mall, London, 6 Feb. 1829.

1st Bart., of Gatton Park, Surrey. cr. 30 Oct. 1808. Eldest son of Alexander Wood and Jean his wife. Brother of Sir George Wood, q.v. m. Calcutta 17 May. 1786, Rachel, dau. of Robert Dashwood and aunt of Francis Dashwood, q.v. (See also Peter Hay.)

Services: See D.N.B. Sailed for India as Midshipman in the Bute Indiaman 5 Mar. 1770. Apptd. Cadet for Inf. 20 Nov. 1770; to d.d. with Corps of Engrs.; transfd. to Engrs. 17 July 1772. Returned from fur. overland to India Mar.-July 1779, with James Nowland, q.v., and pub. in 1803 an account of this journey. Surveyed Calcutta and the country on the banks of Hooghly R. to the sea, 1780-5. Apptd. Surveyor Gen. Bengal 7 Feb. 1786; Chief Engr. Bengal 27 Nov. 1788; returned to England 1793. Purchased the estate of Piercefield on the banks of the Wye. M.P. Milborne Port 1794; Newark 1796; Gatton 1802-18. Presented to George III in 1795 a model in ivory of Fort William. Reckoned by Joseph Farington (Diary, ii. 94) to have brought from India £200,000. Author of "A Review of the Origin, Progress and Results of the late War with Tippoo Sultaun," 1800, 4to, &c.

Refs.: Burke's Landed Gentry, 13th edn., p. 1928, s.n. Brodie-Wood, of Keithick, Cupar Angus. Burke's Peerage, 1832, p. 642, s.n. Wood, Bart., of Gatton. Memorials of the Woods of Largo, by Mrs. F. M. Montague (1863). D.N.B. E.I.M.C. i. 113. D.I.B. G.M. 1829, i. 276. M.I. Gatton church.

WOOD, Samuel (1764/65-1830). Lieut. Colonel, C.B. 23rd N.I. b. London 1764/65. Cadet 1781. Admitted 28 Aug. 1783. Ensign 29 Sept. 1781. Lieut. 11 July 1782. Capt. 29 May 1800. Major 6 June 1805. Lt. Col. 11 Mar. 1811. Retired 3 Aug. 1816. d. London 24 Jan. 1830.

Of Rowden House, Hoddesdon, Herts. Son of Mary Wood. Brother-in-law of William Harris, *q.v.*, of Mrs. Elizabeth Harris, and of Mrs. Jane Reynolds. *m.* on board the *Busbridge* in Hooghly R., 6 Mar. 1797, Miss Ann Cox. (She died 1 Nov. 1850, aged 79.)

Services: Ensign Bucks. Mil. 28 Mar. 1780. Apptd. Cadet 9 Jan. 1781, aged 16; sailed for India in the *Asia* 13 Mar. 1781. First Mahratta War; Lieut. with Goddard's detachment in W. India. Lieut. 3rd Bengal Eur. Bn. in July 1787. Granted fur. on h.p. 29 Oct. 1788. Lieut. 5th Bn. Sepoys in Oct. 1791. Resigned 14 Dec. 1791; readmitted 11 Mar. 1797. Bt. Capt. 1/8th N.I. in Aug. 1798; transfd. to 12th N.I. 1798; Capt. Lt. do. 21 Apr. 1800. Second Mahratta War; Agra; Laswari; Capt. comdg. 1/12th N.I. Transfd. to newly-raised 1/22nd N.I. Dec. 1803. Comdt. Aligarh fort Aug. 1804 till Dec. 1805. Settlement of Hariana 1809; capture of Bhawani; Major comdg. 1/22nd N.I. Posted Lt. Col. to 1/22nd N.I. 1811. (? Reduction of Kalinjar 1812; Lt. Col. 1/22nd N.I.) Transfd. to 2/23rd N.I. 1812. Fur. 5 Feb. 1814 till retirement. C.B. 4 June 1815.

Refs.: *E.I.M.C.* i. 203-6. Will dated 8 July 1825; proved 27 Oct. 1830. M.I. in St. Augustine's, Broxbourne.

WOOD, Thomas (1765-1834). Colonel, C.B., Engineers. *b.* June 1765. Cadet 1783. Arrived in India 30 Oct. 1783. Ensign 18 May 1785. Lieut. 15 Dec. 1798. Capt. 15 Apr. 1806. Major 1 Oct. 1819. Lt. Col. 28 Sept. 1827. Col. 25 June 1830. *d.* Calcutta 22 Jan. 1834.

5th and youngest son of Robert Wood and Anne his wife, dau. of W. Smythe, of Methven, co. Perth. Cousin-german of Sir George Wood, *q.v. m.* 1st (before 1793), ? *m.* 2nd, Calcutta 30 Oct. 1827, Miss Elizabeth Peirce.

Services: Apptd. Cadet 16 Jan. 1783; sailed for India in the *Vansittart* 11 Mar. 1783. Transfd. from Inf. to Engrs. Dec. 1783. Ordered to proceed to the Coast and join army under Earl Cornwallis 15 Aug. 1791. To proceed with Capt. Welsh's detachment to Assam 9 Oct. 1792. Assam expedn. 1793-4; Ensign Engrs., surveyor. d.d. at Ft. Wm. 16 July 1794; drew map of Irrawaddy R. 1796; apptd. to the field 8 Dec. 1796. 4th Asst. to Surveyor Gen., surveying Ganges R. from Hurdwar to Cawnpore 1797 till Apr. 1801; surveying Nawab of Oudh's W. territory 1801 till 23 Sept. 1802. Operations in Jumna Doab 1803; Sasni; Bijaigarh; Kachaura. To comd. newly-raised Corps of Pioneers 18 Aug. 1803. Second Mahratta War; Agra; assault of Rampura; Bhurtpore; Chief Engr. in the field, directing siege operations.

Engr. at Allahabad 10 July 1806 ; actg. Executive Ofr. at Ft. Wm. 5 Feb. 1807 ; permanent do. 19 Oct. 1807 till 1829. Offg. Comy. of Stores 14 May 1812. Suptg. erection of Art. barracks at Dum-Dum 1813. Fur. p.a. 18 Jan. 1829 till 23 Dec. 1830. Chief Engr. Bengal 1830 till death. C.B. 4 June 1815.

Refs.: Memorials of the Woods of Largo. N. & Q. 12S. ix. 6. *G.M.* 1835, i. 221. *A.J.* N.S. xiv. 201. Will dated 21 Dec. 1831 ; proved 25 Jan. 1834. M.I. in S. Park St. cemetery, Calcutta.

WOOD, William (*d.* 1814). Captain. Infantry. Cadet 1769. Ensign 12 Apr. 1770. Lieut. 14 Mar. 1773. Capt. 11 Jan. 1781. Struck off 1793. *d.* March Hall, nr. Shrewsbury, Feb. 1814.

m. (before 1778) Esther.

Services: A.D.C. to Sir John Clavering, C.-in-C. in India, at the latter's death 30 Aug. 1777 ; apptd. Bk. Mr. at Dinapore 27 Feb. 1778 ; Dy. Judge Advocate at Dinapore 22 Nov. 1781 ; Bk. Mr. at Dinapore in Sept. 1785 till Nov. 1786. Fur. on h.p. 6 Nov. 1786 till struck off. A friend of Charles Fox and of both the Burkes, he gave evidence at the trial of Warren Hastings.

Refs.: G.M. 1814, i. 303.

WOOD, William Henville (1783-1833). Colonel, 25th N.I. Comdg. in Arakan. *b.* London 22 Mar. 1783. Cadet 1798. Arrived in India 22 Nov. 1799. Ensign 27 Nov. 1799. Lieut. 29 May 1800. Capt. 5 Sept. 1811. Major 11 June 1822. Lt. Col. 1 May 1824. Col. 14 Mar. 1833. *d.* Kyaukpyu, Arakan, 29 Aug. 1833.

bapt. St. Martin-in-the-Fields, London, 16 Apr. 1783. Son of Capt. John William Wood and Arabella his wife. Brother of Browne Wood and nephew of Jonathan Wood, *qq.v. m.* Calcutta 12 Jan. 1813, Amelia, dau. of John Anderson (*d.* 1812), *q.v.* (*See also* Archibald Oliver and Browne Roberts.) (She died 28 June 1844, aged 52.)

Services: Posted to 1st Bengal Eur. Regt. 15 Apr. 1801. Second Mahratta War ; Gwalior ; battle and capture of Deig ; Bhurtpore (w. in 1st assault 9 Jan. 1805) ; Lieut. Eur. Regt. Adjt. Bengal Eur. Regt. 1806-9 ; Qmr. do. 26 Feb. 1809 till 10 Dec. 1811. Actg. A.A.G. 24 Apr. 1810. Asst. Sec. to Govt. of Java, Mily. Dept., and A.D.C. to Lt. Govr. 15 Aug. 1812. To take tempy. comd. of Eur. Regt. in Java May 1813. Actg. Resdt. at Macassar 1816. Raised Benares Inf. Levy in Mar. 1818 and comdd. till 1822. Fur. p.a. 25 Dec. 1823 till 20 Oct. 1826. Posted Lt. Col. to 2nd Bengal Eur. Regt. May 1824 ; to 36th N.I. 1825 ; to 68th N.I. 4 Nov. 1826 ; assumed comd. of troops in Arakan 14 Dec. 1826. Transfd. to

47th N.I. 24 Sept. 1828; to 66th N.I. 16 Dec. 1830; to 25th N.I. 24 Sept. 1832, and comdd. from 3 Dec. 1832 till death. Posted Col. to 25th N.I. 29 July 1833.

Refs.: *A.J.* N.S. xiii. 205, 270. Will dated Kyaukpyu 8 Aug. 1833; proved 28 Nov. 1833.

WOODBURN, David (*d.* 1804). Colonel, Artillery. (122) Country Cadet 1770. Admitted 29 Nov. 1770. Fireworker 4 Dec. 1771. Lieut. 5 July 1774. Capt. Lt. 22 Sept. 1779. Capt. 28 Jan. 1784. Major 9 July 1788. Lt. Col. 8 Jan. 1796. Col. 1 July 1801. *d.* Charles St., Berkeley Sq., London, 25 July 1804.

Eldest son of John Woodburn, farmer in psh. of Monkton, co. Ayr. Glasgow Univ.; matric. 1764; expelled in 1769.[1]

Services: Second Mysore War; Lieut. 4th Coy. 2nd Bn., with detachment under Col. T. D. Pearse, *q.v.* Capt. 2nd Bn. Art. in July 1787. Third Mysore War 1790-2; Bangalore; Seringapatam. Fur. 1 Aug. 1793 till 1 Oct. 1798. Posted to 2nd Bn. Art. Oct. 1798. Fur. 4 Apr. 1801 till death.

Refs.: *G.M.* 1804, ii. 699.

[1] *Note:* Expelled for quarrelling with John Robison (*D.N.B.*).

WOODBURN, James (1799-1843). Captain, 9th N.I. *b.* Galston, co. Ayr, 4 Dec. 1799. Cadet 1817. Admitted 15 Aug. 1818. Ensign 14 Mar. 1818. Lieut. 25 Aug. 1818. Capt. 15 Sept. 1833. *d.* Karachi 22 Dec. 1843, on board S.S. *Queen*, off the mouth of the Indus.

bapt. Galston 9 Dec. 1799. Son of John Woodburn, at Aird, and Janet Sellars his wife. Kinsman of David Shaw, *q.v.*

Services: Posted Lieut. to 2/8th N.I.; transfd. to 9th N.I. (late 1/8th) May 1824. Fur. s.c. 1 Jan. 1830 till 24 Nov. 1832. Bde. Major to troops on E. frontier under Lt.-Col. J. H. Littler, *q.v.*, 16 July till 22 Oct. 1839. Comdd. 1st Inf. Levy at Fatehgarh 5 Feb. till 1 Oct. 1842. With Army of Reserve (for Afghanistan) Oct. 1842 till Jan. 1843; Capt. 9th N.I. No record of active service.

Refs.: *The Times*, 12 Feb. 1844.

WOODBURN, John (1803-1841). Captain, 44th N.I. Comdg. Shah Shuja's 5th Inf. *b.* Dalmellington, co. Ayr, 4 Apr. 1803. Cadet 1820. Arrived in India 19 July 1821. Ensign 7 Jan. 1821. Lieut. 11 July 1823. Capt. 2 June 1838. *d.* nr. Ghazni, Afghanistan, 15 (? 23) Nov. 1841: kld. in action.[1]

bapt. Dalmellington 12 Apr. 1803. Eldest son of David Wood-

THE BENGAL ARMY, 1758-1834

burn, of Camlarg Lodge, co. Ayr, and Janet Caldwell his wife.[2] Ed. Edin. Coll.

Services: Posted Ensign to 1/25th N.I. 1821. Adjt. 2/25th N.I. 4 Dec. 1822. Transfd. to 22nd N.I. July 1823; to 43rd N.I. (late 1/22nd) May 1824; to 44th N.I. 1825; Adjt. do. 12 July 1825 till 19 Sept. 1838. Leave s.c. to Mauritius 21 Mar. 1833 till 17 Feb. 1834. Expulsion of marauders from Jhabua, C.I., Mar. 1836; Bt. Capt. 44th N.I. Apptd. to comd. Shah Shuja's 5th Inf. 5 Oct. 1838. First Afghan War 1838-41; Ghazni 1839 (Medal); comdd. force which defeated Duranis under Akhtar Khan nr. Girishk, on left bank of Helmand R., 3 July 1841; Capt. 44th N.I., comdg. Shah's 5th Inf.

Refs.: Lt.-Col. L. R. Stacy's *Narrative,* p. 129. *G.M.* 1842, i. 341. *The Times,* 24 Jan. 1842. M.I. Afghan Memorial Church, Bombay.

[1] *Note:* Murdered in Sydabad fort by a party of Ghilzais whilst proceeding from Ghazni to Kabul with a detachment of 108 invalids.

[2] *Note:* She was granted an annuity of £50 by C.D. on her son's death.

WOODCOCK, Samuel (1781-1823). Captain, 5th N.I. *bapt.* St. Nicholas, Gloucester, 25 July 1781. Cadet 1799. Arrived in India 12 Jan. 1801. Ensign 14 Aug. 1800. Lieut. 28 Oct. 1800. Capt. 3 Dec. 1813. *d. unm.* Fatehgarh 17 May 1823. Eldest son of Samuel Woodcock, of Gloucester, and Elizabeth his wife.

Services: Posted Lieut. to 2/5th N.I. 17 Apr. 1801. Adjt. 2/5th N.I. 15 May 1808 till 1813. Reduction of Kalinjar 1812; Lieut. 2/5th N.I. (? Nepal War 1815; operations in Kumaon Feb.-Apr.; capture of Almora; Lieut. 2/5th N.I.) With 6th Gren. Bn. in Kumaon 1815-16. Third Mahratta War 1817-19; Capt. 2/5th N.I., with Reserve of Grand Army.

Refs.: *Bath Chron.* 11 Sept. 1823. Will dated Fatehgarh 21 Apr. 1823; codicil 14 May 1823; proved 13 June 1823. M.I. Fatehgarh fort cemetery.

WOODFORD, Jonathan (*d.* 1776). Lieutenant, Infantry. Cadet 1772. Ensign 10 Nov. 1772. Lieut. 17 Aug. 1776. *d. unm.* Berhampore 17 Sept. 1776.

Services: N.F.P.

Refs.: Will dated Berhampore 13 Sept. 1776; proved 14 Nov. 1776.

WOODFORD, Robert (1781-1801). Cadet, Infantry. d.d. 5th N.I. b. Leicester 13 Feb. 1781. Cadet 1800. Arrived in India 23 Aug. 1801. *bur.* Calcutta 9 Sept. 1801.

bapt. St. Martin's, Leicester, 18 Feb. 1781. Son of Samuel Woodford and Mary his wife.

Services: To d.d. with 5th N.I. Sept. 1801.

WOODMAN, William (*d.* 1774). Captain, Infantry. Cadet (?) Ensign 29 May 1766. Lieut. 5 Sept. 1767. Capt. 1 Dec. 1772. *d.* Bisauli, U.P., 12 June 1774.

Services: (? First Rohilla War 1774; battle of St. George.)

WOODROOFFE, George Henry (1792-1878). Lieut. Colonel. Artillery. (413) b. Ockley, Surrey, 21 May 1792. Cadet 1808. Arrived in India 19 July 1809. Fireworker 31 Oct. 1809. Lieut. 6 May 1817. Capt. 1 May 1824. Major 25 Mar. 1840. Retired 20 Jan. 1842. Hon. Lt. Col. 28 Nov. 1854. *d.s.p.* Hampstead 24 Dec. 1878.

bapt. Ockley 24 May 1792. 3rd son of Rev. Thomas Woodrooffe, rector of Ockley, J.P. Surrey, and Catharine his 1st wife, dau. of Richard Barbor, of Brentwood. *m.* Stamford 7 Sept. 1848, Charlotte, 3rd dau. of Thomas Graham Arnold, M.D. (She died 9 May 1891.) Ed. Merchant Taylors' Mar. 1805 till Mar. 1806.

Services: To P.W.I. on duty 17 Nov. 1810. Third Mahratta War; Lieut. 1st Coy. 1st Bn. Fur. p.a. 27 Dec. 1820 till 27 July 1824. Siege and capture of Bhurtpore; Capt. comdg. 3rd Coy. 1st Bn.[1] Dy. Comy. Ord., Delhi Mag. 16 Mar. 1835; Comy. Ord. 23 Apr. 1835 till 8 Apr. 1840. Posted to 4th Troop 2nd Bde. H.A. 10 Dec. 1839; as Major to 4th Bn. Foot Art. 13 Apr. 1840. Fur. s.c. 27 Feb. 1841 till retirement.

Refs.: Howard & Crisp, ii. 11, *s.n.* Woodrooffe. *Robinson. The Times*, 28 Dec. 1878.

[1] *Note:* Given thus by *Stubbs*, but his name is not included in either India M.R. or Bhurtpore P.R.

WOODS, James (1809-1848). Lieutenant. 32nd N.I. b. London 13 Jan. 1809. Cadet 1824. Arrived in India 11 June 1825. Ensign 8 Feb. 1825. Lieut. 30 Dec. 1825. Retired 16 Oct. 1834. *d.* 1 Nov. 1848.

bapt. St. Luke's, Middlesex, 26 Feb. 1809. 2nd son of Sir William Woods, Kt., K.H., Garter King of Arms 1839-42, and Elizabeth Blake his wife. Brother of Sir Albert William Woods, G.C.V.O., etc., Garter Principal King of Arms 1869-1904 (*D.N.B.*).

THE BENGAL ARMY, 1758-1834 521

Services: Ensign d.d. 61st N.I. 21 June 1825; posted to 32nd N.I. 1825. Siege and capture of Bhurtpore; Lieut. 32nd N.I. Actg. Intr. & Qmr. 32nd N.I. 26 Mar. 1828; permanent do. 12 Aug. 1828 till 1831. Fur. s.c. 16 Apr. 1832 till retirement. Retired on h.p., viz., 4/- *p.d.*

WOODWARD, Henry. Captain. Infantry. Capt. 26 July 1764. Resigned 6 Aug. 1765.

(*Perhaps* the Henry Woodward, of Kilmackanlow, co. Limerick, whose Will was proved P.C. Dublin, 1797.)

Services: Apptd. in England a Capt. on the Bengal Est. 30 Nov. 1763; sailed for India in the *Northumberland* 20 Feb. 1764. *Probably* transfd. from H.M.S., but not traced.

WOODWARD, Richard (1804-1887). Major. 2nd N.I. *bapt.* Kildrumfertin, co. Cavan, 22 Apr. 1804. Cadet 1822. Arrived in India 5 July 1823. Ensign 11 July 1823. Lieut. 13 May 1825. Capt. 11 Feb. 1835. Retired 1 Aug. 1844. Hon. Major 28 Nov. 1854. *d.* 23 May 1887.

Son of Thomas Woodward, of 31 Upper Pembroke St., Dublin, and Frances his wife.

Services: Posted Ensign to 2nd N.I.; Intr. & Qmr. do. 14 Nov. 1825 till 17 Oct. 1827, and 12 Mar. 1829 till Dec. 1831. S.A.C.G. 19 Dec. 1831; in charge of Natpur timber agency. Leave s.c. 12 mos. to Simla 19 Dec. 1836. D.A.C.G. 2 cl. 12 Apr. 1837; 1 cl. 9 Mar. 1840. Fur. s.c. 1 Feb. 1842 till retirement. No record of active service.

WOODYATT, George Thomas (1789-1806). Cadet, Infantry. *bapt.* Ledbury, co. Hereford, 26 Apr. 1789. Cadet 1805. Never arrived in India. *d.* Dec. 1806, on his passage to India, in the wreck of the *Skelton Castle*. Struck off with effect from 5 Nov. 1806. (See note to David Allan.)

Son of George Woodyatt and Hannah his wife.

WOOLLETT, William (1778-1816). Captain, 12th N.I. *bapt.* Rye, Sussex, 19 Nov. 1778. Cadet 1800. Arrived in India 5 Feb. 1802. Ensign 6 Sept. 1801. Lieut. 13 July 1803. Capt. 23 May 1815. *d.* Calcutta 28 Sept. 1816.

Son of Thomas Woollett and Hannah his wife. *m.* Benares 11 May 1806, Miss Amelia Finney. (She died 26 Mar. 1807.)

Services: Posted Ensign to 12th N.I. Second Mahratta War 1803; Agra (w.); Lieut. 1/12th N.I. Operations in Oudh 1808; Bhadri; Samanpur; Gurha; Lieut. 1/12th N.I. Capt. Lt. 12th

N.I. 18 Oct. 1811. Capt. 1/12th N.I. Nepal War 1816; Capt. 5th Gren. Bn., in 2nd Bde. Left Column.

Refs.: M.I. in N. Park St. cemetery, Calcutta.

WOOLLEY, Benjamin (1792-1825). Captain, 59th N.I. *b.* Nicholl Sq., St. Giles, Cripplegate, 14 Sept. 1792. Cadet 1807. Arrived in India 19 Aug. 1808. Ensign 6 Sept. 1808. Lieut. 1 May 1813. Capt. 9 Dec. 1824. *d.* at sea 2 Sept. 1825, on board the *Hydery.*

bapt. London 10 Oct. 1792. 6th son of John Woolley, clerk in the E.I. House, and Elizabeth his wife, dau. of William Donald Valentine. Brother of George Woolley, *q.v.* Ed. St. Paul's School; admitted 27 Sept. 1806.

Services: Barasat C.C. Posted to 14th N.I. 1809. Nepal War 1814-15; Lieut. 14th N.I., in 3rd Div. Transfd. to newly-raised 1/30th N.I. 1815; Intr. & Qmr. do. 25 Feb. 1820 till May 1824. Transfd. to 59th N.I. (late 1/30th) May 1824; Adjt. do. 17 June till 30 Aug. 1824. Attached to Gren. Bn. 1824; transfd. to 2nd L.I. Bn. 7 Jan. 1825. First Burma War; Arakan 1825; Capt. 2nd L.I. Bn.

Refs.: Family information. *Gardiner.* Will dated 4 Feb. 1825; proved 21 Dec. 1825.

WOOLLEY, George (1783-1860). Lieutenant. 1st N.I. Pensioner on Lord Clive's fund. Subsequently a surgeon in England. *b.* Nicholl Sq., Cripplegate, 1 May 1783. Cadet 1800. Arrived in India 19 Aug. 1801. Ensign 30 Nov. 1801. Lieut. 30 Sept. 1803. Pensioned in England 19 May 1809, with effect from 31 Aug. 1808. *d.* Kensington 30 May 1860.

bapt. London 2 June 1783. 3rd son of John Woolley and Elizabeth his wife. Brother of Samuel Woolley, *q.v. m.* 1808, —— Gell, of Lewes, Sussex. Ed. St. Paul's; admitted 25 July 1793.

Services: Ensign d.d. 2nd Bengal Eur. Regt. 1802; posted Ensign to 1st N.I. 1803. (? Second Mahratta War.) Fur. 21 Feb. 1806 till pensioned. Qualified as a surgeon; M.R.C.S. Lond.; M.D. Abd. 3 Aug. 1849.

Refs.: Family information. *Gardiner.*

WOOLLEY, Samuel (1789-1810). Lieutenant, 9th N.I. *b.* Nicholl Sq., London, 8 Feb. 1789. Cadet 1805. Arrived in India 11 July 1806. Ensign 18 Aug. 1806. Lieut. 28 Aug. 1807. *d.* Pragpur, U.P., 4 Jan. 1810: kld. in action.

bapt. London 8 Mar. 1789. 4th son of John Woolley and Elizabeth his wife. Brother of Benjamin Woolley, *q.v.* Ed. Merchant

Taylors'; admitted Jan. 1801. St. Paul's; admitted 31 Jan. 1801.

Services: Barasat C.C. Posted to 9th N.I. 1807. Operations against Dhundia Khan 1807; Komona; Ganauri; Lieut. 1/9th N.I. Settlement of Hariana 1809; Bhawani, led one of the columns of attack; Lieut. 1/9th N.I. Operations in Oudh 1809-10; Pragpur (kld.); Lieut. 1/9th N.I.

Refs.: Family information. *Robinson. Gardiner.* Will dated 5 Oct. 1809; proved 18 Dec. 1810.

WOORE, John (1805-1879). Captain. 10th L.C. *bapt.* Templemore, Londonderry, 23 Sept. 1805. Cadet 1823. Arrived in India 3 May 1824. Cornet (?) Lieut. 21 Sept. 1824. Capt. 29 Aug. 1832. Retired 8 Dec. 1843. *d.* 21 Nov. 1879.

Son of Thomas Woore and Catherine Davies his wife. *m.* Karnal 28 Mar. 1834, Arabella Georgiana Dickson. (She died Muttra 29 May 1838.) Ed. Foyle Coll.

Services: Posted Lieut. to 3rd L.C.; transfd. to newly-raised 2nd Extra Cav. (became 10th L.C.) 17 June 1825. Siege and capture of Bhurtpore; Lieut. 10th L.C. (? India medal). Fur. s.c. 15 Apr. 1830 till 21 June 1833; fur. p.a. via N.S.W. 22 Mar. 1840. Resigned 10 June 1842 to settle in N.S.W.; subsequently placed on retired list with effect from 8 Dec. 1843.

WORNUM, John Robson (1786-1857). Lieut. Colonel. 51st N.I. *b.* London 13 May 1786. Cadet 1806. Arrived in India 17 Mar. 1808. Ensign 24 Mar. 1808. Lieut. 16 Jan. 1814. Capt. 1 May 1824. Major 10 Jan. 1837. Retired 7 Feb. 1837. Hon. Lt. Col. 28 Nov. 1854. *d.* Phoenix Lodge, Cheltenham, 24 Aug. 1857.

bapt. Marylebone 24 June 1786. Son of Robert Wornum and Elizabeth Robson his wife. *m.* Cheltenham 16 Apr. 1839, Frances Elizabeth, youngest dau. of F. J. Jones, of Seapoint, co. Dublin.

Services: Barasat C.C. 7½ mos. Ensign d.d. 15th N.I. 1810-11; posted Ensign to 26th N.I. 1811; with 2nd Gren. Bn. 1815-16. Third Mahratta War 1818; Dhamoni; Satanwara; Lieut. 1/26th N.I. Transfd. to 51st N.I. (late 1/26th) May 1824. Leave s.c. to Cape 1 Mar. 1827 till 20 May 1829; fur. p.a. 31 Jan. 1832 till 11 Feb. 1835.

Refs.: *G.M.* 1857, ii. 468.

WORRALL, Henry Lechmere (1798-1872). General. Colonel 10th L.C. *bapt.* Bristol 20 Nov. 1798. Cadet 1818. Admitted 10 Feb. 1820. Cornet 16 Aug. 1819. Lieut. 22 May 1822.

Capt. 26 June 1826. Major 12 Jan. 1834. Lt. Col. 12 Nov. 1838. Col. 21 Oct. 1852. Maj. Gen. 28 Nov. 1854. Lt. Gen. 10 June 1862. Gen. 30 Mar. 1869. *d.* Clifton, Gloucs., 8 Dec. 1872, aged 74.

Of The Cottage, Clifton. 2nd son of Samuel Worrall, of Knole Park, Gloucs., barr.-at-law, town clerk of Bristol 1787-1819, and Elizabeth his wife, youngest dau. of Richard Lechmere, of Bristol, and of Boston, U.S.A. *m.* 1st, St. John's, Calcutta, 12 Jan. 1822, Catherine Barron, dau. of William Spottiswoode, of Glenfernate, and widow of Robert (Robertson) Bruce, *q.v.* (*See also* Robert Salusbury Trevor.) (She died Clifton 6 Jan. 1866.) *m.* 2nd, 5 June 1871, Ellen, youngest dau. of Charles Clark. (She died 13 Feb. 1929.) Ed. Westminster; admitted 29 Mar. 1813.

Services: Ensign H.M. 6th Ft. 22 June 1815; h.p. do. 25 Feb. 1816. Posted Cornet to 1st L.C. To join and d.d. with G.G.B.G. until further orders 8 May 1820; to continue so 12 Jan. 1821; Adjt. do. 3 Feb. 1821 till 6 May 1824. Dy. Paymr. at Cawnpore 6 May 1824 till 6 Mar. 1835. Fur. p.a. 15 Jan. 1836 till 17 Dec. 1838. Posted Lt. Col. to 1st L.C. 14 Feb. 1839; to 4th L.C. 27 Jan. 1840; to 9th L.C. 13 Apr. 1843; to 4th L.C. 1 Apr. 1844. Fur. s.c. 10 Mar. 1845 till 7 Mar. 1848. Transfd. to 9th L.C. Jan. 1848; to 4th L.C. 11 Feb. 1848. Fur. s.c. 10 Feb. 1849 till 6 Dec. 1852. Transfd. to 3rd L.C. 1849; to 8th L.C. Nov. 1852; Col. 10th L.C. Jan. 1853 till death. Fur. 22 Dec. 1852 till death. No record of active service. J.P. Bristol 1850; member of the common council of Bristol 1853-63.

Refs.: Burke's *Visitation of Seats & Arms*, 2S. i. 18. *Boase. Westminster School Register.* *V.B.G.* *A.J.* N.S. xi. 101-2. *The Times,* 12 Dec. 1872. M.I. in Clifton psh. church.

WORSHIP, John. Captain. 12th Bn. Sepoys. Country Cadet 1768. Ensign 26 Feb. 1769. Lieut. 17 Sept. 1770. Capt. 31 Aug. 1779. Resigned 3 Feb. 1790.

Services: Apptd. Cadet 15 Dec. 1768. Adjt. of Sepoys, 2nd Bde.; apptd. Qmr. do. 17 July 1778; Capt. 1/1st Bengal Eur. Regt. in Oct. 1779; comdg. 12th Bn. Sepoys in July 1787.

WORSLEY, Sir Henry (1768-1841). Major General, G.C.B. Colonel 10th N.I. *b.* Appuldurcomb, I.W., 20 Jan. 1768. Cadet 1780. Arrived at Madras 10 Jan. 1781. Ensign 1781. Lieut. 26 June 1781. Capt. 1 Nov. 1798. Major 21 Sept. 1804. Lt. Col. 29 Nov. 1809. Col. 12 Aug. 1819. Maj. Gen. 22 July 1830. *d.* Shide, I.W., 17 Jan. 1841.

2nd son of Rev. Francis Worsley, rector of Chale, I.W., and

THE BENGAL ARMY, 1758-1834

Anne his wife, 3rd dau. of Henry Roberts, of Standen. Nephew of William Roberts (1746-1809), uncle of Henry Nelson Worsley, and second cousin once removed of Thomas Worsley, *qq.v. m.* Sarah Hastings (*probably* a relative of the Marquess of Hastings). His dau. *m.* Edward Watt, *q.v.*

Services : See *D.N.B.* Sailed for India in the *Bellmont* 3 Apr. 1780, when he gave his age as 15. Campaign against the Rajah of Benares 1781-2 ; Lieut. 30th N.I. Adjt. 30th N.I. 1783 ; transfd. to 8th N.I. 1785 ; to 32nd Bn. 1786. Served with Vols. in Sumatra 1789 ; to Madras with Vol. Sepoys Aug. 1791 ; transfd. from 32nd to 7th Bn. 27 Dec. 1791. Third Mysore War 1791-2 ; Seringapatam ; Lieut. 7th Bn. Retransfd. to 32nd Bn. 16 Oct. 1794 ; to 1st N.I. 1796. Fur. p.a. 11 Apr. 1797 till 11 Dec. 1800. Transfd. to 15th N.I. 1801. Operations in Jumna Doab 1802-3 ; Sasni ; Bijaigarh ; Kachaura ; Capt. 1/15th N.I. Second Mahratta War 1803-4 ; Koil ; Aligarh ; battle of Delhi ; Agra ; Laswari ; Capt. comdg. 1/15th N.I. Transfd. as Major to newly-raised 21st N.I. 1804. D.A.G. of the Army June 1805 ; A.G., with official rank of Lt. Col., 1 May 1806 till Jan. 1810. Leave s.c. to Cape 23 July 1807 till 26 Aug. 1808. Fur. s.c. 11 Jan. 1811 till 4 Oct. 1813. Pte. Sec. to Earl of Moira, the G.G., 4 Oct. till 17 Nov. 1813. Fur. s.c. 5 Feb. 1814 till Sept. 1818. Mily. Sec. to Govt. 7 Nov. 1818 till 30 Jan. 1819, when he resigned owing to ill health. Fur. s.c. 14 Dec. 1819 till death. Posted Col. to 10th N.I. 29 Nov. 1836. C.B. 4 June 1815 ; K.C.B. 27 Sept. 1831 ; G.C.B. 16 Feb. 1838. Gave £1,000 to the R. Asiatic Soc. in 1837, in recognition of which they placed his bust in their House.

Refs. : Burke's *Commoners*, ii. 188, *s.n.* Campbell, of Gatcombe, I.W. Berry's *Hants Peds.*, p. 142. *Misc. Gen. et Her.* 4S. iv. 216. *D.N.B. D.I.B. E.I.M.C.* i. 130-9. *List of Pte. Secs. to G.G. A.J.* N.S. xxxiv. 169.

WORSLEY, Henry Nelson (1806-1847). Bt. Major, 74th N.I. *b.* Manchester 1 Jan. 1806. Cadet 1821. Arrived in India 19 Aug. 1822. Ensign 10 Mar. 1822. Lieut. 21 Feb. 1824. Capt. 23 May 1836. Bt. Major 9 Nov. 1846. d. Almora, U.P., 15 Dec. 1847.

bapt. St. James's, Manchester, 22 Jan. 1806. Son of Thomas Worsley, of Liverpool (who was younger brother of Sir Henry Worsley, *q.v.*), and Jane his wife, dau. of Francis Armstrong, of Manchester. *m.* Chittagong, 26 July 1830, Emilia Elizabeth, 3rd dau. of Thomas Walford Phillips, indigo planter. (She died 12 July 1864, aged 52.)

Services : Posted Ensign to 9th N.I. 1822 ; transfd. to 10th N.I. 1823 ; to 14th N.I. (late 1/10th) May 1824 ; to newly-raised 6th Extra Regt. (became 74th N.I.) May 1825. Offg. A.D.C. to Maj.-Gen. George Dick, *q.v.*, 19 Oct. 1826. Adjt. 74th N.I. 1 July 1835 till 16 Dec. 1836. Attached to 2nd L.I. Bn. 1842. No record of active service.

Refs. : Misc. Gen. et Her. 4S. iv. 216.

WORSLEY, Thomas (1785-1838). Lieut. Colonel, 28th N.I. *bapt.* Gatcombe, I.W., 15 Mar. 1785. Cadet 1800. Arrived in India 22 Aug. 1801. Ensign 8 Nov. 1801. Lieut. 30 Sept. 1803. Capt. 19 Sept. 1816. Major 8 Sept. 1825. Lt. Col. 2 June 1830. *d.* Meerut 2 Dec. 1838.

Younger son of Rev. James Worsley, rector of Gatcombe, and Ann his wife, *née* Hayles. Kinsman of Sir Henry Worsley, *q.v.*

Services : Ensign d.d. 2nd N.I. in 1802 ; posted Ensign to 4th N.I. (? Second Mahratta War 1803-4 ; Lieut. 4th N.I.) Transfd. to newly-raised 23rd N.I. 1804. Adjt. Allahabad Provl. Bn. 1804-5 ; do. 2/23rd N.I. 1806 till Mar. 1810. Settlement of Hariana 1809 ; Bhawani ; Lieut. 2/23rd N.I. Transfd. to 1/23rd N.I. Bde. Major Bundelkhand 20 Mar. 1810 till 1817. Capt. Lt. 21 Oct. 1815. Capt. 2/23rd N.I. Dy. Postmr. Kaitha 30 Sept. 1817. Third Mahratta War 1817-19 ; Bde. Major 1st Inf. Bde., Centre Div. A.A.G. Narbada F.F. 6 Nov. 1819 ; D.A.A.G. Presdy. Div. 22 Feb. 1825 till 27 Feb. 1826. Transfd. to 45th N.I. (late 1/23rd) May 1824. To take charge of 51st N.I. 19 Jan. 1828 ; do. 53rd N.I. 8 Feb. 1828 ; do 42nd N.I. 24 Sept. 1828 ; to comd. 45th N.I. 17 Jan. 1829. Posted Lt. Col. to 45th N.I. 7 Jan. 1831 ; to 33rd N.I. 7 Mar. 1831 ; to 24th N.I. 14 Oct. 1831 ; to 65th N.I. 7 Jan. 1832 ; to 28th N.I. 9 July 1834. Took comd. of Meywar F.F. 17 Jan. 1835. Bdr. 2 cl. to comd. 5th Bde., 2nd Inf. Div., Army of the Indus, 10 Sept. 1838 ; cancelled 24 Oct. 1838, owing to disaffection in his Regt.

Refs. : Ruvigny's *Plantagenet Roll of the Blood Royal*, Clarence Vol., p. 517. Burke's *Commoners*, ii. 188, *s.n.* Campbell, of Gatcombe, I.W. Berry's *Hants Peds.*, p. 140. *A.J.* N.S. xxviii. 224, 256-7.

WORTHAM, Arthur (1790-1836). Captain, Invalid Est. 19th N.I. *b.* Aspeden, Herts., 13 Apr. 1790. Cadet 1810. Admitted 21 Jan. 1812. Ensign 18 Dec. 1813. Lieut. 15 Apr. 1816. Capt. 16 Dec. 1830. Invalided 6 Jan. 1832. *d.* Delhi 11 May 1836.

bapt. Aspeden 2 Aug. 1790. 2nd son of Hale Young Wortham,

Gent. Usher to George III, Lt. Col. Herts. Mil., and Anne his wife, dau. of Thomas Proctor, of Bengeo Hall, Herts. *m.* Fatehgarh 10 Nov. 1818, Miss Fanny Mullins. (*See also* T. A. Hepworth.) (She *re-m.* George Salter, *q.v.*) Christ's Coll., Camb., 1807-11; B.A. 1811. Admitted Pensioner 26 Feb. 1807; admitted Scholar 5 Mar. 1807.

Services: Posted Ensign to 1/3rd N.I. Dec. 1813; transfd. to 2/3rd N.I. 1818; Adjt. do. 5 Oct. 1818 till May 1824. Apptd. to tempy. charge of Gardner's Horse 10 Oct. 1820. Transfd. to 19th N.I. (late 2/3rd) May 1824; Adjt. do. June 1824 till 14 Apr. 1830. No record of active service. Resided at Delhi from Sept. 1834 till death.

Refs.: Cussan's *Herts.*, i. 133. *Graduati Cantab. A.J.* N.S. xxi. 189.

WOTHERSPOON, John Corse (1791-1839). Captain. 70th N.I. *b.* Glasgow 7 Dec. 1791. Cadet 1806. Arrived in India 21 July 1807. Ensign 12 Aug. 1807. Lieut. 1 June 1813. Capt. 3 Oct. 1824. Retired 1 July 1836. *d.* Bridge of Allan, co. Stirling, 20 July 1839.

Son of John Wotherspoon, manufacturer, and Jean Corse his wife.

Services: Barasat C.C. 8 mos. Posted Ensign to 21st N.I. 1808; Intr. & Qmr. 1/21st N.I. 1 July 1814 till May 1818; Adjt. do. 25 May 1818 till 12 June 1823. In service of Rajah of Nagpur 7 June 1823 till 24 Sept. 1824, and 1825 till Feb. 1830. Transfd. to newly-formed 31st N.I. July 1823; to 61st N.I. (late 1/31st) May 1824; to newly-raised 2nd Extra Regt. (became 70th N.I.) May 1825. Leave s.c. to Cape 4 June 1827 till 27 Jan. 1829; fur. s.c. 5 Feb. 1830 till 20 Oct. 1833.

Refs.: A.J. N.S. xxix. 341.

WRAY, George (1785-1838). Lieutenant. Bengal Eur. Regt. *b.* W. Witton, Yorks., 12 June 1785. Cadet 1806. Arrived in India 3 Oct. 1807. Ensign 30 Oct. 1807. Lieut. 2 July 1813. Struck off 18 Jan. 1822. *d.* Cleasby, nr. Darlington, 22 Nov. 1838.

bapt. W. Witton 11 Aug. 1785. Eldest son of George Wray, of Thoralby Townhead, and Ann his wife, dau. of Thomas Fawcet, of Marrick. *m.* 16 Feb. 1819, Isabella, 2nd dau. of his cousin and guardian, Christopher Wright, of Cleasby. (She died 8 Feb. 1848.)

Services: Barasat C.C. Posted Ensign to Bengal Eur. Regt. 1808. Served at Amboyna 1811-13 and 1814-15; Resdt. at Peling I., Celebes, in 1816. Fur. 19 Nov. 1817 till struck off.

Refs.: Genealogist, iv. 285. *A.J.* N.S. xxvii. 340. M.I. in Wray chapel, Aysgarth church.

WRAY, Henry (*d.* 1809). Lieut. Colonel. Infantry. Cadet 1764. Ensign 1 Nov. 1765. Lieut. 16 Jan. 1767. Capt. 26 June 1771. Major 17 Jan. 1781. Lt. Col. 19 Jan. 1788. Resigned 9 July 1790. *d. unm.* 1809.

Of Rostrevan, co. Down. (*Perhaps* of the family of Wray, of Oak Park, co. Donegal.)

Services: Apptd. Cadet May 1764; sailed for India in the *Speke* 14 Apr. 1765. Posted to 2nd Bde. 1766. To comd. 1st Regt. Cav. 7 Aug. 1777. First Mahratta War till Jan. 1779, when he took leave to Calcutta and resigned comd. of 1st Cav. To comd. 3rd Cav. 17 Aug. 1779; Capt. 2/2nd Bengal Eur. Regt. in Oct. 1779; apptd. to comd. 11th Regt. Sepoys at Fatehgarh 1 Jan. 1781. Dismissed by C.M. Sept. 1783; sentence quashed; restored to the Service Feb. 1784. Comdd. 23rd N.I. Jan. 1785 till 31 May 1786; comdg. at Dinapore in Apr. 1785; Major 1st Eur. Bn. in July 1787; Lt. Col. comdg. 4th Bde. Sepoys and comdg. Midnapore in Dec. 1788.

Refs.: *Hickey,* iii. 311. Will dated 12 Mar. 1791; proved 11 Sept. 1829; proved P.C. Dublin, 1809.

WRIGHT, Alexander (1792-1854). Captain. 72nd N.I. *b.* Falkirk 19 Oct. 1792. Cadet 1810. Admitted 22 Oct. 1811. Ensign 15 Aug. 1813. Lieut. 16 July 1815. Capt. 20 May 1829. Invalided 11 June 1832. Retired 1 Aug. 1834. *d.* 25 Apr. 1854.

bapt. Falkirk 4 Nov. 1792. Son of David Wright, of Ceres, co. Fife, Lieut. h.p. R.N., and Agnes Cleugh his wife. *m.* Chinsura, Bengal, 15 Oct. 1823, Johanna Leonora Christina, widow of John Gordon (1787-1822), *q.v.* Father of William Wright, the orientalist (*D.N.B.*). Ed. St. Andrews Univ.[1]

Services: Cadet d.d. 12th N.I. 1811-12; posted Ensign to 20th N.I. 1813; transfd. to 2/12th N.I. 10 Feb. 1815. Nepal War 1816; Lieut. 2/12th N.I., in 3rd Bde. Centre Column (India medal). Siege and capture of Hathras 1817; Lieut. 2/12th N.I. Third Mahratta War; Dhamoni; Lieut. 2/12th N.I. Operations against the Bhattis of Hariana 1818; Lieut. 2/12th N.I. Transfd. to 12th N.I. (late 1/12th) May 1824; to newly-raised 4th Extra Regt. (became 72nd N.I.) May 1825; actg. Adjt. Left Wing do. 28 Apr. 1826. Leave s.c. 18 mos. to N.S.W. 5 Sept. 1828; s.c. 2 yrs. to Tasmania 9 Nov. 1832 till 30 Apr. 1834. After retirement he settled in Tasmania. Pub. Calcutta, 1829, a volume of Poems.

Refs.: Burke's *Colonial Gentry,* ii. 628, *s.n.* Overbeek.

[1] *Note:* His name is absent from the Matric. Roll.

WRIGHT, Charles (1805-1883). Major. 1st N.I. *b.* London 14 Jan. 1805. Cadet 1824. Arrived in India 24 Feb. 1826. Ensign 6 Sept. 1825. Lieut. 13 July 1827. Capt. 26 May 1843. Retired 1 Apr. 1851. Hon. Major 28 Nov. 1854. *d.* 17 Aug. 1883.

bapt. St. Giles-in-the-Fields, Middlesex, 10 Mar. 1805. Son of Charles Cummins, of the Exchequer Office, by Elizabeth Wright.

Services: Posted Ensign to 3rd N.I. 1826; transfd. to 1st N.I. 18 June 1832; Intr. & Qmr. do. 26 Jan. 1838; Adjt. do. 8 Feb. 1838 till 4 Sept. 1843. Second Sikh War; no actions; Capt. 1st N.I., in garr. at Fort Govindgarh, Amritsar (Medal).

***WRIGHT, David.** Bt. Ensign. Infantry. Bt. Ensign 4 Oct. 1779.

Services: Promoted Bt. Ensign from Sergt. after 18 yrs. service in the ranks. N.F.P.

WRIGHT, George (*d.* 1807). Major. Infantry. Cadet 1767. Ensign 15 Sept. 1767. Lieut. 22 Sept. 1769. Capt. 10 May 1777. Major 28 July 1781. Struck off 1793. *d.* Upper Grafton St., London, 16 Jan. 1807.

m. St. George's, Hanover Sq., London, 25 July 1790, Mrs. Sarah Fraser, of Brock St., Bath. (? Ed. Merchant Taylors' Jan. 1755 till Apr. 1756.)

Services: Sailed for India in the *Lord Holland* 16 Dec. 1766. Lieut. 21st Bn. Sepoys in Jan. 1771. Fur. s.c. 1771-2. With Nawab-Wazir of Oudh's troops in Apr. 1777; tempy. comdg. 3 of Nawab's Bns. at Lucknow in Oct. 1777. Capt. 1/2nd Bengal Eur. Regt. in Oct. 1779; to comd. a Sepoy Bn. 14 Oct. 1779; do. 14th N.I. 29 Mar. 1782; Major 19th Bn. Sepoys in July 1787. On fur. in Dec. 1788.

Refs.: *M.M.* 1807, p. 185. *S.M.* 1807, p. 159.

WRIGHT, James (*d.* 1805). Captain, 6th N.I. Cadet 1783. Admitted 17 Sept. 1783. Ensign 19 Jan. 1785. Lieut. 15 Mar. 1791. Capt. 30 Sept. 1803. *d.* Edinburgh 25 Feb. 1805.

Services: Apptd. Cadet 18 Dec. 1782; sailed for India in the *Lascelles* 11 Mar. 1783. Posted to 3rd Bengal Eur. Bn. 5 Feb. 1790; to 31st Bn. Sepoys 9 Sept. 1791; from 25th Bn. Sepoys to d.d. 4th Eur. Bn. 22 Oct. 1792. Fur. 7 Dec. 1792 till 3 Mar. 1797. Lieut. 14th N.I. in 1798; transfd. from 2/6th to 1/6th N.I. 2 Oct. 1800. Disturbances in Ganjam, Madras, 1801; Lieut. 1/6th N.I. Fur. 1803 till death.

Refs.: *S.M.* 1805, p. 237. *G.M.* 1805, ii. 879.

WRIGHT, James (1784-?). Lieutenant. 10th N.I. b. Norwich 14 Mar. 1784. Cadet 1803. Arrived in India 1 Dec. 1804. Ensign 5 Nov. 1804. Lieut. 5 Nov. 1804. Resigned 23 Mar. 1810.

bapt. St. Mary-at-Coslany, Norwich, 16 Mar. 1784. Son of Cotton Wright and Judith his wife, *née* Walne. (*Probably* cousin-german of Randall Walne Lloyd, *q.v.*)

Services: Posted Lieut. to 10th N.I. 1805. (? Second Mahratta War 1805-6; pursuit of Holkar; Lieut. 10th N.I.) Fur. 24 Feb. 1807 till resignation.

WRIGHT, Richard Robinson (1794-1809). Cadet, Cavalry. b. Dundee 31 Jan. 1794. Cadet 1808. Never arrived in India. d. at sea 18 Nov. 1809: kld. on board the *Windham* in action with the French frigate *La Manche*.

bapt. Dundee 20 Feb. 1794. Son of James Wright, merchant, and Camilla Elizabeth his wife, sister of William Campbell (*d.* 1803), *q.v.*

WRIGHT, Robert (1811-?). Lieutenant. 26th N.I. *bapt.* St. Mary Extra, Southampton, 9 June 1811. Cadet 1826. Arrived in India 29 Nov. 1827. Ensign (26 July 1827) 20 Feb. 1828. Lieut. 21 Jan. 1829. Resigned 2 Nov. 1836.

Son of John Wright and Charlotte his wife.

Services: Posted Ensign to 15th N.I. 22 Jan. 1828; transfd. to 26th N.I. 20 Feb. 1828. Fur. p.a. 28 Feb. 1836 till resignation. No record of active service.

WRIGHTSON, John (or Johnston) (d. 1771). Lieutenant, Infantry. Cadet 1768. Ensign 17 Jan. 1769. Lieut. 16 May 1770. d. Dinapore 24 Aug. 1771, of fever.

Son of John Battie (afterwards Wrightson), of Warmsworth, Yorks., and Isabella Wrightson, of Cusworth, Yorks., his wife.

Services: N.F.P.

Refs.: Burke's *Landed Gentry*, 13th edn., p. 1944, *s.n.* Battie-Wrightson, of Cusworth. *Macpherson*, p. 71.

WROE, Benjamin (1734/35-1783). Major, comdg. 11th N.I. b. Leeds 1734/35. Cadet 1763. Ensign 18 Mar. 1764. Lieut. (?) Capt. 15 Aug. 1768. Major 30 Nov. 1780. d. Calcutta 5 Nov. 1783.

6th and youngest son of Joseph Wroe, of Leeds, and Sarah his wife, dau. of Richard Lester, of Leeds. Brother of John Wroe, cutler in Leeds. Cousin-german of John Roebuck, M.D., the

THE BENGAL ARMY, 1758-1834

inventor (*D.N.B.*), and related to Benjamin Roebuck, *q.v. m.* Bombay 19 Jan. 1777, Miss Elizabeth Storer. (She died 10 Mar. 1780, aged 27.)

Services: Lieut. newly-raised 109th Ft. 19 Oct. 1761; h.p. do. 1763 till death. Permitted to proceed to Bengal as a Cadet 21 Dec. 1763, "to be preferred in the Corps of Horse when a vacancy happens"; sailed for India as an Ensign in the *Vansittart* 4 Mar. 1764, aged 29. Apptd. Adjt. of Black Cav. 11 Jan. 1765; to d.d. in Black Troop of Guard 10 May 1765. Requested leave to resign on 29 Jan. 1766, being then a Lieut. Transfd. as Capt. to Bengal Est. (M.C. 1 Sept. 1768). Ordered to Allahabad with one of the Nawab's Bns. 4 Feb. 1773; apptd. to comd. the Select Picket 24 June 1773, and joined from Allahabad 1 July. Capt. 1st Bengal Eur. Regt. Placed in general charge of all guards, camp equipage, etc., with the mission to Poona 1775-6 under Col. John Upton, *q.v.* Given comd. of 8th Bn. 21 Oct. 1776, on the death of Capt. William Fenwick, *q.v.*; vacated comd. Nov. 1780; posted to 1st Regt. Cav. 14 Dec. 1780. First Mahratta War 1781-3; Major comdg. 1st Cav., with force under Goddard. Apptd. to comd. 11th N.I. Oct. 1783.

Refs.: Harleian Soc. lxxxv (1936), p. 25. *Macpherson*, pp. 136, 233. Will dated 3 Nov. 1783; proved 7 Nov. 1783.

WROE, Samuel. Lieutenant. 7th N.I. Pensioner on Lord Clive's fund. Cadet 1779. Ensign 16 Oct. 1779. Lieut. 25 May 1781. Resigned on pension 19 Jan. 1787.

(*Probably* nephew of Benjamin Wroe, *q.v.*) *m.* Liverpool 31 July 1788, Miss Williamson, of Liverpool.

Services: Apptd. Vol. by Col. Thomas Goddard, *q.v.*, 9 June 1779; to act as Ensign 22 Mar. 1780. First Mahratta War; Lieut. with Goddard's detachment in W. India. Lieut. 7th Bn. Sepoys. Granted fur. s.c. to Cape, and if necessary to Europe, 19 Jan. 1787; fur. 9 Jan. 1788. Submitted a Memorial, dated Chapple Town (Chapeltown), Sheffield, 5 Jan. 1789, praying for a pension and stating that he has served 10 yrs. in E.I.C.S. and has never left his bed for nearly 3 yrs. Pensd. on Lord Clive's fund June 1789.

Refs.: Walker's Hibernian Mag. 1788, p. 500. *G.M.* 1788, ii. 750.

WROTTESLEY, Hugh (1782-1830). Lieut. Colonel, Invalid Est. 15th N.I. *b.* Tetenhall, Staffs., 23 July 1782. Cadet 1799. Arrived in India 12 Jan. 1801. Ensign 6 Oct. 1800. Lieut. 6 Aug. 1801. Capt. 16 Dec. 1814. Major 1 May 1824. Lt. Col. 29 June 1827. Invalided 21 Mar. 1828. *d.* Allahabad 18 Oct. 1830.

bapt. Tetenhall 24 July 1782. 3rd son of Sir John Wrottesley,

8th Bart., Maj. Gen. in the Army, M.P. for co. Staffs. 1768-87, and Hon. Frances Courtenay his wife, 2nd dau. of William, 1st Viscount Courtenay, of Powderham Castle, Devon. Younger brother of John, 1st Baron Wrottesley. *m*. Jaunpur 3 Nov. 1811, Miss Emma Matthews.

Services : Posted Ensign to 2/4th N.I. 17 Apr. 1801. Second Mahratta War 1803-4 ; Aligarh ; battle of Delhi (w.) ; Lieut. 2/4th N.I. Transfd. to newly-raised 21st N.I. 1804. Second Mahratta War 1805-6 ; pursuit of Holkar ; Lieut. 1/21st N.I. Adjt. 1/21st N.I. 1805 till Jan. 1810. Transfd. to newly-raised 1/28th N.I. 1815. Third Mahratta War 1818 ; Dhamoni ; Capt. 2/28th N.I. Transfd. to 56th N.I. (late 2/28th) May 1824. Posted Lt. Col. to 15th N.I. 18 Feb. 1828. To comd. Agra Provl. Bn. 27 June 1828 ; do. 1st Bn. Native Invalids 8 Nov. 1828 till death.

Refs. : Burke's *Peerage*, 1923, p. 2369, *s.n.* Baron Wrottesley of Wrottesley, Staffs. *Genealogist*, N.S. xix. 362, 403. *G.M.* 1831, i. 478. M.I. Kydganj cemetery, Allahabad.

WROUGHTON, Francis Charles (*d*. 1806). Captain. 6th N.I. Country Cadet 1779. Admitted 20 Mar. 1779. Ensign 2 Sept. 1779. Lieut. 20 Apr. 1781. Capt. 1 July 1798. Resigned 31 Dec. 1799. *d*. (? *s.p.*) Nator, Bengal, Mar. 1806.

3rd and youngest son of Rev. William Wroughton, rector of Welbourn, Lincs., and Dorothy his wife, youngest dau. of Sir Christopher Musgrave, 5th Bart. Uncle of Henry Francis Wroughton, *q.v.*

Services : Leave s.c. to sea 5 Aug. 1785. Lieut. 9th Bn. Sepoys in July 1787 and Dec. 1788. Apptd. Adjt. 16th Bn. Sepoys 5 Oct. 1792. After resigning the Service he became a trader at Rangpur, Bengal.

Refs. : Burke's *Peerage*, 1923, p. 1639, *s.n.* Musgrave, Bart., of Edenhall, Cumberland. Ruvigny's *Plantagenet Roll of the Blood Royal*, Mortimer-Percy Vol., p. 216. Will dated Rangpur 6 Jan. 1806 ; proved 2 Apr. 1806.

WROUGHTON, Henry Francis (1790-1864). Captain. 30th N.I. *b*. Newtown, Hants, 4 Dec. 1790. Cadet 1806. Arrived in India 3 Oct. 1807. Ensign 27 Oct. 1807. Lieut. 20 Oct. 1811. Capt. 1 May 1824. Retired 29 Aug. 1823. *d*. 30 Mar. 1864.

bapt. Newtown chapel 1 Mar. 1791. Son of George Wroughton, of Belmont, Wantage, Berks., formerly Coy.'s atty. at Calcutta, and Diana Elizabeth his wife, dau. of Rev. Thomas Denton, rector of Ashtead, Surrey, and of Sebergham, Cumberland. Brother of

Robert Wroughton, q.v., and of the wives of James Eckford and William Percival, qq.v.

Services: Barasat C.C. Posted Ensign to 15th N.I. 1808. Capture of Mauritius 1810-11 ; Ensign 1st Vol. Bn. Intr. & Qmr. 1/15th N.I. 1 July 1814 till Feb. 1820. Third Mahratta War 1819 ; Asirgarh ; Lieut. 1/15th N.I. Fur. 25 Feb. 1820 till end of 1824, when he retired with effect from 29 Aug. 1823. Transfd. to 30th N.I. (late 1/15th) May 1824.

WROUGHTON, Robert (1797-1850). Major, Invalid Est. 69th N.I. *b.* Adwick-le-Street, Yorks., 2 Aug. 1797. Cadet 1816. Ensign (?) Lieut. 1 Aug. 1818. Capt. 26 Aug. 1829. Major 29 July 1848. Invalided 31 July 1849. *d.* Fatehgarh 14 Feb. 1850. *bapt.* 3 Aug. 1797. Son of George Wroughton, of 25 Berners St., London, Lt. Col. Comdt. 3rd W. York Mil., and Diana Elizabeth his wife. Brother of Henry Francis Wroughton, q.v., and nephew of Francis Charles Wroughton, q.v. *m.* Berhampore 31 Dec. 1819, Miss Sophia Eliza Amelia Wright, dau. of Col. Wright. (She died Kensington 9 Nov. 1880, aged 82.) Addiscombe Cadet 1813-16 ; Chatham till Dec. 1816.

Services: Selected for Engrs. 13 Nov. 1815 ; removed to Inf. Dec. 1816 ; restored to Engrs. 19 Jan. 1819, but remained with Inf. Ensign d.d. 1/15th N.I. 1818 ; posted Lieut. to 9th N.I. 1818 ; d.d. 1/20th N.I. 1 Mar. 1820 ; posted to 1/20th N.I. 3 Oct. 1820 ; transfd. to newly-raised 32nd N.I. 1823 ; to 63rd N.I. (late 1/32nd) May 1824 ; to newly-raised 1st Extra Regt. (became 69th N.I.) May 1825. First Burma War ; Arakan 1825-6 ; Lieut. 63rd N.I., S.A.C.G. Asst. to Surveyor of Gorakhpur 1 Nov. 1821 ; Revenue Surveyor 12 Feb. 1824, and spent the remainder of his service in the Survey Dept. Dy. Surveyor Gen., and Supt. Revenue Surveys, 16 Dec. 1843 till invalided.

Refs.: Ruvigny's *Plantagenet Roll of the Blood Royal*, Mortimer-Percy Vol., p. 211. *I.M.* 2 Apr. 1850, p. 186. *G.M.* 1850, i. 558. Will dated 6 July 1849 ; proved 9 Apr. 1850. M.I. Fatehgarh fort cemetery.

WYATT, Charles (1758/59-1819). Captain. Engineers. Afterwards M.P. for Sudbury. *b.* Stafford 1758/59. Cadet (Inf.) 1780. Arrived in India 1782. Ensign (Inf.) 1780. Lieut. (Inf.) 8 June 1781. Lieut. (Engrs.) 3 Sept. 1781. Capt. 10 Dec. 1800. Retired 8 Oct. 1806. *d.* Kentish Town 13 Mar. 1819, aged 60. Of Foley House. Nephew of James Wyatt, the architect (*D.N.B.*). *m.* Calcutta 29 Oct. 1787, Charlotte, *née* Greentree, widow of George Drake, Bo. Marine.

Services: Apptd. Cadet for Inf. 25 Apr. 1780; sailed for India in the *Mount Stuart* 27 June 1780, aged 21. Captured by combined fleets of France and Spain 9 Aug. 1780; returned to England and sailed again in the *Blandford* 26 June 1781, with rank as Practitioner Engr. Called upon in 1798 to prepare plans for the new Govt. House in Calcutta. His design, adapted from the plan of Kedleston Hall, co. Derby, was accepted, and building commenced under his direction Feb. 1799. Apptd. a Comr. of Police May 1800. Supt. of Public Works in June 1803, when apptd. a member of a committee to report on Calcutta improvements. Fur. 4 Mar. 1804 till retirement. Subsequently represented Sudbury, Suffolk, in two successive Parliaments, 1812-18.

Refs.: Lord Curzon's *British Govt. in India. A.J.* vii. 461. *G.M.* 1819, i. 377.

WYATT, Edgar (1781-1851). Major General. Colonel 67th N.I. *bapt.* Tamworth 14 Sept. 1781. Cadet 1798. Arrived in India 6 Mar. 1801. Ensign 8 Dec. 1799. Lieut. 29 May 1800. Capt. 5 Mar. 1813. Major 1 May 1824. Lt. Col. 7 Mar. 1826. Col. (18 June 1831) 8 Oct. 1836. Maj. Gen. 3 Nov. 1841. *d.* London 15 Mar. 1851, aged 69.

Son of Thomas Wyatt and Mary his wife.

Services: Posted to 2/10th N.I. 15 Apr. 1801. Apptd. Asst. Supt. Pusa Stud 14 Apr. 1803, and remained in the Stud Dept., with only two short breaks, for the next 24 yrs. Went to Cutch, Basra and Persia to buy remounts, May 1813 till Mar. 1814; established a Stud in N.W.P. 1819. Transfd. as Major to 16th N.I. (late 2/10th) May 1824. Removed from his appt. as Asst. in Stud Dept. on promotion 28 May 1824. Supt. Hapur Stud 18 June 1824 till 21 May 1827, when he resigned. Posted Lt. Col. to 52nd N.I. 7 Dec. 1826; to 4th Extra Regt. 22 Apr. 1828. Leave s.c. to Singapore, China and Cape 19 May 1828 till 1 June 1830; fur. p.a. 26 Mar. 1831 till 22 June 1833. Transfd. to 8th N.I. 22 Aug. 1833; to 45th N.I. 15 Oct. 1833; to 22nd N.I. 23 Sept. 1834. Shekhawat expedn. 1834; Bdr. 2 cl. comdg. 1st Inf. Bde. of Rajwara force 18 Nov. till 31 Dec. 1834. To comd. troops in Shekhawat with rank of Bdr. 2 cl. 1 Apr. 1835. Posted Col. to 23rd N.I. 29 Nov. 1836; 67th N.I. 1838 till death.

Refs.: Boase. *G.M.* 1851, i. 565.

WYATT, Thomas (*d.* 1786). Lieutenant, Infantry. Country Cadet 1781. Ensign 31 July 1782. Lieut. 22 Jan. 1785. *d.* Calcutta 6 Nov. 1786.

THE BENGAL ARMY, 1758-1834

Services: Apptd. Cadet 22 Nov. 1781. Granted fur. on h.p. 2 Oct. 1786, but did not live to embark.

WYE, Henry (*d.* 1779). Ensign, 2/1st Bengal Eur. Regt. Cadet 1778. Ensign 1778. *d.* Cawnpore 29 Sept. 1779.
m. Mary. (She died 18 Apr. 1786.)
Services: Apptd. Cadet in India 27 Feb. 1778. N.F.P.

WYKES, Ambrose (1760-1784). Lieutenant, Infantry. *b.* Northants 1760. Cadet 1781. Ensign 17 Mar. 1781. Lieut. 12 July 1782. *d.* Jaunpur, U.P., 25 Aug. 1784.
Son of Rev. Ambrose Wykes, of Haslebeach, Northants. Hertford Coll., Oxon.; matric. 16 Dec. 1778, aged 18.
Services: Ensign Oxfordshire Mil. 1 June 1780. Apptd. Cadet 9 Jan. 1781, aged 20; sailed for India in the *Chapman* 13 Mar. 1781. N.F.P.
Refs.: Alumni Oxon.

WYLDE, Charles Vincent (1798-1828). Lieutenant, 14th N.I. *b.* 14 Feb. 1798. Cadet 1819. Ensign 4 Mar. 1820. Lieut. 1 May 1823. *d.* Lucknow 19 Oct. 1828.
bapt. Barrington, Somerset, 26 Jan. 1799. Youngest son of Rev. Sydenham Teast Wylde,[1] rector of Barrington, and Ann his wife. His sister *m.* William Hill Jackson, *q.v. m.* Cawnpore 27 Mar. 1826, Miss Margaret Lock. (She died London 12 July 1875, aged 68.)
Services: Posted to 1/17th N.I. 1820; transfd. to 10th N.I. July 1823; to 14th N.I. (late 1/10th) May 1824; Adjt. do. 26 Oct. 1824 till death. (? First Burma War; Cachar 1825; Lieut. 14th N.I.)
Refs.: G.M. 1829, i. 381. M.I. at Lucknow.
[1] *Note:* Matric. Pembroke Coll., Oxon., 1774, as Wilde.

WYLLIE, Arthur Moss (1811-1829). Ensign, 11th N.I. *b.* Thames Ditton 19 Apr. 1811. Cadet 1827. Ensign 21 Mar. 1828. *d.* Barrackpore 24 Oct. 1829.
bapt. St. Olave's, Jewry, 15 Mar. 1812. Son of Alexander Wyllie, of Thames Ditton and Conduit St., London, and Harriot his wife.
Services: Ensign d.d. 51st N.I. 8 Sept. 1828; posted to 11th N.I. 4 Nov. 1828. No record of active service.

WYLLIE, John (1797-1826). Lieutenant, 49th N.I. *b.* Kilmarnock 11 Jan. 1797. Cadet 1820. Ensign 7 Jan. 1821.

Lieut. 11 July 1823. *d.* Partabgarh, Rajputana, 14 Oct. 1826 : assassinated by an Indian fanatic.[1]

bapt. Kilmarnock 16 Jan. 1797. Eldest son of John Wyllie, of Holmhead House, Kilmarnock, carpet manufacturer and surveyor of taxes, and Elizabeth his wife, dau. of William Brown, of Kilmarnock. Brother of Robert Wyllie, *q.v.*, and of Gen. Sir William Wyllie, G.C.B. (*D.N.B.*). Ed. R. Marine Art. Acad. at Fort Monckton, nr. Gosport.

Services: 2nd Lieut. R.M. Art. 19 May 1813 ; on h.p. do. in 1815 ; full pay 1817-21. Posted to 2/12th N.I. 1821 ; transfd. to 25th N.I. July 1823 ; to 49th N.I. (late 1/25th) May 1824. Adjt. Rampura Local Bn. 1822 till death.

Refs.: *A.J.* xxiii. 530. Admon. ; P.C.C. 16 Jan. 1829. M.I. Partabgarh.

[1] *Note:* His nephew, Sir W. H. Curzon Wyllie, K.C.I.E., was assassinated in London by an Indian student in 1909.

WYLLIE, Robert (1807-1872). Lieut. Colonel. 6th N.I. Dy. Sec. to Govt., Mily. Dept. *b.* Kilmarnock 23 Apr. 1807. Cadet 1823. Arrived in India 3 Sept. 1824. Ensign 13 Apr. 1824. Lieut. 13 May 1825. Capt. 1 Mar. 1844. Major 31 Dec. 1850. Retired 5 May 1851. Hon. Lt. Col. 28 Nov. 1854. *d.* Sandgate 7 Oct. 1872.

9th child of John Wyllie and Elizabeth his wife. Brother of John Wyllie, *q.v.* *m.* 1st, Agra 10 Apr. 1834, Lucy Martha, eldest dau. of N. Dennys, of Savage Gdns. (She died Simla 24 July 1840.) *m.* 2nd, 6 Apr. 1843, Catherine Maria, dau. of Humphrey Herbert Jones, of Llynon, controller of customs, Holyhead. (She died Dorking 30 Oct. 1888, aged 67.)

Services: Posted Ensign to 6th N.I. Siege and capture of Bhurtpore ; Lieut. 6th N.I. (India medal). Adjt. 6th N.I. 8 May 1826 till 30 July 1832. Bde. Major Cawnpore 31 July 1832 till Mar. 1839. Offg. A.A.G. Cawnpore Div. 28 Aug. 1833 ; offg. A.A.G. of the Army 15 Nov. 1838. Bde. Major Meywar F.F. 29 Mar. 1839 ; do. Meerut 17 Oct. 1840. Fur. s.c. 4 Feb. 1841 till 10 Dec. 1843. Offg. Asst. Sec. to Govt., Mily. Dept., 11 Dec. 1843 ; 1st Asst. Sec. do. ; Dy. Sec. do. (with official rank of Major) 21 Feb. 1848 till retirement.

Refs.: *Peds. of Anglesey and Carnarvon Families*, by J. E. Griffiths, p. 153. Boase. *The Times*, 10 Oct. 1872.

WYMER, Sir George Petre (1788-1868). General, K.C.B. Colonel 38th N.I. (Col. 107th Regt.) *b.* Reepham, Norfolk, 19 Aug. 1788. Cadet 1803. Arrived in India 15 Aug. 1804.

Ensign 15 Aug. 1804. Lieut. 21 Sept. 1804. Capt. 1 Aug. 1818. Major 11 July 1828. Lt. Col. 26 Sept. 1833. Col. 10 June 1845. Maj. Gen. 20 June 1854. Lt. Gen. 8 June 1856. Gen. 9 Sept. 1863. *d.* Craven Hill Gdns., Hyde Pk., London, 12 Aug. 1868.

Of St. John's Lodge, Ryde, I.W. *bapt.* ptely. 25 Aug. 1788. Son of George Wymer, of Reepham, and Elizabeth (? Mary) his wife, eldest dau. of Col. Varlo. *m.* 1st, Calcutta 19 June 1811, Mrs. Johanna Maria Litton (*probably* widow of Benjamin Litton, *q.v.*). (She died Chinsura 14 Mar. 1824.) *m.* 2nd, Nimach 1 Dec. 1832, Emily, dau. of Charles James Fox Champion Crespigny.[1] (She died 21 May 1891.)

Services: Posted Lieut. to 3rd N.I. 1804. (? Second Mahratta War 1805.) Nepal War 1814-15; Lieut. 2/3rd N.I., in 1st Div. (India medal). Actg. Adjt. 2/3rd N.I. 1815; permanent do. till 7 May 1816. Capt. Lt. 15 Apr. 1816. Capt. 2/3rd N.I. Transfd. to newly-raised 31st N.I. July 1823; to 61st N.I. (late 1/31st) May 1824. Posted Lt. Col. to 61st N.I. 18 Apr. 1834; to 27th N.I. 21 Feb. 1835. Apptd. Bdr. for Army of Indus 23 Jan. 1839. Transfd. to 38th N.I. 14 Feb. 1840 and assumed comd. in Dec. First Afghan War 1839-42; operations of Kandahar force under Nott; action at Ilmi against Sultan Mohd. Khan 29 May 1841 (*Cal. Gaz.* 7 July 1841); comdd. 38th N.I. in engagement nr. Kandahar 12 Jan. 1842; comdd. Bde. against Prince Safter Jang Mar. 1842 (*Lond. Gaz.* 6 Sept. 1842); apptd. Bdr. to comd. 1st Inf. Bde., Kandahar force, 14 May 1842; relief of Kalat-i-Ghilzai May-June 1842 (*ib.* 24 Nov. 1842) (Medal). Offg. Bdr. comdg. Gwalior Contingent Dec. 1844; permanent do. 25 Apr. 1845 till Feb. 1848. Posted Col. to 38th N.I. Sept. 1845. Fur. 10 Feb. 1848 till death. Col. 107th (Bengal Inf.) 1862. C.B. 24 Dec. 1842; K.C.B. 2 Jan. 1857. Durani 3 cl. 26 July 1844. A.D.C. to Queen (with rank of Col. in E.I.) 23 Dec. 1842 till 20 June 1854.

Refs.: Family information. *Walford. Boase. I.L.N.* liii. 211. *The Times,* 20 Aug. 1868.

[1] *Note:* Cousin-german of Sir William Champion de Crespigny, 2nd Bart., but dropped the 'de' from his surname.

WYMES, John. (*See* **WEMYSS, John.**)

WYNDHAM, Charles (1807-1841). Captain, 35th N.I. *b.* Wishford, Wilts., 13 July 1807. Cadet 1824. Arrived in India 1 June 1825. Ensign 11 Dec. 1824. Lieut. 20 Nov. 1827. Capt. 17 Feb. 1841. *d.* Jagdalak, Afghanistan, 29 [1] Oct. 1841: kld. in action.

bapt. Wishford 10 Oct. 1807. Youngest son of George Wyndham, of Roundhill Grange, Somerset, stockbroker, and Elizabeth his wife, dau. of George Dominicus, of E. Farleigh, Kent. Cousin-german of Markham Kittoe, *q.v. m.* Lucknow 15 Apr. 1836, Harriet Anne, dau. of J. G. Bruce, of Kalpi.

Services : Ensign d.d. 2nd Bengal Eur. Regt. 11 June 1825 ; posted to 35th N.I. 1825. Siege and capture of Bhurtpore ; Ensign 35th N.I. Adjt. 2nd Nassiri Bn. 27 July 1829 ; do. Patna Provl. Bn. 26 Apr. 1830. d.d. 58th N.I. 23 Jan. till 1 Nov. 1830. Actg. Intr. & Qmr. 11th N.I. 14 Nov. 1833 till 25 Nov. 1834 ; do. 7th L.C. 4 Mar. 1836 till 8 Sept. 1838 ; do. 37th N.I. 10 Dec. 1838. First Afghan War 1838-41 ; Ghazni 1839 (Medal), Lieut. d.d. 37th N.I. ; actg. Adjt. 35th N.I. 10 Oct. 1840 ; actg. Intr. & Qmr. do. 17 Apr. till 28 July 1841 ; operations against Ghilzais Oct. 1841 ; forcing of Jagdalak Pass (kld.—*Lond. Gaz.* 11 Feb. 1842) ; Capt. 35th N.I., with Sale's Bde.

Refs. : Burke's *Landed Gentry*, 13th edn., p. 1947, *s.n.* Wyndham, of Dinton, Wilts. Burke's *Colonial Gentry*, i. 305, *s.n.* Wyndham, of Leconfield, N.S.W. *Seaton*, i. 236, 245. *G.M.* 1842, i. 341. *The Times*, 11 Jan. 1842. M.I. Afghan Memorial Church, Bombay.

[1] *Note :* Kld. 12 Oct., according to Eyre's *Journal.* The Ghilzais cut off his head and set it up for a mark to throw stones at. (*Seaton*)

WYNDHAM, Henry (1808-1833). Ensign. 2nd N.I. *b.* Cromer 16 July 1808. Cadet 1828. Arrived in India 27 Aug. 1829. Ensign 5 June 1829. Resigned in India 8 July 1831. *d.* Brighton 21 Oct. 1833.

Younger son of George Wyndham, of Cromer Hall, Norfolk, and Mary Anne (Marianne) his wife, dau. of Col. Philip Bacon, of Ipswich. Ed. Winchester.

Services : Posted Ensign to 2nd N.I. 26 June 1830. No record of active service.

Refs.: Burke's *Commoners*, ii. 244, *s.n.* Wyndham, of Cromer. *G.M.* 1833, ii. 477.

WYNNE, Frederick (1791/92-?). Ensign. 17th N.I. *b.* 1791/92.[1] Cadet 1809. Ensign 25 Apr. 1812. Resigned in India Nov. 1814.

Services : Barasat C.C. Cadet d.d. 25th N.I. 1811 ; posted Ensign to 17th N.I. 1812. No record of active service.

[1] *Note :* Aged 16 in 1808. He was probably the author of "Sketches in India . . . written in the years 1811-14 . . .," pub. anonymously in London in 1816.

WYNNE, John (or Joseph) (*d.* 1765). Lieutenant.[1] Cadet (?) Ensign (?) Lieut. (?) *bur.* Calcutta 10 Mar. 1765.

Brother of George Wynne. *m.* Calcutta 7 Dec. 1764, (Cecilia) Sarah Oudley. (She was pensioned on Lord Clive's fund 8 Oct. 1772.)

Services : N.F.P.

Refs. : Will dated 2 Mar. 1765 ; proved 22 Mar. 1765.

[1] *Note :* Captain in the burial register.

X

*XIMENES, Henry Jackson (1807-1832). Lieutenant, Pension Est. 20th N.I. *bapt.* Hurst, Berks., 18 July 1807. Cadet 1823. Ensign 14 Dec. 1823. Lieut. 13 May 1825. Pensioned in India 3 Oct. 1828. *d.* in the General Hospital, Calcutta, 6 Jan. 1832.

Son of Daniel Ximenes, of Hurst Grove, Berks., and Catherine his wife, only dau. of Rev. J. Jackson, of Ospringe, Kent. Nephew of Lt.-Gen. Sir David Ximenes, K.C.H., of Bear Place, Berks. Addiscombe Cadet 1822-3.

Services : Posted to 20th N.I. 1824. No record of active service.

Refs. : Burke's *Landed Gentry*, 12th edn., p. 2090, *s.n.* Ximenes, of Bear Place, Berks.

Y

YALLAND or YOLLAND, John. Lieut. Fireworker. Artillery. (III.-3) Cadet 1764. Lieut. F. 27 Dec. 1764. Resigned 1765 (? Dismissed 3 Apr. 1766).
Services : Apptd. by Major Hector Munro on 12 Dec. 1764, to be a Lt. F. " till the Govr.'s pleasure is known." Confirmed by the Govr. Jan. 1765. Apptd. Conductor of Art. stores to 2nd Coy. Art. 27 Aug. 1765.
Note : He is clearly identical with John Jelland, *q.v.*, although both *Stubbs* and *D. & M.* give two distinct individuals, Jelland and Yalland. His name appears as Yolland throughout Army Orders of 1764-65.

YARDE, John (*d.* 1777). Captain, Infantry. Cadet 1767. Ensign 15 Sept. 1767. Lieut. 15 Apr. 1769. Capt. 7 Apr. 1777. *d.* Dinapore 2 Aug. 1777.
Of the Churston Ferrers family.
Services : Sailed for India in the *Calcutta* 31 Dec. 1766. N.F.P.
Refs. : Will dated 11 July 1771 ; proved 3 Feb. 1778.

YATES, George (1781-1805). Capt. Lieutenant, 22nd N.I. *b.* Clerkenwell, London, 10 Jan. 1781. Cadet 1795. Arrived in India 3 Apr. 1797. Ensign 27 Oct. 1797. Lieut. 30 Oct. 1797. Capt. Lt. 5 June 1805. *d.* Agra 23 Sept. 1805.
bapt. 27 Feb. 1781. Eldest son of Thomas Yates, of Lansdowne Pl., London, tobacco manufr., and Margaret Gittens his wife, relative and ward of Sir Walter Farquhar, Bart., M.D. (*D.N.B.*). Brother of Walter Alexander Yates, *q.v.*, and of Frederick Henry Yates, the actor (*D.N.B.*). Ed. Charterhouse ; admitted Feb. 1793.
Services : Second Mahratta War 1803-4 ; Adjt. & Qmr. 13th N.I. Transfd. to newly-raised 22nd N.I. 1804 ; Adjt. & Qmr. do. till death. Second Mahratta War 1804-5 ; battle and capture of Deig ; Bhurtpore ; Lieut. 2/22nd N.I., Bde. Qmr.
Refs. : E.I.M.C. iii. 243. *G.M.* 1806, i. 181 ; ii. 775.

YATES, John (1775-?). Lieutenant. 5th N.C. *b.* Edinburgh 26 June 1775. Cadet 1799. Arrived in India 12 Jan. 1801. Cornet 11 Apr. 1801. Lieut. 11 Mar. 1805. Resigned in India 2 Feb. 1808.
bapt. New North Kirk psh., Edinburgh, 30 June 1775. Son of

John Yates, merchant, and Katharine Yeoman his wife. Brother of William Yates, *q.v.*

Services : Served throughout with 5th N.C. (? Second Mahratta War ; Cornet 5th N.C.)

YATES,[1] **Thomas.** Lieutenant. Infantry. Cadet 1779. Ensign 12 Feb. 1780. Lieut. 17 Mar. 1781. Resigned 13 Dec. 1786.

A native of Gloucs. *m. c.* Mar. 1795, Susanna Anna Maria Verkerk, a Dutch lady, widow of Pieter Brueys. (She died, his widow, Chinsura 12 May 1809, aged 66.)

Services : According to William Hickey he was well known on the turf at Newmarket and elsewhere. He had formerly owned a handsome estate in Gloucestershire, " which he run out, and then like many undone heroes took refuge in the plains of Hindustan, being at that period at least forty-five years of age." Apptd. Cadet 14 Oct. 1778 ; sailed for India in the *Norfolk* 7 Mar. 1779. Having been detained on duty at Madras on first arrival in India he did not reach Calcutta till Mar. 1781. Apptd. Persian Intr. to Edward Wheler, the V.P., 12 July 1781, " he not knowing a single word of the language." (*Hickey.*) Apptd. A.D.C. to Wheler 25 July 1782. He subsequently settled as a merchant nr. Chinsura, his name appearing for the last time in *E.I.R.* of 15 Aug. 1816.

Refs. : Hickey, iii. 358-9.

[1] *Note :* The name usually appears as Yeates during his service in the Bengal Army, and his christian name as Joseph.

YATES, Walter Alexander (1784-1853). Colonel, C.B., 51st N.I. *b.* Clerkenwell, London, 9 Aug. 1784. Cadet 1802. Arrived in India 5 Sept. 1803. Ensign 9 Sept. 1803. Lieut. 13 Sept. 1804. Dismissed by G.C.M. 19 Nov. 1809. Restored by C.D. 21 Sept. 1811. Arrived in India 14 Oct. 1811. Capt. 1 Aug. 1818. Major 21 May 1829. Lt. Col. 29 Nov. 1834. Col. 30 Jan. 1846. *d.* Cawnpore 5 June 1853, of heart disease.

bapt. St. John's, Clerkenwell, 8 Mar. 1785. Son of Thomas Yates and Margaret his wife. Brother of George Yates, *q.v. m.* Eliza. (She died Lucknow 22 Nov. 1852.)

Services : Ensign d.d. 12th N.I. 1804. Second Mahratta War ; Monson's retreat ; assault of Dhalra 21 Mar. 1805 (w.) ; Lieut. 12th N.I. (*Cal. Gaz.* 18 Apr. 1805). Transfd. to 18th N.I. 1805. Operations in Bundelkhand 1809 ; Rajaoli ; Ajaigarh ; Lieut. 1/18th N.I. Nepal War 1816 ; Lieut. 1/18th N.I., in 1st Bde. Rt. Column (India medal). Adjt. Patna Provl. Bn. 2 Jan. 1816 till 1818. S.A.C.G. 22 May 1818 ; do. 2 cl. 6 Mar. 1822 ; D.A.C.G.

2 cl. 12 Dec. 1823 ; 1 cl. 28 May 1825 ; A.C.G. 2 cl. 27 Mar. 1826
till 11 Sept. 1829. Transfd. to 34th N.I. July 1823 ; to 67th N.I.
(late 1/34th) May 1824 ; to 5th Extra Regt. (became 73rd N.I.)
May 1825. Posted Lt. Col. to 73rd N.I. 21 Feb. 1835 ; to 67th
N.I. 2 Mar. 1835 ; to 51st N.I. 19 July 1836. Apptd. to comd.
1st Bde., 1st Div., Army of Exercise, with rank of Bdr. 17 Nov.
1843. Gwalior campaign ; Paniar (s.w.) ; Lt. Col. 51st N.I., Bdr.
(*Lond. Gaz.* 8 Mar. 1844) (Bronze star). Col. 51st N.I. 1846 till
death. Bdr. 2 cl. comdg. at Lucknow 5 May 1847 till 26 Jan. 1852.
C.B. 22 May 1844.

Refs.: Boase. Stubbs, i. 240. *I.M.* 5 Aug. 1853, p. 445. *G.M.*
1853, ii. 426.

YATES, William (1778-1812). Lieutenant, Invalid Est. 8th
N.C. *b.* Edinburgh 17 Mar. 1778. Cadet 1799. Arrived in
India 12 Jan. 1801. Cornet 10 Apr. 1801. Lieut. 11 Mar. 1805.
Invalided 1 Mar. 1812. *d.* Serampore 9 Aug. 1812.

bapt. 25 Mar. 1778. Son of John Yates, of Edinburgh, merchant,
and Katharine Yeoman his wife. Brother of John Yates, *q.v.* *m.*
Calcutta 25 Jan. 1811, Miss Marian Ferryman.[1]

Services : Operations in Jumna Doab 1803 ; Sasni ; Bijaigarh ;
Kachaura ; Cornet 4th N.C. Second Mahratta War 1803 ;
Laswari ; Cornet 4th N.C. Transfd. as Lieut. to newly-raised
8th N.C. 1805.

[1] *Note :* After his death she innocently went through a form of
marriage with John William Foster Brown, who had a wife then
living.

YEANDLE, Matthew (*d.* 1791). Lieutenant, 2nd Bn. Sepoys.
Country Cadet 1781. Ensign 12 Apr. 1781. Lieut. 3 Aug. 1782.
d. Chunar 14 Mar. 1791 : drowned.

Son of Matthew Yeandle, of Calcutta, jailer,[1] and Mary his 1st
wife.

Services : Was a Lieut. of Marines in the Privateer *Death or
Glory* c. 1780. Apptd. Cadet 27 Mar. 1781. Lieut. 6th Bengal
Eur. Bn. in July 1787 ; 2nd Bn. Sepoys in Dec. 1788.

Refs.: B.: P.P. iv. 498 *n.*

[1] *Note :* Had the custody of Nuncomar.

YEATES, F—— Robert. (*See* **YATES, Thomas.**)

YORKE, Martin. Major. Infantry. Capt. 14 Dec. 1757.
Major 1761. Resigned 23 Dec. 1761.

m. Calcutta 15 July 1760, Anna, dau. of John Zephaniah Holwell
(*D.N.B.*), and widow of William Rider, sheriff of Calcutta 1757.

Services : Ensign H.M. 39th Ft. (?); Lieut. do. 21 Sept. 1757; h.p. do., on reduction, 25 Dec. 1758 till death.¹ Battle of Kasipur 5 Feb. 1757 ; gallantly saved one of the guns ; Ensign 39th Ft., under Clive. Transfd. as Capt. to Bengal Army. Was one of 11 signatories to a Memorial, dated Calcutta 28 Aug. 1758, complaining of supersession by John Gowin, *q.v.* Storm of Masulipatam 8 Apr. 1759 (w.); " Captain Yorke fell with a ball through each of his thighs, and each of the black drummers was killed at his side." Operations in Birbhum and Burdwan Nov.-Dec. 1760.

Refs. : Forrest's Clive, i. 359 ; ii. 113. *Hill,* iii. 45. *Forde.*

¹ *Note :* His name is still in *A.L.* of 1801 as Lieut. h.p. 39th Ft., but not in 1803.

YOUNG, Adam (1790-1808). Lieutenant, Bengal Eur. Regt. *b.* Dalkeith 27 May 1790. Cadet 1805. Arrived in India 11 July 1806. Ensign 2 Sept. 1806. Lieut. 30 Apr. 1808. *d.* Calcutta 25 Dec. 1808.

bapt. 4 June 1790. Son of Adam Young, of the psh. of Dalkeith, portioner, and Christian Scott his wife.

Services : Barasat C.C. Posted Ensign to Bengal Eur. Regt. 1807. No record of active service.

YOUNG, Andrew (*d.* 1829). Lieut. Colonel. 25th N.I. Country Cadet 1779. Admitted 3 Dec. 1779. Ensign 18 Sept. 1780. Lieut. 30 May 1781. Capt. 31 Aug. 1798. Major 21 Sept. 1804. Lt. Col. 15 Aug. 1809. Retired 28 Apr. 1812. *d.* Cheltenham 1 May 1829.

Of Teignmouth, Devon, later of Cheltenham. Brother of Mary Warren, of Glasnevin, nr. Dublin, of Margaret Hamerton and Elizabeth Wolf. Uncle of Eliza Sarah Lodge (late Geale), widow. *m.* Susan.

Services : (? First Mahratta War 1780-4.) Fur. s.c. 1785-7. Lieut. 12th Bn. Sepoys in Dec. 1788. Apptd. Adjt. & Qmr. 1st Bde. 15 Nov. 1794. Capt. 2/3rd N.I. in June 1798. Transfd. as Major to newly-raised 25th N.I. Oct. 1804. Operations against the Rana of Gohad 1806 ; capture of Gohad ; Major 2/25th N.I. Posted Lt. Col. to 25th N.I. Fur. 9 Feb. 1811 till retirement.

Refs. : G.M. 1829, i. 476. Will dated Cheltenham 17 Feb. 1829 ; proved 27 Oct. 1837.

YOUNG, Frederick (1786-1874). General. Colonel 66th or Gurkha Regt. (now 1st K.G.O. Gurkha Rifles). *b.* Green Castle, Moville, co. Donegal, 30 Nov. 1786. Cadet 1801. Arrived in India 19 July 1802. Ensign 12 July 1802. Lieut. (17 July

1804) 18 Mar. 1805. Capt. 23 Sept. 1821. Major 21 July 1826.
Lt. Col. 1 Nov. 1830. Col. 3 Oct. 1842. Maj. Gen. 20 June
1854. Lt. Gen. 18 Feb. 1856. Gen. 28 Mar. 1865. *d.* at his
residence, Albany, nr. Dublin, 22 May 1874.

bapt. Lower Moville 10 Dec. 1786. 2nd son of Rev. Gardiner
Young and Catherine Richardson his wife. Brother of Gardiner
Young, *q.v. m.* Meerut 20 Oct. 1825, Jeannette Jamesina, dau.
of John Jenkins Bird, *q.v.* (*See also* Aynott Chitty.) (She died
Dinapore 10 Apr. 1852.)

Services: Barasat C.C. 1802-3. Apptd. to 1st Vol. Bn. 7 Oct.
1803. Second Mahratta War 1803-5 ; reduction of Cuttack 1803-4 ;
capture of Balasore ; Ensign 1st Vol. Bn. ; posted to 12th N.I.
1805 ; Bhurtpore ; Lieut. 12th N.I. Transfd. to 13th N.I. 1806 ;
Adjt. & Qmr. do. 8 May 1806 till 1 July 1814 ; Intr. & Qmr. 2/13th
N.I. 1 July 1814 till 1815. Nepal War 1814-15 ; Kalanga ;
Nahan ; Jaithak ; Lieut. 2/13th N.I. (India medal). Taken
prisoner during Nepal War. Comdd. newly-raised Sirmoor Bn.
26 Aug. 1815 till 2 Jan. 1843. Third Mahratta War 1817-18.
Operations against the freebooter Kowar Singh in Saharanpur
district 1824 ; assault of mud fort of Kunjawa (w.) ; Capt. comdg.
a detachment of 350 of Sirmoor Bn. Transfd. to newly-raised
34th N.I. July 1823 ; to 68th N.I. (late 2/34th) May 1824. P.A.
at Dehra Dun 13 June 1833 till Nov. 1842. Posted Lt. Col. to
35th N.I. 10 Sept. 1831 ; to 58th N.I. 22 July 1834. Bdr. 2 cl. to
comd. 4th Bde. 2nd Inf. Div., Army of Reserve (for Afghanistan),
6 June 1842 ; to comd. troops in Bundelkhand 14 Oct. 1842.
Posted Col. to 74th N.I. 21 Jan. 1843 ; to 65th N.I. 17 Apr. 1845 ;
66th (Gurkha) Regt. (late Sirmoor Bn.) May 1855 till 1869. Fur.
p.a. 17 Mar. 1844 till 1846. Bdr. comdg. Ferozepore 5 Jan. 1847 ;
Bdr. Gen. comdg. Dinapore Div. 20 Sept. 1849 till 10 Nov. 1854.
Fur. p.a. 5 Jan. 1855 till death.

Refs.: Burke's *Landed Gentry of Ireland,* p. 784, *s.n.* Young,
of Culdaff House, co. Donegal. *Gen. Frederick Young,* by his dau.,
L. Hadow Jenkins, 1923 (portrait by J. Reynolds Gwatkin, 1839).
Boase. *The Times,* 29 May 1874, p. 5.

YOUNG, Gardiner (1791-1809). Ensign, Infantry. *b.* co.
Londonderry 26 June 1791. Cadet 1806. Arrived in India
17 Mar. 1808. Ensign 25 Mar. 1808. *d.* Karnal 6 May 1809 :
kld. by a fall from his horse.

3rd son of Rev. Gardiner Young and Catherine Richardson his
wife. Brother of William Young (1794-1816), *q.v.*

Services: Barasat C.C.

Refs.: Burke's *Landed Gentry of Ireland*, p. 784, *s.n.* Young, of Culdaff House, co. Donegal.

YOUNG, Gavin (1785-1841). Major, 70th N.I. *b.* Aberdeen 7 Dec. 1785. Cadet 1804. Arrived in India 10 Sept. 1805. Ensign 20 Sept. 1805. Lieut. 21 Sept. 1805. Capt. 11 July 1823. Major 10 Apr. 1836. *d.* Calcutta 6 Mar. 1841.

bapt. St. Nicholas, Aberdeen, 9 Dec. 1785. 3rd son of James Young, merchant, and Elizabeth his wife, sister of Peter Black, *q.v.* Brother of Peter Young (1788-1818), *q.v. m.* Calcutta 3 Jan. 1818, Eliza, dau. of Richard Humfrays, *q.v.* (*See also* W. F. Beatson.) (She died Southborough, Kent, 2 Oct. 1844, aged 49.) His dau. *m.* Charles O'Brien, *q.v.* Ed. Aberdeen Grammar School 1795-9.

Services: Posted Lieut. to 17th N.I. 1806. Apptd. Bde. Qmr. Inf. Bde., Benares Div., for Nepal 15 Nov. 1814. Nepal War 1814-15; Jitpur; Lieut. 2/17th N.I., Bde. Qmr. Transfd. to newly-raised 2/28th N.I. 1815. A.D.C. to Maj.-Gen. John Sullivan Wood, H.M.S., comdg. 3rd Benares Div., 1815-17. D.J.A.G. to troops at Dinapore and Benares 11 Nov. 1817 till 15 Jan. 1821. Joint Sec. to Mily. Board, and Accountant in Comst. Dept. on creation of that post, 18 Nov. 1820 till 1827. Transfd. to 56th N.I. (late 2/28th) May 1824; to 2nd Extra Regt. (became 70th N.I.) May 1825. Leave u.p.a. 6 mos. to Cape 7 Mar. 1827. Actg. D.J.A.G. Presdy. Div. 28 Aug. 1828 till 2 Jan. 1829. Sec. and Accountant to Mily. Board 21 Dec. 1830 till 15 Sept. 1835; offg. J.A.G. 16 Mar. 1835; permanent do. 15 Sept. 1835 till death. M.M.B. 26 Jan. 1836. Pub. Calcutta, 1822, "An Inquiry into the Expediency of applying the Principles of Colonial Policy to the Govt. of India"; 1832, "An Essay on the Mercantile Theory of Wealth," 12 mo.

Refs.: Memoir of James Young . . . (1894 edn.), p. 39. M.I. St. John's church, Calcutta.

YOUNG, George (*d.* 1787). Captain, 33rd Bn. Sepoys. Cadet 1767. Ensign 9 Feb. 1769. Lieut. 15 May 1770. Capt. 6 Jan. 1779. *d.* Chunar 30 Nov. 1787.

Services: Sailed for India in the *Ankerwyke* 21 Mar. 1768. Comdd. one of the Bns. raised in 1776 for the service of the Nawab-Wazir of Oudh. On its transfer to the Coy. the following year this Bn. was numbered 26th and called after him "*Ung-ki-Paltan.*" It became 19th N.I. in May 1824, and was disarmed and disbanded at Barrackpore 31 Mar. 1857. Fur. s.c. 8 Jan. 1778 till 1783. Apptd. to comd. 33rd Bn. Sepoys 31 May 1786.

Refs.: Williams, p. 92. *Cardew*, p. 40. Will dated 1 Dec. 1786; admon. 8 Aug. 1789.

YOUNG, George (1789-1860). Colonel. 38th N.I. *b.* Ashburton, Devon, 15 Nov. 1789. Cadet 1804. Arrived in India 10 Dec. 1805. Ensign 1 Nov. 1805. Lieut. 17 Sept. 1806. Capt. 11 July 1823. Major 30 May 1836. Lt. Col. 26 Aug. 1842. Retired 10 Dec. 1847. Hon. Col. 28 Nov. 1854. *d.* Leamington 14 May 1860.

Of Waye House, Ashburton. *bapt.* Ashburton 5 Jan. 1790. Son of William Young, of Ashburton, surgeon, and Elizabeth his wife. *m.* Ashburton 19 Aug. 1852, Winifred Emma, younger dau. of Rev. William Eales, of Ashburton, sometime chaplain E.I.C.S. (who was cousin-german of John Eales, *q.v.*), and niece of Henry Tilman Raban, *q.v.* (She died Ashburton 22 May 1887, aged 76.) Ed. Blundell's 29 Jan. 1801 till 29 June 1804.

Services: Posted Lieut. to 24th N.I. 1806. Lieut. 2/24th N.I. Transfd. as Capt. to newly-raised 34th N.I. July 1823; to 68th N.I. (late 2/34th) May 1824. First Burma War; Arakan 1825; Capt. 68th N.I. (? India medal). Offg. D.A.Q.M.G. to force in Arakan 24 Dec. 1825; do. S.E. Div. 26 June 1826. Fur. s.c. 27 Nov. 1826 till 4 Dec. 1829. Operations in Malwa under Lt.-Col. John Holbrow, *q.v.*, against marauders from Jhabua, Feb.-Mar. 1836. Comdd. 68th N.I. 3 Aug. 1836 till Jan. 1844. Comdg. in Arakan from 10 Aug. 1842. Posted Lt. Col. to 68th N.I. 21 Jan. 1843. Fur. p.a. 9 Jan. 1844 till 1846. Transfd. to 35th N.I. 1846; to 38th N.I. Dec. 1847.

Refs.: Burke's *Family Records*, p. 236, *s.n.* Eales. *Howard & Crisp (Notes)*, ii. 75, *s.n.* Eales. *Blundell's School Register*. *G.M.* 1860, i. 646. M.I. at Ashburton.

YOUNG, James (1782-1848). Major. Artillery. (315) Subsequently a merchant and banker in Calcutta. *b.* Glasgow 2 Oct. 1782. Cadet 1797. Arrived in India 25 Oct. 1801. Fireworker 12 Sept. 1798. Lieut. 24 Feb. 1802. Capt. Lt. 29 May 1805. Capt. 11 Dec. 1810. Major 1 Sept. 1818. Resigned in India 7 Nov. 1818. *d.* Boulogne-sur-Mer 17 Aug. 1848.

2nd son of John Young, professor of Greek at Glasgow Univ. (*D.N.B.*), and Jean Lamont his wife. Brother of Robert Rayner Young, *q.v. m.* Bundi, Rajputana, 18 Apr. 1807, Jane Frances, dau. of Richard Humfrays, *q.v.* (*See also* William Fergusson Beatson.) Glasgow Univ.; matric. 1793. Woolwich Cadet 5 Sept. 1798 till 31 Dec. 1800.

Services: Served with 1st Troop H.A. 1803-5. Second Mahratta

War; capture of Deig; Bhurtpore; Lieut. H.A. Agent for gun carriages 3 Nov. 1807 till 1817. Hon. A.D.C. to G.G. 1817. Sec. to Govt. in Mily. Dept. (with official rank of Lt. Col.) 19 Aug. 1817. Third Mahratta War 1817-18; Capt. 5th Coy. 2nd Bn., Mily. Sec. to Govt., with the G.G. After resigning the Service he joined the firm of Alexander & Co., bankers and agents in Calcutta, till 1832, when he became editor of the *Bengal Hurkaru*, the leading liberal newspaper in Calcutta. Later he became Sec. of the Union Bank, Calcutta. Sheriff of Calcutta 1838-9. One of the six original proprietors of the Bank of Hindostan.

Refs.: I.N. 1848, p. 405.

YOUNG, Keith (1806-1862). Bt. Colonel, C.B., 50th N.I. J.A.G. Bengal. *b.* London 2 Feb. 1806. Cadet 1823. Arrived in India 19 May 1824. Ensign 16 Jan. 1824. Lieut. 13 May 1825. Capt. 14 June 1844. Major 19 May 1858. Bt. Lt. Col. 12 Oct. 1857. Bt. Col. 1 Jan. 1862. *d.* Simla 18 May 1862.

bapt. St. John's, Hackney, 19 June 1812. Son of James Young, of Percy St., Bedford Sq., London, architect, and Elizabeth his wife. *m.* Simla 2 Sept. 1852, Frances Mary, dau. of Henry Barkley Henderson, *q.v.*, and grand-dau. of Thomas Hawkins, *q.v.* Father of Col. Sir Arthur Henderson Young, G.C.M.G., Govr. of Straits Settlements, 1911-19.

Services: Posted Ensign to 50th N.I. 12 Aug. 1824. Fur. s.c. 26 Nov. 1830 till 3 Oct. 1833. Intr. & Qmr. 50th N.I. 21 Dec. 1833 till Jan. 1838. Fur. p.a. 5 Jan. 1838 till 12 Feb. 1841. D.J.A.G. Sirhind Div. 2 June 1841. Insurrection in Bundelkhand, Saugor & Narbada territories 1842-3; Capt. 50th N.I. Transfd. as D.J.A.G. to Presdy. Div. Mar. 1843. Civil Judge Advocate in Sind 29 July 1843 till Apr. 1852. Offg. J.A.G. of the Army Apr. 1852; permanent do. (with official rank of Lt. Col.) 4 Aug. 1854 till death. Mutiny campaign 1857-8; as J.A.G. of Army with Delhi F.F. May-Sept. 1857; Badli-ki-Serai; capture of Delhi; siege and capture of Lucknow Mar. 1858 (Medal with 2 clasps). Fur. Mar. 1860 till Jan. 1861. C.B. 18 June 1858. His Diary and Correspondence relative to the siege, assault, and capture of Delhi, 1857, was pub. 8vo 1902, edited with introduction by Gen. Sir H. W. Norman and Mrs. Keith Young.

Refs.: De Rhé-Philipe. *Scinde in the Forties*, ed. A. F. Scott, 1912 (portrait). Boase. *G.M.* 1862, ii. 234. *The Times*, 14 July 1862. M.I. in new cemetery, Simla.

YOUNG, Peter (1788-1818). Lieutenant, 12th N.I. *b.* Aberdeen 30 Sept. 1788. Cadet 1804. Arrived in India 10 Sept.

THE BENGAL ARMY, 1758-1834 549

1805. Ensign 14 Oct. 1805. Lieut. 9 Feb. 1806. *d*. Dinapore 18 Oct. 1818.

4th son of James Young, of Aberdeen, merchant, and Elizabeth Black his wife. Brother of Gavin Young, *q.v.*, and cousin-german of the wife of his uncle, Peter Black, *q.v.* *m*. Bhagulpur 29 June 1816, Maria, dau. of Peter Littlejohn, *q.v.* (*See also* Ivie Campbell.) (She died 25 Apr. 1875, aged 77.) Ed. Aberdeen Grammar School 1798-1803.

Services: Posted to 12th N.I. 1806. Operations in Oudh 1808; Lieut. 12th N.I. Adjt. Hill Rangers 1812-15. Operations against insurgent Maghs 1812. Adjt. 2/12th N.I. 29 July 1815 till death. Nepal War 1816; Lieut. 2/12th N.I., in 3rd Bde. Centre Column. Siege and capture of Hathras 1817; Lieut. 2/12th N.I. Third Mahratta War 1817-18; Bde. Major 4th L.I. Bde., Rt. Div.

Refs.: *Memoir of James Young* (1894 edn.), p. 44. *Aberdeen Journal*, 18 Aug. 1813. *S.M.* 1819, i. 584. *G.M.* 1819, i. 485. Will dated 16 Oct. 1818; proved 7 Dec. 1818.

YOUNG, Peter Martyn (1749-1778). Lieutenant, Artillery. (118) *b.* London 31 Mar. 1749. Cadet 1771. Fireworker 1 Dec. 1771. Lieut. 30 Jan. 1774. *d.s.p.* in Bengal 1 Jan. 1778.

Eldest son of Peter Young, of Exeter, and Salome his wife and cousin-german, only child of Thomas Martyn, of Kenton, Devon.

Services: Resigned in order to go home on fur. 27 Jan. 1772; readmitted 30 Nov. 1775. N.F.P.

Refs.: Vivian's *Visitations of Devon*, p. 555, *s.n.* Martyn, of Oxton. *Misc. Gen. et Her.* N.S. i. 389, 396.

YOUNG, Robert (*d.* 1781). Lieutenant, Infantry. Country Cadet 1778. Ensign 15 May 1779. Lieut. 19 Jan. 1781. *bur.* Calcutta 25 May 1781.

Services: Apptd. Cadet 11 Aug. 1778. In Comy. Gen.'s office.

Refs.: *India Gazette*, 2 June 1781.

YOUNG, Robert (*d.* 1795). Lieutenant, 30th Bn. Sepoys. Country Cadet 1779. Ensign 21 Aug. 1779. Lieut. 16 Apr. 1781. *d.* Balygautty (? Balliaghata, nr. Calcutta) 8 Feb. 1795.

Services: Apptd. Cadet 19 Aug. 1779. First Mahratta War 1781; action of 9 May 1781 (w. in foot by a rocket); Lieut. 34th N.I., under Col. Grainger Muir, *q.v.* Lieut. 4th Bn. Sepoys in July 1787; transfd. to 5th Eur. Bn. 9 Sept. 1791; to 25th Bn. Sepoys 9 Nov. 1792; Adjt. 30th Bn. at death.

Refs.: *India Gazette*, 9 and 16 June 1781.

YOUNG, Robert (1774-1804). Captain, 8th N.I. *b.* 20 Mar. 1774. Cadet 1794. Arrived in India 2 Feb. 1797. Ensign 4 Dec. 1795. Lieut. 30 Oct. 1797. Capt. 27 Aug. 1804. *d.* 24 Dec. 1804 : kld. in action at the assault of Deig.

bapt. Cleish, co. Kinross, 24 Mar. 1774. Son of Harry Young, of Cleish Castle, Kinross (of Warrock), and Margaret Chalmers his wife. Brother of William Young, of 3 New St., Bishopsgate, London.

Services : Apptd. Cadet 29 July 1795 ; sailed for India in the *Gen. Goddard* 12 Apr. 1796. Operations in Jumna Doab 1802-3 ; Sasni ; Bijaigarh ; Lieut. 1/8th N.I. Second Mahratta War 1804 ; capture of Deig (kld.) ; Capt. 1/8th N.I.

Refs. : Burke's *Landed Gentry*, 9th edn., p. 1662, *s.n.* Young, of Cleish. *G.M.* 1805, ii. 677. Will dated camp nr. Sasni, 17 Jan. 1803 ; proved 7 Nov. 1805.

YOUNG, Robert Rayner (1788-1819). Bt. Captain, 27th N.I. *b.* Glasgow 25 Jan. 1788. Cadet 1803. Arrived in India 3 Dec. 1804. Ensign 17 Nov. 1804. Lieut. 17 Nov. 1804. Bt. Capt. 8 Jan. 1818. *d.* Calcutta 14 July 1819.

bapt. Glasgow 6 Feb. 1788. 3rd son of Professor John Young and Jean his wife. Brother of James Young, *q.v.* *m.* Kidderpore, Calcutta, 25 July 1818, Sophia Charlotte, dau. of —— Hickey, R.N., and cousin-german of Francis Thomas, *q.v.* Glasgow Univ. ; matric. 1802.

Services : Posted Lieut. to newly-raised 27th N.I. 1805. Operations against Dhundia Khan 1807 ; Komona ; Ganauri ; Lieut. 2/27th N.I. Adjt. 2/27th N.I. 1808 till Jan. 1811. Operations in Oudh 1810. Adjt. & Qmr. 27th N.I. 21 Jan. 1811 till July 1814 ; Intr. & Qmr. 2/27th N.I. 1 July 1814 till Dec. 1815. Nepal War 1814-15 ; Lieut. 2/27th N.I., in 2nd Div. S.A.C.G. 22 Dec. 1815 till death. Offg. Asst. Sec. to Govt., Mily. Dept., 7 July 1817 till death.

Refs. : *S.M.* 1819, i. 284. *A.J.* ix. Will dated Calcutta 13 June 1819 ; proved 26 Aug. 1819. M.I. in S. Park St. cemetery, Calcutta.

YOUNG, Thomas (1787-1832). Major, 54th N.I. *b.* Perth 27 July 1787. Cadet 1803. Arrived in India 27 Sept. 1804. Ensign 27 Sept. 1804. Lieut. 27 Sept. 1804. Capt. 6 Nov. 1818. Major 3 Sept. 1827. *d.* Bhagulpur 6 Jan. 1832.

bapt. Perth 8 Aug. 1787. Son of John Young, of Bellwood, merchant in Perth, and Isabella Ross his wife.

Services : Posted Lieut. to newly-raised 27th N.I. 1805. Operations against Dhundia Khan 1807 ; Komona ; Ganauri ; Lieut.

THE BENGAL ARMY, 1758-1834   551

27th N.I. Nepal War 1814-15; Lieut. 27th N.I., in 2nd Div.
With 5th Gren. Bn. 1815-16. Suptg. construction of the *cutcherry* [1]
at Dehra Dun 10 Jan. 1817 till 13 Jan. 1818. Third Mahratta
War 1818; Madhurajpura; Lieut. 1/27th N.I. Fur. s.c. 20 Feb.
1821 till 20 Oct. 1825. Transfd. to 54th N.I. (late 2/27th) May
1824. Was on his way from Benares to Calcutta on sick leave
when his death occurred.
Refs.: *A.J.* N.S. viii. 111. M.I. at Bhagulpur.
[1] *Note*: Court House.

YOUNG, Thomas (1809-1852). Major, 2nd N.I. *b.* Perth
9 July 1809. Cadet 1826. Arrived in India 8 June 1827.
Ensign (16 Feb. 1827) 3 Jan. 1828. Lieut. 19 May 1830. Capt.
1 Jan. 1843. Major 17 Feb. 1851. *d.* at sea 22 Mar. 1852, on
board the *Agincourt*.

bapt. 25 July 1809. Son of John Young, of Ardberry or Ardbinnie,
and Elizabeth Donaldson his wife. *m.* Simla 16 Oct. 1846, Mary
Anne, dau. of Lawford Tronson, of Newry, and widow of William
Egerton, *q.v.* (*See also* Bruce Boswell.) (She died Portobello
1 July 1871.)

Services: Posted Ensign to 40th N.I.; transfd. to 2nd N.I.
3 Jan. 1828. Fur. s.c. 26 July 1828 till 29 Aug. 1831. (? Operations against the Kols 1832; Lieut. 2nd N.I.) Actg. Adjt. 2nd N.I.
25 Dec. 1837. Offg. Bde. Major 3rd Bde., Army of Indus, 29 Jan.
1839. First Afghan War 1840-2; operations against Ghilzais 1840;
against Duranis Dec. 1840-Jan. 1841, with detachment 2nd N.I.
under Capt. H. W. Farrington, *q.v.*; action at Landi-nawa 3 Jan.
1841 (s.w.); Kandahar; Ghazni; Kabul; Bt. Capt. 2nd N.I.,
with Nott's force (Medal). Adjt. 2nd N.I. 16 July 1842 till 14 Feb.
1843. Granted a gratuity of 6 mos. pay for wound. Bde. Major
3rd Bde. 2nd Inf. Div., Army of Exercise, 17 Nov. 1843. Gwalior
campaign; Maharajpur (*Lond. Gaz.* 8 Mar. 1844); Capt. 2nd N.I.,
Bde. Major (Bronze star). Bde. Major Stacy's Bde. 22 Jan. 1844.
Comdt. 7th Inf., Gwalior Contingent, 8 Mar. 1844 till 28 July 1851.
Fur. 1852 till death.

YOUNG, William (1794-1816). Ensign, 9th N.I. *b.* psh. of
Moycosquin (?), co. Londonderry, 26 Mar. 1794. Cadet 1811.
Ensign 7 Feb. 1814. *d.* Cawnpore 2 Oct. 1816: kld. by a fall from
his horse.

Youngest son of Rev. Gardiner Young and Catherine Richardson
his wife. Brother of Frederick Young, *q.v.*

Services: Posted Ensign to 1/9th N.I. 1814. No record of active
service.

Refs.: Burke's *Landed Gentry of Ireland*, p. 784, *s.n.* Young, of Culdaff House, co. Donegal.

YOUNG, William (1809-1885). Captain. 38th N.I. *b.* Banff 4 Nov. 1809. Cadet 1825. Arrived in India 3 Feb. 1827. Ensign 12 Sept. 1826. Lieut. 21 Dec. 1831. Bt. Capt. 12 Sept. 1841. Capt. 1843. Retired 5 July 1843. *d.* 1 Aug. 1885.

bapt. Banff 8 Nov. 1809. Son of Archibald Young (afterwards Young-Leslie), 12th laird of Kininvie, co. Banff, writer, and Jane his wife, dau. of James Donaldson, of Kinnairdy. Requested permission to assume surname of Leslie in addition to that of Young (M.C. 1 Sept. 1841).

Services: Ensign d.d. 57th N.I. 20 Feb. 1827; posted to 38th N.I. 10 May 1827. Fur. s.c. 27 Aug. 1829 till 9 Sept. 1832. Operations against Chuars 1832; comdg. a detachment of 38th N.I. at Huldeepokur in Dec. 1832 when Bhima Singh, a Chuar chief, surrendered. Adjt. 38th N.I. 31 Oct. 1837 till 26 Apr. 1839. Offg. Asst. to P.A. in Upper Sind 14 June 1839; permanent do. 26 Nov. 1839. Fur. s.c. 6 Jan. 1841 till retirement.

Refs.: Burke's *Landed Gentry*, 13th edn., p. 1084, *s.n.* Leslie, of Kininvie.

YOUNG, William Oliver (1810-1843). Bt. Captain, Artillery. (581) *b.* Calcutta 6 Feb. 1810. Cadet 1825. Arrived in India 7 July 1826. 2nd Lieut. 16 Dec. 1825. Lieut. 28 Jan. 1833. Bt. Capt. 16 Dec. 1840. *d.* Erinpura, Rajputana, 6 June 1843.

bapt. Calcutta 10 Mar. 1810. 3rd son of Henry Young, of Fowler's Park, Kent, M.D., Bengal Medical Est., and Elizabeth his wife, sister of Archibald Oliver, *q.v. m.* Nasirabad 3 June 1830, Eliza Harriette, eldest dau. of James Patrick Fagan, *q.v.* (She died 25 Mar. 1893.) Ed. Charterhouse Sept. 1821-Dec. 1823. Addiscombe Cadet 1824-5.

Services: Actg. Adjt. & Qmr. 2nd Bn. Foot Art. 12 Apr. 1834 and 7 Oct. 1835. Adjt. & Qmr. Nimach Div. Art. 21 July 1835 till 19 Jan. 1836. Offg. Comy. Ord. 8 Dec. 1835; Dy. Comy. Ord. 12 Jan. 1836; posted to charge of Ajmer mag. and lead mines 26 Jan. 1836. On field service in Marwar Aug. 1839. Comy. Ord. at Ajmer 4 Mar. 1840 till death.

Refs.: Burke's *Landed Gentry*, 13th edn., p. 1963, *s.n.* Keays-Young, of Eylesden, Kent. *Charterhouse School List. G.M.* 1843, ii. 334. *The Times*, 10 Aug. 1843. M.I. in St. Stephen's, Dum-Dum, and Erinpura cemetery.

YOUNGER, John Robertson (1809-1890). Lieut. Colonel. 56th N.I. *b.* Huddersfield 5 Jan. 1809. Cadet 1825. Ensign

THE BENGAL ARMY, 1758-1834   553

12 Oct. 1825. Lieut. 2 Nov. 1826. Capt. 24 Jan. 1845. Bt. Major 11 Nov. 1851. Retired 9 Mar. 1852. Hon. Lt. Col. 28 Nov. 1854. *d.* Willow House, High Rd., Stamford Hill, 1 Dec. 1890.

bapt. Huddersfield 17 May 1809. Son of Rev. Ralph Younger, minister at Huddersfield, and Mary his wife, late Robertson. *m.* Claines, Worcs., 5 Jan. 1853, Julia Anne, dau. of Lancelot Blackett. (She died Southend 1 Sept. 1902.)

Services : Posted to 56th N.I. 1826 ; Intr. & Qmr. do. 17 Dec. 1832 till 11 Jan. 1844. Fur. s.c. 9 Jan. 1844 till 1846. Offg. D.J.A.G. Punjab Div. 15 Dec. 1847 ; D.J.A.G. Cawnpore 10 Mar. 1848 ; do. Lahore ; do. Meerut Div. 27 Nov. 1850 till retirement. Second Sikh War ; no actions ; Capt. 56th N.I., D.J.A.G. (Medal).

Refs. : *I.M.* 18 Jan. 1853, p. 20. *The Times,* 4 Dec. 1890.

YOUNGHUSBAND, Astley George Francis John (1807-1866). Major General. 35th N.I. *b.* Belford, Northumberland, 18 June 1807. Cadet 1823. Arrived in India 19 May 1824. Ensign 16 Jan. 1824. Lieut. 21 Apr. 1825. Capt. 13 Oct. 1839. Major 27 June 1857. Bt. Lt. Col. 20 June 1854. Bt. Col. 3 Dec. 1857. Retired 13 Sept. 1859. Hon. Maj. Gen. 13 Sept. 1859. *d.* Elm House, Charlton Kings, 24 June 1866.

Of Elm House, Charlton Kings, nr. Cheltenham. *bapt.* 22 June 1807. Only son of George Younghusband, of Elwick, later of Twyning Park, Gloucs., formerly Lieut. 3rd D.G. and Major in the Spanish Service, and Maria his wife, 2nd dau. of Francis John Astley, of Dukinfield, co. Chester. Cousin-german of Oswald John Younghusband, *q.v. m.* 1st, 1835, Marie Françoise, 4th dau. of Pierre Beaufite (? Beaufils), of Port Louis, Mauritius. (She died at sea on board the *Madagascar* 12 Sept. 1839.) *m.* 2nd, Karnal 15 Feb. 1843, Ernestine Mary Amelia, 2nd dau. of John Oliver, *q.v.* (*See also* Robert Campbell (1800-1889).) (She died Ealing 14 Nov. 1888, aged 64.)

Services : Posted to 35th N.I. 1824. Siege and capture of Bhurtpore ; Lieut. 35th N.I. (India medal). Leave s.c. to Tasmania 13 Sept. 1833 till Oct. 1835 ; fur. p.a. 27 Jan. 1837 till 11 Nov. 1839. First Afghan War 1840-2 ; Bamian (*Lond. Gaz.* 9 Jan. 1841) ; forcing of Khurd Kabul Pass (s.w.) (*ib.* 11 Feb. and 9 Aug. 1842) ; defence of Jalalabad (Medal) ; Capt. 35th N.I. Granted gratuity of 1 yr.'s pay for wound. Offg. Comst. Ofr. at Karnal 25 Aug. 1842 till Jan. 1843. Bde. Major at Agra 26 Dec. 1843 ; offg. A.D.C. to Maj.-Gen. James Alexander, *q.v.*, comdg. Benares Div., 5 Nov. 1844.

Fur. s.c. 9 Mar. 1851 till 30 Nov. 1854, and 1858 till retirement. Durani 3 cl. 7 Sept. 1841.

Refs.: *Genealogist,* ii. 61. Burke's *Royal Families,* ped. lxii. Boase. *G.M.* 1866, ii. 273. *The Times,* 27 June 1866.

YOUNGHUSBAND, Oswald John (1808-1879). Lieutenant. 60th N.I. Subsequently of the Foreign Office. *b.* Stonebridge, Middlesex, 26 May 1808. Cadet 1827. Arrived in India 10 Dec. 1828. Ensign 21 July 1828. Lieut. 18 June 1834. Retired 13 Mar. 1837. *d.* Shanklin, I.W., 16 Dec. 1879.

2nd son of William Younghusband, of Beadnell, Comdr. of the *Lord Castlereagh,* East Indiaman, and Anne his wife, 2nd dau. of Thomas Younghusband, of Tuggall. Cousin-german of A. G. F. J. Younghusband, *q.v. m.* Brit. Embassy, Paris, 12 Nov. 1853, Mary, dau. of Henry Heyward, of Aylesbury. (She died 15 Oct. 1894, aged 81.)

Services : Ensign d.d. 24th N.I. 14 Jan. 1829; posted to 60th N.I. Leave s.c. 18 mos. to Cape 31 July 1830; s.c. 7 mos. to China 27 June 1832. d.d. 35th N.I. 23 Jan. till 1 Oct. 1833. Fur. s.c. 11 Apr. 1835 till retirement. Retired on h.p. of Lieut., viz., 4/- *p.d.* No record of active service.

Refs.: *Genealogist,* ii. 58. *The Times,* 22 Dec. 1879.

YULE, Thomas Newte (1803-?). Ensign. 63rd N.I. *b.* London 20 Sept. 1803. Cadet 1825. Ensign 26 Dec. 1825. Resigned 12 Feb. 1830.

bapt. Marylebone 15 Feb. 1804. Son of John Yule, Capt. R.N., of Branscombe, Devon, and Elizabeth his wife, *née* Carslake. Sandhurst Cadet.

Services : Posted to 63rd N.I. 1826; actg. Adjt. do. 17 Nov. 1829. No record of active service.

YULE, Udny (*d.* 1830). Colonel, C.B., 18th N.I. Cadet 1782. Admitted 20 Sept. 1783. Ensign 13 Mar. 1785. Lieut. 30 May 1793. Capt. 13 July 1803. Major 19 May 1808. Lt. Col. 11 Apr. 1814. Lt. Col. Comdt. 4 Sept. 1823. Col. 5 June 1829. *d.* Edinburgh 4 Mar. 1830.

Of Ballencrieff, E. Lothian. Son of George Yule and Elizabeth his wife, dau. of Rev. James Rose (of the family of Kilravock), Episcopal minister of Udny, co. Aberdeen. Brother of William Yule, *q.v.,* of Marion, mother of Patrick Dudgeon, *q.v.,* and of Mary, wife of Thomas Cleghorn, of Weem.

Services : Apptd. Cadet 19 Dec. 1782; sailed for India in the *Duke of Kingston* 11 Mar. 1783.[1] Posted to 2nd Bengal Eur. Bn.

15 Feb. 1790. Lieut. 5th N.I. in June 1798; transfd. to 2nd Eur.
Regt. 1798; Qmr. Marine Regt. (became 20th N.I.) in 1803. Fur.
22 Dec. 1805 till 21 Oct. 1809. Capture of Java 1811; Major
1/20th N.I.; comdd. a Bde. at capture of Cornelis (gold medal),
and afterwards acted as Resdt. under Sir Stamford Raffles (*Lond.
Gaz.* 20 Jan. 1812). Posted Lt. Col. to 11th N.I. 1814; to 1/24th
N.I. 1815; to Bengal Eur. Regt. 1816. Comdg. at Bantam. Fur.
24 Mar. 1818 till 1822. Transfd. to 10th N.I. 1822. Lt. Col. Comdt.
40th N.I. (late 2/20th) May 1824. Fur. 1824 till death. Transfd.
to 18th N.I. 1828; Col. do. 1829 till death. C.B. 4 June 1815.

Refs.: Memoir of Sir Henry Yule prefixed to the *Book of Ser
Marco Polo*, 1903 edn., by his dau., Amy Frances Yule. *G.M.*
1830, ii. 477. Will dated Edinburgh 5 Feb. 1828; proved 19 Aug.
1831.

[1] *Note*: She was burnt at sea off Ceylon 20 Aug. 1783. " After
keeping himself afloat for several hours in the water, he was rescued
by a passing ship and taken back to Mauritius, whence, having lost
everything but his Cadetship, he made a fresh start for India."
(*Memoir.*)

YULE, William (1764-1839). Major. 19th N.I. *b.* 1764.
Cadet 1780. Admitted 17 Sept. 1781. Ensign 29 July 1781.
Lieut. 27 Oct. 1782. Capt. 14 Dec. 1802. Major 28 Oct. 1806.
Retired 7 Sept. 1808. *d.* 25 Regent Terr., Edinburgh, 6 Oct.
1839.

Of Inveresk. Son of George Yule and Elizabeth his wife.
Brother of Udny Yule, *q.v. m.* Edinburgh 1811, Elizabeth, eldest
dau. of William Paterson, of Braehead, and sister of William
Paterson (1791-1819), *q.v.* Father of Sir Henry Yule, K.C.S.I.
(*D.N.B.*).

Services: Apptd. Cadet 21 Dec. 1780, aged 16; sailed for India
in the *Chapman* 13 Mar. 1781, aged 16. Lieut. 36th Bn. Sepoys
in July 1787; Bt. Capt. 5th N.I. in June 1798; Lieut. and Bt.
Capt. 16th N.I.; Capt. Lt. do. 29 May 1800. Postmr. at Lucknow
in 1800. Transfd. as Capt. to 19th N.I. Asst. to Lt.-Col. William
Scott, Resdt. at Lucknow, *q.v.*, and comdg. his escort 25 Feb. 1804;
afterwards Asst. to Lt.-Col. D. Ochterlony, *q.v.*, Resdt. at Delhi.
Fur. 18 Feb. 1806 till retirement. Was offered appt. of Lt. Govr.
of St. Helena. Pub. privately, 1837, a litho. edn. of the *Apothegms
of Ali*, in the Arabic, with an English translation.

Refs.: *Book of Ser Marco Polo*, 1903 edn. *A.J.* N.S. xxx. 263.

Z

***ZIEGLER,**[1] **Alexander** (1723/24-1758). Captain, Infantry.
b. Schaffhausen, Switzerland, 1723/24. Capt. 12 Feb. 1752.
d. (? at sea) 20 Nov. 1758.

Services : Ordered to raise a Protestant Swiss Coy. for Bombay, with Commission as Capt. dated 12 Feb. 1752. Expedn. against Gheria under Clive Feb. 1756 ; comdg. Swiss Coy. of Bombay Eur. Regt. Comdg. do. on detachment in Madras 1754-5. Apptd. in England in Mar. 1758, a Capt. on the Bengal Est., to rank from 12 Feb. 1752 ; sailed for India in the *Prince George* Mar. 1758, aged 34.

Refs. : *Schweizersöldner im dienste der Englisch-Ostindischen Kompanie,* von Dr. J. E. Kilchenmann (Grüningen, 1911). *Hist. of the Bombay Army,* by Sir Patrick Cadell (1938), pp. 59, 60.

[1] *Note :* His name sometimes appears as de Ziegler.

APPENDIX A
LOCAL OFFICERS

THE following list, unfortunately far from exhaustive, has been included as it was felt that a work of this nature would be incomplete without some recognition, however meagre, of the services of a deserving class of soldier, many of whom, as in the two Great Wars, joined up in order to 'do their bit' in response to their Country's call.

Local Officers were those who, belonging only to the Irregular Corps, did not hold a King's Commission as did the officers of the Coy.'s regular service. In other words, they were appointed by, and received their Commissions from, the Governor General in India, not from the Court of Directors at the India House. Most of these Irregular or Local Corps came into existence only during the years 1815-17, several of them being disbanded during the period of peace which followed the Third Mahratta War.

The officers with whom we are now about to deal fall, broadly speaking, into four classes. Firstly, those who left the service of Indian princes on the outbreak of the Second Mahratta War in 1803, and transferred their allegiance to the Coy. They were experienced officers who had already made a name for themselves whilst serving with the irregular troops of their former masters. This class, which includes men of pure European descent (*e.g.*, W. L. Gardner, Meiselbach, Pohlman), and of mixed descent (*e.g.*, James Skinner, 'the Father of Irregular Cavalry,' and H. Y. Hearsey), received a pension and employment from the British Govt. on quitting that of their Indian employers.[1]

The second class consists of the sons, by Indian mothers, of some of those who have appeared in the earlier pages of this List. Not being of pure European descent, they were in consequence ineligible to hold a regular Commission; but their knowledge of the manners, customs, religions and language of the men whom they commanded

---

[1] Those who wish to learn more of these soldier-adventurers are referred to two interesting books on this fascinating subject: *European Military Adventurers in Hindustan*, by Herbert Compton, pub. in T. Fisher Unwin's Adventure Series; and *Hindustan under Free Lances, 1770-1820*, by H. A. Keene, C.I.E., London, 1907. These works will hereafter be cited as *Compton* and *Keene*. The latest book on the subject is *European Adventurers in Northern India, 1785 to 1849*, by C. Grey and H. L. O. Garrett (Lahore Govt. Press, 1929). This will be referred to as *Grey & Garrett*.

pre-eminently fitted them for such service. The Martindells, Forsters and Penningtons are examples of this class.

The third class comprises both Departmental Warrant Officers and subordinate officials of the Coy. (*e.g.*, Babonau, Clarke, Ireland, Radcliffe) as well as the sons of indigo planters, or themselves planters (*e.g.*, Cave and Babington). The majority of this class were presumably of unmixed European descent.

The last and smallest class consists of those (*e.g.*, Picard and William Smith) who had previously held a Commission in H.M.S.

Most of these men were discharged in June 1822, Government having decided to officer Local and Irregular Corps more extensively from the Line, and to dispense with the services of Local Officers as much as possible in the future.

AIRD, G—— D——. Local Sub-Lieut., Cuttack Legion, 4 July 1817. N.F.P.

AIRD, Robert Abercrombie (1796-?). Local Sub-Lieut., Cuttack Legion, 4 July 1817. *b.* 22 Apr. 1796; *bapt.* Calcutta 3 June 1796.

Son of Alexander Aird, Conductor of Ord., and Susanna his wife. His sister *m.* Patrick Grant Matheson, *q.v.*

Services: N.F.P.

ALLAN or ALLEN, Peter (*d.* 1853). Bt. Captain. Ord. Dept. Local Sub-Lieut. 13 Sept. 1816. Retired 7 June 1837. Bt. Capt. 7 June 1837. *d.* 13 Dec. 1853.

Services: Sent out in 1816 by C.D. to teach the use of Congreve's rockets. Apptd. Dy. Comy. Ord. and posted as Local Sub-Lieut. to Rocket Troop on its formation (G.O. 13 Sept. 1816). Rank cancelled by G.G. and ordered to return to Europe (G.O. 27 Sept. 1816). These orders countermanded, and he was restored to his rank (G.O. 8 Nov. 1816). Served with Rocket Troop till 1822. Asst. Comy. Ord. 19 May 1818; Dy. Comy. Ord. at Allahabad 1 Aug. 1828 till retirement. First Burma War; Asst. Comy. Ord. (India medal).

BABINGTON, Charles Lucas (1794/95-1843). Local Ensign. Ramgarh Bn. Afterwards Executive Ofr., P.W.D. *b.* 1794/95. Local Ensign 25 Aug. 1818. *d.* Sambalpur, B. & O., 25 May 1843, aged 48.

m. Cuttack 23 Nov. 1835, Miss Harriot Robinson. (She died 28 Aug. 1873, aged 65.)

Services: Served with Ramgarh Bn. till after 1822. (? Operations against the Larka Kols Feb. 1821.) Was an indigo planter at Mudhobun, Sambalpur, in 1826; latterly Postmr. of Sambalpur and Executive Ofr. in charge of the Raipur road.

Refs.: *I.M.* 3 Aug. 1843, p. 117. Will dated 1 Mar. 1841; proved 29 June 1843. M.I. at Sambalpur.

BABONAU, Henry (1765-1834). Local Cornet. 2nd (Borlase's) Rampura Local Cav. Afterwards Dy. Comy. of Ord. *b.* 15 May 1765. Asst. Comy. Ord. 19 May 1818. Local Cornet 11 Aug. 1818. Dy. Comy. Ord. 8 Apr. 1823. *d.* Calcutta 10 Sept. 1834.

m. 1st, 18 Sept. 1814, Miss Maria Parlby. (She died 9 Aug. 1821.) *m.* 2nd, Dinapore 6 June 1822, Mrs. Mary Loane.

Refs.: *A.J.* N.S. xvi. 196. Will dated 30 Aug. 1834; proved 16 Sept. 1834. M.I. in Bhowanipore cemetery, Calcutta.

BELL, Charles Clarke (1797/98-1833). Local Lieutenant. 4th (Sneyd's) Local Horse. Afterwards Comdr. of the barque *Mercury*. *b.* 1797/98. Local Lieut. 1 Jan. 1817. *d.* Calcutta 26 Oct. 1833, aged 35.

Brother of Richard Clarke Bell, indigo planter. *m.* Anne, late Moore, of Calcutta.

Refs.: *A.J.* N.S. xiii. 270. Will dated 30 Aug. 1831; proved 5 Nov. 1833.

BEVERIDGE, J——. Local Cornet, 4th (Sneyd's) Horse, 28 Nov. 1818. Transfd. as Ensign to Sirmoor Bn. 21 Aug. 1819. Out of the Service before Dec. 1821.

Perhaps identical with William Beveridge (Vol. i. p. 137).

BROWNRIGG, John Boyle (*d.* 1804). Local Major, comdg. a Corps of Levies. *d.* 19 Feb. 1804 : kld. in action nr. Sirsa, Hariana district.

An Irish officer in the Mahratta service. Raised an independent corps for Daulat Rao Sindhia; captured fort of Kolapur, nr. Poona, 1799. Repulsed Holkar in July and Oct. 1801; quarrelled with Perron 1802. Confined by his own men in Agra Fort after the outbreak of war with the British 1803. After the fall of Agra he entered the British service, received comd. of some irregular levies, and was employed against Jaswant Rao Holkar. His widow was granted an annual pension of £60 by the C.D. in 1805.

Refs.: *Compton*, appendix.

BURROWES, J—— E—— (*d.* 1820). Lieutenant and Adjt., Gardner's Horse. Local Lieut. 1 July 1817. *d.* Saugor 21 Sept. 1820.

Services : Was d.d. Gardner's Horse in 1816 ; Adjt. do. before July 1817 till death.

Refs. : *A.J.* xi. 511.

BUTTERFIELD, Edward (1772-1832). Local Ofr. in Gardner's Horse. *b.* 1772. *d.* Agra 12 Sept. 1832, aged 60.

Reputed son of Capt. Edward Butterfield, *q.v. m.* Martha. (She died Agra 2 May 1857, aged 77.)

Services : Joined Sindhia's army in 1788, which he quitted before long for employment under the Rajah of Karaoli, and afterwards that of Durjan Sal, a Rajput chief. Returned to Sindhia's service *c.* 1792, and by 1794 had risen to the rank of Capt. Served under Ambaji Inglia against Lakwa Dada. Left the Mahratta service in 1799, and was subsequently pensioned as Capt. by the Brit. Govt. In Dec. 1814, applied for employment during the Nepal War and served with Gardner's Horse.

Refs.: *B.: P.P.* No. 84, pp. 93-6. *Compton,* pp. 235, 344. M.I. Agra Cantt. cemetery.

CAMERON, Alexander Macquarrie (1800-1819). Local Ensign, Champaran L.I. *b.* 1 Nov. 1800. Local Ensign 25 Aug. 1818. *d.* 19 July 1819 : kld. in action at the storm of Aligarh, aged 18.

Natural son of the late Capt. A. Cameron, H.M. 76th Foot, by Annette Smith, *née* Mitchell. Half-brother of Lucius Horton Smith, *q.v.*

Refs.: *A.J.* ix. 73.

CAMPBELL, W——. Local Ensign, Champaran L.I., 25 Aug. 1818. Out of the Service before Dec. 1821.

CARNEGIE, George (*d.* 1805). Captain, Pension Est.

4th son of George Carnegie, of Pitcairn, Scotland ; brother of Susan and Ann Carnegie. *d. unm.* Delhi 15 July 1805, of liver disease.

Services : Granted a pension of Rs. 500/- *p.m.* by Brit. Govt. on leaving the Mahratta service. Second Mahratta War ; defence of Delhi Oct. 1804 ; Capt. in Corps comdd. by Alexander Harriott, *q.v.* " After surviving several severe campaigns in India, both in the service of the Mahrattas and that of the Coy., in which he uniformly acquitted himself in the noblest manner, and with the fairest prospect of higher preferment, he fell a victim, in the prime of life, to the disease of the country, a complaint of the liver." (*M.M.*)

Refs.: *Calcutta Monthly Journal,* Nov. 1804. *M.M.* 1806, i. 194.

LOCAL OFFICERS

G.M. 1806, i. 180. Will dated camp before Bahadurgarh 8 Jan. 1805; proved 8 Feb. 1806.

CAVE, John Jefferson (1799/1800-1860). Local Lieutenant. 2nd Nassiri Bn. Afterwards an indigo planter. *b.* nr. London 1799/1800. Local Cornet 1 Feb. 1817. Local Lieut. 28 Nov. 1818. *d.* Purnea 9 Apr. 1860, aged 60.

Services : Posted Local Cornet to 4th (Sneyd's) Horse Feb. 1817; transfd. as Local Lieut. to 2nd Nassiri Bn. 21 Aug. 1819. Became an indigo planter at Purnea.

Refs. : *I.M.* 28 May 1860. Will dated 11 Nov. 1857; proved 25 June 1860. M.I. in old protestant cemetery, Purnea.

CLARKE, H——. Local Ensign, Gorakhpur L.I., 30 Jan. (? 6 Mar.) 1819.

Services : Permitted to return to his former situation as a Sub-Conductor in Ord. Dept. (G.O. 26 Aug. 1831). (? Was an indigo planter at Jessore in 1846.)

Note : Henry Clarke *d.* Calcutta 5 Oct. 1855, aged 59.

COLLIS, Robert (*d.* 1818). Local Ensign, Ramgarh Bn., 25 Aug. 1818. *bur.* Benares June 1818.

Note : The authorities were unaware of his death when the appt. was made. John Collis was a shopkeeper at Benares in 1816.

COMYN, Robert Powell (1804-?). Admitted to the Service with rank of Local Lieut. and Adjt., and posted to 8th Local Horse 18 Feb. 1825. N.F.P.

bapt. Dinapore 13 Aug. 1804. Natural son of Powell Thomas Comyn, *q.v.*, by Jane De Courcy.

CUMBERLEGE, William. Local Lieutenant, Agra Najib Bn. (In *A.L.* of 1 July 1820 and 5 Jan. 1822. Not traced further.)

CUMINE, G—— (? *d.* 1834). Local Ensign, Champaran L.I., 19 June 1819. Out of the Service before Dec. 1821.

CUSSONS, Roderick. Local Cornet, Baddeley's Horse, 20 June 1817. Sometime of Skinner's Horse. Served in Third Mahratta War.

(*Perhaps* son of Thomas Cussons or Cozens, *q.v.*)

CUSSONS, Thomas. Local Lieutenant, 4th (Sneyd's) Horse 1 Feb. 1817. N.F.P.

(*N.B.*—Mr. T. Cussons, missionary, *m.* Berhampore 22 Jan. 1835, Miss Sarah Jones.)

DARE, William (*d.* 1820). Local Lieutenant, Rangpur Local Bn. Local Ensign 25 Aug. 1818. Local Lieut. (?) *d.* Titalia, Bengal, 9 Nov. 1820.

Refs.: A.J. xi. 512.

d'CAMERA d'NORONHA, Joseph Joachim (1766-1819). Local Captain. Gardner's Horse. *b.* Dec. 1766. Local Capt. (?) *d.* Patna 3 June 1819, aged 52½.

Son of Dom M. d'Camera d'Noronha, of a very old Portuguese family. *m.* (before 1803) Dona Francisca ———. (She died Patna 31 Dec. 1877, aged 95.)

Services: "In the flower of life, he entered the army and served 8 years with great satisfaction as a cavalry officer in the service and Goa dominions of His Most Faithful Majesty the King of Portugal. After this he served as Captain under several Princes of Hindustan. Finally, being pensioned by the English Government, he retired to Patna; but, some time after, he was appointed Capt. in the Irregular Cavalry under the command of Col. W. L. Gardner." (Translation of M.I.)

Refs.: M.I. erected by his widow on the front of the R.C. Church at Patna.

DICK, Robert (*d.* 1835). Local Lieutenant. Skinner's Horse. *d.* 1835.

Natural son of Maj.-Gen. Sir Robert Henry Dick, K.C.B. (*D.N.B.*), by an Indian woman.

Services: Originally an officer in the Gwalior forces, then, till 1831, Local Lieut. in Skinner's Horse. He next entered the service of Shah Shuja, and finally that of the Amir of Sind.

Refs.: Grey & Garrett, pp. 311-13.

DOUGLAS, William (*d.* 1827). Local Ensign, Gorakhpur L.I. Bn., 4 May 1818; Local Lieut. do. 26 Aug. 1818. (*See* Vol. ii. 76.)

DRING, Robert John (1798-1842). Local Lieutenant. Ramgarh Local Bn. *b.* Calcutta 27 Apr. 1798. Local Ensign, Gorakhpur L.I., 25 Aug. 1818. Local Lieut. 1 Jan. 1819. *bur.* Calcutta 24 Mar. 1842, aged 43.

Son of William Dring, of the firm of Tulloh & Co., Calcutta, agents and auctioneers, and Caroline Harvey his wife. *m.* Calcutta 1 Aug. 1836, Miss Margaret Maclean Todd, dau. of John Todd. (She *re-m.* John Minshull Drake, *q.v.*) Ed. Edinburgh.

Services: Served with Gorakhpur L.I. Sept. 1818 till 26 Feb. 1819, when he was apptd. to the Nagpur service. Was comdg. a

Bn. in the 'provincial' service at end of 1829; discharged with gratuity early in 1830, together with all the remaining Local Ofrs. of the Nagpur service. Returned to Gorakhpur L.I.; given tempy. comd. of a dett. of Ramgarh Bn. at Sambalpur 16 May 1833. Later became an Asst. in firm of Hamilton & Co., jewellers, Calcutta.

DUBOIS, Felix. Local Lieutenant, 2nd Rampura Local Bn., 11 Aug. 1818. N.F.P.

DUFF, James (1799/1800-1834). Local Lieutenant and Adjt., Arakan Local Bn. *b.* 1799/1800. Adjt. Magh Sebundy Corps 29 Apr. 1830; do. Arakan Local Bn. (?) *d.* Akyab 26 Mar. 1834, aged 34.

m. Akyab 3 May 1830, Ann, 2nd dau. of Hugh Augustus Boscawen, *q.v.*

Refs.: A.J. N.S. xv. 100.

EDGAR, W—— G——. Local Lieutenant. Ramgarh Bn. Local Sub-Lieut., 3rd (Baddeley's) Horse, 4 Oct. 1817. Corrected to Local Lieut. from same date (G.O. 6 Feb. 1819). Transfd. to Ramgarh Bn. 21 Aug. 1819. Out of the Service before Dec. 1821.

EDMUND, William. Local Cornet, 1st Rampura Local Cav., 11 Aug. 1818. Out of the Service before Dec. 1821.

EDWARDS, William (1787/88-1840). Local Lieutenant. Champaran L.I. Afterwards Overseer of H.C. Stud at Buxar. *b.* 1787/88. Local Lieut. 19 June 1819. *d.* Calcutta 25 May 1840, aged 52.

Of Loudon St., Calcutta. Son of John Edwards, of I. of St. Mary, Scilly Is., and Mary his wife. *m.* Mary.

Refs.: Will dated 24 Dec. 1827; proved 9 June 1840. M.I. in Scotch burial ground, Calcutta.

FANTHOME,[1] **Bernard** (1770/71-1845). Captain. Gardner's Irregular Horse. Pensioned Ofr. of Mahratta Service. *b.* in France 1770/71. *bur.* Bareilly 25 Nov. 1845, aged 74.

Of French descent.

Services: "He ran away from home probably about the time of the French Revolution. He served first under Raymond in Hyderabad and then migrated to Bhopal, where his brother Jean Baptiste comdd. a Bde. He served under the Maharajah of Jaipur and fought at Madhogarh; he then joined Sindhia's service, but left him with many other officers when war with the British broke out, and joined

Lake, being made a Capt. in Col. Gardner's Irreg. Horse. He retired after the war and lived first at Patna and then at Bareilly, where a market called Faltunganj still commemorates his name. He had studied medicine in his youth and now began to practise it again. On one occasion he was summoned by Metcalfe to attend Shah Alam at Delhi, but the Emperor died before he could even see him. He became physician to the Nawab of Rampur and subsequently his chief minister for a time ; but disagreements followed and he returned to Bareilly, where he again practised medicine. He died somewhat suddenly in 1845." (Blunt's *Christian Tombs in U.P.*) He received a pension as Lieut. from the Brit. Govt. ; but his name is not given in Lewis Ferdinand Smith's list of pensions granted to Mahratta officers and Brit. subjects.

¹ *Note :* The name Fanthome or Fantôme (Phantom) is probably a disguise. (*Blunt*).

FITZROY, Frederick William (*d.* 1843). Local Cornet. Dromedary Corps. Local Ensign, Champaran L.I., 3 Jan. 1817. d. 1843.

Natural son of Hon. Frederick Fitzroy, B.C.S. *m.* Dinapore 8 Oct. 1836, Amelia, widow of John Havell, of Deegah farm, nr. Dinapore. (She died Deegah farm 31 May 1843, aged 43.)

Services : Transfd. to Dromedary Corps 1817 till disbanded 1 Oct. 1821. Supt. of mily. roads, Nagpur. Apptd. a Local Ofr. in Nagpur service 14 May 1823 ; discharged with gratuity, with all other Local Ofrs., in 1830.

Refs. : *Hickey*, iii. 171-2. Intestate ; admon. 21 Feb. 1844.

FORSTER, Henry (1793-1862). Colonel, C.B., Comdt. Shekhawati Bn. *b.* Calcutta 25 Dec. 1793. Local Cornet 1816. Local Lieut. 30 Sept. 1817. Local Major 23 Jan. 1835. Major 19 June 1846. Lt. Col. 20 June 1854. Col. 20 June 1857. d. Calcutta 9 Oct. 1862.

Son of Henry Pitts Forster, B.C.S. (*D.N.B.*), Mint Master at Calcutta, by a Jat woman. His sister *m.* David Mason, *q.v. m.* 1st, Calcutta 9 Sept. 1814, Wilhelmina Elizabeth, elder dau. of Paul Kellner, formerly Lieut. Württemberg Regt., afterwards headmaster of the Lower Orphan School, Calcutta. (*See also* Abraham Fuller.) (She was kld. at Delhi 11 May 1857, aged 58.) Father of Henry Pitts Forster, William Robert Forster, and of the wife of Henry James Michell, *qq.v. m.* 2nd, Nina, an Indian. (She died 1883.) Ed. Ealing Grammar School.

Services : Entered the Mahratta army. Apptd. Local Cornet and Adjt. 1st Skinner's Horse, 13 Apr. 1816 ; Adjt. 2nd Corps

do. 1817-19. Third Mahratta and Pindari War under Sir David
Ochterlony and Sir John Malcolm; Mahidpur (India medal).
Transfd. to Roberts's Horse 1819; rejoined Skinner's Horse as
2nd in comd. 1822. Local Lieut. 10th Rangpur L.I. 22 July 1824.
Raised Rangpur Horse 1826. Adjt. 3rd Local Horse 3 June 1830;
actg. 2nd in comd. do. 15 Apr. 1834. Raised Shekhawati Bde.
(became Shekhawati Bn. in 1847) 1835; Comdt. do. 23 Jan. 1835
till death. Comdd. his Bde. in action against insurgents in
Shekhawat country 1837-40; assault of fort Kaluk, Rajputana,
10 Dec. 1840 (s.w.). First Sikh War; Aliwal (horse shot); Local
Major comdg. Shekhawati Bde. (Medal). Mutiny campaign;
against insurgents in Manbhum and Singhbhum districts. Comr.
of Sambalpur 29 Mar. till 17 Aug. 1858. Fur. to England Aug.
1858. C.B. 27 June 1846.

Refs.: D.I.B. B.: P.P. xxviii. 233. M.I. in Lower Circular
Rd. cemetery, Calcutta.

FORSTER, Henry Pitts (1822-1850). Local Lieutenant and
Adjt. Shekhawati Bde. 1 Dec. 1838. b. Bhopalpore 27 Feb. 1822.
d. Mirzapur, U.P., 26 May 1850.

Son of Henry Forster, q.v.

Refs.: I.M. 1 Aug. 1850, p. 452. Intestate; admon. 1 Aug.
1850. M.I. Mirzapur.

FORSTER, William Robert (1817-1889). Lieut. Colonel
(Unattached). Shekhawati Bde. b. Hansi 21 Feb. 1817. Capt.
and 2nd in comd. Shekhawati Bde. 1 Jan. 1837. Capt. (Unattached)
29 July 1852. Major (do.) 8 Oct. 1860. Retired 1 Jan. 1865.
Lt. Col. 18 July 1865. d. London 16 May 1889.

bapt. Calcutta 15 July 1819. Son of Henry Forster, q.v., and
Wilhelmina Elizabeth his wife. Brother of Henry Pitts Forster,
q.v. m. Bareilly 20 June 1839, Mary Owen Hearsey (*probably* dau.
of Hyder Young Hearsey, q.v.).

Services: Operations in Shekhawat country 1837-40. First
Sikh War; Aliwal; comdg. the Inf. of the Bde. (Medal); Jullundur
Doab 1846. Mutiny campaign 1857-8; operations in Singhbhum
and Sambalpur districts (Medal). Granted an Unattached Commission as Major, " as a testimony of the sense entertained by H.M.
of the meritorious services rendered by Capt. Forster with the
Shekhawattee brigade." (Mily. Dept., 10 Oct. 1860—No. 1,010.)
Comdt. 13th N.I. (late Shekhawati Regt.) 19 Sept. 1860 till 26 Dec.
1862. Fur. s.c. 15 mos. 4 Nov. 1861.

FRANCIS, R——. Local Ensign, Ramgarh Bn., 11 Aug. 1818.
Was still serving in the Bn. in 1822.

(Almost certainly Robert Francis, who was living as an indigo planter at Mudhobun, Sambalpur (where the Ramgarh Bn. was stationed in 1822) in 1850.)

FRASER, William (1784-1835). Senior Merchant, B.C.S. Local Major, Skinner's Horse. *b.* Kirkhill 6 Sept. 1784. Local Major (1 May 1815) 12 Nov. 1817. *d.* Delhi 22 Mar. 1835 : shot by a hired assassin.[1]

2nd son of Edward Satchwell Fraser and Jane his wife, 3rd dau. of William Fraser, of Balnain. Brother of George John Fraser, *q.v.*

Services: See *D.N.B.* Writer, B.C.S., 13 Oct. 1800. Arrived in India Feb. 1802. At Coll. of Ft. Wm. 1802-5. Asst. Sec. to Resdt. at Delhi 1 June 1805. 2nd Asst. to Hon. Mountstuart Elphinstone on his mission to Kabul 1 Oct. 1808 till Oct. 1809. Nepal War 1814-15; Kalanga (s.w. in throat by arrow); Nahan; Jaithak; P.A. with 2nd Div. Apptd. 2nd in Comd., or Asst. Comdt., Skinner's Horse 1815, and on 12 Nov. 1817 was granted local rank of Major with effect from 1 May 1815. Owing to his political and civil duties he only occasionally joined and did duty with the Corps. Comr. for the settlement of Garhwal 15 Oct. 1815 till 1820. Dy. Supt. of Delhi territory 14 Oct. 1820. Siege and capture of Bhurtpore (w.); with Skinner's Horse. Transfd. to 8th Local Horse (late 2nd Skinner's Horse) Feb. 1826; retransfd. to 1st (Skinner's) Local Horse on disbandment of 8th Local Horse 28 July 1829 till death. Comr. in Delhi territory and A.G.G. Delhi 16 Apr. 1832 till death.

Refs.: Burke's *Landed Gentry*, 13th edn., p. 628, *s.n.* Fraser, of Reelick. *Frasers of Lovat. D.N.B. De Rhé-Philipe. D.I.B. Mundy,* i. 378-81. *A.J.* N.S. xviii. 33. *G.M.* 1836, i. 207. Intest.; admon. 7 July 1835 and 30 Nov. 1836. M.I. in St. James's church, Delhi.

[1] *Note:* His assassin, as well as the Nawab of Firozpur, instigator of the murder, were both hanged.

FRITH, Richard (1798-1837). Local Lieutenant. 4th (Sneyd's) Local Horse. *b.* in India Dec. 1798. Local Lieut. 1 Feb. 1817. *d.* Calcutta 3 June 1837, aged 38½.

Son of Richard Frith, *q.v.*, by Shah Begum. Brother of Robert Frith.

Refs.: *A.J.* N.S. xxiv. 209. Will dated 11 June 1835; proved 29 Aug. 1837. M.I. in N. Park St. cemetery, Calcutta.

GARDNER, James Valentine (*d.* 1845). Local Lieutenant, d.d. Gardner's Horse in Dec. 1817. *d.* Chhaoni 14 June 1845.

A Taluqdar and zemindar. Eldest son of William Linnæus
Gardner, *q.v.* *m.* 1st, Bibi Sahiba Banoo. *m.* 2nd, *c.* 1834, the
Nawab Mulka Humanee Begum, dau. of Mirza Sulaiman Shekoh
and niece of the Emperor Akbar Shah.

Refs.: A.J. N.S. xviii. 61. Will dated 22 Apr. 1845; proved
27 Mar. 1847.

GARDNER, William Linnæus (1770-1835). Local Lieut.
Colonel. Comdt. Gardner's Horse (now 2nd Lancers (Gardner's
Horse).) *b.* 1770. Local Lt. Col. 1819. Resigned 15 Feb. 1828.
d. Khasganj, U.P., 29 July 1835.

Son of Major Valentine Gardner and Alida his 1st wife, 3rd dau.
of Col. Robert Livingstone. *m.* by Muhammadan rites (? 1796),
" Nawab Mah Manzil-ul-Nissa, Begum Dehlmi " (? Dehlivi) (aged
13), a princess of Cambay, afterwards adopted as dau. by Akbar
Shah, Emperor of Delhi. (She died Khasganj 31 Aug. 1835.)
Father of James Valentine Gardner, *q.v.*, and grandfather of the
wife of Stewart William Gardner, *q.v.*

Services: See *D.N.B.* Ensign 63rd Ft. 20 Mar. 1783; do.
89th Ft. 23 Apr. 1783; h.p. 89th Ft., on disbandment, 1783.
Ensign 74th (Highland) Ft. 6 Mar. 1789; Lieut. 52nd Ft. 6 Oct.
1789; Capt. of an Independent Coy. of Ft. 2 Jan. 1794; Capt.
30th Ft. 4 Apr. 1794; h.p. of an Ind. Coy. 1796; resigned 1798.
Bt. Major 25 Sept. 1803.[1] On h.p.; rank stationary; left the
Army in 1828. Served under Lord Moira at Quiberon in 1795;
joined 30th Ft. in India in 1796. Entered the service of Jaswant
Rao Holkar in 1798, and raised and comdd. a Bde. of Inf. for him.
Afterwards entered service of Amrit Rao at Poona. Joined Lord
Lake in 1804. Raised at Farrukhabad and Mainpuri in 1809 the
famous cav. corps known as " Gardner's Horse." Served in Nepal
and Rajputana, and in Arakan in 1825 during First Burma War.

Refs.: Burke's *Peerage*, 1923, p. 964, *s.n.* Gardner, B. (Dormant). *D.N.B. D.I.B.* Pedigree in Fanny Parkes' *Wanderings of a Pilgrim*, i. 420. Compton. Keene. *A.J.* N.S. xv, xviii,
xix. Will dated 17 Feb. 1833; proved 23 Nov. 1835.

[1] *Note:* He was rewarded in 1822 with an unattached Majority
in H.M.S., antedated to 25 Sept. 1803.

GREEN, R—— C——. Local Cornet, Baddeley's Horse,
20 June 1817. Out of the Service before Dec. 1821.

GRIFFITHS, Henry Hugh (1801-1831). Local Ensign,
Rangpur Local Bn., 25 Aug. 1818. *b.* 30 May 1801. *d.* Chatteah
indigo factory, Purnea, 22 Aug. 1831.

Sometime of Serampore, and of Luckypore, Jessore, indigo planter. Son of Col. Hugh Griffiths, *q.v.* *m.* Calcutta 18 Aug. 1823 (being then a planter), Miss Eliza Russell.

Refs.: *A.J.* N.S. vii. 159. Will dated 1 Oct. 1830; proved 6 Jan. 1832.

GRUEBER, Richard (1780-1826). Local Lieutenant, 1st (Skinner's) Local Horse. *b.* 1780. Local Cornet 3 Jan. 1816. Local Lieut. 30 Sept. 1817. *d.* Hansi 24 Oct. 1826, aged 46.

Natural son of Col. Richard Grueber, *q.v.* Cousin of Arthur Grueber, Lieut. H.M. 31st Ft.

Services: Apptd. Local Cornet in newly-formed 3rd Skinner's Horse in 1816; Adjt. do. 1 Mar. 1816. Local Lieut. June 1819 with effect from 30 Sept. 1817. Transfd. to 2nd Skinner's Horse on disbandment of the 3rd Corps in 1819; Adjt. do. 1820. Transfd. to Baddeley's Frontier Horse (late 2nd Skinner's) Aug. 1821; Adjt. do. till June 1822, when, in common with the majority of Local Ofrs., he was discharged. Brought back into the Service as Local Lieut. 12 Sept. 1823, and apptd. Adjt. of Skinner's Horse, and granted rank from the date of his former Commission, 30 Sept. 1817. 2nd in comd. Skinner's Horse (became 1st Local Horse) 1 Jan. 1825. Siege and capture of Bhurtpore; 2nd in comd. 1st Local Horse.

Refs.: *De Rhé-Philipe.* *A.J.* xxiii. 674. Will dated camp nr. Bhurtpore, 9 Dec. 1825; codicil dated 11 Jan. 1826; proved 29 Mar. 1827. M.I. at Hansi.

HARRIOTT, Alexander (*d.* 1806). Major. Comdg. a Telinga Bn. *d.* Dinapore 28 Oct. 1806.

Son of Helen Harriott, of (?) Chelsea.

Services: An Officer in Perron's Fifth Bde. in Sindhia's service. Came over to the British on the outbreak of the Mahratta war in 1803, when he was granted a pension of Rs. 400 *p.m.* and was given comd. of one of Sindhia's Bns. which were taken into the Coy.'s service after the war. In comd. of this Bn. he saw some active service in the Hariana district in 1804, including the assault during which James Marshall, *q.v.*, met his death. Defence of Delhi Oct. 1804; Major comdg. Harriott's Corps. (G.O.C.C. 24 Oct. 1804.)

Refs.: *Compton,* p. 362. *Calcutta Monthly Journal,* Nov. 1804. *S.M.* 1807, p. 880. Will dated Diggah, 3 Sept. 1806; proved 16 Jan. 1807.

HEARSEY, Hyder Young[1] (1782-1840). Local Major. *b.* Dec. 1782. Local Major (?) *d.* Kareli, nr. Bareilly, 5 Aug. 1840, aged 57 yrs. 8 mos.

Natural son of Andrew Wilson Hearsey, *q.v.*, by a Jat lady. Half-brother of Sir John Bennet Hearsey, *q.v.* His sisters *m.* J. O. Clarkson, Arthur Owen, and Sir William Richards, K.C.B., *qq.v. m.* Khanum Zuhur-ul-Nissa, a dau. of one of the deposed princes of Cambay. (*See also* William Linnæus Gardner.) (She died Calcutta 13 May 1850, aged 70.) Ed. Woolwich.

Services: Apptd. A.D.C. to Saadut Ali Khan, the last Nawab-Wazir of Oudh, 1798. Entered Sindhia's service under Perron 1799; D.Q.M.G. of Mahratta army. Entered service of George Thomas, the adventurer (*D.N.B.*). Joined Lord Lake in 1803, bringing with him a regt. of cav., in comd. of which he served at capture of Agra, relief of Delhi, battle of Deig. Explored sources of the Ganges 1808; visited W. Tibet and Lake Mansarowar with William Moorcroft (*D.N.B.*) 1812. Nepal War 1815, in comd. of a corps of 1,500 Rohillas which he had raised; s.w. in action 1 Apr., and remained a prisoner in Almora till the surrender of that fortress at the end of the month. Bareilly insurrection 1816; volunteered to take charge of the two guns. Siege and capture of Bhurtpore; afterwards elected Asst. Prize Agent.

Refs.: The Hearseys. *D.I.B. Compton.*

[1] *Note:* His second name is believed to have originally been 'Jung', *i.e.*, 'War', but he subsequently anglicized it into Young.

HEMING, Samuel Bracebridge (1801-1837). Local Ensign. 1st Nassiri Bn. Subsequently Lieut. H.M. 26th or Cameronian Regt. *b.* 1801. Local Cornet 28 Nov. 1818. Local Ensign 28 Nov. 1818. *d.* Madras 24 Feb. 1837, on board the *Java*, of paralysis, aged 36; *bur.* St. Mary's cemetery, Madras, 25 Feb. Son of Rev. Samuel Bracebridge Heming, of Linley, Atherstone, rector of Fenny Drayton, Leics., and Anne his wife and cousin, only dau. of Robert Abney, of Lindley Hall, Leics., high sheriff 1777. *m.* Bolton-le-Moors 29 Mar. 1828, Eliza, dau. of J. Bazley. Ed. Repton; admitted Jan. 1811.

Services: Apptd. Local Cornet in 4th (Sneyd's) Horse 28 Nov. 1818; transfd. as Local Ensign to 1st Nassiri Bn. 21 Aug. 1819, to rank from 28 Nov. 1818, and served with this Bn. till 1821. Transfd. to H.M.S.; Ensign 67th Ft. 1 July 1821; Lieut. 26th Ft. 26 Apr. 1828 till death.

Refs.: Burke's *Landed Gentry*, 5th edn., p. 139, *s.n.* Bracebridge, of Atherstone Hall; p. 1, *s.n.* Abney, of Measham Hall. *Howard & Crisp* (*Notes*), x. 118, *s.n.* Abney. *Repton School Register. A.J. N.S.* xxiii. 320.

APPENDIX A

HENNESSY, ——. Local Ensign, Gorakhpur L.I., 11 Mar. 1818. N.F.P.

HOLLOWAY, Charles. Local Ensign, Bencoolen Local Bn., 22 July 1824. Not in *A.L.* of 1825.

Eldest son of Charles Holloway, Ft. Marlbro' C.S., and Emily his wife. His half-sisters *m.* William Henry Hewitt and Henry William Wilkinson, *qq.v.*

HOLMES, Joseph (1798/99-1836). Local Ensign, 1st Rampura Local Bn., 11 Aug. 1818. (*See* Vol. ii. 470.)

HOY, R——. Local Lieutenant, Gorakhpur L.I., 6 Mar. 1819. Out of the Service before Dec. 1821.

HUTCHINSON, W——. Local Ensign. Gorakhpur L.I. Apptd. Local Ensign, Ramgarh Bn., 25 Aug. 1818, vice Robert Collis, *q.v.*, deceased. Transfd. to Gorakhpur L.I. before 1822. (? *m.* Charlotte, who died his widow at Calcutta 4 Apr. 1836.)

INGLIS, Henry (1803-1860). Local Lieutenant. Sylhet L.I. *b.* 20 July 1803. Local Lieut. 5 Nov. 1832. *d.* 15 Berkeley Sq., London, 31 July 1860.

(*Probably* son of George Inglis, *chunam* [1] merchant, who resided at Chattuck, Sylhet, 1794-1850.) *m.* Calcutta 10 Jan. 1832, Sophia, dau. of F. G. Lister, *q.v.* (She *re-m.* C. S. Guthrie, *q.v.*) (? His sister *m.* J. W. Bennett, *q.v.*)

Services : Apptd. a Local Lieut. in Sylhet L.I. Bn., with the usual salary of Rs. 200/- *p.m.*, 5 Nov. 1832. Asst. to P.A. Khasi Hills, Assam, 11 Feb. 1835, and was still holding this appt. in 1850.

Refs. : Will dated 16 June 1856; proved 4 Jan. 1861. M.I. at Cherrapunji.

[1] *Note :* i.e., prepared lime.

IRELAND, J—— H——. Local Cornet, 3rd (Casement's) Corps of Local Cav., 11 Aug. 1818. (G.O. 25 Aug. 1818.)

Was an Asst. in the Station Bde. Office at Ft. Wm. in 1816.

N.B.—One James Ireland was promoted Condr. of Ord. from Sergt. in Sept. 1804.

JAMES, William (1803- ?). Local Lieutenant, Bencoolen Local Bn., 8 Jan. 1820. (*See* Vol. ii. 545, iv. 379.)

JEFFERSON, D——. Local Lieutenant, 4th (Sneyd's) Horse 1 Feb. 1817. N.F.P.

LOCAL OFFICERS

JOHNSTON, Thomas Andrew. Local Lieutenant and Adjt., Baddeley's Horse, in June 1819. Local Cornet, Baddeley's Horse, 20 June 1817. Local Lieut. do. 30 Sept. 1817. (G.O. 19 June 1819.)

JONES, Charles H—— (*d. c.* 1825). Local Ensign, 2nd Rampura Local Bn., 11 Aug. 1818.

Refs.: Intestate; admon. Sept. 1825.

JONES, William Robert (1788-1857). Local Lieutenant and Adjt. Bundelkhand Najib Bn. in 1815. *b.* 22 Feb. 1788. *d.* Bhuttoneah factory 22 May 1857.

Became an indigo planter at Bhuttoneah, Purnea district. Son of Mostyn Jones, merchant at Cawnpore. Brother of the wife of J. F. Meiselbach, *q.v.*; of Mrs. Sarah Dyce, of Agra, widow; of Mrs. Catherine Bruce, of Banda, widow; and of Mrs. Mary Wilson, of Calcutta, widow. *m.* —— ?

Refs.: Family information. Will dated 2 Mar. 1857; proved 9 Nov. 1857.

KEEN, F——. Local Lieutenant, Ramgarh Bn., 1 May 1819. N.F.P.

KENNY, W—— R——. Local Lieutenant. 1st Rampura Local Bn. Subsequently Local Asst. Surg. in Nagpur service. Local Lieut. 11 Aug. 1818 till July 1822.

(*Probably* related to Michael William Kenny, Asst. Surg. and Surg., H.M. 67th Ft., 1803-28.)

Services: Educated for the medical profession; went out to India *c.* 1816 to serve as a Vol. with H.M. 67th Ft. in the expectation of obtaining a Commn. Third Mahratta War 1817-18; Vol. 67th Ft. Apptd. Local Lieut. Rampura Local Bn. on its formation Aug. 1818, and joined on some date after 1 July 1819; Adjt. do.; discharged with gratuity *c.* July 1822. Apptd. Local Ofr. (Asst. Surg.) in Nagpur service 9 Feb. 1824; discharged with gratuity, with all the remaining Local Ofrs., early in 1830.

KERR, Russell Edward James (1803-1825). Local Cornet, 4th (Sneyd's) Horse, 28 Nov. 1818. (*See* Vol. ii. 592.)

KNOX, William Carnegy (1795-1858). Local Lieutenant. 2nd Rampura Local Cav. *b.* 1795. Local Lieut. 4 May 1818. *d.* Calcutta 21 Dec. 1858, aged 63.

Natural son of Sir Alexander Knox, K.C.B., *q.v.* Father of Caroline, wife of Lieut. John Edward Sharpe, 46th N.I., and of Henry Noble Knox.

Services : Apptd. Local Lieut. & 2nd in comd., 2nd (Borlase's) Rampura Local Cav., May 1818. Resided for many yrs. at Barrackpore, latterly at Entally, Calcutta.

Refs. : Will dated 21 Oct. 1851 ; proved 23 Dec. 1858.

LONG, William (1771-1842). Local Captain, comdg. a Najib Bn., in 1815. *b.* 19 June 1771. *d.* Calcutta 30 Apr. 1842.

" My paternal grandfather *m.* Lady Ratcliffe, dau. and niece of the unfortunate Earls of Derwentwater." (*Autobiog.*)

Services : Entered R.N. and served under Rodney and Parker, 1782. On leaving the Navy he came to India and was apptd. to Col. Robert Sutherland's Bde. in the Mahratta service, eventually obtaining comd. of a Bn. Was present at battle of Indore, 1801. Resigned 19 Aug. 1803 ; joined Lake ; received a pension of Rs. 200 *p.m.* from the British, his rank being then given as Lieut. Was sent with Major Lewis Ferdinand Smith to persuade Sindhia's Bns. to enter the British service. Having volunteered his services, was ordered in Mar. 1815 to proceed to Hapur and assume comd. of a newly-raised corps of Najibs. This order was shortly afterwards cancelled. Was living at Koil as a merchant in 1817 ; afterwards an indigo planter at Mirzapur, at Aligarh, and at Koil. He settled finally in Calcutta. In 1840 published his reminiscences in the *India Review*, vols. I and II.

Refs. : M.I. in Circular Rd. cemetery, Calcutta.

McCABE, H—— W——. Local Cornet and Adjt., 3rd (Casement's) Corps of Local Cav., 1 Jan. 1819. N.F.P.

Note : One Henry McCabe was a watch and clock maker at Calcutta in 1846. His wife, Mary Ann, *d.* 1 Mar. 1844, aged 27.

MACGOWAN, J—— L—— (*d.* 1822). Local Lieutenant, Rangpur Local Bn. Local Ensign, Gorakhpur L.I., 25 Aug. 1818. Transfd. to Rangpur Bn. Local Lieut. do. 13 Feb. 1819. *d.* 15 Apr. 1822.

McGRATH, Charles (*d.* 1821). Local Lieutenant, Gorakhpur L.I. Sub-Lieut., 3rd (Baddeley's) Horse, 11 Nov. 1817. Transfd. to Gorakhpur L.I. 11 Aug. 1818. Local Ensign do. from 11 Mar. 1818. Local Lieut. do. 6 Feb. 1819. *d.* at sea 30 June 1821, on board the *Resource*.

Refs.: A.J. xiii. 489.

McGREGOR, John. Local Sub-Lieutenant, Cuttack Legion, 4 July 1817. Was still serving in this Corps (which became Rangpur Local Bn. in Feb. 1823) in Dec. 1821.

(*Probably* natural son of James Murray MacGregor, *q.v.*)

LOCAL OFFICERS

MACGREGOR, Thomas Paul. Lieutenant, Bengal Auxiliary Cav.[1]

Eldest son of J. A. P. Macgregor, *q.v.* *m.* Glasgow 17 Aug. 1824, Katherine, eldest dau. of William Livingstone.

[1] *Note:* Presumably Local or Irregular Cav.: he has not, however, been traced in any such corps.

McGREGOR, William. Local Lieutenant, 1st Rohilla Cav. Local Sub-Lieut., 3rd (Baddeley's) Horse, 3 Oct. 1817 (G.O. 11 Nov. 1817); corrected to Local Lieut. from same date (G.O. 6 Feb. 1819). Transfd. to 1st Rohilla Cav., with rank as Local Lieut. from 1 Oct. 1817, and was still serving in that Corps in Dec. 1821.

Natural son of R. B. Gregory, *q.v.*

MAILLARD, John Peter [1] (1797/98-1843). Local Lieutenant. Ramgarh Bn. *b.* 1797/98. Local Sub-Lieut., 3rd (Baddeley's) Horse, 5 Oct. 1817; corrected to Local Lieut. from same date (G.O. 6 Feb. 1819). Transfd. to Ramgarh Bn. as Local Lieut., with rank as such from 1 Oct. 1817 (G.O. 21 Aug. 1819), and was still serving with that Bn. in Dec. 1821. He was afterwards in the Preventive Service. *d.* Calcutta 14 June 1843, aged 45 (? 46).

m. Dinapore 23 June 1824, Miss Sarah Humphreys, dau. of Conductor Humphreys. (*See also* John Shipp.)

[1] *Note:* One Jean Pierre Maillard (1799-1826), a native of Vevey, canton Vaud, was a Lieut. in the French service.

MALCOLM, John (1793-?). Local Cornet, Skinner's Horse, 1 Jan. 1819. Was still serving in that Corps in Dec. 1821. *b.* 1793. Apprentice Surveyor, Madras, 1 Apr. 1807; to Java with Colin Mackenzie, Surveyor-Gen., 1811. Returned to Survey Dept. 16 Apr. 1822; pensioned 1829.

MALING, Robert Saunders (*d.* 1843). Local Lieutenant. Arakan Local Bn. "Mr. R. Maling to be attached to Arakan Local Corps, on a monthly allowance of St.Rs. 200, and with rank of Local Lieut." (G.O. 31 Oct. 1833.) He served with this Corps till 1837. Was Supt. of Salt Chowkies at Baugundee, Bengal, at death. *d.* Calcutta 23 Aug. 1843.

m. Calcutta 27 Aug. 1835, Ellen Barons, dau. of John Matthew Dove, of the firm of Cockerell & Co., Calcutta. (She *re-m.* 11 Feb. 1845, A. M. Dowleans, auctioneer in Calcutta.)

MARSHALL, James (*d. c.* 1804). Captain, comdg. a Corps of Levies. *d. c.* 1804 : kld. in action.

Services : Originally a Midshipman in E.I.C.N.S. ; took service with Sindhia and obtained comd. of a Bn. in Hessing's Corps. Granted a pension of Rs. 500 *p.m.* by the Brit. Govt. on quitting the Mahratta service on the outbreak of war in 1803, and was "shortly afterwards apptd. to the comd. of some newly-raised levies, and sent to keep order in the Hariana district. He was shot through the heart about the year 1804, whilst gallantly storming a town, . . ." (*Compton*, p. 372.)

MARTINDELL, C——. Local Lieutenant. 3rd Rohilla Cav. Local Cornet, 3rd Rohilla Cav., 11 Aug. 1818; Local Lieut. do. 28 Nov. 1818; resigned same day.

MARTINDELL, John. Local Lieutenant and Adjt., Agra Najib Bn., 1817-22.

Services : "Mr. J. Martindell, Adjt. Agra Najib Bn., to be Lieut. with Local rank from 26 June 1817." (G.O. 11 Aug. 1818.)

MARTINDELL, Robert (1794/95-1835). Local Lieutenant. 2nd Rohilla Cav. Afterwards an Asst. in Mily. Auditor-Gen.'s office. *b.* 1794/95. Local Lieut. and Adjt. Agra Najib Bn. in 1815. Local Cornet and Adjt. 2nd Rohilla Cav. in Dec. 1817 ; Local Lieut. do. 1818. Out of the Service before Dec. 1821. *d.* Calcutta 19 Feb. 1835, aged 39.

(? Son of H. Martindell.) *m.* 1st, Calcutta 13 Sept. 1823, Miss Maria Duncan Eaton. *m.* 2nd, Calcutta cathedral 30 Aug. 1828 (aged 34), Miss Anne Burns (aged 18).

Services : Served with 2nd Rohilla Cav. during Third Mahratta War.

Refs.: A.J. N.S. xvii. 240. M.I. in S. Park St. cemetery, Calcutta.

MARTINDELL, William (1778/79-1849). Local Lieutenant. Pension Est. *b.* 1778/79. Local Lieut. and Adjt., 1st Corps of Skinner's Horse, 30 Sept. 1817. 2nd in comd. 1st Local Horse ; transfd. to 8th do. 29 Dec. 1824 ; 2nd in comd. 1st Local Horse 18 Nov. 1826. Pensioned 14 Nov. 1840. *d.* Ludhiana 8 June 1849, aged 70.

Son of Sir Gabriel Martindell, *q.v.*, by an Indian woman.

Services : Siege and capture of Bhurtpore ; Lieut. 8th Local Horse.

Refs.: Grey & Garrett, p. 351.

LOCAL OFFICERS

MATHEWS, Albert. Local Cornet, Dromedary Corps, 11 Aug. 1818 till disbanded 1 Oct. 1821. Became an indigo planter in the Shahabad district.

m. Calcutta 13 Mar. 1828, Caroline Adriana, dau. of James Reinier Vos, M.D., police surgeon, Calcutta.

MEISELBACH, Johan Frederick (*d.* 1819). Colonel, comdg. Bundelkhand Najib Bn. *d.* Serampore 15 Oct. 1819; *bur.* at Barrackpore.

A native of Jena. *m.* Cawnpore 8 Aug. 1798, Anne, dau. of Mostyn Jones, merchant, and sister of William Robert Jones, *q.v.* (She died Calcutta 17 July 1834, aged 48.) His daus. *m.* George Byron, P. G. Cornish, C. W. Cowley, William Hodgson, Edward Jackson, and G. W. Moseley, *qq.v.*

Services: Described in the marriage register as "Comdt. in Alli Behadur's Army." Col. in the service of Rajah Himmat Bahadur, of Bundelkhand, and in 1803 was comdg. 3,000 native Mahratta troops in Bundelkhand. Came over to the British on the outbreak of the Mahratta War in 1803, and was given employment with the local rank of Col.

Refs.: Family information. *Cal. Govt. Gaz.* 28 Oct. 1819. Will dated Calcutta, 8 Feb. 1815; proved 30 Oct. 1819.

NELSON, Horatio (Ralph) (*d.* 1839). Local Ensign, 2nd Rampura Local Bn., 11 Aug. 1818. *d.* Dehra Dun 13 Feb. 1839.

Was a land surveyor in Calcutta 1821-6; afterwards Asst. Revenue Surveyor, Meerut district.

Refs.: *A.J.* N.S. xxix. 140 (where he is described as "Lieut. Horatio Ralph Nelson, of the Royal Navy, and assistant revenue surveyor.").

O'BRIEN, Edward (1801 ?-1847 ?).[1] Local Lieutenant. Bencoolen Local Bn. Local Cornet, 1st Rampura Local Cav., 31 May 1819. Local Ensign, Ramgarh Bn. Local Lieut., Bencoolen Local Bn., 27 Jan. 1821 till 1824.

Eldest natural son of Lucius Robert O'Brien, *q.v.* Brother of the next. *m.* Fort Marlbro' 17 Mar. 1823, Mary, dau. of Conductor C. Boardman.

[1] *Note:* Mr. Edward O'Brien *d.* 1 Apr. 1847, aged 45. (M.I. in Howrah cemetery, Calcutta.)

O'BRIEN, William (1802-1863). Local Captain, Pension Est. 8th Inf., Nizam's army. Local Cornet, Sneyd's Horse, 28 Nov. 1818. Local Ensign, Champaran L.I.; do. Bencoolen Local Bn.,

27 July 1819. Local Lieut., Nizam's army, 27 Feb. 1828. Local Capt. 27 Feb. 1840. Pensioned 14 Dec. 1853. *d.* 1863.

Natural son of Lucius Robert O'Brien, *q.v. m.* Frome 11 Oct. 1854 (aged 52) Miss Mary Jane Charles, of Garston House, Frome, dau. of Thomas Charles, manufacturer. Resided latterly at Bath.

Services : Served with Bencoolen Local Bn. 1819-24. Apptd. Local Lieut. in Nizam's army in 1828, and served principally with 8th Inf. Was comdg. Hill Rangers at Buldana in 1852. On 1 Jan. 1854, the Nizam's army was reorganized and became the Hyderabad Contingent, all Local Ofrs. being pensioned with effect from 14 Dec. 1853.

O'DRISCOLL, Thomas. Local Cornet, 1st Local Cav., 11 Aug. 1818. Apptd. a Local Ofr. in the Nagpur service, under the Resdt., 26 Feb. 1819. In 1829 was comdg. a Bn. of the Provl. service ; discharged with gratuity early in 1830.

PEDRON, A—— (*d.* 1821). Local Cornet, Skinner's Horse, 6 Feb. 1819 till death. Formerly a Lieut. in the service of Sindhia. *d.* 31 Aug. 1821.

(*Probably* son of Col. Pedron, a Frenchman in the service of Sindhia, by his wife, dau. of Gen. Pierre Cuiller Perron, of the same service.)

PENNINGTON, Henry Simpson. Local Lieutenant, Pension Est. Local Cornet, 3rd (Baddeley's) Horse, 6 Oct. 1817. Was an indigo planter in 1825.

Son of Henry Pennington, *q.v. m.* 1st, Calcutta 18 Oct. 1824, Miss Catherine Anne Lyons. *m.* 2nd, Calcutta 14 Oct. 1844, Ellen Olivia, dau. of John Bird.

PENNINGTON, William Fawcett (1800-1840). Local Ensign. Champaran L.I. Afterwards Executive Ofr., P.W.D., at Midnapore. *b.* June 1800. Local Cornet 7 Oct. 1817. Local Ensign 12 Jan. 1820. *d.* Calcutta 28 Apr. 1840, aged 39 yrs. 10 mos.

m. 1st, Calcutta 16 Sept. 1823, Miss Charlotte Ann Cunningham. (She died Calcutta 15 June 1838, aged 28.) *m.* 2nd, Calcutta 12 Nov. 1839, Janet McKill, 2nd dau. of James Russell. (She *re-m.* Calcutta 3 Apr. 1845, Henry Driver.)

Services : Posted Local Cornet to 3rd (Baddeley's) Rohilla Horse Oct. 1817 ; transfd. as Adjt. to 2nd (Borlase's) Rampura Local Cav. 4 May 1818 ; as Local Ensign to Champaran L.I. Bn. 12 Jan. 1820. Was an Asst. in Q.M.G. Dept. in Sept. 1823.

Refs. : I.N., No. 2, p. 29.

LOCAL OFFICERS

PICARD, Edward. Local Lieutenant. 3rd (Baddeley's) Horse. Ensign H.M. 17th Ft. 2 June 1804. Lieut. 24th Light Dgns. 5 June 1806. Resigned 3 Oct. 1816. Local Lieut. 1 Oct. 1817. (*d.* or left India before 1849.)

m. Calcutta 6 Aug. 1810, Miss Eliza Rairy. (She died Calcutta 7 May 1817, aged 24.)

Services: Apptd. Sub-Lieut. with local rank in 3rd (Baddeley's) Rohilla Horse 1 Oct. 1817 (G.O. 11 Nov. 1817). " For ' Sub-Lieut.' read ' Lieut.' " (G.O. 6 Feb. 1819). Served during Third Mahratta War. Was an indigo planter at Bareilly in 1845, at Fatehgarh in 1846.

POHLMAN, Anthony (*d.* 1818). Local Lieut. Colonel, Comdt. Agra Najib Bn. Formerly Lt. Col. in the service of Sindhia. *d.* 23 Aug. 1818.

Son of David Pohlman, of Zell, kingdom of Hanover, and Amelia his wife.

Services: Sometime a Sergt. in a corps of Hanoverians in the Coy.'s service, formerly quartered at Madras. Entered De Boigne's Bdes. in Sindhia's service *c.* 1792; Capt. in 1794; comdg. a Najib Bn. in 2nd Bde. at Muttra in Apr. 1795. Apptd. by Perron in 1799 to comd. 2nd Bde.; to comd. 1st Bde. 1802, with which he remained in the Deccan till war broke out with the English. He then entered the Coy.'s service, re-enlisting some of his old soldiers to form an Irreg. Inf. Corps, with which he fought under Capt. W. H. Royle, *q.v.*, at Adalatnagar, 7 Apr. 1805. Subsequently given comd. of Agra Najib Bn. " He is described as an exceedingly cheerful and entertaining character, who lived in the style of an Indian prince, kept a seraglio, and always travelled on an elephant, attended by a guard of Mughals, all dressed alike in purple robes, . . ." (*Compton*)

Refs.: Compton. Will dated 26 June 1818; proved 13 Feb. 1819.

POTE, Thomas (1782-1822). Local Lieutenant. 3rd (Baddeley's) Rohilla Horse. *b.* 9 Mar. 1782. Local Lieut. 11 Aug. 1818. *d.* 13 Oct. 1822.

bapt. Dinapore 5 Apr. 1790. 3rd son of Edward Ephraim Pote, B.C.S., Commercial Resdt. at Patna (who was youngest son of Joseph Pote, of Eton, bookseller), by an Indian mother.

Services: " Thomas Pote, gentleman, to be Lieut. 3rd Rohilla Cav." (G.O. 11 Aug. 1818.) This Corps was transfd. to the service of Oudh by G.O.C.C. of 28 Aug. 1819.

Refs.: Austen-Leigh. B.: P.P. vi. 174-6; xxviii. 67.

RADCLIFFE, Michael Cox (1797-1827). Local Lieutenant. 3rd (Casement's) Horse. *b.* 19 Mar. 1797. Local Cornet 4 May 1818. Local Lieut. 1 Jan. 1819. *bur.* Calcutta 11 Aug. 1827.

m. Calcutta 23 May 1820, Miss Sarah Nicholson. (She died Calcutta 8 May 1845, aged 36.)

Services : Local Ensign Gorakhpur L.I. ; transfd. as Local Cornet to newly-raised 3rd Rampura Local Cav. (Casement's Horse) 4 May 1818 ; Local Lieut. and 2nd in comd. do. 1 Jan. 1819. Afterwards a writer in the office of the Mily. Advocate Gen. in Calcutta.

RATTRAY, Bernard. Local Ensign, Rangpur Bn., 25 Aug. 1818. Out of the Service before Dec. 1821.

RICE, Thomas Benjamin. Local Cornet, 3rd (Baddeley's) Rohilla Cav., 28 Nov. 1818 till disbanded Aug. 1819. Was an indigo planter at Rajmahal 1843-55.

ROTTON, Bernard. Local Ensign, Rangpur Local Bn., 25 Aug. 1818. Out of the Service before Dec. 1821.

(*Probably* son of Lieut. Rotton, formerly an Ofr. in the Mahratta service, who was granted a pension of Rs. 200 *p.m.* by the Brit. Govt.)

ROTTON, Felix. Local Cornet, 3rd (Casement's) Corps of Local Cav., 11 Aug. 1819. N.F.P.

SCOTT, George (? 1784-1822). Local Lieutenant and Adjt., Gardner's Horse, *c.* 1815-17. *b.* in India *c.* 1784. *d.* suddenly 1822.

Son of George Scott (? sometime M.C.S., of the family of Scot's Hall and Nettlestead, Kent). Either he or his father (or both) was formerly an Ofr. in the Mahratta service and was granted a pension of Rs. 200 *p.m.* in 1803.

SEELY, George. Local Ensign, Champaran L.I., 25 Aug. 1818. Local Lieut. do. 1819. Out of the Service before Dec. 1821.

SHEPHERD, James Redhead (1767/68-1813). Local Colonel, Pension Est. Formerly Col. comdg. a Bde. in the service of Ambaji Inglia. *d.* Cawnpore 23 Dec. 1813, aged 45.

Son of Elizabeth Redhead. Brother of Arabella Redhead and Margaret Peverell.

Services : " About 1799 he took service under Ambaji Inglia, for whom he raised a brigade of regular infantry, which numbered five battalions, with 500 cavalry and 25 guns." (*Compton*) Was engaged in the attack on Lakwa Dada's position at Sounda in

1801. "On the breaking out of the war with the English, Shepherd and his party passed over to the Company's service, and he distinguished himself in Bundelkhand in 1804, where he gave the celebrated Free-booter Amir Khan a sound beating at Maltaon Ghaut, and on the 24th of June completed his discomfiture by entirely defeating and dispersing his force near Kunch. Shepherd's corps at this time consisted of 3,180 men, and was highly praised for its efficiency when General Lake reviewed it in 1805." (ib.) Was in receipt of a pension of Rs. 1000/- *p.m.* from Govt.

Refs.: Compton, pp. 388-9. Will dated Cawnpore 16 Oct. 1810; proved 19 Apr. 1814.

SHEETZ, James. Local Lieutenant. Was Intr. & Qmr. and Legion Staff, Bundelkhand Legion (on a salary of Rs. 427/8 *p.m.*), in 1842. N.F.P.

m. Cawnpore 27 Apr. 1842, Frances, dau. of Conductor W. Bryan, Ord. Dept.

SKINNER, Hercules (1814-1866). Captain (Unattached). Comdt. 14th Irreg. Cav. *b.* 1814. Local Lieut. 28 Jan. 1834. Local Capt. 1846. Capt. (Unattached) 16 Jan. 1852.[1] Retired 1 Oct. 1861. *d.* (? in England) 1866.

3rd son of James Skinner, C.B., *q.v.*, by one of his Indian wives. *m.* in England 12 July 1847, Rose Ann, eldest dau. of Samuel Cardozo, of Redruth, Cornwall. Ed. Edin. Acad. 1824-8.

Services: Received a Local Commission in Nizam's army (Hyderabad Contingent) through the influence of Lord William Bentinck. Adjt. 1st Regt. Nizam's Cav. for many yrs. Capture of Fort Jamod 5 Dec. 1841; Local Lieut. 1st Cav. Fur. to Europe 1845. Transfd. as Capt. to 4th Cav. Succeeded his brother James, *q.v.*, as Comdt. 14th Irreg. Cav. 27 Jan. 1852 till it mutinied June 1857. Fur. s.c. to Europe 3 Jan. 1857 till retirement.

Refs.: Compton, p. 396. Burton, pp. 126, 127. *De Rhé-Philipe. Edin. Acad. Register.*

[1] *Note:* "As a mark of our respect for the memory of the late Lt.-Col. Skinner, C.B., we have much pleasure in giving you our authority to confer upon his son, Capt. Hercules Skinner, an unattached commission as capt. in the army of your presidency, . . ." (Mily. despatch from C.D. to Govt. of India, dated 3 Dec. 1851.)

SKINNER, James (1778-1841). Bt. Colonel, C.B., Comdt. Skinner's Horse. *b.* in India 1778. Local Capt. 1803. Local Lt. Col. 1815. Lt. Col. Dec. 1826. Bt. Col. 18 June 1831. *d.* Hansi 4 Dec. 1841.[1]

Son of Hercules Skinner, *q.v.*, by an Indian woman. Brother of Robert Skinner, *q.v.* Father of James Skinner, *q.v.*, Hercules Skinner, *q.v.*, and of the wives of Radclyffe Haldane, *q.v.*, and Peregrine Powell Turner, *q.v.*

Services : See *D.N.B.* Entered Sindhia's service May 1795, as Ensign in a Najib Bn. comdd. by Anthony Pohlman, *q.v.*, and served under Perron till outbreak of Mahratta War in Aug. 1803, when he joined Lake. Entered British Service, with nominal rank of Capt., when elected in Sept. 1803, by the men themselves, to the comd. of a body of 2,000 of Perron's Hindustani Horse which came over to Lake after the battle of Delhi. In comd. of this Corps (now 1st Duke of York's Own Skinner's Horse) he served during the remainder of the Second Mahratta War 1803-5 ; capture of Bhawani 1809 ; Nepal War 1814-15 ; Third Mahratta War 1817-18, with Reserve Div. of Grand Army ; siege and capture of Bhurtpore 1825-6. In Dec. 1826, in recognition of his services, was granted rank of Lt. Col. in H.M.S. in E.I. Apptd. in Nov. 1838, with tempy. rank of Bdr., to comd. a Bde. of Irreg. Horse forming part of the Army of the Indus. This Bde., which did not proceed to Afghanistan, was broken up in Jan. 1839. C.B. 26 Dec. 1826.

Refs. : *D.N.B. De Rhé-Philipe. Compton. Keene. D.I.B.* M.I. in St. James's, Delhi. Portrait (? by W. Melville) in Council ante-room in India Office.

[1] *Note :* In Jan. 1842 his remains were re-interred in St. James's church, Delhi, which he had himself built in 1836, in the discharge of a vow made 36 yrs. before.

SKINNER, James (1808-1861). Hon. Major, Unattached List. Comdt. 14th Irreg. Cav. *b.* in India 13 Dec. 1808. Local Lieut. 18 Feb. 1825. Capt. (Unattached) 27 Nov. 1843. Retired 21 Jan. 1852. Hon. Major 28 Nov. 1854. *d.* Delhi 23 Apr. 1861, of dysentery.

2nd son of James Skinner, C.B., *q.v.* *m.* Hansi 25 May 1829, Miss Sophia Elizabeth Barlow.

Services : Adjt. 1st (Skinner's) Local Horse 18 Feb. 1825 till 11 Jan. 1844. Siege and capture of Bhurtpore ; Lieut. 1st Local Horse (India medal). Apptd. A.D.C. to his father, comdg. a Bde. of Irreg. Cav., 4 Dec. 1838. Apptd. on 2 Jan. 1846 to raise and comd. 13th (became 14th) Irreg. Cav. Second Sikh War ; Capt. comdg. 14th Irreg. Cav., in garr. at Lahore (Medal). Leave 21 Jan. 1850 till retirement.

Refs. : *De Rhé-Philipe.* M.I. St. James's churchyard, Delhi.

SKINNER, Robert (c. 1783-1821). Local Major, Skinner's Horse. b. in India c. 1783. Local Major 1815. d. 7 May 1821.[1]
Son of Hercules Skinner, q.v., by an Indian woman. Brother of James Skinner, C.B., q.v. His dau. m. Henry Milne, q.v.
Services: Entered Sindhia's service as Ensign Nov. 1800; posted to his brother's Bn. in Perron's army. Lieut. comdg. a Bn. in 2nd Bde. under Anthony Pohlman, q.v. On outbreak of Mahratta War in Aug. 1803, he, in common with all other Ofrs. of British origin in Sindhia's army, was dismissed by Perron. Took service with the Begum Somru. Subsequently entered Coy.'s service and was given local rank of Lieut. in the Cav. Corps comdd. by his brother. Second Mahratta War 1805; operations against Amir Khan in Doab and Rohilkhand. Accompanied Elphinstone's mission to Peshawar in 1809. 2nd in comd. of Skinner's Horse and Comdt. of 2nd Corps, with local rank of Major, 1815. In 1819, was granted in perpetuity by Govt. a small *jaghir* in the Aligarh district.
Refs.: Compton.
[1] *Note:* "Skinner's brother, Major Robert Skinner, was the same sort of melodramatic character, and made a tragic end. He suspected one of his wives of a slight *écart* from the path of propriety —very unjustly, it is said—but he called her and all his servants together, cut off the heads of every individual in his household, and then shot himself." (*Up the Country*, by Hon. Emily Eden (3rd edn., 1866), i. 137.)

SMITH, Dudley Robert[1] (1797-1826). Local Lieutenant. Dromedary Corps. b. 31 Dec. 1797. Local Lieut. 3 Jan. 1817. d. Calcutta 10 June 1826.
m. Meerut 28 Apr. 1815, Miss A. C. Tonnochy. (She died Calcutta 26 Sept. 1839, aged 40.)
Services: Apptd. Local Lieut. & Adjt. Gardner's Corps of Irreg. Cav. 3 Jan. 1817; do. Dromedary Corps 1817 till disbanded in Oct. 1821. (? Retransfd. to Gardner's Horse in 1821.)
Refs.: M.I. in S. Park St. cemetery, Calcutta.
[1] *Note:* Or Robert Dudley.

SMITH, R——. Local Cornet, 2nd (Borlase's) Corps of Local Cav., 11 Aug. 1818. N.F.P.

SMITH, T—— B——. Local Ensign, 2nd Nassiri Bn. Local Cornet, 4th (Sneyd's) Horse, 28 Nov. 1818. Transfd. as Local Ensign to 2nd Nassiri Bn. 21 Aug. 1819. Was still serving in this Corps in Dec. 1821.

SMITH, William (*d.* 1823). Local Cornet and Adjt., 1st Rohilla Cav., 11 Aug. 1818. Was still serving in Dec. 1821. Formerly in H.M.S. *d.* Chinsura 25 Aug. 1823.

Refs.: *A.J.* xvii. 464 ("Capt. W. Smith, late of the Rohilla Corps.").

SWINTON, George. Local Lieutenant, Agra Najib Bn., *c.* 1820-2.

(? *m.* 13 Nov. 1819, Miss Anne E. Swinton.)

TETLEY, George. Local Lieutenant, Dromedary Corps, 3 Jan. 1817 till disbanded Oct. 1821.

Son of James Tetley, *q.v.*, by Chaund Bibi.

TURNBULL, James Montague (1801/02-1856). Local Lieutenant, Pension Est. 1st (Skinner's) Local Horse. *b.* 1801/02. Local Cornet 19 June 1819. Local Lieut. 18 Feb. 1825. Pensioned 14 Nov. 1840. *d.* Calcutta 28 Dec. 1856, of dysentery, aged 54.

Brother of John Turnbull and brother-in-law of Dr. Robert Stuart.

Services: Posted Local Cornet to Skinner's Horse June 1819; transfd. as Adjt. to 8th Local Horse (newly-raised by Lt.-Col. Skinner) 18 Feb. 1825. Siege and capture of Bhurtpore; Local Lieut. and Adjt. 8th Local Horse (India medal). On disbandment of 8th Local Horse was retransfd. as supy. to 1st (Skinner's) Local Horse, 17 July 1829 till pensioned.

Refs.: *I.M.* 17 Feb. 1857, p. 115. Will dated 4 Feb. 1853; proved 6 Jan. 1857.

TURNBULL, William (*d.* 1846). Local Lieutenant. Champaran L.I. Local Ensign, Champaran L.I., 25 Aug. 1818. Local Lieut. do. (?) Apptd. Offg. Asst. Surg. 24 June 1819. Struck off 30 Sept. 1820; relieved and discharged 4 Oct. 1820. *d.* at sea 14 Oct. 1846, on board S.S. *Hindostan*, on his passage to Ceylon.

Services: M.D., Edin., 1814; M.R.C.S. 1814.

Refs.: *Roll of I.M.S.*, No. B. 855. *Friend of India*, 12 Nov. 1846.

VALLÉ, Bartholomew (1791-1836). Local Sub-Lieutenant. Cuttack Legion. Afterwards an Asst. in the Judicial Dept., Calcutta. *bapt.* Calcutta 25 June 1793, aged 2 yrs. Local Sub-Lieut. 4 July 1817. *bur.* Calcutta 18 Dec. 1836.

Son of Lazarus (or Lewis) Vallé, *q.v.*

Services: Was still in Cuttack Legion in 1822.

Refs.: *A.J.* N.S. xxiii. 55.

LOCAL OFFICERS

VAN RANZOW, M——. Local Ensign in the Javanese Corps at Sourabaya in 1816. N.F.P. (May perhaps be identified with Lt.-Col. Count Van Ranzow who was living at Sumenep, Madura, Java, in 1829.)

VILLETTE, W—— (d. 1819). Local Lieutenant, Ramgarh Bn. Local Ensign, Ramgarh Bn., 4 Aug. 1818. Local Lieut. do. 1819. d. Hazaribagh 18 Oct. 1819, of jungle fever.
Refs.: A.J. ix. 627.

WADDILOVE, John (1798/99-1836). Local Lieutenant. Cuttack Legion. Afterwards a Pensioner of Govt. b. 1798/99. Local Cornet in Skinner's Horse c. 1816. Sub-Lieut., Cuttack Legion, 4 July 1817. Local Lieut. do. 2 Jan. 1819. Was still serving in that Corps in June 1823, when he was engaged in Singhbhum district in operations against the Kols. *bur.* Cuttack 12 Feb. 1836, aged 37.

WATSON, Henry (1789-1824). Local Lieutenant, Bencoolen Bn. b. 28 Feb. 1789. Local Lieut. 7 Jan. 1820. *bur.* Fort Marlbro' 2 Feb. 1824.
2nd son of Col. Jonas Watson, H.M. 13th Ft., and Harriett Colclough his wife. Brother of Thomas Colclough Watson, *q.v.* m. Estelle, dau. of —— de Guinez d'Illarion de la Bernagerez. (She died 1877.)
Services: Ensign H.M. 87th Ft.; Lieut. 1/87th 16 Sept. 1807. (? Sometime in R.N.) Served with Bencoolen Local Bn. Jan. 1820 till death.[1]
Refs.: Ruvigny's *Plantagenet Roll*, Essex Vol., p. 608. M.I. at Bencoolen.
[1] *Note:* This corps was comdd. by his brother in 1822.

WESTON, Edward. Local Ensign, 1st Rampura Local Bn., 8 Apr. 1819. Discharged with gratuity of Rs. 1,200 from 1 July 1822. Apptd. a Local Ofr. of Nagpur service 27 Sept. 1822; employed in Nagpur Survey c. 1823 till 1 June 1830, when his appt. under Nagpur Rajah was abolished. He was then a Local Capt. Was in Calcutta in 1831.

WHEELER, F—— (d. 1841). Local Lieutenant and Adjt., 3rd or Kohistan Regt., Shah Shuja's forces. Kld. at camp Kahdarrah, Afghanistan, 3 Nov. 1841.
Refs.: Eyre's *Journal*, p. 420. Lady Sale's *Journal*, pp. 55-6. M.I. Afghan Memorial Church, Bombay.

WILLOUGHBY, Francis (1794/95-1823). Local Lieutenant. Gorakhpur L.I. *b.* 1794/95. Local Cornet 3 Jan. 1817. Local Lieut. 26 Feb. 1820. *bur.* Calcutta 7 Sept. 1823, aged 28.

Son of Richard Willoughby, *q.v.*, by an Indian woman.

Services: Cornet & Adjt. Dromedary Corps 1817-19. Third Mahratta War; storm and capture of Jawad Jan. 1818; Cornet Dromedary Corps. Cornet & Adjt. 1st Rampura Local Cav. 1819. With Gorakhpur L.I. Bn. 1820-2. Afterwards an Asst. in the firm of Cruttenden & Co., Calcutta merchants and agents.

Refs.: A.J. xvii. 464. Will dated Calcutta 28 July 1823; proved 9 Sept. 1823.

WOOD, Samuel. Local Ensign, Rangpur Local Bn., 12 Sept. 1818. Was still serving in this Bn. in Dec. 1821.

An Anglo-Indian. *m.* 23 May 1825, Miss Jane Hair.

Services: An Asst. in the Judicial Dept. at Calcutta in 1832.

WOODVILLE, ———. Local Lieutenant. Second Mahratta War; defence of Delhi Oct. 1804; Local Lieut. in Harriott's Corps.

APPENDIX B

SUPPLEMENTARY LIST OF CADETS, OFFICERS, AND BREVET ENSIGNS OMITTED FROM THE MAIN LIST

NONE of these names are given in *Dodwell & Miles*. Those whose eligibility for inclusion is in some degree doubtful, are prefixed with a dagger (†); the remainder should definitely have been incorporated in the body of this work.

ATKINSON, Henry Hugh (1762/63-?). Lieutenant, Infantry. *b.* in Ireland 1762/63. Cadet 1779. Ensign 1780. Lieut. 5 June 1781.

N.B.—The following is conjectural only :—(Eldest son of Rev. Guy Atkinson, of Cangort, vicar of Trim, co. Meath, and Jane his 2nd wife, dau. of Jackson Wray, of co. Donegal. Uncle of Charles Atkinson, *q.v. d.* in India.)

Services : Apptd. Cadet 24 Dec. 1779 ; sailed for India in the *Earl of Dartmouth* 3 June 1780, aged 17. Not in MS. *A.L.* of 1 June 1785.

Refs. : (? Burke's *Landed Gentry of Ireland*, p. 16, *s.n.* Atkinson, of Cangort.)

BATHOE, John (1738/39-1816). Cadet. Infantry. Afterwards B.C.S. *b.* London 1738/39. Cadet 1758. Transfd. to B.C.S. (?) *d.* the Crescent, Bath, 15 Jan. 1816, aged 79.

m. Calcutta 3 Apr. 1771, Mrs. Elizabeth Lindsay, widow. (She died Clifton 1 July 1788, aged 45.)

Services : Apptd. Cadet 1758 ; sailed for India in the *Warren* in 1758, aged 19. Clerk to the Committee of Accounts at Calcutta in 1765 ; Resdt. at Malda in 1770 ; apptd. Export Warehouse Keeper at Calcutta 1 Mar. 1771 ; 3rd at Dacca 6 Feb. 1772 ; Resdt. at Burdwan ; resigned 13 Nov. 1775.

Refs. : G.M. 1816, i. 185. *Bath Chron.* 25 Jan. 1816. M.I. Bath Abbey.

BELSCHES, Anthony (*d.* 1780). Lieutenant, Infantry. Cadet 1769. Ensign (? 27 July) 1769. Lieut. (? 20 Nov.) 1772. *d. unm.* in India 1780.

Stepson of Mrs. Rose Cowie, of Bristol. Cousin of " Lady Jane Belsches, of City of Edinburgh, wife to John Belsches, junr., Esq."

Services: Dy. Judge Advocate to Tempy. Bde. at Fatehgarh in Aug. 1778; Judge Advocate to 1st Bde. in May 1779 and Aug. 1780, when he was granted leave s.c. to sea coast.

Refs.: Will dated 26 Aug. 1780; proved 28 Nov. 1780.

BLUNDELL, Edmund Augustus (1804-1859 ?). Ensign. Engineers. Afterwards Govr. of the Straits Settlements. *bapt.* St. Mary Magdalene, Taunton, 5 Sept. 1804. Ensign 1822. Struck off 18 Apr. 1823. (? *d.* 1859.)

Son of William Blundell, of Lyme Regis, and Mary his wife. Addiscombe Cadet 1818-20.

Services: Apptd. Writer, Penang C.S., Nov. 1820; Comr. Tenasserim; Govr. of the Straits Settlements 1855 till Aug. 1859.

BROOKE, William (1734/35-?). *b.* Norwich 1734/35. Cadet 1758.

Services: Sailed for India in the *Bombay Castle* in 1758, aged 23. N.F.P.

CORNELOUP, James (1734/35-?). *b.* Vevey, Switzerland, 1734/35. Cadet 1758.

Services: Sailed for India in the *Prince George* in 1758, aged 23. N.F.P.

DAVIS, Dudley (1728/29-?). *b.* in Ireland 1728/29. Cadet 1758. Resigned 1759.

m. Calcutta 5 Apr. 1760, Mrs. Eleanor Breswell.

Services: Sailed for India in the *Prince George* in 1758, aged 29. Apptd. Coy.'s atty. in the mayor's court 20 Dec. 1759; requests permission to return to Europe Jan. 1760.

DELAVAL, Henry (1736-1760). Captain. Eur. Gren. Coy. Afterwards Capt. H.M. 79th Regt. *bapt.* 18 Dec. 1736. Capt. 23 Jan. 1759. *d.* Madras Presdy. 27 June 1760 : kld. in action.

7th (twin with George [1]) and youngest son of Francis Delaval, of Seaton Delaval, Capt. R.N., and Rhoda Blake-Delaval his wife, dau. of Robert Apreece, of Washingley, Hunts. Brother of Robert Delaval, *q.v.*, and of John Hussey Delaval, only Baron Delaval, of Seaton Delaval, Northumberland. Ed. Westminster; adm. May 1749, aged 11; in school list 1752.

Services: Ensign 2nd Ft. Gds. 2 Feb. 1754; Capt. 34th (afterwards 73rd) Ft. 2 Sept. 1757. Sailed for India as a Vol. in the *Prince George* May 1758, aged 20. "Resolved that Capt. Henry Delaval be given the comd. of the Coy. raised entirely at the expense of his brother Capt. Robert Delaval who died in his passage to India." (*Pub. Procs.*, Ft. Wm. 23 Jan. 1759.) Went to Madras Sept. 1759, and whilst there accepted a King's Commn. in Col. Draper's Regt. there (79th).

Refs.: *Hist. of Doddington*, by Rev. R. E. G. Cole. *Westminster School Register*. Will dated 4 Nov. 1759; proved (Madras) 5 Aug. 1760.

¹ *Note*: George, refusing to be parted from his twin brother, fell overboard during the voyage and was drowned.

DELAVAL, Robert (1733-1758). Captain, Eur. Gren. Coy. *b.* 5 Mar. 1733. Capt. 26 Apr. 1758. *d.s.p.* 11 Dec. 1758, of a violent fever, shortly before reaching India.

bapt. St. George's, Hanover Sq., London, 5 Mar. 1733. 5th son of Francis Delaval, Capt. R.N., and Rhoda his wife. Brother of Henry Delaval, *q.v.* Ed. Westminster May 1744-1747.

Services: Cornet R.H.G. 29 Apr. 1754; retired 14 Oct. 1755. Agreed with C.D. early in 1758 to raise at his own expense in Northumberland a Coy. of 100 Grenadiers for service in Bengal; sailed for India as a Capt. in the *Prince George* in May 1758, aged 25.

Refs.: *Hist. of Doddington*, by Rev. R. E. G. Cole. *Westminster School Register*. Will dated King's Sq., Soho, 11 May 1758; proved 16 Oct. 1759.

†**EISER, John Christian (or Christopher)** (*d.* 1763). Capt. comdg. Troop of Eur. Hussars. (See Vol. ii. 126.) *d.* in India 1763.

Services: Practitioner Engr. and (rank of) Ensign H.M.S. 9 Sept. 1756; Sub-Engr. and (rank of) Lieut. 17 Mar. 1759; also (at the same time) Lieut. H.M. 79th Ft. 6 Dec. 1757. Rochefort 1757; Mysore 1760. Bde. Major to Coote 11 Sept. 1760, and was with him at taking of Pondicherry, Jan. 1761, and at Patna, June 1761. Apptd. by Coote Capt. Lt. 84th Ft. 21 Feb. 1761; Capt. do. 4 Oct. 1761; his successor apptd. 21 May 1763.

Refs.: *Conolly*, No. 129. Vibart's *Hist. of the Madras Engrs.*

†**ETHERTON, James.** Adjutant with Warrant.

Services: Was Sergt., 15th Bn. Sepoys, in 1778; Fort Adjt. at Buxar in Jan. 1785, when he was recommended by the Comdt. of that fortress for appt. as Ensign; Adjt. with Warrant in 1790.

EVANS, Evan (1733/34-?). Cadet. Infantry. *b.* co. Denbigh 1733/34. Cadet 1758.

Services: Sailed for India in the *Calcutta* in 1759, aged 25. N.F.P.

GIBSON, Thomas (1764/65-?). Cadet. Infantry. *b.* Scotland 1764/65. Cadet 1781.

Services: Apptd. Cadet 18 May 1781; sailed for India in the *Lord Mulgrave* 25 June 1781, aged 16. N.F.P.

HACKETT, John (1734/35-1760). Cadet. Infantry. Subsequently B.C.S. *b.* London 1734/35. Cadet 1758. Resigned 1759. *d.* Moradbag, Bengal, 1760.

Services: Sailed for India in the *Prince George* in May 1758, aged 23. Transfd. to B.C.S.; apptd. Asst. in the Sec.'s office 5 Feb. 1759. "Mr. (Warren) Hastings requiring an Asst. under him at Moraudbaag, and Mr. John Hackett, who came out a Cadet last season, promising to apply himself to the study of the Moor's language and to qualify himself for the business to be done there —Agreed he be permitted to reside at Moraudbaag under Mr. Hastings."

Refs.: Proc. 17 Dec. 1759. Will dated Moradbaug 19 Jan. 1760; proved 26 Sept. 1760.

HARRINGTON, Thomas (*d.* 1771). Cadet, Infantry. Cadet (?) *bur.* St. Mary's cemetery, Madras, 21 June 1771.

Services: N.F.P.

HEREFORD, Charles. Cadet. Infantry. Cadet 1777. Resigned 1778.

Services: Apptd. Cadet 4 June 1777; sailed for India in the *Lord North* 15 July 1777. Writes to the Board in Calcutta from Madras, 10 Feb. 1778, asking leave to resign as he must attend to his affairs in England.

†HORSEFALL, Christopher (*d.* 1793). Captain. Infantry. Afterwards Lt. Col. H.M. 58th Ft. Capt. Sept. 1768. *d.* Blackheath 10 Jan. 1793.

Services: Ensign 80th Ft. (or Regt. of Light Armed Foot in America) 26 Sept. 1760; Lieut. do. 30 Sept. 1763; disbanded on h.p. 1763. Exchanged to 1st Lieut. 23rd R.W.F. 20 Dec. 1764; Capt. do. 15 July 1768. Transfd. as Capt. to Bengal Army Sept. 1768. Major 72nd Ft. (R. Manchester Vols.) 16 Dec. 1777; Major 58th Ft. 19 Nov. 1782; Lt. Col. do. 29 Mar. 1786; Bt. Lt. Col. 19 Feb. 1783. Lt. Col. 58th Ft. 29 Mar. 1786 till 13 May 1789, when succeeded.

Refs.: M.C. 1 Sept. 1768. G.M. 1793, i. 93.

SUPPLEMENTARY LIST 589

HULM, Henry (1801-?). Cadet. Infantry. *bapt.* St. Michael's, Coventry, 27 Dec. 1801. Cadet 1817. Did not proceed to India.

Son of William Hulm, of the city of London, wine merchant, and Elizabeth his wife.

KELLY, James (1727/28-?). Cadet. Infantry. *b.* in Ireland 1727/28. Cadet 1759. Resigned 1760.

Services: Apptd. Cadet Nov. 1759; embarked in the *Onslow* for India in 1760, aged 32, but left her at Plymouth.

MacDOWALL, Michael. Bt. Ensign.

Services: Was Sergt. 39th Bn. Sepoys, with 16 yrs. service on 4 Oct. 1779, when he was apptd. Ensign of Mil., " in consideration of long service and wounds." Was a Bt. Ensign in Apr. 1782; not in List of 1 June 1785.

†MANGIN, Samuel Henry (1737-1798). Capt. Lieutenant. Infantry. Afterwards Lt. Col. 12th (P. of W.) Light Dgns. *b.* 1737. Capt. Lt. (Bengal) *c.* Nov. 1763. *d.* French St., Dublin, 13 July 1798; *bur.* in Huguenot burial-ground, Dublin.

Son of Capt. Paul Mangin (descended from Huguenot ancestors who migrated to Ireland and settled in Dublin) and Anne Henriette his wife (*m.* 26 Aug. 1730), eldest dau. of Henri D'Aulnis, sr. de La Lande et de Lomade. *m.* Sept. 1769, Susanna Corneille, also of French extraction. (She died Dublin 21 Dec. 1824.) Father of Edward Mangin (*D.N.B.*).

Services: Ensign 2/4th Ft. 6 Oct. 1757, which Bn. was formed into 62nd Ft. 21 Apr. 1758. Ensign 84th Ft. 26 Dec. 1758; Lieut. do. 24 Nov. 1759. Apparently transfd. to H.E.I.C.S. *c.* Nov. 1763, but returned to H.M. 84th Ft. in Feb. 1764, when he wrote to the Board from Calcutta refusing the Commission offered him. Capt. Lt. and Capt. 84th Ft. 13 Jan. 1764; h.p. as Capt. 84th Ft. 25 Aug. 1765. Capt. 5th (R. Irish) Dgns. 18 Apr. 1766; Major do. 14 Jan. 1775; Bt. Col. 17 Nov. 1780. Lt. Col. 12th Light Dgns. 19 Nov. 1781 till 25 June 1785.

Refs.: *D.N.B.*, *s.n.* Edward Mangin. *Pedigree Register*, i. 191. *Huguenot Peds.*, by Charles E. Lart, ii. 2.

†MARRIOTT, Randolph (1736-1807). Bengal C.S. *b.* 18 June 1736. Writer, B.C.S., 1753. *d.* 2 June 1807.

Of Leases Hall, Bedale, Yorks. *bapt.* Emberton, Bucks., 27 June 1736. 3rd son of Rev. Randolph Marriott, D.D., Chaplain to George II, and Lady Diana Feilding his wife, 3rd dau. of Basil,

4th Earl of Denbigh. Brother of William Marriott, *q.v.* *m*. 4 Dec. 1769, Elizabeth, 2nd dau. of Rt. Rev. Christopher Wilson, D.D., bishop of Bristol. (She died 27 Feb. 1821.)

Services : " H.E.I.C.S., was transfd. to the Mily. Service and served under Clive with distinction at the battle of Plassey, 23 June, 1757, receiving a gold medal." (*Burke*.)

Refs. : Burke's *Landed Gentry*, 13th edn., p. 1203, *s.n.* Wynne-Marriott, of Avonbank, co. Worcester. *Holzman.*

PALMER, Francis (*d.* 1780). Lieutenant, Infantry. Cadet (?) Ensign (?) Lieut. (?) *d.* 1780.

Brother of John and William Palmer.

Services : Was Dy. Paymr. to Vizier's troops in Rohilkhand in 1778 ; Lieut. and A.D.C. to Gen. Stibbert, *q.v.*, at Calcutta in Sept. 1780, when he requests leave s.c. to sea.

Refs. : Will dated Calcutta 5 Jan. 1780 ; proved 1 Nov. 1780.

PEMBERTON, Henry. Lieutenant. Infantry. Cadet (?) Ensign (?) Lieut. (?)

Services : Was a Lieut. at Calcutta on 13 Sept. 1784, when he applies for leave s.c. to Madras. N.F.P.

PERRY, Charles (1727/28-?). Cadet. Infantry. *b.* in Ireland 1727/28. Cadet 1758.

Services : Sailed for India in the *Bombay Castle* in 1758, aged 30. N.F.P.

POE, John Merton. Cadet. Infantry. Cadet 1778.

Services : Gen. Letter from C.D., dated 17 Apr. 1778 : " . . . John Merton Poe, now in India, is apptd. Cadet."

Refs. : Mily. *Cons.* 19 Dec. 1778.

PUREFOY, H——. Ensign. Infantry. Cadet (?) Ensign (?) (*Probably* brother of William Albert Purefoy, *q.v.*)

Services : Writes from Calcutta, 30 May 1785, to Maj.-Gen. Stibbert, C.-in-C., *q.v.*, requesting permission to be readmitted on the Est. with the usual allowances from the time he ceased to draw them. N.F.P.

PYATT, Robert Thomas. Cadet. Infantry. Cadet 1764.

Services : His name appears in a " List of Cadets apptd. for the Coy.'s Forces in Bengal, with their Rank," dated London, 2 Mar. 1764. N.F.P.

SQUIRE(S), Warr (? *d.* 1796). Ensign. Infantry. Country Cadet 1763. Ensign 20 Sept. 1763. (? *d.* Calcutta 17 May 1796.[1])

Services : " Warr Squire be at liberty to proceed to East Indies to provide for himself in the seafaring way on the Coy.'s usual terms." (Court Min. 15 May 1761.) Ranked as Ensign between Claud Martin and Henry Bevan, *qq.v.* (M.C. 26 Sept. 1763.)

[1] *Note :* One of this name, a Condr. of Ord., *d.* Calcutta 17 May 1796—*G.M.* 1797, i. 356.

TURNER, Alexander. Capt. Lieutenant. Artillery. Afterwards Capt. Lieut. Bombay Art. Cadet (?) Ensign (Bo. Inf.) (?) 2nd Lieut. (Bo. Art.) Nov. 1756. Lieut. (Bo. Art.) Mar. 1758. Capt. Lt. (Bengal Art.) 7 Nov. 1757. Capt. Lt. (Bo. Art.) Feb. 1759. Resigned 1760.

Services : Went to Bengal to serve under Clive in 1756 ; transfd. to Bengal Art. as Capt. Lt. in 1757 ; returned to Bombay ; Adjt. Bombay Art. in 1759.

Refs. : Spring, No. 28.

†WESTON, John (*d.* 1784 ?). Volunteer. Infantry. Afterwards Ensign, Madras Est. Vol. 1780. Ensign (Madras) 8 Dec. 1780. (? *d.* Madras Presdy. 1784.)

Cousin of Orfeur Weston.

Services : Came out as a Vol. in 1780, and served as such with the Bengal detachment during Second Mysore War ; was at Calcutta in Oct. 1781, when he applies to be received with his rank (having accepted a Commission at Fort St. George) on the Bengal Est. His request was refused and he returned to Madras in Nov. 1781.

Refs. : Intestate ; admon. 29 June 1784.

APPENDIX C

MINOR CADETS

UNLESS otherwise stated, all the following were struck off on 2 May 1786, in accordance with orders received from the C.D.[1] (*See* Vol. i. p. xxi.) The appointment of such Cadets was first authorized in M.C. dated 14 Aug. 1777.

ACHMUTY (AUCHMUTY or AHMUTY), Henry Muir.

Son of Major Arthur Forbes Achmuty (i. 6). Apptd. 27 Nov. 1781.

ACHMUTY (AUCHMUTY or AHMUTY), James (1775-1864).

Apptd. 20 Mar. 1780. (*See* i. 6.)

ACHMUTY, John (1772-1836).

2nd brother of the last; *bapt.* nr. Patna *c.* Feb. 1772. Apptd. 20 Mar. 1780. Writer, B.C.S., 1 Aug. 1790; retd. Jan. 1827; *d.* 14 Oct. 1836.

ACHMUTY, Patrick (*d.* 1804).

Son of Major Arthur Forbes Achmuty (i. 6). Apptd. 27 Nov. 1781. Became a merchant in Tipperah district of Bengal; *d.* on his way from Bhies Gong to Comillah, in zillah of Tipperah, 27 Oct. 1804.

ACHMUTY, Richard (1774-1816).

3rd son of Col. Arthur Achmuty (i. 6) and Ursula da Cruz; *bapt.* Calcutta 15 Oct. 1774. Apptd. 20 Mar. 1780. Writer, B.C.S., 24 June 1791; resigned 30 Mar. 1808; *d.* London (? Apr.) 1816.

ACHMUTY, Robert.

Son of Major Arthur Forbes Achmuty (i. 6). Apptd. 27 Nov. 1781.

---

[1] Minutes of Council, 2 May 1786—Extract of a Letter from C.D., dated 21 Sept. 1785 :—Para 11—We have hitherto as an indulgment to our Military Officers tolerated the appointment of their Infant Sons as Minor Cadets; but as We have great reason to believe this indulgence has been much abused and we are thereby put to great expense, We have come to the determination to put a stop thereto, and therefore not only direct that the pay and allowances of all those at present on your Establishment be discontinued from the receipt of these Orders, but expressly forbid any such appointment in future. Whenever you wish to interest yourselves for the Sons of deserving Officers your recommendation of them to the Court of Directors will be properly attended to.

MINOR CADETS

ACHMUTY, Robert (Alexander Gregory) (1770-?).

Eldest son of Col. Arthur Achmuty (i. 6) and Ursula da Cruz; *bapt.* Calcutta 28 June 1770. Apptd. 20 Mar. 1780. Barr.-at-law; admitted Lincoln's Inn 1788; *d.s.p.*

ACHMUTY, Thomas.

Youngest brother of the last. Apptd. 25 June 1781. Cornet 17th Light Dgns. 11 May 1797; Lieut. 27th Light Dgns. (12 Mar. 1799) 5 Feb. 1801.

AITKINS, Robert Ellis.

Son of Lieut. Robert Aitkins (i. 57). Apptd. 17 Jan. 1785.

ANSTRUTHER, Alexander Douglas.

Eldest son of Lieut. Hon. David Anstruther (i. 41) and Mary Donaldson. Apptd. 1 Dec. 1783.

BALFOUR, Francis (1779-1854).

Son and heir of Surg. Francis Balfour (i. 84), V of Fernie, M.D., and his wife, Miss Balfour of Dunbog, Fife; *bapt.* Calcutta 9 Feb. 1779. Apptd. 22 Nov. 1781. VI of Fernie Castle, Fife; served (13 May 1824) heir-male of the body of John, Lord Balfour of Burleigh; *d.* 3 Dec. 1854.

BRISCOE, C—— (or E——).

Son of Maj.-Gen. Horton Briscoe (i. 205) and Millicent Jane Banks his 2nd wife. Apptd. 20 Mar. 1780. *d.v.p.*

BURTON, Richard.

Son of Capt. Richard Burton (i. 264). Apptd. 15 Mar. 1782.

CAMPBELL, J—— E——.

Apptd. 20 Mar. 1780. *d.* before 2 May 1786.

CARRUTHERS, John (1776-1797).

Son of Lieut. John Carruthers (i. 311) and Mary Irvine; *b.* Dalton, co. Dumfries 31 Dec. 1776. Apptd. 28 June 1784. Cadet, Madras Engrs. 1791; *d.* at sea on his passage home 21 Dec. 1797; struck off 17 Dec. 1799.

CLIFTON, Charles.

Son of Major Charles Clifton, Madras Art. (*d.* 1782). Apptd. 22 Nov. 1782.

CRAIGIE, John Adair (1780-1804).

Son of Surg. John Craigie, Bengal Est. (*d.* 10 Feb. 1795), and Jacobina Helena; *b.* Kasim Bazar, Bengal, on or *c.* 23 Sept. 1780. Apptd. 2 Jan. 1782. Writer, Bombay C.S., 1797; *d.* Penang 1804.

APPENDIX C

CRAIGIE, William Charles.
Brother of the last. Apptd. 2 Jan. 1782.

CURFY, Edward John (1774-1800).
Apptd. 19 Aug. 1779 (to rank from 20 Mar. 1779). (*See* i. 433.)

DARE, Hastings (1775-1836).
(*See* ii. 11.)

D'AUVERGNE, Robert (*d.* 1792).
Apptd. 6 Oct. 1780. (*See* ii. 14.)

DAVY, C——.
Son of Major William Davy (ii. 28). Apptd. 28 June 1784.

DAVY, Edwin.
Brother of the last. Apptd. 30 May 1782.

DAVY, William.
Brother of the last. Apptd. 30 May 1782.

EYRES, George Robert.
Only surviving son of Maj.-Gen. George Bolton Eyres (ii. 150) and Anne. Apptd. 14 Jan. 1781. Ed. Eton 1787-92; Trin. Coll., Camb., 12 Apr. 1792, aged 18; B.A. 1796; M.A. 1799; admitted Lincoln's Inn 30 Jan. 1795. Of Lynford Hall and latterly of Cavenham, Norfolk.

EYRES, ——.
Brother of the last. Apptd. 14 Jan. 1781. *d.* before 2 May 1786.

FORD, James Andrew.
Son of Surg. Major James Ford, Bengal Est. Apptd. 30 Aug. 1779.

FORSTER or FOSTER, Frederick Stukeley (*d.* 1780).
(*Probably* son of William Forster or Foster (ii. 208).) Apptd. 20 Mar. 1780. *bur.* (Foster) Calcutta 17 July 1780.

FORTNOM, John (1770-1803).
Eldest son of Col. John Fortnom (ii. 209) and Jane; *bapt.* Calcutta 13 Feb. 1770. Apptd. 30 Aug. 1779; reapptd. 21 May 1781.

FORTNOM, Thomas William (1772-1803).
Apptd. 30 Aug. 1779; reapptd. 21 May 1781. (*See* ii. 209, iii. 779.)

MINOR CADETS

GAHAGAN, Frederick (1779-1815).

Son of Terence Gahagan, M.D., Physician Gen., Madras, and Lucy; *b.* Trichinopoly 1779. Apptd. 18 Mar. 1783. Ed. Westminster; K.S. 1795. Writer, M.C.S., 1796; *d.* Nellore 19 May 1815.

GAHAGAN, Henry (1780-1834).

Brother of the last; *bapt.* 13 Oct. 1780. Apptd. 18 Mar. 1783. Ed. Westminster; K.S. 1795; Ch. Ch., Oxon., matric. 24 June 1799; admitted Lincoln's Inn 26 Mar. 1799; called to the Bar 1805; practised at Madras and subsequently returned to England; *d.* 24 Feb. 1834.

GIBSON, Thomas Samuel (1769/70-1793).

Son of Capt. Thomas Gibson, Madras Est., and Elizabeth, eldest dau. of Thomas Pelling, of the firm of Pelling, De Fries & Co., merchants at Madras. Cousin-german of Walter Palk, *q.v.* Date of appt. not known. Madras Cadet 1788; Ensign; *d.* Cuddalore 4 June 1793, aged 23.

GOODYAR, George Dinely.

Son of Capt. George Dinely Goodyar (ii. 284). Apptd. 3 Apr. 1782.

GRANT, Robert.

Son of Lieut. Robert Grant (*d.* 1779) (ii. 321). Apptd. 18 Dec. 1780.

GREEN, William David.

Son of Lt.-Col. John Green (ii. 327). Apptd. 14 Jan. 1781.

HALL, Montague.

Son of Capt. Thomas Hall (d. 1786) (ii. 365). Apptd. 22 Nov. 1781.

HAMPTON, Charles (1769-1843).

Son of Col. Samuel Hampton (ii. 378) and Sarah his 1st wife; *b.* 28 Jan. 1769. Apptd. 1771. Arrived as a Free Merchant in the *Dutton* Oct. 1785; proprietor of indigo works at Berhampore; *d.* Howrah 9 Nov. 1843.

HAMPTON, James (1784-1821).

Half-brother of the last; *bapt.* Calcutta 25 Nov. 1784. Apptd. 17 Jan. 1785. Madras Cadet 1799; Capt. 7th M.N.I.; *d.* at sea 11 Aug. 1821: lost in the *Lady Lushington*.

APPENDIX C

HAMPTON, Robert (1782-1842).

Apptd. 24 June 1782. (*See* ii. 378.)

HAMPTON, Samuel (1767-1828).

Eldest son of Col. Samuel Hampton (ii. 378) and Sarah his 1st wife; *b.* 16 Feb. 1767. Apptd. 1771. Arrived as a Free Merchant in the *Dutton* Oct. 1785; subsequently of the firm of Palmer & Co.; *d.* Serampore 26 May 1828.

HAMPTON, Thomas (1778-1801).

Half-brother of the last; *bapt.* Calcutta 25 Mar. 1778. Apptd. 6 Oct. 1780. Madras Cadet 1794; Lieut. 1/8th M.N.I.; *d.* 19 May 1801.

HAMPTON, William.

Brother of the last. Apptd. 6 Oct. 1780.

HANSEN, Frederick E——.

Son of Capt. Christian Uldrick Hansen (ii. 385). Date of appt. not known.

HESSMAN, Henry.

Son of Major William Hessman (ii. 438) and Elizabeth. Date of appt. not known.

HESSMAN, Thomas (1772-?).

Brother of the last; *bapt.* Calcutta 27 Sept. 1772. Apptd. 1777.

HESSMAN, William H—— B——.

Brother of the last. Apptd. 1777.

HIGGINS, Edward Hornby (1783-?).

Son of Lt.-Col. Thomas Higgins (ii. 448) and Frances; *b.* Berhampore 16 Aug. 1783. Apptd. 1 Sept. 1783. *d.* an infant.

HIGGINS, Thomas (1781-?).

Brother of the last; *bapt.* Berhampore 8 June 1781. Apptd. 15 Mar. 1782. *d.* an infant.

HODGSON, Robert.

Son of Major Francis Hodgson (ii. 458) and Maria. Apptd. 19 Mar. 1781.

JACKSON, Warren Rowland (1781-1851).

Eldest son of Lieut. Edward Rowland Jackson (ii. 536) and his 1st wife; *bapt.* Calcutta 7 May 1781. Apptd. 21 May 1781.

MINOR CADETS

T.C.D. 3 Nov. 1794, aged 13; B.A. 1798; Fell. Comm. Peterhouse, Camb., 8 Apr. 1804; admitted Lincoln's Inn 16 June 1800. Of Castleview, co. Cork; *d.* 29 Oct. 1851.

KEBLE, George Gilbert (1776-1811).
Son of Page Keble, Marine Storekeeper, Calcutta, and Christian his 1st wife; *bapt.* Calcutta 15 Mar. 1776. Apptd. 5 Feb. 1782. Ed. Harrow 1790-3. Writer, M.C.S., 1794; *d.* Cuddalore 26 Aug. 1811.

KEBLE, John Petrie (1772-1823).
Apptd. 5 Feb. 1782. (*See* ii. 574.)

KELLY, Robert.
Natural son of Major Robert Kelly, Madras Est. (kld. in a duel at Arnee, 29 Sept. 1790, aged 52). Apptd. 12 Nov. 1781. Madras Cadet 1789; Ensign 4 Aug. 1789.

MACGREGOR, John Alexander Paul (1780-1868).
Apptd. 22 Nov. 1781. (*See* iii. 140.)

MACKENZIE, Sir George Steuart, 7th Bart. of Coul (1780-1848).
Only surviving child of Maj.-Gen. Sir Alexander Mackenzie, 6th Bart. (iii. 153), and Katherine; *b.* 22 June 1780. Apptd. Nov. 1784. Father of Major Sir Alexander Mackenzie, 8th Bart. (iii. 153). *d.* Oct. 1848.

MACLEAN, John (? 1770-? 1806).
Son of Lt.-Col. Lachlan Maclean(e) (iii. 174). Apptd. 12 Nov. 1781. (*Possibly* the following:—*b.* Lambeth 29 June 1770; Madras Cadet 1788; Cornet 10 Nov. 1789; Major, 5th M.N.C.; *d.* Madras 1 Aug. 1806.)

McNAMARA, Charles Frederick.
Eldest son of Capt. Edward Comerford William McNamara (iii. 190) and Sally. Apptd. 1 Feb. 1783.

McNAMARA, George.
Brother of the last. Apptd. 28 June 1784.

MACPHERSON, William (1784-?).
Son of Lt.-Col. Allan Macpherson (iii. 192) and Eliza Dell; *bapt.* 28 Sept. 1784. Apptd. 11 Nov. 1784.

MATHEWS, Richard Walter Williams (1773-1800).
Son of Lieut. William Mathews (iii. 254) and Sarah Williams;

b. Westminster 19 May 1773. Apptd. 29 Aug. 1782. Madras Cadet 1790; Capt.; *d.* Amboyna 15 Aug. 1800.

MATHEWS, William Joseph (1778-1864).

Apptd. 29 Aug. 1782. (*See* iii. 255.)

METCALFE, Sir Charles Theophilus, 3rd Bart., Lord Metcalfe, G.C.B. (1785-1846).

2nd son of Major Sir Thomas Theophilus Metcalfe, 1st Bart. (iii. 284); *b.* 30 Jan. 1785; *bapt.* Calcutta 18 Apr. 1785. Apptd. 4 June 1785. Writer, B.C.S., 13 Oct. 1800; *d.* Delhi 5 Sept. 1846. (See *D.N.B.*)

METCALFE, Sir Theophilus John, 2nd Bart. (1783-1822).

Brother of the last; *b.* 19 Sept. 1783. Apptd. 28 June 1784. Ed. Eton. Writer, Canton C.S., 1799; Presdt. of the Select Committee; *d.* 15 Aug. 1822.

MORGAN, Charles (1779-1808).

Son of Lt.-Gen. Charles Morgan (iii. 328) and Hannah; *bapt.* Calcutta 27 May 1779. Apptd. 22 Oct. 1781. Cert. of Corpn. of Surgeons 1797; Surg. *Princess Mary* Indiaman 1799-1805; Asst. Surg. Madras Est., 11 Apr. 1806; *d.* Gazalhati, Mysore, 17 Dec. 1808.

MORGAN, William John (1781-?).

Brother of the last; *bapt.* Calcutta 16 May 1781. Apptd. 22 Oct. 1781. Writer, B.C.S., 1 Oct. 1796; not traced after Nov. 1801.

MURRAY (afterwards MURRAY MACGREGOR), Alexander (1778-1827).

Younger son of Capt. Alexander Murray (1746-1822) (iii. 356) by his 1st wife; *b.* 27 Nov. 1778. Date of appt. not known. Maj. Gen., H.M.S.; *d.* 20 Aug. 1827.

MURRAY, Evan Edmund Hastings Pascal (1777-?).

Brother of the last; *b.* 8 Feb. 1777. Date of appt. not known. *d.* young.

NICOL, Archibald.

Son of Lt.-Gen. James Nicol (iii. 390). Apptd. 22 Oct. 1781.

NICOL, Charles.

Brother of the last. Apptd. 22 Oct. 1781.

NICOL, James (1778-1831).

Apptd. 22 Oct. 1781. (*See* iii. 391.)

PATTERSON, Alexander.
Son of Capt. Alexander Patterson, Madras Est. (*d.* 28 Feb. 1785), who was one of the Madras ofrs. sent to Bengal during the "Batta mutiny" in 1766, and Janet. Apptd. 18 Mar. 1783.

PATTERSON, John.
Brother of the last. Apptd. 18 Mar. 1783.

PEMBLE, James.
Son of Lieut. Charles Pemble (iii. 498). Apptd. 5 Feb. 1782.

PEMBLE, Thomas.
Brother of the last. Apptd. 5 Feb. 1782.

PETRIE, John (1781-?).
Son of Lieut. John Petrie (iii. 513) and Ann; *bapt.* 11 Nov. 1781. Apptd. 27 Nov. 1781.

PLOWDEN, Edward Chicheley (1779-1806).
Eldest son of Richard Chicheley Plowden (1743-1830), B.C.S., Dir. E.I. Co., and Eliza Sophia, dau. of George Augustus Prosser; *b.* 2 Jan. 1779; *bapt.* Calcutta 29 June 1779. Apptd. 20 Mar. 1780. Of no profession; *d. unm.* 14 May 1806.

READ, John Peregrine (1781-1802).
Apptd. 7 June 1781. (*See* iii. 619.)

ROBERTS, Charles Morrissey (1781-1845).
Apptd. 22 Oct. 1781. (*See* iii. 666.)

ROBERTS, William (1780-1851).
Brother of the last; *b.* Cawnpore 11 Apr. 1780. Apptd. 2 Apr. 1781. Lt. Col., R.A.; *d.* Southampton 9 July 1851.

SANDS, William John (1781-1837).
Eldest son of Major William Sands (iv. 16) and Christian; *b.* Calcutta 6 Dec. 1781. Apptd. 18 Apr. 1782. Writer, B.C.S., 9 Oct. 1797; retired 2 Jan. 1827; *d.* Edinburgh 10 Jan. 1837.

SCOTT, Henry (1777-1779).
Eldest son of Major John Scott-Waring (iv. 391) and Elizabeth his 1st wife; *b.* Calcutta 1777. Apptd. 5 Nov. 1777. *d.* Calcutta 3 June 1779, aged 2¼ yrs.

SEARS, ——.
(*Probably* son of Lt.-Col. Samuel Sears (iv. 48) and Mary.)

Apptd. 19 Aug. 1779 (to rank from 20 Mar. 1779). (*Probably* Samuel Montague Sears; Lieut. 76th Ft. 1 Jan. 1796; Capt. h.p. 9th Ft.)

SEWARD, William Philip (1778-?).

Son of Capt. William Seward, Bombay Est. (*d.* July 1803), and Ann Isabella Lewis; *b.* 5 June 1778; *bapt.* Bombay 2 Dec. 1778. Apptd. 2 Jan. 1782.

SHOWERS, Charles Lionel (1780-1815).

Apptd. 26 Nov. 1781. (See iv. 81.)

SHOWERS, Edward Melian Gullifer (1784-1868).

Brother of the last; *b.* Calcutta 29 Feb. 1784. Apptd. 28 June 1784. Madras Cadet 1800; Gen., Madras Art.; *d.* Cheltenham 13 Dec. 1868.

SHOWERS, Hampton Silvester (1781-?).

Brother of the last; *bapt.* Calcutta 12 Apr. 1781. Apptd. 2 Apr. 1781.

SHOWERS, Nathaniel Thornhill (1778-1803).

Half-brother of the last; *bapt.* Calcutta 8 Aug. 1778. Apptd. 20 Mar. 1780. Madras Cadet 1794; Capt. 4th M.N.I.; *d.* England 23 June 1803.

SHOWERS, Samuel Howe (1775-?).

Brother of the last; *bapt.* Calcutta 23 Jan. 1775. Apptd. 20 Mar. 1780.

SKARDON, Samuel William.

Son of Bt. Lt. F. Samuel Skardon (iv. 105) and Mary. Apptd. 22 Feb. 1785.

SKARDON, Warren Hastings.

Brother of the last. Apptd. 28 June 1784.

SMITH, Emilius Felix (1777-1801).

Younger son of Major Lewis (Lucius) Smith (iv. 130); *b.* Rohilkhand 14 Feb. 1777. Apptd. 15 Mar. 1782. Held a Commn. in H.M. 36th Ft.; Capt. in Sindhia's service; *d.* of wounds at Jhajjar 8 Oct. 1801.

SMITH, Lewis Ferdinand (*d.* 1820).

Elder brother of the last. Apptd. 15 Mar. 1782. Permitted to reside at Lucknow as a merchant in 1793; Major in Sindhia's service; received a pension from Brit. Govt. in 1803, of Rs. 1,200 *p.m.*; *d.* 1820.

STAFFORD, John Charles Wynch.

Eldest son of Lt.-Gen. Hugh Stafford (iv. 163) and Thomasine his 1st wife. Apptd. 28 July 1783. *d.* young.

STAMFORD, Joseph.

Son of Ensign William Stamford (iv. 166). Apptd. 23 Oct. 1784.

STAMFORD, William.

Brother of the last. Apptd. 23 Oct. 1784.

STEWART, John MacLean (1767-1816).

Apptd. 12 Nov. 1781. (*See* iv. 189.)

STORMONTH, John (1782-?).

Son of Surg. John Stormonth, Bengal Est.; *bapt.* Calcutta 11 Jan. 1782. Apptd. 2 Jan. 1782.

TOLL(E)Y, Charles Edward (1776-?).

Son of Lt.-Col. William Tolly (iv. 287) by his 2nd wife; *bapt.* Calcutta 21 Sept. 1776. Apptd. 11 May 1780. Capt. H.M. 28th Light Dgns. (4 Apr. 1795) 27 June 1798; casualty in 1799.

TOLL(E)Y, Henry Dunbar (1780-1837).

Brother of the last; *bapt.* Calcutta 21 May 1780. Apptd. 11 May 1780. Ed. Westminster. Lieut. H.M. 4th Ft. 8 Sept. 1796; Lt. Col. 16th Ft. 23 Nov. 1809; Maj. Gen. 27 May 1825; C.B.; *d.* 25 Dec. 1837.

TOLL(E)Y, Joseph George (1779-?).

Brother of the last; *bapt.* Calcutta 21 Feb. 1779. Apptd. 11 May 1780. (? Ed. Westminster.) Admitted Lincoln's Inn 15 May 1795; Cornet H.M. 29th Light Dgns. 21 June 1798; readmitted Lincoln's Inn 15 Nov. 1799. (? Became a shipbuilder at Howrah, Bengal.)

TOLL(E)Y, William (1775-?).

Brother of the last; *bapt.* Calcutta 3 May 1775. Apptd. 11 May 1780.

TOTTINGHAM, John James (1774-?).

Apptd. 29 Mar. 1782. (*See* iv. 295.)

VINCENT, Henry.

Son of Lt.-Col. Henry Vincent (iv. 357) by his 1st wife. Apptd. 15 Mar. 1782.

WATSON, George Eyre.

Son of Lt.-Gen. Samuel Watson (iv. 406) and Mary his 2nd wife. Apptd. 4 June 1785.

WATSON, Richard Augustus Clay (1783-1824).

Apptd. 28 June 1784. (*See* iv. 406.)

WATSON, William Larkins (1784-1852).

Apptd. 4 Nov. 1784. (*See* iv. 409.)

WATSON, William Mitchell (1778/79-1811).

Apptd. 22 Oct. 1783. (*See* iv. 409.)

WHINYATES, Sir Edward Charles, K.C.B. (1782-1865).

3rd son of Major Thomas Whinyates (iv. 442) and Catherine; *b.* Calcutta 6 May 1782. Apptd. 3 Feb. 1783. General, R.A.; *d.s.p.* Cheltenham 25 Dec. 1865. (See *D.N.B.*)

WHINYATES, George Barrington (1783-1808).

Brother of the last; *b.* 31 Aug. 1783; *bapt.* Calcutta 9 Nov. 1783. Apptd. 23 Nov. 1783. Capt., R.N.; *d. unm.* Cheltenham 5 Aug. 1808. (See *D.N.B.*)

WHINYATES, Russell Manners Mertola (1780-1788).

Brother of the last; *b.* Mertola, Portugal, 20 Dec. 1780. Apptd. 3 Feb. 1783. *d.* 1 Aug. 1788.

WHINYATES, Thomas (1778-1857).

Eldest brother of the last; *b.* Stockheld Pk., Yorks., 7 Sept. 1778. Apptd. 3 Feb. 1783. Rear Adm., R.N.; *d. unm.* Cheltenham 15 Mar. 1857. (See *D.N.B.*)

WHITE, Charles.

Son of Col. John White (iv. 450) and Sarah. Apptd. 29 Apr. 1782.

WHITE, George.

Brother of the last. Apptd. 29 Apr. 1782. *d.v.p.*

WHITE, Warren Hastings.

Brother of the last. Apptd. 1 Sept. 1783. Paymr. 2nd Light Dgns., German Legion, 17 Sept. 1812; h.p. do. 21 Sept. 1815; served in Peninsula; still on h.p. in 1842, not in 1856.

WOOD, John Clavering (1778-?).

Son of Capt. William Wood (iv. 517); *bapt.* Calcutta 17 June 1778. Apptd. 30 Aug. 1779.

APPENDIX D

CHANGES OF NAME

			Date of change.
Alderson	formerly	*Lloyd*	11 June 1812
Angelo	,,	*Tremamondo*	Feb. 1818
Bebb	,,	*Lawrell*	7 June 1850
Bird	,,	*Lewis*	15 Dec. 1810
Bostock	see	Rich	
Broadhurst	formerly	*Nichols*	10 Aug. 1809
Brugh	see	Burgh	
Budworth	,,	Palmer	
Burgh	formerly	*Brugh*	—
Carmichael	,,	*Carmichael-Smyth*	17 Aug. 1842
Carpenter	,,	*Cheese*	9 June 1815
Cheere	,,	*Madryll*	12 Feb. 1808
Cheese	see	Carpenter	
Chowne	formerly	*Tilson*	24 Feb. 1836
Cope	,,	*Doolan*	14 June 1844
Halkett-Craigie	see	Craigie-Halkett	
De Montmorency	formerly	*Morres*	5 Aug. 1815
Doolan	see	Cope	
Drummond	,,	Macgregor	
Duppa	formerly	*Hancorn*	1791
Fielding	,,	*Johnson*	1757/58
Gowan	see	Mauleverer	
Craigie-Halkett	formerly	*Halkett-Craigie*	16 Apr. 1856
Hancorn	see	Duppa	
James	,,	Wallace	
Jeffery	,,	Orchard	
Johnson	,,	Fielding	
Jones	,,	Skelton	
Kennedy	,,	Skipton	
Lawrell	,,	Bebb	
Lewis	,,	Bird	
Lind	,,	Thornton	
Lloyd	,,	Alderson	
Lucadou	,,	West	
Macgregor	formerly	*Drummond*	19 Feb. 1777

APPENDIX D

Date of change.

Macgregor	formerly	*Paul*	1784
McPhail	see	Paul	
Madryll	,,	Cheere	
Manners	,,	Tollemache	
Mauleverer	formerly	*Gowan*	13 May 1834
Morres	see	De Montmorency	
Nichols	,,	Broadhurst	
Orchard	formerly	*Jeffery*	13 June 1807
Palmer	,,	*Budworth*	21 Mar. 1812
Paul	see	Macgregor	
Paul	formerly	*McPhail*	—
Read	see	Revell	
Revell	formerly	*Read*	10 Mar. 1809
Rich	,,	*Bostock*	23 Dec. 1790
Skelton	,,	*Jones*	24 Nov. 1772
Skene	,,	*Smith*	1834
Skipton	,,	*Kennedy*	13 Feb. 1802
Smith	see	Skene	
Carmichael-Smyth	,,	Carmichael	
Thornton	formerly	*Lind*	—
Tilson	see	Chowne	
Tollemache	formerly	*Manners*	17 Apr. 1821
Tremamondo	see	Angelo	
Wallace	formerly	*James*	—
West	,,	*Lucadou*	13 May 1816

ADDITIONAL SURNAMES ASSUMED

Date of assumption.

Bernard	became	Bernard-Morland	15 Feb. 1811
Brewster	,,	Brewster-Macpherson	1862
Brown	,,	Brown-Constable	27 Jan. 1853
Conway	,,	Conway-Gordon	12 Aug. 1839
Cooper	,,	Gilbert-Cooper	—
Fergusson	,,	Fergusson-Home	1860
Grant	,,	Grant-Peterkin	1836
Hore	,,	Hore-Ruthven	27 July 1853
Monteath	,,	Monteath-Douglas	18 Dec. 1850
Pollock	,,	Montagu-Pollock	11 Aug. 1873
Rainsford	,,	Rainsford-Hannay	1856
Renny	,,	Renny-Tailyour	16 Nov. 1849
Ross	,,	Lockhart-Ross	17 July 1863
Scott	,,	Scott-Waring	17 Nov. 1798

CHANGES OF NAME

Unsuccessful Applications for Change of Name

Farmer, Charles Finch	To change to C. F. Palmer	4 July 1832
Hodges, Charles Wyndham	To drop Hodges	1819
Lane, Charles Richard William	To change to Mattenby	1824
Young, William (1809-1885)	To add surname Leslie	1841

Pseudonyms

Rover, John	Name assumed on enlistment by	Sir John Horsford
Bateman, George	Name assumed on enlistment by	George Bateman Lawley
"Rambler"	Nom de plume of	Joseph Palmer
"Mentor"	Nom de plume of	Thomas Williamson (II)

APPENDIX E

SCHOOLS, COLLEGES, UNIVERSITIES, AND MILITARY SEMINARIES

THE following Table will give some idea of the pre-Service education of Bengal Cadets down to the year 1834. The list is by no means complete but shows, as far as ascertainable, the numbers educated at nine universities, three military seminaries and 33 of the larger schools in the United Kingdom during the period under review. For 18th-century statistics one is dependent almost entirely upon published school registers, and these differ enormously in the standard of editing and the degree of comprehensiveness attained.

The figure for Cambridge University would undoubtedly have been higher had Venn's *Alumni Cantabrigienses* been published beyond the letter 'F'.

Some names in this list figure under more than one heading.

Aberdeen Grammar School	18
Armagh Royal School	6
Belfast Academy	10
Blundell's	29
Bury St. Edmunds Grammar School	10
Canterbury, King's School	6
Carlisle Grammar School	4
Charterhouse	87
Cheam	6
Christ's Hospital	24
Durham	6
Edinburgh Academy	17
— High School	95
— Military & Naval Academy	15
Elizabeth College, Guernsey	3
Eton	53
Felsted	4
Glasgow Grammar and High Schools	7
Harrow	48
Inverness Royal Academy	19
Manchester Grammar School	7
Merchant Taylors'	32
Perth Academy	14

PRE-SERVICE EDUCATION

Repton	10
Rugby	49
St. Paul's	21
Sedbergh	2
Sherborne	6
Shrewsbury	23
Tonbridge	6
Uppingham	2
Westminster	66
Winchester	39
Aberdeen University (King's Coll. and Marischal Coll.)	20
Cambridge	35
Dublin (Trinity College)	47
Durham	1
Edinburgh	49
Glasgow	32
London (Gower St.)	2
Oxford	56
St. Andrews	25
Marlow Cadet College	34
R.M.C., Sandhurst	47
R.M.A., Woolwich	110

APPENDIX F

LIST OF OFFICERS OF FOREIGN NATIONALITY OR OF RECENT FOREIGN EXTRACTION

Armenian : Emin, J.
Bavarian : Mellish (von Mellisch), D. G. A. F. H.
Belgian : Nollekens, J. J.
Danish : Bie, G.; Bie, J.; Fischer, C.; Hansen, C. U.; Hickland, J.; Knudson, C.
Dutch : Blanckenhagen, H.; De Waal, J.; De Waal, P. H.; De Waal, W.; Hohney, C.; Ramus, W. P.; Tulliken, J. J.; Van Hemert, F.; Van Renen, J. (? Prussian); Van Rixtel, C.; Van Swinden, P. S.; Vanzandt, J.
French : de l'Etang, E.; de Peyron, C. A. M.; Dubois, J. H. V.; Dubois, S.; Lucadou, J. L.; Martin, C.; Mence, C.; Mence, G.; Terraneau, C.; Terraneau, C. C. de; Terraneau, W. H.
German : Chapuset, C. C. F.; Kempel, G. A.; Pfeifer, C. F. J. J.; Reinagle, C. E.; Wilmers, D. A.
Hanoverian : Wilford, F. (? Swiss).
Italian : Tremamondo, A. A. M.
Polish : De Gloss, L. F.; Ritso, G. F.
Portuguese : Carvalho, J.; Queiros, J.
Prussian : Baumgardt, F. R.; Hasenclever, C.; Koehler, G. F.; Neidrick, P.
Sardinian : Roman, J.
Silesian : Engleheart, George.
Swedish : Kiernander, C.; Kiernander, J. S. W.
Swiss : Auberjonois, A. F. L.; Aubert, J. (Geneva); Bonjour, N. A. A. (Vaud); Bourdillon, B. C. (Geneva); Brown (Braun or Brun), B. L. (Bern); Butticaz, G. W. (Vaud); Corneloup, J. (Appendix B) (Vaud); De Budé, H.; De Prelaz, S.; Doxat B.; Doxat, L. (Vaud); Flaction, C. (Bern); Grand, G. F.; Grand, J. E.; Grenier, B. L. (Vaud); Kempt, J.; Levade, C. I. (Vaud); Molitor, J. W. (Grisons); Muller, F. R. (Uri); Parisod, S. (Vaud); Paschaud, J. F.; Paschaud,

FOREIGN NATIONALS

	J. F.; Paschaud, C. F. (Vaud); Perret, H. V. F.; Pillichody, C.; Polier, A. L. H. (French-Swiss); Schalch, J. A. (? German); Schalch, P.; Wild, C. F. (Bern); Winclebeck, T. (Basle); Ziegler, A. (Schaffhausen).
Venetian:	Treves, P.
Nationality uncertain:	Brandt, J.; Brietzcke, C.; De Castro, H.; De Mattos, I.; Eiser, J. C. (Appendix B); Kraft, C.; Vallé, B.; Ximenes, H. J. (? Spanish).

APPENDIX G

LIST OF OFFICERS WHO SERVED IN THE ROYAL NAVY

Baines, G. V.
Bosanquet, F. B.
Bowen, H.
Burnet, James
Campbell, N.
Cowe, J.
Eckford, J.
Grant, C. A.
Hope, Sir William, Bart.
Latter, R. J.
Long, W. (Appendix A)
Macdonald, Cosmo
MacGregor, R. S.
Morland, R. S. B.
Morrison, D.
Nelson, H. R. (Appendix A)
Patton, J. W.
Pott, D.
Rennell, J.
Rice, J. H.
Roberdeau, J. W.
Rosat, D.
Salt, J.
Spear(s), J.
Swinton, W.
Truscott, J.
Vertue, W.
Watson, H. (Appendix A)
Webb, W. S.
Whinyates, G. B. (Appendix C)
Whinyates, T. (Appendix C)

APPENDIX H

LIST, BY REGIMENTS, OF THOSE WHO HELD COMMISSIONS IN H.M. LAND FORCES, INCLUDING THE ROYAL MARINES, COLONIAL AND FOREIGN CORPS, YEOMANRY, CAVALRY, MILITIA, FENCIBLES, AND VOLUNTEER REGIMENTS

The Corps named is the last known one in which that officer served.

CAVALRY

R. Horse Gds.	Browne, Ulysses. Delaval, Robert (Appendix B)
2nd Regt. (Ireland)	Fetherston, Thomas
1st K.D.G.	Scott, George Dennistoun
2nd D.G.	Addison, Henry Robert. Dent, John. Whinyates, Thomas
3rd —	Aitkens, Robert. Everett, Thomas Cooper
6th —	Strachan, Alexander Leigh
2nd Dgns.	Dickson, Richard Lothian
4th —	Macleish, Robert
6th —	Johnston, Francis James Thomas
7th —	Stamford, William
8th Light Dgns.	Pottinger, Thomas. Sneyd, Nathaniel. Wharton, Thomas Ramsay
9th —	Campbell, Alexander (II). Ker, John Baker
10th —	Foreman, James. M'Murdo, Alured Charles
12th —	Mangin, Samuel Henry (Appendix B)
13th —	Hislop, William. Kelso, Fleming
15th —	Horne, Francis Woodley. Wakefield, Edward
16th —	Lovelace, Henry Philip
19th —	Cathcart, James. Monteath, Walter. Verner, James
21st —	Leeson, Joseph
22nd —	Montagu, Robert Copley Rainier
24th —	Alexander, William. Angelo, John. Fisher, John. Ommanney, Cornthwaite.

APPENDIX H

	Picard, Edward (Appendix A). Pillichody, Charles. Queiros, Joseph. Rocke, Frederick Becher
25th Light Dgns. -	Scollay, William. Wade, William Henry
27th — — -	Achmuty, Thomas (Appendix C)

R.A.

Black, Alexander. Broadbridge, John. Burghall, George. Duff, Patrick (I). Hill, Justly. Kindersley, Nathaniel. Martin, Fleming. Pearse, Thomas Deane. Rosat, David. Schalch, Philip.

R.E.

Campbell, Sir Archibald, K.B. Lillyman, James. Tolly, William.

INFANTRY

2nd Foot Guards -	Palmer, Charles
3rd — — -	Skelton, Arnoldus Jones
1st Foot -	Anstruther, Hon. David. (?) Hanbury, George. Steuart, Archibald
3rd — -	Carnac, Scipio
4th — -	Bellingham, Henry Tenison. Cosby, William. Fraser-Tytler, George
5th — -	Grey, Sir John, K.C.B. Morgan, Charles
6th — -	Worrall, Henry Lechmere
7th — -	Hautenville, Alexander Jaffray. Shuldham, Thomas
8th — -	Ashe, Benjamin. Caillaud, John. Edwards, Timothy
9th — -	Pitman, Frederick Cobbe
10th — -	Howard, Thomas Ward
11th — -	Hope, Thomas. Phipps, Thomas. Toone, Sir William, K.C.B.
12th — -	(?) Forbes, John (I). (?) Money, George. Vazeille, John Anthony
13th — -	Popham, William
14th — -	Healey, James. Lambie, John Cosens. Tulliken, James Jones
15th — -	Eden, John
16th — -	Teulon, George
17th — -	Maw, Thomas. Staunton, Philip. Williams, Robert
19th — -	Dalrymple, James. Friell, Simeon Philip. Goddard, Henry. Turnour, Hon. George
20th — -	Cumming(s), James. Monck, Henry Percy

COMMISSIONED IN H.M. LAND FORCES 613

21st Foot	- -	Durham, Hercules. Strettell, Henry Keating
22nd —	- -	Bird, Louis Saunders. Davison, Lewis. Pickersgill, Joshua. Raban, William (II). Ralph, James
23rd —	- -	Torrens, Frederick
24th —	- -	(?) Easson, James. Hawkins, Francis Spencer. Mellis, William
26th —	- -	Birch, John Zephaniah Mill. Heming, Samuel Bracebridge (Appendix A)
30th —	- -	Dundas, Thomas (I). Fraser, Richard. Gardner, William Linnæus (Appendix A). Gibbs, Jonathan Warner. Gould, James (II)
31st —	- -	Hope, Sir William, Bart. Thompson, Primrose
32nd —	- -	(?) Ogilvie, William
33rd —	- -	Shee, John
34th —	- -	Casement, Hugh. (?) Mackay, Hugh (I). Orange, John Edward. Watson, William
35th —	- -	Alves, Gilmour
36th —	- -	Smith, Pooley Molyneux
37th —	- -	Tottingham, John
38th —	- -	Maxwell, William George
39th —	- -	Adnett, Joseph. Broadbridge, John. Carnac, John. Donellan, John. Forde, Edward. Forde, Francis. Nollekens, John Joseph. Powell, Caleb. Yorke, Martin
41st —	- -	Bedingfield, John George. Hickey, William. Tucker, Auchmuty
42nd —	- -	Gascoigne, Peter. Scott, Thomas (I).
43rd —	- -	Denniss, George Gladwin. Lushington, Matthew
45th —	- -	Russell, Lockhart
46th —	- -	Tennison, Richard
47th —	- -	Gordon, Adam Durnford. Peach, Joseph
48th —	- -	Dalzell, Arthur Alexander, Earl of Carnwath. Middleton, Edmund Pytts. Thompson, William Augustus
49th —	- -	Daniell, Averell. Monteath, Archibald Douglas
50th —	- -	Murray, Alexander

APPENDIX H

- 51st Foot - - Dupont, John. Hannay, Alexander. Lock, Henry. Peake, William. Piers, James
- 52nd — - - Peacocke, Sir Joseph Francis, Bart. Rose, Alexander
- 53rd — - - Constable, Charles George. Sempill, Hon. George
- 54th — - - Powell, William
- 58th — - - (?) Clarkson, Robert Graham. Horsefall, Christopher (Appendix B)
- 59th — - - Gibbs, John William. (?) Stewart, Archibald Henry
- 60th — - - Bremer, Thomas Mountsteven. Sears, Samuel (I)
- 62nd — - - Bower, George James. (?) Greatrakes, William
- 64th — - - Broderip, Henry Francis
- 65th — - - Campbell, Robert Macfarlane. Parker, John Neville
- 66th — - - Bailey, Charles Drummond. De Fountain, Angus. Douglas, Patrick John
- 67th — - - Cumberlege, Nathaniel Joseph. Tweedale, James Charles
- 68th — - - Gore, William. (?) Russell, Charles (I). Stainforth, John
- 69th — - - Atkinson, Henry. Hamilton, Sir John, Bart.
- 70th — - - Kennan, Robert. Kinloch, George (I). Palmer, William (I)
- 71st — - - Burrington, George. Ducarel, James Coltee. Forbes, Alexander (II)
- 72nd — - - Mercer, William. Palmer, Joseph. (?) Starkie, Nicholas
- 73rd — - - Ralph, Benjamin
- 74th — - - Bruce, Michael. Graham, John (I)
- 75th — - - Currie, George Alfred
- 76th — - - Leslie, Matthew. Osborn, Thomas Hoadley. Rose, Hugh. Stamford, Bryan I'Anson. Stamford, Thomas. Symes, Michael. Williams, Walter
- 77th — - - Coleman, James. Macnamara, Matthew. (?) Munro, Alexander (I). Robins, John Gregory

COMMISSIONED IN H.M. LAND FORCES

78th Foot - - D'Aguilar, George Thomas. Ferguson, Joseph. Fulton, Thomas. Tod, Suetonius Henry
79th — - - Delaval, Henry (Appendix B). Fryer, George Samuel. Graveley, Thomas Milton. Hogg, Roger. Macnab, Robert. Purefoy, William Albert. (?) Scott, John (I). Seagrave, John. Thomson, William
80th — - - de Peyron, Charles Adolphus Mary
81st — - - Baillie, Alexander Charles
82nd — - - Bainbridge, Thomas Drake. Blood, Michael. Duncanson, William Mayne
83rd — - - English, William
84th — - - Achmuty, Arthur Forbes. Camac, Jacob. Chaigneau, Christopher Theophilus. Crabbe, William Joseph. Cumming, Sir John, Kt. Curtis, Robert Ruddock. Eiser, John Christian (Appendix B). Fielding, Charles John Johnson. Freake, John. Goddard, Thomas. Grant, Henry. Grant, John (I). Hill, Douglas. Irving, John. Knudson, Christian. Long, Charles. Macdonald, Charles (2/84th). Neilson, John. Padman, Selby. Robinson, John Gowan. Roper, Thomas. Skinner, James (I). Witchcot, George
85th — - - Lucas, Richard. Ware, Charles (Crawford's Vols.). (?) Williams, Henry
86th — - - Lloyd, Henry Vereker
87th — - - Barland, Walter. De L'Etang, Eugene. Rattray, George Herbert. Shipp, John. Watson, Henry (Appendix A)
89th — - - Duff, Patrick (I). Forbes, John (I). Macpherson, William (I). Moore, John
91st — - - MacDougall, James Patrick
93rd — - - Kearney, Brydges
94th — - - Muir, Grainger
95th — - - Maynard, Walter. Webber, James
96th — - - Chapman, Charles
98th — - - Thomson, Thomas
99th — - - Gwinnett, John Price. Macharg, James (II)

APPENDIX H

100th Foot	- -	Duncanson, Duncan
101st —	- -	McVeagh, Joseph
102nd —	- -	Griffiths, Joseph
104th —	- -	Lindsay, Sir Alexander, K.C.B. Watson, Henry
106th —	- -	Shrimpton, John
107th —	- -	Gilpin, Martin
108th —	- -	(?) Scott, David
109th —	- -	Scarlin, Roger. Skene, William. Upton, John. Wroe, Benjamin
111th —	- -	Lane, William (I)
112th —	- -	Brereton, Boulter
113th —	- -	Grey, John. Morrison, John (I)
114th —	- -	Macquarie, John
119th —	- -	Nugent, William
121st —	- -	Blair, William
122nd —	- -	Minifie, Burnet
124th —	- -	Callander, Adam

MARINES

Carroll, Thomas. Jones, George. Smith, Frederick Thomas. Spooner, Thomas. Thoms, James. Willis, John. Wyllie, John (R. Marine Art.).

MISCELLANEOUS

Capt. Jonathan Forbes's Independent Coy.	Grant, Alexander (I)
Invalid Coy. - - - - -	MacGregor, Robert
Ordnance Dept. - - - -	Fisher, Thomas
R. Veteran Bn. (11th) - - -	Komblo, Peter
Independent Coy. Invalids (Plymouth)	- Carnac, Scipio

COLONIAL AND FOREIGN CORPS

S. Carolina Rangers - - -	Armstrong, Richard Boswell
Ceylon Regt. (3rd) - - -	Hodges, Alexander
Chasseurs (Swiss)- - - -	Muller, Frederick Rodolphus
Demerara Light Horse Mil. -	St. Clare, Francis
de Meuron Regt. (Swiss) -	Pillichody, Charles
German Vols., Corps of -	(?) Skinner, William Anne
Jamaica Light Horse - -	Park, Alexander
King's German Legion (2nd L.I.)-	Earle, Solomon (II)
New York Standing Mil. - -	Vanzandt, James
W.I. Regt. (3rd) - - -	Frederick, William

COMMISSIONED IN H.M. LAND FORCES 617

Regiment not Known

Arden, Russell. Brereton, William. Burney, James Christian. Calcraft, Henry Fox. Gould, James (I). Grant, Robert (I). Harding, Ralph. Hartle, Anthony. Mackenzie, Sir Alexander, Bart. (I). Macpherson, Samuel. Mills, John. Mordaunt, Henry (I). Ramsay, Jonathan. Ross, Charles (I). Selleck, James. Sturges, Thomas. Woodward, Henry.

Militia

Aberdeen	(?) Gordon, Charles. Gordon, Lord Henry
Antrim-	Macartney, John (I). Morris, John. O'Hara, Brabazon Rawdon
Argyll & Bute	Fergusson, James Alexander Duncan
Armagh	Fulton, Thomas
Beds. -	Comyn, Powell Thomas
Berks. -	Bellasis, Joseph Harvey
Berwick	Somerville, James. Vetch, George Anderson. Vetch, Robert
Brecon -	Chambré, Christopher
Bucks. -	Grant, Charles (I). Wood, Samuel
Carmarthen -	MacClary, William
Cheshire	Kelly, Christopher. Saunders, Samuel John
Devon (N.) -	Robins, John Gregory
(S.) -	Briscoe, John Jessop
(E.) -	Robertson, John (II). Tanner, Samuel
Dumfries	Crichton, David
Edinburgh -	Chiene, Patrick John
(Art.) -	Geddes, William. Walkinshaw, William
Essex -	Harriott, Thomas
(E.) -	Hull, John Watson
(W.) -	Bennett, John William
Forfar -	Carnegy, William. Ogilvy, Hon. Donald. Tandy, John O'Brien
Galloway -	Maxwell, George (I)
Glamorgan -	Jones, William (II). (?) Landeg, John
Gloucs. (N.) -	Jones, John (IV). Taylor, Thomas (III). Wallington, Charles Arthur Granado
(S.) -	Bellingham, Henry
Hants (N.) -	Palmer, Joseph
(S.) -	Missing, John
Inverness -	Grant, James (IV). Grant, John (VI)
Jersey -	Bluett, William Henry Clarke

APPENDIX H

Lanark-	Farie, Allan Scott. Hunter, James (III)
Lancs. -	Berkeley, Henry Nicholas Lionel
Leics. -	Adams, Samuel
London (E.)-	Rich, Robert
Londonderry-	McLaughlin, William. Stirling, Conolly
Meath -	Pepper, Richard
M'sex -	Lennon, James
(E.)	Heard, St. John. Nash, James. Nuttall, Adam. Raban, Henry Tilman
(Westr.)	(?) Van Hemert, Francis
(R. Elthorne)	Grange, Richard George
Northants	Shuckburgh, Henry Adolphus. Squire, Arnott. Turner, William (II)
Northl'd	Leathert, John
Oxford -	Bignell, William Phillips. Wykes, Ambrose
Peebles-	Aitchison, James
Perth -	Maxtone, Anthony. Stewart, Alexander (I)
Renfrew	Kinloch, James John
Ross -	Mackenzie, Roderick. Nicolson, Malcolm (I)
Salop -	Clark, Thomas. Gough, Thomas
Somerset	Langslow, Richard. McDonagh, Eugene
Staffs. -	Harding, Samuel. Osborn, Thomas Hoadley
Stirling-	Erskine, John Francis. Graham, John (V). MacGregor, Robert Stuart. Ramsay, Michael
Suffolk -	Hurring, Thomas. Parker, Windsor
Surrey -	Pearson, Francis Hamilton. Royle, William Henry
(1st) -	Grange, Robert. Lyster, Lyttleton. Scott, George Dennistoun
(2nd) -	Barnes, Walter Richard. Steele, Charles
(3rd) -	Alcock, Thomas
Tower Hamlets	Delamain, James. Delamain, John
Tyrone -	Verner, James
Warwick	Mitchell, William (I). Spiller, Francis John. Stewart, Charles (I)
Waterford -	Roberts, Abraham
Yorks. (N.R.)	Pratt, John Backhouse
— -	Dent, John
Regt. not known -	Hamilton, John (III). Humphreys, Christopher. Leicester, Charles Byrne. Stewart, Archibald Henry. Wishart, Thomas

YEOMANRY

Denbighshire - Lloyd, Sir William, Kt.
E. Devon Legion - Kennaway, Sir John, Bart.
Hants Fenc. Cav. - Everett, Thomas Cooper
Irish - Pollock, Robert McCully. Rainey, William Henry. Scott, Thomas (II)
Bovevagh (Londonderry) Stirling, Robert Gage
Lanarkshire - Lockhart, William

FENCIBLES

Breadalbane (1st Bn.) - Macpherson, Duncan (III)
N. British
   (N. or Gordon Regt.) Gordon, James Cosmo
   (S. Regt.) - Dove, Matthew
   (W. Regt.) - Hook, Lionel
Caithness Legion (2nd Bn.) Hunter, James (II)
R. Clan Alpine - Murray, Alexander (I)
Loyal Durham - Meredyth, Arthur Tisdall
Loyal M'Leod - Parke, Alexander
Northl'd - Thomas, William
Strathspey (1st Highland) Clarkson, Robert Graham. Fraser, Simon. MacInnes, John
Sutherland - Cuninghame, George. Stuart, John Lewis
York - Fulton, Nicholas Graham

VOLUNTEERS

Campbeltown - Macalister, Norman
Carmarthen - Nott, Sir William, G.C.B.
Cinque Port - Kearney, Brydges. Shee, John
Cornwall Rifles (1st Bn.) - Tremenheere, George Borlase
Dysart - Davidson, James
R. Edinburgh (2/2nd) - Reid, Stephen. Sivright, William
Elgin - Grant-Peterkin, Peter
Forfarshire Rifles (1st Bn.) Renny-Tailyour, Thomas
Fraserburgh - Troop, William
Georgeham - Middleditch, John Richard
R. East India (2nd) - Abernethy, Alexander
Loyal London (8th) - Gwatkin, Edward
Middlesex (28th Rifle) - Verner, James Edward
Milford - Roberts, Henry Tufnell
Ross-shire (2nd Bn.) - Mackenzie, John

APPENDIX H

R. Scots (5th Vol. Bn.) - Arnaud, Henry Hawker
I. of Skye (2nd) - - Macdonald, Alexander (III)
Spilsby - - - - Franklin, James
Surrey Rifles (1st) - - McDonald, James Horsbrugh
— (2nd) - - - Campbell, James Hunter
W. Sutherland - - Davidson, Hugh
Regt. not known - - Johnston, Joseph

APPENDIX I

LIST OF OFFICERS WHO SERVED IN THE BOMBAY MARINE, E.I.C.N.S., OR PILOT SERVICE

Bailey, E. J.
Balcetti, J. G.
Barclay, J.
Blanshard, J.
Cowper, I.
Cox, H.
Cranston, A.
Donaldson, J.
Fortnom, T. W.
Grant, Robert (II)
Guthrie, J. (II)
Keir, A.
Kerr, R. E. J.
Laird, C.
Laird, J.
Lewis, T.
Loveday, L. R.
Lownds, L.
Lumsdaine, John (I)
Marsden, F.
Marshall, J. (Appendix A)
Mitchell, J. C.
Naylor, T.
O'Halloran, Sir J.
Parrott, R. L.
Philmore, A.
Powell, John (I)
Pyne, A. T.
Reade, W. B.
Rind, J. N. (I)
Sarney, C. H.
Scotland, J.
Small, J. (?)
Smith, Richard
Stark, J.
Stewart, D.
Swinton, Archibald
Todd, F. B.
Toppin, J.
Walter, J. S.
Wood, Sir Mark, Bart.
Yeandle, M.

APPENDIX J
LIST OF OFFICERS WHO SAT AS MEMBERS OF PARLIAMENT

Baillie, John (II)
Barker, Sir Robert, Bart.
Brownrigg, John Studholme
Carnac, John
Fletcher, Sir Robert, Kt.
Grant, John (I)
Lockhart, William
Maclean(e), Lauchlan
Myers, Thomas
Nowell, Alexander
Ogilvy, Hon. Donald
Parker, Windsor
Prinsep, John
Robinson, Sir George Abercrombie, Bart.
Rumbold, Sir Thomas, Bart.
Russell, Charles (II)
Skelton, Arnoldus Jones
Smith, Richard
Scott-Waring, John
Watherston, Dalhousie
Wood, Sir Mark, Bart.
Wyatt, Charles

APPENDIX K
LIST OF OFFICERS WHO TOOK HOLY ORDERS

Birch, George Roydes
Buck, John
Carte, Edward
Cave-Browne-Cave, Wilmot
Chowne, James Henry
Cornish, Henry Hubert
Craufurd, Charles Henry Gregan
Flemyng, William Henry
Goldfrap, Frederick William
Gordon, John (1811-1853)
Hatch, Thomas
Johnson, Arthur
Johnstone, George Dempster
Littlejohn, William Douglas
Massie, William Henry
Michell, Eardley Wilmot
Oldham, James Oldham
Rainey, Arthur Crowe
Rich, John
Rocke, Thomas James
Shortland, Vincent
Stainforth, Francis John
Wheler, Henry Trevor
Lloyd-Williams, Henry
Eardley-Wilmot, Edward Revell

APPENDIX L
LIST OF AUTHORS, EDITORS, TRANSLATORS, JOURNALISTS, AND POETS

Abbott, George
— Saunders Alexius

Bacon, Thomas
Badenach, Walter
Baillie, John (II)
— William (I)
Barr, William
Bellew, Francis John
Berkeley, Henry Nicholas Lionel
Bracken, Thomas
Broome, Arthur
— Ralph
Broughton, Thomas Duer
Browne, James
Buckle, Edmond
Burney, Henry
Burt, Thomas Seymour
Butler, John (II)

Call, Thomas
Carmichael, Charles Montauban
Caulfeild, James
Conolly, Arthur
Cox, Hiram
Crawfurd, Gavin Ralston
Cunningham, Sir Alexander
— Joseph Davy

Davidson, Charles James Collie
Dixon, Charles George
Dow, Alexander
Drake, John Minshull

Emin, Joseph
Eyre, Sir Vincent

Fenton, Albert
Ferguson, John
Field, George Brydges Plantagenet
Forrest, William
Francklin, William

Galloway, Sir Archibald
Gerard, Patrick
Gladwin, Francis
Goodwyn, Henry
Gordon, Adam Durnford
— George Lawrie
— John (1811-1853)
Grace, Henry
Grand, George François
Greene, Robert

Hadley, George
Hamilton, Alexander (I)
— Charles (I)
Baillie-Hamilton, Ker
Hardwicke, Thomas
Haughton, Sir Graves Chamney
Henderson, Henry Barkley
Henley, William
Herbert, James Dowling
Hodgson, John Studholme
Hollings, George Edward
Horsford, Sir John
Hough, William
Hutton, Thomas (II)

Ironside, Gilbert

Jack, Alexander

APPENDIX L

Jackson, Julian
Johnson, John

Kaye, Sir John William
Keir, Archibald
Kerr, Henry Thomas Coggan
Kirkpatrick, William
Kittoe, Markham
Kyd, Alexander

Lawrence, Sir George St. Patrick
— Sir Henry Montgomery
Lloyd, Sir William
Long, William (Appendix A)
Ludlow, William Andrew
Lumsden, Thomas

Macartney, John (I)
McCulloch, William (II)
Macdonald, John (III)
Macgregor, Robert Guthrie
McKenly, Henry
McNaghten, Robert Adair
Madden, Edward
Martin, William (IV)
Mathews, Arnold Nesbit
Michell, Eardley Wilmot
Morrison, John (I)
Murray, William (III)

Nicolson, Peter
Nuthall, Thomas John

Palmer, Joseph
Parlby, Samuel
Patton, Robert (I)
Pemberton, Robert Boileau
Pester, John
Petrie, John
Pew, Peter Lawrie
Phayre, Sir Arthur Purves
Pickersgill, Joshua

Pogson, Wredenhall Robert
Polier, Antoine Louis Henri

Raban, William (I)
Ralph, James
Rennell, James
Richardson, David Lester
— David Thomas
— Sir John Larkins Cheese
Roberts, Roger Elliot

Salmond, James Hanson
Scott, Jonathan (I)
— Richard
— William (I)
Seaton, Sir Thomas
Shakespear, Sir Richmond Campbell
Sheil, Sir Justin
Shipp, John
Showers, Charles Lionel (II)
Siddons, George Richard
Sleeman, Sir William Henry
Smith, Robert (I)
— Thomas (V)
Carmichael-Smyth, George Monro
Stacy, Lewis Robert
Stephen, Henry Virtue
Stewart, Charles (I)
— Robert (II)
Symes, Michael

Thomas, George Powell
Thompson, David
Thomson, George (I)
— John (III)
Thuillier, Sir Henry Edward Landor
Tickell, Samuel Richard
Tod, James
Torckler, William Young

AUTHORS, EDITORS, ETC.

Trower, Charles Farquhar
Tucker, Henry Tod
Turner, Samuel

Upton, John

Vetch, George Anderson

Scott-Waring, John
Watson, Henry
Waugh, Sir Andrew Scott
Wavell, Arthur Goodall
Webb, William Spencer
Westmacott, George Edward

White, Adam
— William
Williams, John (I)
Williamson, Thomas (II)
Wilson, Roger Williamson
Wood, Sir Mark
Wright, Alexander
Wynne, Frederick

Young, Gavin
— James
— Keith
Yule, William

APPENDIX M
GLOSSARY
(Addenda to list at i. xxix.)

Abkari, a tax on spirituous liquors, collected through licensed vendors in bazaars.

Cutcherry, an office of administration, a court-house.

Ghazi, one who fights against infidels; so a Muhammadan fanatic warrior.

Grassia, "... a term of opprobrium, conveying the idea of a professional robber." (*Hobson-Jobson.*)

Kajahwah (*Kajāwa*), the double litter or pannier on a camel, used by ladies of high rank, and also for packages, etc.

Keddah, "the term used in Bengal for the enclosure constructed to entrap elephants." (*Hobson-Jobson.*)

Maidan, an open space, an esplanade, parade-ground or green, in or adjoining a town or cantonment.

Sirdar-bearer, the head-man of a set of palankin-bearers (lit.), actually the head domestic servant.

Telinga, "This term in the 18th century was frequently used in Bengal as synonymous with *sepoy*, or a native soldier disciplined and clothed in quasi-European fashion, ..." (*Hobson-Jobson.*)

CORRIGENDA

Vol. I

BELLASIS, Joseph Harvey.
  p. 126, l. 11 : *delete* (? Juliana).

BOYD, George.
  p. 191, l. 23 : *delete* (? Became an indigo planter at Nadia, Bengal.) and *substitute* d. at sea off the Cape, 1 Apr. 1793, on the voyage home.

BROWN, Samuel (1774-1805).
  p. 227, l. 15 : *for* d. in England *read* d. nr. Belfast.

Vol. II

D'AUVERGNE, Philip.
  p. 14, l. 16 : *for* 27 Mar. *read* 4 Aug.

FOUNTAIN(E), William Nassau.
  p. 211, l. 18 : *for* D.D., master of a preparatory school for Westminster, at Marylebone. *read* Vicar of Tarrington, co. Hereford.

GRISSELL, Charles.
  p. 342, ll. 7 and 6 from bottom : *delete* (She died Lucknow 23 Aug. 1851.) *m.* 2nd (?)

GRUEBER, Tichbourn.
  p. 346, l. 7 : *for* 1766/77 *read* 1766/67.

HAMILTON, Sir John.
  p. 372, l. 34 : *for* Andrew, Earl of Castle Stewart *read* Andrew Thomas, 1st Earl Castle Stewart.

HODGSON, William Edward John.
  p. 462, l. 32 : *for* Lumsden Strange *read* Thomas Lumisden Strange, M.C.S. (*D.N.B.*).

IRONSIDE, Gilbert.
  p. 528, l. 14 : *for* 1757 *read* May 1758.

JAMIESON, James William Henry.
  p. 546, l. 2 : *delete* (Apparently still living in 1895.)

Vol. III

LANE, John Thomas.
　p. 12, l. 2 from bottom: *for* Comac *read* Camac.

*LANE, Pynsent.
　p. 13, l. 11: *for* Roading *read* Roding.

LAWRENCE, Sir George St. Patrick.
　p. 24, ll. 34 and 36: *for* 1804 *read* 1805.
　Note: Burke, *D.N.B.*, Boase and *D.I.B.* all give the year incorrectly as 1804.

LAWRENCE, Richard Charles.
　p. 28, l. 16: *for* 1875 *read* 1857.

LEWIS, Wynne George.
　p. 50, l. 4: *for* Chok, Kathiawar *read* Chauk, in Thana District, nr. Bombay.

LOVEDAY, William.
　p. 80, l. 21: *for khajawah read kajawah.*

LUMSDAINE, John Charles.
　p. 93, l. 35: *for* John *read* Young.

MACDONALD, Sir John.
　p. 121, l. 2 from bottom: *for* wife *read* mother.

MacGREGOR, Robert.
　p. 142, l. 25: *for* Patparanj *read* Patparganj.

MACKIE, William.
　p. 163, l. 28: *for* 1848 *read* 1846.

MACLEAN, Roderick Norman.
　p. 173, l. 34: *for* Cormorin *read* Comorin.

*MACLEAN(E), Lachlan.
　p. 174, l. 22: *for* 1786 *read* 1768.

MACLEISH, Robert.
　p. 174, l. 35: *for* goal *read* gaol.

MACLEOD, Duncan (1780-1856).
　p. 178, l. 1 from bottom: *for* A.C.I.E. *read* A.I.C.E.

MATHEWS, William.
　p. 254: *delete* last 3 lines and *substitute* d. nr. Bednore, Mysore,

CORRIGENDA

early in 1784 : murdered in the jungle by order of Tippoo Sahib, while a prisoner of war.

p. 255 : *delete* lines 9 to 15 and *substitute Services :* Apptd. Cadet for the Cav. 19 Aug. 1779. Served with force sent from Bombay under his brother for invasion of Kanara and Mysore 1783 ; Q.M.G. with force, and sometimes described as Captain. Sent by his brother to the coast with treasure, and to represent to Bombay Govt. the need for reinforcements, Apr. 1783. Escaped to Goa. Summoned by Gen. Macleod to proceed to Tellicherry ; wrecked on the way with a detachment of Bombay Sepoys under Lieut. Wheldon, Bo. Est. Taken to Tippoo at Mangalore and sent to Bednore, where he and Lieut. Wheldon were murdered by Tippoo's orders, probably early in 1784.

MATTOCKS, John.
    p. 258, l. 11 : *for* 1778 *read* 1788.

MEARES, Robert King.
    p. 272, l. 31 : *for* Mears *read* Meares.

MEDWIN, Henry Clough.
    p. 273, l. 34 : *for* Pinfold *read* Pilfold.

MONTGOMERY, George James.
    p. 317, l. 15 : *for* Agra 23 Aug. *read* Aligarh 24 Aug.

MOORE, Thomas Perring.
    p. 324, l. 18 : *for* Cambell *read* Campbell.

MORGAN, Charles.
    p. 328, l. 30 : *for* Brown *read* Browne.

MOXTON, Charles.
    p. 349, l. 17 : *for* **MOXON** *read* **MOXTON**.

MURDOCH, John.
    p. 355, l. 32 : *for* b. 1781 *read* d. 1781.

NAPIER, John George.
    p. 370, l. 14 : *for* Simpson *read* Symson.

NASH, Sebastian (*d.* 1790).
    p. 375, l. 10 : *for* Shepley *read* Shipley. *Delete Probably.*

OGILVY, Hon. Donald.
    p. 417, l. 5 : *for* Jane *read* Jean.

PALLMER, Hampson Beckford.
    p. 445, l. 21 : after ' Captain ' *delete* the comma and *substitute* a full point.

CORRIGENDA

*QUEIROS, Joseph.
  p. 587, l. 11 : *for* 1828 *read* 1827.

RAWSTORNE, Edward.
  p. 616, l. 3 from bottom : *for* Thomas Ward *read* Thomas Ward Howard.

RICHARDSON, Robert Edward Turnour.
  p. 648, ll. 36 and 37 : *delete* and was comdg. . . . 10 June and *substitute* but had left it before it mutinied at Multan on 31 Aug. 1858, having previously been disarmed on 10 June 1857.

ROBERTS, Charles Morrissey.
  p. 666, l. 21 : *for* Linnee *read* Linnée.

ROSS, Charles George.
  p. 694, l. 10 : *for* Davis *read* David.

BECHER, Charles.
  p. 741, l. 10 : *for* Haselby *read* Hasleby.

BELL, William.
  p. 742, l. 24 : *delete* Ed. Charterhouse 1800-06.

BOILEAU, Alexander Henry Edmonstone.
  p. 746, l. 4 : *for* Todd *read* Tod.

CORFIELD, Frederick.
  p. 760, l. 12 : *for* Paulet *read* Poulett.

FARRINGTON, John James.
  p. 775, l. 4 from bottom : *for* Claus *read* Claus (? Olaus).

GAIRDNER, William John.
  p. 781, l. 23 : *for* Lock *read* Loch.

ADDENDA

Vol. I

ADAMS, John.

p. 8, l. 11 : *add* Son of Joseph Adams, of Ashburton, Devon, and Eleanor (Elinor) his wife, *née* Soper ; *bapt.* Ashburton 20 Apr. 1737. (*See also* Vol. iii. p. 732.)

AINSLIE, John.

p. 14, l. 6 : *add b.* 14 June 1760.
l. 13 : *add* Lillias, eldest dau. of William Walker.
Add to *Refs. Annals of a Border Club,* p. 52.

ANDREWS, James Richard Benson.

p. 36, l. 1 from bottom : *add* Ruth *alias* Caroline, *née* Darling, widow of —— Deacle, then on the Calcutta stage.

BACKHOUSE, Julius Brockman.

p. 66 : *add* to *Refs.* M.I. Deal psh. church.

BEAVOIR, W.

p. 113 : *delete* this biog. and *substitute* the following :

BEAUVOIR, William (1753-1773). Ensign, Infantry. *b.* Canterbury 24 Oct. 1753. Cadet 1771. Ensign 21 Jan. 1773. *d.* Madras Sept. 1773.

bapt. Canterbury cathedral 30 Nov. 1753. 2nd son of Rev. Osmund Beauvoir, Master of Canterbury School, and Anne his 1st wife, dau. of John Boys, of Hode Court, Blean, Kent. Ed. King's School, Canterbury ; adm. 7 Jan. 1760 ; readm. 19 Aug. 1765.
Services : N.F.P.

BEBB, Horatio.

p. 114, l. 6 : *add* and Maria Anne his wife, dau. of John Parsons, F.R.C.P. (*D.N.B.*).

BIRD, Edward.

p. 146 : *add* (*Probably* son of Joseph Bird, of Upton House, Essex, and twin brother of Rev. Godfrey Bird, rector of Little Waltham, Essex.)
Add Refs. : (? Berry's *Kent Peds.,* p. 10.)

BLUNT, James.

p. 170, l. 14 : *add* after 'Bristow' elder natural dau. of John Bristow, B.C.S.

ADDENDA

BRITTRIDGE, Richard Blechynden.
p. 208, l. 2 from bottom: *add* eldest dau. of Richard De Courcy, of Pykeparah (who was natural son of John De Courcy, *q.v.*), and niece of the wife of Powell Comyn, *q.v.* (She died Dehra Dun 22 Sept. 1869, aged 65.)

BROUGHAM, Thomas.
p. 219, l. 27: *add bapt.* Penrith 11 Aug. 1762. Son of Peter Brougham, atty.-at-law, and Matilda his wife, dau. of Thomas Wybergh, of Clifton Hall, Westmorland.
l. 28: *add m.* (settlements dated 19 Oct. 1807) Isabella, 3rd dau. of John Hay of Hopes. (*See also* George Hardyman.)

BROWNE, James Rolfe.
p. 232, l. 17: *add* Son of Alderman James Sladden Browne, of St. George's, Canterbury. Ed. King's School, Canterbury; adm. 26 Jan. 1814; K.S. Dec. 1814 till June 1816, and Aug. 1817 till Dec. 1819.

BURGES, Thomas.
p. 250, l. 9: *add m.* 1st, Joanna ——. (*See also* Vol. iii. p. 751.)

BURNEY, George.
p. 256, l. 3 from bottom: *add m.* 2nd, Dehra Dun 8 Mar. 1869, Amelia, 2nd dau. of Joseph Nash, *q.v.*

CAMPBELL, William Charles.
p. 298: *add* to *Services* Was comdg. 30th N.I. when it mutinied at Nimach 28 May 1857.

CARNEGIE, Nicholas.
p. 307, l. 7: *add* 4th surviving dau. of Robert Boswell of St. Boswells, W.S., Lyon Depute and Clerk.
Add to *Refs.* Will filed 28 Sept. 1825; admon. 23 Nov. 1825.

*CASEMENT, Hugh.
p. 317: *add d.* Ceylon 26 Apr. 1804. Ensign H.M. 34th Regt. 5 Nov. 1802.
Refs.: M.I. St. Peter's church, Fort, Colombo.

CHAMPION, Alexander.
p. 328, l. 20: after 'Nynd' *add* or Nind, dau. and heiress of William Nind, barr.-at-law.
l. 21: after 'Suffolk' *add* (*D.N.B.*)

CHATFIELD, Charles.
p. 334: *add b.* 21 July 1751; *bapt.* Croydon, Surrey, 31 July

ADDENDA

1751. 5th son of Allen Chatfield, of Croydon, distiller, and Mary his 2nd wife, eldest dau. of Robert Osborn, of Croydon, oatmeal maker. Uncle of John Chatfield, *q.v.*
Add to *Refs. Sussex Genealogies*, by John Comber, Pt. II (1932).

CHATFIELD, John.
p. 334, l. 14: *add* 4th son of Robert Chatfield, of Croydon, J.P., Paymr. of seamen's wages to H.E.I. Co., and Ann Storrow his wife. Nephew of Charles Chatfield, *q.v.*
Refs.: Sussex Genealogies (*ut supra*).

CONWAY, John Edward.
p. 376, l. 17: *add* widow of Capt. Archibald Nathaniel Bertram, 17th M.N.I., and dau. of Major Paul Bosc, Madras Est.

COX, Hiram.
p. 400: *add* to *Services* Was a Vol. in Bombay Marine *c.* 1777.

Vol. II

DALSTON, Fletcher.
p. 4, l. 4 from bottom: *add d.* Havre de Grace, France, 6 Apr. 1834, aged 66.
l. 3 from bottom: *add* Of Dalston Lodge, Oulton, Cumberland.
Add Refs.: M.I. Wigton church, Cumberland.

DICKSON, Archibald.
p. 59, l. 23: *add d.* Pembroke Sq., Kensington.
l. 24: *add* Of Chatto. 2nd son of Archibald Dickson, of Housebyres, and Marion his wife, dau. of Andrew Fisher of Housebyres.
Add to *Refs. Annals of a Border Club*, p. 102.

DUNLOP, William (1785-1841).
p. 104, l. 17: *add* 6th son of Walter Dunlop of Whitmuir Hall and Agnes his wife, eldest dau. of Robert Dickson of Hassendeanburn.

DYSON, John.
p. 114, l. 20: *add m.* Jane Hinde, who died 23 Jan. 1877, aged 66. (*See also* Vol. iii. p. 771.)

ELLIOT, William (1740/41-1803).
p. 130: *add* Eldest son of Gilbert Elliot, of Newcastle-upon-Tyne, and Margaret his wife, dau. of Robert Scott of Davington, in Eskdale.
Add to *Refs. Annals of a Border Club*, pp. 159-62. (*See also* Vol. iii. p. 773.)

ADDENDA

FENWICK, John.
  p. 171, l. 33 : *add b.* 26 Mar. 1752. Son of John Fenwick, of Framlington, Northumberland, and Dorothy Lascells his wife.

FORBES, John (*d.* 1808).
  p. 200, l. 13 : His wife, Isabella, was dau. of John Hay, Duncanlaw.
  Add to *Refs.* Will proved P.C.C. 5 Dec. 1808. (*See also* Vol. iii. p. 778.)

FULLARTON, Stewart Murray.
  p. 233, l. 20 : *add* 6th son of Stewart Murray Fullarton of that Ilk, and Rosetta his wife, dau. of Col. Fullarton.
  Add Refs. : Paterson's *Ayr*, ii. 21.

GAUSSEN, David.
  p. 256, l. 5 : *add d.* Dehra Dun, U.P.
  Add to *Refs.* M.I. Dehra Dun.

*GRANT, Alexander (*d.* 1768).
  p. 310 : *add* His wife, dau. of Johannes Zacharias Beck, of Langen-Saltz, was sister of the mother of Jacob Vanrenen, *q.v.* (She *m.* as her 3rd husband, Sir George Buchan-Hepburn, 1st Bart.) (*See also* Vol. iii. p. 786.)

GRAY, James Clarke Charnock.
  p. 324, l. 4 from bottom : *add* (She died Dehra Dun 25 Apr. 1864, aged 63.) (*See also* Vol. iii. p. 788.)

HALL, John.
  p. 365, l. 20 : *add* 2nd dau. of Thomas Thornton, of Coel.

HENDERSON, Henry Barkley.
  p. 428, top line : *add bapt.* St. Mary, Newington, 6 Sept. 1793. Son of James Henderson and Helen his wife.
  l. 2 : *add* eldest dau. of Thomas Hawkins, *q.v.*

HODGSON, James.
  p. 460, l. 6 : *add* Son of Richard Hodgson, of Carlisle. Brother of Sir Richard Hodgson, Kt., mayor of Carlisle.
  l. 7 : *add* (She died Portinscale, nr. Keswick, 1838.)
  l. 9 : *add* Ed. Carlisle Grammar School ; adm. 1773.
  Add to *Refs.* Will dated 26 Nov. 1821 ; proved 15 July 1825. (*See also* Vol. iii. p. 798.)

HODGSON, Richard.
  p. 461, l. 26 ; *add bapt.* 13 Apr. 1760. Youngest son of Thomas

ADDENDA

Hodgson, of Burgh-by-Sands, Cumberland. *Delete* (*Probably brother of James Hodgson, q.v.*)

l. 27 : *add m.* 1st, 1 Oct. 1792, Matilda, widow of George Simpson, of Calcutta. (She died on the way home from India.) *m.* 2nd, Mary, only dau. of John Hetherington. (She died 30 Apr. 1830, aged 41.)

Bottom line : *add* to *Refs.* Will dated 18 Jan. 1828 ; proved 29 May 1830.

HOLLAND, Thomas.

p. 467, l. 18 : *add* Son of Mrs. Jane Thorpe, formerly Holland. Brother of Dr. Samuel Holland, of London.

HOME, James.

p. 472 : *add b. c.* 1727-30.

Add to *Services* Lieut. on Bombay Est. 18 Nov. 1757 ; Capt. do. 22 (or 27) Aug. 1760; transfd. to Bengal Est. Resigned during the "Batta mutiny" and was sent down to Calcutta under arrest; subsequently readmitted.

p. 473, l. 4 : *add* to *Refs. Caraccioli*, i. 247.

HUDSON, George Isaac.

p. 493, l. 11 : *add* 6th son.

Add to *Refs.* Cussan's *Herts.*, p. 186. M.I. Walton church, Herts.

INNES, John.

p. 525, l. 22 : *add* (She died Bognor 12 May 1877.)

JACKSON, John (*b.* 1789).

p. 538, l. 34 : *add d.* Clevedon, Somerset, 21 July 1877, aged 88. *Add* to *Refs. The Times*, 27 July 1877.

JAMIESON, James William Henry.

p. 546, l. 2 : *add d.* Landour 10 Feb. 1866. Left a widow and children.

Add Refs.: M.I. Landour. (*See also* Vol. iii. p. 805.)

JARDINE, Edward Raleigh.

p. 546, l. 32 : *add m.* Hoshangabad 1 May 1824, Miss Charlotte Matilda Mullins. (*See also* Vol. iii. p. 805.)

JENNINGS, William Robert.

p. 553, l. 4 : *add m.* 1st, Bengal 10 Feb. 1814, Miss Mary Anne Malone. (She died Bencoolen 22 Apr. 1818, aged 28.) *m.* 2nd, Patna 16 Feb. 1829, Henrietta Maria, eldest dau. of Peter Jeremie, *q.v.* (*See also* Henry Walter Bellew.)

ADDENDA

JOHNSTONE, James.
   p. 563, top line: *add d.* 27 June 1852.
   Add Refs.: M.I. New Calton burial ground, Edinburgh.

JOHNSTONE, Peter.
   p. 563, l. 16: *add d.* 21 Mar. 1865.
   Add Refs.: M.I. (*ut supra*).

KENT, Arthur Brown Sober.
   p. 588, l. 19: *add m.* Charles church, Plymouth, 4 June 1828, Miss Frances Mary Weir.

KINLOCH, Francis Peregrine.
   p. 598, l. 5 from bottom: *add to Refs.* Will undated; proved 2 Sept. 1806.

KOEHLER, George Frederick.
   p. 611, l. 9: *add* Father of Capt. and Bt. Col. George Frederic Koehler, R.A. (*D.N.B.*).

Vol. III

*LANE, Pynsent.
   p. 13, l. 12: after 'wife' *add* dau. of Michael Impey, of Hammersmith, and

LOCKETT, Abraham.
   p. 71, l. 22: *delete probably*

LOMER, William Humphrey.
   p. 76, l. 5: *add d.* at his residence, S. Norwood Pk.
   Add Refs.: The Times, 27 Mar. 1877.

LUMLEY, James Rutherford.
   p. 91, l. 25: *add* (She died Benares 3 Feb. 1841, aged 24.)

MACALLY or McCALLY, Andrew.
   p. 106, l. 8: *add m.* Tranquebar 30 May 1797, Christina Paulina Bredstrup.

MACFARQUHAR, Hugh.
   p. 132: *add Refs.:* M.I. at Tavoy.

MEDWIN, Henry Clough.
   p. 273, l. 35: *add* 2nd cousin of Percy Bysshe Shelley (*D.N.B.*).
   Add to *Refs. Misc. Gen. et Her.* N.S. iv. 85, *s.n.* Pilford, of Sussex.

MIDDLETON, Peter.
   p. 291: *add b.* July 1797. Natural son of Samuel Middleton, B.C.S., and nephew of Charles Middleton, *q.v.*

ADDENDA

MORGAN, Thomas (1760/61-1814).
 p. 330, l. 22 : *add* 3rd son of James Morgan and Sarah his wife, dau. of Thomas Forman, of Waltham-in-the-Wolds, Leics.
 Add to *Refs.* Family information.

MORRIS, John.
 p. 337, l. 20 : *add* Nephew of John Morris, of Toome Bridge, co. Antrim.
 Add to *Refs.* Will dated Toome Bridge, 17 Apr. 1805 ; proved 26 Oct. 1814.

MYERS, Thomas.
 p. 366, l. 28 : *add d.* Norwood 1 Oct. 1835 : *bur.* Kensal Green cemetery.
 l. 37 : *add* M.P. for Harwich 1802.

NASH, Joseph.
 p. 374, l. 4 : after ' wife ' *add née* Ware.
 l. 7 : *add* (She died Mussoorie 16 June 1876, aged 73.) His dau. *m.* as 2nd wife George Burney, *q.v.*
 Add to *Refs.* Family information. M.I. Dehra Dun and Christ Church, Mussoorie.

NASH, Sebastian (*d.* 1790).
 p. 375, l. 10 : *add* Son of John Nash and Jane (Jeanne) his wife, dau. of Sebastian de Laire or de Loire (*anglice* Loy). Stepson of Peter Abraham de Brissac.

NICHOLL, Thomas.
 p. 389 : *add b.* 24 Sept. 1796. Ed. Charterhouse Jan. 1809-Dec. 1810.

NICOLSON, James.
 p. 393 : *add* to *Refs.* M.I. Landour.

NICOLSON, John.
 p. 393, l. 29 : *add* Son of Rowland Nicolson (or Nicholson) and Barbara Munkhouse his wife.

NUNN, James.
 p. 406, l. 35 : *add* (She died Stranraer 29 Oct. 1889, aged 90.)
 Bottom line : *add* to *Refs.* M.I. Anwoth churchyard, co. Kirkcudbright.

OAKES, John.
 p. 409, l. 29 : *add* (She died Rajpore, U.P., 19 Jan. 1866.)
 Refs. : M.I. Benares.

ORMSBY, William Carleton.
p. 434 : *add* to *Refs. The Times*, 19 June 1875.

PEARSON, James (1752/53-1826).
p. 491, l. 30 : after ' Edmondson, *q.v.*' *add* and dau. of Joseph Ware, of Crayford, calico printer.

PUDNER, John.
p. 582 : *add b.* 1761 ; son and heir of Gilbert Pudner and Dorothy Norton his wife.
Add to *Refs.* Family information.

RIDEOUT, Richard.
p. 654, l. 18 : after ' Isabella Clark ' *add* niece of Robert Macpherson, *q.v.*

ROBERTS, Ralph Gore.
p. 667, l. 34 : *add d.* Orchard Wyndham, Somerset, 21 (*not* 31) Mar. 1876, aged 74.
p. 668, l. 9 : *add* to *Refs. The Times*, 25 Mar. 1876.

ROBERTSON, James William John.
p. 674, l. 20 : *add* His sister *m.* Griffiths Holmes, *q.v.*

ROBINSON, Christopher.
p. 678, l. 33 : *add d.* 7 Dec. 1809.
l. 36 : *add* (His widow, Mary, died 20 Feb. 1834, aged 73.)
Bottom line : *add* to *Refs.* Will dated 31 May 1802 ; cod. 2 Dec. 1809 ; proved P.C.C. M.I. St. Andrew's churchyard, Penrith.

Vol. IV.

TREVES, Pellegrin.
p. 304, l. 20 : after ' Stokes ' *add* natural dau. of Gen. Sir Robert Sloper, K.B., C.-in-C. in India 1785-6.

INDEX

PAINTERS, ENGRAVERS, MINIATURISTS AND SCULPTORS

Alefounder, John (*d.* 1795)	iii. 490
Atkinson, Capt. George Francklin (1822-1859)	ii. 266
Banks, Thomas (1735-1805)	ii. 613
Baugniet, C. (*d.* 1886)	i. 322
Beechey, George D. (*d. c.* 1856)	iv. 113
Bonomi, Joseph (1796-1878)	iv. 81
Brodie, Alexander (1830-1867)	ii. 573
Buchanan, J.	iv. 76
Cardon, Antoine (1772-1813)	iii. 632
Chant, J. J.	iii. 549
Dance, George (1740-1825)	iii. 632
Devis, Arthur William (1763-1822)	iii. 413
Dickinson, Lowes Cato (1819-1896)	iv. 109
Engleheart, George (1750-1829)	iii. 773
Faulkner, Benjamin Rawlinson (1787-1849)	iii. 404
Francis, J. D.	iii. 404
Fry, William Thomas (1789-1843)	iv. 76
Gainsborough, Thomas (1727-1788)	iii. 777
Gauci, M.	iv. 116
Gordon, Sir John Watson, Kt. (1790-1864)	iii. 262, 426, 537
Grant, Colsworthy (1813-1880)	iii. 189
	iv. 284
Grant, Sir Francis, Kt. (1810-1878)	i. 215
	iii. 371, 549
Gwatkin, John Reynolds (1807-1877)	iv. 545
Hickey, Thomas (1740?-1822)	ii. 602
Hobday, William Armfield (1771-1831)	i. 231
Hodges, Charles Howard (1764-1837)	ii. 91
— Joseph Sydney Willies (1829-1900)	i. 174
Home, Robert (*c.* 1750-*c.* 1836)	iv. 19
Jones, Sir Thomas Alfred, Kt. (1823-1893)	iii. 517
Kettle, Tilly (*c.* 1740-1786)	iii. 804
Legoux, ———	iii. 238
Lupton, Thomas Goff (1791-1873)	ii. 266
Maclean, Thomas Nelson (1845-1894)	iii. 517
Masquerier, John James (1778-1855)	iv. 391, 392
Mercier, Capt. Charles	iii. 371
Meyer, Henry (1782-1847)	iii. 413
Millar (? Miller, William) (*c.* 1740-*c.* 1810)	iii. 385
Mottram, Charles (1807-1876)	iii. 371
Nollekens, Joseph (1737-1823)	i. 328
Palmer, G. G.	iv. 274
Payne, G. T.	iii. 404
Pound, D. J.	iii. 741
Prattent, T. (*fl. c.* 1790)	iv. 404

INDEX OF PAINTERS, ETC.

Raeburn, Sir Henry, Kt. (1756-1823)	iii. 776
	iv. 17, 224
Renaldi, F.	iii. 238
Reynolds, Sir Joshua, Kt. (1723-1792)	ii. 79, 195
Romney, George (1734-1802)	i. 281
	ii. 91, 625
	iii. 428, 608
Scott, Edmund (c. 1746-c. 1810)	iii. 632
Seton, Thomas John	iii. 192, 197
Shee, Sir Martin Archer, Kt. (1769-1850)	iii. 557
Smart, John (c. 1741-1811)	iii. 765, 766
	iv. 404
Tomkins, C. J.	iii. 371
Turner, James (*fl.* 1760-1806)	iv. 392
van Loo, Carlo (1705-1765)	iii. 672
Virtue, James Sprent (1829-1892)	iv. 490
Walker, James (1748-?1819)	ii. 69
Ward, George Raphael (1798-1879)	i. 215
Watts, George Frederick	ii. 319
West, Benjamin (1738-1820)	iii. 493
	iv. 221
Whitaker, W.	iv. 116
Wilson, Benjamin (1721-1788)	ii. 137
Zoffany, Johann (1733-1810)	ii. 281, 334, 425
	iii. 238, 452, 530, 547, 726, 766, 804
	iv. 162, 302

INDEX

REFERENCES TO *THE DICTIONARY OF NATIONAL BIOGRAPHY*

Vol. I

1	3	4	12	39	43	52	56	63	67
73	80	84	92	101	109	110	126	143	144
145	160	177	194	205	215	216	218	221	234
235	237	239	240	242	244	259	263	264	274
275	276	281	305	322	325	327	329	336	337
341	352	362	365	370	373	379	380	384	391
396	406	407	422	431	435				

Vol. II

3	10	11	26	34	35	63	69	73	76
78	79	83	89	90	97	99	100	101	108
111	136	138	139	140	145	150	156	161	167
173	190	200	203	211	213	214	217	244	254
257	259	260	265	271	278	284	308	319	321
326	336	344	353	360	362	367	368	369	372
405	456	459	461	462	463	469	471	473	474
482	485	496	500	508	511	520	522	528	534
544	548	549	553	558	573	577	582	602	609
610	612	613							

Vol. III

10	14	25	26	28	53	60	69	94	96
115	117	119	122	138	143	147	162	163	178
182	189	195	196	199	214	217	235	245	246
258	266	270	273	274	287	289	290	324	329
349	352	355	360	370	372	384	394	400	403
408	410	412	418	423	430	438	439	440	448
449	450	454	457	481	486	490	494	496	497
500	503	514	516	521	536	537	548	551	553
557	561	570	577	583	592	602	621	622	630
631	646	663	664	665	667	685	703	705	706
707	713	734	739	740	751	752			

Vol. IV

4	12	17	38	49	52	54	56	60	64
70	73	76	91	94	109	110	113	116	121
127	131	134	142	143	145	149	157	161	166
178	185	193	195	211	227	231	237	240	246
249	256	265	273	276	283	284	288	294	302
304	310	315	326	330	331	340	352	357	362
367	385	392	395	404	408	413	422	423	432
438	443	445	453	468	469	470	476	479	490
500	512	515	518	520	525	528	531	533	536
541	543	547	555	562	564	566	567	569	580
589	598	602	627	631	632	636			

INDEX OF NAMES

N.B.—Before consulting the Index it is advisable to read the following carefully.

THIS Index records only the names of persons mentioned in the genealogical section of each biography. It does not record the names of relatives of any officer bearing the same surname as that officer.

Wives and mothers will be found under their maiden name, when known, as well as under that of a former or subsequent husband. Sisters and other married female relations will be found under their married surname.

No distinction is made between such various forms of christian name as, Eliza and Elizabeth; Ann, Anna, Anne, etc.

No entry has been made of the name of any officer whose biography appears (in dictionary order) in this work, since a reference to such biography will at once furnish full cross-references to any other place where his name may be found.

To take a concrete example : suppose that it is desired to trace an Alexander Fraser. First turn to the Fraser entries in the body of this work (ii. 214-22) and read through them, when a biography of one Alexander will be found on p. 214, a second on p. 215, mention of a third on p. 216, a fourth and fifth on p. 219, a sixth and seventh on p. 220.

It will next be necessary to consult the Index, *s.v.* Fraser, where, under the sub-heading Alexander, four more references are furnished. On turning these up they may often be more certainly identified by their respective territorial designations (*e.g.*, Fairfield, or Torbreck), which are given in every case when known. In order to limit the size of the Index all territorial designations (except in the case of Peerages and Baronetcies), distinctions, name or number of Regiment, etc., have been omitted.

A

Abbey, Henry, ii. 183 ; Mary, ii. 183
Abbot, Edmund, iii. 743 ; Martha, iii. 743
Abbott, Adèle, iv. 53 ; John, iv. 53
Abercromby, Sir George, Bt. of Birknbog, iii. 259 ; Helen, iii. 259
Aberdeen, 2nd Earl of, *see* Gordon, William
Abergavenny, 2nd Earl of, *see* Nevill, Henry
Abney, Anne, iv. 569 ; Robert, iv. 569
Aboyne, 3rd Earl of, *see* Gordon, John ; 5th Earl of, *see* Gordon, George
Ackland, Mary, ii. 41, 44
Acton, William, i. 178

Adair, Barbara, iii. 406
Adams, Catherine Eliza, iii. 295 ; Cordelia, iii. 372 ; Lydia Rachel, iii. 569 ; Sarah Coker, i. 118 ; Simon, i. 118 ; Thomas, iii. 372, 569 ; William, *see* Aveline
Adderton, Dorothy (*née* Taylor), i. 352 ; Jeremiah, i. 352
Addison, Mary, ii. 470
Adeane, Gen. James Whorwood, iii. 22, 436 ; Jane, iii. 22 ; Margaret, iii. 436
Affleck, Katharine Maria, iv. 509 ; Sir Robert, 6th Bt., iv. 509
Agg, Maria, ii. 159
Agnew, Gen. Sir Andrew, Bt. of Lochnaw, iii. 749 ; Mary, iii. 749
Ahmuty, Fanny, i. 175
Aiken, Ann, iv. 134

INDEX OF NAMES

Aird, Alexander, iii. 252; Hannah Mills Butler, iii. 252
Aislabie, Benjamin, iii. 10; Louisa, iii. 10
Aitchison, Jean, iii. 398
Aitkin, Mrs., iv. 488
Akbar Shah, Emperor of Delhi, iv. 567
Albemarle, 5th Earl of, *see* Keppel, Augustus Frederick
Albert, Augusta, i. 391
Alcott, Elizabeth, iii. 762
Aldersey, Eliza Stephens, iv. 398; T. S., iv. 398
Aldous, Eliza Isabella, i. 125; Pamela, i. 149
Aldwell, Rev. John, iii. 507; Margaret, iii. 507
Aldworth, Hon. Caroline Catherine Letitia, i. 17; Hon. Elizabeth, i. 71; Mary, iii. 542; St. Leger, 1st Viscount Doneraile, i. 17, 71
Alexander, Anne, i. 433, iv. 168; James, 1st Earl of Caledon, ii. 628; James, i. 409; Mary, iv. 68; Rt. Rev. Nathaniel, iv. 168; Regina(h), iv. 376; Robert, iii. 769; Sarah, ii. 271; Sir William, 1st Bt., iv. 68; William, iv. 68
Alison, Sir Archibald, 1st Bt., ii. 260; Rev. Archibald, ii. 260; Dorothea Montague, ii. 260
Allan, Mrs. (*née* Welsh), iv. 427
Allanby, William, ii. 194
Allen, Anne (*née* Taylor), iii. 618; Elizabeth, ii. 471, iv. 2; John Bartlett, iv. 422; Louisa Jane, iv. 422; Mappe, iii. 666; Maria Louisa, iii. 666; Sarah, i. 162; William, iii. 618; William Taylor, iii. 618
Alley, Grace, ii. 542; Jerome, ii. 542
Alleyne, H. G., ii. 204; Maria Louisa, ii. 204
Allnut, C. B., ii. 108; Emily Augusta, ii. 108
Allsop, Catherine, ii. 514; Lewis, ii. 514
Allsopp, Lewis, ii. 263; Lucy, ii. 263
Alston, Fred, iii. 70; Janet, iii. 131
Altermatt, Marguerite, i. 184
Alves, Elizabeth Montague, iv. 265
Ameerun, Mussamat, iv. 273

Amesbury, Caroline F., i. 145; J., i. 145
Amyatt, Charlotte, ii. 582; James, ii. 582
Ancaster, Dukes of, *see* Bertie
Anderson, Alexander, iv. 15; Alison, iii. 454; Amelia, iv. 517; Catherine, i. 37, 262; Deborah, iii. 414; Elizabeth, iii. 277; Elizabeth Cecilia, iii. 627; Elizabeth Oswald, iv. 15; Harriet, iii. 150; Isabella, iv. 119, 138; Isobel, iii. 553; Sir James Caleb, 1st Bt. of Buttevant, iii. 627; Jane (*née* Sutherland), iv. 213; Jane, iv. 352; Janet, iii. 363; Jean, ii. 94; John, iii. 534, 789; Surg. John, iii. 553; John M., i. 37; Julia, iv. 233; Katherine Maria, iv. 86; Margaret Ann, iv. 106; Maria Anne, ii. 554; Mary, iii. 114, 534, iv. 397; Mary Anne, iii. 335, iii. 789; Mary Gleig, ii. 274; Patrick, ii. 274; Robert, iii. 277; Susan, iii. 81; Theodosia Dorothy, iv. 354; Thomas, iii. 363; Surg. Thomas, iii. 454; Major Thomas Ajax, iii. 389; Victoria Maria, iii. 389; Sir William, 6th Bt. of Broughton, iv. 86; Rev. Sir William, Bt. of Lea, iv. 354; William, ii. 554, iii. 414, iv. 352; of Linkwood, iv. 106
Andrew, Henrietta, iii. 685; T., iii. 685
Andrews, Albina Grace, iv. 255; Charlotte, iv. 238, 241; Eleanor, iii. 506; John, iii. 506; Margaret, ii. 6; Mary, iv. 386; Rev. Robert, iv. 238; Robert, ii. 6
Angelo, Domenico, iv. 302
Anglesey, 6th Earl of, *see* Annesley, Richard
Ankerville, Lord, iii. 694
Annand, Helen, iii. 33; John, iii. 33
Annandale, Marchioness of, iv. 153
Annesley, Anne, iv. 386; Arthur, iv. 386; Lady Dorothea, ii. 89; George, 2nd Earl of Mountnorris, iii. 760; Richard, 6th Earl of Anglesey, ii. 89
Annoot, Mrs. Maria, iii. 513
Anselme, Mrs. E. H. D., iii. 809
Anslie, Barbary (*sic*), iv. 348

INDEX OF NAMES

Anson, Anne, iii. 65; Gen. Sir George, iii. 809; Sophia, iii. 809; Thomas, 1st Viscount Anson, iii. 65
Anster, John Fitzgerald, i. 299; Mary Anne (*née* Meredyth), i. 299
Anstruther, Rt. Hon. Sir John, Bt., ii. 623, iii. 746; Louisa Ann, ii. 454; William, 3rd Lord Newark, i. 41
Antrim, 5th Earl of, *see* Kerr, Mark
Anwer, Bibi Hannah, i. 273
Apperley, Frances, iv. 302; Thomas, iv. 303
Apreece, Rhoda, iv. 586; Robert, iv. 586
Aratoon, Mary (*née* Stephanos), ii. 498; Michael, ii. 498; Sarah, iii. 585; Mrs. Sophia, iii. 585
Archer, Anne, iv. 216, 329; Edward, ii. 405; Jane, ii. 405; Robert, iii. 7; Rosamond, iii. 276; Thomas, Lord, iv. 329; William, iv. 216; Capt. William, iii. 276
Arden, Christopher, iii. 423; Jane, iii. 423; Mary, iii. 423
Argentini, Vincenza Ruina, ii. 392
Armit, Anne, iv. 507
Armour, Jean, i. 258, ii. 350
Armstrong, Francis, iv. 525; Harriet, iii. 203, iv. 280; Harriet Amelia, ii. 424; Jane, iv. 525; Rebecca, i. 431; William, i. 431
Armytage, Barts., family of, iii. 378
Arniston, Lord, ii. 101
Arnold, Gen. Benedict, iii. 524; Charlotte, iv. 520; Charlotte Jane, iv. 432; Sophia Matilda, iii. 524; Thomas Graham, iv. 520
Arnott, Anne, iv. 507
Arrowsmith, Eleanor (*née* Smith), iv. 138
Arthington, Catherine, iii. 358; Thomas, iii. 358
Ashbourne, Anna Maria, iii. 182
Ashburton, 1st Baron, *see* Baring, Alexander
Ashe, Benjamin, i. 234; Caroline, i. 234; Laura Elizabeth, iv. 394; Robert Hoadley-, iv. 394; Sophia Hoadley-, i. 198
Assey, Surg. Charles Chaston, ii. 1; Sophia Isabella, ii. 1

Asteley, Catherine, i. 234; Thomas, i. 234
Astley, Elizabeth, iv. 479; Francis John, iv. 553; Maria, iv. 553
Aston, Anna Sophia, ii. 457, iii. 728; Henry Hervey, iii. 728
Athanass, Sophia, i. 407
Atherton, Henrietta Maria, iii. 566; Robert Vernon, iii. 566
Athill, Maria, iv. 322; Samuel B., iv. 322
Atholl, 3rd Duke of, *see* Murray, John
Atkinson, Major Adam, iv. 230; Arthur, iv. 24; Charlotte, iii. 536; Elizabeth, iv. 24; Elizabeth F., iii. 116; Elizabeth Gore, iii. 547; Fanny Wilson, iii. 473; Surg. Henry, iii. 473; Isabella Eliza, iv. 230; James, iv. 83; John, iii. 547; Julia, i. 15, iv. 83; Matthew, i. 15
Atwood, Mrs. Catherine, i. 142
Auckland, 1st Baron, *see* Eden, William
Auriol, Charlotte (*née* Russell), iii. 577; James, iii. 577; Jean Louis, iii. 577; Sophie Elizabeth, iii. 577
Austen, Anne, iv. 38; Rev. Daniel, iv. 38; Eleanor Margaret, iii. 623; Samuel, iii. 623; Major, iii. 372
Austin, Adam, iii. 137; Anne, iii. 137; Mary, iii. 32
Axtell, Mary, iii. 390
Aylmer, Sir Gerald George, Bt., ii. 460; Matthew, 5th Baron Aylmer, iv. 24
Ayton, James, ii. 191, iii. 52; Margaret (*née* Burges), ii. 191; Mary, iii. 52
Aziz Khan, i. 355

B

Babbs, Catherine, i. 62
Babington, Catherine, ii. 414, iii. 795; Humphrey, iii. 795; Margaret, iii. 471; William, iii. 471
Backhouse, Eliza, ii. 151; Mary, iii. 566
Bacon, Anthony, i. 322; Frances, i. 322; Francis, ii. 210; John, ii. 558; Maria, ii. 558; Mary, ii. 210; Mary Anne, iv. 538; Col. Philip, iv. 538

646 INDEX OF NAMES

Badman, Mrs. Elizabeth, ii. 172
Baggally, C., iii. 501; Elizabeth, iii. 501
Baggott, Susan, iv. 441
Bagnell, Alexander, iii. 228; Eleanor, iii. 228
Bagot, John, iii. 261; Mrs. Susannah, iii. 261
Bagshaw, Catherine, iv. 366; John, iv. 366
Bagwed, Hannah, iii. 108
Bagwell, Isabella, i. 411; John, ii. 594; Margaret, ii. 594; William, i. 411
Bailey, Capt. Edward Seymour, R.N., iii. 689; Mary, iii. 403; Phillis, iii. 689
Baillie, David, iii. 786; James Evan, iii. 236; Col. John, iii. 691; Katherine, iii. 691, 786; of Dunain, family of, iii. 786
Baily, John, iii. 287; Sapphira Seymour, iii. 287
Bain, Mrs. Margaret, ii. 299
Bainbridge, Maria, iii. 79
Baird, Eliza, i. 109; John, i. 109
Baithe, Eliza, iii. 165
Baker, Elizabeth Helen, iii. 585; George, iii. 44; Georgiana Mary, i. 357; John, iv. 415; Capt. Joseph, R.N., i. 368; Josephine Puget, i. 368; Maria, iii. 805; Maria Elizabeth, iii. 44; Marianne, iv. 415; Sarah, ii. 590; Rev. Thomas, i. 357, iii. 585
Balcarros, 5th Earl of, see Lindsay, James
Baldock, Agnes, ii. 153; Christopher, ii. 153, 612; Mary, ii. 612
Baldwin, Grace, iii. 40; Mary, iii. 701; Richard, iii. 40; Sarah Jane, iv. 175; William John, iv. 175
Balfour, Ann Stewart, iv. 191; Catherine, ii. 325; Charles, iv. 482; Elizabeth, i. 289, iii. 393; Emilia, iii. 739; Francis, iii. 54; Henry, iv. 191; Isabella, iv. 482; (of Burleigh), John, Lord, iv. 593; John, i. 289; Thomas, iii. 393
Ballantine, Patrick, ii. 507; Sarah, ii. 507
Ballantyne, Sarah, iv. 427
Baller, Matty, ii. 139

Ballingall, Helen, iii. 470
Banks, Millicent Jane, i. 206, iv. 467, 593; Sutton, iii. 747
Bannerman, John Alexander, i. 257
Banoo, Bibi Sahiba, iv. 567
Baptiste, Frances Jane, ii. 279
Barber, Mary, ii. 386
Barbor, Catharine, iv. 520; Richard, iv. 520
Barclay, Charlotte, i. 367; David, i. 367; Elizabeth, iv. 388; Frances Webb, iii. 548; Harriet Geldart, i. 116, iii. 717; John, iii. 548, iv. 37; Sir Henry Steuart-, Bt., i. 84
Baring, Alexander, 1st Baron Ashburton, iv. 201; Rt. Rev. Charles, iv. 47; Sir Francis, 1st Bt., iv. 164; Francis Thornhill, 1st Baron Northbrook, iv. 47; Lydia, iv. 201; Maria, iv. 164
Barker, Eliza (née Stewart), iv. 203; Capt., iv. 203
Barlow, Sir George Hilaro, 1st Bt., iv. 134; Harriet, i. 271; Laura Emily, iv. 296; Mary, iii. 214; Adm. Sir Robert, i. 271; Sophia Elizabeth, iv. 580; Thomas, iii. 214, iv. 296; Miss, iii. 504
Barnard, Andrew, ii. 437; Gen. Sir Andrew Francis, iii. 672; Anna, ii. 525; Rev. Henry, iii. 672; Sarah (née Robertson), iii. 672
Barnes, Rosa (née Brook), ii. 517; Juliana Speke, ii. 603; Samuel, ii. 603; Rev. W. H., ii. 517
Barnet, Rev. John, iii. 224; Margaret (née Marley), iii. 224
Barnett, Jane Brady, i. 331; Mary (Bailey), iii. 71; Hon. William, i. 331
Barr, Eliza, iv. 235
Barrett, Charles, iii. 450; Rebecca Carter, iii. 450; Sarah, iii. 464; William, iii. 464
Barrow, Charlotte, i. 211; Elizabeth Fanny Catherine, i. 180; Lieut. Thomas James Raikes, R.N., i. 180
Barrs, Mary, ii. 351; William, ii. 351
Bartels, Petronella Jacquemina, iii. 781
Bartholomew, Sarah, ii. 439
Bartley, Jessey Eliza, iv. 275; Maj.-Gen. Sir Robert, iv. 275

INDEX OF NAMES 647

Barton, Amelia, i. 355; Colette (*née* Addison), i. 10; Elizabeth, ii. 597; F., iii. 351; Nelly, iii. 351; Gen. Sir Robert, i. 10; Rev. Royston, i. 355
Barwell, Charles, iii. 14; Mrs. Susan (*née* Middleton), iii. 291
Bass, Michael Arthur, 1st Baron Burton, i. 47
Bassett, Joseph Davie, iv. 57; Mary, iii. 493
Bate, Harriet Meredith, iii. 702; James, iii. 702
Bateman, Anne, iii. 212; Colthurst, iii. 212; Elizabeth Grace Charlotte, ii. 51; John, ii. 544; Rebecca, ii. 544
Bathurst, Emily Jane, i. 391, iii. 760; Robert, iii. 760
Batley, Ann, iii. 217
Batsford, Charles, ii. 473; Susan, ii. 473
Batten, Amelia Frances (*née* Plowden), i. 336; George Maxwell, i. 336
Battie, John, iv. 530
Battley, Elizabeth Georgina Belvidere, iii. 17; Thomas Cade, iii. 17
Battye, Frederica Elizabeth, iv. 394; Elizabeth, iv. 69; George, iv. 394
Baugh, Benjamin, iv. 272; Elizabeth, iv. 272
Baumgardt, Eliza Hardinge, iii. 21; Johanna Elizabeth, iii. 325; John Pieter, iii. 21, 325
Baverstock, Elizabeth, iii. 283; Thomas, iii. 283
Bawtree, Jane, iv. 327; John, iv. 327
Bayley, Elizabeth, iii. 633; Mary Ann, iv. 331; Stephen, iv. 331
Baylis, Maria, iv. 129; Thomas, iv. 129
Bayly, Frances, iii. 418; Henry, Earl of Uxbridge, iii. 418; Col. Nicholas, iii. 418
Baynes, Penelope, i. 374; Robert, ii. 441; Sophia Maria, ii. 441; Rev. William, i. 374
Bayntun, Annica Susan, ii. 278; Edward, ii. 278; Adm. Sir Henry William, ii. 278
Bazley, Eliza, iv. 569; J., iv. 569
Beach, Charles, ii. 270; Matilda M., ii. 270

Beale, Eleanor, ii. 77
Beamish, Ursilla (*née* Smith), iv. 128
Bean, Elizabeth, iii. 502; Eliza Clara, ii. 131; F., i. 207; Frances Sibley, i. 207; Henry, ii. 131; Sylvester Prior, iii. 502
Beardsmore, Eliza, iii. 16, iv. 52; Isaac, iii. 16, iv. 52
Beatson, Barbara, i. 220; Robert, i. 220
Beattie, Alexander, iv. 63, 108; Margaret, iv. 108
Beaty Ann, ii. 24; Catharine, iv. 470; Henry, iv. 470; Mrs. Mary, ii. 31; Commodore Thomas Dade, ii. 31
Beaufite (? Beaufils), Marie Françoise, iv. 553; Pierre, iv. 553
Beaumont, Ann Eliza, ii. 515; Hannah (*née* Hawkins), ii. 409; Rev. Thomas, ii. 515
Beauvais, Susan, iii. 716
Becher, Anne, iv. 143; Charlotte, iii. 227; Harriet, ii. 301; iv. 30; John Harman, iv. 143; Margaret, iii. 528; Maria, ii. 605; Richard, iii. 227, 479, iv. 30; Richard Turner, iii. 528
Beck, Catharine, iv. 488; Catharina Christina, iv. 343; Jane, ii. 245; Johann Zacharias, iv. 343, 634; Margaretha Henrietta, iii. 786
Becker, Francis, iii. 697; Wilhelmina Louisa Frederica, iii. 697
Beckett, Harriette, iii. 593
Beckley, Jane, iii. 667; Thomas, iii. 667
Bedford, Duke of, family of, iii. 577
Bedingfield, Catherine, i. 366; John, i. 366
Beere, Anne, ii. 536; Rose Anne (*née* Williams), iv. 476; William, ii. 536, iv. 476
Begbie, Elizabeth, ii. 415; Isabella Victoria, iii. 651; Peter, iii. 651
Begby, Margaret, i. 391
Beggs, Elizabeth Elinor, ii. 161
Belford, Priscilla Martha, ii. 566; Capt. William, ii. 566
Belhaven and Stenton, Baron, *see* Hamilton
Bell, Mrs. Adolphina, ii. 40; Anne, ii. 234; Catharine, iii. 361;

INDEX OF NAMES

Christina, i. 433; Daniel, ii. 380; Elizabeth, i. 134, ii. 380; Harriot, iv. 281; Helen, iii. 558; Henry, ii. 234; James, iv. 115; Jane Mary Consett, iii. 270; Jean (*née* Leith), iii. 41; Jonathan, i. 433; Maria Constantia Parker, iii. 496; Rev. Robert Barker, iii. 496; Thomas, iii. 100; William, iii. 270; W. Gillison, iii. 774

Bellamy, Anna Martha, iii. 446; George Anne, i. 274; Rev. Gervas, iii. 446

Bellew, Brianna, ii. 186; Patrick, ii. 186

Belmore, 1st Earl of, *see* Corry

Belsches, John, iv. 421; Mary, iv. 421

Belvidere, 1st Earl of, *see* Rochfort, Robert

Bennet, Harriet Pye, iv. 392; Mrs., ii. 204

Bennett, Florence Harriet Charlotte Burlton-, iii. 601; William Robert Burlton-, iii. 601

Benson, Anne, iv. 236; Rev. Edward, iv. 236; Elizabeth Anne, iii. 499; Ven. Trevor, iv. 236

Bent, Miss, ii. 46

Bentall, Elizabeth, i. 7

Bentinck, Lord William, ii. 119; William Henry Cavendish, 3rd Duke of Portland, ii. 370

Benton, James, i. 233; Sarah Eleanor, i. 233

Beresford, Francis, iii. 244; George De La Poer, 1st Marquess of Waterford, iii. 116; Harriet, iv. 438; John Claudius, iii. 116; Richard, iv. 439; Selina, iii. 244

Bergh, Egberta Sophia Petronella, ii. 308; Egbertus, ii. 308, iii. 766

Bergier de Rovereaz, Marianne, iv. 433; Sebastian, iv. 433

Bergier du Mont, Jeanne Marie, iv. 434; Joseph Samuel, iv. 434

Berkeley, H. J. F., i. 116; Phoebe Letitia Cecilia, i. 116

Berner, Mary Anne, ii. 147, iii. 722

Berners, 9th Baron, *see* Wilson, Robert

Berriman, Frances, iii. 706; James, iii. 706

Bertie, Sir Albemarle, Bt., ii. 41; Mary, ii. 41

Bertram, Capt. Archibald Nathaniel, iv. 633; Mrs. Paulina Anne, i. 376, iv. 633

Bessborough, 1st Earl of, *see* Ponsonby, Brabazon

Besseterre, Jessy, i. 381

Bessis, Hester Elizabeth (*née* Wilson), ii. 258; Pierre Armand, ii. 258

Bestandig, Charles, iii. 17; Ellen Maria Johanna, iii. 17

Beswick, Mrs. Sarah, iv. 351

Bethune, Anne, iv. 41; Catherine Munro, ii. 134; David, i. 371; Rev. H., ii. 134; Mary, i. 371

Bettesworth, Harriet, ii. 193

Beveridge, Catherine, iv. 267

Bevis, Hannah, iii. 810

Bidard, Emilie M. A., i. 236

Bidgood, " Aunt ", iii. 54

Biggs, Sarah Jane, iv. 73; Rev. Thomas Hesketh, iv. 73

Bignell, Caroline, ii. 543; Richard, ii. 543

Bigot, Margaret, i. 106

Bill, Harriot, iv. 296

Billing, Anne, iii. 612; Robert, iii. 612

Bineford, Sophia, ii. 35

Binfield, Caroline Charlotte, iv. 428; Eliza, iii. 99; Rev. (? Henry), iii. 99, iv. 221, 428; Louisa, iv. 221

Bingham, Maria Matilda, i. 91; Comdr. Parker Duckworth, R.N., ii. 490; William, i. 91

Bingley, Caroline, ii. 229; William, ii. 229

Binks, George, iv. 77; Gertrude, iv. 77

Binney, Elizabeth, iii. 259; William, iii. 259

Binnie, Elizabeth, i. 300; James, i. 300

Binny, Clementina, iv. 419, 420

Birch, Elizabeth, iii. 582; Emma Eliza Neville, iv. 107; Emma Marianne, ii. 465; Frederick William, iv. 309; George, ii. 328, iii. 582; Hannah, iii. 723; Mary, ii. 178, iii. 723; Mary Ann, i. 83; Olympia (*née* Langrishe), ii. 328; Rose Maria, iii. 628; Major Stephen, i. 83, iii. 628

INDEX OF NAMES

Bird, Elizabeth, iii. 293, 530; Ellen Olivia, iv. 576; Francis, iv. 486; Rev. Godfrey, iv. 631; John, iv. 576; Joseph, iv. 631; Margaret, iv. 486; Sarah, iv. 348; Shearman, iii. 293, 666, iv. 348

Bishop, Ann, ii. 463; Charlotte Louisa Elizabeth, iv. 208; Edward, i. 59; Elizabeth, iv. 439; Emma Jane, iii. 150, 230; Emily, iv. 468; Harriet, iii. 76; Jane (née Atkinson), i. 59; William, iii. 76, iv. 208, 439, 468

Biss, Catherine, iv. 300; John, iv. 300

Bisset, Adam, iii. 144; Helen Kea, iii. 144; Sarah, iii. 469; S., iii. 469

Black, Anne Wemyss, iv. 443; Arabella, iii. 329; Elizabeth, iii. 400; Rev. Dr. E., ii. 124, iii. 772; James, iv. 443; Margaret (née Minter), ii. 124; William, iii. 400

Blackburn, Bethia, i. 276; Charles Collinson, iii. 392; John, i. 276

Blacker, Barbara, iii. 429; Eliza, ii. 103; William, ii. 103, iii. 429

Blackett, Julia Anne, iv. 553; Lancelot, iv. 553

Blackney, James, ii. 612; Jane, ii. 612

Blackrie, Alexander, v. 392; Elizabeth, iv. 392

Blackwell, Jean (née Fortune), ii. 209; Richard, ii. 209

Blackwood, Hon. Hans, ii. 373; Harriet, ii. 373

Bladen of Ketton Hall, family of, iv. 157

Blair, Anne Persode, ii. 10; Charles, ii. 376; Ellen, ii. 396; Emma Matilda, ii. 376; Frances Charlotte, ii. 359; John, iv. 196; Rev. Dr. John, ii. 10, 520; Margaret, ii. 601; Maria, ii. 26; Mary, i. 23; Sarah, ii. 520; Thomas, ii. 359, 396; Col., ii. 601

Blake, Ann, iii. 248; Elizabeth, iv. 520; Margaret, iii. 330; Miss N., iv. 147; Peter, iii. 330; Robert, iii. 234; Sarah, iii. 234; Susan, iii. 221

Blanc, Mary Victorie, ii. 292

Blanchard, Georgina Matilda, ii. 177; Mary Amanda, iv. 478; William, ii. 177, iv. 478

Bland, Dorothea (Mrs. Jordan), iv. 302; Edward, iv. 302; Elizabeth Martha, i. 37, iv. 302; (or Blane), Jean, i. 122

Blane, Janet, iii. 104; (or Bland), Jean, i. 122

Blanshard, Betty, ii. 388; Rev. Thomas, ii. 388

Blaydes, Hugh, ii. 591; Louisa Anne, ii. 591

Blechynden, Charlotte, iv. 393; Lydia Emma, iii. 12

Blenkinsop, Amelia, iv. 418; Harriet, ii. 188; Rev. ——, Canon of Windsor, ii. 188

Blood, Frederica, ii. 276; Jane Maria (née Shaw), iv. 67; Richard, iv. 67; Thomas, ii. 276

Blosse, Charlotte Lynch- (née Richards), iii. 642; Sir Robert Lynch-, 8th Bt., iii. 642

Blount, Lady, iii. 424

Blunt, Capt. C. D. M., ii. 425; Lydia Julia, iii. 199

Boardman, Ann Grisel, i. 30; Conductor C., iv. 575; Mary, iv. 575; Robert, i. 30

Boddam, Eliza Maria, iv. 317; Maria, ii. 366; Rawson Hart, ii. 366, iv. 317

Bogaardt, Johanna Adriana, iv. 343

Bogle, Lawrence, iii. 122

Boileau, Alicia, iv. 64; Ann, iii. 625; Anne Charlotte, iii. 780; Harriet, iii. 496; Henrietta, ii. 26; Sir John Peter, 1st Bt., iii. 755; John Peter, i. 312; Maria Jane, ii. 275, 276; (de Castelnau), Simeon, iii. 780; Simeon Henry, iv. 64; Solomon, ii. 26, iii. 625

Boisy, seigneur de, see De Budé

Bolt, Andrew, ii. 534; Grace, ii. 534

Bolton, Ann, iii. 783; Col., ii. 22

Bonar, T., iv. 203

Bond, Caroline, iii. 431; Harriet, iii. 539; Capt. Henry, iii. 539; John, iii. 431

Bondfield (Bonfield), Philadelphia, iii. 463; William, iii. 463

Bonner, Elizabeth, ii. 109; Capt. William, ii. 109

Booth, Anna Maria, i. 119; Sarah, ii. 385; William, i. 209

INDEX OF NAMES

Boott, Elizabeth Sophia, iii. 789; Thomas, iii. 789
Booty, Benjamin, iii. 570
Boreman, Elizabeth Caroline, i. 314
Borrow, John Arthur, i. 14; Mary Susanna, i. 14
Bosanquet, Eleanor Eliza, iii. 271; William George Ives, iii. 271
Bosc, Major Paul, iv. 633; Paulina Anne, i. 376
Bossum, John, iii. 577; Sarah, iii. 577
Bostock, Rev. Charles, iii. 637
Boswell, Alexander, iii. 703; Sir James, Bt. of Auchinleck, ii. 262; Margaret Catherine, i. 307; Mary (Hutteman), iii. 703; Robert, ii. 126, iv. 632; Sibella, ii. 126
Bouberg, Olymphia Maria, iv. 499; S. J., iv. 499
Boughton, Sir Edward, 6th Bt., ii. 68; Theodosia, ii. 68; Sir Theodosius, 7th Bt., ii. 68
Boularot, Françoise, ii. 50, 443
Boulton, Grace Carey, i. 378
Bourchier, Anne, iv. 240; Rev. Edward, iii. 63; Elizabeth, iii. 63; Rev. Jonathan, iv. 240
Bourmaster, Harriet, ii. 60; Adm. John, ii. 60
Bouverie, Hon. Charlotte, iii. 725; Sir Jacob, 1st Viscount Folkestone, iii. 725
Bowden, Anne, i. 362, i v. 124; Roger, i. 362
Bowen, Catherine, ii. 356; Charlotte, iii. 29; Charlotte Anne, iii. 522; Frances, iii. 561; Capt. Hugh, ii. 356, iii. 29; John, iii. 561; Lucy Eleanor, ii. 604; Capt. Thomas, iii. 522; Capt. William, ii. 604
Bower, Alexander, i. 307; Edmond, iii. 311; Freeman, ii. 536; Henrietta Priscilla, ii. 536; Margaret St. Clair, i. 307; Philadelphia, iii. 311
Bowerbank, Margaret, ii. 203; Thomas, ii. 203
Bowey, Mary, iii. 69; William, iii. 69
Bowie, Jane (Jean), iii. 222
Bowles, Capt. Charles, ii. 534; George, ii. 617; Harriet, ii. 617, iii. 734; Martina (née Grant), ii. 534

Bowman, Mary, iv. 88
Boxwell, Francis, M.D., iv. 59; Jane, iv. 59
Boyce, Lieut. William Nettleton, R.N., iii. 571
Boyd, Alexander, iii. 323; Christina, iv. 95; Hugh, ii. 82; Mary Anne, iii. 323; Sarah Catherine, ii. 82
Boyé, Anne Charlotte, ii. 132; Lt.-Gen. Charles, ii. 132
Boyes, Isabella Miller, i. 99; Thomas, i. 99
Boyle, Anna Frances, iii. 559; Armor, i. 303; A., iii. 559; Elizabeth, i. 303
Boyne, 4th Viscount, see Hamilton, Richard
Boys, Anne, iv. 631; John, iv. 631
Brabazon, Anthony, 8th Earl of Meath, i. 235, iv. 32; Lady Arabella Barbara, iv. 32; Lady Katherine, i. 235; Miss, i. 213, iii. 718
Braddell, Anna Maria, iv. 234
Braddon, Mary Maynard, i. 340; William, i. 340
Bradley, Mrs. Elizabeth Jane, i. 263; H., i. 263; Isabella Hay, ii. 200; Mary, iii. 678
Bradshaigh, William Harden, ii. 623
Brady, Elizabeth, i. 188; Isabella, i. 247; Mary Ann, iii. 376; Philip, iii. 376
Braham, Elizabeth, iii. 510; John, iii. 510
Brampton, Baron, see Hawkins, Sir Henry
Brandon, Daniel, ii. 242; Rebecca, ii. 242
Branthwayt, Rev. Arthur, i. 122; Jane, i. 122
Bredstrup, Christina Paulina, iii. 106, iv. 636
Breeze, Mary Ann, ii. 556
Bremer, Capt. James, R.N., i. 274; Marianne Elizabeth, i. 274
Bremner, Hugh, iv. 15; Jessie, iv. 15
Brendli, Elizabeth, iii. 516; John Jacob, iii. 516
Brereton, John, ii. 385; Thomas, ii. 385; William, ii. 385
Breswell, Mrs. Eleanor, iv. 586
Breton, Mary, iii. 769

INDEX OF NAMES

Brett, Frederick, iv. 157; Surg. Frederick Harrington, iv. 157
Brettingham, Jane, iv. 471
Brewster, Sir David, iii. 199
Bricklade, Edward, iv. 255
Bridge, Robert, iii. 543
Bridges, Elizabeth, iii. 241
Brietzcke, Caroline, iv. 456
Briggs, Christian, iii. 438; Elizabeth, iv. 305; Rev. John, iv. 305; Penelope, iii. 506
Bright, Edward, ii. 499, iii. 801; Martha, ii. 499, iii. 801
Brignall, Jane, ii. 49
Briones, Eulalia, ii. 63; Don Stephen, ii. 63
Briscoe, Mary, iii. 284; Surg. Robert, iii. 284
Brison, Marion, i. 410
Bristow, Charlotte, i. 361; Elizabeth Georgiana, ii. 102; Lt.-Col. George, ii. 9, 102; Harriet, iv. 113; John, iv. 113, 631; Lucy Anne, ii. 9; Mary, i. 170, ii. 85; Mary Anne, iii. 185; Major Roger, ii. 85; Rev. Skeffington, iv. 487; Sophia, iv. 487; W., iii. 185
Britain, Esther, ii. 4
Britten, Charlotte, i. 386; Olive, ii. 272; Thomas, ii. 272
Broadhurst, Mary Anne, iv. 254; Rev. Thomas, iv. 254
Broadwater, Jane, ii. 507; Col., ii. 507
Brock, Catherine Sarah, *see* Brook, Catherine Sarah; Rev. C. A., *see* Brook, Rev. Charles Abraham; Martha, iii. 42; William, iii. 42
Brockman, Rev. Ralph Drake-, i. 65; Sarah Drake-, i. 65
Broderip, Edmund, iii. 81, iv. 34; Elizabeth Charlotte, iii. 81; Frederica Harriet, iv. 34; Margaret, iii. 81
Brodie, Elizabeth, 5th and last Duchess of Gordon, iv. 73
Broff, Lavinia, iii. 748; William, iii. 748
Bromley, Thomas, iii. 804
Brook, Catherine Sarah, ii. 493, iii. 728; Rev. Charles Abraham, ii. 493, iii. 728; John Savery, ii. 517; Rosa, ii. 517

Brooke, Anne (*née* Patton), iii. 481; Catherine, iv. 364; Eugenia, iii. 540; Henry, iv. 364; Jane Anne, iii. 479; Robert, ii. 601; Rev. Robert Parkinson, iii. 479; Sarah, ii. 601; Sophia, iii. 334; Major William, iii. 540; William Augustus, iii. 540
Brookman, Mary, iv. 39
Brooks, Henry, iii. 408; Margaret Mackenzie, iii. 408
Brough, John, i. 320; Mary, i. 320
Brougham, Adèle (*née* de Momet), ii. 215; Henry, 1st Baron Brougham and Vaux, i. 219; James Peter, M.D., ii. 215
Broughton, Henrietta, iv. 299; Rev. Sir Thomas, Bt., iv. 299
Broun, Anne, i. 242; George, i. 242
Brown, Agnes, iii. 474; Ann, iv. 48, 301; Ann Martinez, i. 52; Bridget, iii. 132; Cecilia, i. 220; Rev. Charles, i. 347; Rev. David, i. 148, 396; Edith, iii. 152; Elizabeth, iii. 665, iv. 536; Frances, i. 293; Frances Elizabeth, iii. 681; Frances Rice, i. 347; Georgiana Fortescue, ii. 516; Harriet, i. 266; Henry, i. 52, iii. 176; Isabella, iii. 61; Capt. James, ii. 302; Rev. James, iv. 301; Jane, i. 148, ii. 302; John, i. 293, iii. 474; Surg. John, ii. 516; John William Foster, iv. 543; Joseph Thomas, iv. 76; Major J., iii. 547; Louisa, iii. 176; Maria Jane, iii. 88; Marion (*née* Morrison), iii. 340; Mary, iv. 10; Mary (*née* Shipton), iv. 76; Mrs. Mary, i. 423; Matilda Frances, i. 290; Mildred, iii. 109; Murdoch, iii. 88; Susanna Robiniana, ii. 163; Thomas, iii. 340, iv. 48; William, iv. 10, 536; Col. William Tod, iii. 293
Browne, Amelia St. George, iii. 59, iv. 141; Andalusia, ii. 7; Lt.-Col. Arthur, ii. 7, iii. 59; Catherine, iv. 449; Charlotte, i. 235; Charlotte Isabella, iii. 25; Eliza Harriet, ii. 10; Col. Fielding, iii. 10; May, ii. 492; Rebecca, ii. 235; Rev. Thomas Adderley, iv. 141; Valentine, 2nd Baron Cloncurry,

iii. 328; William, i. 235, iv. 449; Major, ii. 10
Brownell, Jane Margaretta, ii. 596; R. C., ii. 596
Brownlow, Anne, ii. 203; William, ii. 203
Brownrigg, John, iii. 415; Maria, iii. 415
Bruce, Caroline Anne, iii. 65; Mrs. Catherine, iv. 571; Christian, i. 298; David, iii. 807; Elizabeth (née Wood), iv. 514; Harriet Anne, iv. 538; Ismeney (? Ismay), iii. 445; James, iv. 514; Janet, iii. 807; Surg. John, i. 108; J. G., iv. 538; Louisa Colebrook, i. 108; Mrs. Margaret Tyndale- (née Stuart), iii. 750; Capt. William, iii. 65
Brueys, Pieter, iv. 542
Brumell, Col. William, iv. 60
Brunton, John, iv. 304
Brutton, Major Nicholas, iii. 587
Bryan, Frances, iv. 579; William, iii. 7; Condr. W., iv. 579
Buchan, Agatha (née Cumming), i. 426; 10th Earl of, see Erskine, Henry David
Buchanan, Ann, iv. 151; Elizabeth, i. 49, ii. 288; Helen, iv. 400; Capt. James, i. 49; John, iv. 400; Ralph, iv. 151; Thomas, ii. 288
Buck, Mary, iv. 15; Sarah (Lady Erskine), ii. 139
Buckingham, 1st Marquess of, see Grenville, George
Buckinghamshire, 3rd Earl of, see Hobart, George
Buckland, Mary, iii. 805; Richard, iii. 805
Budd, William, iii. 234
Bukhsh, Bibi Faiz, i. 54
Bulkeley, Augusta, ii. 602; Philip, ii. 602
Bull, Frances (née Hardwicke), ii. 387; Mary, ii. 326; Mary Bruce, ii. 591, iii. 808; Capt. Samuel, iii. 808; William, ii. 326
Buller, James, iv. 245; Mary, iv. 245
Bullock, Rev. Charles Penry, iv. 112; Edward, iv. 220; H., iii. 261; Jane Georgina, iv. 112; Mary Anne, ii. 11, iv. 220; Thomas, ii. 11

Bunbury, Abraham, ii. 504, iii. 264, 665; Christian Elizabeth, ii. 504; Isabella, iii. 264, 665; Jane, ii. 331; Thomas, ii. 331
Bunn, Paymr. Benjamin, ii. 307; Sophia, ii. 307
Bunnoo, Bibi, iv. 156
Buntein, Janet, ii. 119
Burdekin, Elizabeth Ann, ii. 112
Burden, Capt. George P., i. 145; Mary, i. 145
Burdett, Rev. John, ii. 29; Louisa, ii. 29
Burdon, Harriet, iii. 207; John, iii. 207
Burges, Alicia, iii. 3; Daniel, iv. 300; David, ii. 191; Rev. Dr. David, iii. 274; Elizabeth, iii. 274; Eliza Mary, iv. 300; Rev. Jonas, iii. 3; Margaret, i. 63, ii. 191; Ynyr, i. 63, ii. 191, iii. 5; Mrs. Ynyr (née Mee), iii. 274
Burges, Sir John Smith-, Bt., iv. 136
Burgess, Francis, iv. 261; Mary, iv. 287
Burgett, Anne, ii. 201; Charles, ii. 201
Burgh, Mary, ii. 17, 19
Burke, Edmund, iii. 746
Burn, Ellen Mary, ii. 396; Robert, R.N., ii. 396
Burne, Eleanor Elizabeth Lumley, i. 205; Rev. Henry Thomas, i. 205; Marianne Thérèse, iv. 323; Richard Leyburn, iv. 323
Burnet, Mary, i. 404
Burnett, George, ii. 96; Hay, iii. 90; Isabel, iii. 244; James, i. 271; Jean, ii. 96; John, iii. 96; Katherine, ii. 173; Margaret, i. 271; Mary, iv. 169; Samuel, iii. 244
Burney, Dr. Charles, i. 219; Charlotte, i. 219; Fanny, see D'Arblay, Mme.
Burns, Anne, iv. 574; Jane, iv. 266; Robert, ii. 350; Rev. Thomas, iv. 266
Burrel, Bathurst, iv. 267
Burrington, Nancy, iv. 475
Burrough, James, iii. 737; Thomasin, iii. 737
Burrow, James, iv. 273; Julia, iv. 273

INDEX OF NAMES 653

Burrowes, Jane, iii. 583; Thomas, iii. 583
Burrows, Anne Elizabeth, iii. 447
Burrup, John, ii. 36; Martha, ii. 36
Burton, Anne Catherine, ii. 187; Catherine, ii. 2, iii. 763; Rev. Edward, iii. 763; Capt. Joseph, ii. 2; Major Thomas, ii. 187; 1st Baron, see Bass, Michael Arthur
Burwell, Mary Anne (née Higgott), ii. 449
Bury, Bridget, ii. 444, 445; Elizabeth, iv. 456; John, ii. 444, 445; Capt. William, iv. 456
Bush, Catherine, iii. 392; Sarah, iii. 796
Bushby, Wilhelmina, iv. 176; William, iii. 355
"Bussahor, Vizier of," iv. 367
Bute, 3rd Earl of, see Stuart, John
Butler, Anna Jemima, i. 354; Caroline Ann Sophia, iii. 509; James, i. 354; Louisa Elizabeth, i. 299; Robert, iii. 378; Miss, i. 372
Butt, Elizabeth, iii. 233; William, iii. 233
Butter, Elizabeth, iii. 776
Butterworth, Jane, iv. 51; Mary Grace, iii. 408; Thomas, iv. 51
Byng, Hon. Anna Maria Bridget, iii. 790; John, 5th Viscount Torrington, iii. 791
Byrn, Maria (née Arnold), i. 53
Byrne, Catherina, iv. 347

C

Caddell, Richard, i. 57; Sarah, i. 57
Cade, Catherine, iv. 24; Philip, iv. 24
Cadell, Lt.-Gen. Alexander Tod, iii. 746
Cadogan, Adm. George, 3rd Earl Cadogan, i. 309
Cairnes, Anne, i. 128; John, i. 128
Caithness, 12th Earl of, see Sinclair, Sir James
Caldecot, Lloyd, iv. 4; Sarah Strangham, iv. 4
Caldwell, Anne, ii. 120; Janet, iv. 519; Sir John, Bt., ii. 120
Caledon, 1st Earl of, see Alexander, James

Callander, Agnes, ii. 105; Lt.-Col. George, ii. 105; Harriet, i. 197; Harriet Fordyce, iii. 279; Kenneth, i. 197; Dr., iii. 279
Callender, Grizel, iii. 735; Sir John, Bt. of Westertown, iii. 807
Callwell, Ann (née Trevor), iv. 304
Calton, Ellen, iii. 591; Rev. William, iii. 591
Calvert, Felix, iv. 431; Jane, iv. 431
Camac, Alicia, ii. 314; John, iii. 14, iv. 40; Letitia, iv. 40; Margaret, iii. 14
Cambay, Nawab of, ii. 249
Cameron, Campbell, iv. 141; Catherine, iii. 193; Elizabeth Balfour, iii. 54; Elizabeth Genesa, ii. 269; Sir Ewen, of Fassifern, Bt., iii. 120, 193; Harriett, iv. 141; Jane, iii. 677; Capt. John Mackenzie, ii. 269; Judith, iii. 103; Mary, iii. 120; Mary Aleyne, iii. 103; Thomas, M.D., iii. 103
Campbell, Adelaide, ii. 244; Gen. Alexander, iv. 101; Surg. Alexander, ii. 276; Alexander, ii. 381; Rev. Alexander, ii. 7; Alicia (née Kelly), ii. 578; Amelia, ii. 273; Ann, iii. 196; Ann Livingston, ii. 56; Anne Penelope, ii. 48; Arabella, iv. 182; Archibald, ii. 48, iv. 107, 377; Augusta, iii. 249; Bathia, ii. 89; Beatrice, ii. 313; Camilla Elizabeth, iv. 530; Catherine, iii. 194, 353; Charlotte Isabella, ii. 127; Charlotte Marion, iii. 621; Maj.-Gen. Colin, i. 208; Colin, M.D., ii. 127, 245, iii. 52, iv. 353; Adm. Donald, iv. 344; Donald, ii. 254; Duncan, i. 381, iv. 182; Lt.-Col. Duncan, ii. 17; Elizabeth, iii. 52, 164; Elizabeth Binning, iv. 58; Elizabeth Constantia (née Pryce), iii. 333; Euphemia, iv. 494; Flora, i. 433; Frederica (née Blood), ii. 276; Grace, ii. 17; Hannah, iv. 41; Harriet, ii. 371; Harriot Catherine, iv. 344; Hugh, iv. 494; Sir Ilay, 1st Bt. of Succoth, Lord Succoth, iv. 231; Isabella, i. 208, ii. 7; Isabella Augusta, ii. 254; Sir James, 3rd Bt. of Aberuchill, iii. 492; Sir

INDEX OF NAMES

James, Kt., of Inverneil, iii. 249; Jane, i. 109, iii. 492, iv. 101, 107; Jane (*née* Stewart), iv. 183; Janet, iii. 695, 696; Jean, iii. 129, iv. 377; Jessy, ii. 245, iii. 107; John, ii. 56, 302, iv. 41, 58; Capt. John, ii. 244, iv. 183; Surg. John, ii. 254; J., iii. 621; Lt.-Gen. John Douglas, iv. 183; Dr. Lionel, ii. 476; Louisa Colebrooke, iv. 353; Lucy Anne, iii. 578; Margaret, ii. 164, iii. 134; Mary, ii. 197, iii. 405; Mary Florence, ii. 381; Murdoch, i. 109; Neil, ii. 313, iii. 129; Niel, i. 250; Philadelphia, iii. 187; Robert, iii. 578; Capt. Robert, R.N., iii. 333; Robert Henry Scott, iii. 523; Susan, iv. 231; Violet, iii. 169; Walter, ii. 371; William, iii. 107, 187; of Achtyre, iii. 194; of Blythswood, *see* Douglas, James; of Cariebank, ii. 210; Mr., iv. 186

Candell, Mary (*née* Mathews), iii. 254

Canning, Rt. Hon. George, iii. 622; George, iii. 622

Capper, Jane, iii. 226; Peter, iii. 226

Carbery, 4th Baron, *see* Evans, George

Cardozo, Rose Anne, iv. 579; Samuel, iv. 579

Carew, Adm. Sir Benjamin Hallowell, ii. 367; Eliza Jane, iii. 251; Major William Marcus, iii. 251

Carey, Anne, ii. 425; Catherine, i. 82, 83, iii. 738; Elizabeth, ii. 45; John, iii. 738

Carleton, Lt.-Col. Hon. Christopher, ii. 566; Dorothea, iii. 624; Gen. Sir Guy, 1st Baron Dorchester, ii. 566; Hugh, Viscount Carleton of Clare, iii. 624; John, iii. 624; Priscilla Martha (*née* Belford), ii. 566

Carlisle, Jane Louisa, iv. 124

Carlyle, Adam, iii. 21; Rachel, iii. 21

Carmac, Richard, iii. 253

Carmichael, Michael, iii. 708; Rebecca Thomas, iii. 708

Carnaghan, Emma, iii. 17

Carnegie, Isabella, iii. 704; Mary Elizabeth Lindsay-, ii. 286; William, 7th Earl of Northesk, ii. 286; William Fullerton Lindsay-, ii. 286

Carnell, Jane, iii. 338; John, iii. 338

Carnwath, 9th Earl of, *see* Dalzell, Robert Alexander; 11th Earl of, *see* Dalzell, Harry Burrard

Carpenter, Mary, ii. 565; Richard, ii. 565

Carr, Elizabeth, i. 28; Rebecca Ann, iii. 767; Thomas, iii. 767; William Ogle, ii. 58

Carrick, Louisa, i. 88

Carrington, Catherine, iii. 370; Codrington, iii. 370; 1st Baron, *see* Smith, Robert

Carruthers, Henrietta, iii. 263; Susan, iii. 302

Carslake, Elizabeth, iv. 554

Carss, Mary, iv. 123; William, iv. 123

Carstairs, John, i. 335; Margaret, i. 335

Carter, Anna Maria, ii. 323, 420; Benjamin, i. 205; Caroline Helena, iii. 416; Henrietta, iii. 308; Henrietta Priscilla Caroline, i. 142; Isabella Barbara, ii. 597; Laura Elizabeth, iii. 256; Mary Georgiana, i. 205; Michael, iii. 308; Lt.-Col. Samuel George, ii. 597, iii. 416; Comdr. Samuel Thomas, R.N., iii. 256; Sarah, iii. 256; Wilhelma, ii. 451

Cartwright, Mr., ii. 342

Carvalho, Mary, ii. 314, iii. 787

Cary, Henry, i. 157; Letitia, i. 157

Casamaijor, Elizabeth Rebecca, 1. 235; James Henry, i. 235

Case, Edward, iii. 782; Lydia, iii. 782; Phillis, iii. 689; Samuel Bartholomew, iii. 689

Casement, Eleanor, iii. 84; Hugh, iii. 84

Cashel, Henrietta Emilia (*née* Knipe), i. 129; M.P., i. 129

Cassan, Alicia, iv. 95; Richard Sheffield, iv. 95

Castelli, Eliza, i. 316; Don Marianna, i. 316, iii. 544; Rebecca, iii. 544

Castello, John, i. 362; Louisa (*née* Houlton), i. 362

Castle Stewart, 1st Earl, *see* Stewart, Andrew Thomas

INDEX OF NAMES

Caswall, Anna Maria, ii. 360; John, ii. 360
Catherock, Ann, iv. 184
Cattell, John, iii. 320; Sarah, iii. 320
Catts, Charlotte, ii. 194; Eleanor, i. 302, iv. 136; Robert, i. 302, ii. 194, iv. 136
Caulfeild, Anna Julia, iv. 504; Col. John, iv. 504
Cauty, Marianne, i. 69; Sophia Augusta, i. 337
Cavell, William Malston, ii. 471
Chadwick, Arabella, i. 191; Elizabeth, i. 155; Sarah, i. 317; Sophia Carden, i. 123; Susannah, iii. 296; Thomas, i. 123, 155, 191, 317; William, iii. 296
Challoner, Rt. Rev. Bp. Orchard, iii. 254
Chalmers, Capt. Alexander Bishop, iii. 278; Ann, iv. 506; A., iii. 151; Anna Maria, iv. 122; Euphan, iv. 389; James, iii. 795; Margaret, iii. 795, iv. 550; Matilda Fanny, iii. 151; Major, iv. 122
Chamberlain, Catherine Mary, i. 381; Robert, i. 381
Chamberlayne, Margaret, ii. 412
Chambers, Ann Palmer, iii. 301; Brooke, i. 192, iii. 480; Emily Mary Ann, ii. 197; Frances (née Wilton), iii. 82; Frances Maria, iii. 122; Isabella, i. 192; Jane Mary, iii. 480; Mary, ii. 378; Richard, ii. 378; Sir Robert, iii. 82, 122, iv. 140, 500; Sir Samuel, ii. 197
Chamier, Georgiana Sophia, i. 221; John (Ezechiel), i. 221
Chantrey, Maria, iii. 315
Chaplin, Amos, ii. 471; Sarah, ii. 471
Chapman, Frances, iii. 449; Georgiana Agnes Joselyn, iii. 384; J., iii. 384
Charles, Jane, iii. 793; Mary Jane, iv. 576; Thomas, iv. 576
Charlotte, Princess of Wales, i. 186; Queen, i. 397, iv. 43
Charnier, A., iv. 149
Charnock, Charles, ii. 397; Isabella, ii. 397
Charteris, Elizabeth, ii. 62; James, ii. 62
Charters, Margaret, ii. 156; Samuel, ii. 156
Chase, Laura Maria, iv. 309; Mary, i. 194; Rebecca, iv. 53; Richard, i. 194; Thomas, iv. 309
Chatfield, Elizabeth, iii. 801
Chatto, Agnes, iii. 710; J., iii. 710
Chauncy, Charles, iii. 28; Frances, iii. 28
Chaund, Bibi, iv. 582
Chaundy, Rev. John Amyatt, iv. 357; Mary Amelia, iv. 357
Cheape, Henry, iii. 52
Cheney, Dorothy, iii. 706; Richard, iii. 706
Cherry, George Frederick, i. 201
Chester, Jane Seymer, ii. 431; Rev. William, ii. 431
Chesterfield, 5th Earl of, see Stanhope, Philip
Chetwood, Rev. John, iv. 262; Mary Frances, iv. 262
Chicheley, Harriot Catherine, ii. 438
Chilcott, Susan, iv. 197
Child, Barbara Henrietta, ii. 214; Charles, iii. 165; Elizabeth, iv. 202; Elizabeth Anna, ii. 411; Henrietta Louisa, iii. 165; Robert, iv. 491
Chippendale, Thomas, ii. 491, iv. 281
Chisholm, Catherine, iii. 167; Emilia Colina, iii. 168; Lilias, ii. 220; Roderick, The Chisholm, ii. 220; William, The Chisholm, iii. 605; Dr. William, iii. 168
Cholmeley, Mary Elizabeth, ii. 562; Sir Montague, Bt. of Easton, ii. 562
Christian, John, iv. 167; Julia, iv. 167
Christiana, Amelia, iii. 377; Charles, iv. 248; Henrietta, iii. 619; H.L., iii. 619; Maria Jane, i. 229; Sophia, iv. 248
Christie, Eliza, ii. 171; Isobel, iii. 177; Jane, iii. 121; Adm., ii. 171; Dr., iii. 178
Christopher, Emma Octavia, i. 322; George, i. 322, iv. 269; Selina Maria, iv. 269
Church, Susannah, i. 91; William, i. 91
Churchill, Emily, i. 405; Henry, i. 241, 405; Mary Anna, i. 241

Clack, Sarah, iii. 446; Thomas, iii. 446
Clancarty, 1st Earl of, *see* Trench, William Power Keating
Clapperton, Andrew, iii. 671; John, iii. 671; Robert, iii. 671
Clark, Anna, iii. 742; Catherine, iii. 230, 233; Charles, iv. 524; Christian Mercy, iii. 269; Ellen, iv. 524; Isabella, iv. 638; Jane, iii. 263; John, iii. 263; Capt. John, iii. 795; Martha, iii. 763; Matilda, ii. 415, 418; Matilda Hay, iii. 795; Rev. Thomas, iii. 742
Clarke, Ann, iii. 631, 799; Anne Frances, ii. 467; Charles John, iv. 286; Edmund, iii. 798; Elizabeth Maria, i. 169; Rev. Henry, iv. 350; Isabella, iii. 654; James, iii. 127; Jane, iii. 798, iv. 350; John, i. 169, 173; Laura Faith, ii. 124; Margaret (*née* Kilpatrick), ii. 595; Mary, i. 173, ii. 154; Sarah, i. 60; Susannah Hawley, iii. 127; Rev. Thomas, iii. 799; Gen. Tredway, iii. 377; T. E., ii. 124; Capt. Thomas Pickering, R.N., ii. 154; William, ii. 595; of Chudleigh, iii. 631
Claydon, Elizabeth Ann (*née* Smith), iv. 139
Clegg, Thomas, ii. 503
Cleghorn, Mary (*née* Yule), iv. 554; Thomas, iv. 554
Cleland, Catherine, iii. 499; David, iii. 499; Guthrie, ii. 350; Helen, ii. 350; Margaret (*née* Guthrie), ii. 350
Clements, John, ii. 293; Mary, ii. 293, 294; ——, iii. 412
Clerc de Virly, ii. 308
Clerk, Elizabeth, iii. 576; Sir John, of Penicuik, 2nd Bt., iii. 576
Cleugh, Agnes, iv. 528
Cleveland, 1st Duke of, *see* Vane, William Harry
Cliffe, Eleanor, iv. 226; Rev. John, iv. 294; Loftus, iv. 226; Sarah, iv. 294
Clinton, Augusta, ii. 31; Gen. Sir Henry, ii. 31
Clive, Anne, iv. 51; Richard, iv. 51; Robert, 1st Lord Clive, iv. 51

Cloase, ——, iv. 220
Clode, Sarah Phillis, i. 196; William, i. 196
Cloete, Catharine Dorothy, iv. 85; Daniel Johannes, iv. 85; Elizabeth Maria, iii. 744; Henry, iii. 744
Cloncurry, 2nd Baron, *see* Browne, Valentine
Clonmell, 1st Earl of, *see* Scott, John
Close, Isabella, iv. 439; John, iv. 439
Clubley, Mrs. Margaret, iii. 596; W.A., iii. 596
Clunes, Margaret, ii. 525
Clutterbuck, Henry, iv. 283; Julia, iv. 283; Mary, iii. 778; Peter, ii. 199; Thomas, iii. 778
Coape, Frances, iv. 121; John, iv. 121
Coates, Susannah Sarah, iii. 448
Cochrane, Catharine, i. 214; Peter, i. 214
Cock, James, iii. 600; Rachel, iii. 600
Cockayne, Thomas Aston, iii. 60
Cockburn, Isobel (*née* Bruce), i. 238; James, i. 238, iii. 435; John, ii. 625; Margaret, iii. 806; Mark, iii. 806; Mary, iii. 435; Capt. Sir William, Bt., iii. 757
Cockerell, Sir Charles, 1st Bt., iv. 222
Cocks, Virginia (*née* Pattle), 3rd Countess Somers, ii. 44
Cocksedge, Letitia, iv. 227; Thomas, iv. 227
Coffin, Isabella, iii. 187; John, iii. 187; Susannah, i. 405
Coghlan, Margaret, ii. 437
Coker, Elizabeth, ii. 181
Colclough, Harriett, iv. 408, 583; Rev. Thomas, iv. 408
Cole, C., i. 184; Elizabeth, i. 184, ii. 583, iii. 202; George, iv. 510; Rev. Henry, ii. 583; Margaret, ii. 536; Maria, iv. 510
Colebrooke, Sir George, 2nd Bt., ii. 50; Mary, ii. 50
Coleman, Dr. Charles, i. 207; E. S. West, i. 101; Louisa, i. 207; Professor, i. 101
Coles, Edward, iv. 354; Emily, iv. 354
Collett, Sophia, iii. 401; Rev. William, iii. 401

INDEX OF NAMES

Collie, Dr. James, ii. 213, iii. 563; Jennett, iii. 563; Marian Hastings, ii. 213

Collins, Ann, i. 380, iii. 322, 396; Caroline, i. 384, iv. 462; Charles Henry, iii. 387; Claudine, ii. 21; George, iii. 396; John, i. 380; Mary, iii. 387, 439

Collison, Brown, iii. 293; Ellen, iii. 293

Colquhoun, Sir George L. A., Bt., ii. 527; Sir James, 4th Bt. of Luss, i. 74; Lucretia, i. 319; Margaret, i. 74; Robert, i. 320

Colvile, Amy Letitia, iii. 584; Rev. Nathaniel, iii. 584

Colvin, Anna Maria, i. 367; David, i. 426; Elizabeth, i. 22; James, i. 367, ii. 537; John, i. 426

Comber, Henrietta Matilda (née Peach), iii. 486

Comberbach, Benjamin, iii. 206; Harriet, iii. 206; Louisa, iii. 206; Roger, *see* Swetenham

Compton, Sir Herbert Abingdon Draper, i. 194; Louisa, i. 194

Concannon, J., ii. 150; Mary, ii. 150

Coningsby, George Capel-, 5th Earl of Essex, ii. 393

Connell, Arthur, iii. 771; Clara Jessy, iv. 395; Mrs. Elizabeth Camilla, iii. 771

Connely, Eleanor, iii. 202

Connor, ——, iii. 288

Conron, Elizabeth, ii. 332

Consett, Matthew, iii. 270

Considen, Dennis, iii. 761

Constable, Rachel Mary Anne, iv. 8; Archdeacon Thomas, iv. 8

Contes, Delia, ii. 427; Graham, ii. 427

Conway, Catherine, ii. 293

Conyers, Elizabeth Charter, iii. 707; Helena Lydia, i. 81, iii. 738; J.D., iii. 738; Susanna, ii. 426

Cooke, Ann, iii. 462; Eliza Douglas, iii. 131; Louisa (née Hough), iii. 497; Mary, iv. 336; William, iii. 398

Cookes, Alicia Mary, iii. 111; Rev. Thomas, iii. 111

Cooksey, John, ii. 141; Mary Anne, ii. 141

Coombs, Matthew, iii. 483; Susannah, iii. 483

Cooper, Arthur, iii. 664; Christopher, iv. 255; David, R.N., iii. 645; Elizabeth, i. 282; Eliza Raper, iii. 664; Mary, iii. 645, iv. 255, 423

Coore, Frederick R., iv. 70; Harriet, iv. 70

Cope, Catherine, ii. 287; Sir Charles, Bt., ii. 287; Henry, iv. 72

Copland, Martha, iii. 631

Copley, Mary Elizabeth, iii. 314; Thomas, iii. 314

Cop(p)lestone, Charlotte, ii. 35, iii. 765; Richard, iii. 765

Corall, Sarah, iv. 36

Corbett, Mrs. Ann, iv. 187

Corfield, Anna Margaretta, ii. 506; Augusta, iii. 280; Caroline, iv. 49; Charles, iii. 280, iv. 49; Charlotte Emily, i. 183; Maria Frances, ii. 157

Corneille, Susanna, iv. 589

Cornut, Anthoinaz, iii. 466; Jean Gamaliel, iii. 466

Cornwall, George, iii. 782; Mary, iii. 782

Cornwallis, Charles, 1st Marquis, iv. 105

Corry, Dorothea, iii. 235; Rt. Hon. Isaac, iii. 235

Corsane, Janet, iii. 114; Robert Rae, iii. 114

Corse, Jean, iv. 527

Corson, Charlotte Christiana, ii. 332

Cort, Elizabeth, iv. 327; Harriet, ii. 79

Cosby, Jane, ii. 445; Thomas, ii. 445

Cosnahan, Catherine, i. 318; Julius, i. 318

Cossart, Elizabeth, i. 80, 303; John, i. 303; Peter, i. 80

Cossens, Amelia Ann, i. 422

Costello, Jordan, iii. 622; Mary Anne, iii. 622

Cottam, Charles, iii. 299

Cotterell, Charlotte, iii. 48; Sir John Geers, 1st Bt. of Garnons, iv. 242; Mary, iv. 242; Adm., iii. 48

Cottnam, Hannah Barbara, iii. 170

Cotton, Alathea, i. 47; Frances Anne (née Turton), iv. 332; Rev. George William, iv. 332; Robert, i. 47

INDEX OF NAMES

Coulson, Robert, ii. 121
Coulthard, Elizabeth Mary, iii. 796
Coúperús, Jacobina Maria, iv. 319
Courage, Mrs. Frances, iii. 477
Courtayne, Lucy Maria, iii. 434; Thomas, iii. 434
Courtenay, Hon. Anne, iii. 760; Frances, Viscountess, iii. 446; Hon. Frances, iv. 532; William, 1st Viscount, iv. 532; William, 2nd Viscount, iii. 760
Coventry, Elizabeth, i. 187, iii. 746; George William, 7th Earl of, i. 94; Lady Georgiana Catherine, i. 94; James, iii. 746
Cowell, Harriett Elliot, ii. 329; William Wickham, ii. 329
Cowie, Mrs. Rose, iv. 585
Cowing, Margaret, iii. 11
Cox, Agnes, iii. 323; Albina, i. 190; Ann, iv. 516; Christiana, iii. 486; Frances, i. 1; Frances Deborah, ii. 37; Harriet, iii. 124; Howard, iii. 486; Jane, i. 244, iii. 750; Mary Elizabeth, iii. 468; Richard Waite, ii. 359; Sophia, ii. 358; Thomas, i. 190; Lt.-Col., i. 1, ii. 37
Coxon, Barbara, iv. 285
Coxton, Mary Anne, i. 181; T., i. 181
Coyley, Mary, iii. 126
Cozens, George Harrison, iii. 7
Cracroft, Frances, iii. 555; Walter, ii. 407; William, iii. 555
Craggs, Elizabeth Henrietta, i. 416
Craig, James Gibson, iii. 500; Lilias, ii. 573
Craigdallie, Jane, iii. 117
Craigie, Col. Charles Halkett, iv. 17; Christian Smith (Smyth), iv. 17; Maria Sophia, iii. 195
Cramond, Lord, family of, iii. 647
Crane, Charlotte, ii. 422; Miss, ii. 14
Cranston, Jane, iii. 61; Hon. William Henry, iii. 61
Crash, Susannah, iv. 367
Craster, Lt.-Col. Edmund, iii. 651; Eliza Catherine, iii. 651
Craufurd, James, iii. 178; Margaret, iii. 178
Crawford, James Henry, iii. 126; Mary, iii. 126
Creagh, Sarah, ii. 629

Cree, Christian, iv. 190; Patrick, iv. 190
Creed, Emma M., i. 48; Thomas, i. 48
Creedland, Mary Heriot, ii. 88, iii. 721; Capt. Simonides, iii. 721
Creighton (Crichton), Anne, iii. 35; Martha Cordelia, i. 159; Thomas, iii. 35
Crespigny, Charles James Fox Champion, iv. 537; Emily, iv. 537
Creswell, Catherine Grace, i. 229; John, i. 229
Creswick, Henry, iii. 495
Creutzer, Elizabeth Ann, iii. 757; Col. Henry Frederick, iii. 757
Crichton, Helen Cunningham, iv. 370; Susan Hay, iii. 607; W.B., iv. 370
Crickett, Sophia Alexander, iii. 798
Cringletie, Lord, see Murray, James Wolfe
Crofton, Rev. M., iii. 450
Cromartie, 1st Earl of, see Mackenzie, George; 2nd Earl of, see Mackenzie, John; 3rd Earl of, see Mackenzie, George
Crommelin, Charles Russell, iv. 76
Crooke, Elizabeth, iv. 395
Crosbie, Major John, iii. 797
Crosby, Eleanor (née Teasdale), iv. 244
Cross, John, iv. 170
Croucher, Mary, iv. 314; Robert, iv. 314
Crouvezierl, Anne Antoinette, iii. 532; Marie Jeanne, iii. 532
Cruden, Henrietta Elizabeth, i. 128; Capt. William, R.N., i. 128
Cruikshank, Elizabeth, ii. 292; Patrick, ii. 292
Crump, Anne, iv. 332; Charlotte, iv. 280; Letitia, ii. 15; Robert, ii. 15, iv. 280, 332
Crutwell, Lieut. J. W. S., iv. 252; Mary Hurst, iv. 252
Cullen, Margaret, iv. 144; Patrick, iv. 144
Culliford, Mary, iv. 117
Culloden, Jane, i. 117, iv. 17
Cumberlege, Elizabeth Mary, i. 250
Cumin, Charles Anne, iii. 20; George, iii. 20

INDEX OF NAMES

Cumming, Alexander, iii. 691; Caroline, ii. 53; Frances, iii. 763; Jane, iii. 691; Sir John, ii. 53; Mrs. (*née* Shaw), iv. 67
Cummins, Charles, iv. 529; Mary, iii. 31; N. Marshall, iii. 31
Cuninghame, Jean, iii. 785; John, iii. 802; William, iii. 785
Cunningham, Charlotte Anne, iv. 576; Eliza, i. 339; Helen, i. 219; Louisa, ii. 479; Margaret, iv. 147; Mrs. Mary, iii. 775; Lieut., i. 339, ii. 479
Cunninghame, Mrs. Jane Maria, iii. 469
Cunnison, Ann, ii. 89
Cunyngham, Sir Robert Keith Dick-, Bt., ii. 55
Cupola, Catherine (*née* Graham), iv. 377
Cuppage, John, ii. 71; Margaret, ii. 71; Maria, iv. 485
Curling, Mary, iv. 373; William, iv. 373
Currie, David, ii. 530, iv. 58; Elizabeth, iv. 58; Jane, ii. 530; Leonard, i. 354
Curtis, Dorothy, i. 145; James, i. 145; Rev. John Adey, ii. 421
Curty, Margaret (*née* Andrews), ii. 6
Curzon, Hon. John Henry Roper-, ii. 460

D

Dacres, Philip Milner, iv. 467; Rebecca (*née* Wilding), iv. 467
da Cruz—*see also* D'Cruz and de Cruz
da Cruz, Ursula, i. 6, iv. 592, 593
Daffy, Anthony, iv. 220
Dale, Jane, iv. 476
Dalgleish, Jane, iii. 537; William, iii. 537
Dalhousie, 8th, 9th, 12th Earls of, *see* Ramsay, George
Dallas, Elizabeth, iv. 104; William, iv. 104
Dalrymple, Lady Anne, iii. 20; Jean, ii. 618; North, 9th Earl of Stair, iii. 20; Wilhelmina Ramsay, iv. 246; Dr. William, iv. 246
Daly, Capt. Cuthbert Fetherstone, R.N., iii. 517; Eliza, iii. 517
Dalyell, Elizabeth, i. 335; John, i. 335
Dalzell, Allen, iv. 25; Mary Elizabeth, iv. 25; Robert Alexander, 9th Earl of Carnwath, iii. 338
Dana, Frances Harriet, iv. 514
Daniel, Catharine, ii. 328; Francis, ii. 328; James, ii. 328
Daniell, Ann Helena, ii. 300; Janetta, iv. 182; Ralph Allen, iv. 182; Thomas, iii. 436; Capt. Sir William, R.N., iv. 182
Dansey, Ellen, iii. 454; Richard Dansey, iii. 454
D'Arblay, Mme (Fanny Burney), i. 219, 256
d'Arboine, Marie, iii. 41
Darby, Amelia (*née* Turner), iv. 325
Darell, Clarissa, iv. 63; Sir Lionel, 1st Bt., iv. 63
Darke, Ann Maria, iii. 297
Darling, Asst. Surg. David, ii. 393; Elizabeth Ann, ii. 393; Mary, iii. 806; Ruth (*als* Caroline), iv. 631; William Chambers, *see* Bagshawe
Darragh, John, i. 365; Mary, i. 365; Rachel, ii. 627
Darrell, John, ii. 481; Rebecca Mary (*née* Doran), ii. 481
Dart, Rev. P., iv. 182; Sarah Harriet, iv. 182
Dartmouth, 4th Earl of, *see* Legge, William
Dashwood, Lydia Diana, i. 143; Rachel, iv. 515; Robert, ii. 417, iv. 515; Samuel Francis, i. 143; Sarah, ii. 417
D'Aulnis, Anne Henriette, iv. 589; Henri, iv. 589
D'Auvergne, Mary, iv. 235, 476
Davey, Emma, iv. 229; Sir Horace, 1st Baron Davey, iv. 229; Peter, iv. 229
David, Aga, ii. 137; Thangoomkhatoon, ii. 137
Davidson, Surg. Alexander, iii. 326; Emma Gordon, ii. 276; Finella, iv. 325; Isabella Margaret, iii. 371; Dr. James, iv. 389; James, ii. 305; Jane, iii. 673; John, ii. 512; Leith Alexander, ii. 36, 276, 299; Margaret, i. 419, ii. 361, iv. 389; Margaret E., ii. 36; Mary,

ii. 219, 299; Mary Anne, iii. 326;
Mary Ann (*née* Login), ii. 305;
Patrick Moir, R.N., iii. 609;
Robert, ii. 361, iii. 371; Sophia,
iii. 609; of Newton, iii. 673
Davie, Eustatia, iv. 57; Frances
Mary, i. 112; John, iii. 240, iv.
57; Margaret, iii. 240; Rev.
William, i. 112
Davies, Caroline, iii. 397; Catherine,
iv. 523; Rev. Dr. D., iv. 367;
Elizabeth, ii. 314; Frances, iv.
367; Gilbert, ii. 314; Mary Towgood, i. 80; Rev. Richard, i. 80;
Surg. Maj. Thomas, iii. 757;
William, iii. 397
Davis, Esther, iv. 23; John Ford, iv.
493; Louisa, iv. 493; Samuel, ii.
577
Dawes, Mrs. Anne, ii. 131; Bennett,
i. 18; Louisa, iii. 470; Capt., i. 18
Dawn, Catherine, iii. 592; Rev.
George, iii. 770; Marjory, iii. 770
Dawney, Anne, iii. 485; Thomas, iii.
485
Dawson, Ann, i. 103; Betty, i. 143;
Ellen Jacob, iii. 464; Harriot, iv.
58; Henry, iii. 464; Hon. James
Massy, i. 177; Maria, i. 177; Capt.
William, iv. 58
Day, Anne, ii. 182; Benedetta (*née*
Ramus), iii. 608; Jane, iii. 620;
John, iii. 409; Ralph, ii. 182
D'Cruz, Domingo, ii. 316; Rose, ii.
316
Deacle, Ruth, *als* Caroline (*née*
Darling), i. 36, iv. 631
Deacon, Maj.-Gen. Sir Charles, i.
290; Harriet (*née* Speck), iv. 152;
Henry, iv. 152
Dealtry, Sarah, iii. 337
Dean, Richard Betenson, i. 203
Deane, Anne, i. 55; Cecilia (*née*
Knudson), ii. 608; Rev. George
Henry, iii. 95; Grace, ii. 412;
John, i. 356; John Berkeley, ii.
608; Mary, i. 356; Sir Robert, 5th
Bt., ii. 412; Rosamond Harriet,
iii. 95
Deare, Elizabeth, ii. 424; Philip, ii.
424
De Bacquencourt, Anthony Vinchon,
ii. 51

de Baumbach, of Hesse, Baron, iii.
277; Emilie Marie Louise Wilhelmina, iii. 277
de Beaufre, Elizabeth, ii. 351;
Joseph, ii. 351
de Beaurepaire, Comte, iii. 524;
Henrietta, iii. 524
de Beausset, Maria Emilie, iv. 329;
Cardinal Duc, iv. 329
de Bessy, Gaston, ii. 201; Maria
Eudoxie, ii. 201
De Blaquiere, Eleanor, iii. 38; John,
1st Baron, iii. 38; Peter Boyle, iii.
38
Debnam, Charlotte, iv. 194; Jane,
i. 202; Major Robert Joseph, i.
202, iv. 187, 194; Sophia, iv. 187
Debonnaire, Jane Louisa, iii. 646;
John, iii. 285, 646, iv. 126;
Susannah Sophia Selina, iii. 284,
iv. 126
de Bons, Mlle, iii. 768
de Brissac, Peter Abraham, iv. 637
de Brosses, Jeanne Françoise Moreau,
iii. 546
De Bruhl, Mary, Countess, i. 340
de Cere, Blanche Coralie, i. 236
de Chalon, Amélie Josephine, iv. 113;
Comte Blaudin de Fontenne, iv. 113
de Clonard, Comte, *see* Sutton,
Thomas
De Coetlogon, Rev. C. E., ii. 254;
Charlotte, ii. 254
De Courcy, Elizabeth, ii. 13; Eliza
Jane, i. 208; Jane, iv. 561; John,
26th Baron Kingsale, ii. 13;
Richard, iv. 632
de Crespigny, Sir William Champion,
2nd Bt., iv. 537
de Cruz, Maria, iii. 134
Dee, Mrs. Mary, iv. 184
de Fouchy, Charlotte Estelle, iv. 79;
Eleanor Mary, iv. 481; Eliza
Maria, iii. 427; Emilie, ii. 459;
Jacques Grand-Jean, ii. 459, iii.
427, iv. 79, 481
De Gennes, Col. John Daniel, iii.
381; Louisa, iii. 380
de Haller, Albertine, i. 222;
Albrecht, i. 222
de la Bernagerez, Estelle de Guinez
d'Illarion, iv. 583; — de Guinez
d'Illarion, iv. 583

INDEX OF NAMES

de la Fontaine, Gen. Mottet, ii. 471; Virginie, ii. 471
de Laire, *see* Loy
Delamain, Jane Amelia (*née* Youngson), iii. 239; Jesse (*née* Waugh), iv. 414
de la Metrie, Catherine, iii. 565; Quintan, iii. 565
de Lapeijre, Dr. Arnaud, i. 135; Louise Caroline Clementine Deli Bertrand, i. 135
de Lareste, Marie Louise Antoinette Lenferna, iii. 186
de Latre, Major Philip, iv. 1
de la Tremouille, Francis, *see* L'Herondell
De Laval, Maria, i. 323; Marie Hyacinth Oclanis, iii. 43
Delawarr, Lord, iii. 797
de l'Etang, Chevalier Antoine, ii. 522; Julia, ii. 522
Delisle, Mary, iii. 599; Philip, iii. 599
Delmar, Hannah (*née* Alldin), i. 23
de Loire, *see* Loy
Delpierre, Octave, iv. 313
Delpratt, Charlotte Helen, iv. 241; Samuel, iv. 241
de Mazar, Bergetta Maria (*née* Knudson), ii. 608; F., ii. 608
de Miller, Gurtruy, ii. 388
de Momet, Adèle, ii. 215; J., ii. 215
de Montmorency, 1st Viscount Frankfort, *see* Morres, Lodge Evans
de Moor, Anne Cecilia, iii. 785; Pieter Arendt, iii. 785
De More (Demoor), Cara Beata, i. 346
Dempster, Cathcart, ii. 626, iii. 756; Helen, i. 259; Jane, i. 341; John, i. 259; Margaret, i. 341, ii. 626, iii. 756
Den, Patrick, ii. 574
Denbigh, Earl of, *see* Feilding, Basil
Deneys (de Nys), Adrian Christian, iv. 343; Yda Johanna, iv. 343
Denholm, Sarah, ii. 593, iii. 809; Capt. William, iii. 809
Denman, Thomas, 1st Baron Denman, iv. 354
Dennett, Elizabeth, i. 360; Henry, i. 360
Dennilon, Helen Eliza, i. 375; Capt. Rowland, i. 375

Dennis, Col. James, i. 355; Sarah, i. 355
Denniss, Eleanora Sophia, iii. 181; Janet Frances, i. 271
Dennistoun, James, i. 74; Mary, iii. 734; Mary Lyon, i. 74
Dennys, Lucy Martha, iv. 536; N., iv. 536
de Noailles, Mary, iii. 781
Denson, Anne, iv. 387; Susan, i. 107; Thomas, iv. 387
Dent, Caroline, i. 28; Charlotte, iv. 19; Rear-Adm. Sir Digby, iv. 19
Denton, Diana Elizabeth, iv. 532; Matilda, ii. 271; Mrs. Sarah, ii. 255; Rev. Thomas, iv. 532
de Paiba, Bathsheba, iv. 304; Moses, iv. 304
de Panouilhère, Emily Prospère, iv. 118
de Plessis, Mlle, iii. 768
de Poellnitz et de Montricher, Baron, iii. 465
de Pontcarré, Mrs. Eliza, ii. 593
de Revaro, Catharina, ii. 227
De Rinzy, Annesley, i. 172; Hannah, i. 172
De Rozario, Anna, iii. 800
Derwentwater, Earls of, iv. 572
de Saran, Dubois, i. 78; Miss M. L., i. 78
Desbrisay, Mary, iii. 399; Capt. Theophilus, iii. 399
Des Champs, *see* Chamier
De Seden, Viscountess, ii. 51
Despard, Col. Henry, ii. 3; Sophia Elizabeth, ii. 3
de Stein, Baron F., of Kochberg, i. 187
de Trachswald, Dame Catherine Marguerite Mary, iv. 466
de Treytorrens, Barbille Marguerite, iii. 466; Pierre Abram, iii. 466
Devaynes, Harriott Augusta, iii. 312; William, iii. 312
Devereux, Richard, ii. 454
De Verinne, Jean, iii. 24; Mary Jane Antoinette, iii. 24
Devril, Elizabeth, ii. 183
Dewes, Arthur, iii. 684
de Wet, Johanna Hillegonda, iv. 349; Oloff Godlief, iv. 349
Dicas, Helen, iii. 306; John, iii. 306

INDEX OF NAMES

Dick, Abercrombie, i. 282; Anne, ii. 591, 592; Charlotte Susan, i. 282; Isobel, iii. 20; Jane, ii. 304; Quintin, iii. 464; Vice-Adm. Thomas, ii. 304; Thomas, ii. 591, 592; William, iii. 20

Dicken, Barbara, iv. 448

Dickens, Jane (*née* Debnam), i. 202; Maria (*née* Bridgman), i. 202; Theodore, i. 202

Dickerson, Mary, iii. 573; R., iii. 573

Dickson, Agnes, iv. 633; Ann, iv. 201; Arabella Georgiana, iv. 523; Rear-Adm. Sir Archibald Collingwood, Bt., ii. 72; Charlotte, iv. 375; Elizabeth, iii. 791, 793; Isobel, i. 142; James, ii. 508; Jean, ii. 508; John, iii. 791, 793; Mary, iii. 754; Mary Magdalen, ii. 72; Robert, iv. 633; William, iii. 754

Digby, Edward St. Vincent, 9th Baron, i. 399; Adm. Sir Henry, i. 399

Diggle, Diana Frances, iv. 155; Henry Wadham, iv. 155

Dillon, Harriet, iii. 792; Col. John, iii. 341; Penelope, iii. 341

Dimock, John, iii. 798; Sarah, iii. 798

Dingwall, Agnes, iv. 264, 265, 267; Alexander, i. 32, iv. 265; Anna, iv. 265; Elizabeth, i. 32; John, iii. 435, iv. 267; Sarah, iii. 435

Dinorben, 1st Baron, *see* Hughes, William Lewis

Dinwiddie, Elizabeth, iii. 72; Robert, iii. 72

di Pescara, Francisca, iv. 302

Dixie, Sir Beaumont, Bt., iv. 409

Dixon, Joseph, ii. 176; Mary, ii. 176

Dobbie, Katharine, ii. 324, iii. 725; Mary Amelia, ii. 554; Sarah Catharine, iii. 725; Capt. William Hugh, R.N., ii. 324, 554

Dobbin, Harriet, iii. 580; Capt. William, R.N., iii. 580

Dobbs, Conway (Richard), i. 191, ii. 449; Frances Millicent, i. 191; Olivia Nichola, ii. 449

Dobbyn, Grace, iii. 669; William, iii. 669

Dobie, D., i. 92; Eliza, i. 92

Dobree, Isaac, ii. 294; Judith, ii. 294, iii. 738

Dobson, Jane, i. 103; Robert, i. 103

Docker, Rev. John, ii. 12; Sophia, ii. 12

Dodd, Ellen Theresa, iv. 128

Dodgson, Alexa, ii. 506; Rev. John, ii. 506

Doigly, Elizabeth Ann, ii. 575

Dolbel, Charlotte, ii. 579; John, ii. 579

D'Olivier, Capt. Antoine Louis, ii. 411; Eliza, ii. 411; Sarah S., ii. 411

Domina Jan, iii. 415

Dominicus, Elizabeth, iv. 538; George, iii. 810, iv. 538; Harriet Eliza, iii. 810

Domvill, Mary, ii. 427

Domville, Elizabeth, iv. 153; John, iv. 153

Don, Isabella, i. 307; Jean, iii. 658; Lilias, iii. 55; William, i. 307, iii. 55

Donald, Jean, ii. 375

Donaldson, Capt. Andrew Henderson, iii. 236; Elizabeth, iii. 278, iv. 551; James, iv. 552; Jane, iv. 552; Mary, i. 41, iv. 593; Mary Anne, iii. 236

Doneraile, 1st Viscount, *see* Aldworth, St. Leger

Donnithorne, Mary, iv. 396; Rev. Thomas, iv. 396

Doolan, Lt.-Col. Richard, i. 385

Doran, Morris, ii. 481; Roboooa Mary, ii. 481

Dorchester, 1st Baron, *see* Carleton, Gen. Sir Guy

Dore, Capt. Peter Luke, iii. 403; Rosa Wilson, iii. 403

Dormer, Charles, 8th Baron Dormer, ii. 70

Dorril, Elizabeth, iv. 351; Adm. G., iv. 351

Dost Muhammad Khan, iv. 385

Doucett, Maria Agnes, iii. 291; Robert, iii. 291

Doughty, Henry, iii. 41; Mary, iii. 41

Douglas, Archibald, Duke of Douglas, iii. 315; Col. Archibald, ii. 242;

INDEX OF NAMES

Mrs. Archibald (*née* Stuart), iv. 205; Barbara, iii. 187; Campbell, iii. 315; Rev. the Hon. Charles, iii. 317; Elizabeth, ii. 348, iii. 802; George Sholto, 17th Earl of Morton, iii. 317; Helen, iv. 481; Henrietta, iv. 221; Isabella, ii. 242, iv. 198; James, iv. 221; Janet (Jean), iii. 315; Jean Ann, i. 351; John, iii. 315; John Cuppage, M.D., iv. 496; Julia Mary, iii. 317; Maria Esperança, iii. 432; Mary, iv. 496; Robert, iii. 315; William, iii. 117; Lt.-Col., iii. 802

Dove, Ellen Barons, iv. 573; Capt. Henry Francis, R.N., iv. 481; John Matthew, iv. 573; Sarah, iv. 481

Dowleans, A. M., iv. 573

Dowling, Gertrude, iii. 802

Down, Emma, iii. 309; John, iii. 292; Mary, i. 246; Richard, i. 246, iii. 309

Downing, Elizabeth, iii. 794

Doyle, Margaret, ii. 422

D'Oyly, Sir Charles, 7th Bt., i. 171; Edward, ii. 257; Emma, ii. 257; Sir John Hadley, 6th Bt., i. 250; 8th Bt., i. 207, ii. 169

Drake, Frances Mervyn, ii. 304; George, iv. 533; Henry, i. 213; Katherine, i. 213; Zachary Hammett, ii. 304

Draper, Mary (*née* Hurring), ii. 510; William, ii. 510

Drew, Francis, M.D., ii. 422; Margaret, ii. 422

Dring, Charlotte Anne, iii. 761; Cornelia Harvey, iii. 534; Margaret McLean (*née* Todd), ii. 84; R.S., ii. 84; William, iii. 535, 761

Driscoll, Charles, ii. 212; Mary Anne, ii. 212

Driver, Bella, iv. 428; Catherine, iv. 234; Henry, iv. 576; William, iv. 234

Drought, John Armstrong, i. 97; Phoebe, i. 97

Droz(e), Charlotte, i. 153; Charlotte Mary, i. 233; Elizabeth, ii. 410; Henry, i. 233; Maria Magdalena, ii. 410; Simeon, i. 153, ii. 410, iii. 736

D'Rozario, Johanna, iii. 626

Drummond, James, iii. 308; Janet, iii. 308; Sir John Forbes, Bt., iii. 282

Drury, Cecilia, i. 113; Rev. Henry, i. 113

Drysdale, Elizabeth (*née* Pew), iii. 515; Sir William, iii. 515

Dubois, Ann, iv. 459; Ellen, iii. 791; Jane, iv. 491; Mary Ann, iii. 536

Duckett, Richard, iii. 464

Duckle, Kitty, iv. 318

Duddingston, Fotheringham, iii. 425; James, iii. 425

Duff, Alexander, ii. 95; Anne Olivia, iv. 459; Archibald, iv. 459; James, ii. 95, 289; Janet, ii. 598; John, iii. 671; Magdalen, iii. 131; Margaret Ogilvie (*née* Dunbar), ii. 95; Sophia Henrietta, iii. 210; William, 1st Earl Fife, ii. 598; Major, iii. 210

Dufferin, 3rd Baron, *see* Blackwood, Hans

Duguid, Margaret, i. 222

Duke, Henry, iv. 52; Mary, ii. 234, iv. 52

Dumaresq, Frances, iii. 40; George, iii. 40

Dun, Mary, i. 414; William, i. 414

Dunbar, Sir Alexander, 4th Bt. of Northfield, i. 393; Barbara, ii. 349; Catherine Wedderburn, iii. 139; Charlotte Fullarton, iii. 58, iv. 371; Elizabeth, ii. 217, 219, iii. 317, 677; Isabel, ii. 221; James, iii. 58, iv. 371; Jane Rabina, iii. 145; Jean, i. 393; Mary Maxwell, iii. 394; Thomas, ii. 349, iii. 139, 317, 394, 677; William, iv. 145

Duncan, Adam, 1st Viscount Duncan, Adm. R.N., ii. 174; Rev. Dr. Andrew, i. 236, iii. 316; Ann, i. 367; Ann Walker, iii. 156; Charlotte Anna Maria, iv. 444; Hannah, iii. 316; Helen, ii. 259; Hon. Henrietta, ii. 174; John, ii. 259; Govr. Jonathan, iii. 289; Margaret, i. 236; Mary French, i. 176; Thomas, iii. 156; W. J., iv. 444

Dundas, Anne, ii. 73; Christian, ii. 370; Elizabeth (*née* Rannie), iii. 633; George, ii. 370; Henry, 1st

Viscount Melville, iii. 633; James, ii. 73
Dunkin, Letitia, iii. 188; Matilda, i. 372; Sir William, i. 59, 372, iii. 188
Dunlap, Mary Ann Milligan (née Gwilt), ii. 510; Asst. Surg. William Leman, ii. 511
Dunlop, Janet, iii. 150
Dunmore, 4th Earl of, see Murray, John
Dunn, John, ii. 527; Judith, ii. 527; Mary, ii. 286
Dunning, Sarah, iii. 636
Dunsmure, Janet, iii. 434; John, iii. 434
Du Pré, Cornelia Anne, iv. 298; Josias, ii. 125, iv. 298; Rebecca, ii. 125
Durell, Mary, ii. 553
Durham, Frances Eliza, iv. 25; William Hall, iv. 25; 1st Earl of, see Lambton, John George
Durie, Ann, i. 120; Charlotte, iii. 435; Elizabeth Margaret, ii. 338; Katherine Cecilia, iii. 625; Major Robert, i. 120, 172, ii. 338, iii. 435, 625; Sarah, i. 172
Durnford, Harriet, iii. 654; Susanna, iii. 540; Rev. Thomas, iii. 540
Dutton, Eliza, ii. 242
Duval, Rev. David, iv. 429; Mary Anne, iv. 429
Dwarris, Sarah Elizabeth, iv. 85; William, iv. 85
Dwyer, Constantia Harvey, iv. 378; Francis, iv. 378; Sophia, iii. 542
Dyce, Agnes, iii. 39; Alexander, iii. 39; Ann May, iv. 310; Charlotte, ii. 248; Col. George Alexander David, iv. 310; Mrs. Sarah, iv. 571; William, M.D., ii. 248
Dyer, Bridget, iv. 51; Harriet, iv. 477; Phebe, iii. 533; Sir Thomas Swinnerton, 8th Bt., iv. 477; William, iv. 51
Dyke, Harriet, iii. 299; Sir John Dixon, Bt., iii. 299
Dyne, Edward, i. 206; Mary, i. 206
Dyott, John P., ii. 273
Dysart, 8th Countess of, see Tollemache, Maria Elizabeth

E

Eager, Major Francis Russell, i. 132; Matilda Anne, i. 132
Eales, Rev. William, iv. 547; Winifred Emma, iv. 547
Eames, Lydia, i. 235
Earnshaw, Benjamin, iii. 738; Elizabeth, iii. 738
East, Anna Eliza, i. 413; Sir Edward Hyde, 1st Bt., i. 413, iii. 764; Mary, iii. 764
Eastcourt, Frances, ii. 366
Eaton, Maria Duncan, iv. 574
Eccles, Elizabeth, iii. 734; Margaret, iii. 51; Martin, M.D., iii. 51, 734; Mary, i. 324, ii. 143; William, i. 324, ii. 143
Eckford, Janet (Jessy), iv. 96
Eddie, Mary, ii. 348
Eddy, Asst. Surg. Henry Charles, iii. 544
Eden, Dorothea, iii. 285; Higgins, ii. 144; Sir John, 4th Bt., iii. 285; William, 1st Baron Auckland, ii. 120
Edgecumbe, Grace, iv. 461
Edgerton, Margaret, iii. 766
Edmond, Janet, iii. 787
Edmonston(e), Elizabeth, iv. 185
Edmondstoune, Henrietta, iii. 9
Edmund, Mary (née Nollekens), iii. 400
Edward Augustus, H.R.H. Prince, iv. 408
Edward, David, iv. 420; Isobel, iv. 420; Madelina, ii. 488
Edwardes, Maj. Gen. Sir Herbert, iv. 287
Edwards, Ann, i. 179; Ann Matilda, iii. 700; Elizabeth, iv. 460; John, iv. 460; Thomas Dyer, iv. 63
Eggleston, Nanny, iv. 473
Eglinton, 12th Earl of, see Montgomerie, Hugh
Egremont, 4th Countess of, see Wyndham, Jane
Elchies, Lord, see Grant, Patrick
Elderton, Lt.-Col. Charles Augustus, iii. 457; Gertrude, iii. 457
Elias, Magdelina, i. 108, iii. 740; Mr. Nasier, iii. 740
Eliot, Elizabeth, iv. 169; Samuel, iv. 169

INDEX OF NAMES

Eliott, Sir Daniel, iii. 708, 799; George Augustus, 1st Baron Heathfield, ii. 371; Georgiana Mary, iii. 799

Ellenborough, 1st Baron, see Law, Edward

Ellerker, Eliza, iii. 2

Ellicombe, Gen. Sir Charles Grene, iii. 486; Mary (née Peach), iii. 486

Elliot, Elizabeth, iv. 360; George, ii. 67, iv. 360; Georgiana King, ii. 67; Helen, ii. 14, 16, 19; John, iv. 94; Lettice, iv. 360; Margaret, iv. 94; Rev. Philip, iv. 360

Elliott, Alexander, iii. 754; Margaret, iii. 754

Ellis, Ann, ii. 166; Margaret, iii. 276

Elmsall, Anne (née Kyd), ii. 613; William, ii. 613

Elphingston, Jean, iii. 806

Elphinston, John, iii. 118; Maria, iii. 118

Elphinstone, Alexander, iv. 223; Anne, iv. 223; Charles, 10th Baron, iii. 677; John, 11th Baron, ii. 139; Hon. Keith, ii. 139; Marion Dalrymple-Horn-, iii. 221; Gen. Robert Dalrymple-Horn-, iii. 221

Elrington, Amelia, iv. 20; Frances, ii. 284; Major, iv. 20

Elton, Emma, iii. 651

Elwood, Mrs. Melesina, ii. 483

Emerson, James William, iii. 283

Emes, Anne, iii. 790; Fulke, iii. 790

Emlyn, Ann, iii. 73; Henry, iii. 73

English, Helen, iii. 283; William, iii. 283

Ernst, Augusta Elizabeth, ii. 535, iii. 803; G., i. 386

Errington, George, iii. 809; Isabella, iii. 809

Erskine, David, iii. 470; Davie, iii. 470; Col. Henry, ii. 52; Henry David, 10th Earl of Buchan, ii. 105; Jacoba Helena (née De Waal), ii. 52; John Francis, 7th Earl of Mar, ii. 141; Margaret, iii. 201; William, Lord Kinneder, ii. 140; Col., iii. 201

Esmonde, Frances, ii. 611; Laurence, ii. 611

Essex, 5th Earl of, see Capel-Coningsby, George

Esten, Lieut. James, R.N., iv. 392

Ethelstone, Eleanor, ii. 242

Evance, Lucy, ii. 331; Capt. Samuel Baker, iii. 782; Sarah, ii. 255, iii. 782

Evans, Anne, iii. 658; Caroline, ii. 289; Elizabeth, iii. 589, 591; Emily, iv. 425; George, 4th Baron Carbery, iv. 404; George, iii. 589; James, ii. 214; Rev. James Harington, ii. 289; Margaret Maria Clements (née Brown), ii. 214; Mary, iv. 284; Mary Virtue, ii. 334; Maurice, iii. 658; Thomas Browne, ii. 334

Everard, Edward, i. 166; Rebecca, i. 166

Eyles, Sabina, iii. 487

Eyre, Anne, iii. 561; Col. Samuel, iii. 561; Mrs. (née Dyer), ii. 112

F

Fagan, Eliza Mary, iii. 647; John, iii. 647

Fair, James, iv. 80; Margaret, iv. 80

Faithful, Maria, i. 108

Faithfull, Mary, ii. 373

Faiz Bakhsh (Faizun-nissa), Bibi Sahiba, iii. 452

Falconar, Alexander, iii. 795; Sarah, iv. 238

Falconer, Eliza, iv. 494; Mary, ii. 15

Fanshawe, John Gascoyne, i. 175; Mary Annetta, i. 175

Farington, Charlotte, iii. 404; James, iii. 404

Farley, Ann, iv. 324; Thomas, iv. 324

Farmer, Euphemia, ii. 87

Farnborough, 1st Baron of Bromley Hill Place, see Long, Charles; of Farnborough, co. Southampton, see May, Sir Thomas Erskine

Farquhar, Rev. Alexander, i. 404; Catherine Dorothy, ii. 24; Elizabeth, i. 404; John, iii. 2; Susannah Lloyd (née Lake), iii. 2; Sir Walter, Bt., M.D., iv. 541

Farran, Ann (née Lambert), iii. 6; Joseph, iii. 6

Farrell, Dr. John, ii. 253; Susanna Anne, ii. 355
Farrington, Sir Henry Maturin, 3rd Bt., i. 423, iii. 220; Louisa Georgiana, iii. 489; Maria Sophia, i. 423
Fawcet, Ann, iv. 527; Thomas, iv. 527
Fawson, Emma Goodenough (née Goddard), ii. 138; Capt. John, ii. 138
Fearon, Ann, i. 6; Elizabeth Hutchinson, i. 87; Maj.-Gen. Robert Bryce, i. 87
Feilding, Basil, 4th Earl of Denbigh, iii. 226, iv. 589; 6th Earl, ii. 548, 553; Lady Diana, iii. 226, iv. 589
Fell, David, iii. 617; Janet, ii. 146
Fellus, Maria, ii. 306, 458
Fendall, Harriet, iii. 347; John, iii. 347
Fennell, Michael, iii. 800
Fenwick, Elizabeth, iv. 412
Ferguson, Cordelia, ii. 565; Elizabeth, iii. 767; James, iv. 492; Jane, iii. 207; Thomas, iv. 258
Fergusson, Benjamin, i. 181, iii. 580; Ellen Maria, i. 181; John, iii. 806; John Hutchison, i. 3; Margaret Ann Harriett, i. 3; Margaret Tierney, iii. 580; Marion, iii. 340; Mary (née Home), ii. 475; M., iii. 303; Susanna, ii. 579; Thomas, iii. 340; William, ii. 579
Fernie, Margaret, i. 246, iii. 750; William, iii. 750
Ferrand, Anne, iv. 362; Rev. Thomas, iv. 362
Ferrar, Samuel, ii. 525; Sarah Eugenia, ii. 525
Ferrier, Elizabeth Hollings (née Waugh), iv. 414; Helen, ii. 599, iii. 809; James, iii. 809; Jane, iii. 652; Capt. Walter, iii. 652
Ferris, Joanna, iv. 323; William, iv. 323
Ferryman, Marian, iv. 543
Fetherston, Anne, ii. 52; Francis, ii. 52; Sir Ralph, Bt., iv. 273; Sarah, iv. 273
Feuilleteau, William, iv. 499
ffolkes, Fanny Maria, iv. 430; Sir Martin Browne, 1st Bt., iv. 430

Field, Barbara (née Stokoe), iv. 199
Fielding, Eleanor, iv. 407
Fife, 1st Earl, see Duff, William
Finch, Jane, iii. 414; Rachel, ii. 122; William, ii. 122
Fincham, Mary Ann, iii. 535
Fincher, Elizabeth Charlotte, iv. 307; Richard, iv. 307
Finlay, Rev. Justice, i. 420; Mary, i. 420
Finney, Amelia, iv. 521
Finnis, Elizabeth, iii. 99; Robert, iii. 99
Fischer, Ann, ii. 291
Fisher, Andrew, iv. 633; Elizabeth, i. 281; James, i. 281; Marion, iv. 633
Fitzgerald, David, iii. 413; Dorothea Anne, iii. 40; Lt.-Col. Edward, iii. 40; Elizabeth, iv. 277; Isabella Barry, iv. 395; John, iv. 277; Marianna, iii. 615; Walter, iii. 665; William Barry, iv. 395
Fitzherbert, Charlotte, ii. 238; Lucy, ii. 70; Thomas, ii. 70, 238
Fitzpatrick, Mary, iii. 5
FitzRoy, Augustus Henry, 3rd Duke of Grafton, ii. 29; Harriett Elizabeth, ii. 29; Adm. Sir William, ii. 29
Fladgate, John, iv. 161; Mary Ann, iv. 161
Flamank, Dennis, iii. 519; William, iii. 519
Fleeming, Isobel, ii. 17; William, ii. 17
Fleetwood, Barbara, iii. 312; John, iii. 312
Fleming, Archibald, ii. 595; Louisa Anne, iv. 314; Richard, iii. 23, 538; Sophia Span, iii. 538; Wilhelmina, iii. 23
Fletcher, Jane Mabel Allenby, iii. 215; Sydney Maria, iv. 217; Lt.-Col. Thomas, iv. 217
Flowyer, Elizabeth, iii. 565; Peter, iii. 565
Floyer, Margaret, i. 389; Rev. William, i. 389
Foldsone, Anne, iii. 274; John, iii. 274
Folkestone, 1st Viscount, see Bouverie, Sir Jacob

INDEX OF NAMES

Folliott, Frances, ii. 489; Capt., R.N., ii. 489
Fombelle, Emma Frances, iv. 245; John, i. 284, iv. 90, 245; Lucy, i. 284; Mary, iv. 90
Fooks, Emma Sophia, ii. 147; T. B., ii. 147
Foquett, Frances, ii. 40; Richard, ii. 40
Forbes, Anne, ii. 322, iii. 94; Barbara, iii. 282; Christian, iii. 328; Helen, i. 90; Hugh, ii. 529; James, 15th Lord Forbes, i. 427; Jean, ii. 529; Sir John (Drummond), Bt. of Hawthornden, iii. 282; Capt. John, i. 90, iii. 94; Mrs. Mackenzie (née Dowie), ii. 80; Mary, iv. 178; Mary (née Hay), ii. 413; Rebecca, iii. 672; Robert, iii. 282; Sophia, i. 427
Ford, Amelia Wilde, iv. 468; Eliza, i. 338; Eliza Caroline, iii. 214; Frances Anne, i. 114; Sir Francis, 2nd Bt., iii. 214; Harriet Milling, iii. 553; Helen, iv. 62; Surg. James, iv. 138; John, i. 338, ii. 126; Adm. John, iii. 206; Mary, ii. 126; Capt. Matthew William, i. 114, iii. 553; Capt., iv. 468
Forder, Elizabeth, iv. 124
Fordyce, Anne, iv. 180; Arthur Dingwall-, ii. 64; Robert, iv. 180
Forester, Major Francis, ii. 196; Julia, ii. 196; Margaret, ii. 244
Forman, Mrs. Elizabeth, iii. 751; Sarah, iv. 637; Thomas, iv. 637; Thomas Seaton, iii. 751
Forrest, Arthur, ii. 119; Major Arthur, i. 430; Louisa, i. 430; Mary, ii. 119
Forster, George Brooks, ii. 225; Henry Pitts, iii. 246; James, iv. 359; Jane, iii. 246; John, iv. 370; Mary, ii. 225; Sarah (née Volham), iv. 359; Sophia Matilda, iii. 288
Forsyth, Eliza, iii. 533; Lieut. Henry George, R.N., iii. 533
Fort, Richard, iv. 131
Fortier, Emily Betsy, iii. 246; J.B., iii. 246
Foster (Forster or Forester), Lucy (née Knox), ii. 606

Fotheringham, Agnes, iii. 791; Helen (née Hamilton), ii. 375; Robert, iii. 791
Fouquet, Nicholas, iii. 778
Fowke, Edward, ii. 469; Randall, ii. 469; Sophia, i. 126, ii. 469
Fowle, E. Mary, iv. 99; Rev. Fulwar Craven, iv. 99
Fowler, John, iv. 104; Sarah, iv. 104
Foxlow, Mary Ann, iv. 21
Francis, Surg. Clement, i. 219; Joseph, ii. 510; Mary Anne, iii. 275; Sophia, ii. 437; Susan (née Hurring), ii. 510
Franco, Solomon, iv. 411
Frankland, Catherine, iv. 442; Adm. Sir Thomas, 5th Bt., iv. 442
Franklyn, George, iii. 716; James, i. 47; Jane Hannah, i. 47
Fraser, Alexander, i. 400, iii. 121, 192; Lt.-Col. Alexander, ii. 57; Ann Dewar, iii. 121; Arthur John, ii. 468; Caroline (née Kingston), ii. 57; Catherine Jane, iii. 553; Lieut. Edward, iii. 288; Eliza, ii. 321, iii. 521, iv. 164; Eliza Dell, iii. 192, iv. 597; Fanny Louisa, ii. 468; Lt.-Gen. Hastings, ii. 189; Hugh, 8th Lord Lovat, i. 400; Gen. Sir Hugh, iii. 155; Col. Hugh, i. 278; James, iii. 692; Lilias, iii. 692; Mary, i. 400, iii. 128; Mary Lydia, iii. 155; Matilda, ii. 189; Mrs. Sarah, iv. 529; Bdr.-Gen. Simon, iv. 340; Capt. Simon, ii. 381; Dr., iv. 164
Frazer, Alexander, Lord Strichen, i. 295; Katherine, i. 295; Thomas, i. 295
Frederick the Great, iii. 350
Freeman, Betty, iii. 444; Charlotte Sophia, ii. 410; Daniel Spencer, ii. 410, 621; Marianne, iii. 612; Thomas, iii. 612; William, iii. 444
Freer, Helen, iv. 483; John, iv. 483; Margaret, ii. 304; Robert, iv. 483
French, Anne, iii. 411; Catherine Louisa, ii. 197; Elizabeth Wellwood, ii. 418; John, ii. 197; Mary, iii. 411; Robert, iii. 411; Selina, iv. 420; Bdr.-Gen., ii. 418; Dr., iv. 420; of Shooter's Hill, iii. 412
Frewen, Anne, ii. 365

Friell, Elizabeth, iii. 794; Elizabeth (*née* Droz), ii. 410; Henrietta Caroline Lestock, iii. 178; Peter, iii. 794
Friend, Fanny, i. 424
Frushard, James, iii. 744
Fry, Elizabeth Jane, iii. 789; Harriet, iv. 416; Rev. Dr. Henry, iv. 416; Joseph, M.D., iii. 789
Fryer, Dorothy, ii. 519; Elizabeth, i. 363; William, i. 363
Fuge, Emmeline, iii. 784; Mary Elizabeth, iii. 523; Robert, iii. 523
Fulcher, R., ii. 190; Sarah, ii. 190
Fuller, Elizabeth Anna, ii. 371; John Trayton, ii. 371
Fullerton, Lt.-Gen. Robert, iii. 749, iv. 482
Fülling, Mary Elizabeth, iv. 323
Fulton, Ann, iii. 272; Anne (*née* Hamilton), ii. 375; Eliza, iii. 561; Jane, iii. 348; John Williamson, iii. 561; Joseph, iii. 272
Furnivall, George Frederick, iv. 403; Louisa Elizabeth, iv. 403
Furvis (? Purvis), Joseph, iii. 363; Martha, iii. 363
Fyffe, Laurence, M.D., iv. 392

G

Gage, Elizabeth, ii. 11; Louisa Elizabeth, i. 163; Sir Thomas, Bt., ii. 11; Gen. Hon. Thomas, i. 163
Gainsford, Eliza, ii. 495; John, ii. 495
Gairdner, Andrew, iii. 499; Rebecca (*née* Penman), iii. 499
Gaitskell, Henry, ii. 245
Gale, Harriet, i. 166; Roger Henry, i. 166
Galhié, Marguerite, i. 372, iii. 759; Stephen, iii. 759
Galloway, Charlotte, i. 397; James, i. 397; Jane, iv. 136
Galway, 2nd Viscount, *see* Monckton, William
Gam, Catherine, iv. 390
Gambier, Adm. James, 1st Lord Gambier, iv. 195; Lt. Govr. John, iv. 195
Gamon, Eliza, (*née* Rutledge), iii. 711
Gane, Maria Cordelia, ii. 543

Garbet, Elizabeth (*née* Ridley), iii. 657
Gardiner, Anne, i. 85, iv. 303; Rt. Hon. Charles, iv. 303; Elizabeth, iii. 766; Emma Lydia, ii. 587, iv. 131; Gertrude Florinda, iv. 286; Luke, 1st Lord Mountjoy, iv. 303; Gen. William, iv. 286
Gardner, Alan, 1st Baron Gardner, ii. 248; Bibi Sahiba Hinga, ii. 248; Catherine Georgiana, iii. 651; Rev. Charles, i. 41; Edith, iii. 733; Elizabeth, i. 41; Rear-Adm. Francis Farington, iii. 651; Harmuzi Begum, ii. 248; James, iii. 733; Susan (*née* Tennant), iv. 246; Miss, iii. 266
Garle, Alicia, i. 133; Richard, i. 133
Garnet, John, iv. 259; Mary, iv. 259
Garnett, Anne, ii. 265; Henry, ii. 265; Louisa Cleveland, iii. 80
Garrett, Rev. William George, i. 8
Garric, Capt. Peter, iv. 249
Garrick, David, iv. 249; Elizabeth (*née* Tetley), iv. 249; George, iv. 249
Garstin, Harriet Caroline, iii. 189; Capt. Jonathan Hayter, i. 1, iii. 190; Sophia Frances, i. 1
Garth, Edward Turnour, *see* Turnour, Edward, 1st Earl Winterton
Gascoigne, Mary, ii. 129
Gaskell, Nathaniel, iv. 51; Sarah, iv. 51
Gaskin, Elizabeth, iii. 447, 452; Rev. Dr. George, iii. 447
Gataker, Anne, i. 218; Thomas, i. 218
Gatty, Margaret, iii. 713
Gauntlett, Anabella, iii. 596
Gawler, Henry, iii. 760; (Ker), John Bellenden, iii. 760
Gayer, Magdalen, iv. 185; Rev. P., iv. 185
Geach, Martha, ii. 107, 380
Geale, Eliza Sarah, iv. 544
Geddes, Archibald, i. 14, ii. 520; Barbara, ii. 452; Margaret, ii. 520; Sarah, i. 14; Capt. William, iv. 100; Miss, iv. 100
Gee, Caroline, ii. 486; Roger, ii. 486

INDEX OF NAMES

Gell, Miss, iv. 522
George II, i. 112, iv. 340, 589
— III, i. 264, ii. 101, 421, iii. 227, 608, iv. 73, 346, 527
— IV, i. 264, ii. 224, iii. 608
George William Frederick, Prince of Wales, iv. 11
Geraldes, Clementina Elizabeth Peres, iii. 528
Geran, Daniel, i. 272; Mary (née Byrne), i. 272
Gerard, Rev. Charles, iv. 434
Gibbon, Ann, iv. 141; Rev. Charles, ii. 151; Eliza, iii. 398; James, iii. 398, iv. 141, 323; Maria, ii. 151; Mary Jane, iv. 323
Gibbons, Mrs. Sarah, iii. 261
Gibbs, Anna Louisa, ii. 306; John, ii. 306; Capt. John, iii. 10; Lucy, iii. 120; Maria, iii. 10
Gibson, Ann, iv. 297; Catherine (née Achmuty), i. 6; Elizabeth, iii. 72, iv. 496; George, iv. 214; Rev. John, iii. 72; Margaret, iv. 214; Samuel, iv. 297
Gideon, Sampson, iv. 304
Giffard, Catherine, i. 299; Peter, i. 299
Gilbanks, Rev. George, i. 58; Mary, i. 58
Gilbert, Alice, iii. 725; Caroline, iv. 258; Rev. Edmund, ii. 443; Ensign Edward, i. 406, ii. 544; Eliza (née Olivier), i. 406; Frances Isabella, ii. 443; J., iv. 258; Marie Dolores Eliza Rosanna (" Lola Montez "), i. 406, ii. 544
Gilchrist, Jane, iii. 5; John Borthwick, i. 264, ii. 463; Mary Anne, i. 264, ii. 463; Thomas, iii. 5
Gildea, Anthony, iii. 421; Charlotte, iii. 421
Giles, Edmund, iii. 810
Gill, D., i. 402; Suzette, i. 402
Gillanders, Eliza, ii. 162; Emily, iv. 219; Harriet, ii. 241; Letitia, ii. 27; Sarah, iv. 233
Gillery, Isabella, iii. 529; Col. Thomas, iii. 529
Gillespie, Margaret, iii. 106; Miss S. H., ii. 167
Gillies, Eleanor, ii. 163; Margaret, ii. 571

Gillman, Catherine (née Bateman), i. 103
Gillmor, Anna, i. 61; Capt. Clotworthy, R.N., i. 61, iv. 252; Leonora Elizabeth, iv. 252
Gilmour, Adam, iii. 166; Flora Anne, iii. 166; Helen, iii. 738; William Little, iii. 738
Gilpin, William, iii. 718
Girdlestone, Rev. Edward, iii. 63
Gisborne, Dorothea, ii. 289; Gen. James, ii. 289
Gittens, Margaret, iv. 541
Gladwell, Dorothea, i. 173; Francis, i. 173
Gladwin, Maj.-Gen. Henry, ii. 107; Mary, ii. 107
Glascott, Beata, ii. 264; John, ii. 264
Glass, Rachel (née Pollock), iii. 550; Thomas, iii. 550
Glasse, Anne Susannah, ii. 223; Rev. John, ii. 223
Gledstanes, George, iii. 508; Sophia, iii. 508
Glegg, Mrs. (née Hamilton), ii. 375
Glenelg, Baron, see Grant, Charles
Gloucester, Prince William, Duke of, ii. 36
Glubb, Emily Warren, iii. 451; Rev. John, iii. 451
Glynne, Frances, i. 411; Sir John, 6th Bt., i. 411
Goddard, Emma Goodenough, ii. 138; John Harvey, ii. 138
Godfrey, Arabella, ii. 32; Sir William, Bt., ii. 32
Godsalve, Ellen, iii. 615; William, iii. 615
Golding, Bailie, iv. 47; Elizabeth, iii. 268
Goldingham, John, iii. 556; Louisa Maria (née Popham), iii. 556
Golightly, Frances Margaret, ii. 303, iii. 785; William, iii. 785
Golledge, Frances, ii. 297; Isaac, ii. 297
Goodchild, Harriot, ii. 539, 541
Goodenough, Henrietta Sarah, iii. 358; Rev. S., iii. 358
Goodman, Ann, iii. 296
Goodrich, Augusta, ii. 55; Bartlet, ii. 55

Goodwin, Susan, ii. 581
Goodwyn, Catherine Laura, iv. 430; Charles Samuel, iv. 430; Elizabeth Amelia, ii. 408
Gordon, Hon. Alexander, Lord Rockville, ii. 431; Sir Alexander, Bt. of Lesmoir, ii. 528, iii. 92; Alexander, iii. 163, iv. 294; Anne, ii. 101, iii. 92, 94, 561; Ann Forbes, iii. 787; Arthur, iv. 51; Catharine, ii. 431, 432, iv. 51; Charles, iii. 637, iv. 106; Diana, ii. 528; Elizabeth, iii. 74, iv. 107, 494; Ellinor, iv. 3; Euphemia, i. 321; George, 9th Marquess of Huntly and 5th Earl of Aboyne, ii. 287; Georgiana, iii. 637; Gilbert, iii. 259; Grace, i. 287, 290; Helen, i. 74; Hugh, ii. 410, iv. 107; Isabella, iv. 294; Isobel (or Elizabeth), iii. 357; Capt. James, iii. 787; Jenny, ii. 320; John, 3rd Earl of Aboyne, ii. 290; Judith Margaretta, iii. 156; Margaret, ii. 410, iv. 106; Margaret Isabella, ii. 539; Mary, iii. 163; Patricia Heron, iii. 259; Sir Robert, Bt. of Invergordon, ii. 101; Robert, iii. 357, 561, iv. 3; Susannah, iii. 535; Rev. Theodore, iv. 494; William, 2nd Earl of Aberdeen, ii. 284, 432; Sir William, Bt. of Embo, iii. 156; last Duchess of, see Brodie, Elizabeth
Gordon, Sir Alexander Penrose Cumming-, Bt., ii. 95, iii. 206; Helen Penuel Cumming-, ii. 95; Margaret Grace Cumming-, iii. 206
Gore, Anne, iii. 667, iv. 504; Capt. Arthur, iv. 504; Eliza Margaret, ii. 186; Vice-Adm. Sir John, iii. 667; Col. John, iii. 667; Selina Elizabeth, i. 287; William, i. 287, ii. 186
Gorges, Hamilton, i. 132; Susan, i. 132
Gort, 1st Viscount, see Prendergast, John
Gorwyn, Mary Lambert, iv. 314; William Lambert, iv. 314
Gosling, James, ii. 281; Julia Harriet, ii. 281
Gossett, Anna Maria, ii. 538

Gough, Dorothy, iii. 657; Elizabeth, iv. 38; Hon. Frances Maria, ii. 319; F. M. Viscount Sir Hugh, ii. 319; Nathan, iii. 657; Rev. Thomas, iv. 38
Gould, Anne, iii. 214; Blissett William, iv. 239; Emma, iv. 239
Goullet, Margaret, i. 208; Peter, i. 208
Govane, Ann, iii. 162; Robert, iii. 162
Gow, Margaret, iv. 125
Gowan, Elizabeth, ii. 176; Juliana, iii. 342; Juliana Catherine, ii. 19; Maria, iii. 377
Gowdy, William, iii. 84
Graeme, see also Graham
Graeme, Alexina, iii. 262; John, iii. 262; Marjory, iii. 262; Patrick, iii. 262
Grafton, 3rd Duke of, see FitzRoy, Augustus Henry
Graham, Alexander, ii. 232, 381, iii. 266; Anne, ii. 235; Anne Jane, ii. 232; Charlotte Cunningham, iii. 270; Elizabeth, ii. 73, 102; Elizabeth Catherine, iii. 112; Elizabeth Susannah, iv. 93; Ellinor Crawfurd, iv. 266; Emma Rose, ii. 20; Frances Anne, ii. 404; Francis, ii. 235; James, 1st Marquess of Montrose, iii. 806; James, i. 239; James, M.D., ii. 204; Major James George, ii. 602; Jane Augusta, ii. 453; Jean, ii. 419; John, iii. 142, 455, 764; Josephine Morison, iv. 413; Margaret, iii. 734; Margaret Campbell, ii. 381; Marion, i. 239; Mary, iii. 455; Phoebe, ii. 204; Sir Robert, 8th Bt. of Esk, ii. 404, iv. 93; Sir Robert, Kt., iii. 767; Robert, ii. 73, iii. 262; Sarah, iii. 142; Sarah Falconer, iv. 238; Thomas, iii. 455; Wilhelmina, iii. 130; William, ii. 20, 102, iii. 130, iv. 238, 377; Dr. William, iv. 413; W., M.D., iii. 112; Col., iii, 270
Grainger, Barbara, iii. 477; John, iii. 477
Granby, Marquess of, see Manners, John
Grand, Eliza, iii. 145

INDEX OF NAMES

Grandison, Mary, ii. 175
Grange, Belinda, i. 104; Maynard Eliza, i. 170; Rev. Richard Chappell, i. 104
Grant, Andrew, iii. 716; Catherine, iii. 716; Charles, Baron Glenelg, ii. 321; Clementina, ii. 97; Elizabeth, iii. 765, 778, iv. 360; Elspeth, iv. 492; George, iv. 337; Grace, iii. 252; Grizel, iii. 146; Helen, iii. 763; Honor, i. 242; Isabella, iii. 807; Sir James, of Grant, ii. 97; James, i. 242, 405; Jane, iii. 500; Jean, iii. 361; Maj.-Gen. John, i. 255; Major John, i. 191; Rev. John, iv. 360; Sir John Peter, iii. 500; Sir Lodovick, Bt., iii. 162; Louisa, iv. 157; Margaret, iii. 722; Margaret Cussans, iv. 337; Martina, ii. 534; Mary, i. 255, ii. 425, iii. 200, 608; Matilda Campbell, i. 191; Rev. Moses, iii. 608; Patrick, Lord Elchies, iii. 716; Patrick, iii. 252; Rev. Patrick, iii. 763, 807; Penuel, iii. 162; Sarah, iii. 765; Suetonius, ii. 425; Susannah (née Coffin), i. 405; Temperance (née Talmage), ii. 425; Rev. William, iii. 146; Surg. William Lewis, ii. 534; of Laggan, iii. 192
Grant, Sir George Macpherson-, 1st Bt., iii. 197
Granville, John, iii. 392; Maria Georgina, iii. 392
Gravatt, Anne, i. 355; Col. William, i. 355
Gravely, Anna Maria (née Carter), ii. 420
Graves, Abigail, iv. 6
Gray, Agnes (née Methven), iii. 286; Hon. Anne, iii. 470; Ann, iii. 363; Catherine, iv. 174; Charles, i. 312; Charlotte Elizabeth, iv. 471; Elizabeth, ii. 504; George, ii. 274; Helen, i. 312, ii. 418; Capt. James, R.N., iv. 471; Jean, ii. 274; John, 11th Lord Gray of Kinfauns, iii. 470; John, iii. 363
Graydon, Anne, ii. 626; George, i. 313; Robert, ii. 626
Greaves, Margaret Ellen, iii. 460; William, iii. 460

Green, Decima, iii. 371; Rev. James Carter, ii. 355; Rev. Jonathan, iii. 371; Mary, ii. 355; Sarah, iii. 701; Susannah, iii. 488
Greene, Georgina Rebecca, ii. 407; Rev. Henry, iv. 165; Mary (née Stainforth), iv. 165; Nuttall, ii. 407
Greenlaw, Alexander, i. 290; Anna, i. 290; Charles Beckett, ii. 202; Sarah, ii. 202
Greentree, Anne, iv. 46; Bridget, i. 309; Charlotte, iv. 533; Capt. Watkin, iv. 46
Greenwollers, Weston, iii. 789
Greer, Harriet D'Oyly, i. 53; William, i. 53
Gregorie, Katharine, ii. 307
Gregory, Ann Margaret, ii. 201, 202, iii. 778; Dr. John, iii. 778
Greig, Fanny, i. 18
Grenville, George, 1st Marquess of Buckingham, iii. 103
Greville, Emmeline Bethea, iii. 769; Robert Kaye, iii. 769
Grey, Francis, iv. 291; George Harry, 5th Earl of Stamford and Warrington, i. 338; Lady Henrietta, i. 338; Sarah Frances, iv. 291
Grieve, Katherine, iv. 89; Johnston, iii. 398
Griffin, Elizabeth, iii. 621; John, iii. 621; Mary, i. 302; Mary Ann, i. 381
Griffith, Catherine, i. 377; Mrs. Eliza, ii. 349; John, i. 377
Griffiths, Maria Louisa (née Exshaw), ii. 148; William, ii. 148
Grifiths, Dorothea, ii. 451
Grimes, Caroline, ii. 84; Capt. Comy. G.H., ii. 84; Maria, iii. 630; Sophia Maria, iv. 162
Grimsdick, John, ii. 124, iii. 376; Maria Louisa, iii. 375; Mary Jordon, ii. 124
Grimston, Hon. George, ii. 123; James Bucknall, 3rd Viscount Grimston, i. 28; Mary, ii. 123
Grosset, Diana, iv. 382; Walter, iv. 382
Grote, Andrew, ii. 335; Caroline, ii. 335
Grounds, Frances (née Trevor), iv. 304; William, iv. 304

INDEX OF NAMES

Grove, Catherine Leslie, ii. 209; Leslie, ii. 209
Groves, Major George, iii. 85; Susan Eliza, iii. 85
Grundgeiger, Lady Rosina Magdalena, i. 331
Grundy, Grace, iv. 513; Samuel, iv. 513
Guest, Jennett (Jeanette), iii. 701
Guise, Elizabeth, iv. 186; Capt. John, iv. 186
Guitton, Elizabeth, iii. 299; John, iii. 299
Gunn, Ann Elizabeth, i. 267
Gunning, Catherine, i. 283; Capt. William, i. 283
Gurley, Sarah, iii. 3
Gurney, Anne, iii. 794; John, iii. 794
Gustavus III, King of Sweden, ii. 50
Guthrie, D. C., ii. 325; James, i. 334; Lilias, i. 334; Margaret, iii. 433
Gwilt, George, ii. 510; Mary Ann Milligan, ii. 510
Gwynedd, Owen, iii. 206
Gwynne, Harriet Rose, iv. 245; Laurence, iv. 245
Gybbon, Emma, iv. 157

H

Haddock, Sarah, iii. 406
Haden, Rev. Alexander Bunn, iv. 312
Hadfield, Ann, ii. 584; John, ii. 584
Hagar, Rev. George, ii. 517; Julia Maria, ii. 517
Haig, Alexander, i. 104, iv. 218; Janet, i. 212; Louisa Eliza Catherine, i. 104; Maria, iii. 424; Maria Isabella, iv. 218; Robert, iii. 424; William, i. 212
Haigs, Mary Ann, ii. 511
Hailes, Henry, iii. 504
Haines, Elizabeth, iii. 92; Thomas, R.N., iii. 92
Hair, Jane, iv. 584
Haldane, George, iii. 720; James Alexander, ii. 119; Janet, ii. 3, iii. 720; Mary, ii. 119; Robert, ii. 3
Hale, Maj.-Gen. John, iii. 48; Mary, iii. 48
Hales, Robert, i. 70

Halfhide, Amelia Margaret, ii. 366; Major Benjamin, i. 193, ii. 366; Sophia Mary, i. 193
Halford, George, iii. 189; Susanna Ann, iii. 189
Halhed, Caroline Alice, ii. 572; Frances Alicia, i. 333; Helena Louisa (née Reybaud), i. 389; Nathaniel Brassey, i. 389; Nathaniel John, ii. 572
Halkett, Christian, iii. 754; Sir John Wedderburn, 4th Bt. of Pitfirrane, iii. 576, iv. 421; Sir Peter, 1st Bt. of Gosford, iii. 754; Sholto Charlotte, iii. 576
Hall, Charlotte, iii. 157; Daniel, ii. 390; Ellen, ii. 378; Emily Octavia, ii. 390; Lieut. J.F.D'E.W., iii. 547; Marion, iii. 764; Mary, iii. 448; Reynold, iii. 783; Ruth, iii. 783; William, iii. 157; Major, ii. 378
Halliday, John, iii. 90
Hallifax, Charlotte, iv. 430; Rev. Robert, iv. 430
Hallowes, Ann, i. 92; Brabazon, i. 92
Halsey, Henry, ii. 128; Matilda Elizabeth, ii. 128
Hamer, Athelstan, ii. 434; Elizabeth, ii. 434
Hamerton, Margaret (née Young), iv. 544
Hamilton, Alexander, iii. 23; Surg. Alexander, iii. 549; Lady Anne, i. 320; Britannia, ii. 326; Celia Black, iv. 142; Charles, ii. 326, iii. 54; Christian, iii. 676; Douglas, 8th Duke of Hamilton, iii. 427; Dunbar Douglas, 4th Earl of Selkirk, ii. 361; Elizabeth, ii. 38, iii. 23, 427, iv. 122; Frances, i. 40; Sir Frederick, Bt., i. 40; Lieut. George, iii. 278, iv. 183; Grizel, iii. 791; Harriette, iv. 183; Mrs. Henrietta Anne, iii. 54; James Martin, iv. 142; Jean, ii. 207, iii. 779; Jemima R., ii. 527; Hon. John, ii. 361; John, iii. 472, 791; Major J., ii. 240; Lady Katherine, ii. 361; Margaret, iii. 549; Mary, ii. 361; Mary Anne, iii. 79; Richard, 4th Viscount Boyne, iii.

INDEX OF NAMES

81; Robert, iii. 779; Sarah Breviter, iii. 278; Hon. Sophia, iii. 81; Capt. Thomas, ii. 527; Ursilla, iv. 128; William, iii. 676; 8th Duke of, *see* Hamilton, Douglas
Hamilton, George Baillie-, 10th Earl of Haddington, ii. 376; Capt. Thomas Baillie-, iii. 521
Hammond, Ann, iv. 83; Mary, iv. 47
Hamond, Adm. Sir Graham Eden, 2nd Bt., iii. 290
Hampden, John, iii. 258
Hampton, Mary Sarah, iii. 447
Hancock, Eliza Douce, iii. 236; William, M.D., iii. 236
Hannay, Jane, ii. 310; Maria, ii. 418
Hansard, Capt. John, iii. 290; Mrs., iii. 290
Hansford, Elizabeth, ii. 509; Capt., R.N., ii. 509
Hanson, Anne, i. 174; Catherine, i. 40; Charlotte, i. 171; William, i. 171, 174
Harbord, Edward, 3rd Baron Suffield, i. 40; Hon. Georgiana Mary, i. 40
Harcourt, Anne, iii. 446; Harriet, i. 420; John, iv. 111; Letitia Sarah Maria, iv. 111; Richard, iii. 446
Hardcastle, Charlotte, iv. 140; Robert, ii. 47; William, iv. 140
Harden, Susannah, i. 83
Hardie, Mrs., iii. 605
Harding, Elizabeth, iii. 271; Major Richard, iv. 48; William, iii. 271
Hardinge, Rev. Sir Charles, Bt., i. 197
Hardwicke, Maria Theresa, ii. 460; Sarah, ii. 64
Hardy, Charlotte Savery, iii. 572; John, iv. 57; Maria Eleanora (*née* Shairp), iv. 57; Susanna, iv. 301; Thomas Carteret, iii. 572
Hardyman, Marianne, iii. 112
Hare, Barbara, i. 280, 288; Lady Mary, i. 81; William, 1st Earl of Listowel, i. 81
Harington, Rev. Edward, ii. 471; Fanny, ii. 471, iii. 85; Frances Sophia, ii. 529; Henry, M.D., iv. 253, 254; Henry Hawes, iii. 636; Sir James, 9th Bt., iv. 175; Rev. John, iii. 85; John Herbert, ii. 529; Mary Charlotte, iii. 636; Susan Isabella, iv. 253, 254

Hariot, Caroline Matilda, i. 164
Harper, Margaret, ii. 232
Harriman, Elizabeth, iv. 49; John, iv. 49
Harrington, 7th Earl of, *see* Stanhope, Charles Wyndham
Harriott, George, iii. 621; Sarah, ii. 407, iii. 699; Sarah Abbott, iii. 621
Harris, Anna, ii. 150; Caroline, iii. 68; Charles, i. 369; Elizabeth, i. 369, iii. 476; Mrs. Elizabeth, iv. 516; Frances Russell, iv. 381; Hamlyn, iv. 381; Henry Braham, iii. 68; Milborough Anne, ii. 517; S., iii. 476; Thomas, ii. 517
Harrison, Eliza, ii. 72, iv. 274; Harriet, ii. 394; H., iii. 288; Sarah Jane, iii. 288; W., ii. 394
Harrop, Caroline Mann, iii. 10; Josiah, iii. 10
Hart, Emma Deborah, iv. 311; Nathaniel Henry, iv. 311
Hartley (or Huntley), Mary Magdalene, ii. 181
Harvey, Anne, iii. 543; Barbara, iii. 7; Caroline, iv. 562; Catherine, i. 40, ii. 618; Elizabeth (*née* Mitchell), iii. 302; Francis, ii. 618; John, iii. 7; Margaret, i. 126; Thomas, iii. 302; Rev. William, i. 126
Hasell, Christopher, iii. 800; Edward, iv. 8; Elizabeth, iii. 800; Jane, iv. 8
Hasleby, Ann, iii. 227, 479, 741; Sarah, iii. 478
Hassard, Catherine, ii. 530; Robert, ii. 530
Hassell, Charlotte Eleanor Mary, i. 49; Richard, i. 49
Hastings, Edith S., iii. 156; Rev. Penyston, ii. 248; Sarah, iv. 525; Warren, i. 331, ii. 11, 248, iii. 436, iv. 81, 326, 451
Hastings, Francis Rawdon-, 1st Marquess of Hastings, iv. 525; Lady, ii. 370
Hatfeldt, Freiheer, ii. 410; Gertruida Christina (*née* Vanrenen), ii. 410
Hathorn, George, i. 335; Margaret, iii. 129; Wilhelmina, i. 335
Hatsell, Elizabeth (*née* Arnold), i. 53

Havell, Amelia, iv. 564; John, iv. 564
Haverham, Mary Anne, i. 320
Havers, Catherine, i. 121; Thomas, i. 121
Hawkes, Lt.-Col. Jeremiah, iv. 200
Hawkesworth, Judith, iv. 164; Sir Walter, 2nd Bt., iv. 165
Hawkins, Anna Maria, iii. 789; Bridget, ii. 503; Catherine, iv. 388; Edward, iv. 388; Elizabeth Magdalene, ii. 428; Rev. Fancis, iii. 789, 794; Harriet, ii. 505, iii. 801; Sir Henry, Baron Brampton, iii. 794; John, ii. 562; Rev. John, ii. 503; Mary, ii. 604; Mary Anne, ii. 562; Thomas, ii. 604
Haworth, Ann, iii. 494; Jonathan, iii. 494
Hay, Agnes Dickson, iii. 808; Gen. Andrew, ii. 91; Catharine, iv. 97; Christian, ii. 388; Clementina, ii. 92; C., ii. 92; Dorothea, ii. 91; Edward, ii. 613; Eliza (née Wagstaff), ii. 613; George, 7th Marquess of Tweedale, iii. 130; Grace, iii. 197, 356; Sir Hector Maclean, 7th Bt., iii. 744; Isabella, i. 219, iii. 746, iv. 632, 634; James, iii. 197, 356; John, 2nd Marquess of Tweedale, iv. 29; John, ii. 388, iii. 130, iv. 632, 634; Margaret, iii. 130; Susan, iv. 29; Thomas, iii. 808; Lord William, of Newhall, iv. 29
Hayes, Barbara, iii. 734; Sarah, iv. 382
Hayles, Ann, iv. 526
Hayley, Dinah, i. 79; George, i. 79
Haynes, H. C., ii. 136; Mrs. Sarah, ii. 136
Haysome, Bridget, iv. 54; Thomas, iv. 54
Hayward, Sarah, iii. 346; Starlina, ii. 212
Hayward, Anne Curtis-, iii. 397
Hazell, Sarah, iii. 452
Head, Elizabeth Lindsay, iv. 168; Sir Francis Bond, 1st Bt., iv. 168; Capt. James, iv. 168; Capt. Michael, R.N., iii. 70
Heale, Julia, iv. 418
Healey, Emma, iv. 291; T., iv. 291

Heapy, Harriot (née Sparkes), iv. 150
Heard, Sir Isaac, Kt., Garter, iii. 412
Hearsey, Hyder Young, i. 348, iv. 565; Mary Owen, iv. 565
Heath, Anne Raymond (née Dunbar), ii. 96; George, ii. 96
Heathcote, Rev. Henry, iii. 249; Jeanetta, iii. 249
Heathfield, 1st Baron, see Eliott, George Augustus
Hebbron, Elizabeth, iv. 9
Heblethwayte, Frances, iii. 534; James, iii. 534
Hedger, Frances Brand, ii. 154; Francis, ii. 154
Helm, Maria, ii. 356, 357
Helsham, John, ii. 229; Rose, ii. 229
Heming, Elizabeth, ii. 566
Henderson, Andrew, ii. 94; Christian, iii. 155, 472; Dorothea, ii. 94; William, iii. 155
Hennes, Alice, iv. 120, 131
Hennessy, Anne, iv. 173; Isabella, iii. 250; Jane, ii. 445; Mathias, iii. 250; Mrs. (née Manley), iii. 219
Henry, Rev., iii. 228
Henshaw, Egerton, iii. 36; Elizabeth, iii. 36
Hensley, Eliza, iii. 567; John T., iii. 567
Henzell, Catherine, i. 242; Philip, i. 242
Hepburn, Ann, i. 225; Helen, iv. 191; John, iv. 191; Sophia, iii. 6
Hepburn, Sir George Buchan-, 1st Bt., iv. 634
Hepburne, Catherine Gordon, iii. 494; Robert, iii. 494
Herbert, Rev. Arthur, iv. 148; Frances Margaret, iv. 148; Louisa (née Middleton), iii. 292; Mary, i. 70; Thomas, iii. 21
Herd, Henrietta, iii. 641
Heron, Capt. George, iii. 565; Mary, iii. 565
Heronshaw, Henrietta, iii. 614; Robert, iii. 614
Hervey, Charlotte, iii. 570
Hesilrige, Sir Arthur, 9th Bt., iv. 471
Hetherington, John, ii. 461, iv. 635; Mary, iv. 635
Hewetson, Anne, iii. 639; Ven. Archdeacon Nicholas, iii. 639

INDEX OF NAMES

Hewett, Fanny Bartholomew, ii. 74 ; William Nathan Wrighte, ii. 74
Hewitt, Elizabeth Henrietta, iii. 796 ; Henry, iii. 796 ; James, 1st Viscount Lifford, iv. 202 ; Hon. William Williams, iv. 202
Hewson, Margaret, ii. 31
Heyland, Alexander Charles, iv. 74 ; Mary Anne, iv. 227 ; Rowley, iv. 227
Heyward, Henry, iv. 554 ; Mary, iv. 554
Heywood, Isabella, iii. 365
Hibbard, Elizabeth, ii. 207, 208
Hick, Sarah, ii. 379
Hickburn, Mary, ii. 35
Hickey, Lucy Young, i. 252 ; Mary, iii. 210 ; Michael, iii. 210 ; Sophia Charlotte, iv. 550 ; William, i. 252, iii. 774, iv. 324 ; ——, R.N., iv. 550
Hickie, Elizabeth, iv. 218
Hickland, Françoise, ii. 50
Hickman, Eliza, i. 407 ; Richard, i. 407
Hicks, Anne, ii. 203 ; Elizabeth, iv. 105 ; John William, ii. 203 ; William, iv. 105
Hickson, Elizabeth, ii. 153 ; George, ii. 153 ; Capt. Theodore, iii. 479
Hiern, John, iv. 510 ; Mary, iv. 510
Higginbotham, Florinda, iv. 393 ; John, iv. 393 ; William, iii. 202
Higgins, Charlotte Julia, ii. 342 ; Frances, ii. 528 ; George, ii. 342
Highmore, Anthony, ii. 548
Hill, Alexander, ii. 207 ; Ann, iv. 232, 292 ; Anne Byam Wyke, iv. 315 ; Caroline, iii. 384 ; Cecilia, iv. 74 ; Daniel, iv. 315 ; Mrs. Diana, ii. 393 ; Eliza, i. 62, 156 ; Elizabeth Ann, iv. 475 ; Sir Hugh, Bt., i. 156 ; James, iv. 94 ; John Montgomery, iii. 384, iv. 74 ; Margaret, iv. 94 ; Mary, ii. 100, iii. 615 ; Miarah, iv. 475 ; Robert, ii. 100 ; Thomas, iv. 292 ; West, M.D., i. 62
Hillhouse, Elizabeth, iv. 379 ; Grace A., iv. 7 ; J. W., iv. 7 ; Martin, iv. 379
Hilton, John, iii. 678 ; Mary, iii. 678
Hinchcliffe, Frances, i. 349 ; Rt. Rev. John, i. 349

Hinde, Jane, iv. 633
Hindmarsh, Elizabeth (*née* Fenwick), ii. 172
Hinds, Caroline, ii. 420
Hinga, Bibi Sahiba, ii. 248
Hintz, Anna Maria Theresa, iv. 287
Hislop, Francis, iv. 77 ; Jane, iv. 77
Hitch, Eloisa, iii. 783 ; Rev. James, iii. 783
Hitchins, Lydia, iii. 95
Hoare, Bridget, ii. 399 ; Hannah Buckler, i. 339 ; John, i. 339 ; Stephen, iv. 153
Hobart, Anne Catherine, iii. 313 ; George, 3rd Earl of Buckinghamshire, iii. 313 ; Hon. Henry, iii. 313
Hobday, Benjamin, i. 16, 269 ; Charlotte Nott, i. 16 ; Maria Mary Anne, i. 269
Hobson, Phoebe, iii. 349
Hockley, Clementina Clara Jane, iii. 81 ; Joseph, iii. 81
Hodge, Eliza, iv. 210
Hodges, Harriet Ann, iii. 47 ; Jenny, iii. 86 ; Mary, i. 424 ; Thomas Twisden, iii. 403
Hodgkinson, Charles, ii. 483 ; Emily, ii. 483
Hodgson, Georgiana, ii. 267 ; G., ii. 267 ; Honoria, iii. 25 ; Joseph, iv. 60 ; Marianne Elizabeth, iv. 60 ; Samuel, iii. 25
Hodson, Charles Harvey, i. 102 ; Marian, i. 102 ; Major William Stephen Raikes, iv. 178
Hogan, Eliza Sophia, iv. 27 ; Frances, iii. 332 ; Mary, i. 388 ; Thomas Cockerell, i. 388, iii. 332
Hogg, Isabella Maria, iii. 323 ; Jonah, iv. 291 ; Jonah John, iii. 323 ; Maria Helen, iv. 291
Holden, Elizabeth, iv. 31 ; George, iv. 31 ; Mary (*née* Keiller), ii. 575 ; Richard Gleadhill, ii. 575
Holder, Ashley, ii. 136 ; H. Evans, M.D., ii. 136 ; John, iii. 758 ; Sarah Phillis, iii. 758
Holgate, Rev. George, iii. 667 ; Isabella, iii. 667
Hollamby, Sophia, iii. 801
Holland, Anne, iv. 185 ; Henry, i. 407 ; Mary Frances, i. 407 ; Rev. Nicholas, iv. 185

INDEX OF NAMES

Hollings, Frances, iii. 225; Sophia, i. 181; Susan, iv. 257; William C., i. 181
Hollingworth, Ann, iv. 152
Holloway, Charles, iv. 471; Maria, iii. 796; Susan Eliza, iv. 471
Holmes, Rev. Gervas, iv. 475; Matilda Martha, iv. 4; William Anthony, iv. 4; Mrs. (née Owen), iii. 441
Holroyd, Maj.-Gen. Charles, iii. 792
Holston, Elizabeth, iv. 459
Holt, Eliza, iii. 735; Harriet, ii. 260; Thomas L., iv. 342; Zillah, iv. 342
Holte, Marianne, iv. 342; Rev. Dr., iv. 342
Holwell, Anna, iv. 543; Elizabeth, iii. 536; James, iii. 536; John Zephaniah, i. 143, 144, iii. 536, iv. 543
Holyland, Mary, i. 305, iv. 142; Thomas, i. 305, iv. 142
Homan, Margaret, ii. 619; Philip, ii. 619
Home, Rev. Alexander, 9th Earl of Home, ii. 376; Lady Charlotte, ii. 376; Elizabeth, iii. 92; Helen, iii. 770; William, iii. 770
Homfray, Ann Maria, iii. 642; Sir Jeremiah, iii. 642; John, iii. 642; Mary (née Richards), iii. 642
Honyman, Helen, iii. 798; Adm. Robert, iii. 798
Hood, Jean, iv. 495; Mrs., iii. 50
Hooker, Anne, iii. 462; Rev. Dr. Thomas Redman, iii. 462
Hooper, Benjamin, iii. 274; Penelope, i. 21; Sarah, iii. 274; William, i. 21
Hope, James, ii. 174; John, 2nd Earl of Hopetoun, iii. 172; Lady Margaret, iii. 172; Margaret, ii. 174; Sarah, i. 70
Hopetoun, 2nd Earl of, see Hope, John
Hopkins, Amelia, iv. 133; Capt. Charles, iv. 133; Charlotte Rozina, ii. 369; R. T., iii. 296
Hopkinson, Caroline, i. 188; Comdr. Simon, R.N., i. 188
Hopper, Capt. Edward, i. 55; Eleanor, iii. 137, 205; Elizabeth, iv. 176; Harriet, i. 55; Henry, iv. 176; Henry Hudson, iii. 137, 205
Hore, Elizabeth, i. 190; Col. Walter, i. 190
Hornby, Rev. Geoffry, i. 329; Lucy, i. 329
Horne, Eliza Kearton, i. 398; John, i. 398
Horner, Katherine Murray, iii. 98; Leonard, iii. 98
Horsford, Bannatyne, ii. 7
Horsley, John, iii. 337
Hough, C., of Monmouth, ii. 466; Rev. George, ii. 466; Rev. George Henry, iii. 95; Mary Anne, ii. 466; Louisa, iii. 497; Samuel, iii. 497; Sarah Swaine, iii. 95
Houghton, Anne, iii. 639; Catherine, ii. 462; Ellen, iii. 529; Henry Thomas, iii. 529, 639, iv. 256; Maria, iii. 485; Maria Frances, iv. 256; William, ii. 462
Hounsom, George, iii. 311; Lucy, iii. 311
Houston, Alexander, iv. 339; Elizabeth Catherine, iii. 87; H., iii. 87; Katherine, iv. 339; Martha Muir, iv. 488
Howard, Maria, iii. 513; Philip, iii. 513; Thomas, 14th Earl of Suffolk and Berks., iii. 680; Capt. Thomas, iv. 89
Howden, James, ii. 415; Magdalen, iii. 783; Margaret, ii. 415; William, iii. 783
Howe, Elizabeth Lacy, i. 207; Emanuel Scrope, 2nd Viscount Howe, iii. 57; Capt. Hon. Thomas, iii. 57; Lt.-Col., i. 207
Howel, Miss, iv. 75
Howell, Miss E. A., iv. 75; Ilted, iii. 638; Rhoda Cecilia, iii. 638
Howett, Eleanor, iv. 484; Maria, i. 206
Howison, Ann, iii. 471; W., iii. 471
Howitson, Sarah, i. 99; Thomas, i. 99
Hudgson, Catherine, iii. 750
Hudleston, John, iv. 254
Hudson, James, iii. 541; Mary Elizabeth Cadoux, iii. 541
Huet, Elizabeth, i. 133
Huffington, Hessy, ii. 457; William, ii. 457

INDEX OF NAMES 677

Hughes, Ann Somerset, ii. 34; Benjamin O'Neill, i. 97; Elizabeth, ii. 401; Georgiana, i. 50; Henry, iii. 360; Margaret, iii. 788; Mary, iv. 392; Mary Anne, i. 97; Mary Dale, iii. 360; Capt. Philip, i. 50; Rev. Pierce, ii. 401; Samuel, iv. 392; Sydney Jane, iii. 228; Sir William Bulkeley, iii. 228; William Lewis, 1st Baron Dinorben, iii. 800; Major, iv. 118

Hull, Mrs. Frances, iii. 47

Hulse, Sir Edward, Bt., ii. 149; Frances, ii. 149

Hume, Elizabeth, ii. 232; Georgiana, ii. 281; Rt. Rev. John, D.D., iv. 87; Joseph, ii. 99; Sophia, iv. 87; Rev. Travers, ii. 281

Humfrays, Charlotte, i. 115

Humphreys, Anne, iv. 76; Julia, iii. 411; Lucy Nice, iii. 336; Condr. Richard, iii. 336, iv. 76, 573; Sarah, iv. 573; William, iii. 411

Humphries, Jean (*née* Ragull), iii. 592; Samuel, iii. 592

Hunt, Elizabeth, iii. 55; James, iii. 55; John, iv. 208; Margaret, i. 384; Mary, iv. 220

Hunter, Agnes, i. 220, ii. 453; Rev. Dr. Andrew, iii. 698; Anne, ii. 325, 473, iii. 213, iv. 258, 511; Charlotte, i. 423; David, ii. 325; Diana, iii. 60; Elizabeth, iii. 602, iv. 293; Elizabeth Ann, iii. 634; Esther, iv. 115; Capt. George, i. 423; Grace, iii. 698; James, ii. 473, iv. 420; Jane, ii. 473; Janet, iii. 652; Jean, i. 275; John, iii. 60; Margaret, i. 290, iv. 420; Mary, iv. 298; Mary Ann, ii. 67; Robert, i. 290, iii. 652; Thomas, iii. 634, iv. 115, 258; Thomas Montgomery, iii. 213; William, i. 220; Surg. William, iii. 602; Major, iv. 298; Mr., iii. 170

Huntley (or Hartley), Mary Magdalene, ii. 181

Huntly, Marquess of, *see* Gordon, George

Huntridge, Miss (? Frances), iv. 8; Richard, ii. 212

Hurst, Frederica Helen, iv. 81; George P., iv. 81

Hussey, Ellen, ii. 190; Laura, i. 246; Peter Bodkin, ii. 190; Rear-Adm. Sir Richard, i. 246

Hutchings, Julia, iii. 559; Rev. Robert Sparke, iii. 559

Hutchinson, Eliza, iii. 511; Grace, ii. 66; Grace Elizabeth, ii. 78; Henrietta Maria, iii. 594; Rev. James, iii. 594; J., iii. 511; Dr. W. W., ii. 78

Hutchison, James, i. 350; Margaret, ii. 172; Mary (*née* Clearihue), i. 350

Hutt, Matilda, ii. 224; Richard, ii. 224

Huttmann, G. H., ii. 533; Mary (*née* Willis), ii. 533

Hutton, Christian, iv. 399; John, iv. 399; Maria, iv. 227; William, iv. 227

Huxham, Capt. George Corham, iii. 653

Hyde, John, iii. 505; Louise, iii. 505; Mary Eliza, iv. 135

Hylton, Catherine, i. 206; John, i. 206

Hyslop, John, iii. 184

Hythe, Catherine, iii. 380

I

I'Anson, John, ii. 237; Mary, ii. 237

Imbert, Catherine Perrin (or Piron), iii. 451

Imlach, Catherine, iii. 316

Impett, Louisa Jane, iv. 457; Capt., iv. 457

Impey, Sir Elijah, iii. 13, 620; Mary (*née* Reade), iii. 620; Michael, iv. 636; Molly, iii. 13

Imrie, Alexander Taylor-, i. 159; Elizabeth Taylor-, i. 159

Ince, Mary, iii. 217

Incledon, John, iv. 417; Mary, iv. 417

Inglefield, Ann, ii. 367

Inglis, George, i. 130; John, *see* Wightman, John; Sarah, i. 130; Sophia (*née* Lister), ii. 350; Stewart Boone, iii. 576

Innes, Alexander, iii. 790; Ann Scollay, iv. 28; John, iii. 43; Violet, iii. 790

Inshaw, Hannah, ii. 165

Ireland, Charlotte, iii. 397; John, iii. 397, 784; Sarah, iii. 784
Ironside, Edward, ii. 448; Frances, ii. 448
Irvine, Margaret, iv. 118; Margaret (née Macqueen), iii. 200; Mary, i. 311, iv. 593
Irving, Lt.-Col. John, iii. 438; Julia Frances, iii. 438
Irwin, Elizabeth Helen, iii. 762; Eyles, iii. 492; James, iii. 492, iv. 493; Sarah, iii. 492; Selina, iv. 493; William, iii. 762
Isacke, Clarissa, iii. 738; Mrs. Eleanor, iv. 293; Capt. William Bazett, i. 76
Isham, Rev. Charles Euseby, iv. 440; Charlotte, iv. 440; Sir Justinian, 7th Bt., i. 203; Susannah, i. 203
Isherwood, Anne, iii. 741
Isted, Ambrose, iv. 149; Mary, iv. 149
Ives, Edward, i. 346; Eliza, i. 346

J

Jackson, Amelia Cole (née Jones), ii. 568; Anne (née Hunt), ii. 503; Catherine, iv. 540; Eliza, iii. 129; Elizabeth Amelia, i. 142; Frances, i. 358; Harriet, i. 369, iii. 389; John, i. 358, iii. 129; Rev. J., iv. 540; Lucas, ii. 503; Postle, i. 44; Rebecca, i. 44; William, i. 142, ii. 389
Jacob, Rev. Alexander, iii. 239; Margaret, iii. 239
Jacques, Amélie, i. 184; Harriet, i. 184; Jane, iv. 222; Rev. Jean Victor Daniel, i. 184; Sarah, ii. 566
Jaffray, Abigail, ii. 406; Alexander, ii. 578; Robert, ii. 406
James, Edith Edgecumbe Hoskins, iii. 551; Ellen, iv. 19; John, iii. 551, iv. 19; Sarah, iv. 408; Sophia, iv. 447; Thomas, iv. 379
Jamieson, Elizabeth, ii. 197
Jardine, John, ii. 516; Mary Dundas, ii. 516
Jarret, Charlotte, iv. 40
Jay, Rose (née Hurring), ii. 510; Samuel, ii. 510

Jeffery, John, iii. 432
Jeffreys, Harriet, iii. 391; Julia Anne, iii. 18; Rev. Richard, iii. 18
Jelfe, Charlotte, ii. 518; Capt., R.N., ii. 518
Jell, Emma, iii. 55; William, iii. 55
Jenkins, Emma Maria, i. 350; Jane, i. 227
Jenner, Anne, ii. 112; Mary Anne, i. 264; Robert, i. 264, ii. 112
Jennings, Charlotte, iii. 230; Capt. Robert, iii. 230; Sarah, iv. 504, 505
Jephson, Philippa, iv. 398
Jepson, Matilda Deborah, iii. 82
Jervis, Mary, ii. 165
Jervis, Sir John Jervis-White-, 1st Bt., ii. 165, iv. 456
Jessop, Ebenezer, i. 171; Leah, i. 171
Jewtoo, Alice, iii. 758
Jobson, Dorothy (née Fenwick), ii. 172; Mark, ii. 172
Jodrell, Francis, iv. 51
Johns, Mary, iv. 19
Johnson, Anne, iii. 659; Clement, ii. 401; Elizabeth, iii. 318; Frances, iii. 710, iv. 412; Francis, M.D., iii. 385; Gabriel, iii. 710; Harriet Maria, iv. 316; Sir Henry Allen, 2nd Bt., iv. 316; Jena Rosalie (née Serguel), ii. 269; John, iii. 777; Jonathan, iii. 659; Lydia, ii. 236; Maria, iii. 777; Mary Bannister, iii. 385; P. A., ii. 269; Rebecca, ii. 401; Dr. Samuel, i. 182; Sarah Anne, i. 240; Thomas, iii. 318; William, iv. 287
Johnston, Adam Blair, ii. 621; Alexander, iii. 128; Anna Frederica Thomasin, ii. 406; Anne, ii. 621; Charles, iv. 153; Charlotte, iv. 153; Christian, ii. 361; Lieut. Colin, iv. 205; D., iii. 801; Eleanor Hester Maria, ii. 369; George, iv. 153; Lt.-Col. George, iii. 770; Harriet Maria, iv. 215; Hugh, ii. 628; Jean, iv. 469; Mabel, ii. 628; Madeline, iii. 801; Margaret, ii. 382; Mary M., iii. 128; Nicholas Weld, i. 100; Oliver Charles, ii. 384; Rev. Patrick, ii. 382; Rhoda, ii. 384; Susannah, i. 100

INDEX OF NAMES

Johnstone, Clara, iv. 101; David, iii. 705; Elizabeth, iv. 188; (*alias* Macalister), Frances, iii. 105; Harriot Margaret, i. 4; Surg. James, i. 4; Rev. John, iv. 101; Margaret Penelope, iii. 352; Marion Fairrie, iii. 705; Gen., iii. 352; of Redacres, iv. 188
Jolliffe, Margaret, iii. 205
Jolly, Alexander, i. 428; Esther, i. 427
Jones, Anne, iv. 575; Anne Charlotte (*née* White), i. 149; Arthur, ii. 120, iii. 742; Catherine, iii. 589; Catherine Maria, iv. 536; Christian, iii. 750; Capt. David, i. 149; Elizabeth, iii. 34, iv. 16, 236; Emilia, ii. 581; Frances, iii. 742, iv. 188; Frances Elizabeth, iv. 523; Frances Sarah Place, iii. 440; F. J., iv. 523; Hannah (*née* Inshaw), ii. 165; Hugh, iv. 16; Humphrey Herbert, iv. 536; Rev. Canon John, iii. 34; John, ii. 165, iii. 807; Major John Lloyd, iii. 353; Lucy Eliza, iii. 353; Margaret, i. 353, iii. 757; Mariana, ii. 120; Mary, iii. 758, 807; Mostyn, iv. 575; Robert, iii. 758; Sarah, iv. 561; William, iii. 589, 793, iv. 236; William Walter, iii. 440
Jopp, Elizabeth Jane, iii. 67
Jordan, Hon. Jacob, iv. 294; Mrs., *see* Bland, Dorothea
Jorden, Mary, ii. 400
Jover, Eliza, iii. 792
Judah, Abraham, ii. 444; Mary Anne, ii. 444
Julius, George, M.D., iii. 44
Justamont, Marianne, iii. 46

K

Kashmir, Maharajah of, iv. 273
Kaulie, Félicieuse Georgette Marie, ii. 559
Kay, John, i. 197; Mary (*née* Bradley), i. 197
Kaye, Col. Wilkinson Lister, iii. 362
Keane, Hon. Georgiana Isabella, iii. 505; Sir John, 1st Lord Keane, iii. 505; John, 3rd Baron Keane, iii. 72; Sir Richard, Bt., iii. 505
Kearnan, Margaret Ursula, ii. 499; Maria Theresa, iii. 404; Thomas, ii. 499, iii. 404
Kearney, Frances, ii. 619; Henry John, ii. 619; John, D.D., ii. 619
Keates, Sophia, i. 386
Keating, Christopher, i. 198; Polly, i. 198
Keble, Ann, iii. 514
Kedslie, Agnes Williamson Thompson, i. 51; Surg. Andrew, i. 51
Keily, Anne, iii. 307; Richard, iii. 307
Keir, Catherine, iv. 469; William, iv. 469
Keith, Capt. Sir George Mouat, Bt., R.N., iii. 345
Kekewich, Robert, iii. 220; Susanna, iii. 220
Kelk, Frances Sanders, iii. 211; John, iii. 211
Kellett, Emily, ii. 408; Henry, i. 386, ii. 408; Mary Augusta, i. 386
Kellner, Anna Amelia, ii. 233; Paul, ii. 233, iv. 564; Wilhelmina Elizabeth, iv. 564
Kelly, Col. Arthur, iii. 341; Mrs. Charlotte Sarah, ii. 74; John, iv. 510; Louisa, i. 137; Mary, iii. 341, iv. 510; Col., i. 137; Miss, iii. 336
Kelso, Archibald, iii. 146; Elizabeth (*née* Macharg), iii. 146
Kelson, Ann, iii. 292; Surg. Thomas Mortimer, iii. 292
Kemmis, Anne, iv. 385; Thomas, iv. 385
Kemp, Eliza, iii. 75; Mrs., wife of Col., iii. 75; Miss, iii. 773
Kempthorne, Charlotte, iv. 88; James, iv. 88
Kendall, Mary (*née* Thorp), ii. 335 Rev. Nicholas, i. 329; Russell, ii. 335; Susan, i. 329
Kennedy, Ann (*née* Snodgrass), iv. 146; Duncan, iv. 146; Eliza Ann Gale, iii. 300; George Crookshank, *see* Skipton; Isobel, ii. 57; John, iii. 110; Lieut. John, iii. 300; Letitia, ii. 501; Maria, iii. 110; Mary, ii. 253, iv. 363
Kennett, Agnes Charlotte, ii. 258; Rev. B., ii. 258

Kent, H.R.H. Duke of, see Edward Augustus, Prince
Kent, Susan, i. 208
Keppel, Augustus Frederick, 5th Earl of Albemarle, iv. 175
Ker, Helen, iii. 45; John Bellenden, see Gawler; Sarah, ii. 481; of Broadmeadows, ii. 414
Kerin, Catherine (née Nicholson), ii. 162
Kerr, Claudine Anne (née Palmer), i. 374; Elizabeth, iii. 751; Marianne, ii. 147; Mark, 5th Earl of Antrim, iv. 144; William, ii. 147; William Drury, iii. 759
Kestell, J., i. 389; Sarah, i. 389
Keys, Frances Lina, ii. 141; John, ii. 141; Margaret, iii. 311; Sarah, iv. 241; Tasker, iii. 311
Khairan, Mussamat, iii. 450
Khanum Sahib, iv. 468
Killick, Mary, iv. 435
Kilmorey, 1st Earl of, see Needham, Francis
Kinchant, Richard, iv. 505
King, Ann, i. 386; Christian, iii. 760; Edward, iv. 213; Elizabeth, iii. 155; Elizabeth (née Hyde), ii. 518; Surg. George, iv. 276; Sir Gilbert, 3rd Bt. of Charlestown, iv. 357; Isaac, iii. 155; John, i. 6; Letitia, ii. 279; Maria, iii. 119; Mary, i. 6; Lady Mary Elizabeth, iii. 272, 273; Robert, 2nd Earl of Kingston, iii. 272; Rev., iii. 119
Kingdon, Elizabeth, iii. 349
Kingsale, Lord, see De Courcy
Kingsley, Catherine, i. 286
Kingston, Barbara, iv. 169; Caroline, ii. 57; Eliza, ii. 337; Henrietta, iv. 148; John, ii. 57; 2nd Earl of, see King, Robert
Kinloch, Sir David, Bt., i. 430; Harriet, i. 430; Sir James, 2nd Bt. of Kinloch, iii. 612; Jean, iii. 612, 614; Lord, see Penney, William
Kinnaird, Charles, 6th Baron Kinnaird, ii. 8, iv. 462; Hon. Helen, ii. 8; Isabella, iv. 487; Hon. Margaret, iv. 462
Kinneder, Lord, see Erskine, William
Kinneir, Cecilia Maria Douglas, iii. 117; Sir John Macdonald, iii. 117

Kirby, Barbara, iii. 236; Martha Anne, iii. 651; Thomas, iii. 236; Rev. William, iii. 651
Kirchoffer, Francis, iii. 432; Sarah, iii. 432
Kirk, Sir William, i. 403; William Mortimer, i. 403
Kirkaldy, Barbara, i. 417
Kirkby, Fanny, iii. 649
Kirke, Ann, iii. 258
Kirkwood, Anne Eliza Montague, iv. 43; Col. Tobias, iv. 43
Knight, Elizabeth, ii. 109; Margaret, iii. 710; Mary, iv. 64; Peppard, iii. 35; Adm., ii. 109; Capt., R.N., iii. 710
Knightery, Ann, iv. 432
Knipe, Anna Maria, i. 252; Henrietta Emilia, i. 129; Lieut. Samuel, iii. 719; Capt. William, i. 252, iii. 719
Knox, Alexander, iv. 197; Catherine Letitia, iii. 25; Christian, ii. 288; Elizabeth, ii. 97, 100; Rev. George, iii. 25; Helen, iv. 225; John, i. 355; Louisa, i. 355; Robert Henry, ii. 288
Knyvett, Emma, ii. 60; Fanny, i. 424; William, i. 424, ii. 60
Kohstein, Johanna Anna, iv. 183
Koonden Kuar Bhaije (Mrs. Fullarton), ii. 232
Krempion, Catherine, ii. 461
Krongeiger, see Grundgeiger
"Kumasin, Rana of," iv. 367
Kyan, John Howard, iii. 434; Mary Theresa, iii. 434
Kyd, James, i. 420; Jane (née Cumming), i. 426; Mary Kyd Duckett, i. 141
Kyffin, Mary, ii. 441
Kyte, Henry, ii. 561; Louisa (née Levade), ii. 561

L

Lacon, Sir Edmund, 1st Bt., iii. 430; Henrietta Maria, iii. 430
Laffan, Sir Joseph de Courcy, iv. 226
Laing, Charlotte, iii. 646; James Bruce, iii. 646
Lake, Hon. Amabel, i. 217; Sir Atwell King, Bt., iii. 440; Gerard, 1st Viscount, i. 217, ii. 310

INDEX OF NAMES

Laker, John, iii. 547
Lamb, Mary Sarah, iv. 271
Lambert, Emma Hutchinson, iv. 488; Gen. Sir John, iv. 49; Maj.-Gen. John, iv. 49; John, iv. 80; Margaret, ii. 477; Mary, ii. 36; Mary Juliana, iv. 80; William, ii. 477, iv. 488
Lamborne, Elizabeth, iii. 318
Lambton, John George, 1st Earl of Durham, i. 417
Lamont, Jean, iv. 547
Lance, Mary, iii. 473; William, iii. 473
Landales, Alice, iii. 756; John, iii. 756
Landels, Christiana (née Watherston), iv. 399
Landon, Anna, ii. 566; Rev. Charles Richard, ii. 566
Lane, Elizabeth, iv. 215 ;S., iv. 215
Laney, Jane, ii. 609; John, ii. 609; Sarah, ii. 609
Langford, Anne, iv. 152; Edward Coplin, iv. 152
Langley, Capt. John, i. 368; Leonora, iii. 219; Mallet, i. 368
Langrishe, Olympia, ii. 328; Robert, ii. 328
Langstaffe, George, iii. 718; Margaret, iii. 718
Lanigan, Mary Mabel, ii. 97
Laprimaudaye, Jane Elizabeth, iii. 48; Stephen, iii. 48
Larkins, Ann (née Bradley), i. 197; Eliza, iv. 372; Georgiana Grueber, iii. 634; John, i. 197; John Pascal, ii. 324; Laura, iii. 784; Louisa Seton, ii. 324; Thomas, iii. 784; Capt. Thomas, iv. 372; William, iii. 634
Larpent, Sir Albert John de Hochpied, 2nd Bt., iv. 66
Lascelles, Frances, ii. 551; Maj.-Gen. Francis, ii. 551
Lascells, Dorothy, iv. 634
Lashmer, George, iv. 444; Mary, iv. 444
Latham, Jane, iii. 209; Capt., R.N., iii. 209
La Touche, Rt. Hon. David Digges, ii. 190; Maria, ii. 190
La Trobe, ——, i. 414

Lauderdale, 6th Earl of, see Maitland, Charles; 7th Earl of, see Maitland, James; 13th Earl of, see Maitland, Frederick Henry
Laurie, Mary, iii. 201
Law, Rt. Rev. Dr. Edmund, iii. 706; Edward, 1st Baron Ellenborough, iii. 22; Joanna, iii. 706; Ven. Dr. John, i. 151; Stephana, i. 151
Lawder, Frederick, iii. 19
Lawless, James, iii. 351; Mary, iii. 351
Lawrell, James, i. 114
Lawrence, Lt.-Col. Alexander, i. 100; Elizabeth, iv. 339; George, R.N., iv. 339; G. W., ii. 171; Harriett, iii. 669; Honoria Angelina, i. 100; Louisa Ann (née Villiers), ii. 171; Marianne, ii. 340; W. Rogers, ii. 340
Lawrie, Alexander, iii. 515; Ann, ii. 286; Rev. George, ii. 286; Margaret, iii. 515
Lawson, Elizabeth, ii. 624; Jean, iv. 213
Lawtie, Eliza, ii. 151; Harriet Sarah, ii. 154; Rev. James, iii. 767; Sarah, iii. 767
Leadbeater, Catherine, i. 424; Elizabeth, iii. 562; Henry, i. 183, iii. 562; Jane, i. 183
Lear, Elizabeth, iii. 15
Leathert, Margaret, i. 368
Le Blanc, Teresa, iii. 587
Lechmere, Elizabeth, iv. 524; Lucy, ii. 52; Richard, iv. 524; Thomas, ii. 52
Leckonby, Mary, iii. 525; William, iii. 525
le Clere, Mary, i. 147, iii. 717
Le Despencer, Thomas (Stapleton), 15th Baron, iv. 169
Ledlie, Margaret (née Levague), i. 332
Ledwell, Boyce, iii. 437; Jane, iii. 437
Lee, Anne Mary, ii. 436; Christian Catherine, i. 255; Elizabeth, ii. 73, iii. 541; Hannah, ii. 239; John, iii. 271; Robert, i. 255; Sarah, iv. 451; Theodosea, iii. 271; Very Rev. Dean Usher, ii. 239; William, ii. 436, iii. 541
Lees, Sarah, iii. 789; William, iii. 789

682   INDEX OF NAMES

Leeson, Lady Cecilia, iii. 17 ; Joseph, 1st Earl of Milltown, iii. 17 ; Matilda (*née* Maddock), iii. 206
le Febvre, Félicité Jeanne, iv. 222
Legge, Lady Frances Elizabeth, iii. 287 ; William, 4th Earl of Dartmouth, iii. 287
Leibbrandt, Diana Margaretha, iii. 374
Leigh, Catherine, ii. 176, iii. 776 ; Edward, iii. 776 ; Joanna (or Ann), iii. 67 ; Margaret, iv. 201 ; Mary, iv. 306 ; Robert, iv. 306 ; Mrs. Susannah, iii. 568
L'Elant, Laurette Françoise, iv. 117
Leman, Frances (*née* Nynd), i. 328 ; Rev. John, iii. 584 ; Lucy, iii. 584 ; Rev. Thomas, i. 328
Le Marchand, Joseph Jeremiah, iv. 436 ; Madelina Elizabeth Maria Frances, iv. 436 ; Michael Joseph, iii. 485 ; Sarah Rebecca, iii. 485
Le Marchant, Carteret, iv. 22 ; Elizabeth (*née* Waugh), iv. 413 ; James, iv. 22
le Mere, Stephanie, ii. 155
Le Mesurier, Paul, iii. 664
Lemmal, Mette Margarethe, iii. 743
Lemon, Robert, iv. 131
Lennard, Mary, iii. 775 ; Samuel, iii. 775
Lennon, Elizabeth Ann, iii. 283
Lennox, Clotworthy, i. 368 ; Sarah, i. 368
le Sacq, Mary Anne, iii. 400
Leslie, Alexander, iv. 308 ; Ann, iv. 308 ; Archibald Young-, iv. 552 ; Catharine Elizabeth, iv. 41 ; Charles Henry, iv. 300 ; Christian, iv. 183 ; Dorothea, iii. 471 ; George, iii. 680 ; Helen, iii. 104 ; Rt. Rev. Dr. James, iv. 41 ; Jessy, ii. 96 ; Margaret, iii. 680 ; Mary, iii. 744 ; Mary Peacocke, iv. 300 ; Rev. Matthew, iii. 471 ; Sarah, iii. 226 ; Rev. William, ii. 96
Lester, Richard, iv. 530 ; Sarah, iii. 643, 644, iv. 530
Lever, Darcy, iii. 372 ; Kitty Alderson, i. 18 ; Mary Isabella, iii. 372 ; Thomas, i. 18
Leveret, Mary (*née* Treadwell), iv. 301

Levett, Mary Anne, i. 40 ; Rev. Richard, i. 40
Levi, B., iii. 770 ; Elizabeth, iii. 770
Levington, Mrs. Frances, *see* Hull
Lewin, Fawcett James, iii. 309 ; Mary Emma Weller, iii. 309
Lewis, Ann Isabella, iv. 600 ; Catherine, i. 155, iii. 717 ; Fanny Maria, iii. 97 ; Frances, iii. 747 ; John, iv. 435 ; John Hampton Hampton-, ii. 377 ; Matthew, iii. 97 ; Sarah, iv. 435 ; Thomas, ii. 520, iii. 747 ; W., i. 155, iii. 717
Leycester, Emily, i. 292, iii. 40 ; William, i. 292, iii. 40
L'Herondell, Anne, ii. 213 ; Francis, i. 147, iii. 717 ; Marie, i. 147
Liddell, Andrew, ii. 480 ; Rose Amelia, ii. 480
Lidderdale, Elizabeth, iv. 482 ; Margaret, iii. 749
Liddington, Anne Louisa, iii. 598
Liddle, Margaret, ii. 527
Lifford, 1st Viscount, *see* Hewitt, James
Lightfoot, Hannah, i. 63 ; Harriette Matilda, ii. 517 ; Mary Jane, i. 387 ; Surg. Samuel, i. 387
Lillingstone, Anne Agnes, iii. 505 ; Charles, iii. 505
Limerick, Charlotte Cameron, iii. 103 ; Rev. Dr. Paul, iii. 103
Lind, James, M.D., iv. 73 ; Lucy Maria, iv. 73
Lindesay, Henry, ii. 61 ; Mary Anne, iv. 115 ; Rachel, ii. 61 ; William, iv. 115
Lindsay, Benjamin, i. 342 ; Charles, iii. 380 ; Charlotte, iii. 380 ; Charlotte Augusta, i. 343 ; Colin, i. 343 ; Mrs. Elizabeth, iv. 585 ; Hon. Hugh, ii. 432, 437 ; James, 5th Earl of Balcarres, ii. 437 ; Margaret, i. 342
Lindsell, Alice Caroline Catherine, ii. 606 ; Robert, ii. 606
Linley, Mary, iv. 276 ; Thomas, iv. 276
Lisle, 2nd Baron, *see* Lysaght, John
Lister, Isabella, iv. 469 ; James, iv. 469 ; Janet, ii. 618
Listowel, 1st Earl of, *see* Hare, William

INDEX OF NAMES

Little, Mary Hicks, iii. 595; Thomas, iii. 595
Littledale, Catherine, ii. 242; Henry, ii. 242
Livesey, Frances, i. 29; John, i. 29
Livingstone, Alida, iv. 567; Sir James, Bt., of Glentirran, i. 277; Jane, iii. 685; Katherine, iv. 573; Mary, i. 277; Col. Robert, iv. 567; William, iv. 573
Llandaff, 1st Earl of, see Mathew, Francis
Llewellyn, Ann, iii. 800
Lloyd, Charlotte, ii. 144; Edmund, ii. 565; Edward Pryce, 1st Baron Mostyn, iii. 65; Elizabeth, iii. 804; Joanna, ii. 565; Comdr. John, R.N., iv. 389; J., iv. 348; Mary, iv. 348; Priscilla Amelia, iv. 389; Thomas, ii. 144; Col. Verney, iii. 804
Loane, Mrs. Mary, iv. 559
Loch, Agnes, iii. 481; Ann Ellitson, iii. 781; Christiana, i. 87; James, i. 87; John, iii. 781
Lock, Margaret, iv. 535
Locke, Harriet, i. 210; Louisa (née Elliot), iii. 773; Capt. Robert, ii. 129, iii. 773; Rev. Thomas, i. 210
Lockett, Mary (née Barnett), i. 94
Lockhart, Caroline, iii. 671; Clementina, ii. 290; George, ii. 290; James, iii. 671; Jane, i. 135; John, iii. 436; Olivia, ii. 93, iii. 133; Sir William, 3rd Bt., i. 135
Lockwood, Sarah, i. 325
Lodge, Eliza Sarah (née Geale), iv. 544
Loftie, Rev. John, ii. 254; Mary, ii. 254
Logan, Catherine, ii. 225; Robert, ii. 225
Login, John, ii. 305; Mary Ann, ii. 305
"Loiseau, Count," i. 147
"Lola Montez," see Gilbert, M. D. E. R.
Long, Beeston, iii. 313; Charles, 1st Baron Farnborough, iii. 313; Charlotte Tilney, iv. 285; Fanny Teresa, iv. 379; Harriette, iii. 228; Jane, ii. 464; Johanna, i. 241; Col. John, i. 241; Rev. John, ii. 476; J. W., iv. 379; Maria, i. 20, iii. 313; Peter B., i. 20; Rebecca (née Best), i. 136; Samuel, ii. 464; Sarah, iii. 586; Sophia, ii. 476; Wakeman, iii. 228
Longley, Anna Maria, iii. 69; John, iii. 69
Longridge, Jane, ii. 410; Thomas, ii. 410
Lord, Rev. John, iii. 65; Louisa, ii. 55; Priscilla, iii. 65; Simon, ii. 55
Loring, Ann, iii. 594
Lort, Eliza, iii. 522; John, iii. 522
Loscombe, Maria (née Rawlins), iii. 615
Loughnan, Ludivina, iii. 278; Thomas, iii. 278
Louis, Adm. Sir John, Bt., ii. 602
Louis XIV, iii. 778
Louw, Anna Margaretta, ii. 391
Lovat, 8th Lord, see Fraser, Hugh
Lovell, Abraham, iv. 457; Elizabeth, iii. 247; Langford, iii. 247; Martha Pitman, iv. 457
Loveridge, Elizabeth Langdon, ii. 439; William, ii. 439
Low, Anne, ii. 399; Catharine, ii. 34; Gen. Sir John, ii. 34, iii. 214; Capt. Robert, ii. 34
Lowe, Mrs. Deborah Matilda, ii. 333, iii. 789; Elizabeth, ii. 148; Lucy, iii. 684; Maria Sarah, iii. 343; Samuel, iii. 343; Very Rev. Thomas Hill Peregrine Furye, iii. 684; Capt., iii. 789
Lowis, John, iv. 105, 272
Lowndes, Harriet, iii. 669; William, iii. 669
Lowrie, Anna, ii. 14
Lowry, Elizabeth, i. 90; Hester, ii. 62; Rev. James, ii. 62
Lowther, George, i. 16; Col. James, iii. 779; Mary, iii. 779; Sophia Jane, i. 16
Loy, Jane (Jeanne), iv. 637; Sebastian, iv. 637
Lucadou, John Daniel, iv. 429
Lucas, Alicia Elizabeth, ii. 62; Anne, iv. 41; Rev. Daniel E., ii. 62; Rev. Edward, iv. 41; Leonora, i. 49
Lumsden, Alicia Isabella, ii. 408; Edith, iv. 67; Henry, iii. 203;

John, ii. 408, iv. 67 ; Margaret, iii. 203
Lushington, Georgiana, iv. 437 ; Sir Henry, 3rd Bt., iii. 601 ; Laura, iii. 601 ; Paulina, i. 177 ; William, i. 177, iv. 437
Luxmoore, Eliza, iv. 452 ; Surg. Thomas, iv. 452
Lyme (or Lynd), Sarah, iv. 481
Lynd (Lind), Charles, iii. 608 ; Sarah, iii. 608
Lynd, Grace, iv. 205
Lynd (or Lyme), Sarah, iv. 481
Lynn, Rev. James, iii. 216, 365 ; Laura, iii. 216 ; Sophia Ann, iii. 365
Lyon, Dr. Benjamin, iv. 508 ; Rebekah, iv. 508 ; Lady Anna Maria Bowes-, ii. 555 ; John Bowes-, 9th Earl of Strathmore, ii. 555
Lyons, Catherine Anne, iv. 368, 576 ; Vice-Adm. John, iii. 348 ; John, iv. 368
Lysaght, Hon. Catharine, ii. 366 ; John, 2nd Baron Lisle, ii. 366
Lysons, Sir Daniel, i. 384
Lyster, Elizabeth, iv. 23 ; William, iv. 23
Lyttelton, Sir Thomas, 2nd Lord Lyttelton, iii. 487

M

Mabey, Charles, ii. 511 ; Sophia Croome, ii. 511
Macan, Anne, iii. 200 ; Elizabeth, iii. 646 ; Harriet, iv. 144 ; Margaret, iii. 594 ; Robert, iii. 594 ; Thomas, iii. 200 ; Major Turner, iv. 144
Macartney, George, 1st Earl Macartney, ii. 329 ; George, ii. 281 ; Isabella, iv. 108 ; Capt., R.N., iv. 108
Machell, James, iv. 13 ; Rosetta Hester (née Sanders), iv. 13
Madan, Charlotte, iv. 387 ; Rt. Rev. Spencer, iv. 387
Madden, Anne, iii. 612 ; Robert, iii. 612
Maddox, Dulcibella, iii. 219
Madge, Evelina Jane, ii. 107 ; Wilton Phipps, ii. 107

Madgett, Aurora, iv. 66
Madryll, Charles, i. 336
Magee, Martha Maria (née Stewart), iv. 184
Maher, Matilda, i. 161 ; Capt., i. 161
Mahon, Theodosia, iii. 589
Mahundee, Ellen Charlotte, i. 37
Main, Christian, iii. 613 ; George, iii. 613 ; Margaret, iii. 473
Mainwaring, Anna Maria, ii. 16 ; George, ii. 16 ; George Boulton, i. 309 ; Janet, iii. 708 ; Sophia, i. 309 ; William, iii. 708
Maitland, Agnes, ii. 248 ; Charles, 6th Earl of Lauderdale, i. 53, iii. 212 ; Frederick Henry, 13th Earl, iii. 212 ; Capt. Hon. Frederick Lewis, R.N., i. 53 ; James, 7th Earl, iv. 399 ; Pelham, i. 252 ; Gen. Hon. William Mordaunt, iv. 399
Major, Frances, i. 153
Malcolm, Jane, iii. 5 ; Thomas, iii. 5 ; Wilhelmina, iii. 264, 265
Malley, Maria, iv. 359 ; William, iv. 359
Malone, Eliza, iv. 144 ; Mary, iv. 292 ; Mary Anne, iv. 635 ; Thomas, iv. 292
Man, Gilbert, iv. 175 ; Mary, iv. 175
Manaton, Francis W., iii. 430 ; Martha, iii. 430
Manchester, Dukes of, iii. 312, iv. 441
Mandeville, Jane, iii. 805
Mann, Anna Maria, i. 144 ; John, iii. 706
Manners, Hon. Charles, iv. 286 ; John, 3rd Duke of Rutland, iii. 220
Manning, Beatrice Caroline, iii. 622
Mannington, Elizabeth Palmer, iv. 47 ; John, iv. 47
Manoury, Anne Smith, iv. 165 ; Capt. Isaac, iv. 165
Mansell, Anne, iii. 182 ; Elizabeth, i. 38 ; Capt. John, i. 38 ; William, iii. 182
Mansfield, Grace, iii. 113 ; Rev. Ralph, iii. 113
Manson, Alexander, i. 187, 404 ; Elizabeth, iii. 677 ; George, iv. 151 ; Jane (née Bowie), i. 187 ; Mary, ii. 434 ; Sarah, i. 404, iv. 151 ; William, iii. 677
Maples, Bridget, iii. 772 ; John, iii. 772

INDEX OF NAMES

Mapletoft, Ann Maria, iii. 748 ; Constantia Adriana Sally, iii. 481 ; Rev. Robert, iii. 481
Mar, 7th Earl of, *see* Erskine, John Francis
Marjoribanks, Andrew, iv. 30, 41; Margaret, iv. 30, 41
Marrie, Major James, iii. 519 ; Marianne Henrietta Sophia, iii. 519
Marriott, Elizabeth, i. 275 ; Rev. Dr. Robert, i. 275
Marsh, Isobel, iii. 788 ; Joseph, iii. 788
Marshall, Ann, iv. 52 ; Elizabeth, iii. 276 ; Eliza Cecilia, iii. 456 ; Emma Maria, i. 300 ; Rev. George, iii. 26 ; Honoria, iii. 26 ; Physician Gen. John, i. 300, iii. 101, 456, 460 ; John, iii. 276 ; Phoebe, iii. 460
Marston, Hannah, ii. 83 ; Richard, ii. 83
Martin, Mrs. Charlotte, iii. 469 ; Eliza, iii. 430 ; Everilda, i. 93 ; Harriet Alzelia, iv. 424 ; James, iii. 212 ; Asst. Surg. John Woodhouse, iii. 430, iv. 424 ; Joseph, iii. 269 ; Lydia, iii. 461 ; Mary, iii. 212 ; Sir Mordaunt, 4th Bt., i. 93 ; Newland, iii. 269 ; Sarah, iv. 52 ; Sarah Susannah, iii. 234 ; Ursula (*née* Knowles), ii. 605 ; W., iii. 269
Martindell, Sophia, i. 348
Martyn, Salome, iv. 549 ; Thomas, iv. 549
Mascarier, Mary, iii. 777
Mason, Ann Martinez (*née* Brown), i. 52 ; Capt. Henry, R.N., i. 52 ; Mary, iii. 463 ; Mary Ann, iv. 282 ; Sarah, ii. 108 ; Lt.-Col. William, iv. 282
Massey, Capt. Charles, iv. 436 ; Judith, iv. 436
Massie, George, iii. 767 ; Georgiana, iii. 767
Masson, Isabella Jane, i. 246 ; Sarah, i. 2 ; Capt. Thomas, i. 2 ; Capt., i. 246
Massy, Hugh, 1st Baron Massy, i. 177, iii. 738, iv. 438 ; Hugh, 2nd Baron, ii. 332 ; Hon. Jane, ii. 332 ; Margaret, iii. 738, iv. 438
Masters, Sarah, iii. 753
Mather, Mary Anne, iii. 29 ; T., iii. 29

Mathers, Charlotte Mary, ii. 292 ; Capt. George, ii. 292 ; Mary Hannah, iii. 64
Matheson, Sir Alexander, 1st Bt., iii. 124 ; Catherine, iii. 124 ; John, iii. 124
Mathew, Francis, 1st Earl of Llandaff, iii. 252, 255 ; Marian Emma, iii. 462
Mathews, Elizabeth, iii. 174 ; George, ii. 627 ; Ismay Jane, ii. 627 ; Rev. Philip, iii. 174
Mathias, Andrew, iv. 385
Mattenby, Charles Richard William, iii. 11
Matthew, Rev. John, i. 359 ; Susan Elizabeth, i. 359
Matthews, Decima, ii. 161 ; Emma, iv. 532 ; John Henry, iii. 266 ; Margaret, iii. 739 ; Mary Isabella, iii. 266 ; Philip, iii. 739 ; Phillis Augusta, ii. 341
Mattocks, Mary, iv. 401
Maule, Agnes, iv. 92
Mauleverer, Anne, ii. 298 ; Timothy, ii. 298
Maull, Jane, iv. 219
Maunsell, Rev. Daniel Henry, i. 205 ; Jane, i. 205 ; John, ii. 421 ; Susan, ii. 421
Mawbey, Sir Joseph, Bt. of Botleys, i. 17 ; Mary, i. 17
Maxtone, Helen, iv. 194 ; James, iv. 194
Maxwell, Adam, iv. 160 ; Aurora Catherine, i. 352 ; Catherine, iv. 346 ; Eliza, iii. 184 ; James Homer, iv. 346 ; John, iii. 184 ; Capt. Sir Murray, Kt., R.N., iv. 413 ; Sophia Maria, iv. 160
May, Sir Edward, Bt. of Mayfield, iv. 349 ; Elizabeth, iv. 349 ; Jane, iii. 70 ; Miss M. A., iii. 782 ; Sir Thomas Erskine, 1st Baron Farnborough, iii. 21 ; William, iii. 70
Mayne, William, Baron Newhaven, iii. 270
Mayow, Catherine Anne Wynell-, iii. 63 ; Rev. Robert Wynell-, iii. 63
Mac, Mc, M‘, however spelt.
Macalister, Charlotte Elizabeth, i. 428 ; John, iii. 146 ; Mary, iii. 146
MacAlpine, John, iii. 139

McArthur, Arabella Kezia, ii. 324;
Maria, iv. 463
Macaulay, Alexander, ii. 449; Mary,
ii. 449
McBane, Janet (née Clearihue), i. 350;
Lachlan, i. 350
Macbean, Anne, iii. 166, 168; Donald,
ii. 321; Margaret, ii. 321
McCabe, John, iii. 135; Mary, iii. 135
McCall, Helen, iii. 189; Janet, iii.
767
MacCallum, Anne, iii. 113
MacCarthy, Catherine, iv. 70; Eleanora, i. 392; Ellen, ii. 611;
Thomas, ii. 611
McCarty, Justin, ii. 205; Lydia, ii.
205
McCaskill, Anne, ii. 108; Maj.-Gen.
Sir John, ii. 108
McCaull, Janet, ii. 629
M'Causland, Conolly, iii. 34, iv. 110;
Dominick, ii. 453; Hannah, iii. 34;
Harriet Elizabeth, iv. 150; Letitia,
ii. 453; Rev. Oliver, iv. 150;
Sarah, iv. 110
McClary, Jane (née Morgan), iii. 330;
Capt. John, iii. 330
McClintock, Robert, i. 141; Sophia
Amelia Alphonsina, i. 141
M'Combie, Alexander, iii. 782;
Grizel, ii. 246, iii. 782
McConnell, Charlotte Sarah, iii. 550
Macconochie (M'Onochie), Jane
(Jean), iv. 463; William, iv. 463
McCormick, Dorothea, ii. 4
McCorquodale, Archibald, iii. 113
M'Dermeit, Agnes, iii. 761; Rev.
John, iii. 761
McDermot, Elizabeth, iii. 513
Macdonald, Alexander, iii. 105; Col.
Allan, iv. 27; Angus, i. 99; Anne,
iii. 105; Clementina Jacobina
Sobiesi Stuart, iv. 27; Colin, iii.
173; Daniel, iii. 766; Capt. Ewen,
iv. 283; Frances, iii. 173; Helen,
iii. 675; Isobel, ii. 214, iii. 779;
Sir James, Bt. of Sleat, iii. 153;
Lieut. James Ranald, iii. 105;
Jane, iii. 164; Janet, iii. 141, 153,
356; Jessie, iii. 766; John, iii.
141, 356; Lt.-Gen. Sir John, i.
263, iii. 394; Lt.-Col. John, iii.
105; Capt. John, iii. 164; Louisa,
i. 263, iii. 751; Margaret, iii. 394;
Mary, i. 99, iv. 283; Norman, iii.
394, 751; Penelope, ii. 376;
Ronald, ii. 376; Dr., ii. 221
Macdonnell, Duncan, iii. 605; Elizabeth, iii. 605; Jane, iii. 308; John,
iii. 308
McDougal, James, ii. 204; Margaret,
ii. 204
Macdougall, Alexander, ii. 204;
Charlotte, ii. 204
McDowall, Ellen Ramsay, i. 151;
Bdr.-Gen. Robert, i. 151
McDowel, Frances, iv. 107
Macdowell, Jane, ii. 256
Macevoy, Elizabeth, iii. 448
M'Fadzean, Margaret, iii. 606
Macfarlane, Rev. Edward, iv. 297;
John, i. 284, 295; Lilias Margaret,
i. 284, 295
McFie, Elizabeth, iii. 14
McGildowny, John, i. 317; Mary, i.
317
McGillicuddy of The Reeks, ii. 32;
Margaret, ii. 32
M'Ginniss, Mary, ii. 435, 486
Macgrath, Anna Ellerker, ii. 47; Dr.
William Michael, iii. 609
MacGregor (or Murray), Duncan,
XXI of MacGregor, iii. 483
MacGregor, Mary Drummond, iii.
483; Sarah, iv. 434
MacInnes, Margaret, i. 332
McIntosh, Barbara, iii. 198; Donald,
iii. 110; Janet, ii. 285; Margaret,
iii. 110
McIntyre, Barbara Camilla, i. 367;
Rev. Dr. Joseph, i. 367
Mackay, Alexander, 8th Baron Reay,
iii. 694; Hon. Christian, ii. 139;
Donald, 4th Baron Reay, i. 73;
George, 3rd Baron Reay, ii. 139;
Col. Hugh, i. 73; Jane, iii. 182;
John, ii. 218; Katherine, ii. 368;
Mary, i. 73; Millicent, ii. 218;
William, iii. 182
Mackenzie, Sir Alexander, Bt. of Fairburn, iii. 144; Alice, iii. 55; Ann,
ii. 477; Mrs. Ann, iv. 119; Lady
Augusta, iii. 364; Barbara, iii.
144; Caroline Charlotte, iii. 539;
Charles, iii. 539; Col. Colin, ii. 232,
iii. 781; Rev. Colin, iii. 156; Capt.

Donald, iii. 53 ; Flora Loudon, iii. 53 ; George, 1st Earl of Cromartie, iii. 153 ; George, 3rd Earl, iii. 364 ; Isabella, i. 278 ; James, iii. 615 ; Jane, i. 162 ; Jane Falconer, ii. 266 ; John, 2nd Earl of Cromartie, i. 162 ; Sir John, Bt. of Coul, ii. 477 ; John, ii. 266, iii. 177 ; Margaret, ii. 80 ; Mary, iii. 156, 177 ; Richard Alexander, iii. 121 ; Hon. Roderick, i. 162 ; Sarah (*née* Allen), i. 162 ; Gen., iii. 289

McKerrell, Elizabeth, iii. 629 ; Jean (Jane), ii. 235 ; John, i. 410, ii. 235, iii. 629 ; Margaret, i. 410

Mackeson, Capt. John, iv. 195 ; Olive Ann, iv. 195

Mackie, Emily Adelaide, iii. 684 ; Maj.-Gen. George, iii. 684

McKillican, Isobel, iii. 165

Mackinnon, Elizabeth, ii. 216 ; William, ii. 216

Mackintosh, Anne Farquharson, iv. 73 ; Lachlan, iv. 73

Maclaren, Helen Hay, ii. 483 ; John, ii. 483

Maclean, Alexandrina, iii. 195 ; Alice, iii. 199 ; Ann, iv. 109 ; Charles, iv. 109 ; Donald, iii. 199, 454 ; Elizabeth, iii. 454 ; John, iii. 195 ; Sir Lachlan, iii. 387 ; Mary, iv. 391

McLeish, Christian (*née* Knox), ii. 288 ; Robert, ii. 288

Maclennan, Mary, i. 151

Macleod, Alexander, ii. 485 ; Anne, iii. 141 ; Bannatyna Wilhelmina, ii. 485 ; Christian, iii. 127 ; Claus (*Qy*. Olaus), iii. 775 ; Donald, iii. 154, 173 ; Isabella, ii. 485 ; Jane, ii. 166 ; Janet, iii. 105 ; Jessie, iii. 173 ; Margaret, i. 293 ; Mary, iii. 154, iv. 58 ; Norman, iv. 58 ; Olaus (*Qy*. Claus), iii. 775 ; Roderick, iii. 141 ; William, i. 293

Macmahon, Eliza Ellen, iii. 410 ; Sophia, iv. 259

MacManus, Bryan, iii. 420 ; Honoria, iii. 420

MacMillan, Margaret, ii. 531 ; Peter Laurie, ii. 531

McMorran, Jean, i. 296

McNab, Alexander, iii. 125 ; Jane, iii. 125

Macnabb, Donald, iii. 194 ; Eliza, iii. 194

Macnaghten, Jane, iii. 44 ; John, iii. 44 ; Sir William Hay, Bt., i. 373

Macnamara, Mrs. Honora, iii. 380 ; Phoebe, ii. 459

MacNeill, Anne, i. 192

McNish (McNeish), Catherine, iii. 609

Macniven, Margaret, iii. 538

M'Onochie, *see* Macconochie

Macpherson, Agnes, i. 336 ; Ann, iii. 165 ; Annie Charlotte, iv. 273 ; Surg. George Gordon, iii. 269, iv. 273 ; Helen, iii. 109 ; Isobel, iii. 147 ; James, iii. 147 ; Sir John, Bt., iii. 180 ; Lachlan, iii. 165 ; Maria E., iii. 269

Macqueen, Angus, iii. 180 ; Jane, iii. 180 ; Mary, iv. 15 ; Patrick, iv. 15

McRitchie, Ann, ii. 524, 525

McVeagh, Catherine, iii. 96 ; Hugh, iii. 96 ; Jane Maria, iv. 67 ; Letitia, ii. 287 ; Simon, iv. 67

M'Vean, Christian, iii. 148 ; Rev. John, iii. 148

McWhinnie, Elizabeth, iii. 370

MacWilliam, Jean, ii. 287

Meacham, Major John Cathcart, iv. 17

Mead, Jane, iv. 226

Meade, Mary, ii. 383 ; Dr. Robert, ii. 383

Meadowbank, Lord, *see* Welwood, Alexander Maconochie-

Meadows, Arthur, iii. 7 ; Mary Ann Romer, i. 152 ; Lt.-Col., i. 152

Means, Mary, iii. 739

Meares, George, iii. 260 ; Sarah, iii. 260

Mearns, Surg. Archibald, iv. 480 ; Janet Elizabeth Rosalie, iv. 480

Meath, 8th Earl of, *see* Brabazon, Anthony

Medcalf, Elizabeth, iii. 279 ; Parker, iii. 279

Meggat, John, iv. 53 ; Rebecca, iv. 53

Mehindee Khanum, iv. 235

Meik, Surg. James, i. 190, iv. 26 ; Jean Charlotte, i. 190 ; Mary Anne Catherine, iv. 26

Meiningen, George, Duke of Saxe-, iii. 277

Meiselbach, Anne M., ii. 462; Catherine, i. 396; Georgiana Caroline Barbara, i. 272, iii. 210; Col. Johan Frederick, i. 272, 390, 396, ii. 462, 536, iii. 342; Mary Anne, i. 390; Sophia, iii. 342; Susan Elizabeth, ii. 536

Meldrum, Euphemia, iii. 286

Melhado, Sarah, iii. 452

Mellar, Joseph, iii. 543; Mary, iii. 543

Mellis, Eliza Helen, ii. 3; Surg. James, ii. 3

Mellor, Sarah, iii. 378

Melville, Helen, i. 348; James Moncrieff, iii. 54; Jane, ii. 6; 1st Viscount, see Dundas, Henry; Major, ii. 6

Mendes, Mrs. Marcellina Antonia, ii. 376; Peter, ii. 376, iii. 523

Menethy, ——, iii. 705

Menzies, Amelia, iii. 776; Grace, iv. 192; Capt. James, iii. 776; Jean, iv. 190; Joanna, iii. 42; Robert, iii. 42, iv. 192

Mercer, Anne, iii. 369; Eliza, iii. 662; Dr. Graeme, iii. 628; Janet, ii. 289; Laurence, iii. 369; Samuel, ii. 344; Sarah, ii. 344

Meredyth, Frances, iv. 456; Sir John, 1st Bt., i. 299, iv. 456; Mary Anne, i. 299

Metcalfe, Sir Charles Theophilus, 1st Baron Metcalfe, iv. 140

Metford, E. B., iv. 407; Hannah Nickleson, iv. 407

Meulh, Lieut. William, iv. 124

Mexteed, Mrs. Hester, ii. 169

Meysey, Mary, iv. 330; Rev. Thomas, iv. 330

Michael, Anne Maria, ii. 162; J., ii. 162

Michel, Caroline Mary, iii. 785; Lt.-Gen. John, iii. 785

Michell, Major Charles Cornwallis, iv. 130; Julia Anne, iv. 130

Middleton, Anne, iv. 79; Samuel, iv. 131; Barons Middleton, family of, iv. 486

Mildmay, Anne, i. 352; Carew, i. 352

Millar, Andrew, iii. 97; Margaret, ii. 437; Susan, iii. 554

Millard, Anna Maria, iv. 489; Rev. Charles, iv. 489

Miller, Ann, i. 275; George, ii. 431, iii. 727; Isobel, iv. 206; Mrs. Primrose Ann, i. 254

Millett, Caroline, iv. 300; George, iv. 300

Millie, David, ii. 67

Milliken, Antonia, i. 209

Mills, Major Arthur Samuel, i. 251; Charlotte Maria (née Salmon), i. 251; Elizabeth, ii. 438; George G., iii. 712; Susanna, iii. 797; Thomas, iii. 797; William, iii. 236

Milltown, 1st Earl of, see Leeson, Joseph

Milne (Mylne), Caroline, ii. 101; Robert, ii. 101

Milward, Charlotte, ii. 282; John, ii. 282

Minet, Isaac, ii. 113; Millicent, ii. 113

Minifie, Elizabeth Bridget, iii. 578

Minshull, Elizabeth Louisa, iv. 322

Minter, Margaret, ii. 124

Mirtle, Helen, iii. 736; William, iii. 736

Mirza Sulaiman Shekoh, iv. 567

Mitchell, Ann, i. 426, iii. 763, iv. 131, 560; Elizabeth, iv. 247; Frances, ii. 618; Sir John, 1st Bt. of Westshore, iii. 763; Capt., iv. 247

Mitchelson, Archibald Hepburn, i. 425, ii. 514; Isabella, ii. 514; Jane, iii. 740; Jane Hepburn, i. 425; John, iii. 715, 735, iv. 223; Margaret, iv. 223, 224; Mary, iii. 715, 735; Samuel, iii. 740

Moinakin, Eleanor Christian, ii. 327, 400

Moir, Rev. Dr. George, iii. 402; Janet, iii. 402

Molesworth, Caroline, ii. 349; Capt. Robert, ii. 349

Molineux, Ann, iii. 558

Molyneux, Rt. Hon. Sir Capel, Bt., ii. 618; Henrietta, ii. 618; Pooley, iv. 132

Monck, Emily Sophia, ii. 372; George Paul, ii. 372; Marcus, 1st Earl of Tyrone, ii. 372

Monckton, Hon. Frances Charlotte, i. 130; William, 2nd Viscount Galway, i. 130

INDEX OF NAMES 689

Moncrieff, Barbara, iii. 198; Rev. William, iii. 198
Money, Augusta, ii. 78; Wigram, ii. 78
Monneruit, Maria Josephine, iv. 134
Monro, Daniel, iv. 376; Isabella, iii. 83; Jean, iv. 376; John, iii. 83
Monsell, Harriet Augusta Hayes, iv. 160; Margaret Olympia, i. 389; Thomas Ephraim, i. 389, iv. 160
Montagu, Laura Caroline, iii. 550
Monteath, Colin, ii. 76; Thomas, ii. 76
"Montez, Lola," pseud. of M. D. E. R. Gilbert, *q.v.*
Montgomerie, Alexander, ii. 375; Charlotte Molyneux, i. 303; George Molyneux, i. 303; Hugh, 12th Earl of Eglinton, ii. 375, iii. 315, 316; Lilias, ii. 375; Martha, ii. 57
Montgomery, Harriette, iv. 259; J., iv. 259; Louisa Caroline, iii. 345; Matilda, i. 317; Nathaniel, iii. 323; William Richard, iii. 345
Montrilli, Mary Ada, iii. 273
Montrose, 1st Marquess of, *see* Graham, James
Monypenny, William Tankerville, iv. 369
Moodie, Major James, iii. 394; Janet Dunbar, iii. 394
Moor, Anna, i. 31; Elizabeth, iv. 119; Georgina, ii. 231; Henry Isaac, ii. 231
Moorcroft, Mary, i. 260
Moore, Anne, ii. 63, iv. 559; Catherine, i. 314; Charlotte Jane, iii. 561; Henrietta, iii. 506; Hester, i. 308; James, iii. 561; John, ii. 217; Richard, iii. 506; Robert, i. 308; Wilhelmina, ii. 217; William, ii. 63; Major William, ii. 387
Moorhead, Mary, iii. 364
Mordaunt, Charles, 4th Earl of Peterborough, iii. 327; Charles Henry, 5th Earl, iii. 327
More, Catharine, iii. 189; J. S., iii. 189; (or McKay), Margaret, iv. 100
Moreau, *see* Morrow
Morfett, Sarah, iv. 127

Morgan, Elizabeth, iv. 112; Helen, iii. 125; Mary Magdalen, iii. 85; Sarah Anne, i. 213; Susannah, iv. 312; William, iii. 85
Morison, Andrew, iii. 113; Margaret, iii. 113
Morland, Harriet, iii. 331; William, iii. 331
Morley, Catherine, iv. 200; James, iii. 416, 417, iv. 179; John, iv. 200; Louisa, iv. 179; Maria, iii. 417; Sarah, iii. 416
Mornington, Earl of, *see* Wellesley, Marquess
Morrell, Mary, i. 31
Morres, Lodge Evans, 1st Viscount Frankfort de Montmorency, ii. 45; Reymond Hervey, ii. 45
Morris, Ann Maria, i. 19; Caroline, ii. 406; Eliza, ii. 290; Elizabeth Dobree, ii. 610; Eliza Howard, iv. 372; F., ii. 594; George, iii. 421; Henrietta, iii. 488; Jane Lucy, ii. 594; Sir John, Bt. of Clasemont, iii. 488; John, i. 19, ii. 610; Mary Johanna, iii. 108, 421; Robert, ii. 290, 406, iv. 205; Sarah, iv. 205
Morrison, James, ii. 204; Janet, ii. 204; Margaret, iii. 175; Capt., i. 260
Morrissey, Elizabeth, iii. 670; James, iii. 670
Morrow (*Qy.* Moreau), Rose, iv. 126
Morse, Ann Frances, iii. 292; Robert, iii. 292; Sarah, i. 320
Morton, Edwin, iv. 157; Sophia (*née* Arnold), i. 53; Susan, ii. 104; 17th Earl of, *see* Douglas, George Sholto
Mosley, Elizabeth, iii. 250; Sir John Parker, Bt., iii. 250; family of, iv. 451
Moss, D., iii. 542; Ellen, iii. 542
Mostyn, 1st Baron, *see* Lloyd, Edward Pryce
Mouat, Emily Ahmuty, ii. 150
Mouat(t), Capt. Stephen Peter, R.N., i. 140
Moule, Elizabeth Jane, ii. 153; Fanny Elizabeth, ii. 437; Frederick, ii. 437; George, ii. 153
Mount, Mary Christian, iii. 756; William, iii. 756

INDEX OF NAMES

Mountain, Major Armine Simcoe, iii. 410; Jane (*née* O'Beirne), iii. 410
Mountjoy, 1st Viscount, *see* Gardiner, Luke
Mountnorris, 2nd Earl of, *see* Annesley, George
Mountsteven, Catherine Saumarez, i. 199; Thomas, i. 199
Mowatt, Isabella, i. 288, iii. 668; Capt. James Ryder, i. 288, iii. 668
Muckle, Mary Anne, i. 384
Mudge, John, iii. 216; Mary, iii. 216; Adm. Zachary, iii. 216
Muir, Janet, iv. 450; Mary, ii. 506
Muirhead, Rev. Dr. James, iv. 110; Jane, iv. 110
Muirson, Col. Benjamin Wolsey, iii. 745, iv. 59; Louisa Caroline Tobin, iv. 59; Mary Anne Wolsey, iii. 745
Mulcaster, Ann, iv. 315, 316; Maj.-Gen. Frederick George, iv. 315; Sarah, iv. 379
Mulder, Julia, iv. 81
Mulgrave, Martha Sophia, 1st Countess of, iii. 215
Mullins, Charlotte Matilda, iv. 635; Eliza Frances, iii. 409; Fanny, iv. 9, 527; Jane Lydia, i. 90; Jane Sophia, ii. 433
Mundy, Edward Miller, iii. 740
Munkhouse, Barbara, iv. 637
Munro, Eliza, i. 280, 294; Rev. James, iv. 31; Margaret, iv. 31, 319
Munt, Louisa, iii. 461; Sarah, iii. 320
Murchison, Kenneth, iii. 144
Murdoch, Elizabeth, ii. 289; James, ii. 289; Lilias, iii. 354
Murphy, Catherine, iv. 320; J. C., iv. 320
Murray, Alexander, iii. 255; Catherine Theresa, i. 379; Charles, iv. 91; Lady Charlotte, ii. 87; Christian, ii. 303; Sir David, Bt. of Stanhope, ii. 417; Elizabeth, ii. 138, iii. 621, 799; Evan, iii. 141, 144; Harriet, iv. 91; Henrietta Augusta, iii. 215; James, iii. 799; James Wolfe, Lord Cringletie, ii. 527; Jane Wemyss, i. 283, iii. 214; Jean, iii. 676; Johanna Maria, iv. 189; John, 3rd Duke of Atholl, iii. 360; John, 4th Duke, ii. 87; John, 4th Earl of Dunmore, i. 283; Capt. John, R.N., iii. 621; Hon. Leveson Granville Keith, i. 283; Margaret, ii. 417, iii. 352; Marianne Lloyd, ii. 527; P., i. 379; Robert, ii. 303; William, iv. 189; Col. William, iii. 676
Musgrave, Sir Christopher, 5th Bt., iv. 532; Dorothy, iv. 532
Myles, Hannah, i. 233
Mylne, George, iii. 727; Helen, iii. 148, 149, 150
Mytton, Anne, ii. 450; Richard, ii. 450

N

Nagle, Miss, ii. 429
Nail, Anne, iii. 729; Herman, iii. 729
Nairne, Helen (*née* Kyd), ii. 613; Dr. James, ii. 613
Napier, Francis, 5th Baron Napier, ii. 558; Hon. Hester, ii. 558; Isabel, iii. 212; Jane McDowell, ii. 577; Marcia Anne, iii. 417; Maj.-Gen. Hon. Mark, iii. 212, 417; of Merchiston, 6th Baron, *see* Scott, Francis; Col., ii. 577
Napper, Mary Anne, iv. 335; Samuel, iv. 335
Nares, Sir George, iii. 568; Sophia, iii. 568
Nash, Capt. Alexander, iv. 289; Andrew John, ii. 482; Anne, iii. 730; Anne Frances, ii. 161; Clara Wilkin, ii. 455, iv. 271; Mrs. Emma, iii. 55; Jessie, iv. 289; Robert, iii. 730; William, ii. 161
Nasmith, Elizabeth, iv. 99
Nasmyth, Alexander, ii. 211
Navall, Janet, iii. 600
Nawab Manzil-ul-Nissa, Begum, iv. 567
Nawab Mulka Humanee, Begum, iv. 567
Naylor, Emily Todd, ii. 241; J. Todd, ii. 241; Lucy Eliza, i. 189
Neale, Caroline Barbara, ii. 176; Denis, iv. 203
Neate, Louisa (Eleanor), i. 38; Major, i. 38

INDEX OF NAMES 691

Needham, Francis, 1st Earl of Kilmorey, i. 324; Joseph, M.D., iv. 237; Sarah, iv. 237
Neil, Miss, ii. 527, iii. 729
Neill, Bdr.-Gen. James George Smith-, iv. 157
Neilson, Dr. Francis, iv. 336; Isabella, iv. 336; Joanna (Jacky), iv. 483; John, iv. 483
Neish, Mary, ii. 327
Nelson, Susannah, i. 101
Nesbitt, Francelina, iii. 112, 113; James, iii. 112, 113
Ness, Charlotte, iv. 458; James, iii. 140; James Burdett, iv. 458; Jane, iii. 140
Nevill, Henry, 2nd Earl of Abergavenny, iii. 366; Lady Mary Catherine, iii. 366
Neville, Catherine, iii. 458; John, iii. 458
Newark, 3rd titular Lord, *see* Anstruther, William
Newell, William, ii. 430
Newhaven, Baron, *see* Mayne, William
Newhouse, Lt.-Col. William Charles, iii. 214
Newman, Anne, iii. 729, iv. 29; Charles, iii. 729
Newport, Arthur, iii. 189; Jane, ii. 328; William, ii. 328
Newton, Elizabeth, ii. 211; Isabella, i. 308; John, ii. 211; William, i. 308
Nicholls, Sir George, iii. 217; Martha, ii. 389; Capt. Robert, ii. 389
Nichols, Elizabeth, iv. 361; John, iv. 361
Nicholson, Caroline Alicia, iii. 272; Catherine, ii. 162; Charles, ii. 162; Frances, ii. 332, iii. 783; Isabella Maria, i. 3; James, i. 3, iii. 272; John, iii. 783; Joseph, ii. 332; Sarah, iv. 578
Nickle, Col. Sir Robert, iii. 381
Nicol, Euphemia, ii. 73
Nicolay, Frederick, iii. 680; Laura Maria, iii. 680
Nicolls, Anne Sarah Maria, i. 244; Lt.-Gen. Sir Jasper, i. 244
Nicolson, Mary, ii. 538, iii. 729
Nightingale, Capt. Edward Herbert, i. 313; Florence, iv. 121; Asst. Surg. Manby, iv. 81; Sophia (*née* Blackall), i. 313
Nimmo, Maria, ii. 333, iii. 725
Nind, *see* Nynd
Nixon, Elizabeth, iv. 25; Euphemia, ii. 495; George, ii. 495; Mary, iv. 16; Richard, iv. 25; Capt. Richard James, iv. 79
Noble, Caroline Sarah, iv. 361; Vice-Adm. James, iv. 361; Major Jerome, i. 154, iii. 562; Margaret, i. 154, ii. 374; Prudentia, iii. 562
Nooran Begum, iv. 242
Norman, Florinda, ii. 135
Norrah, Pheannah, ii. 498
Norris, Hannah Mary, ii. 42; Louisa Maria, ii. 507; Mary, iii. 6; Matilda Emily Ann, ii. 392, 460; Thomas, ii. 42, 392, 507
Northbrook, 1st Baron, *see* Baring, Francis Thornhill
Northesk, 7th Earl of, *see* Carnegie, William
Norton, Dorothy, iv. 638
Nott, Ann, ii. 42
Nourse, Dorothea Mary, iii. 269; Joseph, iii. 269
Nuzzeer Begum, i. 355
Nynd, Frances, i. 328; William, iv. 632
Nyss, Mary Ann, ii. 180

O

Oakley, Sir Charles, 1st Bt., iii. 627; Louisa, iii. 627
O'Brien, Edmund, ii. 191; Edward, ii. 619; Eleanor, ii. 619; James, 3rd Marquess of Thomond, ii. 485; Kate, ii. 10; Margaret, ii. 342; Mary Ann, ii. 191; Matthew, ii. 10; Peter, M.D., ii. 342
O'Callaghan, Sarah, ii. 583
O'Casey, Mary, iii. 418
Ochterlony, Sir Charles Metcalfe, 2nd Bt., iii. 155; David, iii. 771; Mary, iii. 771; Roderick Peregrine, iii. 155
Odell, Isabella, iii. 683; John Osborne, iii. 683
Ogden, Ann, ii. 12; James, ii. 12
Ogilvie, Emily Charlotte, i. 112; Letitia K. (*née* Spence), iv. 153; William, i. 112

INDEX OF NAMES

Ogilvy, Catherine, iv. 445 ; Margaret, iii. 775 ; (or Ogilvie) Margaret, iv. 96 ; (or Ogilvie) Peter, iv. 96 ; Susan, ii. 521 ; William, iv. 445
O'Hara, Hester, iii. 266 ; Lawrence, iii. 83, iv. 105 ; Robert, iii. 266
Okes, Rev. Dr. Holt, iii. 479 ; Isabella Clara, iii. 479
Oldershaw, Cecilia Elizabeth, iii. 39 ; James, iii. 39
Oldfield, Christopher, iii. 108 ; Elizabeth, i. 323 ; William, i. 323
Oliphant, George, ii. 598 ; Isabel, ii. 598 ; Janet, iii. 362 ; John, Lord Oliphant, iii. 362
Oliver, Bridget, iii. 771 ; Margaret, i. 239 ; Dr. Robert, i. 239 ; Violet, iii. 644 ; William, iii. 644, 773
Olivier, Eliza, i. 406
O'Neal, Dr., iii. 598
Onslow, Lucie (*née* Webber), iii. 804 ; Lieut. Robert Thorpe, iii. 804
Oram, Alfred, iii. 614 ; Georgiana, iii. 614
Orange, Mary, iii. 381 ; Thomas, iii. 381
Oranmore and Browne, Barons, family of, iii. 176
Orchard, Sarah Baker, i. 389 ; William, i. 389
Ord, Eliza, ii. 550 ; Mary, ii. 219, iii. 724 ; Mary Prudence, iv. 392
Orde, B., iv. 393 ; Sarah Caroline, iv. 393
O'Reilly, Anne, iii. 37 ; Anthony Alexander, iii. 37 ; Catherine, iii. 712 ; Philip, iii. 712
Orfeur, Charles, iii. 477 ; Margaret, iii. 477
Orford, 1st Earl of, *see* Walpole, Sir Robert
Orme, A. C., i. 398 ; Mrs. Mary Elizabeth, i. 398 ; Robert, ii. 492
Orr, John, iii. 114 ; Rebecca (*née* McCulloch), iii. 114
Osborn, Mary, iv. 633 ; Mary (*née* Willett), iv. 473 ; Robert, iv. 633
Osborne, Henry, ii. 149, iv. 121 ; Louisa (*née* Twentyman), ii. 149 ; Margaret, iv. 121
Ostlife, Francis, i. 120 ; John, i. 119, iii. 741 ; Mary, iii. 741

Otter, Dorothy, iv. 261 ; Rev. Edward, iv. 261
Ottley, Jane, ii. 485 ; Thomas, ii. 485
Ouchterlony, Mary Ann, i. 130
Oudley, (Cecilia) Sarah, iv. 539
Ouseley, Eliza Martha Maria, i. 196 ; Julia Frances, iv. 37 ; Sir William, i. 196, iv. 37
Overbeek, Daniel Anthony, ii. 53, 292 ; Jacoba Maria Johanna, ii. 53 ; Johanna Leonora Christiana, ii. 292, iv. 528
Ovington, Ann, ii. 568
Owen, Henry, iii. 412 ; Mary, iv. 366 ; Sophia (*née* O'Brien), iii. 412
Owens, Sarah, ii. 425
Oxenden, Flora Elizabeth, iii. 138 ; Sir Henry, 7th Bt., iii. 138 ; Rev. Montagu, iii. 138
Oxley, Ellen, ii. 481 ; Thomas, ii. 481

P

Pacifico, Dr. Emanuel, iv. 346
Padbury, John, ii. 446
Pagan, Catherine, i. 285
Page, Frances (*née* Cartwright), i. 314 ; Mary, ii. 540 ; William, i. 314
Paget, Anna Aletheia Elizabeth, iii. 517 ; Rev. John, iii. 517 ; Sarah Maria, iii. 343 ; William, iii. 343
Pain, Ellen, iv. 322 ; Matilda, iv. 322 ; Rev. Richard, iv. 322
Pairman, Helen, i. 150, iii. 744 ; Rev. William, i. 150, iii. 744
Palm, Maria, iv. 415 ; Thomas, iv. 415
Palk, Sir Robert, 1st Bt., iv. 425
Palliser, Sir Hugh, 2nd Bt., iii. 72 ; Mary Jane, iii. 72
Palmer, Anne, iii. 305 ; Anna Bazett Catherine, iii. 551 ; Caroline, iv. 439 ; Catharina (*née* Catlyn), i. 320 ; Charles Finch, ii. 162 ; Claudine Anne, i. 374 ; Elizabeth, iii. 439, 449 ; John, i. 374, ii. 352, 551, iii. 767 ; Louisa, ii. 58, iii. 767 ; Roger, iii. 449 ; Theophila, ii. 352 ; Ursula, iii. 10 ; William, i. 218, 320 ; Rev. William, iii. 439, iv. 439
Palmerston, Lord, *see* Temple, Henry

INDEX OF NAMES

Palmes, George, iii. 54
Panna Purree, iii. 490
Paris, Ann, iv. 279
Parke, Emily, i. 15; Rev. Gilbert, iv. 480; Rt. Hon. Sir James, Baron Wensleydale, iii. 739; Louisa, iv. 480; William, i. 15
Parker, Anne, ii. 50; Eliza Anne, ii. 268; Harding, ii. 50, 268; Sophia Amelia Alphonsina (*née* McClintock), i. 141; William A., i. 141
Parkhouse, Hannah, i. 396; Philip, i. 396
Parkinson, Sally, iii. 190
Parkyns, Frances Ann Hamilton, ii. 82, iv. 88; Levitt Broadley, ii. 82, iv. 88
Parlby, Maria, iv. 559
Parmenter, Elizabeth, iii. 12
Parr, Rachel, ii. 293; Thomas, ii. 293
Parratt, Eliza Sophia, i. 287; Thomas, i. 287
Parry, Anne, iii. 397; Caleb Hillier, M.D., iv. 488; Elizabeth Emma, iv. 488; Mary, ii. 298; Mary Anne Catherine Eliza, iii. 520; Owen Henry, iii. 520; Robert, iii. 397; Rev. William, iv. 506
Parsloe, Caroline, iii. 97
Parson, Rev. Joseph, ii. 387
Parsons, John, iv. 631; Maria Anne, iv. 631; Penelope, iv. 331; Richard, iii. 548; Sarah Homeria, iii. 548
Partridge, Catherine, i. 399; Joseph, i. 42; Rev. Thomas Esbury, i. 399
Pascal, Major (? Edmund), iii. 356; Frances, iii. 356
Paschaud, Mary Ann, iii. 463
Pasley, Eliza, i. 286; Dr. Gilbert, i. 286; Helen, iii. 58; James, iii. 58
Paterson, Agnes, iii. 459; Col. Daniel, ii. 11; Harriet, ii. 11; Jemima Janet, i. 282; William, iii. 459
Patey, Elizabeth Weekes, iv. 397
Paton, Janet, iii. 733
Pattenson, Ann Louisa, ii. 485; Charles, ii. 485
Patterson, George, i. 84; Janet, i. 84; Dr. John, iii. 598
Pattison, Isabella, iv. 34; Rev. John, iv. 34

Pattle, Lydia Sarah, iv. 370; Sarah Susannah, iii. 684
Patton, Mrs. Isabella, i. 216; James, iii. 748
Pattullo, Ann, iv. 73; Capt. Archibald Erskine, iv. 73
Pau, John, iv. 372
Paul, Ann Maria, ii. 276
Pawson, George, ii. 602; Maria Seaton, ii. 602; William, ii. 602
Paxton, Susan, iii. 566
Payne, Sir Gillies, 2nd Bt., ii. 573; J., ii. 502; Louisa, ii. 287; Mary Anne, ii. 502; Susannah, ii. 573; Capt. William, R.N., iii. 397
Payter, Emily, i. 282; J. W., i. 282
Peach, Capt., ii. 574
Peacock, Ann (or Frances), iv. 384; Emily Edwards, iii. 745; Francis, iv. 384; Rev. William, iii. 745
Pearce, Rt. Hon. Sir Edward Lovett, iv. 256; Esther, ii. 17; Mary, iv. 256
Pearse, Anne Sarah, iii. 370; George, M. D., iii. 370
Pearson, Eliza, ii. 519; Louisa, ii. 133; Sophia, iv. 66; Walker, ii. 133, iv. 66
Pechell, Jacob, iii. 752; Mary, iii. 752; Sir Paul, 1st Bt., iii. 752
Peckwell, Selina Mary, ii. 344; Rev. Dr., ii. 344
Pedron, Ellen, iii. 709; Col. iii. 709
Peel, John, iii. 299; Sir Robert, 1st Bt., iii. 299
Peirce, Elizabeth, iv. 516
Peers, Henry Stackpole de Linnée, iii. 666
Pelling, Catherine, iii. 445; Elizabeth, iv. 595; Thomas, iii. 445, iv. 595
Pemberton, Benjamin, iii. 790; Frances, iii. 270; William, iii. 270
Penfold, Ann (*née* Norton), iii. 402; James, iii. 402
Penneck, Catherine, iii. 618; Rev. Richard, iii. 618
Penney, Florena Charlotte, ii. 217; William, Lord Kinloch, ii. 217
Pennick, Charles, iii. 673; Mrs. Julia, iii. 673

Pennington, Isabella, i. 415; Rev. Thomas, i. 415
Peppere, Powle, iii. 427; Susannah, iii. 427
Pepys, Edmund, iv. 70; Eliza, iv. 70
Perceval, Elizabeth, iii. 499; Major, iii. 499
Perchard, Marguerite, ii. 472, 475
Percival, Anne, ii. 410; Robert, ii. 411
Percy, Elizabeth, iii. 271; Col. Hon. Henry, ii. 108; Rt. Rev. Thomas, iii. 271
Peret, Georgiana, ii. 263
Perfect, John, ii. 241; Lucy Julia, ii. 241
Perham, Elizabeth, iii. 675; John, iii. 675
Perigoe, Maria, iii. 55
Perreau, Daniel, ii. 536; Frances, ii. 536; Robert, ii. 536
Perron, Gen. Pierre Cuiller, iii. 709, iv. 576
Perrot, Mr., iv. 452
Perry, Angel, i. 214; Anna Margaret, iv. 232; Capt. Edward, i. 214; James, ii. 200; Jane, ii. 421; Capt. Robert, ii. 421; Rev. William, iv. 232
Pery, Sophia, iv. 308; William, iv. 308
Peterborough, 4th Earl of, *see* Mordaunt, Charles; 5th Earl of, *see* Mordaunt, Charles Henry
Peterkin, James, iii. 513; Mary Anne, iii. 513
Peterson, Eliza, i. 280; Susannah, ii. 473
Peto, Anne, ii. 342; James, ii. 342
Petre, Sir George Glynn, iv. 145
Pettingall, Mary Ann, i. 151
Pettiward, Frances, ii. 149
Pettus, Sir Horatio, 6th Bt. of Rackheath, iv. 153
Peverell, Margaret, iv. 578
Phelips, Elizabeth, iii. 512; Rev. William, iii. 512
Philipps, Catherine, iv. 290; James, iv. 290
Philips, Georgina, i. 205; Rev. Henry George, i. 205
Phillips, Charlotte, iv. 244; Eliza Douce (*née* Hancock), iii. 236;
Emilia Elizabeth, iv. 525; Frances, ii. 199; Rev. George, ii. 199; Henrietta Wynetta, iii. 587; Miss H. G., iii. 523; Capt. Richard, iii. 587, iv. 244; Thomas Walford, iv. 525; Dr., ii. 274; Miss (Mrs. John Davis), ii. 25; ——, ii. 436
Phillipson, Eliza, iii. 431; W. B., iii. 431
Pickersgill, Emma, ii. 372; Harriet, iv. 72
Picton, Catherine, iv. 392; Lt.-Gen. Sir Thomas, iv. 392; Thomas, iv. 392
Piding, Ann, iv. 55
Pierce, Emilia, ii. 194, iii. 777; Capt. Richard, iii. 651, 777; Sophia Sarah Jane, iii. 651
Pigott, Agnes, ii. 248; Emma, iv. 274; John, i. 221; Mary, i. 221; Sarah, i. 136; William, iv. 274; Rev. William, i. 136
Pigou, Capt. Harry, ii. 94; Henry Minchin, iii. 593; Louisa, ii. 94; Louisa Hester, iii. 593
Pilcher, Jemima, iv. 226; Paul, iv. 226
Pilfold, John, iii. 273, iv. 629; Mary, iii. 273, iv. 629
Pinkerton, George, iv. 180; Mary, iv. 180
Piovene di Vicenza, Contessa, iii. 253
Pipe, Anne, iv. 406
Pirner, Matilda Elizabeth, iii. 714; W., iii. 714
Pitman, Dorothy Hannah (*née* Harriott), ii. 391
Pitt, Honour, ii. 337, 338; James, iii. 558; John, iii. 396, 558; Joseph, iii. 663; Sarah, iii. 396
Plaitt, Ensign John, iii. 535
Playfair, Ann, ii. 443; Surg. George, ii. 443, iv. 434; Jessie Macdonald, iv. 434
Plestow, Eliza Maria, ii. 439; T. B., ii. 439
Plowden, Amelia Frances, i. 336; Frances Sophia Pattle, i. 35; Trevor John Chicheley, i. 35, 336
Plumbe, Fanny, iv. 232
Plumer, Marianne, iv. 330; Sir Thomas, iv. 330

INDEX OF NAMES

Plusker, Jacob, i. 167, iii. 683, 703; Johanna Christina, i. 25; Johanna Margaritta, i. 167; Surg. Johannes, i. 25; Margaretha Louisa, iii. 683; Sophia Jacoba, i. 167, iii. 703
Podmore, Frances Matilda, ii. 342; Maj.-Gen. Richard, ii. 342
Poë, Annie Blanche, iv. 59; Robert Waller, iv. 59
Pogson, Bedingfield, iii. 146; Mary Elizabeth, iii. 146
Poingdestre, Marie, i. 39
Polehampton, Emily Augusta (née Allnut), ii. 108; Rev. Henry Stedman, ii. 108
Polkinghorne, Lieut. John, iii. 805; Mrs. Lydia Maria, iii. 805
Pomeroy, Elizabeth, iii. 512; John, iii. 512
Ponsonby, Brabazon, 1st Earl of Bessborough, iv. 228; Dorothy, iv. 174; Frederick, iv. 228; John, iv. 174
Poole, Ann (née Hurring), ii. 510; Elizabeth, iii. 522; John, ii. 510
Poor Begum, iv. 240
Pope, Maria, iii. 655; Susannah, i. 301
Popham, Anne, ii. 500; Adm. Sir Home Riggs, ii. 469, 500, iv. 471; Joseph, ii. 500; Lady, ii. 469
Popkin, Frances, iv. 299; John, iv. 299
Popplewell, James, i. 78; Mary Anne, i. 78
Porson, Professor Richard, ii. 200
Porteous, Rt. Rev. Beilby, ii. 459
Porter, Anne, iii. 183; Mrs. Mary, ii. 386; Thomas, iii. 54
Porterfield, Ann, iv. 321
Portland, 3rd Duke of, see Bentinck, William Henry Cavendish
Portner, Elizabeth Ann, iii. 523; Melchior, iii. 523
Pott, Bertha Russell, iv. 232; Katherine (née Reid), iii. 559; Percivall, iii. 781; Robert, iv. 232; Sarah, iii. 781
Poulett, Lord, iii. 760
Povoleri, Marchese Domenico, iii. 253; Countess Elizabeth Francesca, iii. 253
Powditch, Margaret, i. 272; Thomas, i. 272
Powell, Anna Maria Selina, iii. 71; Anne, iii. 33, 781; Fletcher, iii. 33; Francis, iii. 71; Harriott, iv. 405; John, iii. 781; Mary, iii. 781; Richard, iv. 405
Power, Sarah (née Smalpage), iv. 115
Powney, Anne, ii. 320; George, ii. 320
Powrie, Rev. J., ii. 523; Louisa Maria (née Loveday), ii. 523
Prager, George, iii. 570
Pratchet, Sarah, iii. 399
Pratt, Edward, i. 26; Lucy, i. 26
Pratten, ——, iii. 527
Précoure, Joseph, iii. 136; Josette, iii. 136
Prendergast, John, 1st Viscount Gort, iv. 203; Teresa, i. 306
Prentice, Charlotte Carse, ii. 120; Edmund Samuel, ii. 120
Prestidge, Hannah, i. 137; H., i. 137
Preston, C. R., i. 177; Elizabeth, ii. 188; Frances Elizabeth, i. 177; Rev. Plunket, ii. 188
Prevost, Lt.-Gen. Sir George, 1st Bt., ii. 308
Prhys, Clopton, iv. 503; Margaret, iv. 503
Price, Clara, i. 168; Jocelyn, i. 168; Mary, i. 348; Richard, iii. 496
Prichard, William, iii. 805
Prickett, Paul, iii. 645; Sarah, iii. 645
Priddle, Anne Phoebe, iii. 575; William, iii. 575
Prince, John, iii. 48
Pringle, Anna Ludivina, i. 392; Elizabeth Leonora, i. 21; Emma, iv. 346; George, iv. 346; Joseph, i. 21
Prinsep, Augusta Emily, i. 118; Augustus, i. 118
Printzling, Conradine, ii. 188; C. H. G., ii. 188
Proby, Letitia, ii. 45; Rev. Narcissus Charles, ii. 45
Probyn, Caroline, iii. 592; Very Rev. John, iii. 592
Proctor, Ann, ii. 271, iv. 527; Cecily, iii. 6; Janet, ii. 288; John, iii. 6; Margaret, iii. 797; Mary Anne, iv. 275; Richard, M. D., iv. 275; Thomas, iv. 527

INDEX OF NAMES

Prosser, Elizabeth Sophia, iii. 540, iv. 599; George Augustus, iii. 540, iv. 599
Pryce, Diana, iii. 774; Elizabeth Constantia, iii. 333; Sir John Powell, 6th Bt., iii. 774; Richard, iii. 333
Puckle, Mary Catherine, ii. 572; Thomas, ii. 572
Pugh, Elizabeth (née Mackenzie), iii. 155; James, iii. 155
Purcell, Richard, iii. 675
Purlewent, Mary, iv. 27; W., iv. 27
Purvis, Capt. George, R.N., iii. 490; (Qy. Furvis), Joseph, iii. 363; Martha, iii. 363, 490
Pybus, Anne, ii. 195; John, ii. 195
Pye, Elizabeth, iv. 369, 375; Capt. William, iv. 369, 375
Pyefinch, Eliza, ii. 403
Pyott, Helen, iii. 97

Q

Queiros, Ann Cordelia, iii. 544; Emily Mary, ii. 62; Joseph, iii. 381, 544; Theresa, iii. 381
Quienchant, Elizabeth, iv. 506; Capt. Jean Jenvre, iv. 506
Quin, Margaret, ii. 480
Quinchant, see Kinchant and Quienchant

R

Raban, Anne, i. 234; Emma Maria, ii. 447; Mary Elizabeth, i. 76; Robert, ii. 614; Thomas, i. 234, ii. 447, 614
Rabeholm, Elizabeth, iv. 2; N., iv. 2
Rae, Sir David, 1st Bt. of Esk Grove, ii. 413; Helen, ii. 413
Raffles, Sir Thomas Stamford, ii. 496, iv. 166; Lady, ii. 497
Raggett, John, i. 402; Sarah, i. 402
Raglan, 1st Baron, see Somerset, Lord FitzRoy James Henry
Raikes, Martha, ii. 597; Sophia, ii. 487; Thomas, ii. 487; William, ii. 597
Raincock, Rev. John, ii. 192
Rainey, Eliza, ii. 39; Maggy Ellen, iv. 465
Raining, Sarah, ii. 596

Rainsford, Capt. Thomas, ii. 384
Rairy, Eliza, iv. 577
Raitt, Helen Hay, i. 109; John, i. 109
Rajendra, Mary Anne, i. 415
Ralston, Annabella, i. 410; Gavin, i. 410
Ramsay, Sir Alexander, Bt. of Balmain, iv. 230; Allan, i. 281; Amelia, i. 281; Hon. Andrew, iii. 281; Anne Finlay Anderson, ii. 146; Elizabeth, iv. 230, 485; Elizabeth Balfour, iv. 389; George, 8th Earl of Dalhousie, ii. 419; George, 9th Earl, iii. 281; George, 12th Earl, iii. 599; Helen, ii. 346; Henrietta, iii. 683; James, iv. 111; Jean, iv. 512; Lt.-Gen. Hon. John, ii. 146; Col. John, ii. 22, iii. 683; Katharine, iii. 153; Margaret, iv. 179; Lady Mary, ii. 419; Mary, ii. 22; Robert, iii. 153, iv. 179, 512; Robert Balfour, iv. 389; of Banff, family of, iv. 512
Ramsden, George, iii. 631
Ramus, Maria, i. 135
Rand, Frances, iii. 527, 528
Randall, Benjamin, iii. 401; Mary Susan, iii. 401; Susan, ii. 70; W., ii. 70
Ranken, Agnes, iii. 471; Elizabeth, iii. 770; George, iii. 471, 695; Janet, iii. 695; Jessie, i. 326
Rankine, Henrietta Janet, iii. 614; John, iii. 614; Robert, iii. 603
Rannie, Elizabeth Bayley, iii. 633
Raper, Catherine Charlotte, i. 231, ii. 217
Ratcliffe, Lady, iv. 572
Rathay, Christina, iv. 278
Rattray, Christian, iii. 603; David, M.D., iv. 421; Eliza, iv. 421
Rauly, Mrs. Carten, iii. 726; Perrette, iii. 726
Ravenhill, G., iv. 5; Maria, iv. 5
Ravenscroft, Elizabeth, ii. 550; George, ii. 549, 550, iii. 536; Harriet Constantia, ii. 549
Rawstorne, Eliza Helen, ii. 526; Sophia, ii. 489
Rayner, Susannah, iii. 677; Thomas, iii. 678
Raynsford, Louisa Sophia, iii. 70; Nicolls, iii. 70

Read, Anne, iii. 631, iv. 421; Henry, iii. 633; Capt. John, iv. 421; John, iii. 120; Mary Ann, i. 293; Sarah, iii. 555
Reay, 8th Baron, *see* Mackay, Alexander
Reddall, Anne, iv. 480
Reddie, Catherine, iv. 37; Capt. John, iv. 37
Rede, Elizabeth, iv. 327; Thomas, iv. 327
Redford, Mary (*née* Hyde), ii. 518
Redhead, Arabella, iv. 578; Elizabeth, iv. 578
Reed, Eleanor, iii. 802, iv. 89; Jean, i. 292; Lydia, iii. 741; Mrs. Mary, iv. 89
Reeder, Surg. Thomas Anthony, iii. 316
Rees, Charles Goldney, iv. 448; Joanna, iv. 448
Reid, David, i. 109, 110, iii. 559; Davidson, i. 109, 110; Eliza, i. 414; Frances Charlotte, iii. 281; Capt. Hugh Atkins, ii. 224; Mrs. Jane, i. 93; John, i. 429, iv. 185; Surg. John, iii. 281; Katherine, ii. 368, iii. 559; Margaret Mary Ann, ii. 224; R. H. S., i. 93; Sarah, i. 429; Lieut. Thomas, iii. 724; Surg. Maj., ii. 240
Reilly, Surg. Bernard, ii. 275, iv. 351; Harriet, ii. 275; Helen Maria, iv. 428; James, iv. 428; Mary, iv. 351
Remington, Frances Vic, iv. 512; John, iv. 512; Margaret, i. 380; Mary, iv. 288; William, i. 380
Rendlesham, 1st Baron, *see* Thellusson, Peter Isaac
Renfrew, Annabella, iii. 434
Rennell, Rose, ii. 117; Rev. Thomas, ii. 117
Rennie, Veronica, iii. 575; Miss, i. 368
Renny (Rainey), Jean, iii. 626; Capt., iii. 626
Revell, Anne Eliza, i. 120; Anne Matilda, ii. 45; Emily, iii. 81; Frances Catherine, iii. 468; Henry, i. 120, ii. 45, iii. 81, 468
Reybaud, Emily, i. 389
Reynolds, Anne Maria, iii. 521; Anna Sophia, iii. 146; Georgiana, Emma, iii. 657; Jacob Foster, iii. 146; Mrs. Jane, iv. 516; John, iii. 657; William, iii. 521
Rhoades, Rev. Edward James, iv. 155
Rhodes, Ann, ii. 603
Rhus Khan, iii. 21
Rice, Ann Davidson, iv. 420; Mary, iii. 810; Robert, iii. 810
Rich, Ann, iv. 201
Richards, Mrs. Sarah, iii. 373; Capt., R.N., iii. 373
Richardson, Agnes, iii. 492; Anne, iv. 224; Anne Mervyn, ii. 601; Catherine, iv. 72, 545, 551; Col. Francis, iii. 73; Jean, iii. 697; John, ii. 416; Capt. Joseph, iv. 279; Katharine Elizabeth, iv. 41; Ker, iv. 72; Letitia Niel, iii. 73; Margaret, ii. 416; Maria, iv. 279; Mary, ii. 61; Samuel, iv. 224; Thomas, iv. 98; Rev. Thomas, iv. 41; Sir William, Bt. of Augher, ii. 601; William, iii. 492
Rickards, Augusta Catherina, i. 169; Hester M., i. 75; John, i. 169; R., i. 75
Ricketts, Charlotte Adeline Judith, i. 163; Fanny, ii. 189; Frances Isabella, iii. 665; George Poyntz, iii. 665; Mordaunt, i. 163, ii. 189
Rider, Jacob, ii. 615, iii. 800; Sally, ii. 558; Selina Cecilia, ii. 491, iii. 800; William, iv. 543
Ridgard, Helen, i. 70; Nathaniel, i. 70
Ridges, Clementina Diana, ii. 242
Ridgeway, James Leech, iii. 516; Maria, iii. 516
Ridley, Viscounts, family of, iii. 656
Rigg, Ann, iii. 599, 603; James, i. 219; Margaret, i. 219
Riggs, Mary, iii. 557
Ringrose, Elizabeth, iv. 200; Capt. Thomas, iv. 200
Ritchie, Christian, i. 14
Rivett, Elizabeth, i. 305; Thomas, i. 305
Robarts, Abraham, iv. 252; Sabine, iv. 252
Robbins, Elizabeth, iii. 101; William, iii. 101

Roberts, Major Allen, iv. 222; Anne, iv. 525; Eleanor, iii. 148; Elizabeth Anne Peel, iv. 222; Eliza Morrissey, iv. 216; Emma, iii. 189; Eugenia, iii. 495; Frances Eliza, ii. 312; Frances Isabella (*née* Ricketts), iii. 665; Frederick Sleigh, 1st Earl Roberts, ii. 312; Harriot, i. 393; Henry, iv. 525; Laura Henrietta, iii. 189; Loetitia, ii. 528; Maria Bellett, i. 233; Martha (*née* Ellithorne), ii. 135; Rev. Robert, ii. 528; Rosamond, iii. 283; Capt. William, iii. 189; William, i. 393, iii. 148; Rev. William Hayward, iii. 283

Robertson, Anne, ii. 235, 502, iii. 750, 777; Catherine, iv. 488; Colin, ii. 272; C., iii. 73; Elizabeth, iii. 742; George, iii. 320; Georgiana, ii. 272; Mrs. Harriet D'Oyly, i. 152; Isabella, ii. 101; Surg. James, ii. 469, iv. 10; Jean, iii. 320; Jean (*née* Hay), ii. 413; Jemima Haldane, iv. 10; John, i. 204, iii. 750; Margaret Haldane, ii. 469; Marion, iii. 79; Mary, ii. 520, iv. 553; Mary Lauderdale, i. 204; Robert, ii. 235, 502, 520; William, ii. 101; Lieut., iii. 79

Robinson, Ann, iii. 687; Bellinda, iv. 93; Elizabeth, iv. 416; Ellen Anne, iii. 572; Euphemia, ii. 140; Frances, iv. 160; Harriot, iv. 558; John, ii. 578, iv. 161; J., iii. 572; Maria, ii. 578; Mary (*née* Ellithorne), ii. 135; Sarah, i. 258; William, iv. 160, 416

Robison, John, iv. 518

Robson, Elizabeth, iv. 523; Col. Francis, iv. 43; Henrietta, iv. 43; James, iv. 331; Jane, iv. 331

Roche, Anne, iii. 78; Capt. David, ii. 173; Stephen, iii. 78

Rochford, Ann, ii. 129

Rochfort, Mary, iii. 785; Robert, 1st Earl of Belvidere, iii. 683, 785

Rocke, Rev. Thomas, iii. 454

Rockville, Lord, *see* Gordon, Hon. Alexander

Roddy, Ann Mary, iii. 737

Rodger, Hugh, iii. 100; Margaret, iii. 100

Rodney, George Brydges, 1st Baron Rodney, i. 326, iii. 352; Hon. Jane, i. 326; Hon. Sarah Brydges, iii. 352

Roe, Catherine, iii. 760; John (or William), iii. 760

Roebuck, Elizabeth Louisa, iv. 245; Henry Disney, iv. 245; John, M.D., iv. 530

Rogers, Fanny Beaumont, iii. 675; Sir Frederick Leman, 5th Bt., iv. 245; Jane, iv. 479; Lewis, iv. 479; Mary, iv. 245

Rolland, Elizabeth, iv. 308; Mary, iii. 361

Rollo, James, 7th Baron Rollo, ii. 507; Hon. Jane, ii. 507

Romer, John, iii. 807; Margaret, iii. 807

Romney, Mary Anne, iii. 646

Rorke, John, iv. 333; Maria Katharine, iv. 333

Rose, Christian, iii. 359; Elizabeth, iv. 554; Hugh, iii. 674; Rev. James, iv. 554; Janet, iii. 674; Margaret, ii. 16; Mrs. Marian, iii. 659; of Kilravoch, family of, iv. 554

Rosie, Catherine, iv. 100

Ross, Anne, iii. 538; Capt. Daniel, iv. 49; Eliza, iv. 49; George, i. 333; Grace, i. 285; Isabella, iv. 550; Isabella Rose, ii. 265; James, iii. 50, 289; Jane, i. 85, 256, iv. 142; John, ii. 600, iii. 538; Maria Ann, iv. 363; Mary, ii. 600, iii. 358; Bailie Nicholas, iii. 358; Lt.-Col. Robert, iv. 303; Sarah Aglionby, i. 333; Major Thomas, ii. 265; of Invernethie, i. 85

Rosselet, Sophia, iii. 511

Rouband, Matilda Elizabeth, iv. 386

Roughsedge, Jane, i. 310; Rev. Robert Hankinson, i. 310

Roundell, Rev. Danson Richardson, ii. 486; Mary Anne, ii. 486

"Rover, John," pseud. of Sir John Horsford, *q.v.*

Rowe, Elizabeth, iii. 16; Elizabeth Grace, iii. 680; Milward, iii. 680; Richard, iii. 16; Sarah, i. 176

Rowlands, Samuel, iii. 554

Rowley, Clotworthy, iv. 356; Adm. Sir Josias, Bt., iv. 357; Mary, iv. 356

Royle, Jane Anne, ii. 36
Rozento, Maria, iii. 276
Ruddiman, Alison, iv. 193; Thomas, iv. 193
Ruddle, Francis, i. 107; Mary, i. 107
Rumball, Emma, ii. 423; Thomas, ii. 423
Rundell, Maria, iii. 743; Thomas, iii. 743
Rush, Rev. Henry John, ii. 85; Mary Anne, ii. 85
Russell, Anne (née McRoberts), iii. 202; Caroline, iii. 243; Charlotte, see Auriol; Eliza, iv. 568; James, iii. 795, iv. 576; Janet McKill, iv. 576; John, iii. 202; Mary, i. 45; Sarah, iii. 795; Sophia, i. 144; Sir William, 1st Bt. of Charlton Park, i. 144, iv. 75; (afterwards Kempe), William, ii. 580; W., iii. 389; Sir William Oldnall, i. 45
Rutherfurd, Alice, iii. 90; David, iii. 90; Jane, iii. 426; John, iii. 426
Ruthven, Elizabeth Sutherland, iii. 552; E. S., iii. 419; James, 6th Lord Ruthven, iii. 711; Louisa Alexander, iii. 419; Mary Elizabeth Thornton, Baroness Ruthven, iii. 711
Rutland, 3rd Duke of, see Manners, John
Rutledge, Eliza, ii. 245, iii. 711; Miss H., ii. 409
Rutter, Isabella, iv. 173
Ruttledge, Dorothea, ii. 607; Peter, ii. 607
Ruxton, Henry Thomas Bellingham, i. 21; Martha, i. 21
Ryan, Honorae, ii. 176
Ryley, Rev. John, iii. 37; Martha, iii. 37
Rynd, Christopher, iii. 19; Rebecca, iii. 19

S

Sabine, Diana Amelia, ii. 297; Joseph, ii. 297
Sadleir, Richard, ii. 377; Wilhelmina, ii. 377
Sadler, Elizabeth, iii. 487; Thomas, iii. 487
Sadur, Rose, iv. 216

St. Albyn, Anne, ii. 551; Langley, ii. 551
St. George, Amelia, i. 230; Edward, i. 230
St. Leger, Ellen, ii. 206; Lt.-Gen. William, ii. 206
Sale, Alexandrina, iv. 211; Caroline Catherine, ii. 453; Henrietta Sarah, i. 204; Julia Elizabeth, ii. 114; Mary Anne (née Denby), ii. 46; Mary Harriet, i. 240; Col. Sir Robert Henry, i. 204, 240, ii. 114, 453, iv. 211
Salmon, George, iii. 122; Nancy Scott, iii. 122
Salmond, Euphemia, iv. 270
Salter, Rev. John, iv. 442; J., iii. 431; Margaret, iv. 442; Mary, iii. 431; Samuel, i. 300; Sarah, i. 300
Sampson, Henry Morse, iii. 17; Mary Anne, iii. 17
Samuelson, als Macpherson, John, iii. 191
Sandby, Cornelia Paulina Henrietta, i. 234; Thomas, i. 234
Sandeman, Letitia, iv. 7; Mary, i. 181; William, iv. 7
Sanders, Harriet, ii. 284
Sand(e)s, Marcia, iii. 3; Rev. Patrick, iii. 3
Sandford, Caroline, iii. 614; E. M., iii. 614; Humphrey, iv. 34; Mary, iv. 34
Sandham, Surg. Backshall Lane, iv. 284; Marian, iv. 284
Sandys, Rev. Abraham, iii. 665; Anne, iii. 665; Philippa, iv. 443; William, iv. 443
Sanford, Frances, i. 340; William, i. 340
Sanxay, Rev. James, iii. 486; Jane, iii. 486
Sardinia, Charles Emmanuel III, King of, iii. 688
Satchwell, Elizabeth, i. 182; Richard Murcott, i. 182
Satterthwaite, Ann, iii. 389; Benjamin, iv. 445; Jane, iv. 270; John, iii. 389, iv. 270; Mary, iv. 452
Saumarez, Hon. Thomas Le Marchant, iii. 287
Saunders, Edward, iv. 363; Mrs. Elizabeth Ann, iv. 232; Helen, iv.

INDEX OF NAMES

363; Joseph, iii. 319; Margaret Lilias (*née* Murray), iii. 357; Martha Louisa, iv. 480; Morley Pendred, iv. 480; Sarah Gray, iii. 319

Savage, Hannah, iii. 378; William, iii. 378

Savary, Elizabeth Sophia, iv. 233; J., iv. 233

Savery, Catherine Elizabeth, iv. 198

Sawrey, John Gilpin-, iii. 783

Sayer, Anne, iii. 14; Mary, iv. 281

Schaw, Frances, iii. 710; John Sauchie, iii. 710

Schneeberg, Elizabeth, iv. 336; Count, iv. 336

Scobie, Mary, iv. 338

Scoones, Charlotte, iv. 202; William, iv. 202

Scott, Agnes, iv. 401; Alexa, ii. 66; Rev. Alexander John, iii. 713; Anne, iii. 321, iv. 150, 401; Archibald, iv. 401; Barbara, iii. 275; Charles, i. 377; Christian, iii. 474, iv. 544; Sir David, 2nd Bt. of Dunninald, iv. 8; David, i. 306, iv. 8; Elizabeth, i. 237, ii. 73; (*als* Macalister) Flora, iii. 105; Francis, 6th Baron Napier of Merchiston, iii. 370; Harriette, i. 377; James, ii. 161; Jane, i. 306, ii. 161; Jean Hay, ii. 484; John, 1st Earl of Clonmell, iii. 321; John, iv. 135; Louisa, iv. 8; Margaret, iii. 140, 354, iv. 375, 633; Marian Isabella, ii. 524; Mark, iii. 321; Mary, iii. 366; Melissa, iii. 773; Robert, iii. 474, 742, iv. 401, 633; Capt. Robert, R.N., ii. 73; Samuel, iii. 366; Sir Walter, iv. 185; Capt. William, R.N., ii. 66

Scriven, Anne, iii. 109; Edward, iii. 109

Scully, "Aunt," ii. 333

Sealy, Agnes, i. 97; John Nathaniel, iii. 19; Samuel, i. 97

Seaton, Elizabeth, ii. 106, iv. 135; Jean, ii. 70

Seck, John, iv. 342; Marian, iv. 342

Segar, Charlotte Elizabeth, i. 238

Selby, Rev. Robert Hele, ii. 426

Selkirk, 4th Earl of, *see* Hamilton, Dunbar Douglas

Sellars, Janet, iv. 518

Sellon, Elizabeth Anna, iv. 448; Rev. William, iv. 448

Sempill, Lord, iii. 137

Semple, Mary, iv. 221; Rev. Samuel, iv. 221

Senhouse, Jane, ii. 532; John, ii. 532

Senior, Ascanius William, iv. 254; Nevillia, iv. 254

Sergeant, Emma, i. 339

Serguel, Emanuel, ii. 269; Jena Rosalie, ii. 269

Seton, Margaret, iii. 735; R. A., ii. 372

Sewell, Rebecca, i. 195

Seymour, Lady Anna Maria, iv. 287; Edward Adolphus, 11th Duke of Somerset, iv. 287

Shadwell, Marianne, ii. 403

Shah Begum, iv. 566

Shakerley, Sir Charles Peter, 1st Bt., iv. 33

Shakespear, Henry, ii. 449; John, iii. 428; John Talbot, ii. 529; Louisa Mary Anne, ii. 449; Marianne Eliza Sparks, ii. 529; Mary, iii. 428

Sharp, Agnes, iv. 352, 353

Sharpe, Caroline, iv. 571; Dorothy, iii. 790; Lieut. John Edward, iv. 571

Shaw, Agnes, ii. 322; Alexander, ii. 322; Elizabeth, ii. 494, iii. 701, iv. 423; Hannah, iii. 516; Sir James, Bt., iii. 14; James, iv. 16; Jane, iii. 390, iv. 16; Jane Maria, i. 108; John, i. 435; Margaret Hannah, iv. 458; Marion, ii. 383; Mary Grace, i. 435; Rev. Samuel, iii. 516; Capt. Thomas, i. 168

Shea, Anna Maria, i. 400; Daniel, i. 400

Sheeles, John, iii. 215; Martha, iii. 215

Sheldrake, Catherine, iii. 765

Shelley, Percy Bysshe, iv. 202, 476, 636

Shepheard, Elizabeth, i. 275; E. W., i. 275

Shepherd, Ann (*née* Ovington), ii. 568

Sheppard, Alice Ordidge, iii. 258; Samuel, iii. 763; Sarah, iii. 763

INDEX OF NAMES

Sheridan, Eleanor, iv. 140; Louisa (*née* Addison), i. 10; Lt.-Gen. Sir William, i. 10
Sherin, Mrs. Charlotte Frederica, i. 356
Shield, Miss (? Louisa Maria), ii. 41
Shiers, Ann, iii. 495; William, iii. 495
Shippen, Edward, i. 52; Margaret, i. 52
Shirtley, Lydia, iii. 766
Shore, Lady Charlotte (*née* Cornish), i. 389; John, 1st Baron Teignmouth, i. 389; John, iv. 464
Shortt, Elizabeth Jane, iii. 519; Major, iii. 519
Shout, Miss, ii. 621
Shrubb, Rev. Henry, iv. 463
Shubrick, Capt. Richard, iii. 173
Shute, Harriet, i. 341; Samuel, i. 341
Sibthorpe, Elizabeth, i. 177; Stephen, i. 177
Siddons, Rev. ——, ii. 437
Sidney, Emma, iv. 287; James, iv. 287
Siegruhn, Augusta Wilhelmina, ii. 341
Sim, Agnes, iii. 392; J., iii. 392
Simpson, Anne, ii. 89; Catherine (*née* Read), ii. 122; Charles, iii. 764; Charles Robert, iv. 171; David, iv. 329; Eleanor, iv. 171; Euphemia, iv. 329; Frances Roupell, i. 80, iii. 738; George, iv. 635; Hannah, iii. 243; Harriet, iii. 785; James, i. 80, iii. 613, 785; James Alexander, iii. 738; Mrs. Jane, iii. 557; John, ii. 89, 122, iii. 557; Julia, iii. 613; Margaret, ii. 601, iv. 500; Mary, ii. 463; Mrs. Matilda, iv. 635
Sims, Anna Maria, i. 179; John, i. 179
Simson, George, iii. 29; Margaret, iii. 29
Sinclair, Lady Charlotte, iii. 137; Sir James, 12th Earl of Caithness, ii. 96, iii. 137; Janet, ii. 215; Rebecca, ii. 38
Sirrell, Joseph, ii. 313; Mary, ii. 313
Skeete, Helen, i. 273; Hon. John Braithwaite, i. 273

Skelley, Catherine Maria, ii. 336; Rev. John, ii. 336
Skene, John, iv. 139; Margaret, iv. 139
Skinner, Catherine, ii. 146; Cortlandt, i. 89; Elizabeth, ii. 357; Euphemia (or Efiginia), i. 89; Joseph, ii. 146; Samuel, ii. 146; Miss, ii. 484
Skipton, Easter, ii. 113; George Crookshank Kennedy, ii. 113
Skirving, Elizabeth, ii. 431; William, ii. 431
Skoulding, Amy, iv. 1
Skyring, Col. George, ii. 13; Jane, ii. 13
Slade, Benjamin, ii. 78; Mary, ii. 78
Slane, Lord, iii. 777
Slater, Barbara, iii. 298; Gill, iii. 298
Slator, Henrietta Dorothea (*née* Thomas), iv. 256; Rev. James, ii. 156, iv. 256; Maria (Mary Anne), ii. 155
Sleigh, Sarah, iv. 373; William, iv. 373
Slessor, Harriet, ii. 252; Major, ii. 252
Sloane, Catherine Margaretta, i. 68; Margaretta Bruce, i. 82
Sloper, Gen. Sir Robert, iv. 638
Small, Beaumont Dixie, ii. 230; Mrs. Caroline Honoria, ii. 230; Joseph, i. 401; Mary, i. 401
Smallwood, Rev. Charles, i. 301; Lydson, i. 301
Smerdon, Martha, ii. 115; Thomas, ii. 115
Smillie, Mrs. Ann, ii. 180; Robert, ii. 180
Smith, Alexander, ii. 428, iii. 533; Anne, iv. 436; Anna (*née* Lowrie), ii. 14; Anne (*née* Burrell), i. 259; Mrs. Anne Catherine, iii. 387; Anna Charlotte, iii. 524; Anna Hester, iv. 503; Aurora Catherine, iii. 265; Benjamin, iii. 89, 384; Burton, iv. 18, 159; Catherine Osborne, i. 207; Charles, i. 190; Charlotte Maria, iii. 107; Cordelia, i. 388; Edward, iv. 163; Egerton, i. 194; Eliza (*née* Harrison), ii. 72; Elizabeth, ii. 385, iii. 793, iv.

313; Ellen, ii. 242; Esther, iii. 502; Felix Vaughan, iv. 503; Folliot, ii. 620; Frances, i. 382, iii. 98; Frances (*née* Scotney), iv. 44; Frances Georgina, iii. 304, iv. 116; Georgiana Margaret, iii. 547; Major Hadden, ii. 148; Harriet, iv. 18, 159; Helen, ii. 523; Henrietta, ii. 428; Henry, ii. 72; Hercules, ii. 109; Isabella, ii. 109; Isabella Leigh, iii. 89; Jacobina, iii. 316; James, ii. 242, iv. 407; Jessie, ii. 325; Capt. John, i. 319; John, iii. 276, iv. 314; Lt.-Col. John Carrington, i. 346; Joseph, i. 88, ii. 352; Joseph Barnard, iii. 201; Lt.-Gen. Sir Lionel, Bt., iii. 384; Louisa, i. 123; Louisa (*née* McQuhae), i. 326; Lucy, iii. 384; Margaret, iii. 533; Martha Rose Diana, iv. 429; Mary, i. 211, ii. 261, 262, iv. 163; Mary (or Ann Maria), iii. 286; Mrs. Mary, i. 319, iii. 280; Mary Adelaide, i. 190; Mary Egerton, i. 194; Mary Garratt, iv. 414; Mrs. McRae, ii. 247; Mercy, ii. 262; M., iii. 547; Nathaniel, iv. 295; Penelope, i. 88, ii. 352; Robert, 1st Baron Carrington, iv. 133; Major Robert, iii. 524; Rose, iii. 201; R., iii. 286; Samuel, i. 207, 326; Sarah (*née* Exshaw), ii. 148; Sir Sidney, iv. 184; S., i. 382; Thomas, iii. 98; Thomas Assheton, i. 211; Thomas Currie, i. 259; Lieut. Thomas Francis, ii. 14; William, ii. 325, iv. 414; William Towers, iii. 107; Capt., iv. 391

Smithwick, Peter, iii. 506; Miss, iii. 506

Smyth, Ann, iii. 545; Elizabeth, iii. 134; Elizabeth Ann, iii. 360; Ellis (or Elisha), iii. 253; James, iii. 254; John, iii. 634; John Greatrix, iii. 489; Joseph Brewer Palmer, iii. 360; Lionel, 5th Viscount Strangford, ii. 127; Hon. Louisa Sarah Sidney, ii. 127; Mary Ann, iii. 634; Sir Skeffington Edward, 1st Bt., iii. 254; Thomas, iii. 419, iv. 203; William, iii. 134; Adm. William Henry, iii. 360

Smyth, Georgiana Christina Carmichael-, ii. 206; James Carmichael-, M.D., ii. 206

Smythe, Anne, iv. 516; Louisa Harriet, iii. 40; Nicholas, iii. 40; William, iv. 516

Sneyd, Jeremy, iii. 382; John, iii. 236; Rosamond, iii. 236

Snodgrass, Alexis, ii. 546; Christina, iii. 629; Neil, iii. 629

Snowden, George, ii. 345; Louisa Eliza, ii. 345

Solomon, Saul, iii. 213

Solomons, Israel Levin, iii. 773; Louisa, iii. 773

Soltau, Maria Louisa, iii. 531; William, iii. 531

Sombre, David Ochterlony Dyce-, ii. 111, iv. 310

Somers (or Sommers), Ann, ii. 209; William, ii. 209

Somers, 3rd Countess, *see* Cocks, Virginia

Somerset, Major Arthur William FitzRoy, iii. 277; F.M. Lord FitzRoy James Henry, 1st Baron Raglan, iii. 277; Duchess of, iv. 11; 11th Duke of, *see* Seymour, Edward Adolphus

Somerville, Henrietta, iv. 146; Judith, i. 279; Rev. William, i. 279

Somru, Begum, ii. 111, iv. 310

Soper, Eleanor (Elinor), i. 8, iv. 631

Southwell, Margaret, iii. 679, 680

Sowerby, John, i. 366; Maria, i. 366

Sowers, Catherine, iii. 585; John, iii. 585

Sowley, Susannah, iii. 747

Spankie, R., iv. 154

Sparks, Luke, iv. 275; Sarah, iv. 275

Sparlen, Susan Conordriade, ii. 40

Sparling, Miss, iii. 500

Sparrow, Elizabeth, iii. 505; Richard, iii. 505

Spedding, James, iv. 365; Sarah, iv. 365

Speeler, Ann, iii. 64

Spelissy, John, M.D., iii. 307; Mary, iii. 307

Spence, Frances Ingram, ii. 4

Spencer, Harriet, iv. 163; Knight, i. 418; Sarah, iv. 463; Susannah

Elizabeth, i. 418 ; Lt.-Col. William, iv. 163

Spooner, Mary, ii. 229 ; Thomas, ii. 229

Spottiswoode, Agnes Anne, iii. 149 ; Catherine Barron, i. 238, iv. 524 ; Hugh, iv. 18 ; Mary, iv. 305 ; William, i. 238, iii. 149, iv. 305, 524

Spry, John, iv. 113 ; Mary, iv. 113

Squire, Mary Margaret Woolmer, iii. 643 ; Capt. Tristram Charnley, iii. 643

Squyre, Jean, iii. 749 ; Rev. John, iii. 749

Stackhouse, Margaret, iv. 286 ; Mary, i. 304 ; Nathaniel, iv. 286 ; William, i. 304

Stacy, Ann Maria, i. 2 ; Rev. Henry Peter, i. 2, ii. 481 ; Sarah Arabella, ii. 481

Stafford, Ann, iii. 220 ; Caroline, iii. 541 ; Edward, iii. 220 ; Elizabeth, ii. 454 ; Rev. William, iii. 541

Stair, 9th Earl of, see Dalrymple, Sir North Hamilton, Bt.

Stamford and Warrington, 5th Earl of, see Grey, George Harry

Stamfordham, Baron, see Bigge

Stanger, James, iii. 365

Stanhope, Charles Wyndham, 7th Earl of Harrington, ii. 457 ; Margaret, iv. 116 ; Philip, 5th Earl of Chesterfield, iv. 116

Stanley, Charlotte, iii. 809 ; Rev. Dr. Thomas, iii. 809

Stansfeld, Adelaide Mary Anne, iv. 297 ; William, iv. 297

Stanwix, Gen. John, ii. 463

Staples, Harriet Charlotte, i. 370

Stark, (Ann) Catherine, ii. 33 ; Elizabeth, iv. 497 ; Margaret, i. 97 ; Rev. Thomas, ii. 33, iv. 497

Starling, Rev. Anthony, iii. 582 ; Catherine, iii. 582

Stedman, Ann Holland, i. 290 ; Catherine, ii. 447 ; George, i. 290, ii. 307 ; John, ii. 447 ; Margaret Reid, ii. 307 ; Sophia Maria, ii. 430

Steedman, Andrew, ii. 289 ; Caroline (née Evans), ii. 289

Steele, Anne, iii. 605 ; Dorothea, i. 268 ; Rev. Dr. James, iii. 605 ; Rev. John, i. 256 ; Margaret, i. 256 ; Sir Richard, 1st Bt., i. 268 ; Capt. (? Richard Charles), ii. 337 ; Sophia, ii. 337

Steer, Rev. Charles, iv. 297 ; Elizabeth, iv. 297 ; Henry William, iv. 273

Stehelin, Alethea Rosamond, i. 380 ; Capt. Francis William, i. 380

Stenton, Dr. George, ii. 167

Stephanos, Mary, ii. 498

Stephens, Rachel, iii. 458

Stephenson, Elizabeth Jane, ii. 236 ; George, ii. 236 ; Mrs. (née Duncan), ii. 100

Steuart, Elizabeth, iv. 12 ; Fanny, i. 378

Stevens, Ann, iii. 402 ; John, iii. 135

Stevenson (Stephenson), John, iii. 348 ; Margaret, iii. 348

Stevenson, Maria (née Maddock), iii. 206

Stewart, Rev. Alexander, iv. 115 ; Mrs. Alexander (née Macpherson), iii. 194 ; Mrs. Allan (née Macpherson), iii. 194 ; Andrew Thomas, 1st Earl Castle Stewart, ii. 372, iv. 205 ; Ann, iv. 17, 101 ; Anne (née Agnew), i. 13 ; Anna Elizabeth Buchanan, i. 431 ; Cecilia, ii. 491 ; Rev. Dugald, iv. 17 ; Duncan, iv. 101, 192 ; Rev. Duncan, iii. 807 ; Eleanor, ii. 372 ; Elenor Howel, i. 125 ; Mrs. Elizabeth, iii. 747 ; Emily, iv. 79 ; Col. Francis Philip, i. 161 ; Helen Olympia, iv. 60 ; Capt. Henry, iii. 60 ; Isabella, iii. 115, 279, 778 ; Lt.-Col. James, iii. 41 ; James, i. 125 ; Janet, i. 111, iii. 687 ; Jean, ii. 18, iv. 115, 405 ; (Steuart), Sir John, 3rd Bt. of Allanbank, iii. 804 ; John, iii. 60, 746, 778 ; Louisa, ii. 572, iii. 807 ; Margaret, ii. 541, iii. 804 ; Mary, i. 125 ; Mrs. Mary (née Lyster), i. 161 ; Rev. Dr. Matthew, iv. 17 ; Susannah, iii. 169 ; Williamina Helen, iii. 41 ; of Fasnacloich, family of, iv. 101 ; of Langholm, Mrs., iii. 644 ; of Lisburn, Miss, iii. 762 ; Mrs. (née Stalker), iv. 165

Stiles, Phyllis, iii. 255

Still, Elizabeth, iii. 456 ; James Charles, iii. 456

Stilwell, Agnes (*née* Pearson), iii. 492; Frances Charlotte (*née* Blair), ii. 359; James, ii. 359

Stinton, Isabel, iii. 421

Stirling, Alexander, iii. 672; Sir James, Bt., iii. 672; Sir John, 5th Bt. of Glorat, iii. 764; Margaret, iii. 672; Mary, iii. 426; Sarah, iii. 764; Sir William, Bt. of Ardoch, iii. 426

Stirling, Lt.-Gen. Alexander Graham-, of Duchray, ii. 303

Stocker, Elizabeth, iv. 20

Stokes, C., iii. 623; Harriet Anne, iii. 623; Hetty, iv. 304

Stokoe, Mary, ii. 448

Stone, Elizabeth, ii. 161; George, iv. 1; William Lowndes, ii. 161

Stonestreet, George Griffin, iv. 313; Mary, iv. 313

Stonhouse, Emily Mary, iii. 308; Sir Timothy Vansittart, Bt., iii. 308

Stopford, Caroline Georgiana, iv. 310; Charles, iv. 310

Storer, Elizabeth, iv. 531

Storrow, Ann, iv. 633

Stowey, Harriet, iii. 16; Philip, iii. 16

Strachey, Sir Edward, Bt., iv. 140

Strange, Euphemia, iv. 203; Lawrence, ii. 313; Robert, iv. 203; Thomas Lumisden, ii. 462, iv. 627

Strangeways, Mary, iii. 5

Strangford, 5th Viscount, *see* Smyth, Lionel

Strathmore, 9th Earl of, *see* Lyon, John Bowes-

Strengthfield, Lydia, iii. 533; William, iii. 533

Strettell, Anna (*née* Greenlaw), i. 290; Charles G., i. 290

Stretton, Lucy, iii. 802

Strichen, Lord, *see* Frazer, Alexander

Strode, Capt. Nathaniel Nugent, ii. 537; Phillis Sophia, ii. 537

Strong, Asst. Surg. Francis Pemble, ii. 554; Helen Martin Ann, ii. 554

Stroud, Fanny Rose, iv. 222; John, iv. 222

Struth, Charles, iv. 140; Emma, iv. 140

Stuart, Ann Maria, i. 215; Prince Charles Edward, iii. 777, iv. 188; Clementina, ii. 413; Elizabeth Clara, ii. 107; John, 3rd Earl of Bute, iv. 11; Margaret (*née* Bruce), i. 237, iii. 750; (Stewart) Paulina, iv. 222; Dr. Robert, iv. 582

Studdert, Elizabeth, iv. 380; George, iv. 380

Sturges, Mary Anne, iv. 94; William, iv. 94

Sturmer, John, iii. 468

Sturt, Eliza Bizarre, i. 269; Capt. Henry Evelyn, R.N., ii. 336; Humphrey, i. 269; Rosa Josefa Louisa, ii. 336

Succoth, Lord, *see* Campbell, Sir Ilay, Bt.

Suffield, 3rd Baron, *see* Harbord, Edward

Suffolk, 14th Earl of, *see* Howard, Thomas; Maria, iv. 367

Sullivan, Albinia, iv. 430; Rev. H., iv. 163; Thomasine, iv. 163

Sulyarde, Edward, i. 316; Sophia, i. 316

Sunbolf, Charlotte, iv. 313; Eliza Augusta, iv. 232; Lieut. George, iv. 232, 313

Suter, Lieut. Andrew, iii. 662

Sutherland, Alexander, i. 72; Barbara, iii. 762; Elizabeth, i. 72; Helen, iii. 748; Lt.-Col. James, iii. 161; James, ii. 498, iii. 748; Katharine, iii. 161; Louisa, ii. 498; Margaret, iii. 161; Robert, iii. 161; Col., iii. 797

Sutton, Elizabeth, iii. 788; Phillis, ii. 612; Thomas, Comte de Clonard, ii. 612

Swaine, George Hoare, ii. 437; Rose Emeline, ii. 437

Swainson, James, i. 397; Mary, i. 397

Swan, Elizabeth, iii. 282; George, iii. 282

Swanston, Rebecca (*née* Lambert), iii. 5

Sweetman, Catherine, iii. 187

Sweney, Mary, iv. 291; Owen, iv. 291

Swetenham, Maria, iii. 464; Roger, iii. 464

Swiney, John, M.D., iii. 702
Swinhoe, Hannah, iii. 388; Henry, i. 230, iii. 388, 403; Jane Catherine, iii. 376; Letitia, iii. 403; Sarah, i. 230; Thomas Bruce, iii. 376
Swinton, Anne E., iv. 582; Charlotte Isabella, iii. 749; Joan, iii. 807; John, ii. 18, iii. 807
Switzer, Dorothea, iii. 693
Sword, James, iv. 192; Margaret, iv. 192; Mary, iv. 192
Syder, Isabella Mingay, ii. 250
Syme, Harriet, iii. 515; John, iii. 515
Symes, Margaret, ii. 264; Mitchelbourne, ii. 264
Symmers, Mrs. Margaret, iii. 167
Symonds, Capt. George Clarke, i. 215; Margaret Louisa, i. 215
Symons, Louisa, iv. 509; William, iv. 509
Sympson, John, iv. 368
Sympson, Col. Edmund Walcott-, iv. 368
Symson, Alexander, iii. 370, iv. 629; Margaret, iii. 370, iv. 629

T

Taap, Ann, iii. 748
Tait, Elizabeth, iv. 399; Elizabeth Watherston, iii. 505; Capt. Robert, R.N., iii. 505; William, iv. 399
Tallyrand, Prince, ii. 308
Talmage, Temperance, ii. 425
Tambs, Susan, ii. 74; Thomas, ii. 74
Tanner, Col. Edward, ii. 244
Tappen, John, iii. 519; Mary, iii. 519
Tate, Eliza, iii. 408
Taylor, Alexander, iv. 125; Anne, iii. 618; Cecilia Philippa, i. 385; Dora Louisa, ii. 249, 272; Dorothy, i. 352; Elizabeth, iii. 276, 316; Frances, iii. 421; Henry, ii. 272; James, iv. 18; James Corbett, iii. 473; Jane, ii. 192; John, i. 25, 352, iii. 316; Joseph Henry, iv. 46; Margaret, iii. 159; Mary, i. 25, iv. 364; Mary Anne, ii. 301; Peter, ii. 192; Gen. Reynell George, iii. 514; Sarah Emma, iv. 46; Capt. Shawe, i. 385; Susan Crayford, iv. 18; Rev. Dr. Thomas, iii. 159; Walter, iii. 421; ——, ii. 433
Tees, Mrs., ii. 451
Teichmeyer, Amélie, i. 222
Teignmouth, 1st Baron, see Shore, John
Temple, Anne, i. 127; Henry, 2nd Viscount Palmerston, ii. 50, iii. 274; Mary, Viscountess Palmerston (née Mee), iii. 274; Simon, i. 127
Templer, Anna Sophia, i. 246; James, i. 246; John William, iv. 277; Maria Georgiana, iv. 277
Templeton, Eliza Sophia, ii. 406; Margaret (née Skinner), iv. 108; Margaret Elizabeth, iv. 513; Thomas, iv. 108, 513
Templetown, 1st Baron, see Upton, Clotworthy
Tenison, Elizabeth, i. 128; Jane, iv. 117; Richard, i. 128
Terraneau, Emily Maria, ii. 185
Terrot, Rt. Rev. Dr. Charles Hugh, iii. 206
Terry, Elizabeth, iii. 794; Mary Ann, ii. 351; Thomas, iii. 794
Tett, Honor, iii. 692
Thackeray, Jane, iii. 631; Richmond Makepeace, iv. 143; Archdeacon Thomas, iii. 631; William Makepeace, iii. 324, iv. 143
Theed, Mary Anne, iv. 106; Thomas, iv. 106
Thellusson, Peter Isaac, 1st Baron Rendlesham, iv. 252
Thomas, Alicia (née Ranken), iii. 608; Anne, iii. 293, 556; Caroline, iii. 604; Mrs. Elizabeth, i. 31; Evan, iii. 608; Sir George, 3rd Bt. of Yapton, iii. 556; Jane Campbell, iv. 403; Marie Anne, iii. 656; Mary, iii. 557; M., iii. 293; Mary Anne, ii. 212; Robert Moseley, iii. 389, iv. 403; Sarah Ann Russell, ii. 389; Sophia, iii. 796; S., iii. 604; Capt. Vigors, R.N., iii. 797; Sir William, 2nd Bt. of Yapton, iii. 557; Lt.-Gen. William, ii. 443
Thomason, Charles Simeon, ii. 87; Eliza Harington, ii. 513; Esther, iv. 178; James, iv. 178; Rev. Thomas Truebody, ii. 513, iv. 178

INDEX OF NAMES

Thomond, 3rd Marquess of, *see* O'Brien, James

Thompson, Ann, iii. 349; Ann Eliza, ii. 553; Caroline, iii. 63; Elizabeth Caroline, iii. 790; Eliza Millbank, i. 354; George Powney, iv. 60; Henry, ii. 486, iii. 63, iv. 306; Isabella, iv. 80; Lieut. James George, R.N., ii. 54; John Deas, iii. 297; Laura Isabella, iv. 306; Maria Elizabeth, ii. 486; Marion Sophia, iv. 60; Samuel, i. 198; Lieut. Thomas, R.N., ii. 54; William J., M.D., i. 354

Thomson, Jean, iii. 161; Rev. John, ii. 233; Mary (*née* Fullarton), ii. 233

Thoresby, Lucy, iv. 445; Thomas, iv. 445

Thornhill, Cornelia, ii. 623

Thornton, Harriet, ii. 365; Martha, ii. 141; Mary, i. 92, 218; Sarah, i. 412; Thomas, iv. 634; William, i. 92

Thoroton, Mary, iii. 784; Robert, iii. 784

Thorp, Mary, ii. 335; Rev. Thomas, ii. 335

Thorpe, Mrs. Jane, iv. 635

Thrale, Cecilia Margaretta, iii. 344; Henry, iii. 344

Thresher, Elizabeth, i. 361; John, i. 361

Thurlow, Edward, 1st Baron Thurlow, i. 432

Thursby, Honor Frances, iii. 36; Capt. Walter Harvey, iii. 36

Tibbets, Margaret, iii. 145; Thomas, iii. 145

Tichborne, James, iv. 89; Mary Ann Sarah, iv. 89

Tierney, Elizabeth, iii. 524, 776; Frances, iii. 182; James, iii. 524; John, iii. 182; Sir Matthew John, 1st Bt., iii. 182

Tighe, Elizabeth, ii. 6; Robert, ii. 6

Tilby, Mr., iv. 135

Tinker, Caroline, iv. 157; Cornelia, i. 242; Commodore, i. 242

Tobin, Gen. James, i. 265, iii. 752

Tod, Archibald, iii. 146; Cecilia, iii. 146; Mary (*née* Heatly), ii. 425

Todd, Anne, ii. 361; Charles, iii. 705; Eleanor, iii. 214; Grace Bell, iii. 705; James Ruddell, iii. 705; John, ii. 84, iv. 562; Margaret McLean, ii. 84, iv. 562; Mary Ann, iii. 608; Sarah, iii. 568; William, ii. 361; Capt. William D'Arcy, iii. 214

Tollemache, Maria Elizabeth (*née* Toone), 8th Countess of Dysart, iv. 291

Toller, Richard, iii. 388

Tollet, George, ii. 385, iii. 792

Tomkins, Rev. Chichester, iv. 290

Tomkyns, Mary, iv. 472

Tompkins, Ann, iii. 296

Tonnochy, Miss A. C., iv. 581

Topham, Anne, iii. 691; Charlotte, i. 265; Henry, iii. 691

Torrane, Cecilia Mary, iv. 339; Col. George, iv. 339

Torriano, Capt. Charles, ii. 488; Dorothea Sarah, ii. 488

Torrington, 5th Viscount, *see* Byng, John

Tottenham, Henry Loftus, ii. 288; Mary Harriet, ii. 288

Tovey, Alexander, i. 171; Anne Armstrong, iv. 253; Lt.-Col. James Dunbar, iv. 253; Matilda Grace, i. 171

Towell, Beata, iv. 365; Surg. James, iv. 365

Townley, Rev. John, iii. 664; Mary, iii. 664

Townsend, Elizabeth Becher, iv. 148; Hannah, ii. 330; Harriot, ii. 239; John, ii. 239, iv. 148

Townshend, Hon. Anne, iv. 493; Rt. Hon. Charles, iv. 493; Edward V., iii. 248; George, 1st Marquess Townshend, iv. 493; Hester Lee, iii. 248

Tozer, Aaron, ii. 582; Frances, ii. 582

Tracey, Andrew, ii. 129; Catherine Charlotte, ii. 129

Trail, Christian, ii. 363, 364

Traill, William, ii. 50

Trant, Alice, i. 178; Clara (or Clarissa), iii. 437; Mary, ii. 31; Patrick, ii. 31; Thomas, iii. 437

Trapaud, Lt.-Gen. Elisha, iii. 457

INDEX OF NAMES

Trasdale, Harriet, iv. 204
Tredgold, Elizabeth, iii. 595
Trench, Anne Power, i. 355; Frances, iii. 450; Nicholas Power, iii. 450; William Power Keating, 1st Earl of Clancarty, i. 355, iii. 450
Trimble, Henrietta L., iii. 424
Tritton, Catherine Louisa, i. 304; Charlotte, ii. 193; Georgina, ii. 177; Capt. John, i. 304, ii. 177, 193, 397; Mary Anne, ii. 397
Tronson, Anne, i. 182; Lawford, i. 182, ii. 126, iv. 551; Mary Anne, ii. 126, iv. 551
Trood, Melloney Grace Schobel, ii. 581
Trotter, Archibald, ii. 389; Charlotte Knox, ii. 607; Laura Anne, ii. 389; William, ii. 607
Trouille, Jeanne, iii. 284
Troup, Jane Helen, i. 121; John, i. 121
Trueman, Robert, iii. 542
Tucker, Charles, iii. 292; Dorcas, ii. 258; Elizabeth Lucy, i. 380; Honora, iv. 419; Col. John Goulston Price, i. 380; Martin, iii. 777; Mary (née Stokoe), iv. 199; Tomasin, iii. 777
Tufnell, Elizabeth, iii. 670; Samuel, iii. 670
Tulleken, Jemima, iv. 105, 319; Col., iv. 105, 319
Tullekens; Tullikens, see Tulleken
Tulloh, William, iv. 479
Turnbull, Catherine, iv. 12; Frances, iii. 231; Isobel, iii. 396; John, iii. 396; Margaret Ann, ii. 5; P., ii. 5; Thomas, ii. 483; Violet, ii. 483
Turner, Benjamin, iii. 774; Diana Wroughton, ii. 15; Elizabeth, ii. 625, iii. 753; Mrs. E., iii. 231; Frances, ii. 165; Mrs. Frances D., i. 313; G., i. 313; Harriet Albina, iv. 357; Henrietta, ii. 143, iii. 774; Jacob, iii. 753; Jane Baily, ii. 143; Jean, ii. 285; Rev. John, ii. 143; John, ii. 165; Margaret Louisa, iii. 231; Matilda Henrietta, iii. 384; Richard, iii. 133; Theophila Louisa, iii. 133; Thomas, M.D., iv. 322; Capt., iii. 384

Turnley, Catherine, i. 190; Francis, i. 190
Turnour, Edward, 1st Earl Winterton, iii. 643; Elizabeth, iii. 643
Turton, Frances, i. 129; Sir Thomas, Bt., i. 129
Tuting, Eliza, iii. 362; Martha, ii. 440; Phoebe, ii. 536; Sarah, iii. 30
Tweedale, 2nd Marquess of, see Hay, John; 7th Marquess of, see Hay, George
Twemlow, Elizabeth (née Hamilton), ii. 375; Thomas, ii. 375
Twentyman, J. H., ii. 149; Louisa, ii. 149
Twine, Sarah, iv. 54; Capt., iv. 54
Twiss, John, iv. 334; Sarah, iv. 334
Tydd, Charlotte Catherine, iv. 85; Thomas, iv. 85
Tyler, Andrew, iii. 412; Henry Huey, iv. 11; Katherine, iii. 412; Marion, iv. 11
Ty Moti, iii. 233
Tyrone, 1st Earl of, see Monck, Marcus
Tyrrell, Mary, iii. 551; Richard, iii. 551
Tytler, Ann Christiana, iii. 124; Jane Anne, ii. 319; Robert, M.D., iii. 124; William Fraser, ii. 319

U

Udny, George, iii. 217
Unett, Charlotte, ii. 583; Henry, ii. 583, iv. 367; Mary Jane, iv. 367
Uniacke, James, i. 409; J., iii. 181; Mary, i. 409; Maria Isabella, iii. 181
Upton, Clotworthy, 1st Baron Templetown, iv. 338
Urmston, Ellen, iii. 373
Urquhart, Surg.-Maj. David, iv. 72; Euphemia, iv. 72; Mary Ann, iv. 196; William Alexander, iii. 614
Usher, S., iii. 369
Ussher, Capt. Arthur, iv. 87; Rev. Hemsworth, iv. 218; Judith, iv. 87; Julia Anne Catherine, iv. 218
Uvedale, Harriet, iv. 149; Ralph, iv. 149
Uxbridge, Earl of, see Bayly, Henry

INDEX OF NAMES

V

Vacossin, Mlle, i. 212
Vaginay, Ann, iii. 237
Valentine, Elizabeth, iv. 522; William Donald, iv. 522
van Berchem, Anne Rose Louise Berthoudt, iii. 546; Baron Jacob, iii. 546
van Coehoorn, Adriana Wiertz, iv. 173; Baron Menno, iv. 173
Van Cortlandt, Eliza, iv. 240; Mary Ricketts, i. 33; Col. Philip, i. 33, iv. 240
Vander Byl, Elizabeth, iv. 91; Philip, iv. 91
Vander Hoff, Catherina Maria, iv. 378; H. C., iv. 378
Vane, William Harry, 1st Duke of Cleveland, ii. 196
Vanheyden, Helena, ii. 53
Vansittart, Elizabeth, iii. 652; Vice-Adm. Henry, iii. 652
Van Straubenzee, Catherine, ii. 248; Charles, ii. 248
Varley, Sarah, iii. 225
Varlo, Elizabeth (? Mary), iv. 537; Col., iv. 537
Vassall, Catherine Spencer Alicia Beresford, iii. 287; Lt.-Col. Spencer Thomas, iii. 287
Vaughan, Charlotte, iii. 613; George, iii. 803; Harriet, iii. 302; James, iii. 44; Sarah, iii. 803; Thomas, iii. 302
Veale, Emilia Cumming, ii. 186; William, ii. 186
Veitch, Dorothea, ii. 475; Hugh, ii. 475
Venables, Mr., ii. 213
Vere, Margaret, iv. 208; Mary, ii. 48; Peter, ii. 48, iv. 208
Vereker, Julia, iii. 67; Thomas, iii. 67
Verkerk, Susanna Anna Maria, iv. 542
Verlée, Noel Catherine, ii. 308; Pierre, ii. 308
Verney, Sir Ralph, 2nd Earl Verney, iii. 448
Vernon, Eliza, i. 19; Frances, iii. 304; John, iii. 304; W., i. 19
Vertue, Hannah, iii. 772

Veysie, Ann (née Arnold), i. 53
Vicaradge, Frances, iv. 43; John, iv. 43
Vickers, Elizabeth, ii. 404; Joseph, iii. 518
Victoria, Queen, iii. 608
Villiers, George, ii. 171; Louisa Ann, ii. 171
Vincent, Rev. John, ii. 184; Lucy, ii. 184; Mary, iii. 83
Vine, Charles, iii. 595
Viner, Mary, iv. 16
Violett, John, iv. 146; Sarah, iv. 146
Virtue, Mary, iv. 244
von Graffenreid, Julia Catharina, iv. 466
von Hahn, Count of Mecklenburg-Strelitz, i. 386
von Wild, Francis Samuel, iii. 350; Maria Albertina Charlotte, iii. 350
Vos, Caroline Adriana, iv. 575; James Reinier, M.D., iv. 575
Vowe, Hester, iii. 462; Capt. Hungerford, iii. 462
Vrignon, Gabriel, iii. 587; Rozalia, iii. 587

W

Wadden, Barrett, iii. 509; Emily, iii. 509
Waddington, Anne Maria, ii. 364
Wade, Augusta Katharine, ii. 538; Eleanor (née Mathews), iii. 254; John Peter, M.D., i. 311; Rachel (née Carruthers), i. 311; Col., ii. 538
Wagentreiber, Elizabeth (née Skinner), ii. 357; George, ii. 357
Wagstaff, Elizabeth, ii. 613, iii. 810; Hannah, iii. 328; William, iii. 328, 810
Wainwright, Harriet, iv. 189
Waite, Jane, ii. 608; John, ii. 608
Wake, Marianne, iii. 669; Sir William, 8th Bt., iii. 669
Waldegrave, Rebecca, i. 402
Waldener, J. N. Orth, iii. 351; Louisa Orth, iii. 351
Wales, Frederick Louis, Prince of, iii. 227; Caroline, Princess of, iv. 92; Charlotte, Princess of, i. 186

INDEX OF NAMES

Walker, Surg. Adam, iv. 275; Agnes Hart, ii. 272; Rev. Andrew, iv. 469; Surg. Andrew, ii. 272; Anne, ii. 413, 416, iii. 793; Anne Maria, iii. 39; Elizabeth, iii. 616; Ellen, ii. 407; James, ii. 475, iii. 158; Jane, iv. 399; Jane Anne, ii. 475; Jean, i. 143, 431; John, iii. 8; Lillias, iv. 631; Margaret, iv. 469; Margaret Scott, iv. 275; Maria Rachel (née Moulton), iii. 347; Mary, iii. 158, 576; Richard Onebye, iii. 39; Samuel, iii. 616; Sophia, iii. 209; Rev. Thomas, iv. 399; Thomas, iii. 209, 347; William, i. 14, iv. 631

Wall, Mrs. Eliza H., i. 361; J. J., iii. 309; Martha, iii. 309; Mary, iii. 101; Selina, iii. 583; Thomas, iii. 101, 583

Wallace, Amelia Ann, i. 132; Mrs. Eliza, iii. 55; Elizabeth, iv. 321; Hugh, ii. 489; Margaret, ii. 489; Thomas, Baron Wallace of Knaresdale, iv. 377; William Cook, iii. 55

Waller, Elizabeth, ii. 439; Jane (Joanna), i. 205; Joseph Conway, i. 205

Wallich, Hannah Sarah, i. 138; Nathaniel, M.D., i. 138

Walmesley, Emma, iii. 590

Walne, Judith, iv. 530; Susannah, iii. 68

Walpole, Sir Robert, 1st Earl of Orford, iv. 500

Walrond, Catherine, iii. 102; Maine Swete, ii. 196, iii. 102; Sarah, ii. 196

Walshman, Roger, iv. 341

Walter, Philip, iii. 794; Sarah, iii. 794

Walters, Ellen, i. 282; Henry, i. 282

Warburton, Lucinda, iii. 136; Rev. Richard, iii. 136; Capt. Richard, iii. 136

Ward, John, iv. 312; Katherine Elizabeth, iv. 335; Margaret Jean, ii. 82; Mary, i. 69, iv. 312; Mary (née Hickburn), ii. 35; Mary Jane, iii. 633; Seth Stephen, iv. 335

Wardell, George, iii. 241

Warden, Jane, ii. 215, 220

Wardlaw, Sir Henry, Bt. of Pitreavie, iv. 421; Mary, iv. 421

Ware, Joseph, iv. 638; Mary, iii. 372, 374, iv. 637; Sarah, ii. 121, iii. 491

Wareing, Anne, iii. 369; Elizabeth, iii. 700; Joshua, iii. 700; Samuel, iii. 369

Waring, Elizabeth, iii. 782; Jane, iii. 807

Wark, James, iv. 488; Jean, iv. 488

Warner, Fanny, iii. 617

Warren, Anne, iv. 326; Isabella, iv. 370; Mary (née Young), iv. 544; Susan, iv. 170; Thomas, iv. 326; Mrs., ii. 480

Warton, Rev. Joseph, iii. 329; Mary, iii. 329

Waterford, 1st Marquess of, see Beresford, George De La Poer

Waters, Anne, i. 75; Morgan, i. 75

Watkinson, Harriet, iii. 293

Watson, Agnes, iii. 759; Ann (née Hadaway), ii. 353; Anne, ii. 542; Anna Theresa, i. 61; Dorothy, i. 12; Harriet Anne, ii. 305; Horace, i. 61, iv. 331; Isabella, i. 421; Gen. Sir James, ii. 305; Sir James, Kt., i. 51; James, i. 421; Mrs. Jane, iii. 278; Commodore John, ii. 496, iv. 366; Lt.-Col. John Popham, ii. 496; Dr. John William, ii. 353; Margaretta, i. 51; Marian Charlotte, iv. 366; Marie, iv. 331; Martha Lewis, ii. 379; Mary, ii. 22; Sophia, iv. 63; Major Thomas Samuel, ii. 22; William, iv. 63; Mrs., iv. 186

Watton, Eunice (née Lake), iii. 2; William, iii. 2

Watts, Edward, iii. 208; Elizabeth, iii. 208; Major Harry Hall, iv. 88; James, i. 18; Jane, ii. 618; Mrs. Mary Anne, i. 18; William, ii. 618

Waugh, Andrew, iii. 513; Margaret, iii. 513

Wayne, Frances Augusta, iii. 71; Thomas Moore, iii. 71

Webb, Amelia, iv. 251; Ann (née Stubbins), iv. 207; Lt.-Col. Richmond, iii. 324, iv. 251; Sarah, iii. 324

Webber, Elizabeth, ii. 399; Maj.-Gen. Henry, iii. 804; John, iii. 608; Lucie, iii. 804; Mary, iii.

INDEX OF NAMES

608; Lieut. William Charles, R.N., iii. 247
Webster, Sir Godfrey, Bt. of Battle Abbey, iv. 444
Wedderburn, Sir Alexander, 4th Bt. of Blackness, iv. 45; Alexander, i. 311; Elizabeth, i. 311; Henry, i. 426; Katharine, iv. 45; Mary, i. 426; Sir Peter, *see* Halkett
Weir, Frances Mary, iv. 636; Mary Margaret, i. 379; Dr. Thomas, i. 379
Welland, Frances Kennaway, ii. 464; Rev. Robert Palk, ii. 464
Wellard, Anne Jigon, ii. 307; Capt. Robert, R.N., ii. 307
Wellesley, Richard Colley, Marquess Wellesley, iii. 661
Wells, Edward, i. 48; Elizabeth, i. 48
Wellwood, Katherine, iii. 308; Robert, iii. 308
Welsh, Margaret, i. 1, 4; Shirley, iii. 734
Welwood, Alexander Maconochie, Lord Meadowbank, ii. 389; Anne, ii. 389
Wemyss, Caroline Charlotte, i. 283; James, i. 283; Margaret, i. 153; Maria, iii. 202
Wensleydale, Baron, *see* Parke, Rt. Hon. Sir James
Wentworth, Mary Maria, iv. 79
Werlée, *see* Verlée
West, Piercy, iii. 797
Westcote, Charlotte Georgiana, iii. 49
Westfield, Crosby, R.N., ii. 291; Sarah, ii. 291
Westmorland, Mary, i. 324; Rev. Thomas, i. 324
Weston, Anne, iv. 406; Charles, ii. 236, iii. 281, iv. 406; Margaret, iii. 281
Westropp, Lt.-Col. Lionel John, iv. 155; Penelope Clarine, iv. 155; Sarah, iii. 561; Thomas, iii. 561
Wetherall, Emily Elizabeth, ii. 361; John, ii. 361
Wetherell, Catherine, iii. 586; Jane, iv. 472; Simon, iii. 586
Wewitzer, Miss, iv. 340
Whalley, Grace, i. 56; Robert, M.D., i. 56

Whatman, James, i. 180; Laetitia Philippa, i. 180
Wheat, Lieut. Thomas Clifton, iv. 356
Wheeler, Capt. Hugh, iii. 738; Miss, iii. 747
Wheler, Sir Charles William, Bt., i. 138; Sophia, i. 138
Whish, Alicia Mary, i. 431; Harriet Mary Benyon, ii. 450; Katherine Elizabeth, iv. 150; Mrs. Lucinda Florence, ii. 76; Lydia, iii. 579; Maria Eliza, i. 391, iii. 760; Martin, iii. 760, iv. 150; Martin Thomas, i. 431, ii. 450; Mary (*née* Dixon), ii. 64
Whitaker, Clara Emma, ii. 186; James, ii. 186; Sarah, iii. 404; Thomas, iii. 404
Whitcombe, Anne, i. 360; Charles, iii. 520; Henry Robert, iii. 187; Robert, i. 360; Rosa Maria, iii. 520; Sarah Anne, iii. 187
White, Ann, ii. 595; Anne Charlotte, i. 149; Ann Hall, i. 249; Frances, i. 51; Major Henry, iii. 98; Jane, ii. 260; Capt. John, R.N., iii. 809; Asst. Surg. John, i. 149; Rev. Dr. Joseph, iv. 326; Marianne, iii. 809; Victoria Hannah, iii. 98; (or Wight), Dr., ii. 260
Whitefoord, Barbara, i. 160; Sir John, i. 160
Whitehead, Hannah, iii. 739; Jane, ii. 402; Rev. Robert, ii. 402
Whitesmith, Mary, iv. 250
Whitmore, Charles, iv. 56; Elizabeth, iv. 376; Elizabeth Sophia, iv. 56; William, iv. 376
Whittell, Anna Maria, ii. 434; Joshua Francis, ii. 434
Whittle, Mrs. Mary, iii. 402
Whitworth, Anna Barbara, iii. 707; Catherine, i. 63; Sir Charles, Earl Whitworth, iii. 707; Sir Charles, Kt., i. 63, iii. 707
Wickstead, Jemima, *see* Wicksted
Wicksted, Jemima, ii. 596
Wigg, Prudence, i. 266
Wiggins (Wiggens), Georgiana Olivia, ii. 548
Wight, Alexander, iv. 108; Andrew, iv. 371; Wilhelmina, iv. 371; (or White), Dr., ii. 260

INDEX OF NAMES

Wightman, Charlotte, iii. 337; (Inglis), John, iii. 332; (Inglis), Rachel Ann, iii. 332; Robina, ii. 589, 590
Wigmore, Elizabeth Margaret (*née* Thompson), ii. 54
Wigram, Sir Robert, 1st Bt., i. 211
Wild, Frederick David, iii. 511
Wilkes, John, iv. 127
Wilkins, Anne, iii. 268; John, iii. 268; Mary, ii. 585
Wilkinson, Alicia, i. 139; Amelia, iv. 103; Ann, ii. 243; Anna Maria, iv. 299; Arabella, ii. 296, iii. 91; Caroline, iii. 90; Charlotte, i. 225; Christopher, i. 139; Elizabeth, ii. 1, 452; Frances, iv. 504; G., iv. 299; Sir Jacob, iv. 498; James, ii. 170; Jane Elizabeth, i. 399; Joseph, ii. 1; J., ii. 243; Capt. J. B., iv. 504; Mary Elizabeth, ii. 170; Thomas, ii. 452; Rev. Thomas Chambers, iii. 91; Lt.-Col. William, iv. 103
Wilks, Col. Mark, i. 12
Willasey, James, iii. 271; Mary Jane, iii. 271
William IV, iii. 608, iv. 302, 322
William, Prince of Orange, iv. 319
Williams, Anne Dering, ii. 212; Catherine, ii. 159; Catherine White, iii. 214; Charlotte, i. 418, ii. 84, iii. 66; Sir Edward, Bt. of Gwernyfed, iv. 513; Eliza, iv. 239; Eliza Anne, iii. 133; Elizabeth, ii. 422, 543; Elizabeth Mary, i. 262; Fleetwood, iii. 155; Frances, ii. 158; Frances Sophia, i. 434; G., i. 262; Harriet Augusta, iii. 106; Helen Maria, ii. 609; Henry, ii. 84, 609, iii. 133; H., i. 434; James, iii. 802; Capt. John, iv. 355; Rev. John, iii. 284; Juliana, iv. 355; Margaret, iii. 284; Martha, ii. 513, iii. 802; Mary, ii. 353, iv. 513; Rev. Richard, i. 418; Capt. Robert, iv. 355; Sarah, i. 126, iii. 255, iv. 597; Stephen, iii. 212; Rev. Thomas, i. 353; Capt. William, iii. 66, iv. 239; Capt., i. 126
Williams, (Eliza) Anne Griffies-, ii. 317; Rev. Sir Erasmus Griffies-, Bt., ii. 340; Sir George Griffies-, 1st Bt., ii. 317, 340
Williamson, Christian, i. 296; Mrs. Henry (*née* Hicks), ii. 446; Surg. James, i. 292; Miss, iv. 531
Willington, Mary (Eleanor), i. 312
Willis, Agnes, iii. 786; Rev. George, iii. 786; John, i. 279; Mary, ii. 533; Matilda Ann, i. 417; Thomas, M.D., iv. 423; William, i. 417
Willmott, Sarah Anne (*née* Noke), iii. 400; Thomas, iii. 400
Willoughby, Sir Christopher, 1st Bt. of Baldon House, iii. 736; Elfrida Cassandra, iii. 501; George Heorald Railton, ii. 502; Harriet Georgina, ii. 502; Juliana, iii. 736
Wills, Elizabeth, iii. 301; Godfrey, iii. 301; Sophia, iv. 130
Willson, Eliza Sophia, iii. 229; James, iii. 229
Wilmer, Sarah (*née* Stokoe), iv. 199
Wilmot, Charlotte, iii. 754; Henry, iii. 754; Louisa, i. 324; Sir Robert Mead, Bt., i. 324
Wilson, Agnes, ii. 628; Alice, iii. 204; Andrew, M.D., iv. 211; Anne, i. 345, iii. 531, 756; Ann Tamer, iii. 424; Barbara, iii. 201; Charles Child, iii. 756; Rt. Rev. Christopher, iv. 590; Cuthbert, iii. 174; Eleanor, iv. 214; Elizabeth, iii. 165, 428, 472, iv. 590; Ellen, iii. 587; Emma, ii. 351; Francis Vernon, i. 374; George, iv. 465; Hester Elizabeth, ii. 258; H., i. 173; Jane, i. 173, iii. 506, iii. 84; Janet, iii. 650; Jannette, iv. 211; John, iii. 531; John Taylor, ii. 351; Joseph, iii. 204; Margaret, i. 88, 374; Mrs. Mary, iv. 571; Col. N., ii. 258; Patrick, i. 88; Robert, 9th Baron Berners, iv. 489; Robert, iii. 201; Sarah, iii. 375; Susan Jane, iv. 465; Thomas, iii. 424; Lieut. Thomas Fourness, iv. 489; William, iii. 587
Wilton, John, iv. 433
Wiltshire, Anne Martha, iii. 304; Charles, iii. 304; Susannah Elizabeth, i. 394, iii. 448

Windsor, Anne, iii. 461; William, iii. 461
Wing, Emma, ii. 145; Thomas, ii. 145
Wingate, Margaret, iii. 231
Winsmore, Edward, iii. 375
Winter, Anna Maria Sarah, iv. 382; Martha, iv. 33; Samuel Pratt, iv. 382; Thomas Bradbury, iv. 33
Winterton, 1st Earl, see Turnour, Edward
Wiseman, Margaret, iv. 5
Wishart, Jane, ii. 240; Patrick, ii. 240
Witham, Sarah, i. 73, 75
Withington, Elizabeth, i. 8
Witts, Apphia, iii. 487; Broome, iii. 487
Wolf, Elizabeth (née Young), iv. 544
Wollaston, George Hyde, iii. 548; Henrietta, iii. 548; Surg. William, ii. 352
Wolleston, see Wollaston and Woolaston
Wolseley, Sir William, 6th Bt. of Wolseley, iii. 424
Wood, Rev. Alexander, iv. 339; Andrew, iv. 155; Bethia, iv. 155; Catherine, iii. 360; Charles Boynton, ii. 254; Charlotte, ii. 268; Eleanor, iv. 506; Emily Jane, ii. 509; F. M. Sir Evelyn, i. 327; Sir George, iii. 740; Rev. G., iv. 250; Maj.-Gen. Sir George Adam, ii. 553; Henry B., ii. 404; (Jane) Ellen, i. 262; John, ii. 268, iii. 360; Rev. Sir John Page, 2nd Bt., i. 327; Maria, i. 327; Mary, ii. 404, iv. 175, 250; Mary (née Jervis), ii. 553; Robert, ii. 509; William, i. 262
Woodley, Rachel (née Yeamans), iii. 709
Woodman, Dr. James, i. 150; Matilda Mary Linning, i. 150
Woodson, Mary, iv. 105
Woodward, Sarah, iii. 304; Susannah, i. 385
Woolaston, Elizabeth, i. 305
Wooldridge, Amelia, iii. 383; Anne Emily, i. 255; Capt., R.N., i. 255
Woolhouse, Mary, ii. 42
Woollen, W., iii. 523

Woolsey, Mary Anne, i. 164
Wordsworth, Anne, iii. 366; James, ii. 212; Richard, iii. 366
Wormald, Jenny (née Rotton), iii. 699; Richard, iii. 699
Worsley, Mary Catherine, iii. 739; Gen. Vaughan, iii. 739
Worsop, Esther (Hester) Arthur, iii. 459; John Arthur, iii. 459
Wortham, Charlotte, iii. 794
Wotherspoon, John, i. 409
Wotton, Joanna (née Maverley), iii. 261; Samuel, iii. 261
Woulfe, Mary Leonora, iv. 70; Rt. Hon. Stephen, iv. 70
Wrangham, Charlotte, i. 365; Elizabeth, ii. 102; William, i. 365, ii. 102
Wray, Jackson, iv. 585; Jane, iv. 585
Wright, Alexander, iii. 686; Col. Alexander, iii. 718; Anne, iii. 718; Charlotte, iii. 686; Christopher, iv. 527; Capt. Fortunatus, ii. 144; George, iv. 257; Helen, ii. 351; Isabella, iv. 257, 258, 527; Maria, iv. 296; Maria Ann, ii. 436; Mary, i. 143; Philadelphia (or Philippa), ii. 144; Sarah, i. 213; Sophia Eliza Amelia, iv. 533; Sophronia Rebecca, iv. 195; William, ii. 351; W., iv. 443; Col., iv. 533
Wrottesley, Amelia Julia, ii. 122
Wroughton, Diana Denton Turner, ii. 119; Elizabeth, iii. 508; George, ii. 119; James, iii. 312; Sophia, iii. 312
Wyatt, Miss, iii. 754
Wybergh, Matilda, iv. 632; Thomas, iv. 632
Wye, Elizabeth, iv. 5; George, iv. 5
Wylde, Albinia, ii. 541; C. E., ii. 608; Dorothy, i. 435; Jane (née Waite), ii. 608; Rev. John, i. 435; Rev. Sydenham Teast, ii. 541
Wynch, Alexander, iii. 204, iv. 486; Florentia, iv. 4; George, iv. 4; Margery, iii. 204
Wyndham, Caroline, ii. 457; Hon. Charles, ii. 457; Charles, ii. 458; Jane, 4th Countess of Egremont, iii. 667
Wynn, Sir William, iii. 77

INDEX OF NAMES

Wynne, Anne Maria (*née* Mapletoft), i. 216, iii. 748; Elizabeth, i. 43; Jane, ii. 339; Robert, ii. 339; William, i. 43

Wynox, Harriet, ii. 273

Y

Yates (or Yeates), Anna, ii. 346

Yates, Anna Maria, i. 146; Caroline, iii. 394; John, i. 146; Margaret, iv. 121; Maj.-Gen. Richard Hassells, iii. 394

Yeamans, William, iii. 709

Yeates, Jane, ii. 209

Yeld, Ellen Mary Frances Margaret, i. 327; Dr. Thomas, i. 327

Yelloly, Adam, iv. 406

Yeoman, Katharine, iv. 542, 543

York, Prince Edward, Duke of, ii. 36; Mary, ii. 329; Rev. Philip, ii. 329

Young, Ann, i. 120; Catherine, ii. 255, iii. 502, 782; Christian, ii. 106, iii. 771; Dorothy, i. 48, ii. 618; Elizabeth, ii. 306; Ellen, iii. 375; James, iii. 172; Lt.-Col. James Robert, iv. 245; Jane, i. 154, iii. 744; John, ii. 306, iii. 771; Margaret F., iii. 35; Mary, iii. 172; Mathew, ii. 618; Penelope, ii. 3, iii. 720; Robert, iii. 741, 782; Sarah, iv. 234; Capt. Stephen, ii. 3, iii. 720, iv. 46; Thomas, iv. 234; Adm. Sir William, ii. 136; William, i. 154, iii. 744

Younge, Harry, i. 33; Lucy, i. 33

Younghusband, John, ii. 496; Martha, ii. 496; Capt. Robert, iii. 672

Youngson, Elise, ii. 142; Ellen, iii. 28; Jane Amelia, ii. 43; Col. William, ii. 43, 142, iii. 28

Yule, George, ii. 90; Sir George Udny, iii. 497; Col. Sir Henry, iv. 453; Marion, ii. 90

Z

Zara, Jane, i. 133

Zinzan, James, ii. 395; Susanna Harriot, ii. 395

Zuhur-ul-Nissa, Khanum, iv. 569

www.ingramcontent.com/pod-product-compliance
Lightning Source LLC
Chambersburg PA
CBHW061930220426
43662CB00012B/1863